# Lecture Notes in Computer Science 11863

More information about this series at http://www.springer.com/series/7409

Erik van der Spek · Stefan Göbel ·
Ellen Yi-Luen Do · Esteban Clua ·
Jannicke Baalsrud Hauge (Eds.)

# Entertainment Computing and Serious Games

First IFIP TC 14 Joint International Conference, ICEC-JCSG 2019
Arequipa, Peru, November 11–15, 2019
Proceedings

 Springer

*Editors*
Erik van der Spek [iD]
Eindhoven University of Technology
Eindhoven, The Netherlands

Ellen Yi-Luen Do [iD]
University of Colorado Boulder
Boulder, CO, USA

Jannicke Baalsrud Hauge [iD]
KTH-Royal Institute of Technology
Södertälje, Sweden

Stefan Göbel
TU Darmstadt
Darmstadt, Germany

Esteban Clua [iD]
Fluminense Federal University
Niteroi, Rio de Janeiro, Brazil

ISSN 0302-9743          ISSN 1611-3349  (electronic)
Lecture Notes in Computer Science
ISBN 978-3-030-34643-0          ISBN 978-3-030-34644-7  (eBook)
https://doi.org/10.1007/978-3-030-34644-7

LNCS Sublibrary: SL3 – Information Systems and Applications, incl. Internet/Web, and HCI

This Springer imprint is published by the registered company Springer Nature Switzerland AG
The registered company address is: Gewerbestrasse 11, 6330 Cham, Switzerland

# Preface

With pride we present the conference proceedings of ICEC-JCSG 2019, a collaboratively hosted event that marked the 18th edition of the IFIP International Conference on Entertainment Computing (IFIP-ICEC) and the 5th edition of the International Joint Conference on Serious Games (JCSG). Both conference series share the mission to bring together researchers and practitioners from diverse backgrounds in the fields of entertainment computing and serious games. Consequently, they decided to bring both networks together for this conference event. In addition, there is a continuing desire to create a real global community, connecting researchers from all parts of the world to further the science of entertainment computing and serious games. Therefore, after hosting ICEC 2018 at the IFIP World Computer Congress in Poland and previous conferences in Japan (ICEC 2017) and Austria (ICEC 2016), and hosting JCSG 2018 in Germany, as well as before that in Spain (JCSG 2017) and Australia (JCSG 2016), this time the ICEC-JCSG shared conference was held in Arequipa, Peru, at the Catholic University of San Pablo (UCSP). As a further connection with industry, the conference was colocated with the local games industry conference COIDEV.

Entertainment computing and serious games operate on the multidisciplinary intersection of Design, Art, Entertainment, Interaction, Computing, Psychology, and numerous Serious Application Domains, and brings together researchers in all these fields. Two workshops were organized: "Towards Inclusive Co-creation of Inclusive Games" and "Designing Serious Mobile Location Based Augmented-Reality Games." The shared conference received a total of 88 submissions, and after an extensive review-process, 26 full papers, 5 short papers, 11 poster papers, 2 demonstrations, and 3 workshop papers were selected. The ICEC-JCSG 2019 Program Committee was composed of 41 experts from 16 different countries, comprising a unique representation of the global entertainment computing and games communities. We thank all the members of this committee and all the additional external reviewers for their work and commitment. The importance and credibility of these proceedings are sustained by the competence and dedication of these professionals.

The conference program was furthermore enriched by three keynote speakers: Prof. Magy Seif El-Nasr of Northeastern University, USA, who gave a keynote on "Game User Research: Building Games That Make Social and Educational Impact"; Renzo Sanchez of ArtiGames, Peru, who gave a keynote on "How To Produce a AAA Independent Game in Peru"; and Prof. Soraia Raup Musse of Pontifical Catholic University of Rio Grande do Sul, Brazil, who gave a keynote on "Crowds Behavior Analysis and Simulation".

Next to the keynotes, we would like to thank the local chair Alex Cuadros-Vargas for hosting and taking care of the local organization with the help of others at the Universidad Catolica San Pablo, the university itself, our sponsors, the Peruvian government and the ICEC and JCSG steering groups, without whom this unique shared conference would not have been possible.

September 2019

Erik van der Spek
Stefan Göbel
Ellen Yi-Luen Do
Esteban Clua
Jannicke Baalsrud Hauge

# Organization

## General Chairs

Esteban Clua      Fluminense Federal University, Brazil
Jannicke Baalsrud Hauge      KTH, Sweden, and BIBA, Germany
Alex Cuadros-Vargas      Universidad Católica San Pablo, Peru

## Program Chairs

Erik van der Spek      Eindhoven University of Technology, The Netherlands
Stefan Göbel      Technische Universität Darmstadt, Germany
Ellen Yi-Luen Do      University of Colorado Boulder, USA

## Workshop Chairs

Paolo Ciancarini      University of Bologna, Italy
Erick Gomez-Nieto      Universidad Católica San Pablo, Peru

## Doctoral Consortium Chair

Helmut Hlavacs      University of Vienna, Austria

## Demonstration Chairs

Javier Gomez Escribano      Autonomous University of Madrid, Spain
Marc-Antoine Le Guen      Universidad Católica San Pablo, Peru

## Tutorial Chairs

Artur Lugmayr      Curtin University, Australia
Johan Baldeon      Pontifical Catholic University of Peru, Peru

## Publicity Chairs

Letizia Jaccheri      Norwegian University of Science and Technology, Norway
Minhua Eunice Ma      Staffordshire University, UK

## Program Committee

Mariano Alcaniz      Universitat Politècnica de València, Spain
Per Backlund      University of Skövde, Sweden

# Contents

## Interaction Technologies

## Measurement and Effects

## Serious Game Applications

## Demonstrations

## Designing Serious Mobile Location-Based Augmented Reality Games

# Workshops

# Mixed Reality

# Diminished Reality Based on 3D-Scanning

Erwin Andre and Helmut Hlavacs[✉]

Faculty of Computer Science, Entertainment Computing Research Group,
University of Vienna, Vienna, Austria
helmut.hlavacs@univie.ac.at

**Abstract.** In this paper a new method for diminished reality is explored, which uses a 3D model of a room to fill in missing regions when removing objects in real time on a video. The room is scanned before, so it is possible to recreate missing pieces in all their detail. The proposed method allows freedom in movement and rotation and is demonstrated with an application on a mobile device, detailed results are shown.

## 1 Introduction

Diminished reality (DR) aims at *removing* visual objects (a.k.a. *targets*) from our field of view. DR is thus considered to be the opposite of Augmented Reality (AR) [8], since AR aims at *adding* visual objects to our field of view. There are two common methods for removing targets from videos or images: the first one fills in the missing regions by using readily available background images or essential information captured beforehand, the other one uses the information around the target or the similarity of textures to artificially produce the filling content (usually using some deep learning technique), an approach also known as image inpainting.

Both methods have their limitations. For the first approach, it might be infeasible to capture the visual information used for filling in image regions occluded by the target, for instance in live video situations. In the inpainting approach, it may not be possible to correctly guess the occluded image information from the surrounding pixels, e.g. if the background contains many details.

In this paper a new method for diminished reality is explored by using 3D scans as stored information to remove targets from *live* video feeds produced by the camera of a mobile device. 3D scanning analyzes objects or whole environments (in this paper: whole rooms) by capturing depth data to reproduce the structure of objects and color data to reproduce their appearance. 3D models can be created by mapping these data correctly. As a consequence, the camera producing the video feed where targets are removed may move freely in 3D space, and also chose its orientation freely (resulting in 6 degrees of freedom), because the 3D room scan can be rendered from arbitrary positions and angles. Currently none of the existing DR techniques for live video streams from mobile

Published by Springer Nature Switzerland AG 2019
E. van der Spek et al. (Eds.): ICEC-JCSG 2019, LNCS 11863, pp. 3–14, 2019.
https://doi.org/10.1007/978-3-030-34644-7_1

devices allows this much freedom in movement and rotation during the diminishing process.

## 2   Related Work

Diminished reality and image inpainting have been topics of research over the past few years and there are already many different approaches [10]. Most are not used in live video feeds, but show how to remove targets from images or videos off-line.

Kawai et al. [7] discuss different approaches on removing targets, both inpainting and diminished reality methods. They also present their own method, which is a mix of diminished reality and inpainting. In their method they have to manually select a visual target and then use SLAM (Simultaneous Localization and Mapping) to track feature points. SLAM is also used in the work presented in this paper. Kawai et al. start with initializing the camera pose and feature points. Afterwards a target region is selected manually by the user and the image is analyzed and divided into multiple images to improve the inpainting quality.

Hackl et al. [3] explore a method for removing targets from live video feeds and show their results with an android application. They use previously captured images to remove objects, images are stored in a large data structure called the frame store. However, the authors only achieve change or orientation, a translation of the mobile device is not allowed.

Yagi et al. [14] present a method on how to remove pedestrians from videos taken with a hand-held camera. This method can only be executed after the video was taken and is not supposed to remove pedestrians in real time. First, the pedestrians get detected and marked. After that a 3D model of the background is created from the video frames with SfM (Structure from Motion) to replace objects later on, by projected 2D frames from this model. Afterwards the camera positions are estimated and frames from the model are extracted. Finally, the original and projected images are blended together and frames with removed objects (pedestrians) are generated. It has to be mentioned that the color of a hidden pedestrian is different from the rest of the image.

Broll et al. [5] propose a method which removes objects from a live video stream. This approach consists of two main tasks: object selection and tracking as well as image completion. Objects are manually selected by drawing a contour e.g. with a mouse on a laptop, then a mask is generated. Image completion uses a patch based inpainting algorithm to fill in the selected area. The quality of such a method is reliant on the input and the area around the target that will be removed. This was one of the first applications on a mobile device which was able to remove targets. The removal quality is not affected by the area around the target, which is the same in this paper's implementation.

All these different methods remove targets from videos or images, but only a few are able to perform this in real time. It is even more difficult to run diminished reality applications directly on mobile devices, like [11], who proposed a similar app like ours, but rely on the AR toolkit Vuforia.

# 3 The Structure Sensor

3D room scans can be created with various devices but for our work it was required to run the application on a mobile device. The recently launched Google ARCore does not have the capability to create 3D room scans, so the only feasible possibilities left were Google Project Tango and the Structure Sensor (cf. Fig. 1).

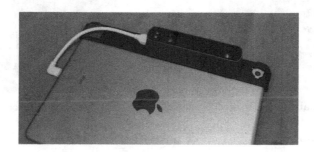

**Fig. 1.** The Structure Sensor mounted to an iPad

At first Google's Project Tango looked promising, but it did not match the scanning quality of the Structure Sensor [6], this also might be due to the fact that the Lenovo Phab 2 Pro that we used is already 3 years old. Furthermore Tango has been discontinued by Google, and so is no longer an option.

When comparing scans from both sensors (cf. Fig. 2) there are some significant differences. The textures of the scan with the Tango device are blurry and rendered images from this mesh would be a bad replacement for removed targets. When comparing both images, the scan with the Structure Sensor looks much better since it does a very good job on capturing plane surfaces. On complex structured surfaces, however, there are some white holes, meaning that the sensor did not capture textures there. The holes, though, can significantly be reduced with better lighting. Overall, the above comparison favours the use of the Structure Sensor for the task at hand.

In more detail, the Structure Sensor is a commercial depth sensor designed to work with iOS devices, e.g. an iPad or iPhone, but there are possibilities to run the sensor on other devices as well (with OpenNI). The device consists of a NIR laser-projector and a NIR camera [9] which work together with the native camera of an iOS device to add 3D vision. The recommended range for the sensor is between 0.4 and 3.5 m, longer ranges are possible but are hurting the sensor's accuracy. At a range of 0.4 m the accuracy is within 0.5 mm and at a range of 3 m within 30 mm. The sensor features two resolutions for capturing depth data, either 640 × 480 or 320 × 240. For our implementation the resolution of 320 × 240 is used.

(a) Lenovo Phab 2 Pro (Project Tango)     (b) iPad 6th Gen. (Structure Sensor)

**Fig. 2.** Comparison of a Google Project Tango room scan and a scan with the Structure Sensor

## 4   The Proposed Method

The main idea of our method is to use the 3D scan of a room to create a 3D model and remove real world targets by filling in missing regions with projected images from the 3D model. The quality of this method depends heavily on the quality of the 3D scan which depends on lighting and how steady the device is moved while scanning. For a good scan a well-lighted room and no harsh movement during the scan are required. The pipeline for this diminished reality approach consists out of five core parts:

1. **3D Scanning:** The first step to diminish objects is to create a 3D model of the room with 3D scanning enabled by the Structure Sensor. It is not necessary to scan a whole room, it is possible only to scan parts of a room.
2. **Positional Tracking:** For each synchronized depth and color frame output by the sensor the position are updated with the SLAM engine of the Sensor's Structure SDK.
3. **Object Detection:** Detection of objects which will be removed later on with either color or face detection.
4. **3D to 2D Projection:** This is used to render a 2D image from the 3D room model at the current camera's position and orientation, which is required for replacing the detected target.
5. **Stitching:** The current camera image is blended together with the extracted 2D image from the 3D model.

The above points are discussed in the following.

## 4.1  3D Scanning

Before any target can be removed the first step is 3D scanning the room and creating a 3D room model. A full room scan is not needed but possible. Objects will be removed only if that area was scanned before. Just before the scanning is started, the camera position is initialized. After that, the sensor data and camera data are used to store point clouds and keyframes during the scanning process. While calculating the 3D mesh the sensors need to be stopped, which only takes a few seconds. Before the sensors are stopped, the current position is saved to later initialize the tracker with this position, so the camera and the mesh are matched. The device should not be moved during the rendering. Unfortunately basic hand movement cannot be prevented 100 %, but since the projected image gets aligned with the camera image later on, this does not influence the overall quality too much. The triangle-mesh is calculated with the depth data and colorized with the color data stored in the keyframes. For the 3D scanning the SLAM engine of the sensor's Structure SDK is used, which includes 3D mapping, tracking and scanning features. For communicating with the sensor, the SDK's sensor controller is used, which allows to start and stop the sensor and to get the status of the sensor.

## 4.2  Positional Tracking

The positional tracking is always active if the sensor is running, since the projected image should have the same viewpoint as the iPad's camera, in order to match the current camera's view as closely as possible when replacing targets. The position is updated with each synchronized depth and color frame output by the camera of the iPad and the Structure Sensor. This process also uses the SLAM engine and is driven by the SDK.

## 4.3  Object Detection

For each frame output by the video camera, either color detection or face detection are applied to the image. In our app, the detection type can be chosen by the user. Multiple objects can be detected and removed at once and the shape and size of the objects can vary. A binary mask is generated during that process which is needed to remove the targets. In such a mask, targets that should be removed are shown with white pixels, while the rest of the mask are black pixels, meaning they do not get removed. When using face detection, if a face is detected, a circle is drawn around the found face and filled with white pixels In case of color detection, if the object color is detected it will be replaced by white pixels.

## 4.4   3D to 2D Projection

To extract the image from the mesh two matrices are needed: the camera extrinsic parameters (e.g. translation, rotation), which describe the coordinate system transformations from 3D world coordinates to 3D camera coordinates and the camera intrinsic parameters which represent the characteristics of the iPad's camera (e.g. focal length, image sensor format) [4,13]. Both matrices are needed to render the image from the same position as the camera. The projection image is the same size as the camera image which is important to stitch them together later. The 3D to 2D projection is described by the following equations [6]:

$$P^2 = P^3 \times M \tag{1}$$

$P^2$ being the 2D image and $P^3$ being the 3D model which is transformed by $M$, the perspective projection matrix.

$$M = K \times R\,(I - C) \tag{2}$$

$M$ is defined by the camera extrinsics $K$, the camera intrinsics $R$ and the coordinate matrix of the camera origin $C$ in the world coordinate frame ($I$ is the identity matrix).

## 4.5   Stitching

Due to inaccuracies in the tracking process, after a target is detected and the frame is extracted from the mesh, the camera image and the mesh image need to be aligned. This is done in order to blend both images together and make them look like one image. The alignment uses feature detection to find matching feature points, then a transformation matrix is calculated from the matches. After the projected image is transformed both are stitched together using the binary mask which is created during the object detection. One single image is created with the target object being removed.

## 4.6   Implementation

Since the Structure Sensor is designed to work mainly with iOS, we developed an iOS app using Xcode. The app is written in objective C and C++, the latter was needed to use the OpenCV library [1]. OpenCV 3.4.4 is used to manipulate the images from the camera and generate a binary mask to remove targets. OpenGL is used together with the Structure SDK to render the 3D mesh, render the color image from the camera to the view or to render an image from a specific position from the 3D model.

For detecting colors, color keying is used by the inRange method provided by OpenCV. Therefore, the image needs to be converted from RGB to HSV, because it is hard to define a range of colors in the RGB color space. In the HSV color space it is easier to define a range of similar looking colors. The inRange method specifies a color range between two HSV scalars. After the inRange method has been used, the image still has some white and black holes which are unwanted. That is why multiple morphological transformations are applied to the image. Before applying morphological transformations to the image it is downscaled to half the size which speeds up the mask generation tremendously (being about 70 % faster than without the downscaling), after all the transformations the image is upscaled again. A binary mask is created which is used later during the stitching process (Fig. 3).

(a) input image                              (b) binary mask

**Fig. 3.** Mask creation from green colored objects (Color figure online)

For detecting faces OpenCV's Haar feature-based Cascade Classifiers [12] are used. There is another option available with LBP-based Cascade Classifiers but the Haar feature-based Cascade Classifiers are usually more accurate. Before the detect MultiScale method is applied to the image, it has to be converted to a greyscale image. The detected objects are marked with a circle (Fig. 4).

 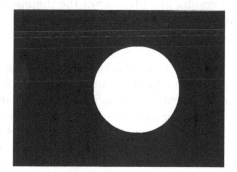

(a) input image                              (b) binary mask

**Fig. 4.** Mask creation from a detected face

## 4.7    User Interface

The User Interface is kept very simple, so it is easy to use and understand. Anybody should be able to use the application after watching a demonstration video of the app. There are no complex settings or preferences implemented which the user can choose from. After starting the application, a short information message is shown to the user welcoming him and explaining what he can do with this app. Before the scanning is started, the range of the scan can be adjusted using the slider located at the bottom of the screen. By default it is set to 5 m which is already a long range considering the sensor works best between 0.4 and 3.5 m. A range between 0.5 and 10 m can be selected. The scanning range makes sure that no objects further away than the selected range can be scanned.

## 5    Evaluation and Discussion

In this section the results and the quality of the target removal of our application are evaluated. We provide a comparison to inpainting and a case study on the iPad in this section.

### 5.1    Removal Quality

The quality of the application's target removal capabilities seem good when compared to other solutions like inpainting or the application of Hackl et al. [3], but there are some factors which determine the quality of the diminished images. Since room scanning is very instrumental for this method, the quality of a room scan is also important to the whole method. For a good room scan the user has to stand on one position and scan the whole room from this position, also the handling of the device is important since harsh or too fast movements result in a bad scan. Blurry scans or cuts in the textures of the scan tremendously reduce the effectiveness of the feature matching algorithm used to align both images and results in stuttering of the diminished output video. That is why a steady hand movement can make a huge difference although it has to be mentioned that the sensor is very fast and when something unexpected happens the scan can be restarted easily.

Another factor for the quality of the removal is the light, there needs to be good lighting in order for the application to achieve optimal results. Faint light makes the color detection very hard because under different light the HSV values do not match anymore and for instance no green color may be detected.

Lastly the structure of the scanned environment is also important to the generated 3D model and influences the removal quality. The more complex the structure of the environment is, the more clunky the scanned 3D model seems to be, this might be caused by the fact that a lot of data has to be processed at once. Object scans are a lot more accurate in comparison to a room scan because only a single object is being scanned.

In Fig. 5b, problems of the Structure Sensor can be seen, caused by scanning complex surfaces. The sensor has difficulties creating an accurate 3D model. At the top of the replaced texture the book seems to be curved a little bit, although it should be straight if compared with the input image (cf. Fig. 5a). In general the textures at the top do not match properly, but that is because of the inaccurate scan.

As mentioned before scanning should be done from only one position, but it is possible to change position during the diminishing process and still receive accurate textures although the angle has changed. Of course textures which are hidden during the scanning will not be there during the diminishing process. Changing positions is made possible thanks to the 3D model which can be rendered from different view points. Obviously this is also having limitations on giving good results, there are around 45° in each direction from the originally scanned position where the rendering of the transformed viewpoint works well. That means there are at least 90° overall where the object removal works good.

## 5.2   Comparison to Inpainting

In this section the results of the proposed method are compared to inpainting, providing the input image and the results of both methods. For this comparison the inpainting functionality of Affinity Photo is being used which is similar to the inpainting from Adobe Photoshop.

When both outputs of the images from the face detection are compared, inpainting is not able to reproduce the textures hidden by the face and a wrongly inpainted image is created (cf. Fig. 5c). The proposed method however is able to fill in the missing regions quite accurately (cf. Fig. 5b).

## 5.3   Case Study

The purpose of this case study was to find out if people recognize that there are two images stitched together in the diminished view. For someone who knows the application spotting some stuttering in the replaced region is easy although it is difficult to be seen. The research question was: Does someone who does not know what the app does notice the stuttering caused by minimal inaccuracies in the filled in region?

We captured a short video sequence (approx. one minute) using color detection and moving around the iPad. Minimal stuttering in the diminished view can be noticed. The video was shown to the participants telling them to mention everything they notice during the video immediately. 10 people participated, saw the video, and should mention it the second they saw something out of the ordinary.

When looking at the table (cf. Table 1) it is interesting that 5 people did not notice the filled in region at all, which means 50 % did not notice it. However from this group all are older than 46 years and 2 participants are in their mid 70s. To some extent not noticing any stuttering might be caused by visual perception, which worsenes when getting older [2]. Three people could spot the diminishing during the first 10 s of the video. Surprisingly one person was able to spot the stuttering after three seconds. It can be said that 70 % of the participants did

(a) Input image
(b) Proposed method

(c) Affinity Photo Inpainting
(d) Stuttering

**Fig. 5.** Comparing face detection to inpainting, and stuttering

not spot the diminishing in the first 40 s of watching the video. Between 37 to 40 s there is some stuttering in the video, which can be seen in the images (cf. Fig. 5d) but it is easier to notice when watching the video because it looks like something is moving. It is also noticeable that there is a trend that people with less visual acuity spot the difference faster than people with higher visual acuity. It must also be mentioned that most participants were really concentrated, showing higher attentiveness to small video artefacts than usual viewers might show.

In summary it can be said that it seems to be difficult to detect the stuttering artefacts when watching the video for the first time. However, highly concentrated and focused viewers can identify it to some extent.

During 3D scanning the app runs with 30 fps, when targets are removed the fps drop, depending on the target detection method used. For color detection, the performance is between 10 and 12 fps which is not completely smooth, but good enough to use the application to demonstrate this method. When using face detection, between 6 and 7 fps are possible. When comparing the application to

**Table 1.** Case study data

| Age | Sex | Visual acuity (in diopters) | Time to recognized (s) |
| --- | --- | --- | --- |
| 24 | Male | 0 | 10 |
| 27 | Male | 0.75 | 40 |
| 27 | Female | 0 | 6 |
| 39 | Female | 0 | 41 |
| 46 | Male | 6 | – |
| 49 | Male | 0.75 | 3 |
| 51 | Male | 0 | – |
| 52 | Female | 3.5 | – |
| 74 | Female | 3 | – |
| 77 | Male | 2.5 | – |

the one developed during the work of Hackl et al. [3], similar speed is achieved with this prototype.

The calculation of the 3D model takes around 0.5 to 3 s depending on how much was being scanned. This is very fast when comparing to the Lenovo Phab 2 Pro were the calculations took up to a minute, but this device is also 3 years older than the iPad.

## 6   Conclusion and Future Work

During this project a method was explored, which uses 3D scanning for diminished reality. Our application is able to remove target objects from live video feeds recorded on a mobile device by using a previously created 3D model of the environment to replace them. Diminished reality is a field where already some methods have been published over the last years, but no method so far has utilized 3D scanning. The proposed method delivers good results and compares favourably when compared to existing diminished reality methods, especially due to its 6 DoF for the mobile device, and the real time use case. Furthermore, the case study shows that the quality of the replaced image is very good and a difference between the real image and the diminished image is hard to spot.

Though our results are promising, there is still room for improvement regarding the application's performance. Currently all the image manipulations are calculated by the CPU which slows down the application a lot. If OpenCL would be available for iOS, parallelization could be used to make this application much faster. Maybe on other platforms it is easier to use the GPU. Although the performance is the biggest weakness of the prototype, the application can still be used to demonstrate this method.

The next step to improve this diminished reality method could be to use surface or pointcloud matching. Surface matching matches 3D data, e.g. depth data from the sensor and the 3D mesh. No more alignment would be needed, only the mask needs to be applied to the images. The tracking is not needed too, incoming depth data will be matched with the 3D mesh. Also storing the last position during the calculation will not be necessary. Surface matching would be hard to do if implemented with the Structure SDK because the pointclouds from the depth frames cannot be accessed easily. Some conversion methods would be needed in order to use surface matching algorithms. OpenCV for example provides a surface matching algorithm.

# References

1. OpenCV library. https://opencv.org/. Accessed 09 Jan 2019
2. Faubert, J., Dixon, P.E., Bennett, P.J.E.: Visual perception and aging. Can. J. Exp. Psychol./Rev. Can. Psychol. Exp. **56**(3), 164–176 (2002)
3. Hackl, A., Hlavacs, H.: Diminishing reality. In: International Conference on Entertainment Computing (IFIP ICEC 2018) (2018)
4. Hartley, R., Zisserman, A.: Multiple View Geometry in Computer Vision, 2nd edn. Cambridge University Press, Cambridge (2004)
5. Herling, J., Broll, W.: Advanced self-contained object removal for realizing real-time diminished reality in unconstrained environments. In: 2010 IEEE International Symposium on Mixed and Augmented Reality, pp. 207–212, October 2010
6. Kalantari, M., Nechifor, M.: Accuracy and utility of the structure sensor for collecting 3D indoor information. Geo-Spat. Inform. Sci. **19**(3), 202–209 (2016)
7. Kawai, N., Sato, T., Yokoya, N.: Diminished reality based on image inpainting considering background geometry. IEEE Trans. Vis. Comput. Graph. **22**(3), 1236–1247 (2016)
8. Kawai, N., Sato, T., Yokoya, N.: From image inpainting to diminished reality. In: Shumaker, R., Lackey, S. (eds.) VAMR 2014. LNCS, vol. 8525, pp. 363–374. Springer, Cham (2014). https://doi.org/10.1007/978-3-319-07458-0_34
9. Kersten, T.P., Przybilla, H.-J., Lindstaedt, M., Tschirschwitz, F., Misgaiski-Hass, M.: Comparative geometrical investigations of hand-held scanning systems. Int. Arch. Photogr. **01**, 507–514 (2016)
10. Mori, S., Ikeda, S., Saito, H.: A survey of diminished reality: techniques for visually concealing, eliminating, and seeing through real objects. IPSJ Trans. Comput. Vis. Appl. **9**(1), 1–14 (2017)
11. Queguiner, G., Fradet, M., Rouhani, M.: Towards mobile diminished reality. In: 2018 IEEE International Symposium on Mixed and Augmented Reality Adjunct (ISMAR-Adjunct), pp. 226–231 (2018)
12. Viola, P., Jones, M.: Rapid object detection using a boosted cascade of simple features. In: Proceedings of the 2001 IEEE Computer Society Conference on Computer Vision and Pattern Recognition, vol. 1, p. I (2001)
13. Wikipedia. Camera resectioning - Wikipedia. https://en.wikipedia.org/wiki/Camera_resectioning#Parameters_of_camera_model. Accessed 18 Jan 2019
14. Yagi, K., Hasegawa, K., Saito, H.: Diminished reality for privacy protection by hiding pedestrians in motion image sequences using structure from motion. In: 2017 IEEE International Symposium on Mixed and Augmented Reality, pp. 334–337, October 2017

# Measuring Preferences in Game Mechanics: Towards Personalized Chocolate-Covered Broccoli

Irene Camps-Ortueta[(✉)], Pedro A. González-Calero,
María Angeles Quiroga, and Pedro P. Gómez-Martín

Universidad Complutense de Madrid, Madrid, Spain
{icamps,pagoncal,maquirog,pedrop}@ucm.es

**Abstract.** When developing educational games we face the problem of finding the right design for making the learning activities as intrinsic to the game mechanics as possible. Nevertheless, in many cases it is not possible to fully integrate the learning content into the game play, resulting in the well known "chocolate-covered broccoli" game design.

The long term goal of the work presented here is to determine whether a personalized selection of game mechanics for the playful part, the game mechanics around the learning part of the game, can improve the satisfaction of the player and therefore make the whole learning experience more enjoyable. The first step towards that goal is to obtain a model for the preferences of game mechanics for a particular type of game, and later use that model to guide the selection of game mechanics.

In this paper, we present *Enigma MNCN* a treasure hunt for mobile devices designed for the National Museum of Natural Sciences of Spain and some experimental results intended to identify preferences for game mechanics in that type of game across demographic variables. The main finding of these experiments is that preferences in game mechanics get shadowed when combined with a mostly disliked learning mechanic.

**Keywords:** Serious games · Informal learning · Games in museums · Games for education · Augmented Reality

## 1 Introduction

The current challenge for museums is how to successfully turn their institutional knowledge and authority into meaningful, engaging experiences by leveraging the appropriate technological media in the context of their physical settings, and for heterogeneous audiences [10]. In order to solve this problem, a growing number of initiatives integrating serious games, gamification, augmented reality and virtual reality through mobile devices have appeared in the last years [6,9].

In this paper we present results from a project that intends to promote informal learning in a natural history museum through a treasure hunt type of game.

© IFIP International Federation for Information Processing 2019
Published by Springer Nature Switzerland AG 2019
E. van der Spek et al. (Eds.): ICEC-JCSG 2019, LNCS 11863, pp. 15–27, 2019.
https://doi.org/10.1007/978-3-030-34644-7_2

The game incorporates image recognition, mini-games, 3D virtual reconstructions and augmented reality elements, being part of a growing number of initiatives that seek to exploit the use of augmented reality and related technologies in informal science learning sites [4].

As designers of educational games we face the problem of designing just a new version of the well known "chocolate-covered broccoli", a term first introduced by Amy Bruckman in a presentation at the Developers Game Conference in 1999 [1]. Actually, she used the term "dipped-covered broccoli" for an approach used when combining learning content with gameplay where the gaming element of the product is used as a separate reward or sugar-coating for completing the educational content. This is an intrinsic problem of educational games. Although digital games may be capable of providing activities which are intrinsically motivating in their own right, it is critical to consider the effect of adding learning content to an intrinsically motivating game [5].

Ideally the learning goals in an educational game should be attained through activities that are intrinsic to the game play. For certain subjects or learning goals the use of intrinsic game mechanics with learning purposes can be straightforward, for example when the game serves as some kind of simulator of the target content. On the other hand, some types of learning content are very hard to turn into game mechanics, such as factual knowledge, as the one we want to include in our game for a Natural History museum. Therefore, either we accept that games are just adequate for certain types of learning content or we accept some broccoli in our game recipes.

*Enigma MNCN* is a treasure hunt for mobile devices designed for the National Museum of Natural Sciences (referred to by its Spanish acronym MNCN) in Madrid, one of the oldest museums of Natural History in Europe and the most important in Spain. This is the second game in the Enigma saga[1], after *Enigma Galdiano* released in 2016 and designed to be played at the Lázaro Galdiano Museum in Madrid [2].

*Enigma MNCN*, described in more detail in Sect. 2, is designed for kids from 8 to 12 years old. The kid plays as a Paleontologist apprentice who has to find some objects in the collection and solve some puzzles and quizzes along the way. The learning content in the game is provided through a field notebook with images and textual information about pieces in the museum, which pages are revealed as goals in the game are fulfilled. In order to make the reading of the field notebook more intrinsic to the game, we include quizzes which answer is included in one of the pages of the notebook, usually the last one that was revealed.

*Enigma MNCN* includes a number of mini-games and treasure hunt mechanics, the *chocolate*, in order to cover a reading task, the *broccoli*. The long term goal of the work presented here is to determine whether a personalized version of the playful part, the game mechanics around the learning part of the game, can improve the satisfaction of the player and therefore make the whole learning experience more enjoyable. Keeping up with the metaphor, we want to deter-

---

[1] http://www.padaonegames.com/enigma/.

mine whether a personalized chocolate recipe can make the chocolate-covered broccoli taste better. The first step towards that goal is to obtain a model for the preferences of game mechanics for this particular type of game, so that we can later use that model to guide the selection of game mechanics.

In this paper we present the different game mechanics included in *Enigma MNCN* and the results of several experiments trying to determine the preferences for those game mechanics among kids from 8 to 12, based on age and gender. We run experiments with two different versions of the game, the full version including the learning component (field notebook), and a reduced one without the learning component, in order to measure the variability in preferences for game mechanics in a treasure hunt game versus an educational version of the game. The main finding of these initial experiments is that preferences in game mechanics get shadowed when combined with a mostly disliked learning mechanic. We can detect significant differences in preferences for game mechanics when evaluating those preferences in the purely playful version of the game, but those differences get blurred when measured in the educational version, with broccoli (i.e., reading tasks) added in.

The rest of the paper runs as follows. Next Section describes the game mechanics in *Enigma MNCN*. Section 3 details the experimental set-up along with the results from the experiments and our conclusions about those results. Finally, Sect. 4 presents related work and concludes the paper.

## 2    Enigma MNCN

*Enigma MNCN* is a treasure hunt for mobile devices designed to be played at the National Museum of Natural Sciences of Spain, in Madrid. The players, kids between 8 and 12 years, are committed to become the new assistant of Dr. Anning, one of the paleontologist in the museum, helped by two of her current assistants: Pérez and Neand. The three of them, depicted in Fig. 1 will alternatively propose new challenges that will let the kid to demonstrate her merits to join the team. The theme of the exposition where the game is played is the evolution of life on Earth, from the first micro-organisms to Homo Sapiens, through a collection of fossils, skeletons, reconstructions and illustrations that recreate the life on Earth at different points in time.

The core game mechanic in Enigma uses the camera of a mobile device to recognize an object in the museum (we use Vuforia$^{TM}$ and Unity 3D$^{TM}$ as underlying technology). The object to be found is indicated to the player with its scientific name, such as *Brachiopoda Strophonema*, *Calamopora Spongites* or *Ammonitida Ammonitina Perisphinctidae*. We want the kids to pay attention to the signs in the exposition and make sense of the organization of the objects, where, for example, every fossil from the *Ammonitida* family is in the same showcase. Once the name of the object to be found has been read, the mobile turns into "search mode" becoming the "Paleo lens" in the game, as depicted in Fig. 2.

In some search tasks of the game just one object has to be found while in others we provide up to three different names of objects that have to be found

**Fig. 1.** Enigma MNCN characters

in any order. Depending on the complexity of the search we can also provide a hollow silhouette of the target object in order to facilitate its identification. Since the player will typically forget the exact name of the object, she can ask Pérez, our friendly sloth, to remind her the name (see the sloth in the right bottom of Fig. 2).

As an additional clue, we can also provide the time depicted in the showcase of the object to be found. The exposition uses the well known metaphor of mapping the history of Earth into 24 h, so for example first fossils appear at 5:36 am and humans at 11:58 pm. Once the camera is pointing at the target object, it will be recognized and the task will have been fulfilled. We do not used QR codes but the actual objects in the collection. Since kids are usually unfamiliar with this technology, the game begins with a tutorial explaining: how the Paleo lens can be used to recognize objects in the museum; that you can ask Pérez to remind you the name of the object; and that it is possible to give up and quit a search if you can not make the Paleo lens to see it (kids almost never give up in their searches).

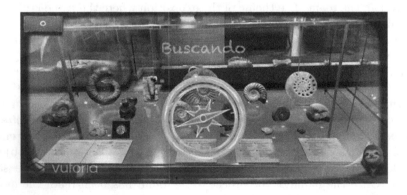

**Fig. 2.** Paleo lens while searching

In addition to the Paleo lens searches we have 4 different types of mini-games in *Enigma MNCN*: Packaging, Skeletons, AR Hunt and Magic Fields. Every mini-game comes after a Paleo lens search and usually relates somehow to the object just found. This serve to give some context for the mini-game, since we know where is the kid in the museum and we can use in the mini-game those elements in front of her.

*Packaging*, Fig. 3 left, is a puzzle game where the kid has to put all the pieces appearing to the right of the box, inside of the box. Following the narrative of the game, the kid is helping the museum by packaging some fossils that need to be sent to another museum. The fossils in the mini-game are similar to those in the showcase in front of the kid.

*Skeletons*, as *Packaging*, also require visual-spatial skills to be solved. As shown in Fig. 3 right, a partial skeleton is provided on the left with some missing bones on the right. The goal is to place the bones at the right positions. To provide and contextualize the task, the game has taken the kid in front of that same skeleton in the museum (a *Deinotherium* in the example of Fig. 3), so that she can look at the original to get inspiration.

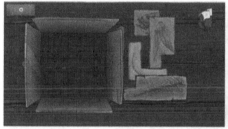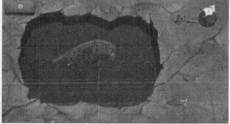

**Fig. 3.** Packaging and skeletons

*Magic fields* are 3D reconstructions of prehistoric life. The Museum already displays large panels with illustrations of prehistoric life (an example is depicted in Fig. 4 left). A *magic field* is a 3D scene that is loaded after a search task that has led the player in front of the illustration panel, making that illustration come alive. The goal in the mini-game is to move around the 3D scene, through the gyroscope of the mobile device, and find a particular prehistoric animal, which usually corresponds to an skeleton we have seen before in the game.

*AR hunts* use augmented reality technology to insert an image of a prehistoric animal into one of the illustration panels of the museum, as shown in Fig. 4 left where a *Meganeura*, an extinct insect from the Carboniferous period, is moving around the illustration as seen through the camera of the device. The goal is to capture the moving animal by tapping it.

For the educational version of the game we add two more elements: the field notebook and the quizzes.

**Fig. 4.** AR hunt and magic field

The field notebook plays the role of the notebook of Dr Anning, where the paleontologist is writing down some of the main facts about the pieces she find, which are actually the ones that we found in the game. After every search, one more page, as the one showed in Fig. 5 left, is added to the initially empty notebook. In order to motivate the kids to read the contents of the notebook we include a new game mechanic: the quizzes.

The quizzes, as the one showed in Fig. 5 right, are multiple choice questions with a humorous tone where there is only one right answer. There is time limit to answer the question of 30 s, but the kid can stop the timer by opening the field notebook and reading it. Every time, the right answer to the quiz is provided in the notebook.

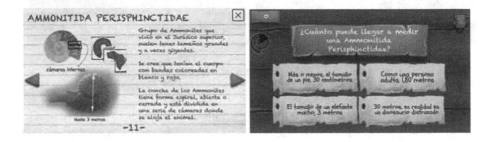

**Fig. 5.** Field notebook and quiz

The first version of the game used for the experiments consists of 8 stages, where each stage includes a search or multi-search and a mini-game, roughly including two mini-games of each type. In average it takes between 20 and 25 min to complete this version of the game. The educational version includes, in addition, 4 quizzes, every 2 or 3 stages, and adds between 7 and 8 more minutes to the gameplay time.

# 3  Experiments and Results

## 3.1  Experimental Set-Up

The experiments are run in the museum, when it is closed to the general public. In every run of the experiment we have a group of between 10 and 14 kids playing the game individually, using the same type of device, a Lenovo$^{TM}$ TAB3 10 Plus, provided by the museum. The choice of the size of the group seeks to find a balance between the effort to run the experiments and the bias from having more people playing the game at the same time. Imagine that if you see five kids pointing their devices at the same point then maybe you should be pointing there too. In our experience, the variability in the time that the kids need to find the first objects alleviates this bias, and they quickly distribute among the different searches.

In the game we collect metrics obtained during game play, including data such as the time spent in every task, whether the task is successful or not, and how many times did the player make use of the help. Although the game is implemented in Unity 3D which offer some functionality for metrics collection, we have developed our own system that collects the metrics of interest and send them, at the end of every task in the game, as JSON files to a server where they are made persistent. The opinion of the kids about the game play mechanics are collected at the end of the game, and also made persistent as metrics in the server for later analysis.

For the experiments described in this paper, satisfaction is our main variable. We collect satisfaction data through a questionnaire integrated at the end of the game. On the questionnaire there is a question for every mechanic included in the game, with an image from the game to remind the kid what mechanic is she being asked for (see Fig. 6). Answers are given by selecting among a smiley, a neutral or a sad face, to make it more appealing for kids. Since most of the answers were smiley faces, we decided to dichotomize the answers into "positive" (smiley face) and "negative" (sad or neutral face), in order to increase the power in our analysis.

**Fig. 6.** Satisfaction questionnaire

We ran two sets of experiments. The first one with the treasure hunt game without learning mechanics (quizzes and field notebook), and the second one with the full version of the educational game.

## 3.2   First Experiment: Treasure Hunt game

The sample of the first experiment consisted of 30 subjects with an average age of 9.4 years (SD = 0,56; 17 subjects of 9 years and 13 of 10 years). Of the 30 subjects, 14 were boys and 16 girls. We consider it a specially homogeneous sample since they all attended fourth grade at the same school. Due to the small size of the sample on this experiment, we decided to run only non-parametric analysis.

Average satisfaction was above 80%, an encouraging result for the game, but our main goal was to determine whether we can detect differences in preferences for the different mechanics. For this purpose we have analyzed differences in preferences based on gender, Fig. 7, and age, Fig. 8.

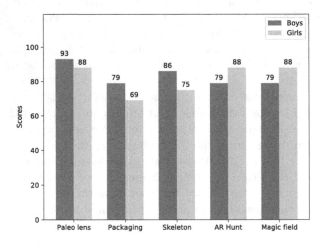

**Fig. 7.** First experiment: differences by gender

Although results are not statistically significant (p values higher than .05 for each chi square analysis run), we can observe that boys have a larger preference than girls for the Paleo lens, packaging and skeletons mechanics, while girls tend to prefer AR hunt and magic fields. Considering the type of activities in the game mechanics we can conclude that boys prefer instrumental activities, focused on action, while girls tend to prefer expressive activities, focused on aesthetics and emotion. It is interesting to see this tendency, usually observed in adults [11], to appear in young kids.

Regarding age, even with such a little age difference, we can observe some differences between 9 and 10 year old kids, as shown in Fig. 8 right. Again not

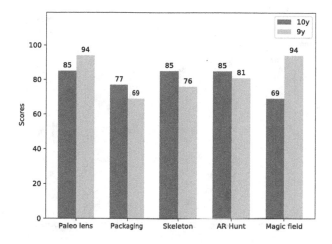

**Fig. 8.** First experiment: differences by age

statistically significant results point in the direction that 9 year old kids find more enjoyable less complex mechanics, such as Paleo lens and magic fields, while 10 year old kids tend to prefer skeletons or packaging that require a more complex problem solving abilities.

These initial results make us think in the possibility of finding some correlation between game mechanics preferences and demographic data such as age and gender.

### 3.3  Second Experiment: Educational Treasure hunt

A total of 213 children participated in the second experiment. A part of them did not finish the game ($N = 28$, which is 13%), and from the remaining 185 an additional 20% ($N = 36$) were outside of the established age range. Therefore, the results refer to a sample of 149 subjects, in the age range from 8 to 12 ($M = 9.60$, $SD = 1.17$). Of these 73 were boys and 76 were girls.

Average satisfaction is again above 80%, as shown in Fig. 9, except for the additional learning mechanic: quizzes. Regarding differences based on gender we can observe in Fig. 10 that differences are at most of 3% points, or 4 in the case of quizzes, what does not introduce any significant difference.

Higher variability can be observed when considering age differences, as shown in Fig. 11. Nevertheless, again the differences are not statistically significant, as shown by the results of Pearson's chi-squared test ($\chi^2$) in Table 1.

Our hypothesis is that although differences in preferences for game mechanics can be observed just by considering demographics data as study 1 shows, such differences mostly disappear when adding a mechanic that has a much lower acceptance value, and therefore make the rest of mechanics equally acceptable in comparison.

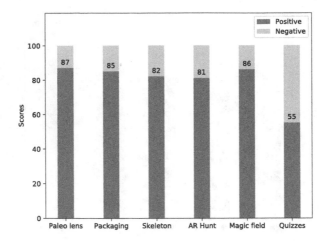

**Fig. 9.** Satisfaction by game mechanic

**Table 1.** Pearson's chi-squared test ($\chi^2$) on age differences

|             | 8y  |     | 9y  |     | 10y |     | 11–12y |     | $\chi^2$ | p   |
|-------------|-----|-----|-----|-----|-----|-----|--------|-----|----------|-----|
|             | Pos | Neg | Pos | Neg | Pos | Neg | Pos    | Neg |          |     |
| Paleo lens  | 10  | 3   | 33  | 2   | 43  | 9   | 23     | 2   | 4.26     | .23 |
| Packaging   | 11  | 2   | 29  | 6   | 45  | 7   | 21     | 4   | 0.24     | .97 |
| Skeleton    | 9   | 4   | 31  | 4   | 43  | 9   | 21     | 4   | 2.56     | .46 |
| AR Hunt     | 10  | 3   | 31  | 4   | 41  | 11  | 20     | 5   | 1.63     | .65 |
| Magic field | 10  | 3   | 31  | 3   | 44  | 8   | 23     | 2   | 2.52     | .47 |
| Quizzes     | 4   | 9   | 20  | 15  | 29  | 23  | 16     | 9   | 3.98     | .26 |

## 4  Related Work and Conclusions

Research on personalized content for serious games is a growing area of interest. Once it has been accepted that digital games are an appropriate instrument for applications beyond pure entertainment, in training and communication, the question of how to personalize serious games is being raised to increase their effectiveness. In this sense, we find works that show that the effectiveness of serious games improves with personalization in adults, and others that advance in the definition of instruments to facilitate such customization.

In [7] some initial results are provided showing the importance of tailoring games for change in the context of a game designed to improve healthy eating habits. Tailoring the game design to players' personality type improved the effectiveness of the game, as was later shown in [8] with a large-scale study of more than 500 participants where their results reveal that people's gamification user types play significant roles in the perceived persuasiveness of different strategies in serious games.

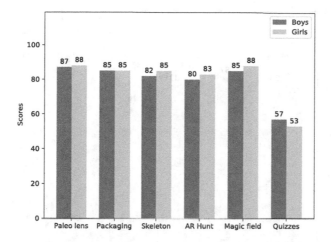

**Fig. 10.** Second experiment: differences by gender

Regarding related work on instruments designed to facilitate the construc-
tions of customized games, in [13] a conceptual framework of player preferences
based on game elements and game playing styles is presented. Such framework
can be used by designers to create games that are tailored to their target audience. Applying these ideas to serious games, [12] presents a general framework
for personalized gameful applications using recommender systems, by describing the different building blocks of a recommender system (users, items, and
transactions) in a personalized gamification context.

In this paper we have presented some initial results of experiments conducted
in order to determine whether a model for game mechanics preferences can be
found for an specific type of games: treasure hunts in museums with educational
purposes for children. We have experimentally analyzed differences in preferences
based on demographics, which are easier to measure than other potentially more
informative differences such as temperament or cognitive capacities that we plan
to measure in the future. Accepting that in some situations it is not possible to
find an intrinsic game mechanic that serve the learning purposes of an educational game, our goal is to find if by tailoring the selection of accompanying
game mechanics we can improve the whole educational experience.

For this purpose, we first ran a set of experiments with a non educational
version of the game, and obtained initial values of variability in preferences
along age and gender axes. Although not statistically significant, we found some
indication of the existence of a preference model.

In a second run of experiments, with a larger population, we measured again
preferences for game mechanics, but using the full educational version of the
game. In this case differences in preference for game mechanics were hardly
measurable, invalidating our initial results.

Our hypothesis is that although differences in preferences for game mechanics
can be observed just by considering demographics data, such differences mostly
disappear when adding a mechanic that has a much lower acceptance value,

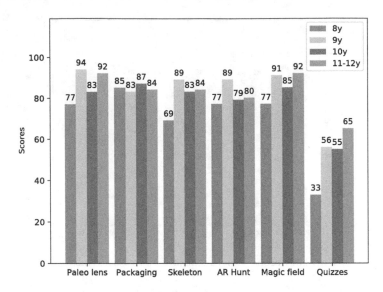

**Fig. 11.** Second experiment: differences by age

and therefore make the rest of mechanics equally acceptable in comparison. This effect resembles the "contrast effect" from Psychology, or the "contrast principle" as defined by [3]. We need to collect additional data in order to test this hypothesis, and we will do in future work.

Also as future work, we want to measure the effect of the time spent with the educational content, in our case reading the field notebook in the game, both in terms of the quality of the answers for the quizzes in the game, and for the general satisfaction of the player. It would be a positive result if we could demonstrate that making use of the educational content in the game promotes learning, and does not decrease the quality of the playful experience.

**Acknowledgments.** We are very grateful to the personnel at the National Museum of Natural Sciences in Madrid for their support and assistance in designing and evaluating *Enigma Ciencia*, in particular to Luis Barrera and Pilar López. We also thank the anonymous reviewers for their insightful comments and suggestions.

This work is partly supported by the Spanish Ministry of Economy, Industry and Competitiveness (TIN2017-87330-R and DI-16-08520).

# References

1. Bruckman, A.: Can educational be fun? In: presented at the Game Developers Conference 1999, San Jose, CA (1999). http://www.cc.gatech.edu/~asb/papers/bruckman-gdc99.pdf
2. Camps-Ortueta, I., Rodríguez-Muñoz, J.M., Gómez-Martín, P.P., González-Calero, P.A.: Combining augmented reality with real maps to promote social interaction in treasure hunts. In: CoSECivi. CEUR Workshop Proceedings, vol. 1957, pp. 131–143. CEUR-WS.org (2017)

3. Cialdini, R.B.: Influence: The Psychology of Persuasion. Revised Edition. Harper Business (2006)
4. Goff, E.E., Mulvey, K.L., Irvin, M.J., Hartstone-Rose, A.: Applications of augmented reality in informal science learning sites: a review. J. Sci. Educ. Technol. **27**(5), 433–447 (2018). https://doi.org/10.1007/s10956-018-9734-4
5. Habgood, J., Ainsworth, S.: Motivating children to learn effectively: exploring the value of intrinsic integration in educational games. J. Learn. Sci. **20**, 169–206 (2011). https://doi.org/10.1080/10508406.2010.508029
6. Koutsabasis, P.: Empirical evaluations of interactive systems in cultural heritage: a review. Int. J. Comput. Methods Herit. Sci. **1**(1), 100–122 (2017)
7. Orji, R., Mandryk, R.L., Vassileva, J.: Improving the efficacy of games for change using personalization models. ACM Trans. Comput.-Hum. Interact. **24**(5), 32:1–32:22 (2017). https://doi.org/10.1145/3119929
8. Orji, R., Tondello, G.F., Nacke, L.E.: Personalizing persuasive strategies in gameful systems to gamification user types. In: Mandryk, R.L., Hancock, M., Perry, M., Cox, A.L. (eds.) Proceedings of the 2018 CHI Conference on Human Factors in Computing Systems, CHI 2018, Montreal, QC, Canada, 21–26 April 2018, p. 435. ACM (2018). https://doi.org/10.1145/3173574.3174009
9. Paliokas, I., Sylaiou, S.: The use of serious games in museum visits and exhibitions: a systematic mapping study. In: 8th International Conference on Games and Virtual Worlds for Serious Applications, VS-Games (2016)
10. Roussou, M., Pujol, L., Akrivi, K., Angelik, C., Sara, P., Vayanou, M.: The museum as digital storyteller: collaborative participatory creation of interactive digital experiences. In: MW2015: Museums and the Web (2015)
11. Sonja, S., Rigotti, T.: Instrumentality and expressiveness at work. Organisation-spsychologie **3**, 111–124 (2014)
12. Tondello, G.F., Orji, R., Nacke, L.E.: Recommender systems for personalized gamification. In: Bieliková, M., Herder, E., Cena, F., Desmarais, M.C. (eds.) Adjunct Publication of the 25th Conference on User Modeling, Adaptation and Personalization, UMAP 2017, Bratislava, Slovakia, 09–12 July 2017, pp. 425–430. ACM (2017). https://doi.org/10.1145/3099023.3099114
13. Tondello, G.F., Wehbe, R.R., Orji, R., Ribeiro, G., Nacke, L.E.: A framework and taxonomy of videogame playing preferences. In: Schouten, B.A.M., Markopoulos, P., Toups, Z.O., Cairns, P.A., Bekker, T. (eds.) Proceedings of the Annual Symposium on Computer-Human Interaction in Play, CHI PLAY 2017, Amsterdam, The Netherlands, 15–18 October 2017, pp. 329–340. ACM (2017). https://doi.org/10.1145/3116595.3116629

# Augmented Reality Museum's Gaming for Digital Natives: Haunted Encounters in the Carvalhal's Palace

Valentina Nisi[1](✉), Vanessa Cesario[2], and Nuno Nunes[3]

[1] ITI/LARSyS, U. Madeira. Campus da Penteada, 9020-105 Funchal, Portugal
Valentina.nisi@gmail.com
[2] ITI/LARSyS, U. Nova Lisboa, Campus da Penteada,
9020-105 Funchal, Portugal
vanessa.cesario@m-iti.org
[3] ITI/LARSyS, IST - U. Lisbon, Avenida Rovisto Pais,
1049-001 Lisbon, Portugal
nunojnunes@tecnico.ulisboa.pt

**Abstract.** *Memories of Carvalhal's Palace – Haunted Encounters* is an Augmented Reality (AR) location-based game which involves players in uncovering the mystery behind the haunted aspects of a museum premises. The game deployed at the Natural History Museum of Funchal makes use of mobile interactive AR and gaming strategies to promote the engagement of teenage visitors (digital natives) in museum experiences. Through this game, the audience embarks in a journey through the museum spaces, collecting scientific information about selected exhibits, while interacting with their tridimensional (3D) AR models. The audience's interactions with the museum exhibits are rewarded with pieces of a map, which will guide them to a hidden location, the scientific library of the museum. There participants can finally unlock the mysteries they have been summoned to solve. The game's goal stems from the fact that digital native teenagers are identified as an audience group that is often excluded from a museum's curatorial strategies [1] and as consequence, they appears to be generally disinterested in what museums might offer [2]. In this article, we present the description and rational behind *Memories of Carvalhal's Palace: Haunted Encounters* mobile gaming application and then discuss the results of first empirical tests performed to evaluate the usefulness and usability of the game.

**Keywords:** Museums and cultural heritage · Digital natives · Gaming · Augmented Reality · Interactive storytelling

## 1 Introduction

As museums move away from being places where exhibits are collected and displayed, they become spaces where people can actively engage in personalized discoveries and challenges [3]. Traditionally, support for museum visits was limited to audio guides and interactive kiosks. However, the fast and wide uptake of interactive and mobile

© IFIP International Federation for Information Processing 2019
Published by Springer Nature Switzerland AG 2019
E. van der Spek et al. (Eds.): ICEC-JCSG 2019, LNCS 11863, pp. 28–41, 2019.
https://doi.org/10.1007/978-3-030-34644-7_3

technologies is making audiences more eager to engage in active experiences. Museums are trying to keep up this challenge and enhancing their context to provide more engaging opportunities to interact with the exhibits secured behind glass shelves [4]. Many studies underline the importance of providing museums with improved user experiences both at individual and cooperative levels [5]. Games and narrative elements are proven to ameliorate engagement, motivation and learning within edutainment environments [6]. Moreover, Falk reports on museums experiences that "one size does not fits all" [7], in particular when addressing the "digital natives" generation (currently 15–19 years old), whose beliefs and behaviors are quite different from their previous generations [8]. While museums often offer guided tours for children and adults, very little is designed for the digital natives [1].

Here we present *Memories of Carvalhal's Palace – Haunted Encounters (MoCP-HE)*, a location-based game which involves players in uncovering factual and fictional elements of a museum premises and collection. We designed *MoCP-HE* as treasure hunt experience which makes use of AR in order to engage digital native teenagers in pursuing scientific knowledge about the museum exhibits. The goal of this project is to use gaming and narrative elements to influence our target group engagement with the museum content. The experience is currently being studied in order to understand teenage dynamics and preferences in museums providing a way to analyze the complex relationship between context of use, technological solutions, engagement and learning effectiveness. In the rest of this paper we first discuss related work, including museums related location-based games and stories. Then we describe the game mechanics and technological platforms used in *Memories of Carvalhal's Palace: Haunted Encounters*. Lastly, we report on some first preliminary user testing carried out with young gamers and users and provide some concluding remarks and indications for future work.

**Fig. 1.** The opening screen of the *Memories of Carvalhal's Palace game (right side)* and a screenshot of the two main characters that call the player for action *(left side)*

# 2  State of the Art

## 2.1  Mobile and Context Aware Guides for Cultural Heritage

The evolution of smartphones and tablets with technologies like GPS, gyroscopes, accelerometers and AR enables the development of a new generation of games with great potential to be applied in location-based experiences [9]. For instance, gamified tour experiences can be tailored to visitors by calculating their position and orientations. Referred to Long et al. [10], as the position-aware handheld intelligent tour, these mobile apps are capable of orienting visitors around public spaces and provide them with custom-fit information [10]. Support and gamified elements of the tour can be accomplished and delivered by interpreting the user behaviour; physical movement within the space and how they interact with the object or artefact of an exhibit, a monument, or another element of interest [11]. The user's information combined with HCI concepts and location-aware systems can augment the engagement of the user, support their everyday activity and gain more effectiveness in the mobile delivery of information (links, audio messages, images, videos, 3D models) [11]. Exploration and enhancement of environments with 3D and 360VR modelling, allow the exploration of reconstructions of public spaces. Examples include, Mehringplatz neighbourhood in Berlin [12] or the convent of São Francisco in Funchal [13] helping not only in the narrative of the stories but also facilitating acquisition of knowledge in regards to the physical space. In addition, many experiences are designed to work using different platforms that complement the participant interaction within the physical space, making connections between displays, context-aware, storytelling, and historical events [9]. Recently several research projects developed around context-aware experiences and personalising edutainment in cultural heritage grounds. Personal Experiences with Active Cultural Heritage (PEACH), aims at developing educational and entertaining experiences (edutainment) tailored to the user background, needs and interest of the audience [14]. Immersive experiences like 360° Mobile Reality (MVR) are more accessible thanks to the devices affordance and advancement in mobile technology. The rapid growth of these technologies creates new research and design opportunities widely desirable and enjoyable by a wide range of users [14]. Nevertheless, in order to be widely adopted in public settings we need to overcome several design and technical challenges [13]. As a consequence several guidelines for the development of interactive context-aware systems in physical spaces, especially, those devoted to tourism and cultural heritage have been identified: (1) flexibility to enable visitors to explore and learn in their own way, controlling their own pace; (2) content-aware information tailor to their context (personal and environmental); (3) Support for dynamic information – aware of changes in venues, times, menus, opening and closing hours of events, need always to be updated; and (4) Remote access to interactive (online) services [15].

## 2.2    Serious Games in the Cultural Sector

Several projects in the area of serious games in the cultural sector are supported by museums. Examples include, Yong's China *Quest Adventure* [16]; *The China Game* [17] about Chinese traditions; *Fascinating Egyptian Mummies* about the spiritual beliefs of the ancient Egyptians; *The Great Bible Race* [18] dealing with the religious roots of the Western civilization; and, the *Mosaica project* [19] developed a Jewish heritage game. In the past few decades, a variety of game-based applications were designed for different media platforms and visitor types [20]. Those games are frequently entailed with the goal of using mobile devices to guide families' explorations through solving mystery and treasure hunting [21, 22].

Cabrera and colleagues [21] built an interactive museum guide called *Mystery in the Museum*, deployed at historical/cultural museums, which allowed students to play and perform tasks related to certain artifacts while stimulating their imagination. The game mechanics involves exhibits related puzzles such as scrambled images of specific exhibits and verses from manuscripts of the museum. The study revealed that some of the users (13–19 years old teenagers) lost interest in the interactive guide due to the complexity of the tasks, while others switched the focus from the displayed artifacts to the handheld computers.

*Ghost Detector* [23] is a story-driven location-based museum game for children. In this game, ghosts of various museum artefacts appear on the screen of the visitors' mobile device and challenges them to find the artefacts that the ghosts are representing. While evaluating this game, children were observed running through the corridors, paying attention to the feedback on the smartphone as well as the artefacts surrounding them. This study highlights how the introduction of the ubiquitous game undoubtedly influenced that level of excitement and engagement with the museum premises.

*Intrigue at the museum* [24] is a plot-driven mobile game for children structured around exploration and tasks performance. It is a single-player game, and its plot invites visitors to search for a thief in the museum among a set of virtual characters. Clues are given to the players and as they solve riddles after scanning tags deployed in the building. Following a constructivist approach, the game allows children to explore the museum environment freely, according to their interests and agenda. Moreover, AR gaming and storytelling and cultural sector experiments are proliferous and date back to the beginning of the new millennia [25, 26] [ref]. From the related work reported, location-based mobile games seem to represent a relevant learning tool and offer potential for further research and improvements.

## 2.3    Gaming as a Strategy to Involve Teens in Museum Experiences

While gaming and narrative as strategies to engage young audiences has been extensively studied, the particular application of these techniques to engage teenage public in museum is somehow still in development. Teenagers and participatory design within museum studies are covered by some papers in the Interaction Design Children

(IDC) Community. For instance, the study *Digital Natives* [27] where teens (currently 15–19 years old) collaborated with designers, programmers, anthropologists and museum curators to create four digital installations for an exhibition. The case study *Gaming the Museum* [28] is another example that started from everyday practices where children's (14–15 years old) everyday engagement was strong and thus computers games and online communities were chosen to start a process of creating a game for a museum.

According to formal studies about teenage preferences regarding museum engagement, Cesário et al. [29, 30] identified that mobile experience for museum's teenage audiences should first and foremost include (1) Gaming and storytelling aspects, secondarily teens look for (2) Interaction elements, (3) and Social media connections and last but not least (4) Museum and exhibits relevant information. Based on these findings and in accordance with the museum goals, the authors in collaboration with a team of creatives and developers, designed Memories *of Carvalhal's Palace – Haunted Encounters,* an interactive mobile game experience, engaging teens in solving a mystery thorough exploring the museum and its embalmed species collection.

## 3   The Mobile Game Experience

The *Memories of Carvalhal's Palace – Haunted Encounters* is a location-specific non-linear game deployed at the Natural History Museum of Funchal (NHMF). The museum was once the residence of a noble Madeiran family, the Carvalhal's, before being donated to the city municipality in order to be transformed into a museum. The game builds on the historical backstory of the building enhanced by the embalmed species. The game suggests the premises are haunted by mysterious forces which are disturbing the status quo. At the beginning of the game, two characters ask the player to help them solve the mystery behind the upsetting circumstances in which the museum verses (Fig. 3). Through a game of shadows, the audience is challenged to find and interact with the exhibits displaced around the museum as they match the shadow presented to them on the screen (Fig. 2). By finding the correct animal, the players unlock an AR 3D model of it (Fig. 4, left side) and are prompted with a multiple answers quiz style question that require them to closely check the species in display. As the players progress in their quest, they are rewarded with pieces of a map that will lead them to find the hidden scientific library of the museum. There they are encouraged to look for a treasure chest. inside which they will find the final answers to satisfy their pleading senders (Fig. 5).

**Fig. 2.** One of the 12 Rune marker *(right side of the figure)* used to unlock the 3D model of the Butterfly. Each Rune is related to a different exhibit. This specific rune is related to the Butterfly, as it signifies "change". Screenshot of the game of shadows interface *(left side of the figure)*.

### 3.1  Game Mechanics

The game unfolds encompassing a series of game mechanics which are described below in details.

- *Call for action.* Upon launching the app (Fig. 1), two fictional characters – Meara and Isabel – ask the user for help (Fig. 1). Two different museum tours and game endings are delivered, depending on which character the players chooses to help. Meara leads the player to explore the marine species collected the museum, while Isabel steers them to get to know the terrestrial fauna. One character will lead the audience to discover a ghost, who has been haunting the museum for almost a century, while the other will haunt the players herself with a malignant turn of events.

- *Game of shadows.* For the player to uncover the truth about the haunting of the museum he/she needs to interact with the species in display on the glass shelves. The players engage in a game of shadows (Fig. 2), where they have to match museum exhibits with the silhouettes proposed by the application, one at the time. By identifying the correct species from its shadow, the players gain some scientific knowledge about the animal and an Augmented Reality (AR) three-dimensional (3D) model of it, which they can manipulate and examine in detail as if it was outside the protected shelves (Fig. 4, left side). In order to identify the correct species for each shadow the game offers a tip that are available clicking on a help button, on the top right corner of the device. As the players answer quizzes and learn about the marine and terrestrial fauna of the archipelago, the audience is rewarded with pieces of a map for each carried out interaction. Once completed the map will finally disclose where they can find the answer to the mystery they have been engaged to solve.

- *Markers and Augmented Reality Artifacts*. Not all the species in display are part of the game. Twelve special markers (six per different characters journey) have been designed in the shape of Runes (ancient Nordic divining alphabet) to contradistinguish the species that are part of the game. When the user finds the animal that he/she recons corresponding to the shadow displayed on the app, he/she can capture the Rune shaped marker (Fig. 2). If the exhibit is the correct one, the user is rewarded with several scientific facts and curiosities about that animal, and a 3D model of it.

- *The AR 3D model artifact – freeing species from the shelves*. Once the 3D model is triggered, the audience can manipulate it through an AR interface and explore it in details from all its sides by rotating it in all directions, zooming in into its features, complementing the knowledge gained from the observing the exemplar in the glass shelves with the curiosity generated by manipulating the AR 3D model.

- *Quiz*. After capturing the marker and the corresponding AR 3D model, the app asks the audience to answer a quiz related to the taxidermied animal, exhibited in the shelves. The quiz questions are designed to prompt the viewer to look closely at the exhibited species as the quiz is related to some physical details of the animal. After answering the question, either rightly or wrongly, the audience is presented with a text reporting on several additional scientific facts about the animal.

- *The puzzle and the treasure hunt mechanism*. For every completed interaction, from finding the silhouette corresponding animal, to receiving the scientific information, the audience is rewarded with a piece of a puzzle, representing a map. Once completed, the map will guide the players to a hidden location, the scientific library of the museum. In the library, the audience is encouraged to look for a small chest, containing the answer to their search for the truth. The chest is a small wooden box hidden among the scientific publications of the library. Opening the chest, reveals a last Rune, which will lead them to two different ending, depending which character they decided to help in the beginning.

- *Conclusion: exposing the haunting*. When the user finds the treasure box and captures the last marker, the game is completed. If they had been helping Meara, they will uncover the presence of a restless ghost, once landlord of the place, haunting the museum premises (Fig. 5). If, on the other hand, the players were helping Isabel, they will be met by the evil ghost of Isabel herself (Fig. 5). She will deny them any satisfaction, take all of their points, and warn them not to wander about the museum site as it once was her house, and she doesn't like strangers walking around!. To quench her wrath and recover their points, the players are given one last option: they need to rightly answer one last question regarding the museum tour.

- *The reward, a token for later reflection*. In the end, independently from who they have been helping, all the players receive a reward for finishing their quest. They can take a selfie photograph with the encountered ghost and their game punctuation which will be emailed to them. Moreover, they will receive a book (in PDF printable format) containing pictures and scientific facts of the animals that they have interacted with during the tour (Fig. 4). The book also contains the Runa/markers which can be recaptured at any time and release the AR 3D models of the species.

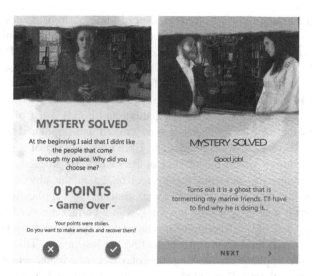

**Fig. 3.** Screenshot of the ending of the game according to the two different characters that open the game: Isabel, (left) and Meara (right).

**Fig. 4.** Left side of the image: user interacting with the 3D model of the Butterfly displayed as Augmented Reality. Right side of the image: two pages of the digital book. It is possible to reload the 3D models of the animals by capturing the rune charms of the book pages.

### 3.2   Implementation

*Haunted Encounters* makes use of the Unity3D engine, chosen for its flexibility and extensive community support. Some widely known applications that are built upon the Unity3D engine are *Pokémon GO* and *Magic Arena*. Unity3D was also chosen for being compatible with the Vuforia Engine, which provides a set of tools such as the use of custom images presented in the real world as in-game triggers, using the custom images' features for recognition.

The Vuforia Engine allows the recognition of these custom images by uploading them to a database and performing a feature extraction process, determining the quality of the image as a marker for Augmented Reality during the process. This results in a black and white image with emphasis on the highest contrast points. As a rule of thumb, an image with a greater number of features provides for a better target for the AR application. In terms of logic, the bulk of it is in the quiz part, where it follows the behaviour of the Factory software design pattern and builds a list of quizzes. While loading, new instances of the quiz *pre-set* are created and populated with the correct information relative to the displayed species. Each quiz consists of a set of questions, related to the species to which the marker is associated. To proceed, the player must select the desired species and find the correct image in the physical environment. Vuforia triggers the image recognition event, causing the application to display a question along with a set of possible answers, with a correct answer being worth full score and a wrong one only a fraction of it. Once all the questions have been answered, a new scene will load, tasking the player to find the last image. This will trigger the ending part of the application, starting the playback of videos while showing the surroundings to the player. The video format chosen was *webm*, for the support of transparency and its light-weight characteristics.

## 4    Evaluation

### 4.1    Pilot Testing and Preliminary Findings

Before the formal evaluation the game was piloted with two young girls of the age of 12. The experimenters followed the users during the trial taking notes and collecting loose feedback. An open-ended interview was made to the players to better understand their perception and experience with the game. With this pilot, we aimed at testing the flow of the game, general usability of the interface and gather some preliminary impressions. A summary of insights from the open-ended interview with the young teens is summarized below.

Both users found the game interesting and engaging ("because we played and understood more about the animals.", C1 and "It was fun to find the animals and take photos" C2). They found the main game challenge (matching the shadow to the correct exhibit and answering quizzes) demanding and referenced the tips as a necessary help ("Not so easy. … the tips helped." C2). C1 mentioned that she'd like to have more tips and take more photos that could then feature in the game ("we should be able to take a photo when we found the animals and put in the game… More hints instead of only shadow…" C1). One of the girls suggested to add a time challenge to the task of finding the animals corresponding to the shadows ("A time challenge that give us finite time to find the animal corresponding to the shadow" C1). They also appreciated the AR 3D realizations of the animals, and the fact that they could manipulate them ("They were cool" C1 and C2…" Specially because you could touch the screen and manipulate them (turn them around)" C2). The treasure hunt was their top favorite element of the game ("Looking around the museum for the animals, the treasure hunt, looking for the chest, and then the ghost thing." C2. They positively remembered the ghostly encounter at the end of the game and the game payoff, in the form of the pdf printable book ("We found a ghost it was cool." C1 and C2. it was cool because we had the book… and could capture the markers again and see the 3D animals. C1). Finally, they mentioned the game enhanced the museum experience ("In this museum, we learned much more than in other museums", C2, "I was in many museum and this idea is very cool", C1) and would recommend to friends and classmates ("Yes, but our class is quite troubling and I don't think they would behave." C1 and 2).

**Preliminary Insights from the Pilot.** The pilot highlighted the positive impact of the game on the young players. They were both highly engaged and had fun, mostly appreciating of the treasure hunt mechanism and learning outcomes. Attention should be paid to balance difficulties of the challenges proposed in the game with the tips given to help solve them. Overall, the flow of the game (the timing, engagement and level of challenge) worked well, but the pilot exposed an interesting addition: a time constrain to some of the challenges. The AR element were also appreciated together with the possibility of re capturing them through the PDF book markers later on. After the pilot study, we proceeded to conduct a more focused evaluation of some of the game features, before deploying an on site study of the game. In the next section, we will describe the usability evaluation carried out after the pilot, while a complete study of the game onsite is being conducted as we speak.

## 4.2    Formative Usability Evaluation

The game was further evaluated with 16 students from a single school (14 male and 2 female – mean age: 17.25; standard deviation: 1.29). After trying the game the students compiled two different questionnaires: the Multimedia Guide Scale, measuring the reactions to the usefulness and usability of multimedia guides [31], and the AttrakDiff [32] measuring the attractiveness of the experience. Due to the constrained protocols and schedule of the school, the tests were set up in our lab premises where we replicated the control conditions found at the museum. This enabled us to gather data on the general usability, learnability, quality of the interaction and attractiveness of the application.

**Procedure.** The users were split into two even groups (8 users per group) who performed the evaluation with the same protocol into two separates but equally sized and equipped rooms. In order to interact with the mobile app., we provided one smartphone shared by every two students. In preparation for the study we photographed and printed A4 sized posters of all the museum exhibits that are covered in the Haunted Encounters game (Fig. 5). These posters contained the picture of the exhibit photographed on the museum shelf and its associated marker on the side. The lab evaluation consisted in the students playing the game in pairs, as they were in the museum, finding the requested exhibit poster and capturing its corresponding marker in order to unlock the content and answer the quiz related to each exhibit. The posters were distributed on a table in the lab room. After the interaction with the mobile app, participants were required to compile two questionnaires one for the Multimedia Guide Scale and the other for the AttrakDiff.

**Fig. 5.** Teenagers using the mobile app. to interact with the poster and capture the markers, during the usability test conducted int the lab.

**Usability Results.** Within the Museum Guide Scale (MGS) scale, the parameter of General Usability scored an average of 2.57 (median: 2.50) out of 5 points. As lower than average values in this parameter indicate participants not finding usability issues. Hence, results show that some usability issues might be at play in the Haunted Encounters Museum game and its usability could be improved.

The parameter of Learnability and Control with the mobile guide scored an average of 3.58 (median: 3.67) out of 5 points. Higher values in this parameter mean participants understood and could control the multimedia guide. Results from our test indicate that users found the application quite easy and intuitive to grasp, and master.

The parameter of Quality of Interaction with the mobile guide scored an average of 3.90 (median: 3.67) out of 5 points. Higher values in this parameter mean participants enjoyed the quality of interaction of the multimedia museum guide. In our test, the Quality of interaction scored relatively high compared to the other measures. In sum, the participants reported enjoying the experience of interacting with the application, also thanks to the intuitiveness of its feature, which helped them overcome the usability issues encountered.

The overall results from the Attrakdiff scale are very positive: this scale scores from $-3$ to 3. Hence, values near 3 are strongly positive. In particular, the Pragmatic quality parameters, describing traditional usability and task related to the design aspects, i.e. efficiency, effectiveness and learnability, scored 2.10 (mean 2.14). The Hedonic quality parameters (identity and stimulation), describing aspects of the product connected to the product qualities, such as originality and beauty for example, scored respectively 2.46 (mean: 2.50) and 2.21 (mean: 2.14). The Attractiveness parameter also scored highly positive with an average of 2.58 (mean: 2.64). The perceived Attractiveness of a product results from an averaging of the perceived pragmatic and hedonic qualities.

With further analysis, a significant relationship between Attractiveness and Hedonic qualities ($p < 0.003$) emerged from the data. Attractiveness was significantly positively related to how well people scored in the Hedonic quality – identity ($r_s = 0.748$, $p = 0.001$) and stimulation ($r_s = 0.564$, $p = 0.023$). We can infer that the high attractiveness of our product is strongly related to its hedonic qualities (originality and beauty). On the other hand, there was not any significant correlation between the results from Pragmatic quality and Attractiveness ($r_s = 0.398$, $p = 0.127$).

# 5   Discussion

In summary, our pilot and usability evaluations gave us an initial encouraging set of highlights and findings to guide us shape further our game and its future evaluations. In general, the game was well perceived, it was confirmed that it adds value to the museum, and encourage teenagers exploring its content. It was interesting to note how the aesthetics qualities and originality of the game, helped users overcome usability issues, and left players with an enthusiastic impression of the experience. These positive results led us to agree with [6], who argued that games are proven to improve engagement, motivation and learning within edutainment environments. Moreover, our preliminary findings echo broader literature in the field of HCI and gamified experiences for teenagers. Our findings echo [33] arguing that it is possible to have a single gamified experience for teens spanning from 12 to17 years old, when the game contains elements that are considered novel by this teens group, such as mobile applications, gamification, 3D models and interaction through AR. Teens value the technology, and appreciate when it is included in museum experiences. However, we are aware of the limitations of our study: the pilot was conducted with a very limited sample, and the usability study constrained by the reproduction of the experience in the lab, instead of the museum itself. For understanding how this mobile intervention could enhance the user experience of teenage visitors in museums, a deeper analysis is needed. The conducted studies encouraged us to continue the evaluation of the game, in particular exploring the effects of the game tested on site, and with a wider and more gender balanced sample.

# 6   Conclusions

This article reports on the design and preliminary testing of Haunted Encounters, a teenage targeted mobile game deployed at the Natural History Museum of Funchal. In the game, the audience is called to solve a mystery by looking for and interacting with the museum exhibits, collecting AR 3D models of the species in display while gaining scientific knowledge about such species. The article reports on some preliminary testing of the game and its findings. The game was piloted with two young teenagers, yielding enthusiastic reception and some suggestions on improvements. The game was then tested with further 16 digital native teenagers evaluating its usability and interaction qualities. The results were extremely positive, despite the limitation of the study which was conducted in the lab, instead of the museum premises. The next phase of our work involves extensively testing this prototype inside the museum's premises in order to validate its flow, game mechanics and overall usability on site. The results from these studies will help us understanding and facilitating the design of engaging interactive museum experiences for the understudied museum teenage audiences.

**Acknowledgments.** ARDITI (Agência Regional para o Desenvolvimento da Investigação, Tecnologia e Inovação) with the PhD scholarship number M14-20-09-5369-FSE-000001. The support of the Beanstalk project team, In particular Research Assitants Rui Trinidade, Sandra Olim and Ana Bettencourt.

# References

1. Tzibazi, V.: Participatory action research with young people in museums. Mus. Manag. Curatorsh. **28**(2), 153–171 (2013)
2. Cesário, V., Coelho, A., Nisi, V.: Teenagers as experience seekers regarding interactive museums tours. In: Proceedings of the 1st International Conference on Design and Digital Communication, Barcelos, pp. 127–134 (2017)
3. Falk, J.H., Dierking, L.D.: Learning from Museums: Visitor Experiences and the Making of Meaning. AltaMira Press, Lanham (2000)
4. Simon, N.: The Participatory Museum. Santa Cruz, Museum 2.0 (2010)
5. Ghiani, G., Paternò, F., Santoro, C., Spano, L.D.: UbiCicero: a location-aware, multi-device museum guide. Interact. Comput. **21**(4), 288–303 (2009)
6. Jemmali, C., Bunian, S., Mambretti, A., El-Nasr, M.S.: Educational game design: an empirical study of the effects of narrative. In: Proceedings of the 13th International Conference on the Foundations of Digital Games, New York, NY, USA, pp. 34:1–34:10 (2018)
7. Falk, J.H.: Identity and the Museum Visitor Experience. Routledge, Walnut Creek (2009)
8. Prensky, M.: Digital natives, digital immigrants part 1. Horizon **9**(5), 1–6 (2001)
9. Fraser, M., et al.: Assembling history. In: Kuutti, K., Karsten, E.H., Fitzpatrick, G., Dourish, P., Schmidt, K. (eds.) ECSCW 2003, pp. 179–198. Springer, Dordrecht (2003). https://doi.org/10.1007/978-94-010-0068-0_10
10. Long, S., Aust, D., Abowd, G., Atkeson, C.: Cyberguide: prototyping context-aware mobile applications. In: Conference Companion on Human Factors in Computing Systems, New York, NY, USA, pp. 293–294 (1996)
11. Petrelli, D., Not, E., Sarini, M., Stock, O., Strapparava, C., Zancanaro, M.: HyperAudio: location-awareness + adaptivity. In: CHI 1999 Extended Abstracts on Human Factors in Computing Systems, New York, NY, USA, pp. 21–22 (1999)
12. Nisi, V., Dionisio, M., Hanna, J., Ferreira, L., Nunes, N.: Yasmine's adventures: an interactive urban experience exploring the sociocultural potential of digital entertainment. In: Chorianopoulos, K., Divitini, M., Hauge, J.B., Jaccheri, L., Malaka, R. (eds.) ICEC 2015. LNCS, vol. 9353, pp. 343–356. Springer, Cham (2015). https://doi.org/10.1007/978-3-319-24589-8_26
13. Dionisio, M., Bala, P., Nisi, V., Nunes, N.: Fragments of laura: incorporating mobile virtual reality in location aware mobile storytelling experiences. In: Proceedings of the 16th International Conference on Mobile and Ubiquitous Multimedia, New York, NY, USA, pp. 165–176 (2017)
14. Stock, O., Zancanaro, M. (eds.): PEACH - Intelligent Interfaces for Museum Visits. Springer, Heidelberg (2007). https://doi.org/10.1007/3-540-68755-6
15. Cheverst, K., Davies, N., Mitchell, K., Friday, A.: Experiences of developing and deploying a context-aware tourist guide: the GUIDE project. In: Proceedings of the 6th Annual International Conference on Mobile Computing and Networking, New York, NY, USA, pp. 20–31 (2000)
16. Yong's China Quest Adventure. https://www.mylearning.org/stories/yongs-china-quest-adventure-game-level-1/resources. Accessed 08 Jan 2019
17. The China Game: Asia Society. https://asiasociety.org/media/asia-society-news/melissa-chiu-interviewed-about-chinese-artist-ai-weiweis-detention. Accessed 08 Jan 2019
18. Great Bible Race. http://greatbiblerace.com/. Accessed 08 Jan 2019

19. 6th EU Framework Program-IST-034984 MOSAICA– Semantically enhanced, multifaceted, collaborative access to cultural heritage. https://cordis.europa.eu/project/rcn/79350/factsheet/en. Accessed 08 Jan 2019
20. Pierroux, P., Bannon, L., Walker, K., Hall, T., Kaptelinin, V., Stuedahl, D.: MUSTEL: framing the design of technology-enhanced learning activities for museum visitors. Presented at the International Cultural Heritage Informatics Meeting (ICHIM07), Toronto (2007)
21. Cabrera, J.S., et al.: Mystery in the museum: collaborative learning activities using handheld devices. In: Proceedings of the 7th International Conference on Human Computer Interaction with Mobile Devices and Services, New York, NY, USA, pp. 315–318 (2005)
22. Dini, R., Paternò, F., Santoro, C.: An environment to support multi-user interaction and cooperation for improving museum visits through games. In: Proceedings of the 9th International Conference on Human Computer Interaction with Mobile Devices and Services, New York, NY, USA, pp. 515–521 (2007)
23. Nilsson, T., Blackwell, A., Hogsden, C., Scruton, D.: Ghosts! A location-based bluetooth le mobile game for museum exploration. ArXiv160705654 Cs, July 2016
24. Xhembulla, J.: Intrigue at the museum: facilitating engagement and learning through a location-based mobile game. In: International Association for the Development of the Information Society (2014)
25. Kretschmer, U., et al.: Meeting the spirit of history. In: Proceedings of the 2001 Conference on Virtual Reality, Archeology, and Cultural Heritage, New York, NY, USA, pp. 141–152 (2001)
26. Spierling, U., Kampa, A.: Structuring location-aware interactive narratives for mobile augmented reality. In: Mitchell, A., Fernández-Vara, C., Thue, D. (eds.) ICIDS 2014. LNCS, vol. 8832, pp. 196–203. Springer, Cham (2014). https://doi.org/10.1007/978-3-319-12337-0_20
27. Iversen, O.S., Smith, R.C.: Scandinavian participatory design: dialogic curation with teenagers. In: Proceedings of the 11th International Conference on Interaction Design and Children, New York, NY, USA, pp. 106–115 (2012)
28. Dindler, C., Iversen, O.S., Smith, R., Veerasawmy, R.: Participatory design at the museum: inquiring into children's everyday engagement in cultural heritage. In: Proceedings of the 22nd Conference of the Computer-Human Interaction Special Interest Group of Australia on Computer-Human Interaction, New York, NY, USA, pp. 72–79 (2010)
29. Cesário, V.: Analysing texts and drawings: the teenage perspective on enjoyable museum experiences. In: 32nd British Human Computer Interaction Conference, pp. 1–3(2018)
30. Cesário, V., Coelho, A., Nisi, V.: Design patterns to enhance teens' museum experiences. In: 32nd British Human Computer Interaction Conference, pp. 1–5 (2018)
31. Othman, M.K., Petrie, H., Power, C.: Engaging visitors in museums with technology: scales for the measurement of visitor and multimedia guide experience. In: Campos, P., Graham, N., Jorge, J., Nunes, N., Palanque, P., Winckler, M. (eds.) INTERACT 2011. LNCS, vol. 6949, pp. 92–99. Springer, Heidelberg (2011). https://doi.org/10.1007/978-3-642-23768-3_8
32. Hassenzahl, M., Burmester, M., Koller, F.: AttrakDiff: Ein Fragebogen zur Messung wahrgenommener hedonischer und pragmatischer Qualität. In: Mensch and Computer, vol. 57, B. G. Teubner (2003)
33. Cesário, V., Radeta, M., Coelho, A., Nisi, V.: Shifting from the children to the teens' usability: adapting a gamified experience of a museum tour. In: Bernhaupt, R., Dalvi, G., Joshi, A., K. Balkrishan, D., O'Neill, J., Winckler, M. (eds.) INTERACT 2017. LNCS, vol. 10516, pp. 464–468. Springer, Cham (2017). https://doi.org/10.1007/978-3-319-68059-0_52

# Virtual and Real Body Representation in Mixed Reality: An Analysis of Self-presence and Immersive Environments

Wesley Oliveira[✉], Michelle Tizuka, Esteban Clua,
Daniela Trevisan, and Luciana Salgado

Computer Science Institute, Universidade Federal Fluminense, Niterói, Brazil
{wesleyoliveira, mmtizuka}@id.uff.br,
{esteban, daniela, luciana}@ic.uff.br

**Abstract.** Over the last decade, most of studies were focused on assessments of presence, degrees of immersion and user involvement with virtual reality, few works, however, addressed the mixed reality environments. In virtual reality, mostly through an egocentric point of view, the user is usually represented by a virtual body. In this work, we present an approach where the user can see himself instead of a virtual character. Different than augmented reality approaches, we only detach the user's body and his/her proxies interfaces. We conducted four experiments to measure and evaluate quantitatively and qualitatively the feeling of presence. We measure and compare the degree of presence in different modes and techniques of representation of the user's body through virtually integrated questionnaires. We also analyzed what factors influence to a greater or lesser feeling of presence. For this study, we adapted a real bike with an haptic interface. Results show that there is not necessarily a better or worse type of avatar, but their appearance must match the scenarios and others elements in the virtual environment to greatly increase the participant sense of presence.

**Keywords:** Mixed Reality · Haptic interface · VR bicycle · Presence

## 1 Introduction

Studies on immersion and presence in Mixed Reality (MR) are not new, but with the continuous evolution of the technologies used, we are increasing the simulation capacity of the developed experiences. An important point of this advancement is the ability to present content more realistically, either graphically or interactively, allowing more immersive experiences to the user [1].

In a recent work [2] we introduced the concept of real egocentric representation: real hands, forearms and legs appearance, capturing images from the Head Mounted Display (HMD) camera and showing tangible interfaces feedback for the user. We define here the concept of real avatar and virtual avatar representation. In the real egocentric representation, the real body and interfaces proxies are shown. For so, image processing techniques are required for extracting the user's body from the background scene. Gestures and movement must be captured in order to become inputs of the

© IFIP International Federation for Information Processing 2019
Published by Springer Nature Switzerland AG 2019
E. van der Spek et al. (Eds.): ICEC-JCSG 2019, LNCS 11863, pp. 42–54, 2019.
https://doi.org/10.1007/978-3-030-34644-7_4

virtual scenario. For the virtual avatar, other techniques must be used for interpreting the user's actions and interfaces (e.g., traditional VR interfaces, depth cameras, tracking systems). In the previous work, we built a real bicycle and an HMD as a MR display using a procedural city as a background scenario. We show that it is the MR that provides a greater sense of presence. However, the work only presents a qualitative analysis. In this work, the same bicycle system was implemented but a new study was carried out in order to collect quantitative data in a systematic way through four experiments: two that simulates a VR mode with a virtual avatar and two others with a MR simulation mode, where the user's real body and the front part of the real bicycle are visualized inside the virtual environment. Each mode has two different types of scenarios, one realistic and one non-realistic, for all participants. Thus, we sought to verify how much the visualization of the body itself in the interactive environment influences the sensation of presence and whether it is better or worse than the feeling of presence visualizing a 3D reconstruction. In this paper, the visualization of one's own real hand, forearms and part of the legs will be referred as a *real avatar*, while the 3D reconstruction virtual hands, forearms and part of the legs will be described as a *virtual avatar*. Besides, we seek to identify the influence of the type of scenario (realistic or non-realistic) in which the participant is involved, according to the representation of his/her avatar, and the effect of Plausibility through features to evaluate reactions of the users during the experiments. The tests were conducted within twenty participants.

On Sect. 2, we discuss related works that influenced and lead to the development of this experiment. After that, in Sect. 3, it is shown the methodology and data measures acquirements. Following Sect. 4 details experiments and the results obtained. Finally, in Sect. 5, the conclusion achieved based on the results is presented.

## 2 Related Works

### 2.1 Presence in Mixed and Virtual Reality

Studies on VR have gained prominence in several areas of knowledge and have a fundamental characteristic: the creation of the sense of presence. According with Witmer et al. [3], presence can be defined as a normal awareness phenomenon that requires directed attention and is based on the interaction between sensory stimulation, environmental factors that encourage involvement and enable immersion, in addition to inherent tendencies to become involved. However, few studies had taken those questions from a real virtual environment evaluation in order to mitigate the effects of interruption to measure presence [4]. Other authors subdivide presence into objective and subjective categories [5] or in different types of personal, social, and local presence [6]. As for [7], the act of being aware of its surroundings is of extreme importance to understand the factors of immersion and presence. Slater et al. [8, 9] argues that the perception of the environment for the participant is still an action that involves his/her whole body, so the more faithful the system can capture the movements or gestures and represent them within the system, the higher is the immersion. Thus, when a VR system is determined immersive, we mean that it possesses the technological capability to meet the sensory needs of a system participant and the immersion can be measured through the hardware's capacity. It is known that to make the user experience immersive, with environments generated through sensorial elements, usually visual, auditory and tactile stimuli and also by the continuous tracking of the surrounding environment, is crucial to track real and virtual world, maintaining their correct positioning during the interaction.

In the case of MR, one of the main characteristics is the ability to permeate between the virtual and the real world [10]. This ability that MR environment is constructed and enriched using real-world information sources that causes extremely intense and immersive feeling has emerged as "pervasive virtuality" [11–13].

When a VR or MR environment is able to present itself in a sufficiently believable way, it can provide the sensation of "Plausibility" described in [8, 15]. For instance, when participants react and try to bypass rapidly approaching virtual objects. Another sensation connected with the sense of presence is the Place Illusion [16], it is presented as the sensation of being in the place shown as it was a real experience. So, when a system effectively manages to replace or alter a person's sensory perception, the consciousness of reality is transformed into an awareness of the virtually created scenario and means that the visual scene visualized could be perceived in a satisfactorily realistic way by the participant's brain.

## 2.2    Virtual and Real Avatars

The 'obvious' distinction between the terms 'real' and 'virtual' is shown to have several different aspects, depending on whether one is dealing with real or virtual objects, real or virtual images, and direct or non-direct viewing of these [10]. In this paper, our concept of a real avatar will be considered the experience of someone viewing one's own real hand directly in front of one's own self, which is defined as quite distinct from a virtual avatar [10], that is, viewing an image of the virtual 3D hand on the HMD, and it's associated perceptual issues.

## 2.3    Interfaces and Interactivity in Virtual Environments

In order to interact with the contents of VR or MR, an interface is needed to meet the requirements of the experience and enable the feeling of presence. Traditionally, physical controls have been used for manipulations of objects in VR interactions, with gesture controls being used on a smaller scale, due to their application being more punctual. However, some authors [17] show that gesture controls have the highest degree of immersion in the system, allowing the interaction between the user and the interface to be done in a more natural way (NUI). In MR, the user can see virtual elements and some of the real features, but one must carefully think about how the interaction with the content will be, since putting a standard control in the user's hands will break the immersion of the system and user presence. One possibility is to use a motion controller disguised as a "prop" with its usability and appearance matching the simulated environment. This allows the user to physically interact with a controller in a more natural way. The use of bicycles with HMD acting as haptic interfaces in VR have also been presented in different works, such as [18]. However, assessments on the interactivity and appropriation of the user's actual body itself with the bicycle are still rare, being most works focused on the body perception restricted to the arms and hands of the users [19, 20]. This implementation of haptic interfaces in virtual systems contributes to increase user presence, but without haptic feedback in the interactions [21, 22], which should be consistent with the actions performed in the real world, in order to avoid the effect of sensory conflicts [23, 24] and possible breakdown of immersion and presence. This was the motivation for [2], who implemented an haptic system using a standard commercial bicycle to allow the interactivity of the experiment to be as close as possible with a realistic situation, since its handlebars can be moved freely with the hands of the participant, either by viewing a real or a virtual avatar. As an extra complement, we developed integrated questionnaires as an alternative to obtain the data, avoiding any possible presence breakdown and increasing the consistency of the data response variance, as based on recent works [25].

## 3  Methodology

The detailed description of the MR builds, and also the chroma key installation have been previously presented in [2]. Basically, it is a standard commercial bicycle supported with a stand to hold the bicycle stable, an Arduino board connected to the sensors, a Hall sensor and magnets attached to the rear rims used to measure the RPM of the rear wheel of the bicycle and a 10 KΩ potentiometer connected through 3D printed gears to the handlebars allowing to capture the turning angle of the bicycle. The software was developed in Unity3D (2017.1.0f3) using Leap Motion Orion (3.2.1) and SteamVR (1.2.3) plugins and using the Arduino sensors data as input on the application. The experiment runs on a Windows PC with an Intel i7 3.10 GHz, 8 GB RAM a Nvidia GTX 1050 and the HTC Vive as the Head Mounted Display.

Exclusively for VR mode, there was a capture of the participant's hands actions and transmission to the simulation, causing the virtual avatar to move hands and fingers faithfully to the user's actual movements. With the positioning data of the participant's hands, we performed the positioning of the front arm through algorithms of inverse kinematics to enable a realistic movement of the arms. This synchronization with the positioning of the real and virtual bicycles allowed the user to move their hands touching the surface of the actual bicycle while visualizing the same occurring in the virtual environment with the hand of his/her avatar and the virtual bicycle. For the MR mode, there was no need to make this positioning since the participant sees his/her own body and the actual bicycle within the simulation. The image captured by the Vive's front facing single camera was positioned inside of the simulation aligned with the point of view from the user.

### 3.1  Scenarios

The scenarios chosen were from two cities: a representative of a nonrealistic environment, in this case, a cartoon style, with vivid colors and a low number of polygons, and another capable of representing a realistic city with a high quantity of polygons, high quality of models and textures. Each city was built following the same pattern for the streets, changing only the appearances and distribution of the buildings and houses between them. The location of the participant's starting point in both cities was the same, close to several corners and intersections of the virtual map, giving him/her different possibilities of exploration.

In Fig. 1, the four generated modes can be seen: A: Cartoon Scenario in MR, with a real avatar (where the participant can see his hands and the real bicycle), B: Cartoon Scenario in VR, with a virtual avatar (where the participant sees the hands of an avatar and a virtual bike), C: Realistic Scenario in MR, with the real avatar and D: Realistic Scenario in VR, with the virtual avatar.

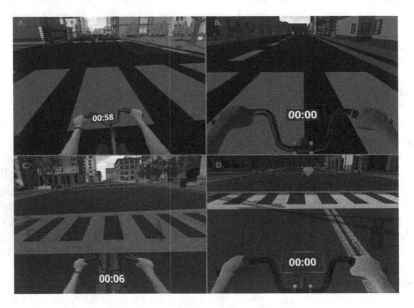

**Fig. 1.** The four modes that composed the experiment.

### 3.2   Participants, Stimuli, Tasks, and Measures

The experiment was performed with 20 participants: 15 were males and five females. The age group ranged from 19 to 32 years, and 50% of the users had no experience with VR, and 70% were not familiar with cycling.

After signing the consent, image, video forms, and also a profile questionnaire to evaluate their experience with HMD and their ability to ride a bicycle, each participant was asked to go up on the real bicycle. After setting up the HMD and being familiarized with the handlebar, the participant was transported to a virtual room where a self-explanatory board presented the objectives of the experiment and how to proceed to answer the integrated questionnaires. After that, he/she started the experiment in one of the four possible modes. The usage time for each mode was fixed (2 min) so that the participant could freely pedal within the presented virtual scene. The order in which the participant experimented was defined following the sampling balancing technique of the Latin Square, used to avoid the learning factor of the participant between the environments [26]. In this study, since the experiment was composed of 4 distinct modes, the Latin Square used was a multiple of 4.

To encourage the movement and exploration in the scenarios, we scattered along with the route objects that should be collected. Each scenario had 20 precious gems that could be collected along the course and a hidden crystal that shifted position to each mode. Also, as part of the scenario, characters were walking through the city and looking at the participant when they approach, to improve the sense of realism.

To analyze the degree of presence, integrated questionnaires were developed during the experiment and adapted inside our virtual environment experiment. Thus, through the ray casting-gaze technique, the participant answered by looking at the desired answer, and after 3 s, the option was confirmed. In total, four questions were proposed at the end of each mode, whose responses were collected through a seven-point Likert scale.

During the course, the evaluator had a real-time aerial view of the city map with the participant's path demarcation. This view allowed the evaluator to interact with the virtual scene through the interface that was presented on the computer, activating events that should draw attention and cause reactions of the participant, such as an explosion that occurred in pre-established locations or a tank of war that fired bullets of cannon toward the participant. These reactions were implemented to analyze the effects of "plausibility" of the virtual system [15]. The explosion was chosen to represent reactions to the unexpected relative to a sudden event, while the bullets fired by the tank served to observe the reflection of the participant when dodging from a virtual object. Each event was performed only once in each mode, and it was adopted that the first attempt of reaction should occur only after one minute of the beginning of the current mode. The order of which event was first activated was alternated with each mode. All sessions were recorded on video.

At the end of the four modes, a final "thank-you" screen was displayed. Finally, we applied a final post-experiment questionnaire with two questions: Which was the scenario remembered in more detail, and if the participant was deconcentrated for some reason during the experiment. A summary of the data collected is presented in Table 1.

**Table 1.** Table showing the data collected at each stage

| Outside of the experiment (Collected once) | Inside of the experiment (Collected for each mode) |
|---|---|
| The affinity with cycling | How much do you feel present at the moment? |
| The affinity with experiences in Virtual or Mixed Reality | Does the appearance of the environment affect your degree of presence? |
| The scenario remembered in more detail by the participant | Does the appearance of your body affect your degree of presence? |
| Degree of concentration | How natural was it to get around in the environment? |
| The experiment total time | If he/she had a reaction to the unexpected event |
| The modes order of execution | If he/she had a reaction to the reflex event |

## 4    Virtual or Real Avatars: Which Is Better?

The 7-point Likert scale responses were considered as an ordinal scale. Thus, these non-parametric data were analyzed following Friedman and Mann-Whitney tests [27], in the statistical analysis program R.

### 4.1    Answers Evaluation for the Sense of Presence

Figure 2 shows the graph of the responses to the first question at the end of each of the four modes of the experiment: "How much do you feel present at the moment?". The data indicates that in the Realistic MR Scenario the number of participants that felt present were higher than when compared with other modes. The Friedman test was performed, and a statistical significance was found (Friedman $X2 = 3.0008$, $p = 0.01439$) only between Realistic MR and Cartoon MR Scenarios, identified by an * in Fig. 2.

It was also observed that the Mann-Whitney test did not show a significant difference between the groups of participants with and without experience in the use of devices of VR (for all groups $p > 0.05$) and with and without experience with cycling (for all groups $p > 0.05$).

In the environment analysis, high notes represent 50% or more, but no significant difference was found between the modes (Friedman $X2 = 2.115$, $p > 0.05$). This analysis indicates that the scenarios are important for the sense of presence due to the high notes, but this importance is independent of the visual style of the scenario.

The analyze of the avatar body indicates no significant difference between any of the groups (Friedman $X2 = 1.2702$, $p > 0.05$). However, it is possible to see a reduction in the number of high notes (7 and 6) and an increase in the low notes (1 and 2) when compared to the previous question. These results can lead us to conclude that the body also contributes to the presence.

When analyzing the locomotion scores, there was a constant mean (5.15) among the four modes, but once more, no significant difference was found between these modes (Friedman $X2 = 1.7201$, $p > 0.05$), even though this result was expected, as the locomotion was a constant among the modes tested because there were no changes in how the bike interacted in each mode.

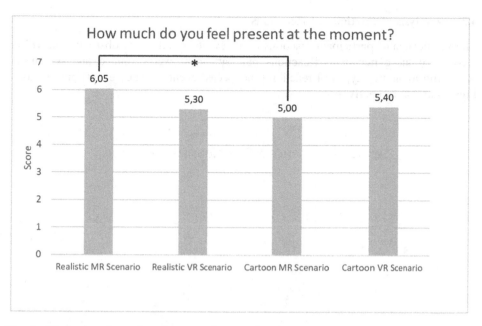

**Fig. 2.** Illustrative chart of responses to the question "How much do you feel present at the moment?"

## 4.2 Complementary Analysis

The combination of the interface in MR together with the Realistic Scenario showed a significant increase in the sense of presence of the participant than when the same interface was applied to the Cartoon Scenario. Visualizing his/her own body within an interactive environment influences the sense of presence. However, this influence can be both positive and negative, as demonstrated by the conflicting results obtained in the Realistic MR and Cartoon MR Scenarios. A plausible explanation for this phenomenon may be the effect of the Uncanny Valley [28, 29] that occurs when a virtual or robotic character tries to replicate human behavior, but imperfectly resemble actual human beings provoke strangely familiar feelings of eeriness and revulsion in observers.

We confirmed that if the participant sees his/her own hands inside the virtual environment and if his/her hands are inside a scenario that does not match a reality similar to the hands (for example, the Cartoon environment), it can cause revulsion and also the rupture of the immersion. This also explains why it does not happen in the MR Realistic Scenario as the real avatar overcome the Uncanny Valley. In the case of Realistic VR and Cartoon VR Scenarios, which use the VR interface, the virtual hand is anterior to the Uncanny Valley because it does not try to faithfully replicate the appearance of a hand in the smallest details and therefore was well accepted by the participants, supported by the similarly researched in [30, 31].

### 4.3  Analysis of Participant Reactions

The verification of participant reactions to the events was done by observing the video records of the experiment. Reactions per participant were counted and organized according to the two types of reaction (unexpected event or reflex event) presented in Figs. 3 and 4, respectively.

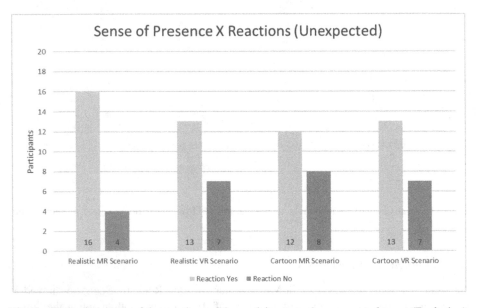

**Fig. 3.** Illustrative graph of the reactions of the participants to the unexpected event (Explosion), divided between groups with and without reactions.

In the graph of reactions to the unexpected event (explosion), we can see that in all modes, the number of users who reacted to the unexpected is greater than those who did not respond with a reaction. However, there is a difference in the number of reactions of users in the Realistic MR Scenario (16) than in the other modes (13, 12, 13). Also, presenting a higher proportion in the difference between the users with the reaction of those who did not present a response.

In relation to the graph of Fig. 4, we noticed that there was less variance in the differences between the users that presented a reaction of those that did not. Perhaps due to the fact that the tank was already visualized by the user and that somehow subconscious could already be predicted that something could happen even without knowing exactly what. Even so, it should be noted that for the same RM Realistic Scenario, there was also a greater amount of reaction than for other scenarios. Once the user visualizes their own hands, parts of the arm and legs and even of the actual bicycle, the feeling of presence and plausibility of being in that place could have caused that when foreseeing a deviation or even a reaction they were more intense. The targeting of bullets towards the user certainly allowed greater credibility of the event that comes in compliance with the predictive effect that the tank can generate when viewed by the user, causing a critical role to maintain the effect of Plausibility Illusion as indicated by Sanchez and Slater in [14, 15].

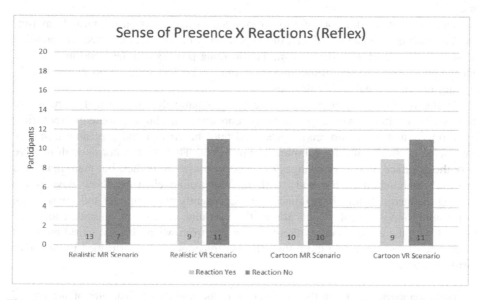

**Fig. 4.** Illustrative graph of the reactions of the participants to the reflection event (Cannon Shot), divided between groups with and without reactions.

These differences of reactions corroborate with the results of the data in the comparison of the degree of presence seen in Fig. 2. We can affirm that both groups with and without reaction of Realistic MR Scenario were more immersed in the virtual environment than the non-reaction group of the Cartoon MR Scenario. This indicates that the act of visualizing their own body within a realistic scenario also brings a sense of presence greater than in a non-realistic scenario. The free comments further support that participants could indicate in the post-test questionnaire ("Which of the four modes do you remember in more detail and why"). In this case, the most outstanding scenario was the MR Realistic Scenario (n = 9), which may indicate that either this is a confirmation of the high degree of presence experienced by the participants or a possible novelty effect. There is evidence that when a person remembers in more detail one scene than another is an indication that the participant was feeling more present in that environment [7, 8].

## 5 Conclusions

In this work, we intend to give an answer for which MR egocentric visualization mode is more immersive: a real image or avatar representation of the user. This work validates preliminary results from a previous study, which proposes strategies of real egocentric images visualization. Also, once again, the comparison of experiments by the users showed the capability of seeing their real body in the MR experiment allowed them to have better handling and balance of the haptic interface being tested. Some of the users liked this improvement due to the capacity that they were able to see their real body.

The fact that we did not have to remove the participant from the virtual environment to each questionnaire reduced the experiment time and also avoided any possible presence of the user with the system. The learning process was fast, and none of the participants presented any difficulty, even those who had little or no experience in cycling or with virtual reality devices.

In the present study it was possible to systematically analyze that there is not necessarily a better or worse type of body representations, but the contents (scenarios, body representations or objects) reproduced must be created and presented in a way they are consistent with the complete environment. That is, it is not enough to have only the interface of MR, or changes of scenery or types of bodies, but there must be a specific combination of the body with its background elements. New devices are starting to emerge, being able to function independently of a computer and can scan the surrounding environment, which allows the user and the content presented to freely interact with the environment without a clear line from where the real world ends and where the virtual begins. In the future, the experiments can be performed in this other form of interfaces.

**Acknowledgments.** We thank the Medialab from the Institute of Computer of the Federal Fluminense University for providing the bicycle and infrastructure required to develop the haptic system and the participants that help by being part of our tests.

# References

1. Slater, M., Usoh, M.: Representations systems, perceptual position, and presence in immersive virtual environments. Presence: Teleoper. Virtual Environ. **2**(3), 221–233 (1993)
2. Oliveira, W., Gaisbauer, W., Tizuka, M., Clua, E., Hlavacs, H.: Virtual and real body experience comparison using mixed reality cycling environment. In: Clua, E., Roque, L., Lugmayr, A., Tuomi, P. (eds.) ICEC 2018. LNCS, vol. 11112, pp. 52–63. Springer, Cham (2018). https://doi.org/10.1007/978-3-319-99426-0_5
3. Witmer, B.G., Singer, M.J.: Measuring Presence in Virtual Environments: a presence questionnaire. Presence **7**(3), 225–240 (1998)
4. Frommel, J., et al.: Integrated questionnaires: maintaining presence in game environments for self-reported data acquisition. In: Proceedings of the 2015 Annual Symposium on Computer-Human Interaction in Play (CHI PLAY 2015), pp. 359–368. ACM Press, London (2015)
5. Schloerb, D.W.: A quantitative measure of telepresence. Presence: Teleoper. Virtual Environ. **4**(1), 64–80 (1995)
6. Heeter, C.: Being there: the subjective experience of presence. Presence: Teleoper. Virtual Environ. **1**(2), 262–271 (1992)
7. Slater, M.: Measuring presence: a response to the Witmer and Singer presence questionnaire. Presence **8**(5), 560–565 (1999)

8. Slater, M., Lotto, B., Arnold, M.M., Sánchez-Vives, M.V.: How we experience immersive virtual environments: the concept of presence and its measurement. Anuario Psicol. **40**, 193–210 (2009)
9. Kilteni, K., Groten, R., Slater, M.: The sense of embodiment in virtual reality. Presence: Teleoper. Virtual Environ. **21**(4), 373–387 (2012)
10. Milgram, P., Kishino, F.: A taxonomy of mixed reality visual displays. IEICE Trans. Inform. Syst. **77**(12), 1321–1329 (1994)
11. Valente, L., Feijó, B., Ribeiro, A., Clua, E.: The concept of pervasive virtuality and its application in digital entertainment systems. In: Wallner, G., et al. (eds.) ICEC 2016. LNCS, vol. 9926, pp. 187–198. Springer, Cham (2016). https://doi.org/10.1007/978-3-319-46100-7_16
12. Artanim: Real Virtuality. http://artaniminteractive.com/real-virtuality. Accessed 21 Apr 2018
13. Silva, A.R., Valente, L., Clua, E., Feijó, B.: An indoor navigation system for live-action virtual reality games. In: 2015 14th Brazilian Symposium on Computer Games and Digital Entertainment (SBGames), pp. 1–10. IEEE (2015)
14. Sanchez-Vives, M.V., Slater, M.: From presence to consciousness through virtual reality. Nat. Rev. Neurosci. **6**(4), 332 (2005)
15. Slater, M.: Place illusion and plausibility can lead to realistic behaviour in immersive virtual environments. Philoso. Trans. Roy. Soc. B: Biol. Sci. **364**(1535), 3549–3557 (2009)
16. Minsky, M.: Telepresence. Omni **2**(9), 45–51 (1980)
17. Emma-Ogbangwo, C., Cope, N., Behringer, R., Fabri, M.: Enhancing user immersion and virtual presence in interactive multiuser virtual environments through the development and integration of a gesture-centric natural user interface developed from existing virtual reality technologies. In: Stephanidis, C. (ed.) HCI 2014. CCIS, vol. 434, pp. 410–414. Springer, Cham (2014). https://doi.org/10.1007/978-3-319-07857-1_72
18. Ranky, R., Sivak, M., Lewis, J., Gade, V., Deutsch, J.E., Mavroidis, C.: VRACK - virtual reality augmented cycling kit: design and validation. In: Virtual Reality. IEEE, Waltham (2010)
19. Argelaguet, F., Hoyet, L., Trico, M., Lécuyer, A.: The role of interaction in virtual embodiment: effects of the virtual hand representation. In: Virtual Reality (VR), pp. 3–10. IEEE (2016)
20. Schwind, V., Knierim, P., Tasci, C., Franczak, P., Haas, N., Henze, N.: These are not my hands!": Effect of gender on the perception of avatar hands in virtual reality. In: CHI 2017 Proceedings of the 2017 CHI Conference on Human Factors in Computing Systems, pp. 1577–1582. ACM, Denver (2017)
21. Lee, S., Kim, G.J.: Effects of haptic feedback, stereoscopy, and image resolution on performance and presence in remote navigation. Int. J. Hum.-Comput. Stud. **66**(10), 701–717 (2008)
22. Sallnäs, E.-L., Rassmus-Gröhn, K., Sjöström, C.: Supporting presence in collaborative environments by haptic force feedback. ACM Trans. Comput.-Hum. Interact. (TOCHI) **7**(4), 461–476 (2000)
23. Mittelstaedt, J., Wacker, J., Stelling, D.: Effects of display type and motion control on cybersickness in a virtual bike simulator. Displays **51**, 43–50 (2018)
24. Carvalho, M.R.D., Costa, R.T.D., Nardi, A.E.: Simulator sickness questionnaire: tradução e adaptação transcultural. J Bras Psiquiatr **60**(4), 247–252 (2011)
25. Schwind, V., Knierim, P., Haas, N., Henze, N.: Using presence questionnaires in virtual reality. In: Proceedings of the 2019 CHI Conference on Human Factors in Computing Systems, CHI 2019, pp. 360:1–360:12. ACM, New York (2019)
26. MacKenzie, I.S.: Within-subjects vs. between-subjects designs: which to use? Hum.-Comput. Interact.: Empir. Res. Perspect. **7**, 2005 (2002)

27. Joshi, A., Kale, S., Chandel, S., Pal, D.: Likert scale: explored and explained. Br. J. Appl. Sci. Technol. **7**(4), 396 (2015)
28. Mori, M., MacDorman, K.F., Kageki, N.: The uncanny valley [from the field]. IEEE Robot. Autom. Mag. **19**(2), 98–100 (2012)
29. Schwind, V., Wolf, K., Henze, N.: Avoiding the uncanny valley in virtual character design. Interactions **25**(5), 45–49 (2018)
30. Schwind, V., Knierim, P., Tasci, C., Franczak, P., Haas, N., Henze, N.: These are not my hands!: Effect of gender on the perception of avatar hands in virtual reality. In: Proceedings of the 2017 CHI Conference on Human Factors in Computing Systems, pp. 1577–1582. ACM (2017)
31. Tauziet, C.: Designing for hands in VR (2016). https://medium.com/facebook-design/designing-for-hands-in-vr-61e6815add99. Accessed 20 Apr 2019

# Virtual Reality

# Effects of End-to-end Latency on User Experience and Performance in Immersive Virtual Reality Applications

Polona Caserman$^{(\boxtimes)}$ ⓘ, Michelle Martinussen, and Stefan Göbel

Multimedia Communications Lab - KOM, Technische Universität Darmstadt,
Darmstadt, Germany
{polona.caserman,stefan.gobel}@kom.tu-darmstadt.de,
michelle.martinussen@stud.tu-darmstadt.de

**Abstract.** Immersive virtual reality (IVR) offers an opportunity to immerse oneself into a virtual world and experience an exciting adventure. However, latency between a user's movement and visual feedback has a big impact on user experience and performance. In this paper, we explore the effect of increased end-to-end latency in IVR applications by conducting a user study. Firstly, in the searching task, we analyze cybersickness level based on simulator sickness questionnaire. Secondly, in the reaching task, we measure the user performance by tracking the time they need to reach a target and the error they make during the execution. Lastly, in the embodiment task, we measure the sense of body ownership, agency, presence, and latency perception when only one body side is impaired by latency. We apply the Friedman test with Conover's test of multiple comparisons as a post hoc test on all dependent variables to find significant results. Results show that the end-to-end latency above 63 ms induces significant cybersickness symptoms. In addition, user performance decreases with increasing delay and with end-to-end latency above 69 ms, the users need significantly longer to complete the task. Results also show that end-to-end latency affects body ownership significant later, namely, not until 101 ms.

**Keywords:** Immersive virtual reality · End-to-end latency · Cybersickness · User experience · Simultaneity perception · Body ownership · Sense of agency · Sense of presence · Full-body motion reconstruction

## 1 Introduction

Many users experience adverse effects such as cybersickness when wearing a Head-Mounted-Display (HMD). The reasons for these symptoms are the subject of research. One possible theory is the mismatch between the senses which provide information about the body's orientation and motion, also known as *the*

© IFIP International Federation for Information Processing 2019
Published by Springer Nature Switzerland AG 2019
E. van der Spek et al. (Eds.): ICEC-JCSG 2019, LNCS 11863, pp. 57–69, 2019.
https://doi.org/10.1007/978-3-030-34644-7_5

*sensory conflict theory* [13]. Thus, increased cybersickness is often reported when the delay between user input and visual feedback is too high [7,17] or when the movements are forced upon the users, e.g., in flight simulations [16]. Shafer et al. [15] argue that with increasing sensory conflict, users will experience a higher level of cybersickness.

High end-to-end latency can induce cybersickness [17]. End-to-end latency in immersive virtual reality (IVR) refers to the time delay between a user's action and when this action is visible on the HMD. High delays also impair user performance and experience. Attig et al. [2] state that the lower limit of 100 ms is too high and suggests to update the guidelines.

In this paper, we want to recommend appropriate end-to-end latency so that the researchers and developers can prevent or minimize cybersickness, maximize user performance, and ensure immersive user experience. Our main contributions in this paper are:

- We aim to identify the lower limit for the end-to-end latency in IVR at which the users report increased symptoms for cybersickness.
- We analyze the impact of end-to-end latency on the sense of body ownership, agency, and presence. It should be investigated which maximal delay the users tolerate without losing the joy of the IVR application.

The paper is structured as follows. In Sect. 2, we present selected related work. In Sect. 3, we describe the IVR tasks to measure the effects of increased end-to-end latency on user experience as well as performance and furthermore propose our hypotheses. We describe the evaluation method in Sect. 4. We show the results in Sect. 5 and discuss them in Sect. 6. Lastly, we conclude in Sect. 7.

## 2    Related Work

The work of Albert et al. [1] reveals that participants, even if instructed to search for artifacts, could not find them if the latency was not higher than 50 to 70 ms. Waltemate et al. [18] stated that motor performance and simultaneity perception are worsened significantly at end-to-end latency above 75 ms, whereas the sense of agency and body ownership only decline at latency higher than 125 ms. However, in their study, the participants performed motor tasks inside a Cave virtual environment and did not use IVE with a HMD. Similarly, Kasahara et al. [6] observe that with an end-to-end latency of 104 ms, the participants lose the sense of body ownership.

Kawamura and Kijima [7] studied the effect of latency on the ability to stand on one foot in IVR. They used a Wii Balance Board to measure the stability of the participants and found that balance decreased with increased latency of already 1 ms. Attig et al. [2] expressed a similar view. The researchers report that the users are indeed able to perceive latencies down to the single millisecond and furthermore state that performance already gets impaired by latencies between 16 to 60 ms.

Increased latency of 450 ms also negatively effects the ability to memorize objects in IVR [12]. Furthermore, Samaraweera et al. [14] investigated the impact of additional latency applied either to the left or right side of the avatar. The researchers found significant differences between the control (with base latency of 45 ms) and experimental group (end-to-end latency of 200 ms). However, only three out of ten participants noticed the added delay. Users in the experimental group walked slower towards the mirror and tried to compensate for the latency by increasing the step and swing time on the impaired side. Likewise, Meehan et al. [10] argue that lower latency of 50 ms compared to 90 ms corresponds to a higher sense of presence.

Stauffert et al. [17] investigated the impact of latency jitter on cybersickness in IVR. In their study, almost half of the participants did not even notice latency jitter and the ones who did, found it to be annoying. The researchers furthermore found a significant correlation between heart rate and cybersickness. Similarly, Waltemate et al. [18] also conclude that the users did not show cybersickness symptoms, even at end-to-end latency above 350 ms. Other works suggest that delays above 40 ms already evoke cybersickness and postural instability [3].

## 3   Experimental Design

### 3.1   Tasks

We want to measure and compare the impact of different latency conditions on user experience and performance. In general, we apply latency to the virtual body and the HMD, controllers, as well as trackers. In other words, player movements are delayed with a certain amount of time. We analyze the impact of tracing delay in IVR to determine the upper latency limit that is still tolerated by users. Therefore, we developed three tasks:

**Searching task** is designed to measure cybersickness through the simulator sickness questionnaire (SSQ) [8]. As proposed by Stauffert et al. [17], the user has to find circular targets (platforms), spawned on the ground in one of three corridors. As soon as the user steps on one platform, a new one randomly spawns in another corridor. Thus, the user has to walk to find the next platform. Only one platform is present in the scene at the same time. The user is exposed to different artificial added delays, between 0 and 100 ms. In each round, the user has to find three platforms, one after another. After that, the user has to state how affected he/she is by each symptom on a four-point Likert scale: "None", "Slight", "Moderate", and "Severe". The scale is converted into integer numbers from 0 to 3. Finally, we calculate the final SSQ scale.

**Reaching task** is designed to measure user performance, in particular, how much time a user needs to touch a cube appearing in a virtual scene and how many errors he/she makes during the execution. Similar to the searching task, we add delays between 0 and 100 ms. As proposed by Ware et al. [19], targets are spawned around the user in the field of view, at a distance so that he/she can reach them. The user has to sit on a stool and should use his/her dominant hand to reach the virtual target. As soon as their hand reaches the target, the virtual object disappears and a new one spawns randomly in the virtual environment. Thus, the users should reach the targets as fast as possible; however, they must avoid making mistakes. The user can access the object only once. If he/she fails, it is considered as an error.

**Embodiment task** is designed to measure user experience while the users can observe themselves in a virtual mirror. As proposed by Samaraweera et al. [14], we apply latency to only one side of the body (either the left leg and left arm or the right leg and right arm). By using a seven-point Likert scale, we measure the sense of body ownership, sense of agency, sense of presence, and latency perception. The users are exposed to different artificial added delays, between 0 and 200 ms. The questionnaire consists of five questions, as listed in Table 1.

**Table 1.** Embodiment questionnaire. Each question was assessed on a seven-point Likert scale: "Strongly Disagree" ($-3$) and "Strongly Agree" ($3$).

| Condition | Question |
| --- | --- |
| Body ownership | It felt as if the virtual body in the mirror was my body |
| Agency | My movements caused the movements of the virtual body in the mirror |
| Presence | I felt as if I was really there |
| Impaired side | I noticed a difference in how the avatar responded to my movements between my left and right side. (If the participant answered the question with a value greater than 0, we furthermore asked which side was delayed. The participant could respond with "left'," "right side" or "not sure.") |
| Simultaneity | The motion of the avatar was simultaneous to my movement |

### 3.2   Hypotheses

Studies on latency in IVR show that users performance may drop and they may notice latency smaller than 75 ms (see Sect. 2). However, studies evaluating the sense of agency and body ownership show that the users in IVR tolerate higher end-to-end latency between 90 and 200 ms.

For our experiment, we pose our hypotheses as follows:

**H1:** Higher end-to-end latency evokes cybersickness.
**H2:** Higher end-to-end latency decreases user performance.
**H3:** Higher end-to-end latency decreases user experience, in particular, sense of embodiment.

The evaluation of H1 is based on the SSQ, as proposed by Kennedy et al. [8]. Another way to detect cybersickness symptoms could be by using an ECG to measure the electrical activity of the heartbeat as proposed in our previous work [5]. To test H2, we measure the time it takes for a user to reach a cube and the errors that the user makes. Furthermore, to test H3, we analyze an embodiment questionnaire on a seven-point Likert scale.

## 4   Method

We recruited 21 participants, aged between 19 to 53 years ($M = 28.6$ years, $SD = 8.79$, six females). At the beginning of the experiment, all participants filled out a demographics questionnaire and were informed about the risks.

The experiment was conducted on a laptop with an Intel i7-7700HQ processor and an Nvidia GeForce GTX 1080. This setup fulfills the minimal hardware requirements of the HTC Vive Pro.[1] The tracking area was approximately 3.1 × 2.9 m large. The application was built with Unity 3D on a Windows 10 system. We used an HTC Vive Pro HMD with two controllers and three trackers to enable full-body motion reconstruction. The users had to bind two trackers to left and right ankle as well as one on the hip. Additionally, they had to hold both controllers in the hands to track arm movements. One additional tracker was bound to a stool so that it can be shown in the IVR application.

Each participant could choose between two virtual bodies (a female and male avatar). After the avatar calibration, the participants then viewed a simple scene with a mirror in from of them and a stool, as shown in Fig. 1. Thus, they could view their avatar from the first-person view, i.e., by looking down towards their body or by observing themselves in a virtual mirror.

(a) Searching task             (b) Reaching task             (c) Embodiment task

**Fig. 1.** The virtual environment, used for our experiment. (a) The search task consists of three corridors, where the users have to find platforms, spawned on the ground in one of three corridors. (b) In the reaching tasks, the users sit on a stool and have to touch virtual targets, spawned around them. (c) In the embodiment task, the users have to observe themselves in a virtual mirror, to find the impaired side. Note that the player can see the virtual body from the first-person view.

---

[1] https://www.vive.com/us/support/vive-pro-hmd/category_howto/what-are-the-system-requirements.html.

The study had a fully within-subjects design. Thus, all participants tested all tasks and all conditions. To ensure that the participants do not adapt to the latency during execution, we randomized the task order as well as latency conditions. The experiment started with a SSQ to provide a baseline measurement. After that, a total of 165 (11 × 3 different platform positions in the searching task, 11 × 6 different cube positions in the reaching task; 11 × 6 tries in embodiment task) randomly conditions were presented. In searching and reaching task, we added a delay between 0 and 100 ms (0 ms, 4 ms, 8 ms, 13 ms, 19 ms, 25 ms, 33 ms, 42 ms, 54 ms, 71 ms, 100 ms). In the embodiment task, we added higher delays between 0 and 200 ms (0 ms, 8 ms, 17 ms, 27 ms, 38 ms, 51 ms, 66 ms, 84 ms, 108 ms, 142 ms, 200 ms).

At the end of each latency condition in the searching task, the participants had to complete the SSQ. The surveyor read the questions and noted the participant's responses. In the reaching task, the participant did not need to complete any questionnaire. Instead, we measured how long each participant needed to grab the cube and how many errors he/she made. In the embodiment task, the participants again had to complete a questionnaire (see Table 1). Note that the order of the tasks and different latency conditions were randomly selected for each participant. Exposure time was approximately 55 min.

## 5    Results

### 5.1    Base End-to-End Latency

We firstly measured the system latency of our setup by using a frame counting approach, as proposed by Friston and Steed [4]. The end-to-end latency is the delay between the player's movement until the corresponding avatar movement is displayed on the HMD. Due to the calculation of inverse kinematics for full-body motion reconstruction, our base latency is slightly higher than those found in related work, which is often between 22 and 36 ms [1,11,17]. Other similar studies using full-body motion capturing reported higher end-to-end latencies, between 45 and 80 ms [6,9,14,18]. We measured end-to-end system latency of approximately 50 ms.

### 5.2    Cybersickness

To evaluate the level of cybersickness, we calculate the final SSQ scores at the end of each sub-task. Figure 2 shows the final SSQ scores for different end-to-end latency conditions. Error bars represent 95% confidence intervals of the mean.

Results of the Friedman test show that higher end-to-end latency has a significant effect on final SSQ scores ($\chi^2(2) = 100.6$, $p \leq .001$, Kendall's $W = .57$). The internal reliability for cybersickness was very high (Cronbach's $\alpha = .922$). Post-hoc analysis with Conover's test and $\alpha = .05$ reveals significant differences between 50 ms and $\geq$75 ms, 54 ms and $\geq$75 ms, 58 ms and $\geq$75 ms, 63 ms and $\geq$83 ms, 69 ms and $\geq$75 ms, 75 ms and $\geq$121 ms, 83 ms and 150 ms, 92 ms and

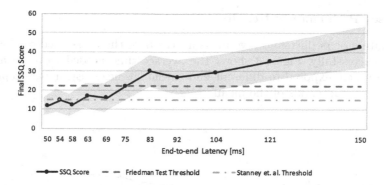

**Fig. 2.** Final SSQ scores at different end-to-end latency conditions. Error bars show 95% confidence interval of the mean. The values above the Friedman threshold contribute to the significant cybersickness symptoms. Indeed, values above Stanney et al. threshold already indicate too high SSQ scores.

150 ms, as well as 104 ms and 150 ms. Thus, the results show that higher latency values tend to correspond to higher final SSQ scores.

The results furthermore show significant lower SSQ score before the users put on the HMD (0 ms) and after they experienced end-to-end latency of 75 ms ($p < .001$). Thus, these findings indicate that users will experience sufficient discomfort at end-to-end latency above 75 ms. As it can be seen in Table 2, the reported final SSQ score at 75 ms is already >22. Stanney et al. [16] also complement these findings, stating that the final SSQ scores of >20 indicate that such a system is troublesome.

**Table 2.** Final SSQ scores prior the users put on the HMD (0 ms) and after each end-to-end latency condition (50–150 ms).

| End-to-end latency [ms] | 0 | 50 | 54 | 58 | 63 | 69 | 75 | 83 | 92 | 104 | 121 | 150 |
|---|---|---|---|---|---|---|---|---|---|---|---|---|
| Mean [ms] | 11.4 | 11.8 | 14.6 | 12.3 | 17.1 | 16 | 22.1 | 30.1 | 26.9 | 29.4 | 35.1 | 42.9 |
| SD [ms] | 13.8 | 11.2 | 13.9 | 13.7 | 15 | 18.2 | 18.2 | 20.2 | 21.3 | 22.1 | 22.4 | 25.7 |

Moreover, Stanney et al. [16] report that users who report symptoms which are already higher than 15 on the SSQ are experiencing sufficient cybersickness. Comparing this value with the measurement results, the users reported increased symptoms at end-to-end latency above 63 ms (see Table 2). Thus, to minimize cybersickness symptoms, end-to-end latency of below 58 ms (<15 on SSQ) is required.

## 5.3   User Performance Results

To evaluate user performance, we measure the time the users need to complete the task successfully. Figure 3 shows the average time needed to reach a cube while users were exposed to different end-to-end latencies. Error bars represent 95% confidence intervals of the mean.

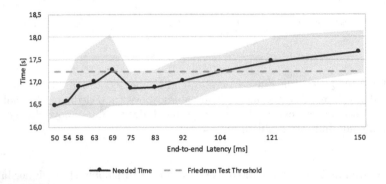

**Fig. 3.** Mean needed time for different end-to-end latency conditions. Error bars show 95% confidence interval of the mean. At values above the Friedman threshold, users need significantly longer to complete the reaching task.

Results of the Friedman test show that higher end-to-end latency has a significant effect on time, needed to complete the task ($\chi^2(2) = 68.71$, $p \leq .001$, Kendall's $W = .658$). The internal reliability of the scale was high (Cronbach's $\alpha = .872$.) Post-hoc analysis with Conover's test and $\alpha = .05$ results in significant differences between 50 ms and $\geq$69 ms, 54 ms and $\geq$92 ms, 58 ms and $\geq$92 ms, 63 ms and $\geq$104 ms, 69 ms and $\geq$121 ms, 75 ms and $\geq$121 ms, 83 ms and $\geq$104 ms, 92 ms and $\geq$121 ms, and 104 ms and 150 ms. In other words, with the minimum end-to-end latency (i.e., 50 ms), users could complete the task faster than with added delay. Thus, the results show that higher latency values tend to require more time to complete the task.

**Table 3.** Mean needed time for each end-to-end latency condition.

| End-to-end latency [ms] | 50 | 54 | 58 | 63 | 69 | 75 | 83 | 92 | 104 | 121 | 150 |
|---|---|---|---|---|---|---|---|---|---|---|---|
| Mean [ms] | 16.5 | 16.6 | 16.9 | 17 | 17.3 | 16.9 | 16.9 | 17 | 17.2 | 17.5 | 17.7 |
| SD [ms] | .7 | .7 | 1.5 | 1.9 | 1.9 | .8 | .9 | 1.2 | .9 | 1.3 | 1.1 |

By observing Fig. 3, we can see that higher delay worsen user performance. Looking at the findings from the post-hoc test indicate that user performance drops at 69 ms. The data in Table 3 shows that mean needed time values at end-to-end latency of 69 ms and 104 ms are nearly the same. Thus, user performance gets worse with increased delay and most users need significant longer to fulfill the task at end-to-end latency above 69 ms.

Even though the users were allowed to touch the virtual cubes only once, we could not identify any mistakes. We believe that the reaching task is very simple to complete and that more complex tasks would lead to higher chances of performance errors.

## 5.4   Embodiment Results

We conducted a user study to furthermore measure the sense of presence, agency, and body ownership at different end-to-end latency conditions. We calculated the median (MED) and Inter-Quartile Range (IQR) for each question, as it can be seen in Table 4 and Fig. 4. Each question was assessed on a seven-point Likert scale: $-3$ for "Strongly Disagree" and 3 for "Strongly Agree."

The internal reliabilities for embodiment measurements are high. Cronbach's $\alpha$ for embodiment ranges between .706 (impaired side), .869 (simultaneity), .953 (sense of agency), .988 (sense of presence), and .992 (sense of body ownership). For the sense of agency (MED = 3) and for the sense of presence (MED = 2), we could not find any significant differences. These findings indicate that end-to-end latency of up to 250 ms does not cause a significantly lower sense of agency or presence.

However, results also show that end-to-end latency above 101 ms will decrease the sense of body ownership (see Fig. 4a). Indeed, body ownership significant decreases for end-to-end latency above 192 ms. Thus, the sense of body ownership decreases with increasing end-to-end latency. Furthermore, with end-to-end latency above 67 ms, one user already noticed different latencies between the left and right side and also correctly specified the impaired side. As expected, with higher end-to-end latency the users not only perceived increased latency but also correctly specified the side (either left or right body side) which was influenced by additional delay (see Fig. 4b). At end-to-end latency of 250 ms, almost half of the users ($n = 10$) perceived the delay and could correctly specify the impaired side. Similarly, with an end-to-end latency of 116 ms and $\geq$158 ms, the users perceived the movements of the avatar not simultaneously to their movements.

# 6   Discussion

With the significant results of the SSQ comparing pre- and post-conditions, we accept hypothesis H1. Thus, increased end-to-end latency will evoke cybersickness symptoms. Stauffert et al. [17] expressed a similar view. The researchers evaluated latency jitter and found that the disorientation sub-scale was higher in the affected group, although nearly half of the users did not notice the repeated lag in the tracking of the HMD. In contrast to Waltemate et al. [18], we found significant results at the end-to-end latency of 75 ms. However, as suggested by

**Table 4.** The table depicts the median (MED) answers for embodiment questionnaire for each end-to-end latency condition. Inter-Quartile Range (IQR) values furthermore indicate the variability of the questionnaire responses.

| End-to-end latency [ms] | 50 | 58 | 67 | 77 | 88 | 101 | 116 | 137 | 158 | 192 | 250 |
|---|---|---|---|---|---|---|---|---|---|---|---|
| MED$_\text{agency}$ | 3 | 3 | 3 | 3 | 3 | 3 | 3 | 3 | 3 | 3 | 3 |
| IQR$_\text{agency}$ | 1 | 1 | 1 | 1 | 1 | 1 | 1 | 1 | 1 | 1 | 1 |
| MED$_\text{presence}$ | 2 | 2 | 2 | 2 | 2 | 2 | 2 | 2 | 2 | 2 | 2 |
| IQR$_\text{presence}$ | 2.5 | 2 | 2 | 2.5 | 2 | 2 | 2 | 2.5 | 2 | 2.5 | 4 |
| MED$_\text{body ownership}$ | 2 | 2 | 2 | 2 | 2 | 1 | 1 | 1 | 1 | 1 | 0 |
| IQR$_\text{body ownership}$ | 2.5 | 3 | 3.5 | 3 | 3 | 3 | 3.5 | 4 | 4 | 3 | 3 |
| MED$_\text{simultaneity}$ | 2 | 2 | 2 | 2 | 2 | 2 | 1 | 2 | 1 | 0 | 0 |
| IQR$_\text{simultaneity}$ | 1 | 1 | 1 | 1 | 1 | 1 | 1.5 | 0 | 1 | 2 | 1 |
| MED$_\text{impaired side}$ | −3 | −3 | −3 | −3 | −3 | −2 | −3 | −2 | 0 | −2 | 2 |
| IQR$_\text{impaired side}$ | 1.5 | 1 | 1 | 1.5 | 1 | 2.5 | 1.5 | 3 | 4 | 5.5 | 5.5 |

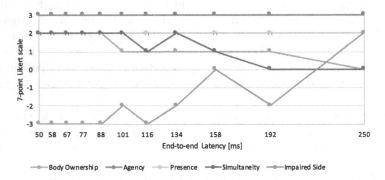

(a) Sense of body ownership, agency, presence, simultaneity, and impaired side.

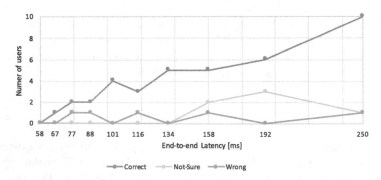

(b) Number of users who identified the impaired side correctly, wrong or were unsure.

**Fig. 4.** Median responses for the embodiment questionnaire at different end-to-end latency conditions.

Stanney et al. [16], we want to satisft the desire of keeping the value beneath 15 on the SSQ. Therefore, we recommend that the researchers and developers should keep end-to-end latency well below 58 ms (see Sect. 5.2). Our guidelines also confirm those proposed by Attig et al. [2], according to which the lower limit of 100 ms seems to be outdated. Moreover, we indeed recommend keeping the end-to-end latency below 20 ms as suggested by DiZio and Lackner [3].

Furthermore, with the significant results for user performance, we also accept hypothesis H2. Thus, with higher end-to-end latency, the user performance will decrease. In particular, users will need more time to complete the task. Compared to Waltemate et al. [18], stating that motor performance is affected by latency above 75 ms, we obtain similar results. The results show that the higher delays worsen user performance (see Sect. 5.3). Although the users typically need more time to complete the reaching task with increased end-to-end latency, we could not identify significant differences until 69 ms.

Hypothesis H3 cannot be accepted. We found no significant results for the sense of agency and presence. However, with increased end-to-end latency, body ownership and simultaneity perception will decrease. As already noted by Waltemate et al. [18], the delay affects body ownership significantly later, between 125 ms and 210 ms. Our results show that the sense of body ownership decreases earlier, already at 101 ms; however, we could not find significant differences until 192 ms. Similarly, Waltemate et al. [18] stated that simultaneity perception was affected by latency above 75 ms. Our results show that simultaneity perception dropped at latency values higher than 116 ms.

In contrast to work from Kondo et al. [9], not all our participants were able to identify the impaired side even not in the 250 ms end-to-end latency condition. Nevertheless, with the increased delay, more and more users identified the impaired side correctly. With end-to-end latency of 67 ms only one user and with an end-to-end latency of 250 ms total of ten users were able to specify the impaired side correctly.

# 7   Conclusion

This study aimed to gain insight into the effect of latency on user experience and performance in IVR by artificially increasing the end-to-end latency. We designed three different tasks to evaluate which impact increased latency has in IVR. For quantitative results, we used the Friedman test with Conover's test of multiple comparisons as a post-hoc test. We found significant differences when comparing final SSQ scores between several end-to-end latency conditions. Increased latency negatively affects user experience, e.g., users reported significant cybersickness symptoms with end-to-end latency above 63 ms. Thus, to ensure final SSQ scores of <15 and minimize cybersickness symptoms, the researchers and developers should ensure end-to-end latency far below 58 ms.

Furthermore, also user performance decreases with higher end-to-end latency. The results show that latency above 69 ms causes significant longer execution time. The results suggest that the sense of body ownership does accept higher latency values than user performance and cybersickness before significant results can be found. Sense of body ownership decreases with end-to-end latency above 101 ms; however, significant results were not found until 192 ms. We could not find any significant results for the sense of presence and agency. In general, with increasing end-to-end latency, user experience decreases and user performance worsens. We conclude that latency between perceived and physical head movements does not only contribute strongly to cybersickness but also decrease user performance and sense of embodiment.

In future work, we will focus on physiological data, such as ECG to measure the electrical activity of the heart. We believe that this will detect the cybersickness symptoms easier than subjective measurements of a SSQ. Furthermore, the task complexity and duration should be increased and breaks should be included between latency conditions, to avoid carry-over effects.

# References

1. Albert, R., Patney, A., Luebke, D., Kim, J.: Latency requirements for foveated rendering in virtual reality. ACM Trans. Appl. Percept. **14**(4), 25:1–25:13 (2017)
2. Attig, C., Rauh, N., Franke, T., Krems, J.F.: System latency guidelines then and now – is zero latency really considered necessary? In: Harris, D. (ed.) EPCE 2017. LNCS (LNAI), vol. 10276, pp. 3–14. Springer, Cham (2017). https://doi.org/10. 1007/978-3-319-58475-1_1
3. DiZio, P., Lackner, J.R.: Motion sickness side effects and aftereffects of immersive virtual environments created with helmet-mounted visual displays. Technical report, Ashton Graybiel Spatial Orientation Laboratory, Brandeis University (2000)
4. Friston, S., Steed, A.: Measuring latency in virtual environments. IEEE Trans. Vis. Comput. Graph. **20**(4), 616–625 (2014)
5. Garcia-Agundez, A., Reuter, C., Caserman, P., Konrad, R., Göbel, S.: Identifying cybersickness through heart rate variability alterations. Int. J. Virtual Reality **19**(1), 1–10 (2019)
6. Kasahara, S., et al.: Malleable embodiment: changing sense of embodiment by spatial-temporal deformation of virtual human body. In: Proceedings of the 2017 CHI Conference on Human Factors in Computing Systems, pp. 6438–6448. ACM, New York (2017)
7. Kawamura, S., Kijima, R.: Effect of HMD latency on human stability during quiescent standing on one foot. In: 2016 IEEE Symposium on 3D User Interfaces (3DUI), pp. 141–144 (2016)
8. Kennedy, R.S., Lane, N.E., Berbaum, K.S., Lilienthal, M.G.: Simulator sickness questionnaire: an enhanced method for quantifying simulator sickness. Int. J. Aviat. Psychol. **3**(3), 203–220 (1993)
9. Kondo, R., Sugimoto, M., Minamizawa, K., Hoshi, T., Inami, M., Kitazaki, M.: Illusory body ownership of an invisible body interpolated between virtualhands and feet via visual-motor synchronicity. Sci. Rep. **8**(1), 7541 (2018)
10. Meehan, M., Razzaque, S., Whitton, M.C., Brooks, F.P.: Effect of latency on presence in stressful virtual environments. In: Proceedings of the IEEE Virtual Reality, pp. 141–148 (2003)

11. Niehorster, D.C., Li, L., Lappe, M.: The accuracy and precision of position and orientation tracking in the HTC vive virtual reality system for scientific research. i-Perception **8**(3), 0–23 (2017)
12. Papadakis, G., Mania, K., Coxon, M., Koutroulis, E.: The effect of tracking delay on awareness states in immersive virtual environments: an initial exploration. In: Proceedings of the 10th International Conference on Virtual Reality Continuum and Its Applications in Industry, pp. 475–482 (2011)
13. Reason, J.T., Brand, J.J.: Motion Sickness. Academic Press, Cambridge (1975)
14. Samaraweera, G., Perdomo, A., Quarles, J.: Applying latency to half of a self-avatar's body to change real walking patterns. In: 2015 IEEE Virtual Reality (VR), pp. 89–96 (2015)
15. Shafer, D.M., Carbonara, C.P., Korpi, M.F.: Factors affecting enjoyment of virtual reality games: a comparison involving consumer-grade virtual reality technology. Games Health J. **8**(1), 15–23 (2018)
16. Stanney, K.M., Kennedy, R.S., Drexler, J.M.: Cybersickness is not simulator sickness. In: Proceedings of the Human Factors and Ergonomics Society Annual Meeting, vol. 41, no. 2, pp. 1138–1142 (1997)
17. Stauffert, J., Niebling, F., Latoschik, M.E.: Effects of latency jitter on simulator sickness in a search task. In: 2018 IEEE Conference on Virtual Reality and 3D User Interfaces (VR), pp. 121–127 (2018)
18. Waltemate, T., et al.: The impact of latency on perceptual judgments and motor performance in closed-loop interaction in virtual reality. In: Proceedings of the 22nd ACM Conference on Virtual Reality Software and Technology, pp. 27–35. ACM (2016)
19. Ware, C., Balakrishnan, R.: Reaching for objects in VR displays: lag and frame rate. ACM Trans. Comput. Hum. Interact. **1**(4), 331–356 (1994)

# FPVRGame: Deep Learning for Hand Pose Recognition in Real-Time Using Low-End HMD

Eder de Oliveira$^{(\boxtimes)}$ , Esteban Walter Gonzalez Clua,
Cristina Nader Vasconcelos, Bruno Augusto Dorta Marques ,
Daniela Gorski Trevisan, and Luciana Cardoso de Castro Salgado

Fluminense Federal University, Niterói, RJ, Brazil
eder_oliveira@id.uff.br

**Abstract.** Head Mounted Display (HMD) became a popular device, drastically increasing the usage of Virtual, Mixed, and Augmented Reality. While the systems' visual resources are accurate and immersive, precise interfaces require depth cameras or special joysticks, requiring either complex devices or not following the natural body expression. This work presents an approach for the usage of bare hands to control an immersive game from an egocentric perspective and built from a proposed case study methodology. We used a DenseNet Convolutional Neural Network (CNN) architecture to perform the recognition in real-time, from both indoor and outdoor environments, not requiring any image segmentation process. Our research also generated a vocabulary, considering users' preferences, seeking a set of natural and comfortable hand poses and evaluated users' satisfaction and performance for an entertainment setup. Our recognition model achieved an accuracy of 97.89%. The user's studies show that our method outperforms the classical controllers in regards to natural interactions. We demonstrate our results using commercial low-end HMD's and compare our solution with state-of-the-art methods.

**Keywords:** Hand poses recognition · Convolutional neural network · Deep learning · Virtual reality · User interfaces

## 1 Introduction

Head-Mounted Displays (HMDs) are becoming popular and accessible, leveraging Virtual, Mixed and Augmented Reality applications to a new level of consumption. A considerable amount of these market is strongly attached to low-end devices, based on smartphones as displays and computing hardware, enhancing the possibility of users interacting with virtual worlds anytime, anywhere, whether to watch a movie, work or play games [14].

© IFIP International Federation for Information Processing 2019
Published by Springer Nature Switzerland AG 2019
E. van der Spek et al. (Eds.): ICEC-JCSG 2019, LNCS 11863, pp. 70–84, 2019.
https://doi.org/10.1007/978-3-030-34644-7_6

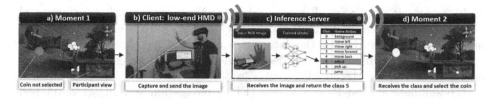

**Fig. 1.** The FPVRGame is a virtual reality environment developed to simulate a first-person view game which allows the usage of the bare hand to control a character. This figure shows the action of selecting a coin and the process involved: capture of the image, the inference of the convolutional neural network and the label send for the execution of the action in the game.

High-end devices, such as Oculus Rift or HTC Vive, provide sophisticated interfaces controllers and tracking systems, allowing powerful and complex interactions with the virtual environment [16]. Due to the lack of these components, mobile-based systems must be projected to be more straightforward and in many cases less immersive solutions.

Visual immersion achieved by the HMDs can generate high interaction expectation among the users. It is common to observe, at interaction time, that the user makes undesired body and hand gestures, moved by a natural body instinct [22].

This body interaction cannot be implemented with regular HMD joysticks and controllers. Thus, research has been conducted to offer a more natural engagement to users. For instance, several body and hand gestures recognition solutions are being presented in the last years, some of them using very different approaches than traditional joysticks: heart rate monitors [28], Coulomb friction model [9], acoustic resonance analysis [32] and even clothing that restricts joint movements [1].

The usage of bare hands is what seems to be the most natural and immersive solution, and some researchers are working on this [24,26]. In this sense, precise and comfortable solutions still require some dedicated hardware, such as depth cameras, structured light-based systems, and even Inertial measurement unit (IMU) based hardware.

In this work, we present an interaction solution based on bare hand interactions, which perform the real-time recognition with 98% accuracy and can be executed indoor and outdoor using ordinary cameras as input devices through low-end platforms, such as smartphones. Our solution is constrained for egocentric point of view and for a specific set of hand poses. It can be easily Incorporated in any application and presents good performance, suitable for low-end VR devices.

The hand pose recognition is a Machine Learning problem modeled as a pattern recognition task. Given that the state-of-the-art algorithms for pattern recognition in images are based on Convolutional Neural Networks (CNNs) [25], we have chosen to use this approach in our work. We adopted three CNNs based architectures (GoogLeNet, Resnet, and DenseNet), with which we conducted several training sessions using two different datasets until we get to the model used in our solution. One of the data sets was created specifically for this work, containing approximately 59,000 Red-Green-Blue (RGB) images of the hand in an egocentric vision [18, 30, 33].

To simulate a First-Person Vision (FPV) navigation system, we developed the FPVRGame (Fig. 1), a Virtual Reality (VR) environment. The FPVRGame design and evaluation process involved three empirical studies. In Study One we specified a preliminary vocabulary containing the hand poses considered more intuitive to represent the actions of a character from an FPV perspective. In Study Two we evaluated the hand poses existing in the preliminary vocabulary and built a new and more comfortable vocabulary, capturing the images required to create the dataset. Finally, in Study Three we validated our results using a low-end HMD and a simple VR environment.

The main contributions can be summarized as:

1. Implementation of a CNN-based method for recognition of user's hand poses captured from an FPV navigation system perspective in any environment (indoor and outdoor) and without any background or lighting constraints;
2. Creation of an open dataset with approximately 59,000 images of hand poses from a FPV navigation system perspective;
3. Generation and assessment of a hand pose vocabulary by using the Wizard of Oz method;
4. Empirical evaluation of user's experience and performance, using the proposed hand posture recognition in comparison to the main interfaces available for HMDs, in both low and high-end systems;

In addition, while we attempted to solve FPV systems, our solution can be trivially extended to any other interaction paradigm, depending only on providing a new image dataset.

The remainder of this paper is organized as follows: Sect. 2 describes the related works. Section 3 presents our CNN based solution for hand posture recognition and describes our Dataset, which we defined as public. Section 4 presents the FPVRGame design and evaluation process, i.e, the hand poses vocabulary construction process; the comparison between the accuracy achieved by our method with other interfaces. Finally, Sect. 6, present the conclusions of our work.

## 2   Related Work

Although there are several precise and functional interface devices for HMD's, we claim that the usage of bare hands is the most natural, intuitive and immersive [24].

Among several works, Son and Choi [27] proposed a hand pose detection approach that is capable for classifications based on raw RGB images. Their method recognizes three distinct hand poses employing a faster R-CNN, capable of identifying the region of interest and classifying one of the three possible poses. The dataset for training the network requires additional annotation for the palm position and fingertip. Their method aims to estimate the bounding box of the hands and identify which hand is in the camera field of view (left or right). In our paper, we consider that the game controller should work similarly for both hands, allowing left-handed and right-handed users to share the same experiences.

Hand gestures are classified in static and dynamic gestures [24]. Different datasets containing images in egocentric vision are available, such as [17,18,30,33]. However, most of them contain dynamic gestures. Dynamic gestures recognition usually exploits spatiotemporal features extracted from video sequences. The evaluation of this type of method usually employs a sliding window of 16 frames or more [4], which introduces a significant input lag corresponding to the time between the 16 frames and the gesture recognition. Our work recognizes static gestures through a CNN, classifying hand poses from a single frame and allowing real-time recognition without the before-mentioned input lag penalty. Furthermore, tests performed in an egocentric dataset [33] shows that our method has a competitive accuracy when taking account gestures similar to our hand poses vocabulary. We created a specific dataset with a limited number of poses but with higher accuracy.

Depth cameras (RGB-D) have the capacity of delivering depth information for each pixel, making possible the use of different techniques for geometry reconstruction and estimation of inverse kinematics bones positioning [24]. In indoor and controlled environments the depth cameras perform very well and are being vastly used. However, depth sensors can generate noisy depth maps, presenting some limitations: restricted field of view and range, near-infrared interference (such as light solar) and non-Lambertian reflections, and thus cannot acquire accurate measurements in outdoor environments [23]. These issues become more critical when the cameras are not fixed.

Yousefi et al. [31] presented a gesture-based interaction system for immersive systems. Their solution makes use of the smartphone camera to recognize the gesture performed by the user's hands. The recognition process is based on matching a camera image with an image in a gesture dataset. The gesture dataset contains images of a user's hand performing one of the 4 available gestures. The images were recorded for both left and right hands under different rotations and a chroma key screen was employed to remove the background pixels. The construction of the dataset is labor-intensive, requiring the manual annotation of 19 joint points for each image in the dataset. At runtime, a preprocessing step is necessary to ensure that only the relevant data is fed to the gesture recognition system. This stage consists in segmenting the hand from the background and crop the image in the region of interest. The gesture recognition system performs a similarity analysis based on L1 and L2 norms to match the camera image with one of the dataset images. A selective search strategy based on the previous camera frame is used to reduce the search domain and efficiently recognize the gesture in real time.

The previous method requires extensive labor-intensive adjustments through the manual annotation of 19 joint points for each sample on the dataset creation process. Furthermore, the segmentation process requires manual adjustments based on the user's environment. As opposed to their approach, our method employs a dataset creation process that automatically annotates the images while the user is experimenting with the application. Furthermore, our recognition system works on raw input images and does not require background extraction, chroma key, and lighting adjustments.

## 3   Hand Pose Recognition Solution

The hand pose recognition is the process of classifying poses of the user's hands in a given input image [24]. We use the recognized pose to perform an action in an interactive game. Since we are using the player's hands like a game controller, the process must be robust to recognize the player's hands in multiple scenarios and different environments. It is important to have a consistent result in the hand recognition since a wrong classification would result in an involuntary movement in the game, potentially harming the user's experience.

The hand pose recognition is a Machine Learning problem modeled as a pattern recognition task. Given that the state-of-the-art algorithms for pattern recognition in images are based on Convolutional Neural Networks [25], we choose to use this approach in our work.

Convolutional Neural Networks are learning algorithms that require a two-step process. A compute-intensive training step executed once, and a fast inference step, performed in the application runtime [24,26]. Considering that our method aims to be executed in a mobile environment, the hand pose recognition must be executed in interactive time even on low spec mobile devices. This requirement makes the Deep Neural Network a suitable approach for our purposes.

The input of our method is an RGB image containing the user's hands (Fig. 4). The output is a probability distribution of the $k$ possible classes. The classes are composed of the specified vocabulary described in Sect. 4, and an additional Background Class, that represents the absence of the user's hands in the input image.

We adopted three off-the-shelf CNN architectures for the hand pose recognition: GoogLeNet [29], Resnet 50 [8], and DenseNet [10].

### 3.1   Datasets

We use two datasets in the CNNs training.

**Dataset 1 (DS1):** We use a pre-training dataset, containing 1,233,067 samples, taken from publicly available sign language datasets [15]. A sample in the dataset consists of a tuple (image, label) where the image portrays an interpreter performing a sign language gesture. Even though this dataset does not contain the correct label for our recognition system, the images of the dataset are employed to precondition the CNN to recognize features related to human hands under different poses.

**Dataset 2 (DS2):** We created a second dataset specially tailored for our recognition system. The dataset consists of 58,868 samples captured in an indoor environment, comprising images of fifteen people (eleven men and four women). To improve our detection for both right-handed and left-handed users, we applied a mirror transformation in the images. The images were manually annotated with one of the seven classes that represent the possible actions of the game, or a class representing the background (Fig. 4).

A preprocessing step in both datasets ensures that the images have the same dimensions (256 × 256 pixels). A bicubic transformation was performed to resize images to adequate dimensions.

## 3.2 CNNs Training Results

Training a CNN from scratch requires a significant amount of labeled data; therefore, we trained three CNNs through a process known as fine-tuning. We loaded a pre-trained model with weights adjusted to the ImageNet dataset [6]; then we fine-tuned our network to the DS2 dataset. Figure 2a shows a summary of the results obtained during the training.

The ResNet architecture obtained a not satisfactory result, with a mean accuracy of 85.46% (test) and 79.25% (validation), with a mean error of 0.854%. Aiming to improve the accuracy of the classification, we performed a second experiment that exploits the features learned from the DS1 dataset.

The second experiment consists in, first, fine-tuning the CNN from the ImageNet dataset to the DS1 dataset, then fine-tuning the resulting model to the DS2 dataset. The result of this experiment for the ResNet architecture results in a mean accuracy of 93.03% (test) and 89,79% (validation) with a mean error of 0.406%. When compared to the first approach, we obtained a significant improvement in the mean accuracy of 8.85% (test) and 13.28% (validation) with a mean error of 0.406%.

While the ResNet highly benefit from the second approach, the GoogleNet and DenseNet obtained only a slight change in the mean accuracy when compared to the first experiment. The GoogLeNet test accuracy improved by a small margin (from 97.47% to 98.05%) while the DenseNet present a small decrease in test accuracy (from 97.89% to 97.23%).

Overall, the GoogLeNet obtained the highest mean accuracy of 98.05% on tests while the DenseNet, trained with the first approach, achieved the lowest mean error on the validation and a better mean accuracy distribution across the different classes. Furthermore, the training process was facilitated due to the usage of the first approach that does not require the finetuning to the DS1 dataset. The mean accuracy across multiple classes can be observed in the confusion matrix depicted in Fig. 2b and c. In our hand pose recognition system, we choose to use the DenseNet implementation due to less associated error across multiple classes and the relative uncomplicated single training process.

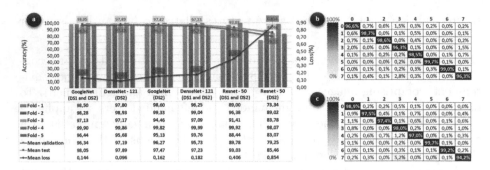

**Fig. 2.** (a) Best results achieved during the training of CNNs, using the two data sets DS1 and DS2. (b) DenseNet's confusion matrix. (c) GoogleNet's confusion matrix.

For validation purposes, we tested our trained CNN against a public available egocentric benchmark dataset, EgoGesture [33]. The dataset contains 2,081 RGB-D videos, 24,161 gesture samples totaling 2,953,224 frames. There are 83 classes of gestures, mainly focused on interaction with wearable devices. Because it is a data set different from ours, we have chosen a subset of gestures that are similar to the poses of our vocabulary. The mapping between the EgoGesture classes and our vocabulary classes is shown in the Table 1. Our GloogleNet model, even though have never been trained with any of the images in the EgoCentric dataset achieved an accuracy of 64.3%. This result is superior to the mean average accuracy of 62.5% in the VGG16 model presented by Cao et. al [4]. On one hand, we could improve our accuracy results by considering spatiotemporal strategies like appending an Long Short-Term Memory (LSTM) network to the output of our last fully connected layer, on the other hand, this introduction would increase the input lag in our application, thus making the model inadequate for VR applications.

**Table 1.** Gesture mapping our vocabulary of hand poses to EgoGesture [33] gestures.

| Our Vocabulary | | EgoGesture | |
|---|---|---|---|
| Class | Gesture | Class | Gesture |
| 1 move left | | 66 thumb toward left | |
| 2 move right | | 65 thumb toward right | |
| 3 move forward | | 83 move fingers forward | |
| 4 move back | | 67 thumbs backward | |
| 5 select | | 29 number 5 | |

Most of the errors associated with our model are the misclassification of gestures as background (class 0), as shown in the confusion matrix depicted in Fig. 3a. This error is associated with the different nature of our training dataset and the tested dataset (video sequences in the EgoGesture vs single frames in our dataset). Frames at the two extremes (beginning and ending) of a video sequence in the EgoGesture dataset contains no identifiable gestures, for example, partially visible hands or the very beginning/ending of a gesture. To test this hypothesis, we tested our model by dropping the few beginning and ending frames of the video sequences. With 4 and 8 frames dropped, the model achieved a notable higher mean accuracy of 76.17% and 78.81%. The improvement in the model's accuracy and the confusion matrix (Fig. 3b and c) confirm our hypothesis.

**(a) 0 frames dropped**

|   | 0 | 1 | 2 | 3 | 4 | 5 | 6 | 7 |
|---|---|---|---|---|---|---|---|---|
| 0 | 0,0% | 0,0% | 0,0% | 0,0% | 0,0% | 0,0% | 0,0% | 0,0% |
| 1 | 32,8% | 61,3% | 0,3% | 3,2% | 1,5% | 0,6% | 0,0% | 0,3% |
| 2 | 26,4% | 0,0% | 63,3% | 2,9% | 4,4% | 0,2% | 0,5% | 2,2% |
| 3 | 29,5% | 0,1% | 0,1% | 63,9% | 1,8% | 0,3% | 0,0% | 4,3% |
| 4 | 31,4% | 0,4% | 0,0% | 6,5% | 60,4% | 0,2% | 0,4% | 0,8% |
| 5 | 20,7% | 0,2% | 0,2% | 2,5% | 1,4% | 73,5% | 1,4% | 0,0% |
| 6 | 0,0% | 0,0% | 0,0% | 0,0% | 0,0% | 0,0% | 0,0% | 0,0% |
| 7 | 0,0% | 0,0% | 0,0% | 0,0% | 0,0% | 0,0% | 0,0% | 0,0% |

**(b) 4 frames dropped**

|   | 0 | 1 | 2 | 3 | 4 | 5 | 6 | 7 |
|---|---|---|---|---|---|---|---|---|
| 0 | 0,0% | 0,0% | 0,0% | 0,0% | 0,0% | 0,0% | 0,0% | 0,0% |
| 1 | 21,7% | 72,8% | 0,4% | 2,8% | 1,5% | 0,6% | 0,0% | 0,2% |
| 2 | 15,6% | 0,0% | 76,3% | 1,4% | 3,9% | 0,3% | 0,6% | 1,8% |
| 3 | 19,4% | 0,1% | 0,1% | 72,7% | 1,9% | 0,4% | 0,0% | 5,4% |
| 4 | 20,2% | 0,4% | 0,0% | 6,0% | 71,8% | 0,2% | 0,5% | 0,9% |
| 5 | 7,7% | 0,1% | 0,3% | 1,7% | 1,0% | 88,3% | 0,9% | 0,0% |
| 6 | 0,0% | 0,0% | 0,0% | 0,0% | 0,0% | 0,0% | 0,0% | 0,0% |
| 7 | 0,0% | 0,0% | 0,0% | 0,0% | 0,0% | 0,0% | 0,0% | 0,0% |

**(c) 8 frames dropped**

|   | 0 | 1 | 2 | 3 | 4 | 5 | 6 | 7 |
|---|---|---|---|---|---|---|---|---|
| 0 | 0,0% | 0,0% | 0,0% | 0,0% | 0,0% | 0,0% | 0,0% | 0,0% |
| 1 | 19,9% | 75,6% | 0,3% | 2,2% | 1,4% | 0,4% | 0,0% | 0,2% |
| 2 | 14,8% | 0,0% | 80,7% | 0,6% | 2,4% | 0,2% | 0,6% | 0,6% |
| 3 | 18,1% | 0,1% | 0,1% | 73,4% | 2,0% | 0,4% | 0,1% | 5,9% |
| 4 | 19,2% | 0,4% | 0,0% | 4,8% | 74,0% | 0,2% | 0,7% | 0,8% |
| 5 | 5,9% | 0,0% | 0,3% | 1,0% | 0,4% | 92,0% | 0,4% | 0,0% |
| 6 | 0,0% | 0,0% | 0,0% | 0,0% | 0,0% | 0,0% | 0,0% | 0,0% |
| 7 | 0,0% | 0,0% | 0,0% | 0,0% | 0,0% | 0,0% | 0,0% | 0,0% |

**Fig. 3.** Confusion matrix: (a) 0 frames dropped, (b) 4 frames dropped, (c) 8 frames dropped. As for classes 6 and 7 we did not find similar gestures. Class 0 does not make its inference because it does not appear in the label of the base EgoCentric.

The CNN training was executed on a DGX-1 machine with the following specification: Intel Xeon E5-2698 v4 2.2 GHz, 512 GB DDR 4, 8 x NVIDIA P100 Graphics Processing Unit (GPU). All the networks are trained using 4 GPUs adopting Stochastic Gradient Descent (SGD) as our solver. We applied 5-fold cross-validation to our model, splitting the dataset into 5 distinct folds [7]. We run the tests for 30 epochs with batch size 96. The learning rate is set initially to 0.01 with the exponential decay (gamma = 0.95).

### 3.3 Inference Server Implementation

The recognition system is based on a client/server system. The FPVRGame, running on a smartphone Moto X4, act as a client that captures the HMD camera image and send them to the inference server application through a TCP/IP protocol. The server feeds the CNN with the received image and carries the recognized hand pose identification back to the FPVRGame. The inference server application (Fig. 1c) was implemented with Python 3.6 using the Caffe framework [11] within an Intel® Core™ i7-7700HQ CPU @ 2.80 GHz, 16 GB RAM and NVIDIA GeForce® GTX 1050 Ti machine and running the DenseNet model performs the inference with an average of 28 ms. Thus, the inference process can run in real-time (35 fps) on any modern GPU enabled devices. Alternatively, it is possible to use our CNN model with third-party inference engines such as NVIDIA TensorRT [20], Clipper [5], and DeepDetect [12].

## 4   FPVRGame - Design and Evaluation Process

FPVRGame is a VR environment developed to simulate an FPV game. Its primary objective is to navigate through the scenario and collect as many coins as possible. For this, it captures the image of the player's hand and forwards the images to the Inference Server, see Fig. 1. As the camera is the single input device, the player has to position his hand inside the camera field. This limitation may require considerable physical effort, and if the hand pose is not the most suitable, may cause pain.

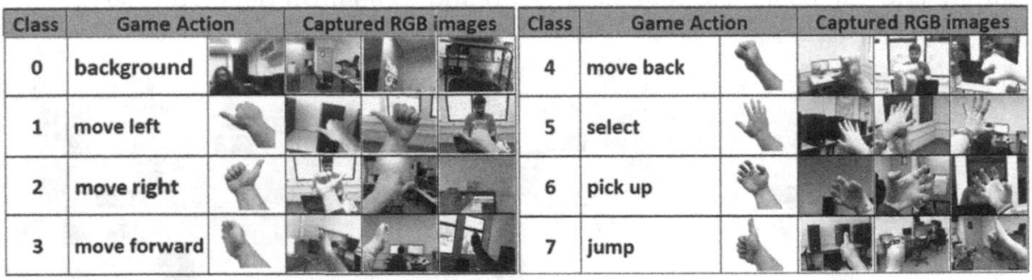

| Class | Game Action | Captured RGB images | Class | Game Action | Captured RGB images |
|---|---|---|---|---|---|
| 0 | background | | 4 | move back | |
| 1 | move left | | 5 | select | |
| 2 | move right | | 6 | pick up | |
| 3 | move forward | | 7 | jump | |

**Fig. 4.** Vocabulary of hand poses used for the player.

Figure 4 shows the vocabulary provided by FPVRGame, built based on two empirical studies, that offer a set of intuitive and comfortable hand poses. Study One included identifying users' preference for the most appropriate hand poses. This study was attended by 173 people, being 105 males and 68 females, aged between 18 and 39 years (M = 25, SD = 4.06), 92.5% and 7.5% left-handers. What resulted in preliminary vocabulary. In Study Two by using the Wizard of Oz method [13], we evaluate the existing hand poses in the preliminary vocabulary and construct a new, more comfortable vocabulary, capturing the images needed to create the data set. This study was attended by 15 people, 11 males, and 4 females, aged 18 to 43 years (M = 26.46, SD = 6.94), all right-handed.

Study Three is aimed at assessing the participant's experience and performance when using our hand poses recognition solution. The primary measures used in this study were the participant's feelings (Easy to learn, Comfort, Natural and Enjoyment) when using different game controllers (joystick, gaze and hand poses) to control a virtual character in the FPVRGame.

Figure 5 shows a summary of the results for questions Q1 - Easy to learn, Q2 - Comfort, Q3 - Natural, and Q4 - Enjoyment, for each game controller. All statistical analyses were performed using IBM SPSS[1] with ($\alpha = 0.05$).

For the item "Q1 - Easy to learn", we find none significant difference between the game controllers (Friedman $X^2_{(2)} = 4.480$, $p = 0.106$).

---

[1]  https://www.ibm.com/analytics/spss-statistics-software.

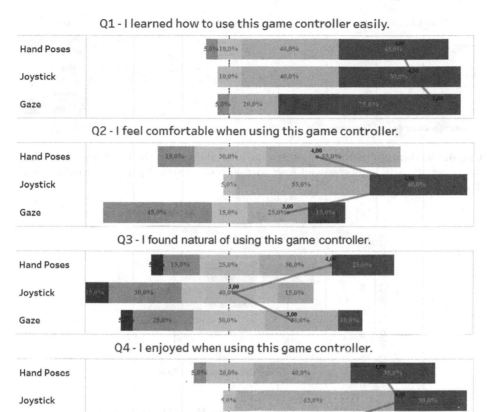

**Fig. 5.** Perceptions of the participants considering all game controllers.

For the item "Q2 - Comfort", there was a significant difference between gaze and joystick controllers (Friedman $X^2_{(2)} = 16.033$, $p < 0.001$). The joystick achieved the highest percentage of positive feelings among the controllers (95%), is significantly higher than the gaze (40%).

For the item "Q3 - Natural", there was a significant difference between the joystick and hand pose controllers (Friedman $X^2_{(2)} = 12.400$, $p = 0.002$). The hand pose achieved the highest percentage of positive feelings among the controllers (55%), is significantly higher than the joystick (15%).

For the item "Q4 - Enjoyment", there was no significant difference between the game controllers (Friedman $X^2_{(2)} = 8.041$, $p = 0.018$, with the multiple comparisons tests with $p$ value adjusted (Gaze-Hand Pose $p = 0.207$), (Gaze-Joystick $p = 0.144$), (Hand Pose-Joystick $p = 1$)).

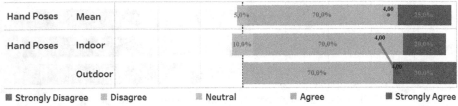

■ Strongly Disagree     ■ Disagree          ■ Neutral          ■ Agree          ■ Strongly Agree

**Fig. 6.** Participants' perception of effectiveness while using the hand pose controller, first row: all participants, second row: participants separated per group (indoor, outdoor).

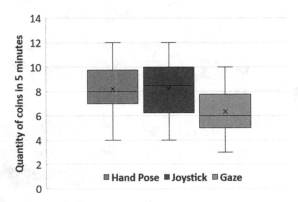

**Fig. 7.** Quantity of coins per game controller: Hand Pose (M = 8.2, SD = 0.46), Joystick (M = 8.25, SD = 0.51) and Gaze (M = 6.35, SD = 0.43).

For the evaluation of "Effectiveness" perception (Fig. 6) the majority of the participants pointed out positive feelings regarding the effectiveness of the hand pose recognition with only 5% of "Neutral" responses. In addition, we found no significant difference between the participants who performed the study in different environments (Mann-Whitney $U = 41.500$, $p = 0.423$).

Concerning the performance of participants using the hand pose controller in indoor and outdoor environments we find none significant difference (t-test $t_{(18)} = 0.631$, $p = 0.536$). This result is in agreement with the evaluation of effectiveness perception.

We also recorded the number of coins collected by participants using each game controller (see Fig. 7). The Shapiro-Wilk test shows that the data follows a normal distribution (Hand Pose: $W = 0.970$, $p = 0.760$, Joystick: $W = 0.958$, $p = 0.499$ and Gaze: $W = 0.952$, $p = 0.396$). Thus, a One-way ANOVA with repeated measures ($\alpha = 0.05$) with *posthoc* and correction of Bonferroni was used ($F_{(2,38)} = 8.218$, $p = 0.001$. We note that the quantity of coins collected while using the hand pose controller was significantly higher when compared to the gaze controller. However, it was not different from the performance achieved while using the joystick.

One limitation of FPVRGame is to use a single input device. The interaction occurs only when the user places his hand within the angle of the camera, which can cause some physical discomfort. Therefore, we evaluated the participants' comfort when using hand pose and surprisingly, such aspect was not a problem for the participants to enjoy and to achieve excellent performance.

## 5  Discussion

Natural User Interfaces (NUIs) is not a trivial definition [19]. Bill Buxton [3] argues that NUI exploits skills that were acquired through a lifetime of living, which minimizes the cognitive load and therefore minimizes the distraction. He also states that NUIs should always be designed with the use of context in mind. Bowman et al. [2] questioned naturalism in 3D interface saying that high levels of naturalism can enhance performance and the overall user experience, but moderately natural 3D UIs can be unfamiliar and reduce performance. Traditional, less natural, interaction styles can provide excellent performance, but result in lower levels of presence, engagement, and fun.

Dealing with this trade-off between naturalism versus performance is still a challenge, and few efforts have been reported about how to explore the design space in order to find the appropriate and natural interaction for a specific context of use. Different from Son et al. [27] and Yousefi et al. [31], our work addresses such issue by using a user-centered design approach to build a hand pose vocabulary for 3D user interaction in an egocentric vision scenario. The Wizard-of-Oz technique used in Study Two shown to be adequate for validating the preliminary vocabulary achieved by Study One and contributing for a good final user's experience with the FPVRGame, as was discussed in Study Three.

In addition, the simulation with the wizard allowed appropriate conditions for recording the images and generating the data set. Before using the simulation we tried to ask the volunteers to perform some hand poses to be captured and used in the CNNs training, using the same method of capturing the databases cited above in related works [17,30,33]. However, in practice, the results were not good, and we assume that it was due to the robotic and not natural movements made by the volunteers without causing oscillations in the poses.

Even with a dataset composed only of images collected indoor, no need for background extraction, chroma key, and lighting adjustments [31] or data augmentation [27], our CNN model was able to generalize the recognition of hand poses, and it works appropriately for both indoors and outdoors environments. Besides that, we observed that the performance of the hand pose interaction with the FPVRGame presented satisfactory results, similar to the joystick in the number of collected coins (Fig. 7).

## 6  Conclusion

Our FPVRGame proposal allows the use of bare hands as a control for VR and Head Mounted Display scenarios, especially for low-end VR devices. Our scenario is focused on egocentric vision and presents a set of natural and comfortable hand poses, considering users' preferences. We developed a public dataset [21], which allows extensions and inclusions of new hand poses. The FPVRGame demonstrates a hand pose interaction solution, based on deep learning, that using a trained CNN model capable of recognizing hand poses, captured at indoors or outdoors environments and without any illumination or background constraint. We achieved an average accuracy of 97.89%, which allowed smooth and comfortable human interaction through different usage scenarios. We demonstrate our results using commercial low-end HMD's and compare our solution with traditional interaction devices.

# References

1. Al Maimani, A., Roudaut, A.: Frozen suit: designing a changeable stiffness suit and its application to haptic games. In: Proceedings of the 2017 CHI Conference on Human Factors in Computing Systems, CHI 2017, pp. 2440–2448. ACM, New York (2017). https://doi.org/10.1145/3025453.3025655
2. Bowman, D.A., McMahan, R.P., Ragan, E.D.: Questioning naturalism in 3D user interfaces. Commun. ACM **55**(9), 78–88 (2012)
3. Buxton, B.: Sketching User Experiences: Getting the Design Right and the Right Design. Morgan kaufmann, Burlington (2010)
4. Cao, C., Zhang, Y., Wu, Y., Lu, H., Cheng, J.: Egocentric gesture recognition using recurrent 3D convolutional neural networks with spatiotemporal transformer modules. In: Proceedings of the IEEE International Conference on Computer Vision, pp. 3763–3771 (2017)
5. Crankshaw, D., Wang, X., Zhou, G., Franklin, M.J., Gonzalez, J.E., Stoica, I.: Clipper: a low-latency online prediction serving system. In: NSDI, pp. 613–627 (2017)
6. Deng, J., Dong, W., Socher, R., Li, L.J., Li, K., Fei-Fei, L.: ImageNet: a large-scale hierarchical image database. In: IEEE Conference on Computer Vision and Pattern Recognition, CVPR 2009, pp. 248–255. IEEE (2009)
7. Fushiki, T.: Estimation of prediction error by using k-fold cross-validation. Stat. Comput. **21**(2), 137–146 (2011)
8. He, K., Zhang, X., Ren, S., Sun, J.: Deep residual learning for image recognition. In: Proceedings of the IEEE Conference on Computer Vision and Pattern Recognition pp. 770–778 (2016)
9. Höll, M., Oberweger, M., Arth, C., Lepetit, V.: Efficient physics-based implementation for realistic hand-object interaction in virtual reality. In: 2018 IEEE Conference on Virtual Reality and 3D User Interfaces (2018)
10. Huang, G., Liu, Z., Weinberger, K.Q., van der Maaten, L.: Densely connected convolutional networks. In: Proceedings of the IEEE Conference on Computer Vision and Pattern Recognition, vol. 1, p. 3 (2017)
11. Jia, Y., et al.: Caffe: convolutional architecture for fast feature embedding. arXiv preprint arXiv:1408.5093 (2014)
12. JoliBrain: Deep detect (2018). https://deepdetect.com. Accessed 20 Sept 2018
13. Kelley, J.F.: An empirical methodology for writing user-friendly natural language computer applications. In: Proceedings of the SIGCHI Conference on Human Factors in Computing Systems, pp. 193–196. ACM (1983)

14. Knierim, P., Schwind, V., Feit, A.M., Nieuwenhuizen, F., Henze, N.: Physical keyboards in virtual reality: analysis of typing performance and effects of avatar hands. In: Proceedings of the 2018 CHI Conference on Human Factors in Computing Systems, CHI 2018, pp. 345:1–345:9. ACM, New York (2018). https://doi.org/10.1145/3173574.3173919
15. Koller, O., Ney, H., Bowden, R.: Deep hand: how to train a CNN on 1 million hand images when your data is continuous and weakly labelled. In: IEEE Conference on Computer Vision and Pattern Recognition, Las Vegas, NV, USA, pp. 3793–3802, June 2016
16. Lee, S., Park, K., Lee, J., Kim, K.: User study of VR basic controller and data glove as hand gesture inputs in VR games. In: 2017 International Symposium on Ubiquitous Virtual Reality (ISUVR), pp. 1–3, June 2017. https://doi.org/10.1109/ISUVR.2017.16
17. Li, Y., Ye, Z., Rehg, J.M.: Delving into egocentric actions. In: Proceedings of the IEEE Conference on Computer Vision and Pattern Recognition, pp. 287–295 (2015)
18. Molchanov, P., Yang, X., Gupta, S., Kim, K., Tyree, S., Kautz, J.: Online detection and classification of dynamic hand gestures with recurrent 3D convolutional neural network. In: Proceedings of the IEEE Conference on Computer Vision and Pattern Recognition, pp. 4207–4215 (2016)
19. Mortensen, D.: Natural user interfaces-what are they and how do you design user interfaces that feel natural. Interact. Design Found. (2017)
20. NVIDIA: NVIDIA tensorrt (2018). https://developer.nvidia.com/tensorrt. Accessed 20 Sept 2018
21. Oliveira, E.: Dataset from egocentrics images for hand poses recognition (2018). https://goo.gl/EEbtcP. Accessed 10 Sept 2018
22. Piumsomboon, T., Clark, A., Billinghurst, M., Cockburn, A.: User-defined gestures for augmented reality. In: Kotzé, P., Marsden, G., Lindgaard, G., Wesson, J., Winckler, M. (eds.) INTERACT 2013. LNCS, vol. 8118, pp. 282–299. Springer, Heidelberg (2013). https://doi.org/10.1007/978-3-642-40480-1_18
23. Proença, P.F., Gao, Y.: SPLODE: semi-probabilistic point and line odometry with depth estimation from RGB-D camera motion. In: 2017 IEEE/RSJ International Conference on Intelligent Robots and Systems (IROS), pp. 1594–1601. IEEE (2017)
24. Rautaray, S.S., Agrawal, A.: Vision based hand gesture recognition for humancomputer interaction: a survey. Artif. Intell. Rev. **43**(1), 1–54 (2015). https://doi.org/10.1007/s10462-012-9356-9
25. Russakovsky, O., et al.: ImageNet large scale visual recognition challenge. Int. J. Comput. Vis. (IJCV) **115**(3), 211–252 (2015). https://doi.org/10.1007/s11263-015-0816-y
26. Sagayam, K.M., Hemanth, D.J.: Hand posture and gesture recognition techniques for virtual reality applications: a survey. Virtual Reality **21**(2), 91–107 (2017). https://doi.org/10.1007/s10055-016-0301-0
27. Son, Y.J., Choi, O.: Image-based hand pose classification using faster R-CNN. In: 2017 17th International Conference on Control, Automation and Systems (ICCAS), pp. 1569–1573. IEEE (2017)
28. Sra, M., Xu, X., Maes, P.: Breathvr: leveraging breathing as a directly controlled interface for virtual reality games. In: Proceedings of the 2018 CHI Conference on Human Factors in Computing Systems, CHI 2018, pp. 340:1–340:12. ACM, New York (2018). https://doi.org/10.1145/3173574.3173914
29. Szegedy, C., et al.: Going deeper with convolutions. In: Proceedings of the IEEE Conference on Computer Vision and Pattern Recognition, pp. 1–9 (2015)

30. Tewari, A., Grandidier, F., Taetz, B., Stricker, D.: Adding model constraints to CNN for top view hand pose recognition in range images. In: ICPRAM, pp. 170–177 (2016)

31. Yousefi, S., Kidane, M., Delgado, Y., Chana, J., Reski, N.: 3D gesture-based interaction for immersive experience in mobile VR. In: 2016 23rd International Conference on Pattern Recognition (ICPR), pp. 2121–2126. IEEE (2016)

32. Zhang, C., et al.: FingerPing: recognizing fine-grained hand poses using active acoustic on-body sensing. In: Proceedings of the 2018 CHI Conference on Human Factors in Computing Systems, CHI 2018, pp. 437:1–437:10. ACM, New York (2018). https://doi.org/10.1145/3173574.3174011

33. Zhang, Y., Cao, C., Cheng, J., Lu, H.: EgoGesture: a new dataset and benchmark for egocentric hand gesture recognition. IEEE Trans. Multimed. **20**(5), 1038–1050 (2018)

# Give MEANinGS to Robots with Kitchen Clash: A VR Human Computation Serious Game for World Knowledge Accumulation

Johannes Pfau[✉], Robert Porzel, Mihai Pomarlan, Vanja Sophie Cangalovic, Supara Grudpan, Sebastian Höffner, John Bateman, and Rainer Malaka

University of Bremen, Bibliothekstraße 1, 28359 Bremen, Germany
{jpfau,porzel,pomarlan,vanja,gud,shoeffner,bateman,malaka}@uni-bremen.de

**Abstract.** In this paper, we introduce the framework of MEANinGS for the semi-autonomous accumulation of world knowledge for robots. Where manual aggregation is inefficient and prone to incompleteness and autonomous approaches suffer from underspecified information, we deploy the human computation game *Kitchen Clash* and give evidence of its efficiency, completeness and motivation potential.

**Keywords:** Serious game · Knowledge accumulation · Framework

## 1 Introduction

Robotic proficiency excels in well-defined tasks and environments [1,4,12], but fails in compensating for missing or too generic information. Human-level world knowledge has been shown to close the reasoning gap [4], yet teaching robots this kind of knowledge remains one of the most challenging tasks for robotic AI research, since autonomous approaches end up with underspecified information and manual accumulation results in incalculable effort. In this paper, we introduce *Kitchen Clash*, a VR human computation serious game for the extraction of human world knowledge in the context of everyday activities. Within the framework of MEANinGS (MALLEATING EVERYDAY ACTIVITY NARRATIVES IN GAMES AND SIMULATIONS), we integrate a combination of information-transforming modules that include finding a proper set of instructions for a given complex task, processing these syntactically as well as semantically to detect underspecified information, autonomously generating testbed scenarios including a variety of decision making affordances and finally solving world knowledge problems by human computation through a serious game aided by physical simulation. In an explorative pilot study, we assessed user experience, appraisal and the overall viability of the presented serious game to report on the findings and demonstrate the feasibility of the approach. To constitute a baseline condition,

E. van der Spek et al. (Eds.): ICEC-JCSG 2019, LNCS 11863, pp. 85–96, 2019.
https://doi.org/10.1007/978-3-030-34644-7_7

we evaluated these findings against a control group executing manual knowledge accumulation, resulting in higher efficiency, increased motivation and considerably higher information retrieval. This paper contributes to the community of serious game research, presenting a successful application advantageous to a real-world problem solving field, as well as to the community of robotic research, exemplifying the practicability of a novel framework to overcome underspecified knowledge.

## 2   Related Work

One of the earliest research programs to study autonomous robots was the Shakey project [12]. Shakey was a mobile robot that used planning to reason about its actions and performed tasks that required planning of paths and actions as well as re-arranging of simple objects. This work was seminal for the fields of classical planning and computer vision. Nevertheless, even in Shakey's simple environment, the limitations of the approach became clear, as the computational complexity of planning problems proved, in general, to be intractable.

Many researchers [4,11–13,18] have worked on providing robotic systems with human-like common sense knowledge so that the robots could, hopefully, avoid costly planning from scratch or trial and error. Dang et al. [3] proposed a method to teach a robot to manipulate everyday objects through human demonstration. The authors asked participants to put on motion capture suits and perform tasks, such as opening a microwave or a slide door, and recorded 3D marker trajectories. These trajectories were used as the input for a chain learning algorithm. Parde et al. [13] developed a method to train robots to learn the world around them by using interactive dialogue and virtual games. The game asked a human player to put some objects in front of the robot and challenge it to guess which object the user has in mind. Through many gameplay sessions, the robot learns about objects and features which describe them and associates these with newly captured training images. Beetz et al. [1,2] proposed the software toolbox for design, implementation, and the deployment of cognition-enabled autonomous robots to perform everyday manipulation activities. To teach the robot, they use a marker-less motion capture system to record human activity data, which is then stored as experience data for improving manipulation program parameters. Programs, object data, and experience logs are uploaded to the openEASE web server, from which they can be retrieved as needed to extend the task repertoires and objects that a robot can recognize.

The representations needed for action knowledge have also been a topic of research, because the symbolic, highly abstract, "actions as black boxes" representations of the Shakey era do not result in robust behaviors in a realistic environment. In general, action knowledge tends to be subsymbolic, and often takes the form of success/failure probability distributions over an action's parameter space [17,19]. Note that the experience the robot learns from doesn't have to be from the real world. Simulated episodes, produced either by a human player of a game or a robot simulating itself, can be used for this purpose. Simulation will of course not provide a complete description of a realistic action, but even

very coarse simulation can already be useful for a robot that needs to validate
its plans and/or pick a better set of parameters [8].

In our work, we propose MEANinGS to use a VR human computation serious game to simulate real-world tasks in realistic environments and situations.
Recorded trajectories can be translated to real-world robotic movements which
are spatially less constrained than motion capturing approaches and accumulated world knowledge can help overcoming underspecified information, which
has the potential to reduce planning computation considerably. Similar to the
aforementioned approach, we contribute to the field of cumulative robotic knowledge by adding resulting symbolical and subsymbolical insights to the openEASE
repertoire.

## 3   Implementation

### 3.1   Framework

Figure 1 demonstrates the flow of information, as well as the impact of and interaction between the particular modules. MEANinGS originated in the context of
everyday household activities and focuses on knowledge accumulation in this
area, while its functionality is not limited to the application field. Offering an
interface to any natural language based instruction set (**retrieval**), the contained
information is **processed** in order to represent subtasks as tuples of manipula-
tive actions and objects acted on or with. When utilizing natural language, the
ontological scope of these objects is often heavily underspecified, since humans
are used to working with generalized information and specifying these in terms
of individual choice, influenced by world knowledge, availability and preference.
Yet, this underspecification does not render all possible objects contained in
a general term as viable (or usual). Thus, in the **specification** layer, human
knowledge is added through *Kitchen Clash*, a serious game presenting a decision
making paradigm within this set of objects. Parallel to this, complementing world
knowledge is derived from physical properties of the objects and their surroundings via simulation. In both approaches, object choices can be quantified and

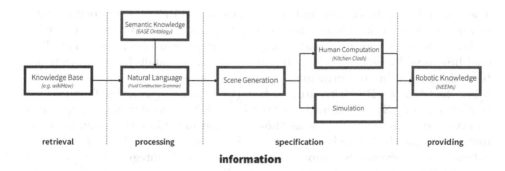

**Fig. 1.** Flowchart of the introduced MEANinGS framework.

thus ranked by efficiency and effectiveness. Within the simulation, this assessment can be realized in a fully autonomous manner, while the serious game offers further qualitative insights, since peer-rated quality measurements are included in the rating process, as well as preference and conventionality measures. Eventually, world knowledge is aggregated with trajectorial and contextual information and **provided** as *narrative-enabled episodic memories* (*NEEMs*) according to the KnowRob [1] paradigm.

## 3.2  Knowledge Base

In order to have a generic, comprehensive framework that is capable of adapting to human data input, our approach does not rely on a single knowledge base, but is designed to handle any set of natural language instructions that are goal-oriented and describe the most crucial subtasks sequentially or hierarchically. In this way, we introduce an interface that manages to grasp verbal commands equally effective as cooking recipes or tutorial websites (e.g. wikiHow). After retrieving the document encompassing the entire task completion, subgoals are derived from the contained sentences or steps and processed in the next module, independently of each other.

## 3.3  Natural Language Processing

In order to flexibly handle natural language input consisting of abstract and underspecified instructions, a deep semantic parser based on the Fluid Construction Grammar formalism [16] is used. Both the lexicon and the analysis itself make use of ontological knowledge described in Sect. 3.4, to guide the extensive search process, disambiguate otherwise unclear instructions and evoke unspecified parameters which need to be inferred by later processing steps of MEANinGS. In this way, natural language commands are transformed into a series of desired actions, accompanied by their parameters and respective pre- and post-conditions.

## 3.4  Ontology

The semantics of the actions and entities involved in the game are defined by a formal ontology. This ontology is designed to provide descriptions for everyday activities in terms of human physiology and human mental concepts, as well as enabling formal reasoning. The ontology supplying the labels for the objects has been designed using the principles proposed by Masolo et al. and is created by using the DOLCE+DnS Ultralite ontology (DUL) as an overarching foundational framework [5,6]. Specific branches of the KnowRob knowledge model pertaining to everyday activities [1], such as those involved in table setting and cooking, have consequently been aligned to the DUL framework. Additional axiomatization that is beyond the scope of description logics is integrated by means of the Distributed Ontology Language [9]. For the task at hand, however, only the taxonomic model is employed to classify events and objects.

## 3.5   Scene Generation

Within the scene generation module, we aim to provide a rich contextual world for the following **specification** methods by preparing a scene that contains sufficient interactable objects to ensure *completeness* (i.e. solvability of each contained subgoal) and to facilitate *variety of choices* (in order to retrieve actual world knowledge through humans' decisive solutions or physical properties of the simulation). Since the **processing** layer results in rather generic, underspecified semantic descriptions of objects required to fulfill the task, this module tries to generate as many alternatives for the respective objects as possible. This can be realized either in a bottom-up (empty scene where only necessary objects and alternatives are generated) or top-down (fully fledged household scene where only objects missing for completion and/or their alternatives are generated) approach. Once a scene meets the conditions of the task, it can be used for both human computation as well as simulation.

Placement of objects in a scene is done in a generate and validate fashion. The qualitative constraints on object placements are first used to select and/or modify probability distributions for object positions. These probability distributions can be learned from a set of training scenes– e.g., what it means for a chair to be "near" a table can be represented as a distribution on relative locations of the chair to the table–, or sometimes inferred from an object's shape; for example, the top of an object corresponds to the fragments of its surface with the highest z-coordinate. Probability distributions resulting from different constraints on the same object are combined via point-wise multiplication. Once constructed, a probability distribution accounting for all qualitative constraints on an object is sampled several times to produce candidate poses, and the first candidate that passes a list of tests– e.g. placing the object there would not result in collisions– is used.

## 3.6   Human Computation

As the primary gap filler for underspecified information, we introduce *Kitchen Clash*, a virtual reality-based, competitive household serious game. Players are challenged with the same set of instructions that stem from the original knowledge base within a virtual household produced by the scene generation module. Each instruction is realized as reaching a subgoal represented by the contained objects and the type of the manipulation (picking up/dropping objects, combining objects with other objects, making use of specific object properties, etc). VR, compared to offline or non-natural interaction approaches, offers the great potential of tracking complete trajectories of hand, head and body movement, as well as the distinctly classified manipulation actions. Players are asked to execute these tasks with optimal efficiency and quality, which is measured by *time spent on a task*, the *number of recognizable actions* and the *number of undesired events* (e.g. breaking dishes or glitching through physical barriers). Additionally, these sessions are assessed qualitatively by peer-rating individual executions from other players, in an either absolute or relative measurement.

Eventually, players are rewarded with a score representing their qualitative and quantitative success.

### 3.7 Simulation

Within MEANinGS, the simulation branch is employed to estimate concrete parameter setting for the ultimate robotic execution of the activities involved. For example, in the case of transporting liquids in various containers from a source to a target location, the game engine physics can be used to simulate different velocities and trajectories and measure the ensuing spill rate in order to find a suitable setting. Ultimately, we see this as a modern extension of the KARMA system [10], in which the complete understanding of an utterance entails a mental simulation thereof. It is also related to "projection" [8], which is light-weight simulation used by a cognitive robot to try combinations of program parameters and/or change sequences of actions quickly, in a simulated world, before attempting them in reality.

## 4    Exemplary Case

To showcase the functional principle of the framework, we present one of the example tasks used in the **Evaluation**, i.e. *to prepare a portion of cucumber salad*.

**Retrieval.** When querying wikiHow as a possible source for natural language instructions, *cucumber salad* will result in a multitude of cucumber salad variants, from which the most basic one will be chosen since no further specifications are asked for. Within this module, the overall task will be divided into subtasks (*Slice the cucumber into thin pieces*, *Place the slices into a bowl* and *Pour dressing over the cucumbers*), which will be forwarded to the **processing** layer.

**Processing.** The natural language parser extracts one action per subtask, each of which should be performed by the discourse addressee - in this case the human player. For the *slicing* action, the undergoer *cucumber* is identified while the obligatory instrument slot is left unspecified. Moreover, the action should result in a goal state that is defined by the changed consistency of the undergoing object. Also, the ontologically equivalent *cutting* action is extracted, to prepare for the case in which only one of these actions is known by the following processing steps. The subsequent *placing* action describes the desired trajectory of the undergoing *slices* to their destination, an undetermined container of type *bowl*. For the final *pouring* action, the poured substance *dressing* and its destination, *the cucumbers*, are identified. Furthermore, the various referring expressions of the main ingredient all resolve to the initial *cucumber* object, in its different configurations.

**Specification.** In order to prepare a suitable testbed, the scene generation module spawns a *cucumber* (since it doesn't find more specific alternatives to the term) and different variants of *cutting objects* (scissors, a kitchen knife, a butter knife, a butcher's knife, etc.).

Within *Kitchen Clash*, a new level is generated that constitutes the challenge and constraints of the overall task. Players entering this level have to find suitable solutions for the presented subtasks and execute these quickly and dexterously, since time, number of actions and the opinion of other players determine the final score. If e.g. a player executes a pickup action on the kitchen knife, triggers a collision between the knife and a cucumber (c.f. Fig. 2), collects the resulting slices, causes them to fall into a bowl and initiates the final collision between dressing and cucumbers, all subgoal constraints have been fulfilled and the main task is completed.

**Fig. 2.** In-game representation of the three tasks. UI has been kept minimal to prevent distraction, action number is counted and required time outlined on a bar with respect to the best and average time targets. In the second screenshot segment, the *cucumber slicing* task is represented, where the required *cutting object* is specified by taking a *serrated utility knife.*

When it comes to simulating the physical properties, the same scene is populated by a robotic agent instead of a human performer, that evaluates the cutting action between all given alternatives and comes up with a quantitative result of the most appropriate parameters and choices.

**Providing.** In the end, trajectories and action choices from the **specification** layer are formulated into the standardized *NEEM* description to generalize and publish the insights to the open robotic community.

## 5  Evaluation

In order to assess the feasibility of the approach, the overall player experience and appraisal, as well as to generate a first data set for further analysis, we conducted an exploratory comparative user study in a laboratory setting. Data was gathered through game protocols, screen capture and a post-study questionnaire. The study was split into two groups in a between-subjects design, where the **VR** group was exposed to *Kitchen Clash* within the associated framework and the **control** group had to accumulate the desired world knowledge manually by depicting the respective tasks in written form.

**Measures.** In-game, we tracked movements from head and hands every second, as well as all of the players' actions, collision events, time measures and attained scores (quantitative and qualitative). The control group submitted instructional data textually. Through the questionnaire, demographics and prior experience in VR were recorded. Using seven-point Likert scales, we asked for players' motivation (using the Intrinsic Motivation Inventory (IMI) [7]), presence (using the igroup Presence Questionnaire (IPQ) [15]), comprehensibility and perceived usefulness of the game. Additionally, participants elaborated on their decision making processes with respect to world knowledge accumulation.

**Procedure.** Following informed consent and a temporally unlimited tutorial that explained the controls and interactions of the game, participants were asked to complete three levels containing complex tasks. In the first level, they had to set a table for two persons, deciding on the type of cutlery and tableware and arranging these in their usual composition. Level two consisted of the formerly explained task of turning cucumbers into a salad. Finally, they were asked to prepare a steak by heating the hotplate, choosing a pan, filling it with oil and cooking the steak until the desired degree of doneness was reached. The tasks did not differ between the VR and control group. They were specifically designed to extract world knowledge about solving underspecified information, providing preferred or conventional items, object target constellations and actual execution trajectories. After completing all levels, the subject was redirected to the final questionnaire.

**Participants.** ($n = 26$) participants took part in the study. (46% male, 54% female, aged 22–58 ($M = 29.9, SD = 8.3$). 72.7% stated having prior experience in VR.

**Results.** On average, subjects of the VR group spent ($M_1 = 150.9, SD_1 = 51.7$; $M_2 = 94.9, SD_2 = 42.3; M_3 = 114.9, SD_3 = 34.2$) seconds on the three respective tasks, whereas the control group required ($M_1 = 244, SD_1 = 108.1; M_2 = 350, SD_2 = 196.3; M_3 = 336.3, SD_3 = 181.4$) seconds. Using a Welch's t test, we found significant or even highly significant effects for required time between the groups in all tasks ($p_1 < 0.05, d_1 = 1.1$), ($p_2 < 0.01, d_2 = 1.8$), ($p_3 < 0.01, d_3 = 1.7$, cf. Fig. 3).

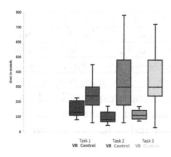

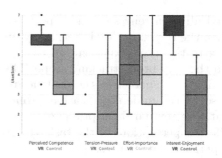

**Fig. 3.** Time required to fulfill the three tasks between VR (blue) and control (green). (Color figure online)

**Fig. 4.** Results of IMI categories Perceived Competence (red), Tension/Pressure (yellow), Effort-Importance (green) and Interest/Enjoyment (blue) between VR (left) and control (right). (Color figure online)

Assessing the IMI, we found no difference for Effort-Importance or Tension-Pressure, but highly significant effects for Perceived Competence ($p < 0.01, d = 1.26$) and Interest-Enjoyment ($p < 0.01, d = 3.13$), showing VR drastically outperforming the control group in terms of motivation (cf. Fig. 4). When asked how descriptive the execution in VR (or in written instructions) can be with respect to the real set of actions, 81.2% of the VR group stated that the execution comes close to the real actions, where from the control group only 40% were convinced that real tasks can be sufficiently expressed in written form. Participants had no trouble following the given instructions (indicated by ($M = 6.27, SD = 0.62$) on a comprehensibility scale). According to the IPQ, VR participants reported a mediocre presence ($M = 4.15, SD = 0.81$) for Spatial Presence, ($M = 4.3, SD = 0.42$) for Involvement, ($M = 3.3, SD = 0.54$) for Realness and ($M = 5.63, SD = 1.15$) for General Presence). Regarding simulation sickness, most participants reported no discomfort at all ($M = 2.1, SD = 1.73$). Most of the subjects stated that they would like to play similar games more often ($M = 5.72, SD = 1.6$). Elaborating on the decision making strategy, 45.4% of the participants stated to select the necessary objects based on the respective task or prior experiences, where 54.6% tended to just take the first available thing.

For the qualitative measurements, subjects reported that VR is *"capable of capturing the most crucial aspects of the tasks"* and *"close to reality"*, despite *"lacking haptic feedback [that] decreases grasping accuracy"* and *"not [being] able to perform fine motor functions"*. Participants of the control group stated that it is *"impossible to find the right level of detail"*, *"implicit knowledge is easily overlooked"*, *"it takes way too long to describe all actions in detail"* and *"you cannot really describe cooking since you don't think at details that will come up in the process"*.

We also assessed the amount of information retrievable from the sessions in both groups. Within VR, all executions managed to complete the tasks and filled all occurrences of underspecified information, since these were needed to finish the respective level. Yet, many unnecessary actions were tracked that trace back to the novel experience of the game, accustoming to VR and the controls and the very broad tracking scope. The amount of unnecessary information was significantly smaller in the control group, but in most of the cases they failed to solve the underspecification problem, even when going into detail. Above that, the textual descriptions deviated considerably in their semantics, due to different perceptions of the task, the projection to their individual environment or personal preferences.

## 6     Discussion and Future Work

Contrasting accumulation of world knowledge manually and in a gamified approach, we have given evidence that human computation can result in significantly higher efficiency, motivation and closeness to the actual execution. Above that, *Kitchen Clash* was able to track complete sequences of actions that describe the fulfillment of tasks both symbolically (registering required operations) as well as subsymbolically (tracking continuous trajectories and contact parameters). Participants enjoyed playing and competing with other players and were interested in continuing the game. Based on these results, we have demonstrated the opportunities and usefulness of human computation for world knowledge aggregation and the feasibility of the overall framework. Yet, this study illustrated that the current implementation suffers from over-collecting unnecessary information and undesirable player choices (e.g. players who take the first object available instead of making an informed decision). Regarding the first issue, we aim to compile large sets of similar task executions using Deep Player Behavior Models [14], offering an optimization paradigm across sessions to extract the necessary core actions needed to fulfill the task probabilistically. When it comes to undesirable player choices, we will evaluate a knockout system of object alternatives that constrains the *variety of choices* of the Scene Generation module in order to force players to overcome obstinate individual preferences and obvious decisions. Furthermore, we are aiming for a narrower interaction between the human computation and the simulation module to generate more elaborate level constellations in *Kitchen Clash* and to make use of the accumulated sequential action knowledge while simulating. Eventually, we are going to open up the game to online multiplayer scenarios where players have to compete against other human players as well as agents representing the aggregated knowledge while learning continually.

## 7     Conclusion

Learning from natural language instructions is a desirable opportunity for robots, but ends up in underspecified information, even when accessing detailed directions. Introducing MEANinGS, we present a potent framework able to break down these instructions syntactically and semantically, before resolving missing or underspecified information with the aid of human computation. With this approach, we have shown to outperform manual accumulation in terms of efficiency, motivation and completeness. This work demonstrates a successful application of a human computation serious game to facilitate research in the context of robotic learning.

**Acknowledgments.** This work was funded by the German Research Foundation (DFG) as part of Collaborative Research Center (SFB) 1320 EASE - Everyday Activity Science and Engineering, University of Bremen (http://www.easecrc.org/), subprojects H2 and P1. We thank all participants.

# References

1. Beetz, M., Bessler, D., Haidu, A., Pomarlan, M., Bozcuoglu, A.K., Bartels, G.: Know Rob 2.0 - a 2nd generation knowledge processing framework for cognition-enabled robotic agents. In: Proceedings - IEEE International Conference on Robotics and Automation, pp. 512–519 (2018). https://doi.org/10.1109/ICRA.2018.8460964
2. Beetz, M., Mösenlechner, L., Tenorth, M.: CRAM–a cognitive robot abstract machine for everyday manipulation in human environments. In: 2010 IEEE/RSJ International Conference on Intelligent Robots and Systems, pp. 1012–1017. IEEE (2010)
3. Dang, H., Allen, P.K.: Robot learning of everyday object manipulations via human demonstration. In: 2010 IEEE/RSJ International Conference on Intelligent Robots and Systems, pp. 1284–1289. IEEE (2010)
4. Kunze, L., Tenorth, M., Beetz, M.: Putting people's common sense into knowledge bases of household robots. In: Dillmann, R., Beyerer, J., Hanebeck, U.D., Schultz, T. (eds.) KI 2010. LNCS, vol. 6359, pp. 151–159. Springer, Heidelberg (2010). https://doi.org/10.1007/978-3-642-16111-7_17
5. Mascardi, V., Cordì, V., Rosso, P.: A comparison of upper ontologies (technical report disi-tr-06-21). Dipartimento di Informatica e Scienze dell'Informazione (DISI), Universitr? degli Studi di Genova, Via Dodecaneso **35**, 16146 (2008)
6. Masolo, C., Borgo, S., Gangemi, A., Guarino, N., Oltramari, A.: Wonderweb deliverable D18, ontology library (final). ICT Proj. **33052**, 31 (2003)
7. McAuley, E., Duncan, T., Tammen, V.V.: Psychometric properties of the Intrinsic Motivation Inventory in a competitive sport setting: a confirmatory factor analysis. Res. Q. Exerc. Sport **60**(1), 48–58 (1989)
8. Mösenlechner, L., Beetz, M.: Fast temporal projection using accurate physics-based geometric reasoning. In: Proceedings of the IEEE International Conference on Robotics and Automation (ICRA), pp. 1821–1827, Karlsruhe, Germany, 6–10 May 2013
9. Mossakowski, T.: The distributed ontology, model and specification language–DOL. In: James, P., Roggenbach, M. (eds.) WADT 2016. LNCS, vol. 10644, pp. 5–10. Springer, Cham (2017). https://doi.org/10.1007/978-3-319-72044-9_2
10. Narayanan, S.S.: KARMA: knowledge-based active representations for metaphor and aspect (1999)
11. Nielsen, R.D., et al.: A platform for human-robot dialog systems research. In: 2010 AAAI Fall Symposium Series (2010)

12. Nilsson, N.J.: Shakey the robot. Technical report, Sri International Menlo Park CA (1984)
13. Parde, N.P., Papakostas, M., Tsiakas, K., Dagioglou, M., Karkaletsis, V., Nielsen, R.D.: I Spy: an interactive game-based approach to multimodal robot learning. In: Workshops at the Twenty-Ninth AAAI Conference on Artificial Intelligence (2015)
14. Pfau, J., Smeddinck, J.D., Malaka, R.: Towards deep player behavior models in MMORPGs. In: Proceedings of the 2018 Annual Symposium on Computer-Human Interaction in Play, CHI PLAY 2018, pp. 381–392. ACM, New York (2018). https://doi.org/10.1145/3242671.3242706
15. Schubert, T., Friedmann, F., Regenbrecht, H.: Embodied presence in virtual environments. In: Paton, R., Neilson, I. (eds.) Visual Representations and Interpretations, pp. 269–278. Springer, London (1999). https://doi.org/10.1007/978-1-4471-0563-3_30
16. Steels, L.: Basics of fluid construction grammar. Constr. Frames 9(2), 178–225 (2017). https://doi.org/10.1075/cf.00002.ste
17. Stulp, F., Fedrizzi, A., Mösenlechner, L., Beetz, M.: Learning and reasoning with action-related places for robust mobile manipulation. J. Artif. Intell. Res. (JAIR) 43, 1–42 (2012)
18. Walther-Franks, B., Smeddinck, J., Szmidt, P., Haidu, A., Beetz, M., Malaka, R.: Robots, pancakes, and computer games: designing serious games for robot imitation learning. In: Proceedings of the 33rd Annual ACM Conference on Human Factors in Computing Systems, pp. 3623–3632. ACM (2015)
19. Winkler, J., Bozcuoğlu, A.K., Pomarlan, M., Beetz, M.: Task parametrization through multi-modal analysis of robot experiences. In: International Foundation for Autonomous Agents and Multiagent Systems, Proceedings of the 16th Conference on Autonomous Agents and MultiAgent Systems, AAMAS 2017, pp. 1754–1756, Richland, SC (2017). http://dl.acm.org/citation.cfm?id=3091125.3091428

# Designing a VR Experience to Reduce the Experience of Pain: Scare, Excite or Relax?

Erik D. van der Spek$^{(\boxtimes)}$ ⓘ and Luuk P. M. Roelofs

Industrial Design, Eindhoven University of Technology, Den Dolech 2,
5612AZ Eindhoven, The Netherlands
e.d.vanderspek@tue.nl, l.p.m.roelofs@student.tue.nl

**Abstract.** Ever since Snow World, there has been a proliferation of Virtual Reality (VR) for pain alleviation in clinical settings. VR provides a relatively low-cost and side-effects free way to distract patients from acute pain. Numerous studies have shown the feasibility of using VR to reduce pain compared with control conditions, however very little research has been done on how the VR experience itself should be designed to optimally distract a user's attention away from the pain. Here, we used the circumplex model of affect as an input to design three affective, wireless, passive VR experiences, viz. a tense experience (horror), an exciting experience (parachuting) and a relaxing experience (nature-walk). In a counterbalanced within-subjects experiment, 14 participants underwent a cold pressor test through three experimental and one control conditions. There was a significant effect of condition, with participants in the tense (horror) condition being able to withstand pain for longer. This may also be due to the anticipation inherent in horror experiences however.

**Keywords:** Virtual Reality · Pain reduction · Affective VR · Game design

## 1 Introduction

### 1.1 VR Based Pain Alleviation

The experience of (acute) pain is a partly physiological but also partly psychological process that serves to direct our attention to a painful stimulus [23]. As it is contingent on attention, directing attention away from the pain experience itself has been found to be a useful strategy to mitigate pain [1], because pharmaceutical analgesics can be costly or have unwanted side-effects. Over the past two decades, the advent of Virtual Reality (VR) technologies as a means to distract patients from pain with entertaining virtual worlds has been shown to be highly effective, both in lab experiments and in clinical settings. VR-based distraction methods typically show statistically significant superior pain reduction compared with control groups or non-VR distraction methods, by large effect sizes [15]. In the US alone, reportedly more than 250 hospitals already employ VR for this purpose [2].

Several theories have been proposed why VR distracts a patient from the pain they are experiencing [14]. One of these theories is based on the Multiple resource theory by Wickens [26]. The Multiple resource theory states that people have a limited amount of

© IFIP International Federation for Information Processing 2019
Published by Springer Nature Switzerland AG 2019
E. van der Spek et al. (Eds.): ICEC-JCSG 2019, LNCS 11863, pp. 97–110, 2019.
https://doi.org/10.1007/978-3-030-34644-7_8

mental resources that can be spent on sensing, perceiving or thinking. If someone is fully focused on one thing, they do not have the mental resources to focus on anything else. In the case of using VR to distract people from experiencing pain, this means that they would use all their mental resources in perceiving and thinking about the virtual environment, and subsequently have no resources left for the pain. Related to this, the degree of presence, or the mediated illusion one is present inside the virtual world, and everything that entails for perception and believability of the virtual world, has been found to be correlated to the effectiveness of pain reduction [11, 23].

## 1.2   Related Work

One of the first well researched and widely publicized VR experiences for pain distraction in hospitals was the VR game Snow World [11]. Here, patients who have to undergo painful burn wound treatments, get to play a game set in a snowy world, where they fly through an icy gorge and throw snowballs at among others penguins and snowmen. The efficacy of Snow World to reduce the experience of pain has been well documented [e.g. 15]. Since then, immersion in VR for analgesic purposes and arguments to its efficacy has been researched for dental pain [10], multiple types of cancer treatment [3], long term fibromyalgia relief [8], and more.

## 1.3   The Design of VR Experiences for Pain Reduction

The research around VR experiences for pain reduction seems to have so far centered on its efficacy compared with other types of pain reduction, the psychological factors surrounding it and explanations for the measured effect. To the best of our knowledge however, very little research has been done on how to design the VR world or VR experience itself in order to engender a reduction in pain. Is the simple act of immersing and distracting enough, as the multiple resource theory for pain reduction would imply [26]? In another paper, Johnson suggests that additionally altering mood, anxiety and arousal next to engaging attention would more effectively reduce pain [12]. In this light Snow World, next to being distracting and arousing in the game mechanics, also appears to have design qualities of being immersive and entertaining, lowering anxiety, while stimulating opposite affective connotations to what originated the pain, i.e. snow instead of fire, and thereby altering mood. While on the surface it seems like a good idea to give patients an environment that is both moderately relaxing and stimulating an opposite affective response, it's less clear what the right affective environment would be for a host of other, less evocative or easy to pinpoint causes of pain. Nor do we get closer to understanding the type of affective experience that best mitigates pain, and why.

Therefore, we propose an experiment with different types of affective experiences, and to measure the amount of time which the experiences can engender people to sustain a simple cold pressor test. In order to delineate different types of affective experiences, the Circumplex Model of Affect by Russell was used [18]. This plots a range of possible affective states in a 2D plane according to the amount of Arousal (vs Boredom), and Valence (Pleasant-Unpleasant) a person experiences; see Fig. 1. With the two axes giving the possibility for both negative and positive scores, four quadrants are formed, with at the extremities Excited, Relaxed, Tense and Depressed. However, given the usual application domain of these kinds of pain alleviation experiences, i.e. hospitals, we considered "Depressed" to be wholly unsuitable, as it could strengthen depressive associations with the procedure, and pessimism generally predicts worse physical health outcomes [17]. A similar argument could indeed also be made for the "Tense" affective setting; however we contend that the popularity of thriller or horror movies and games show that enough people consider these forms of entertainment to be engaging enough to actively seek out immersion in them. Conversely, we think that, given the context, a depressing VR world would not be considered entertaining and therefore the player would be less likely to engage with it.

Most VR for pain reduction research has so far focused on elaborate VR technologies that tether bulky headsets with wires to large gaming PCs. With the advent of low-cost mobile VR, we envision a future where these will be more often used because physicians and surgeons will be able to more easily navigate around them. As general treatments require patients to remain still, we also focused on passive entertaining VR experiences for the purpose of this experiment. The experiences are consequently developed with passive mobile VR in mind.

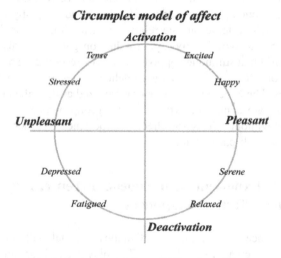

**Fig. 1.** Circumplex model of affect, adapted from [17] and used in the experiment to measure affective states.

## 1.4 Tense, Exciting and Relaxing Experiences

All of the 3 emotions chosen from the Circumplex model of Affect have different reasons for why they could work in distracting the patients of their pain while being immersed in VR entertainment.

For the first one, Unpleasant & Activation ("Tense"), the patient could be distracted from their pain by creating fear for something outside of the real world. Fear can be an overwhelming emotion [24], thus if someone is placed in an immersive world, where a fear is created for something, someone could lose awareness of what happens in the real world. The mental resources would be drawn away from the real world and the pain they are experiencing, to the fear of the experience in the virtual world. This could lead to being distracted from the pain in such a way that they are not experiencing it actively anymore.

For the second one, Pleasant & Activation ("Excited"), the patient could be perceiving so much audiovisual stimuli, that it would be overwhelming for the senses of the patient, and in this way make them focus less on the other senses (cf. Multiple resource theory). In this case enough complexity in audible and visual stimuli could hypothetically overload cognitive processing capacity, making people less aware of haptic stimuli.

For the final one, Pleasant & Deactivation ("Relaxed"), the experience is designed to stimulate an affective response opposite to the stress and anxiety induced by the real world pain, similar to Snow World for burn victims. This could furthermore create a mindfulness experience and give the patient a place which allows them to retreat to their thoughts and ignore the real world. There is some evidence that mindfulness meditation can reduce pain [20], and mindfulness has been stimulated in VR by nature walks in e.g. [5, 7].

As explained above, the three different experiences have very different reasons why they could work in reducing the experienced pain. In addition, by contrasting them directly we may be able to tease out the relative contributions of the factors that were purported to make Snow World a good pain reduction game, viz. distraction, immersion and a game world that stimulates opposite affective responses. Therefore, Russell's circumplex model of affect was used as a guideline in designing the different Virtual Reality Experiences. The experiences are operationalized as described below. The three different experiences are contrasted with a control group, where participants undergo the cold pressor test without a designed affective experience, in order to have a baseline of pain tolerance for each participant.

## 2    Designed VR Experiences to Engender Tense, Exciting and Relaxing Affective Responses

For the *Tense* experience (Unpleasant & Activation) a virtual walk through a moodily-lit creepy hospital was created (see Fig. 2). The player can hear unintelligible whispering voices and two jumpscares (a frightening event where something loud and "in your face" happens to make people "jump" out of their seat), were implemented to cause some distress in the player; first a non-humanlike humanoid creature jumps at the player and at the end the player is surrounded by ghosts with a stroboscope effect. Both non-humanlike humanoids and sounds without an identifiable source are well-known tricks in the survival horror genre to induce fear [22]. Due to the limited graphical output of mobile VR and to make the experience palatable to people who do not like horror movies, the experience was probably more akin to a haunted house theme park than something truly unnerving.

**Fig. 2.** A screenshot of the Horror Virtual Reality experience with the non-humanlike humanoid used in this research.

For the *Exciting* experience (Pleasant & Activation) we had to design something that was thrilling and fun. The initial idea was a rollercoaster or high-speed race, but due to technical limitations with the amount of scenery that could be drawn at the same time at high speeds, these were scrapped for something easier to render. As such, we settled on a skydiving experience, where the player falls downwards towards the ground and cloud particles shoot past the player, as wind sounds fill their ears (see Fig. 3). The cloud particles provided a high amount of visual complexity, while the visual and sound design were intended to create a sense of speed through visual and auditory vection cues [13]. Since vection (the mediated illusion of self-motion) may lead to motion sickness, no rotation or translation was added, and motion sickness was included as a measurement. If the player can hold out long enough to reach the lake on the ground, they would shoot through it and reemerge high above the world. This would be repeated, with a new world rising underneath you every time.

In the third and final *Relaxing* experience (Pleasant & Deactivation), the player had to experience a calm, relaxing and serene environment. For this, a relaxing forest was created (see Fig. 4) (similar to relaxing VR games like [5, 7]). In this forest, the player would walk along a path next to the river with a waterfall, with the sounds of birds chirping, a calming pan flute song and the rushing of the waterfall. There was not much activity in the experience, outside of the waterfall, which was designed to calm the players down and make them as relaxed as possible. Both the Tense and Relaxing experiences were designed to last about three minutes; the Exciting experience could potentially loop forever.

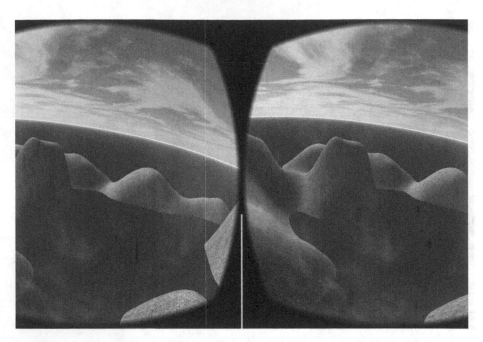

**Fig. 3.** A screenshot of the Exciting Virtual Reality experience used in this research.

**Fig. 4.** A screenshot of the Relaxing Virtual Reality experience used in this research.

## 3    Method

### 3.1    Participants

In total 14 participants (6 Female, 8 Male, Age between 21 and 57, mean age 24.64) participated in a within-subjects design. Because there were four conditions (three experiment groups and one control group), the participants were counterbalanced in a Latin Square design. One person (male, 21 years old) was not able to complete the full experiment due to the equipment malfunctioning, leading to Valid N = 13 for most tests.

### 3.2    Cold Pressor Test and Apparatus

An often used and ethically acceptable way of simulating pain and testing the pain tolerance is the Cold Pressor Test (CPT) [1, 27]. This test asks people to put their hand in cold water at a regulated temperature and times how long someone can hold their hand submerged in the cold water before taking it out. This test is already used in some cases with Virtual Reality [4, 16], and is therefore also used to test the conditions with here.

From other research done with the CPT [16] and testing with water temperatures from 0 °C to 10 °C, a temperature between 6.5 °C and 7 °C was chosen as most useful for this experiment, as anything below 6 °C would lead to the hand being submerged in the water too briefly to experience much of the VR, whereas anything above 8 °C would lead to high variability in the users, compounded by possible disengagement from the designed VR experiences. An important thing to keep into account while doing a CPT is the dangers that are involved in submerging a body part into cold water. The safety prescriptions include prevention of cold-induced tissue damage by setting a maximum time and prevention of an accidental electrical shock [16]. To avoid targeting of the maximum time by the participants, this time was blinded from the participants. The maximum time in this research was set to 2:30 min (150 s) [25]. Prevention of an accidental electrical shock was provided by clearing the area of the water of electrical devices. The water temperature was measured by a safe thermometer with a cord of 1.5 m, the phone used in the Virtual Reality goggles was waterproof and the head-phones were fitted with a well manufactured sealed cord and were too big to fit in the water bucket while the hand was submerged (Fig. 5). Besides this, the participants were watched carefully by a researcher at all times.

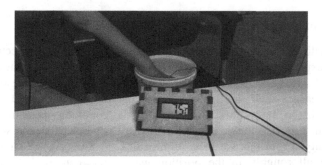

**Fig. 5.** An illustration to show how the Cold Pressor Test was conducted in this research

In between tests, the water was kept between 2 °C and 5 °C in a fridge. It was subsequently taken out and mixed with normal water right before the test to get to 6.5 °C. The water was put in a bucket deep enough to fully submerge the hand in a comfortable way, while not requiring too much cold water. A waterproof thermometer was used in this test, which measured the temperature with a precision of 0.1 °C and a low adoption time, as the longer it takes to measure the temperature, the more the temperature of the water rises.

The Virtual Reality was played on a mobile phone (Samsung S5) which was put in a VR Box Virtual Reality headset. The phone was connected to high quality Sennheiser headphones to make sure the sound was of good quality and canceled out any other sounds.

### 3.3    Materials and Procedure

Upon entry of the lab, the participants were informed about the experiment and told that they were allowed to quit at any time. They were additionally questioned about prior experience with VR and in particular whether they were prone to simulator sickness. After filling out a consent form, they were then administered the conditions in a counterbalanced Latin square order. The water temperature was recorded and the stopwatch started each time they put their hand into the water. At the moment they took their hand out of the water, the time was stopped and the water temperature was recorded again. After every CPT, the participants had time to dry and warm up their hands, and then they were asked to fill in an adapted version of the Visual Analogue Scale (VAS) [6] about the level of experienced pain, the level of nausea experienced and the emotion which was evoked in the Circumplex Model of Affect [18]. For the purpose of filling in, a program was created that presented visual scales on a tablet with a granularity of −400 to +400 where participants could easily visually select how much they agreed/disagreed with the statement. After this, in the three experiment conditions the participants were asked to fill in the Igroup Presence Questionnaire (IPQ) [19], to determine how present they had felt in the virtual environment. After participating in all four conditions in a latin square counterbalanced order, the person was thanked for his or her participation. No reward was provided.

## 4    Results

### 4.1    Validity of VR Experiences

As a general indication, the participants were asked to position their affective response from the VR experience onto the x (valence) and y (arousal) coordinates of the circumplex model of affect. It should be noted that we did not use the official questionnaire to measure their affective response, out of fear we would overload the participants with too many questions for all of the conditions combined. Therefore these results (in Fig. 6) should be taken as a very general indication without much construct validity. From this we may surmise that the Control, Relaxing and Tense conditions are all roughly in the position we expect them to be, and since the participants weren't told where they should be, that the designed experiences portray the mood that we intended. However the same cannot be said for the Exciting condition, which appears not Pleasant enough.

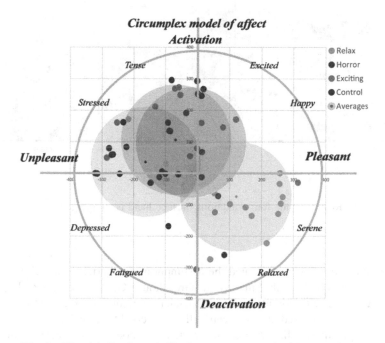

**Fig. 6.** Visual indication of affective responses to the VR experiences

## 4.2   Pain Reduction Expressed in Time

Mauchly's test showed the assumption of sphericity had not been violated $\chi2(5) = 2.14$, $p = 0.83$. A repeated measures ANOVA with the four conditions as within-subjects independent variable and the time the hand was submerged as dependent variable, shows a significant effect of condition on the time the participant was able to submerge their hand $F(3,33) = 5.413$, $p = 0.004$, partial $\eta^2 = 0.33$. A Sidak-corrected post-hoc test attributes this mainly to a significant difference between the Tense condition and the Control condition ($p = 0.014$), with the participants in the Tense condition (M = 48.15, SD = 26.04) being able to keep their hands submerged significantly longer than in the Control condition (M = 34.15, SD = 18.10). A trend was found between the Tense and the Exciting condition ($p = 0.052$), with the participants in the Tense condition being able to keep their hands submerged longer. The other within-subjects differences were not significant. The results of the analysis are shown in Fig. 7. Note that 95% confidence interval whiskers are quite large, meaning there was quite some variability in pain tolerance.

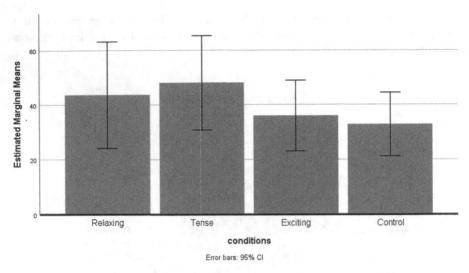

**Fig. 7.** Results of the four conditions on time hand is submerged in water

### 4.3 Presence

The reported presence scores violated the assumption of sphericity (Mauchly's test $\chi2$ (2) = 6.844, $p$ = 0.033), subsequently a Greenhouse-Geisser corrected Repeated-Measures ANOVA with conditions as independent variable and reported presence as dependent variable showed a significant effect of condition, $F(1.394, 26)$ = 8.951, $p$ = 0.004, partial $\eta^2$ = 0.408. A Sidak-corrected post-hoc test showed that the Tense condition induced significantly more presence (M = 0.79, SD = 0.75) than the Exciting condition (M = 0.32, SD = 0.67). No other differences were significant. The experience of presence was significantly correlated with the time a person could submerge their hand for the Relaxing VR condition ($r(13)$ = 0.581, $p$ = 0.037), but not for the other two conditions. Average presence for all three conditions was also not significantly correlated with average time the hand was submerged for all three conditions ($p$ = 0.79).

### 4.4 Experienced Pain and Nausea

A visual analog scale to express the degree of experienced pain from the CPT and nausea from the VR experience was administered, but no significant effects of the conditions were found. This means among others that Passive Mobile VR did not significantly introduce nausea over the control condition and the overall level of experienced pain was about equal (though there were still significant differences in the amount of time the pain could be withstood). There was no correlation between the degree of presence in the Exciting condition and the reported nausea.

# 5 Conclusion and Limitations

In this early exploratory research into the affective design of VR experiences for pain alleviation, we contrasted three conditions, a Tense, Relaxing and Exciting VR experience on their analgesic effect compared with a baseline. It appears that while the use of our VR setup had some analgesic effect in terms of the ability of participants to withstand pain in a CPT (time submerged was higher for all conditions compared with the control condition), only the Tense VR experience was able to cause a significant positive effect on the ability to withstand pain ($p = 0.014$), although the Relaxing setting showed promise ($p = 0.052$). Beforehand we hypothesized that the Tense condition could induce fear, which would overwhelm the attention for the real-world stressor; this could be supported by our findings.

For the Relaxing condition, we hypothesized that the affective response would be the polar opposite to a cold stressor, and the resulting mood change may lead to pain reduction. In addition, we hypothesized that our experience may induce mindfulness, which makes it easier to ignore the pain. Neither can be supported by our findings. However interestingly, here the degree of presence was strongly, positively correlated with the time the hand could be submerged in cold water. Either a natural susceptibility to experiencing presence, a preference for nature walks or the ability to enter a mindful state rapidly may lead to greater success for this type of experience. The latter because brief mindfulness interventions may be ineffective for pain reduction [21]. In any case this should be tested.

For the Exciting condition, we hypothesized that overloading the audiovisual system could draw attention away from the cold stressor, thus lowering the experience of pain. This could not be supported by our findings. On a surface level, this would reject the hypothesis that VR experiences reduce pain solely through stimulus overload from a multiple resource theory standpoint, because the VR condition that would hypothetically have the most audiovisual stimuli, fared the worst.

Before generalizing these conclusions, we should note a number of constraints to the scope. First, the experiment and corresponding results were intended to get an indication of how to design VR experiences, and cannot be easily generalized to affective experiences mediated through other means without additional testing. Second, we focused on distraction through entertainment experiences, since this is one of the main affordances of VR. Other means of distraction, for instance by performing serious tasks, visual noise or through cognitive training could have different effects or influence our results. Lastly, both to serve as a baseline and because it could be more widely applied in real contexts, we focused here on passive VR experiences. However, Snow World is an interactive game, and interaction in an affective game world may lead to differentiated results.

There are some other limitations to consider. Next to the low number of participants and the operationalization of the VR experiences, the Exciting condition did not, on rough visual examination, fall in the expected Excited dimension of the Circumplex model of affect. In addition, even thought the Tense condition created the most presence, there was no ostensible correlation between presence and pain reduction. It could very well be that the low quality of VR experience from mobile VR might not induce enough presence to significantly affect pain experience. This should be quantified in a future experiment, but the notion is supported by Hoffman et al., who found that high quality VR was better at pain reduction than low quality VR [11]. This research is comparatively old however, and current mobile VR may be better than high quality VR in 2004.

## 6 Discussion

Looking at the results, it is rather striking that the VR experience that should be affectively closest to the control condition also creates the largest and only significant difference (NB construct validity of our circumplex model should be low, but we contend that the placement of the two conditions, viz. unpleasant for the control condition and unpleasant and activated for the horror VR experience, make sense). This may indicate that a person can most easily supplant an unpleasant real-world experience with an "unpleasant" VR entertainment experience, which is also supported by the Tense VR condition showing the highest amount of presence. The haptic stressor from the cold pressor test could be more congruent with the audiovisual stressors induced by the tense VR experience, than for the other two conditions.

However, a lack of effect in the other two conditions that are further away from the control condition, could also indicate something else entirely. Namely that designing for specific affective responses in VR has in fact little bearing on pain reduction. A hidden variable may have come to light in the design of the VR experiences that we did not think about beforehand. For the Relaxing condition, we did not want to activate the player and so the experience was sedate and somewhat monotonous throughout. For the Exciting condition, we wanted to create a high-octane experience throughout, making it activating but however also somewhat monotonous. By virtue of creating a Tense experience however, one needs to build up anticipation for an unknown future event (see the design of suspense in a text by Hoeken and Van Vliet [9]), this could have made it so that people were willing to hold their hand in the cold water for longer, just to see 'what was around the corner'. Snow World may be successful not (solely) because of the distraction and the opposite affective setting, but (partly) because of the user wanting to see what comes next. The role that anticipation in immersive VR entertainment may play in mitigating the experience of pain could therefore be a worthwhile avenue for further research.

## References

1. Birnie, K.A., et al.: Systematic review and meta-analysis of distraction and hypnosis for needle-related pain and distress in children and adolescents. J. Pediatr. Psychol. **39**(8), 783–808 (2014)
2. Castanada, R.: How virtual reality can help treat chronic pain. USNews.com. https://health.usnews.com/health-care/patient-advice/articles/2019-01-14/how-virtual-reality-can-help-treat-chronic-pain. Accessed 23 June 2019

3. Chirico, A., Lucidi, F., De Laurentiis, M., Milanese, C., Napoli, A., Giordano, A.: Virtual reality in health system: beyond entertainment. A mini-review on the efficacy of VR during cancer treatment. J. Cell. Physiol. **231**(2), 275–287 (2016)
4. Dahlquist, L.M, McKenna, K.D, Jones, K.K, Dilliger, L., Weiss, K.E., Ackerman, C.S.: Active and passive distraction using a head-mounted display helmet: effects on cold pressor pain in children. Health Psychol. Off. J. Div. Health Psychol. Am. Psychol. Assoc. **26**(6), 794–801 (2007)
5. Damen, K.H.B., van der Spek, E.D.: Virtual reality as e-mental health to support starting with mindfulness-based cognitive therapy. In: Clua, E., Roque, L., Lugmayr, A., Tuomi, P. (eds.) ICEC 2018. LNCS, vol. 11112, pp. 241–247. Springer, Cham (2018). https://doi.org/10.1007/978-3-319-99426-0_24
6. Gould, D., et al.: Visual Analogue scale (VAS). J. Clin. Nurs. **10**, 697–706 (2001)
7. Gromala, D., Tong, X., Choo, A., Karamnejad, M., Shaw, C.D.: The virtual meditative walk: virtual reality therapy for chronic pain management. In: Proceedings of the 33rd Annual ACM Conference on Human Factors in Computing Systems, pp. 521–524 (2015)
8. Herrero, R., Garcia-Palacios, A., Castilla, D., Molinari, G., Botella, C.: Virtual reality for the induction of positive emotions in the treatment of fibromyalgia: a pilot study over acceptability, satisfaction, and the effect of virtual reality on mood. Cyberpsychol. Behav. Soc. Netw. **17**(6), 379–384 (2014)
9. Hoeken, H., van Vliet, M.: Suspense, curiosity, and surprise: how discourse structure influences the affective and cognitive processing of a story. Poetics **27**(4), 277–286 (2000)
10. Hoffman, H.G., Garcia-Palacios, A., Patterson, D.R., Jensen, M., Furness III, T., Ammons Jr., W.F.: The effectiveness of virtual reality for dental pain control: a case study. Cyber Psychol. Behav. **4**(4), 527–535 (2001)
11. Hoffman, H.G., et al.: Manipulating presence influences the magnitude of virtual reality analgesia. Pain **111**(1–2), 162–168 (2004)
12. Johnson, M.H.: How does distraction work in the management of pain? Curr. Pain Headache Rep. **9**(2), 90–95 (2005)
13. Keshavarz, B., Hettinger, L.J., Vena, D., Campos, J.L.: Combined effects of auditory and visual cues on the perception of vection. Exp. Brain Res. **232**(3), 827–836 (2014)
14. Li, A., Montaño, Z., Chen, V.J., Gold, J.I.: Virtual reality and pain management: current trends and future directions. Pain Manag. **1**(2), 147–157 (2011)
15. Malloy, K.M., Milling, L.S.: The effectiveness of virtual reality distraction for pain reduction: a systematic review. Clin. Psychol. Rev. **30**(8), 1011–1018 (2010)
16. Piskorz, J., Czub, M.: Distraction of attention with the use of virtual reality. Influence Level Game Complex. Level Exp. Pain **45**(4), 480–487 (2014)
17. Rasmussen, H.N., Scheier, M.F., Greenhouse, J.B.: Optimism and physical health: a meta-analytic review. Ann. Behav. Med. **37**(3), 239–256 (2009)
18. Russell, J.A.: A circumplex model of affect. J. Pers. Soc. Psychol. **39**(6), 1161 (1980)
19. Schubert, T.: The sense of presence in virtual environments: a three-component scale measuring spatial presence, involvement, and realness. Zeitschrift fuer Medienpsychologie **15**, 69–71 (2003)
20. Sharon, H., et al.: Mindfulness meditation modulates pain through endogenous opioids. Am. J. Med. **129**(7), 755–758 (2016)
21. Smith, K.E., Norman, G.J.: Brief relaxation training is not sufficient to alter tolerance to experimental pain in novices. PLoS ONE **12**(5), e0177228 (2017)
22. Tinwell, A., Grimshaw, M., Williams, A.: Uncanny behaviour in survival horror games. J. Gaming Virtual Worlds **2**(1), 3–25 (2010)

23. Triberti, S., Repetto, C., Riva, G.: Psychological factors influencing the effectiveness of virtual reality–based analgesia: a systematic review. Cyberpsychol. Behav. Soc. Netw. **17**(6), 335–345 (2014)
24. Van den Berg, A.E., Ter Heijne, M.: Fear versus fascination: An exploration of emotional responses to natural threats. J. Environ. Psychol. **25**(3), 261–272 (2005)
25. Vigil, J.M., Rowell, L.N., Alcock, J., Maestes, R.: Laboratory personnel gender and cold pressor apparatus affect subjective pain reports. Pain Resist. Manag. **19**(1), 13–18 (2014)
26. Wickens, C.D.: Multiple resources and mental workload. Hum. Factors **50**(3), 449–455 (2008)
27. Williams, E.: Cold pressor: acceptance, control and expectations. Plymouth Stud. Sci. **6**(2), 98–123 (2013)

# Increasing Learning Motivation: An Empirical Study of VR Effects on the Vocational Training of Bank Clerks

Michael D. Kickmeier-Rust[1($\boxtimes$)], Philipp Hann[2], and Michael Leitner[3]

[1] University of Teacher Education, St. Gallen, St. Gallen, Switzerland
michael.kickmeier@phsg.ch
[2] Graz University of Technology, Graz, Austria
philipp.hann@tugraz.at
[3] Create 21st Century, Vienna, Austria
michael.leiter@create.at

**Abstract.** Virtual reality applications in education are becoming more and more frequent. Empirical, data-based insights in the mechanisms and impacts of VR trainings are still sparse, however. With this quasi-experimental investigation, we compare the effects of a VR training game with a conventional face-to-face presence workshop in the field of vocational training. The training domain is awareness and customer interaction training for bank clerks. The results show that the VR solutions excelled the expectations of participants and the learning motivation was significantly higher as opposed to the conventional training. In the perceived effectiveness, the VR conditions achieved equal results than face-to-face workshops. The results provide evidence that VR solutions are an appropriate approach for vocational training.

**Keywords:** Virtual Reality · Games · Vocational training

## 1 Introduction

Virtual Reality (VR) is increasingly acknowledged as a serious means of education; VR provides powerful immersion and rich interaction [1, 2]. VR learning environments allow students to manipulate objects and parameters, and makes it possible to replace or expand real world learning environments [3]. Students can benefit from VR observing otherwise unobservable phenomena, in virtual worlds that provide a high sense of environmental, physical and social presence [4, 5].

The use of VR goes back to the 1960's in the entertainment industry [6], and, since then, has gained attention in various fields (gaming, flight simulation, higher education, surgery, construction management, weld training, military, etc.) [7–9, 21–23]. Device cost was a problem for a long time, but the high level of immersion that VR provided was considered to increase students' motivation [10], engagement, learning focus and time ever since - including its potential to decrease time for skill mastery, to lower material use, and to gain performance outcomes. However, VR in education is still at its developing stage. Despite years of research, scholars argue it will still take time to

© IFIP International Federation for Information Processing 2019
Published by Springer Nature Switzerland AG 2019
E. van der Spek et al. (Eds.): ICEC-JCSG 2019, LNCS 11863, pp. 111–118, 2019.
https://doi.org/10.1007/978-3-030-34644-7_9

bring VR to the classroom [18]. Educators still need to understand the underlying pedagogical mechanisms and to identify design strategies that enhance learning experiences for broader use [11]. There is a clear lack of empirical evidence showing VR's educational value [3]. Furthermore, the large part of studies focus on acquiring and practicing physical skills; only few studies focus on learning social skills, for example studies on cultural awareness, e.g. in military operations [24], distance counselling [25] and interpersonal problem solving [26].

Literature typically distincts between low immersion and high immersion VR [12]. Low immersion VR is also referred to as "desktop VR". The virtual environment is displayed on a computer display with sound coming through speakers, while the interaction with the virtual world is controlled through a computer mouse [3]. Most studies that investigate educational benefits focus on this type of low immersion or desktop VR [2]. Even though desktop VR cannot provide a fully immersive virtual experience, photorealistic computer graphics have shown to enhance learners' engagement [13]. The use of low immersion VR, in contrast to high immersion VR, is much cheaper because of the drastic reduction in the cost of devices. Empirical studies and meta-analyses have shown desktop VR to result in better cognitive outcomes and attitudes toward learning compared to more traditional teaching methods [2, 14, 15] and to have greater motivational value [16, 17].

High immersion VR is characterized by the use of a head-mounted-display called VR headset, which provides room-scale virtual reality and 360-degree coverage immersion experience [18]. The interaction in the virtual environment is controlled through head-motion. There is little empirical evidence that high immersion VR increases cognitive and motivational outcomes, compared to desktop VR [19, 20]. However, there is limited and inconclusive research regarding the question whether higher immersion leads to greater levels of presence, therefore better outcomes in learning, and transfer than is achieved by desktop VR [2].

The aim of the present study is to investigate the effects of a high-immersion VR training solutions in a field where "soft", interpersonal skills are supposed to be practiced in combination with acquired rather declarative knowledge. The VR solution is compared to a conventional face-to-face (f2f) training solution. The domain is the training of bank clerk's behavior sets to be attentive and engaging with bank customers. We hypothesize that the participants using VR training will be more satisfied, more motivated to learn and will believe to learn more (perceived effectiveness) than participants in traditional f2f trainings.

## 2    A Quasi-experimental Study

### 2.1    Participants

In total, 46 bank clerks of an Austrian bank participated in the study. One group (34 participants) was trained traditionally with a f2f presence workshop (F2F group), while the second group (12 participants) was trained using a high immersion VR training game (VR group). Participants were between 19 and 54 years old ($M = 26.56$, $SD = 8.84$) and there was no significant age difference between the two groups ($t = -.73$, $p = .467$). In the f2f group, 19 participants were female and 14 participants were male, in the VR group, 9 participants were female and 2 participants were male. The participants of the VR group had more average work experience in their current job ($M = 9.18$, $SD = 10.27$) than the participants in the traditional group ($M = 3.24$, $SD = 3.77$; $t_{44} = -2.91$, $p = .006$), but the two groups did not differ in their general work experience ($t_{44} = 0.146$, $p = .885$), which showed an average work experience of about 7 years. Participants were provided through a cooperation with a bank.

## 2.2   Materials and Procedures

The f2f group was trained by traditional learning methods like direct instructions and lectures during a one-day presence workshop. There were three one day classroom trainings, with 10 to 15 participants each (frontal lecture, exercises and role-playing). The VR group was trained by using high immersion VR game. The VR training took place in a bank office. Training was followed by a questionnaire that each participant had to complete, containing some sociodemographic questions followed by the BFI-10 [30] to assess their Big Five personality traits. The next questions assessed the participants' motivation (7 items), their usage of digital media (7 items), what they thought about the training method (46 items), how they prefer to learn (6 items) and what kind of expectations they had about the training session (2 items). The VR group additionally had to complete questions regarding their interaction with the virtual world and the VR-headset (15 items). The answers to all the questions were given with a 5-point Likert scale from "*strongly agree*" to "*strongly disagree*".

## 2.3   The VR Training Game

The VR game was produced by eLearning agency *CREATE.21ˢᵗ century* in collaboration with an Austrian bank. Financial domain experts contributed to the development of training content and game dramaturgy. The game is set in a bank branch. VR learners follow a bank employee taking care of a client (from first contact to contract signing). Learners enter the virtual environment, which is based on a 360° video of a bank branch. Actors take the role of customers and a bank clerk. Learners follow the scenarios in the virtual environment and interact with the actors. Participants are able to make decisions, which are reflected in the interaction between the bank employee and the client. The VR training lasts approximately 30 min. Technically, the scenario has been developed with Unity3D for Oculus Rift.

The VR game's (and the f2f workshop) aim was to improve bank clerks' attention to customers, argumentative skills and sensitivity for cross-selling. Moreover, the training focusses on increasing the declarative knowledge about customer interactions and practicing this knowledge.

**Fig. 1.** Insight the VR glass: Bank clerk attending client. User is feedbacking the action using a joystick

## 3  Results

In a first step, we analysed the background variables of participants. Overall, the majority of the participants use digital media quite often at work and in their private life. Also, the participants strongly believed that digitization has a significant impact on their work ($M = 2.05$ on the 5-point Likert-scale; $SD = 1.06$).

**Table 1.** Learning preferences

|  | Books and texts | Videos and movies | YouTube tutorials | Search engines on smartphone | Direct contact with teachers |
|---|---|---|---|---|---|
| Strongly agree | 15 (32.6%) | 13 (28.3%) | 11 (23.9%) | 32 (69.6%) | 15 (32.6%) |
| Agree | 6 (13%) | 8 (17.4%) | 7 (15.2%) | 8 (17.4%) | 16 (34.8%) |
| Undecided | 14 (30.4%) | 10 (21.7%) | 6 (13%) | 3 (6.5%) | 10 (21.7%) |
| Disagree | 4 (8.7%) | 8 (17.4%) | 11 (23.9%) | – | 1 (2.2%) |
| str. disagree | 3 (6.5%) | 3 (6.5%) | 8 (17.4%) | – | 1 (2.2%) |
| Missing | 4 (8.7%) | 4 (8.7%) | 3 (6.5%) | 3 (6.5%) | 3 (6.5%) |

Participants were also asked about their preferred way to learn (see Table 1). Interestingly the majority of participants indicated that they thought that the most effective way to learn is by being in direct contact with teachers and trainers. The majority of the participants stated that they could not imagine participating only in online/virtual trainings ($M = 3.33$; $SD = 1.57$). There was no difference between the traditional and the VR group regarding this statement ($t_{41} = 1.76$, $p = .087$). In turn, many participants were undecided regarding the question if they see the future of training in the digital or virtual world - a large part agreed with this statement, with a significant difference between the traditional group and the VR group ($t_{41}$= 4.40, $p < .001$). The VR group agreed more with the statement that they see the future of further training in the digital or virtual world ($M = 1.42, SD = 0.90$) than the traditional group ($M = 3.20, SD = 1.28$) (Fig. 2).

**Satisfaction, Expectation and Perceived Effectiveness:** Our main results show three notable differences between VR and f2f groups.

First, the majority of participants stated that their *satisfaction* with the training session were met or even surpassed (see Fig. 1). However, we observed a significant difference between the traditional group and the VR group ($t_{41}$ = 4.34, $p < .001$). The VR group was significantly more satisfied with the training session ($M = 2.46$, $SD = 0.45$) than the traditional group ($M = 2.09, SD = 1.18$).

Second, we analysed the trainings' *perceived effectiveness*. Both groups, VR and f2f, perceived their training as similarly effective. The self-assessed effectiveness was slightly higher in the f2f group, with, however, no statistically significant difference ($p = .135$).

Third, analysing trainees' *expectations* towards their training resulted in a significant difference between VR and f2f groups. This finding is the most distinctive one we observed. In VR groups, participants' expectations were met (and excelled) significantly stronger than in f2f groups ($t_{41}$= 3.22, $p < .001$; cf. Fig. 1).

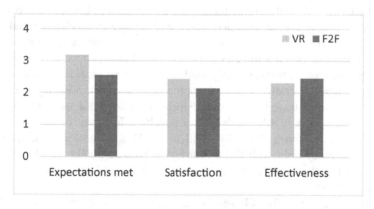

**Fig. 2.** Comparison of VR and f2f groups.

There were no significant differences between the f2f and the VR group in any of the personality traits (Extraversion: $t_{43} = 1.79$, $p = .080$; Agreeableness: $t_{43} = 0.31$, $p = .755$; Conscientiousness: $t_{43} = .35$, $p = .732$; Neuroticism: $t_{42} = 0.18$, $p = .857$; Openness: $t_{42} = 0.562$, $p = .577$). Thus, there is no reason to believe that any of the other examined differences between the two groups in this study are the result of personality differences between the traditional group and the VR group.

**Motivation:** There were significant differences between the f2f group and the VR group in their *motivation* ($t_{42} = 2.38$, $p = .022$) and their thoughts about the training method ($t_{44}$ = 4.82, $p$ < .001). The VR group perceived their training as more motivating ($M$ = 1.48, $SD$ = 0.36) than the f2f group ($M$ = 1.89, $SD$ = 0.55). The VR group also perceived their training as more positive in general ($M$ = 1.43, $SD$ = 0.33) than the f2f group ($M$ = 2.52, $SD$ = 0.75).

## 4   Conclusion and Discussion

The aim of this study was to investigate whether a high immersive VR training game can be a solution for vocational training, by this concrete example, in the banking sector. We hypothesized that VR leads to higher learning *satisfaction*, perceived learning *effectiveness* and *motivation*. Our results show that, in our experimental setup, participants who used VR training were generally more satisfied with their training, were more motivated to learn and perceived their learning outcomes as greater than f2f participants. There are some influencing factors that may explain these results:

First, **personality traits**: For example, one may hypothesize that introverted participants are more satisfied with a training method like VR. In fact, we collected qualitative feedback that hints at such aspects. Some participants reported the typical f2f workshop elements, specifically role-playing acts, can be perceived as displeasing. In the past, they felt uncomfortable when being requested to perform a role-play with others, who were mostly strangers. This can be considered an indicative and important strength of VR training scenarios. When shifting displeasing or disruptive elements of a training into the virtual world. Since there were no differences between the two groups in personality traits, it can be assumed that the difference in motivation and training scores could be attributed to such aspects of the different training methods.

Second, the VR solution's **novelty** may also have had an effect, especially when it comes to trainees' expectations. Blandly said, it is harder to excel the expectations of a f2f training, which is a known standard approach. In contrast, VR may excel expectations easier due to its novelty. However, since VR is not yet a standard approach in vocational training, it is highly likely that a novelty effect may occur across studies with a similar setup. Hence, "novelty" will be a VR attribute for some time being, which may fade away only with the technology's broader uptake in education. Educators may use novelty effect as an attribute to motivate and satisfy learners for their educational purposes.

Third, **learning time**: The VR session lasted 30 min. In contrast, f2f participants spent one day in a workshop room. One may hypothesize that participants are generally more satisfied and motivated when spending less time in trainings, independently from the didactical approach. Our findings, however, show that f2f participants were satisfied with their training and found it effective, too. Furthermore, despite the large difference in training time demand (30 min vs. 1 day workshop), both VR and f2f participants found their training similarly effective. Therefore, we assume that the effects observed as rather independent from training time, but more a result of the training method itself.

In conclusion, it appears that VR training methods are an appropriate means of educational and training. In a medium to long-term perspective, VR and AR will become a serious part of the educational landscape. With the present study, we contribute empirical evidence for the advantageous characteristics of VR solutions. Further research will increase the sample size, evaluate different VR designs. as well as VR trainings transferability to the real world.

# References

1. Cochrane, T.: Developing interactive multimedia learning objects using QuickTime. Comput. Hum. Behav. **23**(6), 2596–2640 (2007)
2. Merchant, Goetz, Cifuentes, Kenney-Kennicutt, Davis: (2014)
3. Makransky, G., Terkildsen, T.S., Mayer, R.E.: Adding immersive virtual reality to a science lab simulation causes more presence but less learning. Learn. Instr. **60**, 225–236 (2017)
4. De Jong, T.: Instruction based on computer simulations and virtual laboratories. In: Mayer, R.E., Alexander, P.A. (eds.) Handbook of Research on Learning and Instruction, 2nd edn, pp. 502–521. Routledge, New York (2017)
5. Makransky, G., Lilleholt, L., Aaby, A.: Development and validation of the multimodal presence scale for virtual reality environments: a confirmatory factor analysis and item response theory approach. Comput. Hum. Behav. **72**, 276–285 (2017)
6. Heiling, M.: Sensorama simulator. Patented August, 28 (1962)
7. Blascovich, J., Bailenson, J.: Infinite Reality. HarperCollins, New York (2011)
8. Greenlight, V.R.: Roadtovr 2016 virtual reality industry report (2016). http://www.greenlightinsights.com/reports/2016-industry-report
9. Youngblut, C.: Educational uses of virtual reality technology. Alexandria, VA: Institute for Defense Analyses (IDA Document D-2128) (1998)
10. Bodekaer, M.: The virtual lab will revolutionize science class (2016). https://www.ted.com/talks/michael_bodekaer_this_virtual_lab_will_revolutionize_science_class
11. Bronack, S.C.: The role of immersive media in online education. J. Contin. High. Educ. **59**(2), 113–117 (2011)
12. Bonde, M.T., et al.: Improving biotech education through gamified laboratory simulations. Nat. Biotechnol. **32**(7), 694–697 (2014)
13. Clark, D.B., Tanner-Smith, E.E., Killingsworth, S.S.: Digital games, design, and learning: a systematic review and meta-analysis. Rev. Educ. Res. **86**(1), 79–122 (2016)
14. Makransky, G., Thisgaard, M.W., Gadegaard, H.: Virtual simulations as preparation for lab exercises: assessing learning of key laboratory skills in microbiology and improvement of essential non-cognitive skills. PloS One **11**(6), e0155895 (2016)
15. Makransky, G., et al.: Simulation based virtual learning environment in medical genetics counseling: an example of bridging the gap between theory and practice in medical education. BMC Med. Educ. **16**(1), 98 (2016)
16. Thisgaard, M., Makransky, G.: Virtual learning simulations in high school: effects on cognitive and non-cognitive outcomes and implications on the development of STEM academic and career choice. Front. Psychol. **8**, 805 (2017)
17. Zhou, Y., Ji, S., Xu, T., Wang, Z.: Promoting knowledge construction: a model for using virtual reality interaction to enhance learning. Procedia Comput. Sci. **130**, 239–246 (2018)
18. Passig, D., Tzuriel, D., Eshel-Kedmi, G.: Improving children's cognitive modifiability by dynamic assessment in 3D immersive virtual reality environments. Comput. Educ. **95**, 296–308 (2016)
19. Webster, R.: Declarative knowledge acquisition in immersive virtual learning environments. Interact. Learn. Environ. **24**(6), 1319–1333 (2016)

20. Sacks, R., Perlman, A., Barak, R.: Construction safety training using immersive virtual reality. Constr. Manag. Econ. **31**(9), 1005–1017 (2013)
21. Stone, R.T., Watts, K.P., Zhong, P., Wei, C.S.: Physical and cognitive effects of virtual reality integrated training. Hum. Factors **53**(5), 558–572 (2011)
22. Bhagat, K.K., Liou, W.K., Chang, C.Y.: A cost-effective interactive 3D virtual reality system applied to military live firing training. Virtual Real. **20**(2), 127–140 (2016)
23. Butt, A.L., Kardong-Edgren, S., Ellertson, A.: Using game-based virtual reality with haptics for skill acquisition. Clin. Simul. Nurs. **16**, 25–32 (2018)
24. Fominykh, M., Leong, P., Cartwright, B.: Role-playing and experiential learning in a professional counseling distance course. J. Interact. Learn. Res. **29**(2), 169–190 (2018)
25. Rammstedt, B., Kemper, C.J., Klein, M.C., Beierlein, C., Kovaleva, A.: Eine kurze Skala zur Messung der fünf Dimensionen der Persönlichkeit: Big-Five-Inventory-10 (BFI-10) (2012)
26. Morch, A.I., Hartley, M.D., Caruso, V.: Teaching interpersonal problem solving skills using roleplay in a 3D virtual world for special education: a case study in second life. In: Proceedings of IEEE 15th International Conference on Advanced Learning Technologies (ICALT), Hualien, Taiwan, 6–9 July 2015, pp. 464–468 (2015)

# Entertainment Algorithms

# Learning How to Play Bomberman
# with Deep Reinforcement
# and Imitation Learning

Ícaro Goulart$^{(\boxtimes)}$, Aline Paes$^{(\boxtimes)}$, and Esteban Clua$^{(\boxtimes)}$

Institute of Computing, Universidade Federal Fluminense, Niterói, RJ, Brazil
igoulart@id.uff.br, {alinepaes,esteban}@ic.uff.br

**Abstract.** Making artificial agents that learn how to play is a long-standing goal in the area of Game AI. Recently, several successful cases have emerged driven by Reinforcement Learning (RL) and neural network-based approaches. However, in most of the cases, the results have been achieved by training directly from pixel frames with valuable computational resources. In this paper, we devise agents that learn how to play the popular game of Bomberman by relying on state representations and RL-based algorithms without looking at the pixel level. To that, we designed five vector-based state representations and implemented Bomberman on the top of the Unity game engine through the ML-agents toolkit. We enhance the ML-agents algorithms by developing an Imitation-based learner (IL) that improves its model with the Actor-Critic Proximal-Policy Optimization (PPO) method. We compared this approach with a PPO-only learner that uses either a Multi-Layer Perceptron or a Long-Short Term-Memory network (LSTM). We conducted several pieces of training and tournament experiments by making the agents play against each other. The hybrid state representation and our IL followed by PPO learning algorithm achieve the best overall quantitative results, and we also observed that their agents learn a correct Bomberman behavior.

**Keywords:** Bomberman · Proximal Policy Optimization · Reinforcement Learning · LSTM · Imitation Learning

## 1 Introduction

Building games with agents that *learn* how to play is a long-standing goal in Game-AI. So far, this has been mainly addressed by Reinforcement Learning (RL) algorithms [1] and, more recently, by combining RL with deep neural networks in the area of Deep Reinforcement Learning (DRL) [2–4]. However, the most remarkable results achieved so far have counted with valuable computational resources to deal with large pixel level-based search spaces.

We would like to thank the Brazilian research agencies CAPES and CNPq, and NVidia.

© IFIP International Federation for Information Processing 2019
Published by Springer Nature Switzerland AG 2019
E. van der Spek et al. (Eds.): ICEC-JCSG 2019, LNCS 11863, pp. 121–133, 2019.
https://doi.org/10.1007/978-3-030-34644-7_10

In this work we take a step in another direction: we focus on the game of Bomberman represented in a grid scenario. Bomberman is a popular and universally pleasurable maze-based strategy video game that requires intelligence. Although at first sight it looks simple, designing an intelligent Bomberman agent faces a number of challenges: a vast search space due to numerous components possibilities (other agents, bombs, blocks, *etc.*), multiplayer mode, strategic reasoning, delayed reward due to the time that the bombs take to explode, and a dynamic environment [5].

Most of the available work addressing Bomberman *learning*-agents has focused on table-based RL without exploring the more general function approximation power of neural networks [6,7]. Only recently, Komerlink *et al.* [8] have used Q-learning coupled with a multi-layer perceptron neural network (MLP), focusing on comparing exploration strategies. Here, we tackle the complexity of the Bomberman game with a combination of Imitation Learning (IL) [2] and the recently developed Actor-Critic Proximal Policy Optimization (PPO) strategy [9], developed within the area of DRL. In IL, an apprentice agent learns to perform a task observing an expert. Arguably, this strategy produces a good starting point for the PPO algorithm. We devised the Bomberman game using the Unity game engine and implemented the combined approach on the top of the ML-Agents toolkit [10], an open-source project to create simulation environments based on ML and using the Unity Editor. Also, we implemented five vector-based state representation, namely: (1) Hybrid One-hot, (2) ZeroOrOne, (3) Binary Flag, (4) Normalized Binary Flag e (5) ICAART.

The Bomberman game we developed holds the capability of representing cells with more than one element, allowing for more than one agent to be in the same cell, as in the original game. Additionally, the only information the agents have from the game is the observation of the environment, in the form of the vector-based state representations and the rewards.

We conducted a series of training sequences and tournament among the agents to compare (i) the five ways of representing the space state, (ii) PPO trained with MLP or Long-Short-Term memory [11] (LSTM), and (iii) the Behavioral Cloning (BC) IL algorithm followed by PPO compared to training these algorithms singly from each other. The results have pointed out that by using the hybrid state representation and aggregating the experiences of several learners in a PPO+LSTM at once is the best general way of reaching an effective Bomberman agent. Our solution is publicly available[1,2], allowing for further improvement and usage.

## 2    Background

Bomberman[3] is a maze-based strategy game franchise, developed by Hudson Soft Company in 1985. The game is based on placing bombs strategically within

---

[1] https://github.com/lorel-uff/pip.
[2] https://github.com/icaro56/ml-agents.
[3] https://en.wikipedia.org/wiki/Bomberman.

the scene, to kill the enemies, and to destroy blocks in the scenario, aiming at opening paths or finding items. In a multiplayer mode, the player's goal is to be the last player alive by killing all its opponents. The explosion of a bomb propagates vertically and horizontally to the neighbor cells, respecting possible obstructions along the way.

Here, we address the Bomberman game with RL algorithms. RL aims at teaching agents by trial and error, mapping states into actions through maximizing a numeric reward. The reward can be positive, when the chosen action leads to the goal, or negative, in the opposite case [1]. To define the interaction between the learner agent and its environment, an RL problem is specified as a Markov Decision Problem (MDP) with a space state $S$, a set of actions $A$, a transition function $Tr(s, a) \rightarrow s'$, a reward function $R(s, a) \rightarrow \mathbb{R}$, and a discount factor $\gamma$. The goal is to find a policy function that maps states to actions.

An RL problem can be modeled as a regression function by mapping the space of states and actions to the reward [12]. The goal becomes approximating such a function using, for example, a neural network [13]. Neural networks can focus on optimizing the policies directly or on learning the value functions from them to infer policies. When the underlying neural network used in an RL problem is deep, we have a Deep Reinforcement Learning (DRL) algorithm [4].

In this work, we rely on a DRL actor-critic method, using either an MLP or an LSTM network and on Imitation Learning. We briefly describe them as follows.

**Proximal Policy Optimization** (PPO) is a DRL policy optimization method that uses a stochastic ascent gradient to update the policy function. PPO has the stability and reliability of trust-region methods [14], it is a model-free, on-policy RL algorithm, it can deal with a continuous space of observation and actions, and it relies on the Advantage operator instead of Q-values. It is based on the *actor-critic* framework that, roughly speaking, encompasses two networks, one to act as an estimator of the function value (the critic) and the other to determine the policy itself (the actor) [15]. Accurately, PPO follows the actor-critic A3C [16] technique allowing that multiple asynchronous agents can be trained simultaneously in a global supervisor network.

**Long Short Term Memory (LSTM)** is a recurrent network (RNN) designed to avoid the problem of long-term dependency [11] encountered by RNNs. The input information that enters an LSTM network may undergo some small linear interactions or move on to the subsequent iterations. LSTM also can add or remove cell status information through gates, composed of Sigmoid layers and multiplication operations.

**Imitation Learning** RL algorithms follow a series of interactions with the environment to achieve the goal, which can make the learning process very slow. To speed up the training time, IL techniques learn from expert demonstrations. Here, we use the Behavioral Cloning (BC), a supervised imitation learning method that maps state/action pairs from expert trajectories to policies without learning the reward function [2]. The BC method works as follows: (i) observe the current state $s$ and the action chosen $a$ by the expert; (ii) choose an action

$a'$ based on the current policy $P$ (initially this policy is selected at random); (iii) compare the chosen action $a'$ with the expert demonstrated action $a$ using an error function; (iv) optimize the policy $P$ using the error function, yielding a policy $P'$; (v) repeats the whole process, now using $P'$ as the current policy.

## 3   Related Work

Previous work has also focused on Bomberman to implement and experiment with ML techniques. Bomberman as an Artificial Intelligence Platform (BAIP) [6] is a Bomberman-based graphical, open-source, agnostic language platform, able to assist in the study and development of new AI techniques. It includes agents based on heuristics, searching, planning, and RL methods. Agents that use RL techniques were not able to play the same version of the game as heuristic and search agents.

In [7] a Reactive, MiniMax, and Q-Learning agents were compared in a discrete-style Bomberman game. The MiniMax-based agent routinely defeats a human player, but it is computationally expensive and unable to run in real-time. The Reactive agent was able to defeat human players most of the time, but cannot beat the MiniMax agent. The best result achieved by their Q-Learning agent was in a static scenario without destructible blocks and with only one enemy standing still.

A Q-learning with MLP strategy was implemented in [8]. An Error-Driven-$\epsilon$ and Interval-Q exploration strategies were compared to five other techniques. As there, we also represent the state of the environment with a vector to feed a neural network. However, we also include other state representations and rely on more sophisticated learning techniques, trying to address the complexity of the Bomberman game.

Pommerman [5] is a multi-agent environment based on the game Bomberman, consisting of a set of scenarios, each one with at least four players and containing cooperative and competitive aspects. Also, it can be used to create methods such as planning, opponent/teammate modeling, game theory, and communication. A competition track at NIPS 2018[4] used Pommerman as a framework. The Pommerman scenarios always have 11 rows by 11 columns and, different from the original game, Pommerman agents cannot occupy the same cell. The environment developed in our work allows cells with more than one state, and agents can occupy the same cell as in the original game. Besides that, we developed using a commercial game engine with a large community of developers.

## 4   State Representation and Imitation-Reinforcement Learning in Bomberman

In this paper, we investigate the influence of five vector-based state representation and four learning algorithms to make an agent learn how to play Bomberman. The Bomberman game implemented here resembles the original gameplay.

---

[4] https://nips.cc/Conferences/2018/CompetitionTrack.

However, we focus on the agent behavior regarding the other agents, the scenario, and its wish to remain alive, disregarding power abilities and not allowing more than one bomb per agent. With that, the agent aims at being the last living agent on the scene to win the match. The game was developed with the Unity game engine, and the algorithms were built on the top of ML-Agents Toolkit.

## 4.1   Dynamic of the Game

The Bomberman scenario has nine rows and nine columns within a 2D grid board. The game computes the time according to the number of interactions between the agent and the environment. Each game may have two, three, or four players battling against each other. The entities in the game are (i) indestructible blocks, (ii) destructible blocks, (iii) agents, (iv) bombs, (v) bomb's fires, and (vi) danger zones. The danger zones are invisible entities that inform the extension of the bomb's fires when it explodes.

At the start of a match, the agents are randomly positioned in one of the four corners, each one in a different position. At each iteration, the agent receives the observation from the environment (detailed next) and takes one action. The agents can put one bomb at a time on the scenario in their current position. After $N$ iterations that the bomb has been activated, it explodes with a range of two cells to each linear direction (up, down, left, and right). It is required to wait for the bomb explosion before putting another one. The fire of a bomb blast is configured to last only one iteration.

Some entities within the range of an explosion obstruct its effect beyond them. Thus, the bomb explosion does not pass through the blocks or other bombs. Thus, in the presence of such entities, the explosion of a bomb is limited to one cell in the direction of the block (or another bomb) if it is on the same side of the bomb. However, the fire of a bomb causes the explosion of other bombs inside the two-cells range.

A match ends when there is only one living agent remaining on the scenario, or when they are all dead (draw). The last existing agent in the scenario is the winner of the game. If we do not have a winner after 300 iterations, then we generate a rain of bombs to force the end of the game.

## 4.2   Bomberman Training as a Markov Decision Process (MDP)

As usual in RL problems, we design the Bomberman problem as a finite and episodic MDP. The MDP problem is composed of (1) *the state set*: the states of all the grid cells in the scenario and the position $(x, y)$ of the agent. The state is encoded as a vector to feed the agent's observation. The vector representation can vary according to the type of representation. (2) *Actions*: the agent can (i) standstill, (ii) go up, (iii) go down, (iv) go left, (v) go right, all of these last four moving a single cell, and (vi) put a bomb. (3) *Transitions*: the transition from one state to another guided by action is determined by the previous state and the action themselves, with no uncertainty caused by the environment. Thus, the agent tries to execute an action and, if it is allowed, the environment perceives its effect. Other entities may also cause a transition from one state to another, such as a bomb that explodes. (4) *Rewards*: The rewards are distributed according to Table 1. After performing one action, the agent receives a reward according to the new state of the game. One or more type of rewards can be applied combined in the same iteration. For example, the agent can kill an enemy *and* destroy a block, or the agent can only stay still and suffers the iteration penalty. Every time an agent gets closer to an enemy, it receives a reward for approaching an opponent (the fifth line in the table). For example, if the distance between the two agents in question is $x$ cells, then the reward will only be given to the agent if he gets closer than that to the opponent, *i.e.*, at least $x - 1$ cells. Rewards for approximating and distancing agents are only given after a successful walking action when the observed state has a new position of the agent. The distances are computed as Manhattan distance.

**Table 1.** Rewards given to the Agent

| State | Reward |
| --- | --- |
| The agent is dead | $-0.5$ |
| An opponent is dead by the agent earning the reward | 1.0 |
| The agent is the last man alive | 1.0 |
| A block has been destroyed | 0.1 |
| The agent is in the closest position so far to an enemy | 0.1 |
| The agent is closer to an opponent than before | 0.002 |
| The agent is farther to an opponent than before | $-0.002$ |
| Penalty per iteration | $-0.01$ |
| The agent is in a cell within reach of a bomb | $-0.000666$ |
| The agent is in a safe cell when there is a bomb nearby | 0.002 |

### 4.3    State Representations

In RL algorithms, the choice of representation for the observed states may influence the agent's learning ability as, if the state is misrepresented, the agent will probably be unable to find patterns and perform coherent actions. Here, the observation of the current state is represented as a vector. The size of this vector depends on the type of the state representation: if we use only the numerical value to represent a cell, then the observation vector has a numerical value to represent each cell of the grid. If we use an array, then the observation vector has the number of elements in this array to represent each cell in the grid.

We devised four possible representations to the environment: Binary Flag, Normalized Binary Flag, Hybrid, ZeroOrOne. Furthermore, we implemented the state representation devised in [8] and named it as ICAART, yielding a total of five state representations. In all of these cases, every cell is first encoded as bit flags. Bit flags are used to store more than one Boolean value in a whole set of bytes, representing the existence of one or more objects of that state type in the cell. Thus, we can inform, for example, that an agent *and* a bomb are in the same grid cell at the same moment. In this case, if the bit flag representing the agent and the bomb are 01 and 10, respectively, then the bit flag representing the grid cell is 11. Eight possible state types are represented by bit flags: empty cell, indestructible block, destructible block, current agent, enemy, bomb, fire, and danger. The five state representations are as follows:

1. **Binary Flag.** In this case, for each cell in the grid, there is a bit flag to represent what is there, plus the position (x, y) of the agent, making the size of the observation vector as the size of the grid plus 2. After composing the observation vector with the bit flags, it is converted to decimal to provide the agent with this information finally.

2. **Normalized Binary Flag.** This representation only normalizes the previous one to stay between maximum and minimum values. Values are in [0.0, 1.0] range.

3. **Hybrid.** The hybrid representation combines the Binary Flag representation with a One-Hot Vector representation. A One-Hot Vector is a $1 \times C$ matrix, where C is the number of possible situations, which consists of 0s in all dimensions except for a single 1 in a dimension used uniquely to identify the class or state type. To represent a cell that has an agent ([1, 0]) and a bomb ([0, 1]) with a One-Hot Vector, the vector dimension must be increased by one, generating a new One-Hot Vector that represents the agent plus the bomb ([0, 0, 1]). This feature makes One-Hot vectors very costly. Thus, we propose a hybrid representation that allows for using a One-Hot vector similar to the Binary Flag representation. For example, to represent bomb and agent entities occupying the same grid cell, we have the Hybrid vector [1, 1] instead of a new vector [0, 0, 1]. Each cell in the grid is represented using a Hybrid vector. Thus, if there are 4 types of state (plus empty), then the size of each Hybrid vector will be 4 (e. g. [1, 0, 0, 1]). Consequently, the size of the observation vector will be the number of cells multiplied by the size of the Hybrid Vector plus position x, y (e.g. $4 \times 4 + 2 = 18$, in a $2 \times 2$ grid). More accurately, a Hybrid vector is a matrix $1 \times H$, where $H$ is the number of possible situations, which consists of numbers 0 in all dimensions, except for numbers 1 in each dimension when their respective state is active.

4. **ICAART.** This is the representation used in [8]. For each cell in the grid, the number 1 is used to represent an empty cell, 0 if it is destructible or $-1$ if it is obstructed (indestructible or bomb). After this step, we have a vector of the same number of cells that we have in the grid. Next, for each cell in the grid, the number 1 is included if the agent is in that position or 0, otherwise. Then, we add 1 to the cell if there is an opponent there, or 0, otherwise. Finally, for each cell in the grid, a float value between $-1.0$ and $1.0$ is included to represent the level of danger of a cell, computed according to the time that the bomb has left to explode (less time to explode means more dangerous). The danger value is negative if the bomb was placed by the agent and positive if it was placed by an opponent or by the environment itself. In this representation, the size of the observation vector is four times larger than the size of the grid.

5. **ZeroOrOne.** This representation closely resembles the Hybrid representation, but, instead of adding one hybrid vector to each grid cell, each observation is added to the observation vector separately, as in the ICAART representation. It increases the size of the agent observation vector by seven times the grid size. The order of addition, considering the value of 1 or 0, respectively, is as follows: (1), free or obstructed cell; (2) destructible or indestructible; (3) the cell contains an agent or not; (4) the cell has an opponent or not; (5) the cell has a bomb or not; (6) the cell is dangerous or not; (7) the cell is on fire or not.

## 4.4 Reinforcement Learning Algorithms

We include four RL algorithms to train Bomberman agents, as follows: (i) the PPO [9] method integrated with a Multi-Layer Perceptron (MLP); (ii)the PPO [9] method integrated with a Long Short-Term Memory (LSTM) network; (iii) the Behaviour Cloning (BC) [2] imitation learning method; and (iv) a novel implementation that runs the PPO after learning with BC, *i.e.*, first, we run the BC, save its model, and start PPO with such a model.

The PPO algorithm approximates the policy function using a neural network. To that, the implementation provided by the ML Agents toolkit allows for using either an MLP or an LSTM as such a neural network. In this last case, we benefit from the memory component of the LSTM to allow for the agent to remember its relevant past experiences. The method keeps saving the iterations of the agent with the environment together with the received rewards to compose the batch of examples. More specifically, during each iteration of the game, the method accumulates the experience of each agent composed of the current state, the executed action, the received reward, and the next state. After a certain number of collected experiences, the network (MLP or LSTM) do its job, by executing the value and the advantage function, computing the errors, and updating the policy.

To train the agent using the BC algorithm, we provide a replay file with the expert interactions. The number of opponents in each match may change according to the replay file. The match in which the expert agent has played is exactly reproduced in the replay file so that the expert can demonstrate to the student how to play the game. When the student is learning, all the opponents' moves and matches are synchronized with the replay file. In this case, its opponents react according to the replay, but the apprentices have made their own decisions. After it dies or the number of iterations per match reaches a maximum limit, the next match in the file is loaded.

We also developed a novel combination of the BC and PPO training, by first training with the BC approach, followed by training with PPO. We save the model trained with BC and load this model to initialize the weights of the PPO network. We use a function that forces the network to load even though they are slightly different. All the nodes in the neural network that have the same name are loaded with the values from the previous training, while all nodes that were not present in the last training are initialized with their default values.

## 4.5   Training Process Loop

The entire training process is composed of several matches, corresponding to the episodes of a traditional RL algorithm. At the beginning of each match, the agents are created and randomly positioned in the grid. Since there is more than one agent per scenario, it is necessary to synchronize their observations, actions, and rewards. In this way, one agent does not have advantage over another one due to getting some information first. At the beginning of each iteration in a match, the state of the bombs is updated, and, if the time has come, they explode. It is also necessary to update the blocks since some of them may have been hit by an explosion. Next, each agent receives the state of the environment and the reward corresponding to the observed state. The learning algorithm also receives state observation and the given rewards to update the policy function. Finally, the living agents act in the environment, according to the action computed by the current policy function. At the end of an iteration, we apply the time penalty reward.

## 5   Experimental Results

In this section, we present experiments and results related to our proposal and conducted to investigate how Bomberman agents learn under (1) the five state representation, (2) MLP versus LSTM, and (3) the learning algorithms.

*General Experimental Setting:* At the beginning of a match, we create at random 2 to 4 agents per scenario. To train the agents, we created and configured ten scenarios that run in parallel in the same 2D environment, simulating different episodes of the RL algorithm. Among them, five are static, meaning that their destructible blocks are recreated in the same configuration at the beginning of the episode, and the other five are configured at random. Table 2 shows the learning algorithms' hyperparameters. After the training phase, we conducted tournaments with the agents composed of a 100 matches (T100) whenever we want to compare agents learning within the same environment and tournaments with 1000 matches (T1000) to compare distinct agents.

To select the most appropriate way of representing states, we train PPO with only one ML-Agents toolkit's brain learning from the experience of all the agents in the scenario. We repeat the training five times for 2M iterations for each one of the five types of state representation (Binary Flag, Normalized Binary Flag, Hybrid, ICAART, and ZeroOrOne). Thus, we have a set of *homogeneous_brain* = {**BF, NBF, H, I, ZO**}, with each element in the set corresponding to one of the five state representations. Each element in *homogeneous_agents* set unfolds into five training sets, *i.e.*, **BF** = {$BF_1, \ldots, BF_5$ }, **NBF** = {$NBF_1, \ldots, NBF_5$}, where the first element corresponds to a whole training execution, the second element corresponds to another independent training execution, and so on. Thus, we have a total of 25 training executions, taking, on average, 20 h of training. The larger is the observation vector, the more time the training takes to finish.

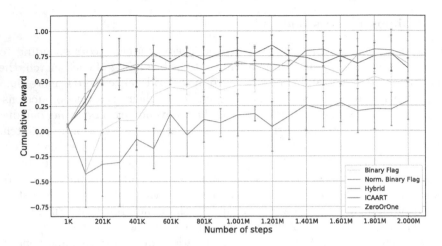

**Fig. 1.** Cumulative rewards in the Bomberman training sessions with the 5 types of state representation. Vertical lines stand for standard deviation.

Figure 1 shows that the cumulative rewards of the Binary Flag and Normalized Binary Flag representations are lower than the other for almost the entire training phase, achieving the average performance of the others only over the end of the training. Meanwhile, the other agents keep all taking the lead until the step 651K, when the ICAART representation gets the best average cumulative reward and surpasses the rest of them until the end of the training. The average cumulative reward of both ZeroOrOne and Hybrid Brains were similar. Note that standard deviation behaves similarly for all Brains.

The behavior of the cumulative rewards of the PPO with LSTM and the BC agents are very similar to the one presented in Fig. 1. Thus, due to lack of space, we do not show them here.

**Table 2.** Hyperparameters used in the learning process

| Name | Value | Name | Value | Name | Value |
|------|-------|------|-------|------|-------|
| Batch size | 128 | # hidden layers (MLP) | 3 | # hidden units (MLP) | 128 |
| Learning rate (MLP) | 0,0003 | Time horizon | 128 | Beta | 0,005 |
| Buffer size (MLP) | 2048 | Epsilon | 0,2 | Gamma | 0,99 |
| Lambd | 0,95 | Max steps | 2M | Normalize | False |
| # epoch (MLP) | 3 | Sequence length (LSTM) | 32 | Memory size (LSTM) | 256 |
| # hidden layers (LSTM) | 1 | Time horizon (LSTM) | 64 | Buffer size (LSTM) | 1024 |

Next, we select four out of the five agents of each representation according to their cumulative rewards (we keep the four agents with the largest accumulated rewards). Then, the selected agents battle against the other agents that learned with the same representation as in a T100. The tournaments are accomplished with four agents because this is the maximum number of agents allowed in the same scenario.

The percentage of wins considering each battle in the T100 tournaments are: $BF_2$ (28.5% of victories), $NBF_1$ (28.2%), $H_1$ (38.5%), $I_4$ (27.2%), $ZO_1$ (29.7%). Next, we would like to make these winners fight against each other in a new tournament. Again, as we have at most four agents in a scenario, we must discard the worst of these five. For so, we rely again on their training accumulated reward. Then, we have a new set composed of the winner agents $W = \{H_1, I_4, ZO_1, NBF_1\}$ as $BF_2$ was the worst of them in the training phase. By analyzing the behavior of the agents in $W$ when battling, we observed that they were able to learn how to play the Bomberman game correctly. They usually put bombs and escape from them, except for $NBF_1$, which only sometimes acts as expected.

Finally, we yield a $T1000$ tournament to make the agents in the set $W$ to battle against each other, aiming at verifying the best state representation for the Bomberman environment. The results are listed in Table 3. We can see that $H_1$ was the one reaching the most significant number of victories (4442), pointing out that this should be the best way of representing the environment.

Next, we experiment with LSTM to approximate the policy function within the PPO algorithm and verify if this would improve the performance of an agent that uses the Hybrid representation (the winner of the previous tournament). As LSTM requires a lot more parameters than MLP, we change some hyperparameters to alleviate the runtime. We trained five models with LSTM and did a T100 with the four models that obtained the best cumulative rewards. The winner of them was the second model generated in the training, achieving 31.4% of wins.

Then, we created another tournament called T1000-LSTM to compare two LSTM agents with two hybrid-MLP agents, the winner of the T1000-representation battle. As can be seen in Table 4, an agent trained with LSTM won the tournament with 61.02%. These results indicate that by activating LSTM in the PPO algorithm, we can induce agents that learn better from their environment to the point of winning other agents. This is due to the memory capacity of LSTMs that allows for the agent learn what to do, even when the reward is in a long way ahead in the future.

**Table 3.** Results of a T1000 tournament that compares agents with different state representations

| Results | No. of Wins |
|---------|-------------|
| Draw | 263 (2,63%) |
| $NBF_1$ | 319 (3,19%) |
| $H_1$ | **4442 (44,42%)** |
| $I_4$ | 1782 (17,82%) |
| $Z_1$ | 3194 (31,94%) |
| Total | 10000 (100%) |

**Table 4.** Results of a T1000-LSTM Versus Hybrid tournament

| Results | No. of Wins |
|---------|-------------|
| Draw | 395 (3,95%) |
| **LSTM 2** | **6102 (61,02%)** |
| $H_1$ | 3503 (35,03%) |
| Total | 10000 (100%) |

Finally, we trained an agent with the BC algorithm and the Hybrid representation and tried to continue its training with PPO. Before training, we recorded 40 matches in a replay file where we play at least three matches in static scenarios and 20 matches in random ones, fighting against others that use LSTM. This replay file acts during the BC training as the expert so that the student agent can learn to play from it. In the BC training, we use the same hyperparameters used in Table 2 except that we changed **max steps** to 100K and set **batches per epoch** to 5. If the learner dies or if the game is taking more than 400 iterations to finish, we reset the scenario and load the next match of the replay file.

After finishing the BC training, we may still improve the policy function of the agent following two ways: (i) (**BC+PPO_Only1**): we run PPO starting from the policy learned by BC to train one agent against enemies already trained with the PPO-LSTM-Hybrid-state setting; (ii) (**BC+PPO_All**): In the second way of continued training, PPO runs after BC as before, but all the agents in the scenario are still learning. We create a series of T100 and T1000 tournaments to observe the BC agents behavior and found out the following: (**A**) (**T1000 BC-vs-LSTM**): The BC agent plays reasonably only when it is in the exact scenarios he has trained before, and when his enemies behave in the same way as in the replay file. When the BC agent battles against the LSTM in a T100 one-vs-one agent tournament, it wins only 9.7% of the matches. (**B**) (**T1000 BC+PPO_Only1 vs LSTM**): In this case, the BC-PPO_Only1 wins the LSTM in 91.3% of the matches. This result shows that it is useful to start from a trained BC agent and refine it with PPO. (**C**) (**T1000 BC+PPO_All vs. LSTM**): Here, the winning agent was the BC+PPO_All with 56.69% of wins against 39.98% of the LSTM agent. These results further confirm that BC provides a good starting point to PPO and that the knowledge acquired in the previous training with BC has not been forgotten. (**D**) (**T1000 BC+PPO_Only1 vs. BC+PPO_All**): The BC+PPO_All won 49.5% of the matches whereas the BC+PPO_Only1 won 42.3% of the matches. This result shows that the agents may learn better when facing other agents that are learning as well. However, this was the most closely results from all the others. Note that the LSTM opponents used in BC pre-training are also used in the BC+PPO_Only1 training. However, in BC+PPO_All training, LSTM opponents are not used, as all the agents are using the same controller and, therefore, the same policy function. This explains why BC+PPO_All wins fewer matches against LSTM opponents than BC+PPO_Only1 as this later becomes an expert at beating LSTM because it trained only with these opponents.

# 6  Conclusions

In this work, we investigated five state representations and four learning algorithms to build Bomberman agents that learn how to play. Regarding the state representations, the results pointed out that our proposed hybrid representation achieves the best results in test time, experimented with tournaments conducted after the learning phase. Regarding the learning algorithms, we experimented with the actor-critic-based PPO algorithm using either an MLP or an LSTM, the BC imitation learning, and a novel approach developed by us that starts with BC and continues the training with PPO from the function learned with BC. The results pointed out that by coupling LSTM within the PPO algorithm produces smarter agents and training beforehand with the BC algorithm can influence subsequent training with PPO. As future work, we would like to enhance the Bomberman agents by giving them the ability to put several bombs at once and acquiring power, variable-size scenarios, multi-players and testing other RL and IL algorithms.

# References

1. Sutton, R., Barto, A.: Reinforcement Learning: An Introduction (2017). (in preparation)
2. Li, Y.: Deep reinforcement learning: an overview. CoRR, vol. abs/1701.07274 (2017)
3. Silver, D., et al.: A general reinforcement learning algorithm that masters chess, shogi, and go through self-play. Science **362**(6419), 1140–1144 (2018)
4. Mnih, V., et al.: Playing atari with deep reinforcement learning. CoRR, vol. abs/1312.5602 (2013)
5. Resnick, C., et al.: Pommerman: a multi-agent playground. In: Joint Proceedings of the AIIDE 2018 Workshops Co-located with 14th AAAI Conference on AI and Interactive Digital Entertainment (AIIDE 2018) (2018)
6. da Cruz Lopes, M.A.: Bomberman as an artificial intelligence platform. Master's thesis, Universidade do Porto (2016)
7. Karasik, E., Hemed, A.: Intro to AI Bomberman (2013). http://www.cs.huji.ac.il/~ai/projects/2012/Bomberman/. Accessed 25 Nov 2018
8. Kormelink, J.G., Drugan, M.M., Wiering, M.A.: Exploration methods for connectionist Q-learning in Bomberman. In: Proceedings of the 10th International Conference on Agents and Artificial Intelligence, ICAART 2018, pp. 355–362 (2018)
9. Schulman, J., Wolski, F., Dhariwal, P., Radford, A., Klimov, O.: Proximal policy optimization algorithms. arXiv preprint arXiv:1707.06347 (2017)
10. Juliani, A., et al.: Unity: a general platform for intelligent agents. CoRR, vol. abs/1809.02627 (2018)
11. Hochreiter, S., Schmidhuber, J.: Long short-term memory. Neural Comput. **9**(8), 1735–1780 (1997)
12. Lapan, M.: Deep Reinforcement Learning Hands-On: Apply Modern RL Methods, with Deep Q-Networks, Value Iteration, Policy Gradients, TRPO, AlphaGo Zero and More. Packt Publishing Ltd. (2018)
13. Hornik, K., Stinchcombe, M.B., White, H.: Multilayer feedforward networks are universal approximators. Neural Netw. **2**(5), 359–366 (1989)
14. Schulman, J., Levine, S., Abbeel, P., Jordan, M., Moritz, P.: Trust region policy optimization. In: International Conference on Machine Learning, pp. 1889–1897 (2015)
15. Lanham, M.: Learn Unity ML-Agents-Fundamentals of Unity Machine Learning: Incorporate new powerful ML algorithms such as Deep Reinforcement Learning for games. Packt Publishing Ltd. (2018)
16. Mnih, V., et al.: Asynchronous methods for deep reinforcement learning. In: Proceedings of the 33rd International Conference on Machine Learning, pp. 1928–1937 (2016)

# Procedural Content Generation of Rhythm Games Using Deep Learning Methods

Yubin Liang, Wanxiang Li$^{(\boxtimes)}$, and Kokolo Ikeda

School of Information Science,
Japan Advanced Institute of Science and Technology, Nomi, Ishikawa, Japan
liang_yubin@yahoo.com
{wanxiang.li,kokolo}@jaist.ac.jp

**Abstract.** The rhythm game is a type of video game which is popular to many people. But the game contents (required action and its timing) of rhythm game are usually hand-crafted by human designers. In this research, we proposed an automatic generation method to generate game contents from the music file of the famous rhythm game "OSU!" 4k mode. Generally, the supervised learning method is used to generate such game contents. In this research some new methods are purposed, one is called "fuzzy label" method, which shows better performance on our training data. Another is to use the new model C-BLSTM. On our test data, we improved the F-Score of timestamp prediction from 0.8159 to 0.8430. Also, it was confirmed through experiments that human players could feel the generated beatmap is more natural than previous research.

**Keywords:** Procedural Content Generation · Rhythm game · C-BLSTM

## 1 Introduction

Rhythm game is a genre of music-themed (action video) game in which players play by taking actions in accordance with rhythm and music [8]. Since music and songs are familiar to ordinary people, it is easy to understand how to play such games. In addition, both of easy stage and hard stage can be created from one music, therefore rhythm game becomes a popular game genre in the whole world.

In many cases, the contents (required action and its timing) of rhythm game are hand-crafted by human designers from music material. Also, there are countless pieces of music, but only a part of them have already been used as game contents. Therefore, to generate contents automatically for rhythm game is required. In this research, two models are used to generate contents from music materials for famous rhythm game "OSU!" [1]. One inputs the audio data, outputs timestamps (timing of action), another inputs the timestamp and outputs action type.

© IFIP International Federation for Information Processing 2019
Published by Springer Nature Switzerland AG 2019
E. van der Spek et al. (Eds.): ICEC-JCSG 2019, LNCS 11863, pp. 134–145, 2019.
https://doi.org/10.1007/978-3-030-34644-7_11

As a Machine Learning task, this approach has some difficulties such as: (1) Because same music may be processed by different authors or has different level settings, one music may have many different beatmaps. (2) Proportion of positive/negative samples is ill. To deal with those problems, in this research we adopt that: (1) Handle the difficulty settings as an input feature. (2) Using fuzzy labels to increase positive samples.

Proposed training methods and new model C-BLSTM are evaluated through F-Score, shows a better performance than previous research on timestamp generation. And from human experiments we can find that beatmaps which generated by purposed method are more natural than beatmaps generated by previous research.

## 2    Background

The system structure of purposed method is shown as Fig. 1. The main workflow is from audio files generating the timestamp, and using those timestamps to generate action type by second model. Combining the generated timestamp and action type, we can obtain beatmap for input music.

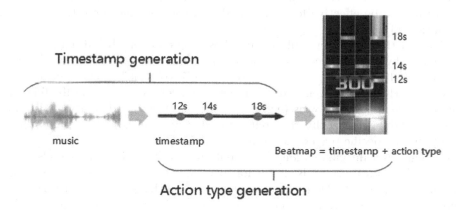

**Fig. 1.** System structure of purposed method.

### 2.1    Rhythm Game: OSU!

To generate the contents of rhythm game, we use open-sourced game "OSU!" which has over 10 million registered users [1] as our test bench.

"OSU!" consists of many types (or mode) of game, but in this research we foucs on the mode called mania 4k. Players are required to push the button when markers are dropping from the top of screen. When players push the correct button, they would get a high score. On the other hand if the timing or required action was incorrect, system would judge this action as missing. By pushing the buttons, players would feel like they are playing this rhythm by themselves.

These required actions (4 types: click, long push start, long push end and none) and their timing consist the game contents. In "OSU!", beatmap records these information. Generally, beatmap are usually hand-crafted by human designers. So even if there are countless pieces of music, the number of contents that can be played in the game is limited. An automatic generation method is needed in this case.

### 2.2    Previous Research

In the field of rhythm game and game contents generation research. There are some previous researches which is essential to our approaches.

Capturing the characteristics of music is an important part in rhythm game content generating. Generally, selection of action timings is based on the sounds or rhythm which can be clearly heard by human. Since the beginning or changing of music is most distinguishable to human, we usually set actions around these timing in rhythm games. To extract these timing, Schlüter et al. proposed an research using deep learning methods to detect the beginning of musical notes (musical onsets) [10]. Their method is used to extract features in our research.

Long Short-Term Memory (LSTM) is a kind of Recurrent Neural Network (RNN) which is effective to suppress gradient vanishing over time [5], and it has been proved to be effective for time-based task such as voice detection [7] and translation [6], etc.

Music or rhythm is generally regarded as a type of time-based data, and in the field of rhythm game content generation, LSTM was used to generate game content of a rhythm game called "Dance Dance Revolution" in Donahue et al.'s research [3]. However, to generate a content which correspond to specify difficult level, or some special patterns (e.g. patterns that player good at or not) is still not so gratifying. Hence, this research is aimed at generating game contents that correspond to specific player's level in rhythm game.

In many rhythm games, long press buttons are basically corresponds to a long sound of music. So it is useful for analyzing the melody to generate the long press properly. In Donahue et al.'s research, although the effectiveness of melody information in action generation is examined, but its application has not been taken yet [3]. In this research, we use the method which propose by Salamon et al. [9], for extracting the main melody of music. By using their method, we can detect long sounds in music and attempt to employ them in long press action generation.

## 3    Preparation of Training Data

### 3.1    Data and Difficulty Definition

In this research, all training data is collected from the homepage of "OSU!" [1] on June, 2017. Considering to use the most popular beatmaps as our training data, only beatmaps which has been played over 100 thousands times will be chosen.

In general, one music file corresponds to various beatmaps depending on the different authors and different difficulties. And players can play a suitable difficulty according to their ability. The statistical information of used training data is shown as Table 1.

**Table 1.** Statistical information of traning data

| Number of authors* | Number of music | Number of beatmap | Number of all action* | Action per second* |
|---|---|---|---|---|
| 300 | 473 | 1655 | 1690000 | 7.85 |

*Approximately.

Since there are various difficulties in the training data, and we aims to generate beatmaps with different difficulties from one music. So a proper definition of difficulty is highly required.

Generally, the difficulty is depending on: (1) Complexity of action combination. (2) Number of actions per second (density of actions). (3) Speed of action marker. (4) The strictness of judging miss (max allowable time difference). (5) Number of miss that could be permitted.

Because (3), (4) and (5) is the more relative to setting of game, we don't consider these factors in this research. Also, individual players have different action combinations that they are not good at, so it is hard to use factor (1) in automatic generation method. More actions in same time means beatmap is more difficult, so in this research we just use density of actions to define the difficulties for each beatmap.

We divide the training data to 10 levels by density, that is (a) number of action under 3 per second is level-0, (b) number of action from 3 to 17 per second is used for level-1 to level-8 equally (e.g. 3 to 4.75 is level-1 and 4.75 to 6.5 is level-2), (c) number of action more than 17 per second is level-9.

## 3.2   Feature Extraction

In order to use the audio data in neural networks, some feature extraction process is needed. Firstly we compute a multiple-timescale short-time Fourier transform (STFT) of every audio file by three window sizes 23 ms, 46 ms and 93 ms and stride of 10 ms as 1 frame (that means there are 100 frames per second). Shorter window sizes preserve low-level features such as pitch and timbre while large window sizes provide more context for high-level features such as melody and rhythm [4].

Then we compute the Mel-scale from 27.5 Hz to 16 kHz with 80 bands of STFT magnitude spectra to better represent human perception of loudness [12].

Finally we prepend and append $n$ frames of past and future context for each frame, so the final audio representation is a 80 * 3 * $(2n + 1)$ tensor.

## 4  Timestamp Generation

### 4.1  Network Structure

Donahue et al. uses C-LSTM to generate timestamp [3], which has the advantage to learn not only the current frame but also the past and future frames. Structure of C-LSTM is shown as Fig. 2. We use 15 * 80 * 3 tensor ($n = 7$) as input. First layer is a convolution layer which has the size of 7 * 3 * 3 and 1 * 3 max-pooling, output 9 * 26 * 10 matrix to next layer. Second layer is a convolution layer which has the size of 3 * 3 * 10 and 1 * 3 max-pooling, output 7 * 8 * 20 matrix. Adding the 10 units one-hot density (which present the level of difficulty), we input the matrix to 2 LSTM layer which have 200 units. After LSTM there are 2 full-connected layer with 258 units and 128 units separately. Finally we output the result by a single Sigmoid unit, which presents the possibility of been chosen as a timestamp. LSTM layers use tanh function as activation function, while other layers use ReLU.

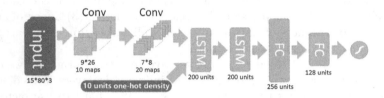

**Fig. 2.** Structure of C-LSTM.

C-LSTM can only use the information "until now". In this research, "OSU!" has a lot of "long push" action, since most "long push start" action is at the onset of long melody, we need to consider not only the information in past, but also information in the future. One way is to use more frames (i.e. make $n$ bigger), but the high calculation cost and performance reduction is unbearable sometimes. Another way to get more future information without increasing frames is using the C-BLSTM [11].

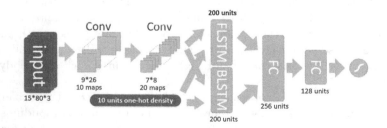

**Fig. 3.** Structure of C-BLSTM.

The structure of C-BLSTM is shown as Fig. 3. C-BLSTM can predict times-tamp using more future information, but has the similar calculation cost as C-LSTM.

### 4.2 Fuzzy Label

There are about 7.85 actions per second in our training data. Since we have 100 frames in 1 s, there are just few positive data (less than 8%). One way to solve this problem is to calculate feature with wider stride. For example using 50ms stride will get 20 frames per second, which will make the rate of positive data to 40%. But longer stride will lose some rhythm or melody information.

In this research a method called fuzzy label that can solve the problem is proposed. Shown as Fig. 4, the original data use 0 (no action in this frame) and 1 (there is action in this frame) label which have a drastic changing. And fuzzy label modify the data using Gaussian distribution, transform the data from "whether the frame has actions or not" to "the possibility that the frame has actions", makes the changing smoother.

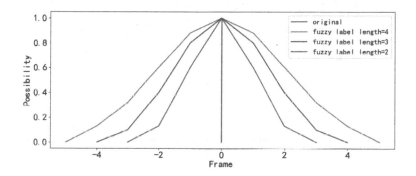

**Fig. 4.** Example of fuzzy label.

### 4.3 Threshold Selection

Output of network is the "possibility whether one frame should have actions". In practice, we need to transform the possibility into a two-value number (0 or 1), to decide whether there should have actions in this frame. Using some rules such as "when possibility is bigger than a threshold $t$, there should have actions" can be helpful for judging.

When threshold was too large, output actions would decrease, and output action would increase when it was too small. Both situations are not good for timestamp selection, so a proper threshold is needed. Some data which called "threshold deciding data" is randomly selected to decide the threshold $t$, which we will test different threshold in the same model by it, to maximize the F-score. The threshold deciding data is independent to training data and will not take part in the training process.

## 4.4   Experiment

Difficulty distribution in original data is biased, there are just few low difficulty data and high difficulty data. Such an ill data distribution is harmful and causing unstable learning [2]. To solve this problem, we copy the training data in low and high difficulty to make original data distribution balanced.

**Validation Experiment.** In this experiment, all model uses $80 * 3 * 15$ (frame length $n = 7$) tensor as input and same learning hyper-parameters. All networks are trained for 25 epochs (1000 batches per epoch), the mean F-score of each epoch is shown as Fig. 5.

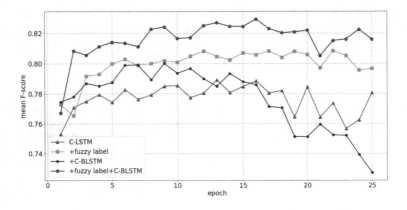

**Fig. 5.** Result of validation experiment.

From the result, we can find that comparing to the C-LSTM, C-BLSTM shows a better performance in the beginning, but suddenly facing the problem of degradation in performance. We also find that training error of C-BLSTM deceasing follow the process. This means C-BLSTM faced a serious overfitting problem in the mid of training.

When comparing the result of C-LSTM to C-LSTM with fuzzy label (label length is 3), we can find that fuzzy label improved the performance dramatically. Moreover, from the result of C-BLSTM with fuzzy label, we can find that fuzzy label not only improved the performance, but also solved the overfitting problem of C-BLSTM.

**Experiment of Different Fuzzy Label.** We also have experiments on different fuzzy label lengths to compare their performance. In this experiment, all models use C-BLSTM and $80 * 3 * 15$ (frame length $n = 7$) tensor as input, also, they use same learning hyper-parameters.

Mean F-score of each epoch is shown as Fig. 6. We can find that our method improved the naive C-BLSTM comparing to the result with no fuzzy label. Also, we find best fuzzy label length is 3 on our data. One possible reason is when length was 3, the rate of positive data would be closed to 50%, which is a well-balanced data distribution.

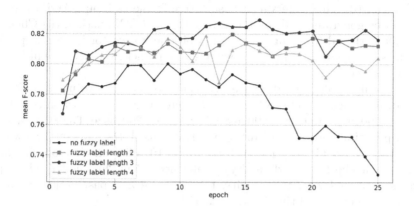

**Fig. 6.** Result of fuzzy label experiment.

**Experiment of Different Frame Length.** In this experiment, all model use C-BLSTM, same fuzzy label length of 3 and same learning hyper-parameters. The only difference is the frame length, which will influence the input tensor size. For example when frame length $n$ was 7, the input size would be $80 * 3 * 15$, and when frame length $n$ was 9, the input size would be $80 * 3 * 19$.

The result of $n = 4$, 5, 6 and 7 is shown as Fig. 7a. We can find that when $n$ is 4, we would get the best performance, and when $n$ is 7 we would get the similar performance to $n = 4$. From Fig. 7b we can find that $n = 7$ showed the best performance. The result shows that we cannot get better performance by simply adding the by frame length.

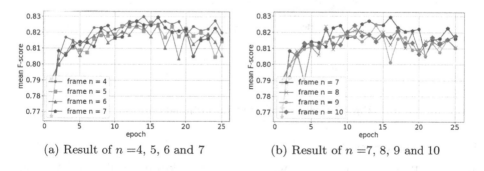

(a) Result of $n = 4$, 5, 6 and 7          (b) Result of $n = 7$, 8, 9 and 10

**Fig. 7.** Result of different frames

# 5   Action Type Generation

## 5.1   Input Feature and Output

In our Action type generation model, we use (1) Action before one frame, (2) Difficulty and (3) Time interval of past/future frame as input. And 4 types of action will be generated and used as input, that is (a) No action, (b) Click, (c) Long push start and (d) Long push end. 4 bit one-hot vector is used to present action on single channel. And since we have 4 channels, the action will be four 4 bit one-hot vectors.

The time interval is the distance between two actions. We use a 8 bit one-hot vector to present it. This 8 bit one-hot vector means the interval is $\sim$50 ms, $\sim$100 ms, $\sim$200 ms, $\sim$400 ms, $\sim$800 ms, $\sim$1600 ms, $\sim$3200 ms and 3200 ms$\sim$. Since both the past time interval and future interval is used, the time interval will be presented as two 8 bit one-hot vector. And a 10 units one-hot density label (which present the level of difficulty) is also needed in this model. The input feature is combined with the density, time interval and past action, so input feature has 7 vectors and the data size is 42 bit.

The output is probabilities of all action combinations. Since we have 4 channels and each channel has 4 types of action, the number of all valid actions is 256 $(4^4)$. Finally we will choose one action combination that have biggest probability.

The example of input feature and output probabilities is shown as Fig. 8.

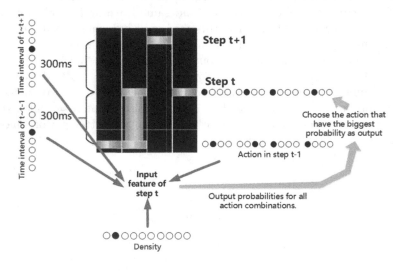

**Fig. 8.** Example of input features and output.

## 5.2   Network Structure

In Action type generation part, we uses the network frame called LSTM64 [3]. Shown as Fig. 9, after input layer the first layer uses 128 LSTM units, and second layer uses 128 LSTM units. Finally this network output 256 probabilities of all valid actions.

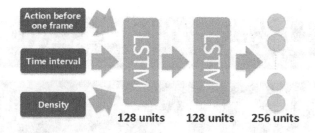

**Fig. 9.** Structure of beatmap generation model.

## 5.3   Experiment of Predict Actions

Same training data as timestamp generation model are used for training this model. Also, since the difficulty distribution in original data is unbalanced, training data in low and high difficulty is copied to make original data distribution balanced.

The finial accuracy of predicting action is 0.4366, which is not a high accuracy. But we find that even in one music, there are different beatmaps. And according to the different designers, the beatmap is various. For example in Fig. 10, we can find that about half actions arc not same between two human designer, even they have used the same music.

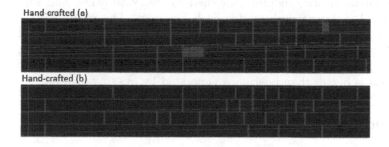

**Fig. 10.** Compare of two Hand-crafted beatmaps.

Figure 11 shows a result of beatmap generated by network and human designer for same music. We can find that even some actions are different, these two beatmaps are similar, which player may not notice the difference. According to these evidence, we think the result that predicting accuracy is 0.4366 is not bad. Prediction accuracy is not enough for estimating how human players can enjoy the generated beatmaps, so it will be an interesting future work to propose such a measurement.

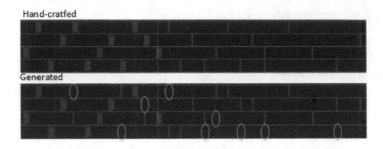

**Fig. 11.** Compare of Hand-crafted and purposed method.

# 6   Evaluation of Naturalness

We conduct a experiment though 10 human subjects. 15 beatmaps (5 of them are hand-crafted by human designer, 5 of them are generated by previous research and 5 of them are generated by proposed method) are used in this experiment. "Purposed method" data and "Existing method" data use same action type generation model, but "Purposed method" data use C-BLSTM model with fuzzy label (length $= 3$), frame size $n$ is 7 to generate timestamp. timestamp of "Existing method" data are generated by C-LSTM without fuzzy label, and frame size $n$ is 7.

All Beapmaps are randomly watched by every subjects, and subjects are asked to judge the naturalness for each beatmap. The result is hand-crafted beatmaps get 4.52 points, existing method get 3.30 points and purposed method get 3.72 points. From the result we can find that even beatmaps which generated by purposed method are not as natural as hand-crafted beatmaps, the naturalness is better than beatmaps generated by existing method.

# 7   Conclusion

Overall, a new method "fuzzy label" is introduced in game contents generation of rhythm game, and new model C-BLSTM is used in our timestamp generation method. We have proofed that purposed method improved the performance of Timestamp generation, and the F-Score is increased from 0.8159 to 0.8460.

Moreover, a generation model from timestamp to beatmap is introduced. And by experiment on human subjects, we have proofed that beatmaps generated by purposed method is more natural than previous research.

**Acknowledgments.** This research is financially supported by Japan Society for the Promotion of Science (JSPS) under contract number 17K00506.

# References

1. Osu! https://osu.ppy.sh/home. Accessed June 2017
2. Buda, M., Maki, A., Mazurowski, M.A.: A systematic study of the class imbalance problem in convolutional neural networks. Neural Netw. **106**, 249–259 (2018)
3. Donahue, C., Lipton, Z.C., McAuley, J.: Dance dance convolution. In: Proceedings of the 34th International Conference on Machine Learning, vol. 70, pp. 1039–1048. JMLR. org (2017)
4. Hamel, P., Bengio, Y., Eck, D.: Building musically-relevant audio features through multiple timescale representations (2012)
5. Hochreiter, S., Schmidhuber, J.: Long short-term memory. Neural Comput. **9**(8), 1735–1780 (1997)
6. Kalchbrenner, N., Danihelka, I., Graves, A.: Grid long short-term memory. arXiv preprint arXiv:1507.01526 (2015)
7. Parascandolo, G., Huttunen, H., Virtanen, T.: Recurrent neural networks for polyphonic sound event detection in real life recordings. In: 2016 IEEE International Conference on Acoustics, Speech and Signal Processing (ICASSP), pp. 6440–6444. IEEE (2016)
8. Pasinski, A.: Possible benefits of playing music video games (2014)
9. Salamon, J., Gómez, E.: Melody extraction from polyphonic music signals using pitch contour characteristics. IEEE Trans. Audio Speech Lang. Process. **20**(6), 1759–1770 (2012)
10. Schlüter, J., Böck, S.: Improved musical onset detection with convolutional neural networks. In: 2014 IEEE International Conference on Acoustics, Speech and Signal Processing (ICASSP), pp. 6979–6983. IEEE (2014)
11. Schuster, M., Paliwal, K.K.: Bidirectional recurrent neural networks. IEEE Trans. Sig. Process. **45**(11), 2673–2681 (1997)
12. Stevens, S., Volkmann, J., Newman, E.: The mel scale equates the magnitude of perceived differences in pitch at different frequencies. J. Acoust. Soc. Am. **8**(3), 185–190 (1937)

# Music Video Clip Impression Emphasis Method by Font Fusion Synchronized with Music

Kosuke Nonaka[✉], Junki Saito, and Satoshi Nakamura

Meiji University, Nakano 4-21-1, Tokyo, Japan
electro0701@gmail.com

**Abstract.** Video content that displays lyrics synchronized with the music in, for example, karaoke or music videos on the Internet is becoming popular. The font can change the impression the users get from the content; therefore, by changing the font according to the content, it is possible to improve the content and the overall experience. We aim to develop a new lyric expression method by blending the existing fonts and synchronizing them with the music. In this study, we propose a method that generates fonts that match music videos by mixing fonts according to the music characteristics. Also, we reveal through experiments whether displaying lyrics in a blended font can emphasize music video impressions compared to displaying them in the existing font.

**Keywords:** Font · Music video · Lyric video · Emphasis impression · Subtitle · Font blending

## 1 Introduction

The content of music lyrics is very important. The function of lyrics is to convey information about thoughts, situations, and scenes to the listeners. Nowadays, there are many ways to read the lyrics, for example, on lyric cards in CDs, in subtitle-guided singing at karaoke clubs, or during music programs on TV.

In recent years, video with lyrics software, which uses the lyrics as the main content and synchronizes them with the music, has become popular. In Japan, there are many lyrics videos, for example, Hold Your Hand (Perfume), Aruku Around (Sakanaction), and Go Go Ghost Ship (Kenshi Yonezu). It is not unusual to see lyrics displayed in music videos created with Vocaloid, voice synthesizer software, because synthetic voices are harder to understand than human voices. Other technologies that support musical text expression are TextAlive [1] and LyricSpeaker [2]. Visualization of lyrics synchronized with the music is an effective way to understand the meaning of lyrics. This visualization provides the user with a fascinating and enjoyable experience.

The font of the lyric texts created by software such as Lyric Video or TextAlive is usually the same throughout the music video regardless of the genre, melody, and content of the lyrics. Lyrics shown as a guide in karaoke also use the same font. On the other hand, on posters and in comics, creators choose appropriate font designs to emphasize the content; they would not use a joyful font for a sad scene in a comic

Published by Springer Nature Switzerland AG 2019
E. van der Spek et al. (Eds.): ICEC-JCSG 2019, LNCS 11863, pp. 146–157, 2019.
https://doi.org/10.1007/978-3-030-34644-7_12

book. Several studies have investigated how the font design can change the impression of the content. We expect that the comprehension of the music, as well as the visual and auditory experience, can be augmented if an appropriate font design is selected to display the content. As a result, kinetic text expression created with, for example, LyricSpeaker or TextAlive may become richer. Specifically, it is thought that music video entertainment will be further enhanced by making the lyrics more enjoyable.

## 2  Related Work

Several studies have proposed various ways to extend the viewing experience by adding other types of stimulation, such as, using vibrations synchronized with the music in an impression emphasis method [3]. Similarly, in our research, we aim to extend the visual and auditory experience by adopting an appropriate font for a music video.

A number of studies have reported that the font designs affect the impression of the content. The visual effects of the shapes of Japanese characters on printed matter have been investigated, and it has been verified that different font designs change visual impressions. Mackwiewicz et al. [4] examined the relation between the font design and human recognition. In the same study, 15 types of fonts were evaluated for 10 types of attributes, and it was clarified that the visual characteristics and design characteristics of the font were related to each other. Also, Caldwell [5] analyzed the emotional response to the Japanese font systematically and revealed a relation between the visual characteristics of the font and the emotional response.

Several studies have investigated how the impressions of the font affect human recognition or emotions. Doyle et al. [6] reported that an appropriately selected font for a product can change human behavior. He focused on the consistency of the font and product because the impressions gained from the font design affect human emotions before the meaning of the words does. Velasco et al. [7] revealed that the shape of the font and the sense of taste are related. For example, angular fonts are associated with "sourness", "bitterness", and "spiciness", while rounded fonts are associated with "sweetness". Karnel et al. [8] studied the relation between product packaging and the consumer's behavior: a consumer with healthy habits tends to perceive a lightweight font as healthy, so this font increases the consumer's intention to buy merchandise.

In a study of the creation of new fonts, Suveeranont et al. [9] proposed a system for creating a new font by blending a base font with any other font. However, the system requires manual corrections when the output font is distorted due to blending fonts with extremely different shapes. Contrary to this, Campbell et al. [10] proposed a method that places fonts on a two-dimensional map so that fonts with similar shapes are close to each other and no distortion occurs when they are fused. Our method also blends some existing fonts. However, unlike in Campbell's method, we expressed the font using a numerical formula as done by Saito et al. [11] and generated blended fonts by weighting and averaging the fonts.

## 3  Proposed Method

In this study, we proposed a method that generates fonts that reflect music video impressions by blending existing fonts. We used six music video impressions as input: five impression classes from MIREX [12] and "cuteness" from Yamamoto et al.'s study [13]. The descriptions of C1–C6 are given in Table 1.

**Table 1.** Impression classes

| Name | Adjectives |
|---|---|
| C1 (grandness) | Grand, sonorous, massive |
| C2 (vigorousness) | Lively, exciting |
| C3 (sadness) | Painful, sad |
| C4 (violence) | Aggressive, violent, exciting, passionate |
| C5 (funniness) | Unique, funny, roguish, whimsical, hilarious |
| C6 (cuteness) | Cute, lovely, adorable |

We applied Saito's method of blending fonts [11]. In this method, fonts are blended by considering strokes and diameters as numerical formulas. We supposed that letters can be represented by the locus of a circle with a changing diameter and express these letters by drawing the trajectory of the circle with its center mapped on the stroke line. Specifically, as shown in Fig. 1, first, we obtained a set of circles for drawing the font, and then, to express the font smoothly, we performed cubic spline interpolation to connect the obtained set of circles as much as possible. After that we generated a circle that fills in the gaps. Next, we calculated the numerical formula, which is a sequence of the centers of the circles, by Fourier series expansion. In Fig. 1, $(f(t), g(t))$ is a point on a stroke of a character of a font, and the distance between the edge of the font and the point is $h(t)$: distance information.

Each calculated stroke can be expressed as a numerical formula of $t$:

$$\begin{cases} x = f_i(t) \\ y = g_i(t) \qquad -\pi \le t \le \pi \\ r = h_i(t) \end{cases}$$

By fusing $N$ fonts using the optional rate $\alpha_1 - \alpha_n$ the numerical formulas of the blended strokes are as follows:

$$\begin{cases} x = \sum_{i=1}^{N} \alpha_i f_i(t) \\ y = \sum_{i=1}^{N} \alpha_i g_i(t) \qquad \sum_{i=1}^{N} \alpha_i = 1 \\ r = \sum_{i=1}^{N} \alpha_i h_i(t) \end{cases}$$

By changing the rate of blending, we can create appropriate fonts. Although the number of impression words when blending is two, we extend the number of words by fusing the aforementioned impression classes C1–C6. In the following section, we describe a preliminary survey for computing the C1–C6 impression values of fonts and music videos.

In our method, we blended fonts by associating music video impressions with font impressions. We conducted preliminary surveys on the impressions of fonts and music videos. The first survey was on the fonts. Nineteen participants evaluated their impressions of 14 fonts (Fig. 2); eight fonts were taken from previous research [11], and six fonts were selected by the authors. We showed text in each font on the web system used for the experiment. In this survey, the participants evaluated each impression class on a scale from −2 to +2 using adjectives and negative words.

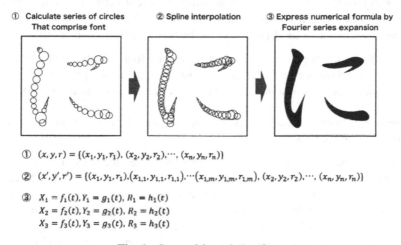

① (x, y, r) = {(x_1, y_1, r_1), (x_2, y_2, r_2), ⋯, (x_n, y_n, r_n)}

② (x', y', r') = {(x_1, y_1, r_1), (x_{1,1}, y_{1,1}, r_{1,1}), ⋯ (x_{1,m}, y_{1,m}, r_{1,m}), (x_2, y_2, r_2), ⋯, (x_n, y_n, r_n)}

③ $X_1 = f_1(t), Y_1 = g_1(t), R_1 = h_1(t)$
$X_2 = f_2(t), Y_2 = g_2(t), R_2 = h_2(t)$
$X_3 = f_3(t), Y_3 = g_3(t), R_3 = h_3(t)$

**Fig. 1.** Steps of formulating fonts

**Fig. 2.** Used fonts

Next, we conducted a survey on the impressions of the music videos. Nineteen participants (university students aged 19–23) watched 18 shortened music videos and evaluated six classes of impressions. The duration of each shortened music video was about 20–30 s. In this evaluation, each impression class was evaluated on a scale from −2 to +2 using adjectives and negative words. Also, the order of the music videos was made random for each participant.

# 4   Experiment

Experiment procedure: We hypothesized that the impression of the music video can be emphasized by using a blended font for lyrics. We conducted experiments to compare a blended font and two fonts created under two conditions.

In our experiment, we verified the usability of a font created by our method by watching a music video that was synchronized with lyrics created in three ways. For generating fonts, we also used two other methods in addition to our method.

1. Blended font: A font generated by adopting the top four neighboring fonts obtained from the impressions of a target music video, weighted averaging, and fusing.
2. Neighborhood font: A font determined to be the closest to the impression of a target music video.
3. Impression_0 font: A font generated by the font fusion method with all six impression class inputs as 0.

In the experiment, the choruses of the same 18 music videos from the preliminary survey were used. A total of 54 types of music videos were generated, and three types of fonts were superimposed on the lower part of the screen. Although there may be important factors for displaying lyrics such as color, size or position, we unified these conditions because subtitles are static throughout the music video in many cases. The generation system was implemented using Processing, open-source graphical library. An example of the generated font is shown in Fig. 3. And examples of the fonts and each impression class are shown in Fig. 4.

**Fig. 3.** Fusion example of each font. From top: fusion font, neighborhood font, and impression_0 font.

**C3(sadness), C6(cuteness)**

| |
|---|
| 私たちあいまいに愛し合ってさあ |
| 私たちあいまいに愛し合ってさあ |
| 私たちあいまいに愛し合ってさあ |

**C2(vigorousness), C6(cuteness)**

| |
|---|
| ああ触れればすぐにまた会えるって言うのに |
| ああ触れればすぐにまた会えるって言うのに |
| ああ触れればすぐにまた会えるって言うのに |

**C1(grandness), C4(violence)**

| |
|---|
| 野放しに突走らうぜ |
| 野放しに突走らうぜ |
| 野放しに突走らうぜ |

**C2(vigorousness), C5(funniness)**

| |
|---|
| この世終わりの日には |
| この世終わりの日には |
| この世終わりの日には |

**C2(vigorousness), C6(cuteness)**

| |
|---|
| 知りたいんだけど怖いから |
| 知りたいんだけど怖いから |
| 知りたいんだけど怖いから |

**C2(vigorousness), C4(violence)**

| |
|---|
| 繋いでいたいとも思わないよ |
| 繋いでいたいとも思わないよ |
| 繋いでいたいとも思わないよ |

**Fig. 4.** Generated font of lyrics and their impression classes. In each music video, from top: fusion font, neighborhood font, and impression_0 font.

Nineteen participants (university students aged 19–23) watched music videos with superimposed lyrics in fonts created under three conditions. Although some of the participants had participated in the data set construction, it was judged to have no influence on the experiment because the font design, music animation and the super-position were considered to be independent from each other. For the experiment, we prepared a web system, which was used to evaluate six impression classes after viewing music videos on a five-point scale steps from $-2$ to $+2$ (Table 1).

Also, even if the impression is emphasized, it is conceivable that the character design would not match the mood of the music video. Therefore, to quantify the degree of matching between the font and the music video, we asked the question "Did the font match the music video?" The answer scale had five steps from $-2$ ("It did not match at all") to $+2$ ("It matched very well"). In addition, the order of music videos was made random for each participant; therefore we concluded that there was no order effect.

### 4.1 Results

Figure 5 shows the degree of matching when the fonts that were created using three different methods were applied to the lyrics of the music videos. Seven music videos were evaluated to be most suitable for the fusion font, nine music videos were evaluated as most suitable for the neighborhood font, and two music videos were evaluated as most suitable for the impression_0 font. From these results, we can assume that a font synchronized with an impression is suitable regardless of fusion, although the most suitable font to be used for the lyrics depends on the music video. Music videos C, F, I, and R had an overall low degree of matching.

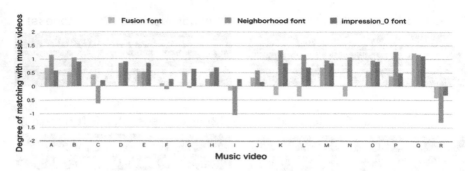

**Fig. 5.** Matching degree of music videos and lyrics for each font.

Figure 6 shows a list of comparisons of the values from the preliminary survey and the experiments for each music video. The blue columns show the values of the preliminary survey, and the green, yellow, and red columns are the values obtained in the experiments. It can be seen that there is variation in impression emphases. The number of evaluation values of any one of the three types of fonts exceeding the value of the pre-survey is 8 for C1, 8 for C2, 14 for C3, 6 for C4, 11 for C5, and 15 for C6. This shows that the impressions of C3 (sadness), C5 (funniness), and C6 (cuteness) are well emphasized.

### 4.2　Analysis

A numerical comparison is performed for each impression class of each music video. From Fig. 6, it can be seen that C3 and C4 in the impression class have a large variation in values for each font, and impression emphasis did not occur as intended. Figure 7 shows graphs in which the impression value data of the font created in the preliminary survey are sorted in ascending order for each of the C1 to C6 impression classes. This graph indicates that C3 and C4 are less than 0, which is the median value in the questionnaire survey, for most of the fonts. In other words, among the impressions of music videos, those with higher C3 and C4 are considered to have the same font each time and do not reflect the impression of the music videos accurately. In addition, the variation in the values of each font is small, and it is considered that a similar font has been generated as a result of font fusion. Furthermore, although the lyrics were added to the lower part of the music video screen this time, if the participants were familiar with the music, it is possible that they could have watched the music video without looking at the lyrics. In the future, we plan to conduct an experiment that takes into consideration the way the viewer sees the subtitles, for example considering karaoke lyrics and TV subtitles.

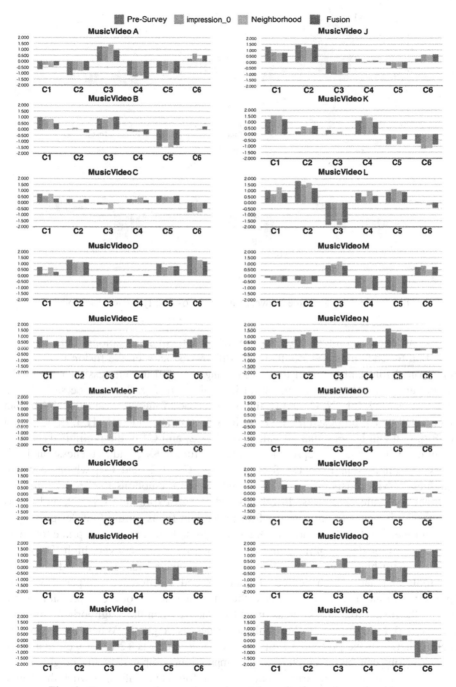

**Fig. 6.** Pre-survey values and experimental results for each music video.

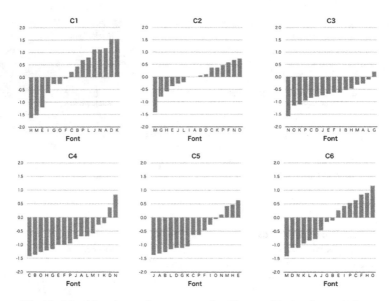

**Fig. 7.** Matching degree between music videos and lyrics for each font

Next, we focused on the differences in impression emphasis among fonts. Figure 8 shows that for each music video, there are differences between the fusion font and the impression_0 font and between the neighboring font and the impression_0 font. The numbers are graphed for each numerical interval. From Fig. 8, it can be seen that in music videos F, H, I, L, N, O, and R, the neighborhood fonts are evaluated higher than fonts created by the proposed method. By looking at music videos F, H, I, L, N, O, and R in Fig. 6, it can be seen that all values of C1, C2, and C4 in the preliminary survey are high. C3, C5, and C6 represent "sadness", "funniness", and "cuteness" and can convey the impression from the font. However, C1, C2, and C4, which represent "grandness", "vigorousness", and "violence", represent emotions that may be difficult to convey by static characters. In other words, when expressing C1, C2, and C4 as characters, it is better to animate the font rather than focus on the font design.

In our method, four fonts are fused, and it is possible that an inappropriate font may be generated if the degree of matching with the music video is not very high. Therefore, to analyze with high degree of matching, we first selected fused fonts and neighborhood fonts that had a high degree of matching and a difference compared with the impression_0 font. Then, we calculated the difference in size of the impression vector between the fusion font and impression_0 font and between the neighborhood font and impression_0 font. Figure 9 shows these values as a graph. When the degree of matching between the presented font and the music video is +2 (very well matched), the fusion font can better emphasize the impression compared to the neighborhood font. However, it can be confirmed that the fusion font is not effective when the degree of matching is +1 (matched). Therefore, it is possible that the font fusion method can greatly emphasize the impression if the degree of matching with the mood in the music video is high. Otherwise, the impression will be suppressed.

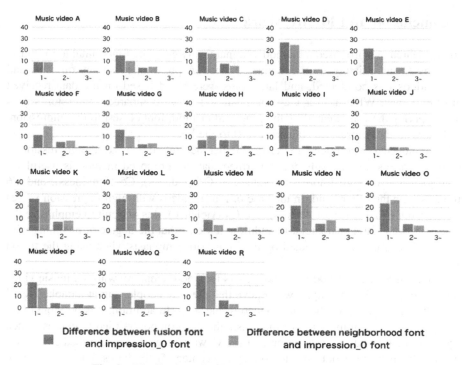

**Fig. 8.** Distribution of differences for each music video.

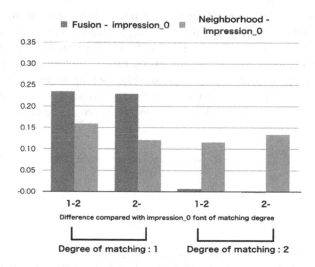

**Fig. 9.** Difference in size of impression vectors.

## 5   Conclusion and Future Work

In this research, we proposed a method to dynamically generate fonts suitable for music videos by fusing existing fonts for music videos. A preliminary survey on fonts and music videos was conducted, and later fonts were fused based on the data received from the survey. When a user views a music video, we compared impression values when applying the font created by the proposed method, font closest to the impression, and font with the impression value set to 0 to the lyrics.

We conducted experiments to verify whether the font emphasizes the impression of the music videos. As a result, we confirmed that the proposed method is useful for music videos with high impression values of C3 (sadness), C5 (funniness), and C6 (cuteness). On the other hand, in the case of music videos with high impression values of C1 (grandness), C2 (vigorousness), and C4 (violence), it is difficult to emphasize the impression with static characters. In addition, it seems that the degree of matching with the music video is greatly affected by the impression emphasis when using the fusion font.

In the future, this method will make users feel more empathy with the music video while watching it. For example, we believe that the way people sing at karaoke would reflect their impression of the music video of the song. In addition, it is possible to fill the gap between the impression of the music that the composers tried to express when they composed it and the impression that the viewers receive. As described above, we consider this method is not only to convey the content of the lyrics, but also to make the lyrics more enjoyable and to contribute greatly to the creation of highly entertaining music and video content.

The limitations of this research are that the impression values of the selected font were uneven, and there was a possibility that the participants viewed the music videos without looking at the lyrics. Therefore, in the future, we plan to have a pre-selection stage to consider the variations in font impression values and then conduct experiments in which the participants watch music videos while looking at the lyrics. Also, in the proposed method, the impression emphases of music classes C1, C2, and C4 did not show the intended results, so we plan to develop an impression emphasis method that uses animation and color.

**Acknowledgments.** This work was supported in part by JST ACCEL Grant Number JPMJAC1602, Japan.

## References

1. Kato, J., Nakano, T., Goto, M.: TextAlive: integrated design environment for kinetic typography. In: Proceedings of the 33rd Annual ACM Conference on Human Factors in Computing Systems, pp. 3403–3412 (2015)
2. Lyric Speaker. https://lyric-speaker.com/index.html. Accessed 16 Aug 2019
3. Yoshida, R., Ideguchi, T., Ooshima, K.: An examination of a music appreciation method incorporating tactile sensations from artificial vibrations. In: Fourth International Conference on Innovative Computing, Information and Control (ICICIC), pp. 417–420 (2009)

4. Mackiewicz, J., Moeller, R.: Why people perceive typefaces to have different personalities. Proc. IPCC **2004**, 304–313 (2004)
5. Caldwell, J.: Japanese typeface personalities: are typeface personalities consistent across culture? In: IEEE International Professional Communication 2013 Conference, pp. 1–8 (2013)
6. Doyle, J.R., Bottomley, P.A.: Mixed messages in brand names: separating the impact of letter shape from sound symbolism. Psychol. Market. **28**, 749–762 (2011)
7. Velasco, C., Woods, A.T., Hyndman, S., Spence, C.: The taste of typeface. i-Perception **6**(4), 1–10 (2015)
8. Karnal, N., Machiels, C.J.A., Orth, U.R., Mai, R.: Healthy by design, but only when in focus: communicating non-verbal health cues through symbolic meaning in packaging. Food Qual. Prefer. **52**, 106–119 (2016)
9. Suveeranont, R., Igarashi, T.: Example-based automatic font generation. In: Taylor, R., Boulanger, P., Krüger, A., Olivier, P. (eds.) SG 2010. LNCS, vol. 6133, pp. 127–138. Springer, Heidelberg (2010). https://doi.org/10.1007/978-3-642-13544-6_12
10. Campbell, N. D.F., Kautz, J.: Learning a manifold of fonts. In: ACM Transactions on Graphics (SIGGRAPH), vol. 33, no. 4 (2014)
11. Saito, J., Nakamura, S.: Fontender: interactive Japanese text design with dynamic font fusion method for comics. In: Kompatsiaris, I., Huet, B., Mezaris, V., Gurrin, C., Cheng, W.-H., Vrochidis, S. (eds.) MMM 2019. LNCS, vol. 11296, pp. 554–559. Springer, Cham (2019). https://doi.org/10.1007/978-3-030-05716-9_45
12. Hu, X., Downie, J., Laurier, C., Bay, M., Ehmann, A.: The 2007 MIREX audio mood classification task: lessons learned. In: Proceedings of 9th International Conference on Music Information Retrieval, pp. 462–467 (2008)
13. Yamamoto, T., Nakamura, S.: Leveraging viewer comments for mood classification of music video clips. In: Proceedings of the 36th Annual International ACM SIGIR Conference on Research and Development in Information Retrieval (SIGIR 2013), pp. 797–800 (2013)

# δ-logit : Dynamic Difficulty Adjustment Using Few Data Points

William Rao Fernandes[(✉)] and Guillaume Levieux[(✉)]

CNAM CEDRIC, Paris, France
{william.rao_fernandes,guillaume.levieux}@cnam.fr

**Abstract.** Difficulty is a fundamental factor of enjoyment and motivation in video games. Thus, many video games use Dynamic Difficulty Adjustment systems to provide players with an optimal level of challenge. However, many of these systems are either game specific, limited to a specific range of difficulties, or require much more data than one can track during a short play session. In this paper, we introduce the δ-logit algorithm. It can be used on many game types, allows a developer to set the game's difficulty to any level, with, in our experiment, a player failure error prediction rate lower than 20% in less than two minutes of playtime. In order to roughly estimate the difficulty as quickly as possible, δ-logit drives a single metavariable to adjust the game's difficulty. It starts with a simple +/−δ algorithm to gather a few data points and then uses logistic regression to estimate the players failure probability when the smallest required amount of data has been collected. The goal of this paper is to describe δ-logit and estimate its accuracy and convergence speed with a study on 37 participants playing a tank shooter game.

**Keywords:** Difficulty · Dynamic difficulty adjustment · Game balancing · Player modeling · Motivation · Video games

## 1 Introduction

Difficulty in video games is a fundamental factor of enjoyment and motivation [14,15,17,21,23]. Flow Theory suggests that one can reach a state of optimal enjoyment when a task level of challenge is set with regard to their own perceived skills [19]. To adjust the balance between challenge and skills, video games can either use static, predefined difficulty levels or rely on Dynamic Difficulty Adjustment (DDA) systems. However, few of these systems can target any level of difficulty, are generic enough and use a small amount of data. In this paper, we introduce and evaluate such a system, that we call δ-*logit*.

First, we want our system to be as **generic** as possible: we want to be able to use it with as many different games as possible and rely on a measure of difficulty that allows comparison between games. Following our previous work,

© IFIP International Federation for Information Processing 2019
Published by Springer Nature Switzerland AG 2019
E. van der Spek et al. (Eds.): ICEC-JCSG 2019, LNCS 11863, pp. 158–171, 2019.
https://doi.org/10.1007/978-3-030-34644-7_13

we model a game as a follow up of *challenges* that can either be won or lost and whose difficulty can be manipulated using a set of variables [3]. Indeed, the notion of success and failure is at the core of video games: in many of them, the players have clear goals and their performance is constantly evaluated. Each of the players' success or failure have an impact on the game's progression and are conveyed to them using audio, visual or haptic feedbacks. We thus propose to start from these events to define a set of challenges, and then track players' failures and successes to estimate their failure probability for these challenges. Such a challenge can be, for instance, jump on a platform, shoot at another player, or win a battle against enemy tanks. We consider that failure probability to these challenges is close to how challenging and difficult a video game is.

Second, we want to be able to choose **any level of difficulty**. As we will see, some simple algorithms only balance difficulty towards a 0.5 failure probability. We, however, want to be able to instantly select any level of difficulty, as many games do not target 0.5 balanced difficulty [1]. Indeed, some imbalance between skills and challenge can lead to desirable emotional states e.g. arousal, control or relaxation [19].

Third, we want to propose a model that uses **as few data points as possible**, gathered from one player only. We record one data point every time the player tries a challenge, and want to predict difficulty using less than 20 points. The two previous goals can be achieved using various techniques, but many of them require a lot of data, either tracked from many players or generated. In this paper, we want our system to handle a cold start and reach a sufficient accuracy within the shortest playtime. This way, our model can be used in offline games, where the only data available can be the data of a single local player starting the game with no tracked data. As an example, therapeutic games often require DDA while having a very complex development process and may not generate enough revenue to maintain live servers capable of storing players data [16]. Of course, we will thus have to define what *sufficient accuracy* means for our game. In this study, we only use the predictive part of our algorithm when the prediction error rate is higher than 40%, as we thus consider that our predictions are too close to randomness to be used. Our experiment shows that we can reach error rates lower than 20% in less than two minutes of playtime, and our actual player failure rates will be close to our targeted failure rates (Fig. 2). Our experiment shows what our δ-logit approach is able to achieve in the context of a shooter game, but it is to note that the required accuracy for a DDA system is still an open question, as perception of difficulty is a very complex matter [6,7].

## 2   Simple DDA Algorithms

One of the simplest DDA algorithms is to slightly raise the difficulty when the players won and slightly lower it when they failed. We call it the $+/-\delta$ algorithm. Constant et al. used this algorithm to study the link between DDA and confidence [6]. In the mainstream video game *Crash Bandicoot*, when the player dies a lot, the game gives them power-ups or checkpoints so their progression is eased, making the game more balanced [10].

Another approach is the rubber band AI, especially prevalent in racing games like Mario Kart [25]. The goal of the rubber band AI is to adjust the parameters of the computer-controlled opponents with regard to their distance to the player as if a rubber band was pulling them towards the player. Opponents ahead of the player will be slowed down, while those behind him will be sped up.

Such simple systems can be manually tuned to provide a balanced play experience using a very small amount of data. However, none of them can't directly adapt the difficulty towards a specific failure probability. Moreover, rubberband algorithm is only suited to games with opponents.

As we will see in Sect. 4, $\delta$-logit uses $+/-\delta$ as a fallback strategy when not enough data is available. But as soon as possible, we need to switch to a more advanced strategy to be able to target any level of difficulty.

## 3     Advanced DDA Algorithms

Other difficulty adaptation methods were developed using learning algorithms. Andrade et al. extended Q learning to dynamically adapt a policy when playing against a human [2]. However, this approach is only possible for games involving some sort of AI that can first play against itself to develop a policy. Spronck et al. propose a similar technique called dynamic scripting, which can be considered close to Q-learning except that actions are replaced by manually authored action scripts [22]. Thus, this DDA policy suffers from similar drawbacks as the previous one. The same goes for DDA systems that rely on Monte Carlo Tree Search (MCTS) to build an adapted opponent [8,11,13], or when real-time neuroevolution of opponents' AI is used [20]. These approaches can only be used when the game features some kind of opponent whose decision can be modeled using either a tree structure or a neural network, and where the game features some kind of synthetic player, allowing the AI to build its strategy while quickly exploring the game space by fighting this player.

Hocine et al. adapt a therapeutic game using a generic DDA system, that can be applied to any video game as long as a success probability can be estimated [12]. They base their evaluation of difficulty on player failure probability, but follow a strategy similar to the $+/-\delta$ algorithm, as they lower the difficulty when the player loses and raise it when they succeed and thus can only target a 0.5 balanced state. Zook et al. use tensor reduction to adapt the difficulty of a custom RPG game [26]. Their approach allows to predict spell effectiveness for a specific player at a specific time but does not provide a more generic measure of difficulty like failure probability. Allart and Constant used a mixed-effect logistic regression to evaluate both commercial and experimental games difficulty [1,6,7]. Logistic regression seems indeed well suited to predict a failure probability from few samples and binary outcomes. In these works, mixed-effect logistic regression was used because these studies had access to the data of many players with repeated trials of the same challenge. In our case, we want to use few data points from the current player only and thus we can only use a fixed effect logistic regression. Also, these studies did not use logistic regression to dynamically balance the game, but to evaluate the difficulty for post-experiment analysis purposes. Thus, they only compute the regression at the end, when all the experiment data is available. We thus still need to experiment whether using logistic regression from the start of the play session, in real time, is a viable option or not.

## 4   δ-logit : DDA Using Few Data Points

### 4.1   A Single Metavariable: θ

Our goal, as explained in the previous sections, is to develop a model that can instantly target a specific failure probability while using as few data points as possible, i.e. while having only observed a few attemps of the player to win the challenge. To do so, we propose to only rely on a single meta-parameter to balance the gameplay, that we name θ. Using this single parameter limits our ability to fine-tune the game's difficulty, but also drastically limits the search space of our δ-logit algorithm.

Following [3], we define a challenge as a goal players are trying to reach, and for which they may win or fail e.g. shoot a target, jump on a platform, finish a mission. We then find a subset of variables that we can modify to change this challenge's difficulty, from one player's try to another. Then, we define two challenge configurations, that is, two sets of values for these variables. Those two configuration have to be defined manually by a designer. The first configuration is the easiest challenge that the algorithm is allowed to create, while the second is the hardest. These extreme configurations prevent us from proposing challenges that we consider undesirable to any player, due to their extreme values. Then, θ is used to linearly interpolate each parameter between the very easy and very

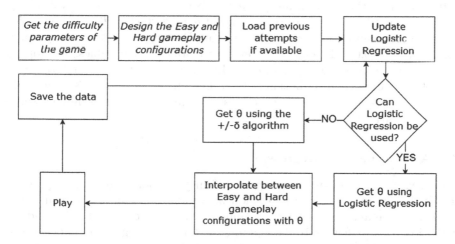

**Fig. 1.** Flowchart of the δ-logit algorithm Steps in italic are design steps that needs to be done manually

hard challenge configurations. $\delta$-logit thus only drives $\theta$ to adjust the game's difficulty for each specific player. $\theta$ varies between 0 and 1, if the parameter is not continuous, we interpolate it and then round it to the nearest integer.

## 4.2   Exploring with $+/-\delta$ Algorithm

When no data is available, as the player starts playing for the first time, $\delta$-logit uses a very simple algorithm to explore the game space while balancing the gameplay. We chose to use the $+/-\delta$ algorithm as it is not specific to a particular game genre and adapts the difficulty using only the player's last result. If the player wins, $+/-\delta$ raises the difficulty by $\delta_{win}$, if they fail it lowers it by $\delta_{fail}$. If $\delta_{win} = \delta_{fail}$, the difficulty eventually oscillates around a gameplay configuration where the player has a 0.5 failure probability.

During this exploration phase, we are just able to drive the difficulty toward a balanced state and can't target a specific failure probability. But if we do not simulate the game in advance using a synthetic player and do not possess any data about the player, this exploration phase is mandatory. We propose to start from the very easy challenge configuration and let the $+/-\delta$ raise the difficulty.

More specifically, we propose to use a $\delta_{win}$ and $\delta_{fail}$ value close to 0.05. Indeed, it is often considered that logistic regression can only be performed with a minimum of 10 to 20 data points per variable [5]. Thus, if we start from the very simple case where $\theta = 0$, we can reach $\theta = 0.5$, just in between the hardest and easiest configuration, if the player wins 10 times and the $+/-\delta$ adds $10 * 0.05 = 0.5$ to $\theta$. This would allow us to have data points spread between $\theta = 0$ and $\theta = 0.5$ as soon as we start to estimate the logistic regression, as it is the case in our experiment. However, this is just a rule of thumb we followed and one may choose to use different values of $\delta_{win}$ and $\delta_{fail}$ to provide players with a slower or steeper learning curve.

It is to note that if $\delta_{win}$ and $\delta_{fail}$ are fixed values, the $+/-\delta$ will always sample a limited set of data points. Indeed $\theta$ may start at 0, then be 0.05 if the player wins and then again 0 if they fail. But we will never sample values between 0 and 0.05. To ensure a better exploration of $\theta$ values, we apply a random uniform noise to $\delta_{win}$ and $\delta_{fail}$. In our experiment, $\delta_{win}$ and $\delta_{fail}$ were drawn from a uniform distribution $\mathcal{U}(0.05, 0.1)$, ensuring that $\delta$ was never under 0.05 but could still vary up to twice this value, allowing us to sample $\theta$ values at a wider, variable range.

## 4.3   Adding Logistic Regression

$\delta$-logit switches to logistic modeling of difficulty as soon as the $+/-\delta$ provided enough data points. Logistic regression allows us to estimate a probability of failure from binary results, in a continuous way, that can start to provide an estimation with as few as 10 data points [5]. Once the regression is performed, the model is able to estimate the value of $\theta$ that corresponds to the desired probability of failure.

To update the logistic regression, we iteratively fit a logistic function to the available data points using the Newton-Raphson method. We adapted the C# code provided by McCaffrey to use it in the Unity Game Engine to perform our experiment [18].

To estimate if we can switch from the $+/-\delta$ algorithm to the Logistic Regression, we perform several tests, summarized in Fig. 1. First, we do not compute the regression if we gathered less than 10 data points, following [5]. Then, as these first data points are mostly sampled on the lowest difficulty levels, we only start to perform the regression if we gathered at least 4 successes and 4 failures. If these basic conditions are met, we perform the logistic regression and check its accuracy using 10-fold cross-validation. Cross-validation is computed by using our logistic regression as a binary predictor[1] of success and failure and by comparing predictions to actual results. In our experiment, we only use the logistic regression if it's estimated accuracy is higher than 0.6. We empirically chose to use 4 successes/failures and a 10-fold cross-validation score higher than 0.6. These values performed well in our experiment but it might be worth running other experiments to investigate different values.

When it has switched to the logistic regression, $\delta$-logit is thus able to estimate the value of $\theta$ that corresponds to a specific failure probability. This value can be driven by any process: for instance, a designer might want to target difficulty values following a curve that oscillate around an 0.5 value, allowing the player to experience a globally balanced gameplay, while having periods of arousal when the difficulty is higher and a feeling of control when it is lower, as suggested by [19].

As for the $+/-\delta$, we want our algorithm to keep exploring different values of $\theta$. To do so, we propose to add noise to the failure probability requested by the game. Empirically, we add a value drawn from a uniform distribution $\mathcal{U}(-0.05, 0.05)$ to the requested failure probability when using the logistic regression to estimate $\theta$. That way, if a designer asks for a difficulty of 0.2, the model will estimate the value of $\theta$ for a difficulty randomly picked between 0.15 and 0.25. This allows us to have values of $\theta$ that always vary and we consider that the player's perception of difficulty is not accurate enough to perceive such a subtle difference [7]. However, difficulty perception is a complex matter and in further studies, we should investigate the impact of this parameter on both perception of difficulty and difficulty estimation accuracy.

## 5 Adapting a Shooting Game

We implemented $\delta$-logit in a tank shooting game (Fig. 2). We started from the Unity Tutorial *Tank Shooter Game* [24], modified the controls so that the player still manipulates the tank using the keyboard arrows but can shoot in any direction using the mouse. We also added AI to the enemy tanks. The flow of the game is very simple: the player and one or two enemy tanks are spawned. They can shoot at each other and move. A tank shell explodes when it hits the ground

---

[1] If $p(fail) > 0.5$, predict failure and predict success otherwise.

or a tank and applies damage to the tanks close to the explosion. If the player kills the enemies they win and if they die they fail. Every time, we record the value of $\theta$ and the game's result, i.e. whether enemy tanks were destroyed or not. At the beginning, we do not have enough samples so $\delta$-logit starts from the easy condition $\theta = 0$ and follows the $+/-\delta$ algorithm. Then, as soon as the logistic regression is ready (see Sect. 4.3), $\delta$-logit uses it to estimate the value of $\theta$ corresponding to the chosen difficulty and spawn the player and the enemy tanks again.

The enemy tanks have different characteristics that can be modified to change the game's difficulty, as shown in Table 1. It is to note that the number of enemies will double as $\theta$ crosses the 0.5 value. We compute the value of $\theta$ with our DDA system and use it to interpolate these parameters between easy and hard settings.

**Table 1.** Easy and hard settings

| Game parameters | Easy setting | Hard setting |
| --- | --- | --- |
| Nb of enemies | 1 | 2 |
| Moving speed | 1.2 | 9.6 |
| Turning speed | 18 | 900 |
| Time between shot | 3 s | 0.5 s |
| Accuracy | 0 | 15 |

Turning speed in degrees.$s^{-1}$. Moving Speed is in unit.$s^{-1}$, a tank's length is 2 units and the game space is 76 units per 47 units. Accuracy: we add a random 2D vector of size 0 to 15 units to the targeted position.

## 5.1 Methodology

Participants played 60 turns, thus spawned 60 times, corresponding on average to less than ten minutes of gameplay. Play sessions were short because we wanted players to stay concentrated, and because the experiment's main goal is to evaluate the accuracy of our model when few data points are available. We use $\delta$-logit described in Sect. 4, starting with no data and thus with the $+/-\delta$ algorithm.

When $\delta$-logit switches to the logistic regression, as described in Sect. 4.3, we target specific levels of difficulty. We chose to evaluate our model for failure probabilities of 0.2, 0.5 and 0.7. The 0.2 difficulty is far from the 0.5 balanced setting that can be reached with the simple $+/-\delta$ algorithm, while still being a bit challenging. It is also close to the average difficulty of some AAA games [1]. We target the 0.2 difficulty until turn 44. Then we test if, having sampled many data points while playing at a low difficulty level, we are able to create accurate difficulty peaks. So from turn 45, we start a cycle of three turns with different difficulties, beginning at 0.2, rising to 0.5, ending at 0.7. We repeat this cycle five times, up to turn 60. Each turn takes on average less than 8 s to complete if the player understands the goal of the game. We follow such a difficulty curve because it follows many game's difficulty pacing: slowly raise the difficulty when the player discovers the game rules, then propose a certain level of challenge, until you reach a difficulty peak, like the *bosses* of many games.

## 6   Results

37 participants played our shooter game (26 male, 11 female), with a mean age of 30 ($\sigma = 8.6$). All participants played 60 turns, for an average of 7 min of playtime ($\sigma = 82$ s). Figure 3 describes the evolution of the difficulty parameter $\theta$ for all the participants.

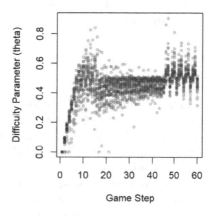

**Fig. 2.** The tank shooting game The player, at the bottom of the screen, is being shot at by an enemy tank.

**Fig. 3.** Evolution of difficulty parameter $\theta$
One can distinguish the $+/-\delta$ phase for 15 turns on average, followed by the 0.2 difficulty phase up to turn 44, and then the 5 difficulty peaks.

We first checked the level of the participants, by using the mean of our difficulty parameter $\theta$ across the whole game session. As difficulty is dynamically adapted to have all players experience the same failure probabilities, best players will have higher values of $\theta$. Players levels are ranging from 0.3 to 0.6 ($\mu = 0.46$, $\sigma = 0.05$).

$\delta$-logit performs logistic regression to estimate the failure probability from the values of $\theta$ and each turn outcome. Figure 5 illustrates this estimation : for most of the participants, the game starts to be challenging when failure probability starts raising, at $\theta = 0.4$ and is very hard when $\theta >= 0.6$ as failure probability is above 0.75.

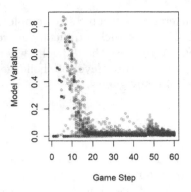

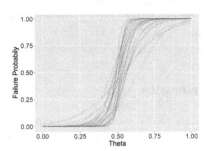

**Fig. 4.** Model's variation for each participant at each step
Logistic regression's variation between each turn. Variability drops when 20 ata

**Fig. 5.** Logistic regression for each participant at the 60th turn
Players always win on the easy setting, always fail on the hard one. Difficulty changes very quickly around $\theta = 0.5$, being still very low at $\theta = 0.4$ and already very high at $\theta = 0.6$.

We then looked at the model convergence[2] speed. We first calculated, for each participant, the number of $+/-\delta$ turns before the model switched to the logistic regression for the first time. The model took on average 15 turns to converge ($\sigma = 1.82$ turns), corresponding to 105 s of gameplay ($\sigma = 24.52$ s).

We also calculated the model variability for each turn. We used the model at turn $t$ to predict the failure probability for 21 values of $\theta$, from 0 to 1 by steps of 0.05. We then computed the root-mean-square error (RMSE) between predictions at step $t$ and those at steps $t - 1$, $t - 2$ and $t - 3$ as given by the Eq. (1). We computed the distance with the last steps to have larger values for models varying in the same direction than for those oscillating around a value.

$$RMSE = \sqrt{\sum_{i=1}^{3} \frac{\sum_{j=0}^{20}(p_t(\theta = j/20) - p_{t-i}(\theta = j/20))^2}{3 * 21}} \qquad (1)$$

The model variability can be examined over time, as shown in Fig. 4. On average, the logistic regression was used after 15 turns, and we can see that from turn 20, the prediction tends to be much more stable. One can also notice a peak of variation after turn 45, corresponding to the difficulty peaks we included in the game. Those peaks forced the model to explore higher values of $\theta$, and thus to readjust accordingly.

Another way to look at the model accuracy and convergence speed is to look at the cross-validation result over time. When logistic regression is used, the obtained accuracy has a mean of 0.82 ($\sigma = 0.06$). Interestingly, it is to note that

---

[2] We consider that our model has *converged* when it is able to use logistic regression to adapt the difficulty.

for 4 out of 31 players, we switched back to $+/$ $\delta$ algorithm even long after the 15 first steps. These players stayed in $+/-\delta$ for an average of 2.75 steps ($\sigma = 2.22$), meaning that the model can occasionally lose accuracy.

We targeted three levels of difficulty ($p(fail) = 0.2$, 0.5 and 0.7) and the model was able to achieve the failure probabilities presented in Table 2. Actual failure probabilities are estimated for all participants by taking the mean of their actual success (1) and failures (0) when the model was either targeting $p(fail) = 0.2$, 0.5 or 0.7. It is to note that the model never exactly targeted these values, as a uniform noise $\mathcal{U}(-0.05, 0.05)$ was applied to them, see Sect. 4.3. Target failure probabilities are centered on 0.2, 0.5 and 0.7, but have a standard deviation of 0.03.

**Table 2.** Actual failure frequencies for each target failure probabilities

| Target difficulty | Objective difficulty |
| --- | --- |
| 0.2 | 0.14 [0.12, 0.16] |
| 0.5 | 0.55 [0.47, 0.62] |
| 0.7 | 0.74 [0.67, 0.80] |

For each target difficulty, we provide the observed failure frequencies. Values between brackets are the 95% CI values given by an Exact Binomial test.

# 7   Discussion

Our algorithm was able to successfully adapt the difficulty of the game to match the difficulty curve wanted by a designer, see Table 2. One can note, however, that for $p(fail) = 0.2$ we are slightly lower (0.14), whereas for $p(fail) = 0.5$ and 0.7 we are slightly above (0.53 and 0.76). This might be explained by the nature of gameplay's progression.

As explained before, we change the difficulty variables all together following $\theta$: tanks become more accurate, faster and come in larger numbers at the same time. On the one hand, this allows us to have a continuous and monotonic difficulty: if we had chosen to first change speed and then accuracy, both these variables may not have the same impact on objective difficulty and create a change in progression when switching from one variable to the other. On the other hand, this approach might have the drawback of compressing objective difficulty in a short range of $\theta$. Indeed, the objective difficulty might grow exponentially with $\theta$ as all the parameters raise at the same time. This can clearly be seen in our difficulty curve mapping $\theta$ to objective difficulty (Fig. 5): the game is very easy when $\theta <= 0.4$ and very hard when $\theta >= 0.6$.

Moreover, we chose to have a gameplay progression variable that has only two values: the number of enemy tanks. We think that this might explain why objective difficulty is lower than the targeted difficulty in the easy setting and higher in the hard setting: when $\theta > 0.5$, meaning there are two tanks to beat, the difficulty rises much faster than when $\theta < 0.5$. A tank at $\theta = 0.49$ is almost as strong as a tank at $\theta = 0.5$, but the number of tanks creates a difficulty peak at $\theta = 0.5$ and changes the slope of the impact of $\theta$ on objective difficulty when $\theta$ crosses 0.5.

Our model takes on average 15 turns (an average 105 s of gameplay) to converge, which is quick enough for our game, allowing players to discover the gameplay during few minutes starting from the easy condition. It is to note that each turn is relatively quick, taking less than 10 s. As we estimate a probability, we need to be able to gather player failures/successes. To have the model converge as quickly as possible, it is thus important to be able to split the gameplay into multiple short challenges, as explained in [3].

During the first steps of $\delta$-logit, we rely on the $+/-\delta$ algorithm. Of course, it is impossible for us to predict the difficulty of the game without having explored the player's abilities a little bit. We tuned the $+/-\delta$ so that it starts with a low difficulty level and slowly raises the difficulty (or lower it when the player fails). This is consistent with self-efficacy theories stating that failure, when a subject discovers a new task, can dampen their motivation [4]. However, $+/-\delta$ might be configured to start from any difficulty level, for instance from a difficulty level chosen by the player. As we designed a very easy and very hard difficulty setting, we could interpolate between them to provide the player with a starting easy, medium and hard difficulty setting. However, when starting from an easy setting, we quickly explore the easy difficulty levels, gaining quickly more information about the player's abilities with low $\theta$ values than if we started from a medium level and adapted toward p(fail) = 0.5.

As long as a game can be expressed as challenges that the player repeatedly tries to achieve and that these challenges are driven by a set of variables that have a monotonic impact on this failure probability, our model could be used to drive these challenges' difficulty. Of course, such challenges can be harder to identify in more complex games. In an open world AAA game like *The Legend of Zelda: Breath of the Wild*, when the player finds a new object, does it only change the difficulty of the current challenge (e.g. for a slightly more powerful weapon), or does it change the gameplay so much that a new challenge is to be defined (e.g. when using a bow instead of a sword) [9]? And if the player rides a horse while using their bow, is it a new challenge or an extension of the bow one? However, as our model uses very few samples, we think that $\delta$-logit could be used to drive these challenges difficulty, when properly identified. We may indeed postulate that few games propose original challenges that the player can't try more than 15 times.

# 8   Conclusion

In this paper, we propose a DDA algorithm that starts with no data and then uses as few data points as possible gathered from a single player. Many models have been proposed to dynamically adjust the difficulty of a game, but none of them really addresses the problem of using very few data from one player while targeting any failure probability.

Our model starts with a $+/-\delta$ algorithm that drives difficulty towards a 0.5 failure probability and then uses logistic regression as soon as possible to follow a specific difficulty curve, described in terms of failure probabilities, with correct accuracy. In our example, a tank shooting game, the model takes on average 105 s to switch from $+/-\delta$ to logistic regression and targets difficulties of 0.2, 0.5 and 0.7, with actual difficulties of 0.14, 0.55 and 0.74. The model's failure prediction accuracy was 0.82 ($\sigma = 0.06$). We evaluate our model in a realistic and challenging setting: shooting is a widely used game mechanic, we adapt enemy's AI number and behavior, and follow a difficulty curve providing a learning phase, a low difficulty plateau and difficulty peaks at levels that were almost never sampled before.

Of course, we discuss that our approach has drawbacks. Having only one metavariable must have an impact on accuracy. Also, our model is continuous and discontinuities in gameplay variables might not be correctly modeled.

We think that our model might be very useful for the design of many games. Even more, we think that by considering any game as a collection of various challenges [3], one may use multiple instances of our model to adapt more complex gameplays.

**Acknowledgement.** This research is part of the *Programme d'investissement d'avenir E-FRAN* project *DysApp*, conducted with *Caisse des Dépôts* and supported by the French Government.

# References

1. Allart, T., Levieux, G., Pierfitte, M., Guilloux, A., Natkin, S.: Difficulty influence on motivation over time in video games using survival analysis. In: Proceedings of the 12th International Conference on the Foundations of Digital Games, p. 2 (2017)
2. Andrade, G., Ramalho, G., Santana, H., Corruble, V.: Extending reinforcement learning to provide dynamic game balancing. In: Proceedings of the Workshop on Reasoning, Representation, and Learning in Computer Games, 19th International Joint Conference on Artificial Intelligence (IJCAI), pp. 7–12 (2005)
3. Aponte, M.V., Levieux, G., Natkin, S.: Measuring the level of difficulty in single player video games. Entertainment Comput. **2**(4), 205–213 (2011)
4. Bandura, A.: Self-efficacy: toward a unifying theory of behavioral change. Psychol. Rev. **84**(2), 191 (1977)
5. Concato, J., Peduzzi, P., Holford, T.R., Feinstein, A.R.: Importance of events per independent variable in proportional hazards analysis. i background, goals, and general strategy. J. Clin. Epidemiol. **48**(12), 1495–1501 (1995)

6. Constant, T., Levieux, G.: Dynamic difficulty adjustment impact on players' confidence. In: Proceedings of the 2019 CHI Conference on Human Factors in Computing Systems, CHI 2019, pp. 463:1–463:12 (2019)
7. Constant, T., Levieux, G., Buendia, A., Natkin, S.: From objective to subjective difficulty evaluation in video games. In: Bernhaupt, R., Dalvi, G., Joshi, A., Balkrishan, D.K., O'Neill, J., Winckler, M. (eds.) INTERACT 2017. LNCS, vol. 10514, pp. 107–127. Springer, Cham (2017). https://doi.org/10.1007/978-3-319-67684-5_8
8. Demediuk, S., Tamassia, M., Raffe, W.L., Zambetta, F., Li, X., Mueller, F.: Monte carlo tree search based algorithms for dynamic difficulty adjustment. In: 2017 IEEE Conference on Computational Intelligence and Games (CIG), pp. 53–59, August 2017
9. Fujibayashi, H., Aonuma, E., Toda, A., Takizawa, S.: The legend of zelda: breath of the wild. Game [Nintendo Switch], 3 March 2017 (2017)
10. Gavin, A.: Making crash bandicoot part 6 (2011). https://all-things-andy-gavin.com/2011/02/07/making-crash-bandicoot-part-6. Accessed 09 June 2018
11. Hao, Y., He, S., Wang, J., Liu, X., Huang, W., et al.: Dynamic difficulty adjustment of game AI by MCTS for the game PAC-Man. In: 2010 Sixth International Conference on Natural Computation (ICNC), vol. 8, pp. 3918–3922. IEEE (2010)
12. Hocine, N., Gouaïch, A.: Therapeutic games' difficulty adaptation: an approach based on player's ability and motivation. In: 2011 16th International Conference on Computer Games (CGAMES), pp. 257–261. IEEE (2011)
13. Ishihara, M., Ito, S., Ishii, R., Harada, T., Thawonmas, R.: Monte-Carlo tree search for implementation of dynamic difficulty adjustment fighting game AIS having believable behaviors. In: 2018 IEEE Conference on Computational Intelligence and Games (CIG), pp. 1–8. IEEE (2018)
14. Klimmt, C., Blake, C., Hefner, D., Vorderer, P., Roth, C.: Player performance, satisfaction, and video game enjoyment. In: Natkin, S., Dupire, J. (eds.) ICEC 2009. LNCS, vol. 5709, pp. 1–12. Springer, Heidelberg (2009). https://doi.org/10.1007/978-3-642-04052-8_1
15. Lazzaro, N.: Why we play games: four keys to more emotion without story (2004)
16. Mader, S., Levieux, G., Natkin, S.: A game design method for therapeutic games. In: 2016 8th International Conference on Games and Virtual Worlds for Serious Applications (VS-Games), pp. 1–8. IEEE (2016)
17. Malone, T.W.: Heuristics for designing enjoyable user interfaces: lessons from computer games. In: Proceedings of the 1982 Conference on Human Factors in Computing Systems, pp. 63–68. ACM (1982)
18. McCaffrey, J.: Test run - coding logistic regression with Newton-Raphson (2012). https://msdn.microsoft.com/en-us/magazine/jj618304.aspx. Accessed 19 Sept 2018
19. Nakamura, J., Csikszentmihalyi, M.: The concept of flow. Flow and the Foundations of Positive Psychology, pp. 239–263. Springer, Dordrecht (2014). https://doi.org/10.1007/978-94-017-9088-8_16
20. Olesen, J.K., Yannakakis, G.N., Hallam, J.: Real-time challenge balance in an rts game using rtNEAT. In: 2008 IEEE Symposium on Computational Intelligence and Games, CIG 2008, pp. 87–94. IEEE (2008)
21. Ryan, R.M., Rigby, C.S., Przybylski, A.: The motivational pull of video games: a self-determination theory approach. Motiv. Emotion 30(4), 344–360 (2006)
22. Spronck, P., Sprinkhuizen-Kuyper, I., Postma, E.: Difficulty scaling of game AI. In: Proceedings of the 5th International Conference on Intelligent Games and Simulation (GAME-ON 2004), pp. 33–37 (2004)

23. Sweetser, P., Wyeth, P.: Gameflow: a model for evaluating player enjoyment in games. Comput. Entertainment (CIE) **3**(3), 3 (2005)
24. Unity: Tanks tutorial (2015). https://unity3d.com/fr/learn/tutorials/s/tanks-tutorial. Accessed 19 Sept 2018
25. Yasuyuki, O., Katsuhisa, S.: Racing game program and video game device (2003). https://patents.google.com/patent/US7278913. Accessed 18 Sept 2018
26. Zook, A., Riedl, M.O.: A temporal data-driven player model for dynamic difficulty adjustment. In: AIIDE (2012)

# Game Design and Development

# A Feature-Based Approach to Develop Digital Board Games

Filipe M. B. Boaventura and Victor T. Sarinho(✉)

Laboratório de Entretenimento Digital Aplicado (LEnDA),
State University of Feira de Santana,
Av. Transnordestina, s/n, Novo Horizonte, Feira de Santana, Bahia, Brazil
fmbboaventura@gmail.com, vsarinho@uefs.br

**Abstract.** Several types of development strategies are available to provide digital games in a reusable way. However, the idea of a "one-size-fits-all" architecture for digital games can be problematic, being preferable to build dedicated architectures for specific game genres. This paper proposes the development of *feature-based* artifacts for the production of digital board games. It presents a subdomain game architecture that represents configurable features of core concepts related to board games (the game *model* and *controller*), and implements feature artifacts capable of being executed in distinct game clients (the game *view*). For validation purposes, two types of classic board games, together with a proposed web client for board games, were developed, consolidating as a result a software product line approach to develop classic board games.

**Keywords:** Feature modeling · Software product line · Board games

## 1 Introduction

Game development is a complex task that requires technical mastery and integration skills from several areas of computer science [26]. In fact, many of the major traditional challenges on software engineering arise during the development of digital games as complex software systems, such as large-scale software engineering, game requirements engineering, game software design, and so on [26]. However, develop digital games is not the same as develop traditional software systems [12], which causes some specific problems during their production.

Regarding digital game development strategies, the reuse of specific components for game development, which can be provided or not by *SDKs*, *frameworks* and *game engines* [14], can reduce the development time and cost [9] to provide desired games. However, reused game components may restrict or predetermine the types of digital games that can be developed [26], changing as a consequence the initial game design idea for adapting purposes, and providing as a result an "unwanted" game project for the game designer.

© IFIP International Federation for Information Processing 2019
Published by Springer Nature Switzerland AG 2019
E. van der Spek et al. (Eds.): ICEC-JCSG 2019, LNCS 11863, pp. 175–186, 2019.
https://doi.org/10.1007/978-3-030-34644-7_14

In this sense, one possible solution would be to separate the core of the game logic (the *G-factor*) from the implementation resources, allowing a game portability between development environments to be reused in distinct game productions [3]. However, the idea of a *"one-size-fits-all"* architecture for digital games can be problematic for many reasons, being preferable to build dedicated architectures for specific game genres [12].

This paper proposes the development of *feature-based* artifacts for the production of digital board games. The objective is to represent configurable features of core concepts related to board games (the game *model* and *controller*), and implement feature artifacts able to execute configured features in distinct game clients (the game *view*). As a result, a simple and scalable digital board game development approach is provided, which can be classified as a Software Product Line [20] able to generates new games through configured board game features.

## 2    Related Work

### 2.1    Feature Modeling and Development

*Features* are aspects or characteristics of a domain that are visible to the user [16], which are used to identify similarities or differences between products in a product line [1], and can be defined as a unit of functionality of a software system that meets a requirement [2].

Kang et al. [16] introduced the concept of *feature*, originally presented as part of *Feature-Oriented Domain Analysis* (FODA). According to them [16], *Feature Modeling* is used to identify system properties during domain analysis, and the *feature model* represents standard features of a family of systems and the relationships between them [16].

*Feature-Oriented Software Development* (FOSD) [2] is a paradigm for the construction, customization and synthesis of large-scale software systems in terms of *features*. According to Apel and Kästner [2], the FOSD is not a single development method or technique but a combination of different ideas, methods, tools, languages, formalisms and theories, connected by the concept of *feature*.

### 2.2    FOSD and Digital Game Development

Regarding the use of feature based approaches in the development of digital games, Zhang and Jarzabek [27] proposed the *RPG Product Line Architecture* (RPG-PLA), a set of common and variable features where any of the four original RPGs, as well as other similar games, could be derived from the RPG-PLA.

Furtado et al. presented the *ArcadEx Software Product Line*, a SPL created for 2D *arcade* games [11]. It is an improvement over the *SharpLudus* project [13], and it uses feature models to describe the commonality and variability of the 2D game domain.

Zualkernan proposed a Feature Modelling Framework for *Ubiquitous Embodied Learning Games* (UELG) [28], which represents educational games where the players interact with an augmented physical environment. It is an approach designed with the intent of reducing the cost and shorten the development life-cycle of such ubiquitous systems, while including features regarding pedagogy and learning concepts [28].

Finally, Sarinho et al. have been obtained some interesting results in the development of digital games by FODA and FOSD paradigms, such as reusable features focused on digital game concepts and implementation aspects (NESI [22] and GDS [25] models), SPL structures to provide digital games by feature configurations (FEnDiGa [23] and MEnDiGa [6]), and feature development for specific game genres and categories (AsKME [24]).

## 2.3   Board Games

*Board games* are a specific group of games where figures are manipulated in a competitive game mode played over a surface according to predefined rules [7]. The expression *board game* is used to refer to games played on a table [8], even those without a board such as classic card games. Board games usually have a delimited surface divided into sectors where a set of pieces, associated with players by shape or color, are moved according to the events of the game [18].

Objectives, rules, strategies and win conditions can be quite diverse on board games, such as conquering the most areas of the board, eliminating pieces of the opponents, achieving the highest score, or gathering the most of some form of currency [18]. Regarding the various mechanics present in board games, the *Board Game Geek* (BGG) is one of the largest and most used forums dedicated to board games on the internet [17]. This site is dedicated to cataloging information about physical board games in order to maintain a database for posterity and historical research [4]. Containing a listing of 99953 board games, 83 categories and 51 game mechanics [4], the BGG database became a source of information widely used by game designers and researchers alike [17].

## 2.4   Board Game Models

Based on available information of the BGG database, Kritz, Mangeli, and Xexéo [17] proposed a board game mechanics ontology, following the concept of mechan-ics presented in the *MDA (Mechanics, Dynamics e Aesthetics) Framework* [15]. MDA is a formal approach to analyzing games, built with the goal of under-standing the concepts that help designers, researchers and scholars to perform the decomposition of games into coherent and understandable parts [15].

Thus, the proposed ontology organizes several board game mechanics [4] into two main concepts: *Algorithm mechanics* and *Data Representation mechanics*. *Algorithm* is the general mechanic for the processes that take place in the game and is subdivided into: *Action*—a set of mechanics that allow the user to interact with the game; *Ruleset*—mechanics that define, among other aspects, the behav-ior of the components of the game; and *Goal* - mechanics that define the various goals to be achieved during the game, such as win conditions or transitory goals.

*Data Representation* is the general mechanic for storing and conveying information in games and is divided into: *Component*—representing the elements of the game that the players can own and manipulate directly; and *Resource*— representing the elements of the game that the player must manage to fulfill goals.

Finally, the *Quiz Board Game Model* proposed a formal model to represent *quizzes* as board games with multimedia appeal [7]. It describes board games as a set containing: objects, positions, functions, actions, rules and effects. The game is presented on a background image, where objects of various types are arranged in positions according to a matrix that describes their initial layout. Quiz questions are distributed according to board game positions, and are presented to the player through multimedia assets as objects reach these positions.

## 3   Methodology

As three main stages of this work: (1) a *feature model* was proposed to represent *features* for the board game domain; (2) a development approach was defined to describe, configure and interpret the proposed board game features; and (3) a board game client was implemented in order to execute configured features.

### 3.1   Features for Board Games

*Feature Models* [16] are used to describe the relationships and dependencies of a set of features belonging to a specific domain [2]. For this work, a feature model was proposed to describe generic software components for the production of digital board games. These features were designed to represent families of board games according to board game concepts found in literature [4,7,17].

The proposed model presents 88 features responsible for describing a *Board Game*, such as the game *Id*, the game logic as a whole (*Game Flow*) and the information that is handled during a gameplay (*Game Data*). *Game Flow* is represented in terms of *Actions*, *Rules* and *Game Events*, while *Game Data* describes the *Component Options*, the *Board Options* and the *Player Options* of the game. A complete diagram of all features proposed by this paper can be found at https://github.com/lenda-uefs/BoardGameEngine.

Regarding the *Game Data* subfeatures, *Component Options* represents the configuration of the objects that can be manipulated by the players during matches [17], such as *Dice* or *Tokens* of different types (*Token Type*) (Fig. 1). A *Token Type* is identified by a *Type Id*, which is referenced by a *Token*, and it configures the visual representation of the *Token* by mapping a *Player Id* to a *Image File*. *Tokens* are positioned on the board according to their *Position Id*. *Dice* appear in two distinct types: the *N-sided Die* represents a common dice, containing a sequence of numbers from 1 to N; and the *Special Die* can be used by the *Game Designer* to represent custom dice, containing a list of custom values (*Value Set*). *Components* can belong to a specific player, identified by feature *Owner Id*.

Still on *Game Data* (Fig. 2), the *Board Options* feature represents the game board, which consists of a *Background Image* and a set of *Positions* which can take on various types of (*Position Type*). *Positions* are identified by a *Position Id*. They have limited bounds defined by the *Area* feature and are located by the *Location* feature, which represent the Cartesian coordinates of the *Position* on the *Background Image*. *Positions* can hold a certain number of *Tokens* according to its *Capacity* feature. The remaining *Position* features are determined by the *Board Type*. On *Grid* boards, *Positions* are organized in a two-dimensional array, with the feature *Grid Index* holding its two-dimensional index. On *Point to Point* boards, *Positions* may point to adjacent positions (*Previous Position* and *Next Position*), forming the path to be traversed by the *Tokens*. Both *Previous Position* and *Next Position* can refer to more than one *Position*, allowing multiple paths to be formed on the board.

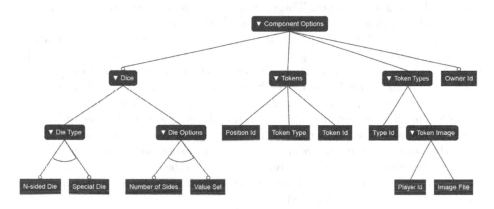

**Fig. 1.** Component Options subfeatures.

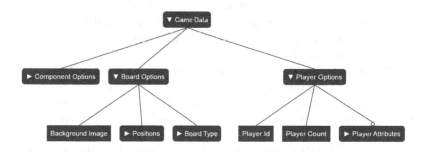

**Fig. 2.** Partial feature diagram for the *Game Data* feature.

Finally, *Player Options* represent the game settings regarding the number of players (*Player Count*), their identifiers (*Player Id*) and their attributes (*Player Attribute*). *Player Attribute* represents a list containing the various types of

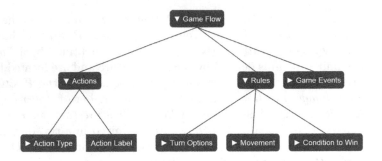

**Fig. 3.** Partial feature diagram for the *Game Flow* feature.

resources that players can accumulate during the game, such as score points and values to be used as currency. These resources are represented by *Name*, *Value*, a textual description (*Description*) and an illustrative image (*Image*).

Regarding the *Game Flow* subfeatures (Fig. 3), the *Action* feature represents the set of actions that can be performed during the game. Each *Action Type* is presented to the player by an *Action Label*, which contains a textual description of the *Action* to be performed. By these actions, the player is able to change the state of the game, manipulating *Components* and/or *Player Attributes*. For example, through the feature *Roll Dice*, the player is able to interact with the *Component Dice* to generate random numbers. *Select Token* and *Select Position* allow the player to mark a *Token* or a *Position* respectively. *End Turn* allows the player to end his movement, giving the turn to the next player. Finally, the feature *Move Token* is used to move *Tokens* between *Positions*, according to the rules that will be discussed ahead.

Performing actions and evaluating rules can trigger several *Game Events*. Currently, these events include: *Dice Event*—triggered when a value is retrieved from a dice roll; *Passing Event* and *Stopping Event*—which are triggered when a *Token*, respectively, passes through or stops on a *Position*; *End Turn* and *End Game*—respectively triggered when a turn or game is completed; *Token Eliminated*—triggered when the player loses a *Token*; and *Token Select*—triggered when the player selects a *Token*.

*Rule* features are responsible for evaluating the execution possibility of *Action* features according to the current state of the game. It also defines the configuration of other aspects of the game, such as *Token Movement*, the player succession policies throughout the turns (*Turn Options*), and the *Conditions to Win* the game.

Regarding turn related rules, *Turn Options* describes the game settings according to the maximum number of turns (*Max Turn Count*), the *Player Order* and the *Action Queue* to be performed during a turn. The succession of players can happen in a *Static Order*, which means *player 3* will always play after *player 2*, *player 2* after *player 1* and so on, or it may vary according to some event (*Dynamic Order*). For example, a game may give the turn to a player who has just finished his turn if he or she has fulfilled any special conditions.

For the *Movement* rules, they are directly affected by the *Board Type* and the organization of the *Positions* on the board. In *Point to Point* boards, where the *Positions* are organized as a trail of interconnected points, the *Tokens* can only move to the *Next Position* adjacent to their current position. This type of movement is known as *Point to Point Movement* [4,17]. If the current position of the *Token* refers to more than one adjacent position, it is necessary to decide which position the *Token* should be moved to. This decision is configured by the feature *Path Selection Rule*, which can be: *Manual*, delegating to the player the task of selecting the desired position; or *Automatic*, where a provided function decides the *Token* location that must be sent.

Regarding the *Position Selection Rule*, it represents an *evaluator* to be provided by the *game designer* to validate a *Position* selected by the player. This method is used in games that use the *Grid Board Type*, since the *Positions* will not hold information on which adjacent *Positions* the *Tokens* can move to.

Finally, *Condition to Win* represents a collection of the winning conditions of the game, as well as their evaluation settings. From the currently available conditions, *Reached Position* refers to the act of moving a *Token* to a position with a specific *Position Type*. *Player Attribute Value* and *Number of Remaining Tokens* are conditions related to numerical values and they refer respectively to: a *Player Attribute*, identified by an *Attribute Name*; or the remaining amount of *Tokens* of a certain *Token Type*. These conditions can be evaluated for the *Highest* value, *Lowest* value or compared with a *Exact* value, as described by the feature *Evaluation Option*. Finally, the feature *Evaluation Event* defines the moment when the evaluation of the conditions is performed. The conditions can be evaluated for every update of the game state (*On Game Update*) or only once per turn (*On Turn End*). In both cases, the game ends if the winner is found. If the game ends without a winner, such as the maximum number of turns was reached, the end game victory conditions (*On Game End*) are evaluated to decide the winner.

### 3.2 Developing Feature Based Board Games

Once the proposed feature model is defined, it is necessary to define a development approach for the implementation of configured board games. Several FOSD [2] approaches have been used successfully for the development of digital games, such as generative programming [25] and SPL instance [12]. For this work, the game development approach consist of the definition of a *Domain-Specific Language* (*DSL*) for the description and configuration of the proposed board game features, as well as a generic *game loop* able to interpret and run the board game configurations.

In this sense, by the proposed feature model, a DSL was defined using *JavaScript Object Notation* (*JSON*), where each feature was used to represent the numeric, textual, and procedural values involved in the configuration of a digital board game. Figure 4 illustrates an example of a partial configuration of the *Game Flow* feature and its subfeatures *Actions*, *Rules* and *Game Events*.

```
gameFlow: {
  actions: [
    {actionType: "rollDice", actionLabel: "Roll Dice"},
    {actionType: "selectToken", actionLabel: "Select Token to move"},
    {actionType: "moveToken", actionLabel: ""}
  ],
  rules: {
    movement: {
      pathSelectionRule: function (GameStatus) {...} // "manual" or a function
    },
    turnOptions: {
      maxTurnCount: null,
      playerOrder: function (GameStatus){...}, // "staticOrder" or a function
      actionQueue:["rollDice", "selectToken", "moveToken"]
    },
    conditionToWin: {
      numRemainingTokens: {tokenType:null, evalOption:"exact", value:0, evalEvent:"update"}
    }
  },
  gameEvents: {
    tokenSelected: function(GameStatus, selectedToken) {
      if (
        selectedToken.position.positionType.includes("Base") &&
        GameStatus.currentPlayer.diceValue != 6 &&
        GameStatus.currentPlayer.diceValue != 1 &&
        GameStatus.currentPlayer.attributes["Active Tokens"] > 0
      ) {
        GameStatus.repeatAction(
          "You got a " + GameStatus.currentPlayer.diceValue}.
          + " You need a 1 or a 6 to move a token into the game."
          + " Please select another token.");
      }
    }, ...
  }
}
```

**Fig. 4.** JSON representation of a partial configuration of a board game.

In order to provide a *game loop* capable of running the proposed features, an interpreter has been developed using Javascript for the purpose of reading and executing game actions and events, and to control the game flow defined in a given JSON configuration file. The interpreter follows the AsKME strategy for initializing and updating configured games, using the *startGameStatus* and *updateGameStatus* functions [24]. The *updateGameStatus* function performs the actions of the game, following the order queued in *Action Queue* (Fig. 4) and triggering the appropriate *Game Events* when necessary. Each performed action is removed from the queue, and, when there are no more actions to take, the turn ends, the action queue is restored and the game identifies the next player.

### 3.3   The Board Game Client

As a presentation layer of configured board game features, a web client (Fig. 5) was initially implemented using *Phaser*, an open source framework for browser games based on *HTML5 Canvas* and *WebGL*. The user interface is divided into three main areas. The left *sidebar* displays the values of the current *Player Attributes*, as well as its illustrative icon and textual description (displayed on a *mouse over* event). The central area displays, among other information, the game board, drawn by *Phaser* on a *Canvas* with a resolution of 800 × 600 pixels. Finally, the right *sidebar* displays the available *Actions* and feedback messages for the player. User inputs are obtained through click events on *hyperlinks* on the right *sidebar*, on the *Tokens*, or on the *Positions* of the board. These events execute the *updateGameStatus* function of the *interpreter* which in turn executes the appropriate *Action* according to the current state of the game. After running the *updateGameStatus*, the *interpreter* notifies the client to update the current *View* with the new values from the current game state.

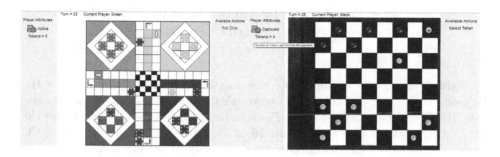

**Fig. 5.** Two screenshots of the *Phaser* client running *Ludo* and *Checkers*.

## 4   Results and Discussion

For the validation of the proposed board game features, two digital versions of classic board games were implemented (Fig. 5). For the *Grid* board, a digital version of the popular game *Checkers* was developed. This version is played by two players on an $8 \times 8$ grid, each starting with 12 *Tokens*. Regular *Tokens* (called *men*) can only move and capture enemy *Tokens* forward. Special *Tokens* (called *Kings*) can both capture and move backwards. Captures are mandatory and can be done in sequence, if possible. The winner is the player who captures all enemy *Tokens*.

For the *Point to Point* board, a digital version of the *Ludo* [5] was implemented. In this game, the players must guide their *Tokens* from their bases to the finish line on the center of the board. The movement is controlled by a simple *six-sided die* that determines how many positions a selected *Token* should move. However, *Tokens* can only move from their starting positions if the *Roll Dice Action* returns a one or six value. Also, if a player roll a six, it gets another dice roll. And if the player roll a six for the third time in a row, the turn ends. If a token stops at a position that contains an opposing token, the latter is "captured" and sent back to its base. If the token occupying the position is not from the opponent, the movement is undone and the turn ends.

Considering the reuse level achieved by FOSD usage in the developed games, some code metrics [10] were collected using the *Plato* code analyzer [21] for the *amount of reused code* and the *cyclomatic complexity*. The *Amount of Reuse* metric is used to evaluate and monitor the reuse improvement effort by tracking percentages of reuse of lifecycle objects over time [10], which can be defined as the number of reused *SLOC* (*Source Lines of Code*) of a given module divided by the total *SLOC* of the system. The *Cyclomatic Complexity* (*CC*) is used to measure the complexity of the code based on the number of execution flows in the source code [19].

**Table 1.** Obtained SLOC and CC metrics for Ludo and Checkers games.

| Game Name | Reused SLOC/Total SLOC | Amount of CC/Total CC |
|---|---|---|
| *Ludo* | $948/(315+948) = 75{,}06\%$ | $120/(23+120) = 83{,}91\%$ |
| *Checkers* | $948/(274+948) = 77{,}58\%$ | $120/(38+120) = 75{,}94\%$ |

Table 1 shows the obtained metrics for the developed games, where the Reused *SLOC* and the total *CC* were calculated by the sum of the respective SLOC and *CC* values for the *Phaser* client, the JSON interpreter and the JSON configuration file. As a result, 76,32% of SLOC reuse and 79,93% of CC reuse, on average, were obtained from the developed artifacts, confirming the game core reusability and mantainability for the developed board games.

## 5    Conclusions and Future Work

This paper presented a feature-based approach for the development of digital board games. It is based on a previous development effort to provide a cross-platform product line architecture for the quiz game domain [24], but in this case providing board game features and artifacts able to manage the game logic represented as a game core of simple board games.

To achieve this objective, a feature model has been defined to represent relevant concepts of the board game domain, along with software artifacts capable of configuring and executing the board game dynamics in a web client. In fact, once the components of a desired board game are identified and configured through the proposed feature model, these can be executed by the implemented artifacts in a client application developed for a specific platform, providing as a result new board games for each new configured JSON file.

Regarding the Javascript interpreter for board game features, it provides an interface to retrieve and modify the state of the board game described by the JSON file. The client application, then, is responsible for querying the interpreter about the information needed and to use the obtained information to present the game using its own components. As a result, the Javascript interpreter works as a game controller facade based on features that communicates with developed cross-platform client applications, such as web, mobile platforms, game engines (Unity3D, Godot) and Arduino (Johnny-Five framework), in order to provide configured board games [24].

Digital versions of the games *Ludo* and *Checkers* were also presented in this work. It is an important verification/validation step of this project as an attempt to show the feasibility of the reusable artifacts to produce digital versions of classic board games. Furthermore, the obtained metrics for the developed software artifacts (SLOC reuse and cyclomatic complexity) presented satisfactory results, with over 76% SLOC reuse and 79% complexity reuse. However, the amount of Javascript functions that need to be programmed in order to configure board game dynamics using the proposed model can compromise the maintainability and scalability of the developed games. Thus, it is necessary to further identify common behaviors between board games in order to build a more detailed board game feature hierarchy. It is also need to develop more games using the proposed artifacts to perform an improved benchmarking of metrics, as well as a better evaluation of their reuse and expansion capabilities.

As future work, it is necessary to expand the proposed feature model to cover more board game mechanics such as trading and collecting cards, for example. The development of new board game clients, such as mobile, Unity3D and embedded systems, along with the support for *multiplayer* matches, will also be performed in the future, in order to provide a *multiplayer* and *multiplatform* SPL for the development of digital board games.

# References

1. Antkiewicz, M., Czarnecki, K.: FeaturePlugin: feature modeling plug-in for eclipse. In: Proceedings of the 2004 OOPSLA Workshop on Eclipse Technology Exchange, Eclipse 2004, pp. 67–72. ACM, New York (2004)
2. Apel, S., Kästner, C.: An overview of feature-oriented software development. J. Object Technol. **8**(5), 49–84 (2009)
3. BinSubaih, A., Maddock, S.: Game portability using a service-oriented approach. Int. J. Comput. Games Technol. **2008**, 3:1–3:7 (2008)
4. BoardGameGeek: Board game mechanics (2018). https://boardgamegeek.com/browse/boardgamemechanic. Accessed 28 July 2018
5. BoardGameGeek: Pachisi—board game (2018). https://www.boardgamegeek.com/boardgame/2136/pachisi. Accessed 20 Jan 2019
6. Boaventura, F., Sarinho, V.T.: MEnDiGa: a minimal engine for digital games. Int. J. Comput. Games Technol. **2017**, 13 (2017)
7. Bontchev, B., Vassileva, D.: Educational quiz board games for adaptive e-learning. In: Proceedings of International Conference ICTE, pp. 63–70 (2010)
8. Duarte, L.C.S., Federal, S.: Jogos de tabuleiro no design de jogos digitais. In: Anais do XI Simpósio Brasileiro de Jogos e Entretenimento Digital, Brasília, DF, pp. 132–137 (2012)
9. Folmer, E.: Component based game development – a solution to escalating costs and expanding deadlines? In: Schmidt, H.W., Crnkovic, I., Heineman, G.T., Stafford, J.A. (eds.) CBSE 2007. LNCS, vol. 4608, pp. 66–73. Springer, Heidelberg (2007). https://doi.org/10.1007/978-3-540-73551-9_5
10. Frakes, W., Terry, C.: Software reuse: metrics and models. ACM Comput. Surv. (CSUR) **28**(2), 415–435 (1996)
11. Furtado, A.W., Santos, A.L., Ramalho, G.L.: SharpLudus revisited: from ad hoc and monolithic digital game dsls to effectively customized DSM approaches. In: Proceedings of the Compilation of the Co-located Workshops on DSM'11, TMC'11, AGERE! 2011, AOOPES 2011, NEAT 2011, & VMIL 2011, SPLASH 2011 Workshops, pp. 57–62. ACM, New York (2011). https://doi.org/10.1145/2095050.2095061

12. Furtado, A.W., Santos, A.L., Ramalho, G.L., de Almeida, E.S.: Improving digital game development with software product lines. IEEE Softw. **28**(5), 30–37 (2011)
13. Furtado, A.W.B., Santos, A.L.M.: Using domain-specific modeling towards computer games development industrialization. In: Domain-Specific Modeling workshop at OOPSLA (2006)
14. Gregory, J.: Game Engine Architecture. AK Peters/CRC Press, Natick (2014)
15. Hunicke, R., LeBlanc, M., Zubek, R.: MDA: a formal approach to game design and game research. In: Proceedings of the Challenges in Games AI Workshop, Nineteenth National Conference of Artificial Intelligence, pp. 1–5 (2004)
16. Kang, K., Cohen, S., Hess, J., Novak, W., Peterson, A.: Feature-oriented domain analysis (FODA) feasibility study. Technical report CMU/SEI-90-TR-021, Software Engineering Institute, Carnegie Mellon University, Pittsburgh, PA, USA (1990)
17. Kritz, J., Mangeli, E., Xexéo, G.: Building an ontology of boardgame mechanics based on the boardgamegeek database and the MDA framework. In: XVI Brazilian Symposium on Computer Games and Digital Entertainment, Curitiba, pp. 182–191 (2017)
18. Lucchese, F., Ribeiro, B.: Conceituação de jogos digitais (2009). http://www.dca. fee.unicamp.br/~martino/disciplinas/ia369/trabalhos/t1g3.pdf. Accessed 12 Nov 2018
19. McCabe, T.J.: A complexity measure. In: Proceedings of the 2nd International Conference on Software Engineering, ICSE 1976, pp. 407, IEEE Computer Society Press, Los Alamitos (1976). http://dl.acm.org/citation.cfm?id=800253.807712
20. Northrop, L.M.: Software product lines: reuse that makes business sense. In: Australian Software Engineering Conference (ASWEC 2006), pp. 1–3, April 2006
21. Plato: Javascript source code visualization, static analysis, and complexity tool (2012). https://github.com/es-analysis/plato
22. Sarinho, V., Apolinário, A.: A feature model proposal for computer games design. In: VII Brazilian Symposium on Computer games and Digital entertainment, Belo horizonte, pp. 54–63 (2008)
23. Sarinho, V.T., Apolinário, A.L., Almeida, E.S.: A feature-based environment for digital games. In: Herrlich, M., Malaka, R., Masuch, M. (eds.) ICEC 2012. LNCS, vol. 7522, pp. 518–523. Springer, Heidelberg (2012). https://doi.org/10.1007/978-3-642-33542-6_67
24. Sarinho, V.T., de Azevedo, G.S., Boaventura, F.M.: AsKME: a feature-based approach to develop multiplatform quiz games. In: 2018 17th Brazilian Symposium on Computer Games and Digital Entertainment (SBGames), pp. 38–3809. IEEE (2018)
25. Sarinho, V.T., Apolinário, A.L.: A generative programming approach for game development. In: 2009 VIII Brazilian Symposium on Games and Digital Entertainment (SBGAMES), pp. 83–92. IEEE (2009)
26. Scacchi, W., Cooper, K.M.: Research challenges at the intersection of computer games and software engineering. In: Conference on Foundations of Digital Games (FDG 2015), Pacific Grove, CA, June 2015
27. Zhang, W., Jarzabek, S.: Reuse without compromising performance: industrial experience from RPG software product line for mobile devices. In: Obbink, H., Pohl, K. (eds.) SPLC 2005. LNCS, vol. 3714, pp. 57–69. Springer, Heidelberg (2005). https://doi.org/10.1007/11554844_7
28. Zualkernan, I.: A feature modelling framework for ubiquitous embodied learning games. In: New Trends in Software Methodologies, Tools and Techniques, vol. 231, pp. 198–216, January 2011. https://doi.org/10.3233/978-1-60750-831-1-198

# Playing with Persiflage: The Impact of Free-Form Dialogue on the Play of Computer Role Playing Games

Bernard Cheng and T. C. Nicholas Graham[(✉)]

School of Computing, Queen's University, Kingston, ON K7L 2N6, Canada
chengb@gmail.com, nicholas.graham@queensu.ca
http://equis.cs.queensu.ca

**Abstract.** Digital games struggle to blend compelling narrative with interactivity. For example, computer role-playing games (CRPGs) allow players the freedom to explore an open world, yet limit their interaction with the world's inhabitants to selecting from pre-determined dialogue choices. In this paper, we explore how players behave when truly free-form dialogue with non-player characters (NPCs) is supported. In the novel *Persiflage* game, players converse with NPCs using speech. NPCs are in turn voiced by a human, allowing truly free-form conversation. Through a study of five groups playing the game, we show how players converse, interact, and play using natural language.

**Keywords:** Game design · Natural language in games

## 1 Introduction

In computer role-playing games (CRPGs), players enter a virtual world in which they can take on different personas and engage in novel experiences. Players can adopt roles as diverse as a renaissance assassin [23], a dragon-slaying adventurer [4], or the commander of a spaceship [5]. Games enable fantasies, allowing players to immerse themselves in new worlds and situations. A large part of these fantasies is the stories that games embody.

In CRPGs, however, players lack the ability to carry out open-ended conversations with the inhabitants of the game world [17]. This restricts the player's ability to use dialogue to learn about the world or to pursue interests beyond those anticipated by the game's designers. Digital games restrict players' interaction with characters they encounter in the world, allowing only what Lessard terms "dialogue trees of pre-defined utterances" [14]. Players are presented with a series of dialogue choices from which they must choose, limiting their ability to truly guide a conversation.

**Electronic supplementary material** The online version of this chapter (https:// doi.org/10.1007/978-3-030-34644-7_15) contains supplementary material, which is available to authorized users.

© IFIP International Federation for Information Processing 2019
Published by Springer Nature Switzerland AG 2019
E. van der Spek et al. (Eds.): ICEC-JCSG 2019, LNCS 11863, pp. 187–200, 2019.
https://doi.org/10.1007/978-3-030-34644-7_15

In this paper, we explore the effect of *permitting truly open-ended conversation with non-player characters in computer RPGs*. Since current AI techniques do not allow automation of open-ended conversation, we introduce "voiced NPCs", non-player characters whose dialogue is provided by a human being. We illustrate this idea in *Persiflage*, a CRPG where players are represented as avatars in a graphical virtual world, using a traditional game controller to explore this world. Unlike traditional CRPGs, however, when talking with NPCs, players speak out loud using unrestricted natural language. Players are unrestricted in what topics they raise with NPCs, and in how they express themselves.

This paper shows the effect of open-ended conversation on play of a CRPG. We explore how players present themselves verbally and engage in storytelling when given the ability to talk in their own voices. To investigate these questions, we conducted a study where five groups of three people were recruited to play through a murder mystery plot in *Persiflage*, where their utterances were recorded and then coded. The groups were split into two players and one *orchestrator*, whose primary job was to give voice to non-player characters. We found that players engaged with the game's goals and used open-ended dialogue to advance the story's plot, sometimes in unexpected ways. Players did not constrain themselves to the game's mediaeval setting, instead opting to import their own humour and anachronisms. We found that permitting open-ended conversation in a CRPG led to vibrant, humorous, and light-hearted interaction, while remaining grounded in the game's setting and goals.

We distinguish this approach of enhancing a CRPG with voiced NPCs from the use of a game master (GM) in traditional pen-and-paper role playing games such as Dungeons and Dragons [12]. Our approach extends CRPGs to have more intelligent NPCs without otherwise changing the presentation or interaction affordances of the game. Voiced NPCs give a hint of how CRPGs would be played if the artificial intelligence directing the behaviour of NPCs were powerful enough to support open-ended conversation using natural language. In contrast, GMs take the much broader approach of narrating and guiding the game as a whole.

In this paper, we first review approaches to improving the flexibility of dialogue in digital games, then describe *Persiflage*, our game incorporating voiced NPCs, and finally present our study of open-ended conversation in CRPGs.

## 2    Related Work

Murray describes the idealized vehicle for interactive narrative as Star Trek's fictional Holodeck [17], where users assume the role of characters in a holographic environment and interact using natural dialogue. Current digital games are far from this ideal, limiting players' interaction with characters in the game to selecting among choices that have been provided by the game's designer.

Clicking through dialogue trees to advance conversations is a form of *hypertext fiction*. A story is created through a combination of fragments (or *lexia*) [19]. Players make decisions by selecting which story-block to follow next. These blocks and the corresponding available choices must be carefully arranged to preserve the logical and temporal consistency of the resulting narrative arc [22]. While the player has agency around the choice of which story-block to select, their choices are limited to the content created prior to delivery, and players lack any true sense of authorship over the resulting creation [25]. This is the state of the art found in popular computer RPGs such as Bethesda's *The Elder Scrolls 5: Skyrim* [4], or Bioware's *Mass Effect* series [5].

Some early explorations have permitted players to interact with games using natural language. In *Facade*, players speak with AI agents using typed dialogue [15]. In a study of three natural language games, Lessard concludes that players have a large degree of freedom to explore humorous interactions if they are willing to forgive the errors and limited knowledge of parsers [14]. While artificial intelligence has helped with personalization of narratives, current techniques are still far from allowing open-ended dialogues supporting compelling narrative progression [15].

Another approach is *game orchestration*, where a human directs the operation of the game at runtime. Crabtree et al., for example, use *orchestrators* to guide the narrative in large-scale pervasive multiplayer game [9]; similarly, in *Egyptian Oracle*, a *puppeteer* controls an avatar that interacts with an audience in an augmented reality performance [11]. In *game sketching*, a designer manipulates the progression of a game in real-time, allowing testing of game ideas before they are fully implemented [1]. For example, in *Raptor*, an orchestrator uses a tabletop interface to manipulate the content of a game world, while a play tester plays in real time [20]. Allison et al. used an orchestrator to implement a helper in the game *Minecraft*, to aid and advise players in building tasks [3]. In these approaches, the orchestrator's role is to enhance the experience of players, allowing open-ended interaction that would not be possible with AI alone.

In multiplayer games, voice interaction is often used by players to rapidly coordinate intense encounters where typing would be too slow [2,6]. During less frantic episodes, players use voice channels to banter and maintain a social environment in game. However, Wadley et al. find that not all players are comfortable with the increased social presence attendant to broadcasting one's voice online, especially amongst relative strangers [24], and tended not to speak in character while using voice technology.

There has been little study into how open-ended dialogue affects play. There has, however, been research into how players interact in traditional pen-and-paper role playing games, such as Dungeons and Dragons [12]. Unlike CRPGs, pen-and-paper RPGs are based on imagination; the game master (GM) describes verbally what players see, and acts out the role of characters they encounter. This affords the open-ended interaction that is absent from digital role-playing games. The voiced NPCs introduced in this paper are best viewed as an enhancement of CRPGs rather than an attempt to digitize the pen-and-paper RPG experience. Nonetheless, it is helpful to review how players interact in pen-and-paper RPGs. Tychsen discusses that control lies mainly with the GM, who has conceived a story from prepared material. The GM is able to retain control whilst

**Fig. 1.** (Left) Players of *Persiflage* are collocated, sharing a couch and TV. In conversation, the orchestrator's voice is played through the television set. (Right) The players' characters are dressed in blue and red in their shared view of Northaven. (Color figure online)

providing an illusion of choice to the players. This is likened to the situation in CRPGs where player choice is limited by the predetermined dialogue structure. Although a GM can impose their will on players, there is always some degree of improvisation and change in plans as the game progresses.

## 3   Open-Ended Dialogue in Persiflage

We designed *Persiflage* to explore the effect of open-ended dialogue in digital games. *Persiflage* is a computer role-playing game where the non-player characters (NPCs) are voiced by a human being. These orchestrators use a special interface to move and animate NPCs and to play the NPC's part in conversations with players. This removes the restrictions of rigid conversational systems, allowing players to express themselves as they choose. *Persiflage* allows us to address our primary research question of, how do players in fact choose to express themselves when such freedom is given?

As shown in Fig. 1, Left, two players each control an avatar using a standard game controller. Players are collocated, sharing a single display. Players view a cartoon-style fantasy village containing streets and buildings (Fig. 1, Right). Players move their avatars using the joysticks on their game controllers, and interact with NPCs and objects using buttons on the controller. Various NPC villagers are located around the fictional village of Northaven. To advance the plot, the players must talk to the villagers to gather information.

An orchestrator sits in another room (Fig. 2, Right), and uses a special interface to control the NPCs (Fig. 2, Left). The orchestrator can draw a path for an NPC to follow, and can trigger NPC animations (e.g., talking, waving) using buttons on the interface. For context, the orchestrator sees an inset view of the players' view (top-right of Fig. 2, Right). Players and orchestrators speak to voice their characters. The conversation is transmitted between the two rooms

**Fig. 2.** (Left) An orchestrator manage NPCs and items, and uses a headset to voice the NPCs. (Right) The NPC in the centre moves along the path traced out by the orchestrator in red. The blue buttons allow the orchestrator to trigger speaking and waving animations. The window inset in the top-right shows the players' view. (Color figure online)

using voice over IP. The orchestrator's voice plays through the speakers on the television, helping to convey that the NPC is talking. Players are aware that a human orchestrator is voicing the NPCs.

*Persiflage* is a murder mystery with story-driven gameplay where players need to question, coerce, and beg the NPCs for information and clues. The players take on the role of investigators that have arrived in Northaven in pursuit of a fugitive named "Helena". They must interact with residents of the town – the voiced NPCs – to find and bring Helena to justice. As the players explore and interact with the townsfolk, they collaboratively build a story with the orchestrator. Northaven is a mediaeval townscape consisting of homes, farms, a church, an inn and a market square. Six NPCs inhabit the town.

### 3.1 Digital Northaven

The townscape is still and lifeless until the orchestrator starts moving the NPCs and responding to the players in conversation. The items in game are deliberately generic and can take on different meanings under different situations. A vial of red liquid might be an ominous sample of blood or a potent truth serum; a bound tome can become Helena's diary or a priest's lost bible. We leave it up to the orchestrator and players to build their own stories using the digital pieces.

The opportunity for open-ended interaction poses a challenge to both the orchestrator and players. The players are invited to be inventive in the portrayal of their characters. The orchestrator on the other hand must be ready to react to unforeseen player requests.

Players can engage NPCs in conversation by walking up to them and pressing the "A" button on their controller. The interface zooms to focus on the NPC's face. The orchestrator can activate talking animations, giving the impression that when the orchestrator talks, their voice is coming from the NPC's mouth.

None of the dialogue in game is scripted outside of notes that the orchestrator has prepared. Players are initially aware only of the fact that they are searching for a fugitive named Helena, and must invent all their conversation on the fly.

The orchestrator must also improvise dialogue during play in response to the players' questioning. This allows players to express their creativity without being restrained by a script.

## 4    Study Method

To explore how players and orchestrators approach open-ended conversations in CRPGs, we performed an exploratory study where we observed play of five groups of three participants. We recruited these participants from the university community using an advertisement posted on Facebook. Participants were asked to form their own groups of three members and to choose who would play the roles of players and orchestrator. Participants ranged from 19 to 27 years in age with a mean of 23 years. 6 participants were female, and 9 male.

The orchestrator attended a training session before the study to become familiar with the story and the orchestrator interface. The orchestrator was presented with a document outlining the murder mystery story: the two players play detectives in pursuit of "Helena", a woman wanted for an unspecified crime. The chase has led them to the town of Northaven where some of the villagers have conspired to fake her death. The document briefly described each of six NPCs, to help the orchestrator in creating dialogue for the NPCs during the game. The orchestrator was shown how to move NPCs, activate their animations, engage in conversation with players, and create, move, and destroy items (Fig. 2). This training session occurred the day before the actual play session.

### 4.1    Play Session

At the beginning of the play session, the game and its user interface were demonstrated to the players, including how to move, enter, and exit a conversation with an NPC, and pick up, drop, and trade items. They were then allowed to experiment and familiarize themselves with the controls, until they reported that they were comfortable. This took approximately five minutes. The players were given the premise of the game, and instructed to solve the mystery as best they could. The play session was allowed to run to its conclusion or for thirty minutes, whichever occurred first.

The session was recorded with two separate video cameras, one for the players and one for the orchestrator. The Skype call between the parties and a screen capture of the orchestrator's screen were recorded. A transcript of their speech during the session was taken from the recordings and coded for interesting behaviours. The transcribed dialogue was split into utterances on which we employed an open coding approach [21] to identify interesting speech patterns.

## 5    Results and Analysis

*Persiflage* was created to enable natural language interactions in CRPGs, enabling open-ended dialogue between players and NPCs. These results show

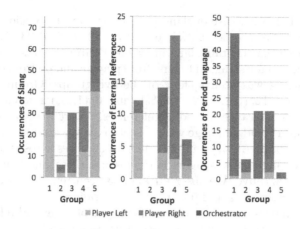

**Fig. 3.** Occurrences of slang, external references and period language

how players and orchestrators exercise this freedom of interaction. We coded *players' choice of language*, indicating how players and orchestrators engage with and invest themselves in this type of gameplay, and the *content of their conversation*, showing the players' engagement with the game's goals and objectives. The following sections present these codes.

### 5.1   How Players Present Themselves Verbally

In *Persiflage*, the opportunity to use natural language in conversation with NPCs allows players to adopt richer personalities in the game. The style and language of players' conversation indicates their attitude toward the gameplay. Just as film and theatre might be comedic or dramatic, the atmosphere of a game can vary as well. By looking at how players and the orchestrator chose to present their characters, we can see the atmosphere and tone they intended in their play of *Persiflage*. We selected three codes as characterizing players' language: the use of *slang, external references*, and *period language*. Figure 3 shows the counts of these codes.

*Slang* indicates that an utterance contains modern vulgarisms or vernacular that are out of place in the mediaeval village in which the game is set. An utterance coded as an *external reference* alludes to knowledge or ideas outside the game world. External references were further sub-classified as *inside jokes, current events*, and *pop culture*. We coded utterances for *period language* when the speaker deliberately used language outside of colloquial norms to suggest a different setting and era. Such language need not be an accurate representation of mediaeval speech; in particular, Reichert has coined the term "RPG-Dialect" to describe faux-period language "that makes liberal use of 'thous', 'thees', and 'mi'lords" [18].

As shown in Fig. 3, the use of slang is by far the most prevalent, and is seen in all five groups. We see 30 (5.6%), 6 (1.3%), 32 (8.2%), 33 (5.2%), and 70 (14.4%) utterances that contain slang in groups 1 through 5 respectively. Of the 171 utterances coded for slang, 111 came from players and 60 from orchestrators. External referencing was seen in four of the five groups. Groups 1, 3, 4, and 5 made 11 (2.0%), 12 (3.8%), 21 (3.3%), and 6 (1.2%) reference utterances respectively. Of 53 utterances coded as references, 7 were made by orchestrators and 46 by players. Period language was present in all five groups, with 33 (6.1%), 7 (1.3%), 23 (5.8%), 31 (3.3%), and 2 (0.4%) occurrences across the five groups. The use of period language was higher in groups one, three, and four, and notably less in groups two and five. We observed 74 of 83 occurrences of period language in orchestrators' utterances and 9 in players' utterances.

The above numbers show that players made use of slang and references more liberally than orchestrators, who in turn were more likely to employ period language. This example from group one shows the players using slang whilst the orchestrator uses more formal language:

**Player Left**: What up?
**Player Right**: ⟨laughter⟩
**Magistrate (voiced NPC)**: What are you doing in my town?
**Player Left**: We're looking for Helena, where she at?
**Player Right**: ⟨stifled laughter⟩ . . . where she at. . .
**Magistrate**: As far as I know, Helena's passed away.

Player Left greets the magistrate using slang, and the orchestrator voicing the magistrate responds sternly, modeling his character's speech to the game setting. Despite the magistrate's suggestion of the game taking place in a past era, the player insists on using another colloquialism, "where she at?". The resulting dialogue is asymmetric, with a comedic dissonance between the player's and NPC's speech. The absurdity of the interaction is not lost on Player Right, as shown by her reactions and laughter during the dialogue.

Another example shows the use of an external reference. Player Left compares an antagonistic authority figure to U.S. president Donald Trump:

**Player Left**: Are you the mayor?
**Magistrate (voiced NPC)**: I'm the magistrate.
**Player Left**: Is your name Donald Trump?
**Player Right**: ⟨laughter⟩
**Magistrate**: Uh, it's actually Rufus.
. . .
**Player Left**: Where's Donald Trump, aww geez, oh.

This example shows Player Left using her knowledge of the outside world to inject humour into the game. The humour is well-received, as shown by Player Right's laughter. The juxtaposition of modern people and ideas with the setting of a sleepy mediaeval village adds levity to the dialogue. The resulting experience is not unlike a pantomime play where a classic story is presented with a modern

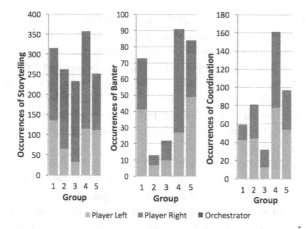

**Fig. 4.** Occurrences of utterances coded for storytelling, banter and coordination

and cheery slant, making liberal use of anachronistic references to current events and culture. Whilst the reference in the example above is anachronistic and introduces knowledge that the character would not possess, it nevertheless relates back to the game world, in this case by drawing an analogue between the fictional character and the real-life politician.

External referencing and slang are both used to provide humour and a personalized game experience leveraged from the modern social zeitgeist. Period language, conversely, indicates a desire to play in character and to provide a more (or possibly mock) authentic game experience. Players overwhelmingly display a higher propensity to use slang and external references than orchestrators, whilst the inverse is true for period language. Orchestrators are more invested in authenticity whilst players are content to make jokes and enjoy the experience less rigidly.

## 5.2  Storytelling

The presence of open-ended dialogue gives players the opportunity to contribute to the story by adding to the story arc, or to step out of the story, e.g., by telling a joke unrelated to the game. Coding revealed that utterances fell into one of three categories, denoted as *storytelling*, *coordination*, and *banter*. Figure 4 shows the counts of these codes.

A *storytelling* utterance seeks to advance the story. These usually take the form of a player posing a question to an NPC, or conversely, the orchestrator responding to a player's question. An utterance that helps participants plan or otherwise coordinate their activities is coded as *coordination*. These mostly involve players summarizing their gathered knowledge, or planning their next step in the adventure. An utterance is coded as *banter* if it represents some form of repartee that does not contribute to the game's goals. This could include inserting a joke or an external reference into conversation.

Of the three categories, storytelling utterances are the most common, accounting for 315 (58.6%), 259 (61.1%), 232 (64.1%), 358 (56.5%), and 251 (51.5%) of total utterances over the five groups. Orchestrators devote more of their utterances towards storytelling than the players, averaging 86.4% and 44.3% of total utterances respectively. Storytelling utterances represent the heart of *Persiflage*, where players interrogate, beg, and intimidate the NPCs for information and clues. The fact that almost half of players' utterances are related to storytelling indicates that despite the levity noted earlier, players were seriously engaged in trying to solve the mystery.

Coordination utterances account for 10.3%, 16.9% 8.3%, 23.0% and 17.1% of all utterances in groups 1 through 5. In theory, these utterances ought to be produced exclusively by players. We expect players to summarize and plan without the involvement of orchestrators, who play exclusively in character as NPCs. However, on rare occasion, we saw orchestrators contributing their own coordination utterances, commenting on players' observations or correcting their erroneous assumptions.

Three groups engaged in significant banter; in groups 1, 4, and 5, banter accounted for 11.9%, 14.5%, and 17.2% of total utterances respectively. The other two groups engaged in little banter, accounting for 3.3% and 5.2% of total utterances in groups 2 and 3. We observed bantering as a behavior more frequently in players than in orchestrators. In all groups, the players made more banter utterances (13.0%) than the orchestrator (4.9%). In the following typical example of banter, the exchange does not advance the story, but stays within context of the game:

**Player Left**: Hey.
**Hamish (voiced NPC)**: Hello again, it's me Hamish.
**Player Left**: Hey Hamish, so what's up?
**Hamish**: Uh, I've just been enjoying that cheese you gave me, it's quite tasty. Although it was a little dusty from the floor you found it on.
**Player Left**: It's not really our fault, it's the only place that people put cheese around here.
**Hamish**: Well it's mostly your fault.
**Player Left**: Quiet now.
**Hamish**: ⟨laughs⟩
**Player Right**: So, we lost the diary?

The orchestrator responds to the open query, "Hey Hamish, so what's up" by recalling a previous interaction and introducing some humour from the absurdity of finding cheese on the floor. This sets off an exchange between Player Left and Hamish which does not advance the story, but adds levity to the conversation. The example concludes with Player Right redirecting the interaction back to storytelling. While banter is humorous and does not advance the story, it remains rooted within the game world. Similarly, players are happy to mix banter and coordination in conversation with each other:

**Player Right**: We're getting mixed stories here. I feel like a real investigator, okay so. . .
**Player Left**: . . . this is not a field.
**Player Right**: This is not a field.
**Player Left**: This just proves that women with cats are crazy.
**Player Right**: He said to our left?
**Player Left**: Maybe [orchestrator] doesn't know directions; I'd believe that also.
**Player Right**: Maybe he's thinking his left?

Here the players have just finished talking with NPC "Annie", and they jokingly comment on the ambiguity of the directions they've recieved. Player Left makes a joke referencing the trope of the "crazy cat lady". In the short excerpt, we see the players seamlessly coordinate their movement, banter about the reliability of the NPCs, and tease the orchestrator on his ability to correctly give directions.

Orchestrators devote most of their play to storytelling, accounting for approximately 85% of their utterances on average. The players ask the NPCs questions, but contribute fewer storytelling utterances. This is not entirely surprising considering that the orchestrator controls all the facts of the mystery and slowly reveals them to the players over the course of the game. Players on the other hand, must interact with their co-player to coordinate in addition to talking with the NPCs. We see that participants are content to mix in banter whilst both progressing the story and coordinating between players. Players drive most of the bantering, which is consistent with our earlier observations that players adopt a less formal manner than orchestrators.

## 6   Discussion

To better understand how players engage with *Persiflage* we can look to the concept of the magic circle. Johan Huizinga coined the term "magic circle" to denote a boundary, not only in space and time, but also as a societal construct, that delimits where and how a game and play occurs [13]. The magic circle establishes behaviours, etiquettes, regulations and their adherent consequences that form the terms of a game, separate from society as a larger whole.

In the context of playing a character, behaviours within the circle are those that an in-game character might exhibit. Behaviours outside of the circle are those that we would expect the player as an individual outside of the game to show, but that their assumed characters could not exhibit. For example, contextually leaving the game and discussing a school assignment breaks the magic circle. Williams et al. argue that roleplay cannot exist without a strong magic circle [26]. However, both Consalvo [8] and Castronova [7] argue that the magic circle can be porous.

In the terminology of Montola [16], *Persiflage* expands the magic circle in the *societal* dimension. Players and orchestrators take on two distinct roles; as a game player as well as an audience to their fellow players' performances. Orchestrators and players, as they were observed in this study, exhibit not only the characters of their game world personas, but also their own personalities. We see this as they incorporate current affairs, private jokes, and shared experiences into their game dialogue. By using the freedom afforded by open-ended natural language, players adapt and modernize *Persiflage*'s environment, expanding the social contract they play under and in turn redefine their shared reality of the game. Fine describes these behaviours in terms of *frames*, defined as distinct worlds of knowledge [10]. Players and orchestrators in *Persiflage* switch fluidly between the primary frame of reality and that of the game world, sometimes within the same sentence. The characters within Northaven maintain an open awareness between the two frames, giving rise to quips about contemporary politics and the use of modern slang and colloquialisms whilst playing in a mediaeval fantasy world. Fine explains that in the informal setting of fantasy gaming, this form of banter and the maintenance of multiple selves is common amongst players and does not usually lead to confusion.

Our findings mirror these observations. Players and orchestrators used natural language interactions in full confidence that they would be understood by the others. Participants were aware that they were playing a game with friends, and felt comfortable stretching the magic circle. They took ownership of the game, incorporating their own ideas, views, and experiences to entertain both themselves and their peers. Rather than finding the magic circle porous, we find it to be expansive and elastic, stretching beyond the borders of Northaven to include colloquial vernacular and references to modern day pop-culture and politics. Yet the magic circle is strong enough that the players and orchestrator stayed rooted in the game for the duration of the play session. Figure 3 shows that players were the principal instigators in stretching the magic circle with jokes and slang, whilst period language originated almost exclusively from orchestrators. The clash of styles makes for humorous dialogue exchanges.

Even though orchestrators are not as active in expanding the magic circle, our examples showed that they played along when the players did so. For example, orchestrators happily acknowledged the absurdity of finding cheese on the ground. Both players and orchestrators committed fully to play. When playing *Persiflage*, all participants gave their full attention to the game. Banter and external references unfailingly alluded to in-game devices or events. We observed no events where players opened topics unrelated to the ongoing game.

As we saw earlier, orchestrators stretch the edges of the magic circle to a lesser extent than players. The banter they engage in is topical to the game setting, providing idiosyncrasies to their characters, and making small talk and gossip that one might expect in a quaint medieval village. Players, on the other hand, incorporate pop-culture and current politics in the service of humour.

# 7   Conclusion

In this paper we have explored the effect on play of computer role-playing games of permitting free-form dialogue between players and NPCs. To study this question, we introduced *Persiflage*, a novel digital RPG that employs a human to voice NPCs. Through open-ended natural language, players deliberately derived humour from the absurdity of mixing modern popular culture with *Persiflage*'s mediaeval setting. The orchestrators who gave voice to the NPCs were more rooted within the game world, using less slang, and more period language, resulting in asymmetric and humorous dialogue.

**Acknowledgements.** The authors wish to thank the Natural Sciences and Engineering Research Council of Canada (NSERC) for its support of this research.

# References

1. Agustin, M., Chuang, G., Delgado, A., Ortega, A., Seaver, J., Buchanan, J.W.: Game sketching. In: Proceedings of DIMEA 2007, pp. 36–43. ACM (2007)
2. Allison, F., Carter, M., Gibbs, M.: Word play: a history of voice interaction in digital games. Games and Culture, pp. 1–23, December 2017
3. Allison, F., Luger, E., Hofmann, K.: How players speak to an intelligent game character using natural language messages. Trans. Digit. Games Res. Assoc. **4**(2), 1–47 (2018)
4. Bethesda: The Elder Scrolls V, Skyrim (2011)
5. BioWare: Mass effect (2007)
6. Carter, M., Allison, F., Downs, J., Gibbs, M.: Player identity dissonance and voice interaction in games. In: Proceedings of the 2015 Annual Symposium on Computer-Human Interaction in Play - CHI PLAY 2015, pp. 265–269. ACM Press, London (2015)
7. Castronova, E.: Synthetic Worlds: The Business and Culture of Online Games. University of Chicago Press (2006)
8. Consalvo, M.: There is no magic circle. Games Cult. **4**(4), 408–417 (2009)
9. Crabtree, A., et al.: The cooperative work of gaming: orchestrating a mobile SMS game. Comput.- Support. Coop. Work **16**, 167–198 (2007)
10. Fine, G.A.: Shared Fantasy: Role Playing Games as Social Worlds. University of Chicago Press (2002)
11. Gillam, R., Jacobson, J.: The Egyptian Oracle Project: Ancient Ceremony in Augmented Reality. Bloomsbury Publishing (2015)
12. Gygax, G., Arneson, D.: Dungeons and Dragons, vol. 19, Tactical Studies Rules, Lake Geneva, WI (1974)
13. Huizinga, J.: Homo Ludens. Routledge (1949)
14. Lessard, J.: Designing natural-language game conversations. In: Proceedings of the 1st International Joint Conference of DiGRA and FDG, pp. 1–16 (2016)
15. Mateas, M., Stern, A.: Procedural authorship: a case-study of the interactive drama Façade, Digital Arts and Culture, p. 27 (2005)
16. Montola, M.: Exploring the edge of the magic circle: defining pervasive games. In: Proceedings of DAC, vol. 1966, p. 103 (2005)
17. Murray, J.H.: Hamlet on the Holodeck. The Free Press (1997)
18. Reichert, D.: Thou art awesome - the failings of 'RPG-dialect' (2013). http://www.thesofaiswaiting.com/2013/08/thou-art-awesome-failings-of-rpg-dialect.html
19. Ryan, M.L.: From narrative games to playable stories: towards a poetics of interactive narrative. Storyworlds: J. Narrative Stud. **1**, 43–59 (2009)
20. Smith, J.D., Graham, T.C.N.: Raptor: sketching games with a tabletop computer. In: Proceedings of the International Academic Conference on the Future of Game Design and Technology (Futureplay 2010), pp. 191–198 (2010)

21. Strauss, A.L., Corbin, J.: Basics of Qualitative Research: Techniques and Procedures, 2nd edn. Sage (1998)
22. Tanenbaum, J., Tanenbaum, K., El-Nasr, M.S., Hatala, M.: Authoring tangible interactive narratives using cognitive hyperlinks. In: Proceedings of the Intelligent Narrative Technologies III Workshop (INT3 2010), p. 8 (2010)
23. Ubisoft: Assassin's Creed II (2009)
24. Wadley, G., Carter, M., Gibbs, M.: Voice in virtual worlds: the design, use, and influence of voice chat in online play. Hum.-Comput. Interact. **30**(3–4), 336–365 (2015)
25. Willerton, C.: Structure problems in hypertext mysteries. In: Proceedings of the eleventh ACM Conference on Hypertext and Hypermedia (HYPERTEXT 2000), pp. 234–235 (2000)
26. Williams, D., Kennedy, T.L., Moore, R.J.: Behind the avatar: the patterns, practices, and functions of role playing in MMOs. Games Cult. **6**(2), 171–200 (2011)

# Strategies for Inclusive End-User Co-Creation of Inclusive Storytelling Games

Franco Eusébio Garcia$^{(\boxtimes)}$ ⓘ and Vânia Paula de Almeida Neris ⓘ

Departamento de Computação, Universidade Federal de São Carlos (UFSCar),
São Carlos, SP, Brazil
{franco.garcia,vania}@dc.ufscar.br

**Abstract.** As gaming acquires new purposes (for instance, entertainment, education and healthcare), game accessibility becomes increasingly important for multiple domains. For broader inclusion, game accessibility encompass both creation and play. Towards this goal, we have defined a framework to enable more people to create and play digital games In this paper, we present strategies resulting from developing and evaluating Lepi, an inclusive end-user tool for co-creation of inclusive storytelling-based games. Adults with heterogeneous interaction needs, levels of literacy and experience with computers used Lepi to co-create their games over ten creation workshops. Using Lepi and following the framework practices, the participants managed to co-create games accessible for themselves and their peers. From this experience, we have identified some strategies (Creation Commands, Interaction Alternatives for Input, Slots, Creation Alternatives, Assisted and Collaborative Co-Creation, Gentle Slopes, Multimodal Features, Playing Commands and Presenting Game Content) which can contribute towards more inclusive practices of game creation and play of storytelling-based games.

**Keywords:** End-User Development · Game development · Game accessibility · Universal Design · Meta-Design · Human-Centered Computing

## 1 Introduction

Game accessibility aims to enable more people to play digital games. Although the Literature provides techniques, guidelines, and strategies (for instance, in [9,12,15,16,29]), developers often ignore game accessibility recommendations, for reasons including efforts (for instance, costs and time), impossibility of application and unfamiliarity [1,23,28]. Developers often makes assumptions of user

---

This study was financed in part by the Coordenação de Aperfeiçoamento de Pessoal de Nível Superior – Brasil (CAPES) – Finance Code 001.

© IFIP International Federation for Information Processing 2019
Published by Springer Nature Switzerland AG 2019
E. van der Spek et al. (Eds.): ICEC-JCSG 2019, LNCS 11863, pp. 201–213, 2019.
https://doi.org/10.1007/978-3-030-34644-7_16

abilities [24], which, in practice, do not always hold true. As a result, people whose abilities were not considered during design might become unable to play.

As gaming expands to new applications and domains, accessibility issues may hinder digital and social inclusion. Besides the traditional entertainment value, domain experts can explore digital games as tools to support their activities. Education and healthcare are two examples of serious domains that have been exploring games to enhance learning, training, therapy and rehabilitation practices [8,13]. In these domains, experts can use games to aid people with heterogeneous characteristics, including age, socioeconomic status, (dis)abilities, skills, interests and knowledge. With such heterogeneity, assumptions of abilities and skills can limit audiences for games in serious domains. However, the people in these domains often possess the knowledge and skills required for inclusion that the original developers lacked. In education, professors and special educators can remove communication barriers for students. In healthcare, therapists can support use without harming their patients. Moreover, in both cases, students and patients could further provide their skills to enable use.

In this scenario, co-creation could provide a different strategy to promote inclusion. To achieve a scenario on which end-users could co-create inclusion, they would have to act as non-professional software developers to improve the original game. Game modification (popularized as "modding") [13] is a popular term to describe End-User Development (EUD) [18] practices in games. EUD provides methods, techniques, and tools to allow end-users to create, modify, or extend software [18]. Game creation and modding expand these practices to game making.

Although, traditionally, EUD is concerned with functional software features, it may be employed to improving non-functional features. In particular, EUD could contribute to co-creation of accessibility and usability, which we have been exploring by the means of a framework to promote inclusive co-creation of inclusive games [10,11]. With the framework, we can implement software without assuming particular interactions, enabling communities of end-users to co-create alternatives to enable use and promote inclusion. This way, the community may provide broader accessibility even if the original developers failed to do so. The community, thus, practices "accessibility modding" towards broader inclusion.

Lepi (Fig. 1) was the first game creation tool developed for the framework, serving both as a proof of concept and a study of a viability. As a proof of concept, Lepi targeted a single genre (storytelling-based games) with a subset of features considering interaction needs of potential creators and players (mainstream audiences, hearing disabilities and low literacy)[1]. Participants with heterogeneous interaction needs (adults with different levels of literacy, computer skills, and emotional characteristics) used Lepi in a public healthcare service during ten collaborative workshops performed at a period of four months at an

---

[1] Although some of these features can assist people with vision disabilities to play, we have not yet addressed creation for these audiences.

(a) Creation interface.                    (b) Linking scenes (graphics).

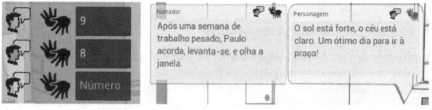

(c) Linking scenes (text).    (d) Slots for text, audio, and sign language video.

**Fig. 1.** Lepi provides interfaces to suit different interactions needs.

alcohol and drugs rehabilitation program[2] [11]. To enable every participant to play every game, participants collaborated to provide accessible content to the game according to their abilities and knowledge. As they were not programmers, we explored an iterative and incremental process to adapt Lepi to suit and support the participants' interaction needs for use and co-creation. In this paper, we have generalized adaptations and features that we have explored into strategies that we had followed to enable the creation and workflow, promoting inclusive end-user co-creating of inclusive storytelling games.

## 2  Related Work

### 2.1  Game Accessibility Strategies

Although enabling end-users to create inclusive game is an incipient practice (for instance, there are solutions to support the development of memory games by blind users under supervision [14] and to form communities of audio game designers [27]), existing studies regarding game accessibility seem to be aimed at professionals developers. For instance, Universally Accessible Games (UA-Games) have techniques to support professionals designing [15,16], and implementing them [9,12].

---

[2] We complied with research ethics protocols throughout the entire evaluation. Certificado de Apresentação de Apreciação Ética from Plataforma Brasil: CAAE: 89477018.5.0000.5504.

Another useful artifact for developers is the game interaction model from [29]. The model defines a finite state machine based on how players interact with a game during play. A player cycles among three states ( "receive stimuli", "determine response", and "provide input") to play. Based on the model, high-level strategies for game accessibility include: enhancing stimuli and replacing stimuli (for the state receive stimuli); reduce stimuli, reduce time constraints and reduce input (for the state determine response); reduce input and replace input (for the state provide input). We have explored these strategies to define the framework's software architecture, as well as to provide interaction alternatives for creation tools and generated games.

## 2.2   Collaboration and Accessibility

Communities are an important element for game modding [5]. In this paper, in particular, we explore communities as receivers and providers of inclusion. This is similar, for instance, to "communistic interactions" ("from each according to their abilities, to each according to their needs") [19] and to accessibility as interdependence [3]. For the former, inclusion should aim for groups of people instead of individuals, and on abilities instead of disabilities. For the latter, interdependence can highlight relations and dependencies between people and things.

We argue that, from a combination of both (individuals and groups, independence and interdependence), communities could start providing and receive support to enable game creation and play by more audiences. To achieve this result, communities would need computational support to co-create.

## 2.3   Storytelling in Game Creation and Modding

Storytelling has been previously explored to promote game creation by end-users. For instance, ScriptEase [6] is a tool to convert text into game scripts for Neverwinter Nights. <e-Game Project> [7] (aimed at writers) describes a documental approach employing a Domain Specific Language (DSL) to create graphical adventure games. Writing Environment for Education Video Games [20] (aimed at educators) provides a methodology for the creation of stories in point-and-click games. As with <e-Game Project>, it also employs a DSL to promote content creation.

However, to the best of our knowledge, intended audiences for existing solutions are literate people. In this paper, we aimed at broader inclusion to support people with low literacy as well other interaction needs (for instance, providing signs for hearing disabilities and audio-description for visual disabilities). We explored for in-game adaptation (created by the end-user acting as non-professional designers/developers) supported by the creation tool (Lepi) itself. This contrasts to current approaches in two ways, which may enable more inclusive creation and result into better quality and experience of use. First, the tool provides features for adaptation (later discussed in Sect. 4 and Sect. 5) to tailor generated games to players during use, potentially enabling new audiences to play. Accessibility features are typically are not available in creation tools [1]), forcing players to resort to external tools (for instance, assistive technologies) which were not considered during design, resulting into low quality of interaction and use [1,29]). Second, creating the tool with the features them allows for defining different ways to promote game creation, potentially enabling new audiences to create. To support this workflow, we fostered community collaborations.

## 3 Research Approach

This paper results from lessons learned from past studies regarding game design and implementation for game accessibility (visual, hearing, motor and cognitive disabilities), and serious games education and healthcare (depression, and alcohol and drugs rehabilitation) [8,9,11,12,26]. We adopted Participatory Design [22] and Organizational Semiotics [4] as research frameworks for design activities, gathering requirements from participatory workshops performed at public schools, hospitals and healthcare services. For use (design and play), we started the research gathering requirements for designing and implementing serious games for these institutions [8,26]. For implementation, we had defined approaches to improve game accessibility [12] based on recommendations from the Literature, which resulted into a game engine [9]. The game engine was simplified to its core architecture [10], which we briefly outline in Sect. 4.

Over time, we have progressed towards end-user co-creation of digital games [10,11]. In our considered domains (students, patients, and educational and healthcare professionals), we found storytelling as a suitable introduction to end-user game creation via visual novels[3]. Lepi was developed to assist inclusive end-user co-creation of inclusive storytelling games. It was designed and initially implemented based on our previous experience, and improved in an incremental and iterative process in participatory activities as research participants created games with it.

Design considerations and evaluation are detailed in [11]. As anticipated in Sect. 1, we have performed co-creation workshops in ten activities over four months. In the workshops, participants co-created their games using Lepi according to their own abilities and preferences. For instance, participants able to write and who had previous experience with computers opted to type their stories. Participants unable to write either recorded their story in audio (then inserted the resulting file into the audio slots of Lepi) or dictated their stories to Collaborators, who either typed the content for them or spelled the characters to the Creators. Likewise, some participants opted to draw or sketch their stories before inserting them into Lepi. Others opted to use Lepi directly (especially on their following creations).

To enable every participant to play every game, Collaborators enhanced the projects with complementary content to fill the other slots in Lepi (performing

---

[3] Reasons included: focus on story over programming; closeness to traditional media (for instance, books and films); potential for introducing programming practices over time [11].

the proposed "accessibility modding"). This included, for instance, voice content for written stories and text content for voiced stories. Therefore, they co-created inclusion together, as a community, based on the skills and abilities of each member. Similarly to the creation, every participant could play the resulting games based on their interaction needs and/or preferences. Without the collaborative enhancements, this would have been impossible: for instance, people unable to read would not be able to play text-only stories. In the remainder of this paper, we described the strategies that we have explored to support broader inclusion for creation and play.

## 4    An Inclusive End-User Development Framework for Tailorable Games

To enable more people to create and play games, we have designed a framework to foster community co-creation of inclusion games [10]. The framework defines (i) a software architecture for game implementation, (ii) a collaborative working model to support co-creation and (iii) game creation approaches to enable end-users to develop their games.

Based on the concept of tailoring [21] (adaptations of software to suit the practices of a user), games implementing the architecture were named "tailorable games". The central idea of the architecture was allowing the implementation of interaction-abstract games, defining commands and semantics of use instead of pre-defined interactions to enable play. This way, developers can define interaction alternatives to suit different abilities and skills from players iteratively, one audience at a time, via "interaction add-ons". These add-ons can be attached to (or removed from) a game, defining how a player sensory perceives the game (for the "receive stimuli" phase of game interaction model from [29]) and controls it (for the "provide input" phase of the game interaction model).

To foster community co-creation, we have defined a collaborative working model around the flexibility of the architecture. The central idea of the model was enabling members of a community to provide accessibility features to a game project. In the same way modding enables a community to improve aesthetics, content and gameplay for games, the collaborative working model promotes "accessibility modding" towards broader inclusion. As with "communistic interactions", members of a community can provide their own abilities and skills to create (or improve) accessibility features (interaction alternatives) to enable new audiences to play. In particular, if these people had support to co-create the game, they could further contribute to improve it. Their own abilities and skills could, potentially, include other new audiences, defining "cycles of inclusion". This way, inclusion could become an iterative and dynamic process, because people who become able to play may further contribute to improve the game.

As end-users are (usually) not programmers, game creation approaches enable and support the co-creation. In special, systems for co-creation can also implement the architecture (for the same benefits) to become tailorable systems *and* implement tailorable games as their projects. From this, it results inclusive end-user creation tools able to define inclusive games – that is, game making tools as well as games that members of a community can improve with content, accessibility and usability features to promote play and inclusion. Lepi was the first tool that we have defined to explore this idea.

### 4.1  Strategies of the Framework to Foster Inclusion

**Decoupled Interaction from Logic.** The architecture simplifies the engine from [9,12] to a few elements – components, entities and subsystems from Entity-Component-Systems (ECS) events and event handlers from Event-Driven Architectures. These elements, combined, allow for modifying game interaction at use-time (run-time). These elements allow developers to change input and output (IO) features of an entity at run-time [9,12], as they can make arbitrary interaction toggle-able. For instance, entities with graphical components are graphically represented into a screen. Once the component is removed, the entity stops being represented (although it still exists). This idea allows swapping ways to control (input to command) and represent (output to convey) an entity, even when the game is already running. For accessibility, particularly useful applications of EDA include providing immediate feedback to players (for instance, with sound, haptic, or graphical effects) and implement game agents able to provide input to the game.

**Interaction-Abstract Implementation.** To achieve interaction-abstract digital games using the architecture, the implementation should not impose any fixed physical-level IO-related interactions for use. Rather, the architecture proposes that developers define semantics of use (that is, define *what* the play can do) first, then provide interaction alternatives (that is, define *how* the player will do it) to allow users to apply the semantic to play. This allows developers to implement interactive systems without assumptions of how a player will use it to, and to interaction alternatives to define physical-level interactions. This way, developers can re-define the "receive stimuli" and "provide input" states from the game interaction model at use-time.

**Commands.** In the architecture, commands abstract the proposed semantics of use. They are implemented as events. Commands define possible actions to express intents of what a user wants to accomplish when using the system. Commands are usually verbs expressing actions available to modify the current state of the system. For instance, in a storytelling game, commands can include "choose an option", "confirm / cancel a choice", "forward / rewind a piece of dialogue". The implementation processes these commands; as they are events, an interaction-abstract implementation reacts to them whenever they are issued. In turn, the system performs the required processing to change its internal state. This makes it easier to implement interaction alternatives for input, input (re-)mapping [17] and provide automation features. For the latter, the system can dispatch a command to provide input on behalf of a player, assisting players

who may need help at the "determine response" and "provide input" states of
the game interaction model.

**Interaction Alternatives for Input.** For human-interaction, developers can
offer multiple implementations of physical-level interactions to map users' abilities into commands to allow for user input. Thus, instead of single, fixed and
predefined mappings, developers can provide users with choice. If a pair consisting of an input device (for instance, controllers, mice, keyboard, microphones,
cameras) and mechanism (for instance, button presses, stick movements, spoken
words, gestures) can be translated into a command, then the pair can be used
to control the game. These pairings can be defined via input (re-)mapping (for
instance, "press ENTER" or "say CONFIRM" perform the command "confirm
a choice").

**Interaction Alternatives for Output.** As the design should not impose any
physical-level IO-related interactions, the concepts of sign and signifier from
Semiotics [4] are useful for the architecture. These concepts enable separating a
message (abstract meanings, conceptions and functions for things in signs) from
its representation (denotation using symbols through signifiers). If game output
is considered as the means to continuously providing message to translate the
current state of the abstract simulation (a sign derived from data) into concrete
representation (signifiers representing information) to a player, then providing
accessible stimuli becomes the task of matching signs to accessible signifiers.
As a result, the final user interface can be a composition of output alternatives
to convey the internal state of the game to the player. This allows modifying
game presentation to support the "receive stimuli" state of the game interaction
model.

## 5    Strategies for Inclusive End-User Co-Creation of Inclusive Storytelling Games Defined in Lepi

The strategies from Sect. 4.1 were applied to the iterative development of Lepi
over the workshops to enable our initial audiences (including people with hearing
disabilities and low literacy) to create and play storytelling-based games. In this
section, we describe how we abstracted from the end-users acting as creators and
players.

### 5.1    Strategies to Enable Inclusive Creation of Storytelling Games

**Creation Commands and Interaction Alternatives for Input.** Lepi, as an
editor, provides commands underlying user interfaces and widgets to perform the
processing (for instance, "add / edit / remove an entity", "add / edit / remove a
piece of dialogue" and "add / edit / remove a new scene"). Creation commands
can be bound to available input devices to enable use. The architecture idea of
interaction add-ons enable combinations of commands to define macros, which
Creators can attach to their software to perform compound commands.

**Slots.** In storytelling games, entities can be characters, places and objects as well as pieces of dialogues and narrations. In Lepi, every game entity can be multimodal. To support the current audiences, entities have text, image, audio and video slots. To abstract the architecture from the Creators, Lepi provides slots to represent different signifiers of a same sign. Creators can attach data and media files into these slots to convey a very same sign in different ways. For instance, entities support text, audio, image and sign language (video) descriptions. Likewise, text, voice audio or sign language video can convey dialogues (Fig. 1d). Once a Creator fills a slot providing its media, the content can be reproduced to players to sensory convey the desired information.

**Creation Alternatives.** Slots featuring multimodal alternatives mean that people with different knowledge, skills, abilities and background can contribute with the development of the project. Thus, people have opportunities to co-create based on their preferences and skills, instead of being unable to contribute based on what they cannot do. For instance, the current slots enable people to collaborate based on writing, speaking, drawing and acting skills. Thus, besides the traditional text composition in storytelling games, Creators can provide content to Lepi by adding voice narrations, drawings, and sign language videos into their slots. Initial prototypes can start with low-level technology (for instance, paper) to explore ideas (such as a sketch of the story in a comic book format). Once the idea is refined, creators can insert their content into Lepi.

**Assisted and Collaborative Co-Creation.** Although independence is often strove in accessibility [3], people can assist one another to co-create. Their abilities can complement each other to overcome barriers that each one could not address individually ("cross-ability cooperation" [3]). In the collaborative work model, Collaborators provide these external assistance whenever Creators cannot satisfy their own abilities – or those from their Players – alone. Collaborators can create and provide accessible media, add support for assistive technologies or even support use (for instance, a therapist can help a patient to perform tasks that he/she would not be able to do on her/his own). Every collaboration contributes to broader inclusion. For creation activities in serious contexts, there will often be people who have skills and knowledge to contribute towards inclusion (for instance, with audio-description or sign language content in inclusive education).

**Gentle Slopes.** Making syntactic errors hard (preferably impossible) and supporting incremental development are desirable features of EUD tools [25]. Practices can also scaffold creation. Creation practices should aim for gentle slopes [2], gently introducing complexity over time. Lepi explores gentle slopes within storytelling activities: Creators can start with small, linear stories and explore more complex features (for instance, branches and decisions for branching storytelling) over time. With slots, this same reasoning applies to media.

**Multimodal Features.** Inclusive creation requires multimodal features. Although visual programming languages and approaches are commonly explored in EUD tools (because they accessible for sighted users), they are not accessible for everyone. Rather, constructs should be multimodal. For instance, instance, in Lepi, Creators can define story branches and decisions with visual (linking connectors in a graph; Fig. 1b) and text constructs (providing the next scene number; Fig. 1c). For content creation, slots allow Creators to co-create according to their needs and skills (written, spoken and acted content, for instance).

## 5.2    Strategies to Enable Inclusive Play of Storytelling Games

**Playing Commands.** As Players' interaction needs can differ from Creator's, the resulting games should be IO flexible as well. The first strategy is similar to "Creation Commands and Interaction Alternatives for Input" in Lepi. Players should be able to use their preferred devices to play the game. In this first prototype, Lepi supports traditional game input devices (keyboard, mice and controllers).

**Presenting Game Content.** The second strategy results from the Slots. Players can choose what slots they want to build the user interface of their games (text, image, audio and video slots). If a combination of available content is slots fulfill the interaction needs of a Player, she/he can play the game.

As, at this time, the interaction alternatives do not conflict with each other, a resulting game can have any combination of slots. For instance, one Player may interact with a traditional storytelling game, composed of text and graphics. Another play with graphics and sign language videos. Finally, a third Player may enable all features to read, listen and watch the game content.

# 6    Concluding Remarks and Current Work

As digital games are becoming increasingly important for different domains and purposes (including entertainment, education and healthcare), it becomes fundamental to enable more people to create and play them. Otherwise, instead of reducing social and digital inclusion, technology would contribute to increase them and to create more barriers.

In this paper, we described some strategies that we have employed towards promoting inclusive co-creation of inclusive storytelling-based games. These strategies resulted from the development of inclusive end-user tool (Lepi) for the creation of inclusive storytelling games. We have briefly described a game framework aimed at game accessibility and its three pillars, with special focus on its software architecture and Lepi, its first co-creation tool. For these pillars, we have described the strategies that we have defined and have been exploring to enable new audiences to co-create and play digital games based on their abilities and skills. The strategies resulted from our experiences in participatory workshops involving participants with heterogeneous interaction needs making games for themselves and for their peers. They focus on the concept of tailoring to adapt software to better suit interaction needs of users – in this case, to promote more inclusive game creation and use practices.

We aim to keep improving the framework. We are currently introducing creation and play features (for instance, text-to-speech and simple voice commands) to Lepi aimed at making it more accessible for visual disabilities. Some of these features should also provide the first resources towards inclusion for motor disabilities. Once we address those, the goal is introducing new mechanics for creation and playing practices, introducing new practices and tools over time.

# References

1. Aguado-Delgado, J., Gutiérrez-Martínez, J.M., Hilera, J.R., de-Marcos, L., Otón, S.: Accessibility in video games: a systematic review. Univ. Access Inf. Soc., 1-25 (2018). https://doi.org/10.1007/s10209-018-0628-2
2. Basawapatna, A.R., Repenning, A., Koh, K.H., Savignano, M.: The consume - create spectrum: balancing convenience and computational thinking in stem learning. In: Proceedings of the 45th ACM Technical Symposium on Computer Science Education, SIGCSE 2014, pp. 659–664. ACM, New York (2014). https://doi.org/10.1145/2538862.2538950
3. Bennett, C.L., Brady, E., Branham, S.M.: Interdependence as a frame for assistive technology research and design. In: Proceedings of the 20th International ACM SIGACCESS Conference on Computers and Accessibility, ASSETS 2018, pp. 161–173. ACM, New York (2018). https://doi.org/10.1145/3234695.3236348
4. Bouissac, P. (ed.): Encyclopedia of Semiotics. Oxford University Press, New York (1998)
5. Burke, Q., Kafai, Y.B.: Decade of game making for learning: from tools to communities. In: Angelides, R.C., Agius, H. (eds.) Handbook of Digital Games, pp. 689–709. Wiley, Cambridge (2014)
6. Carbonaro, M., et al.: Interactive story authoring: a viable form of creative expression for the classroom. Comput. Educ. **51**(2), 687–707 (2008). https://doi.org/10.1016/j.compedu.2007.07.007
7. de Leeuw, K., Moreno-Ger, P., Sierra, J.L., Martínez-Ortiz, I., Fernández-Manjón, B.: A documental approach to adventure game development. Sci. Comput. Program. **67**(1), 3–31 (2007). https://doi.org/10.1016/j.scico.2006.07.003
8. de Souza, P.M., da Hora Rodrigues, K.R., Garcia, F.E., de Almeida Neris, V.P.: Towards a semiotic-based approach to the design of therapeutic digital games. In: Liu, K., Nakata, K., Li, W., Baranauskas, C. (eds.) ICISO 2018. IAICT, vol. 527, pp. 53–62. Springer, Cham (2018). https://doi.org/10.1007/978-3-319-94541-5_6
9. Garcia, F.E.: Um Motor para Jogos Digitais Universais. Msc thesis, Universidade Federal de São Carlos, São Carlos (2014)
10. Garcia, F.E.: An Inclusive End-User Development Framework for Tailorable Games. Phd thesis, Universidade Federal de São Carlos, São Carlos (2019)
11. Garcia, F.E., Brandão, R.P., Mendes, G.C.D.P., Neris, V.P.D.A.: Able to create, able to (self-)improve: how an inclusive game framework fostered self-improvement through creation and play in alcohol and drugs rehabilitation. In: Proceedings of the 17th IFIP TC.13 International Conference on Human-Computer Interaction (INTERACT 2019). Paphos, Cyprus (2019)

12. Garcia, F.E., de Almeida Neris, V.P.: A data-driven entity-component approach to develop universally accessible games. In: Stephanidis, C., Antona, M. (eds.) UAHCI 2014. LNCS, vol. 8514, pp. 537–548. Springer, Cham (2014). https://doi.org/10.1007/978-3-319-07440-5_49
13. Gee, E.R., Tran, K.M.: Video game making and modding. In: Handbook of Research on the Societal Impact of Digital Media, pp. 238–267. Information Science Reference, Hershey (2015)
14. Giannakopoulos, G., Tatlas, N.A., Giannakopoulos, V., Floros, A., Katsoulis, P.: Accessible electronic games for blind children and young people. Brit. J. Educ. Technol. 49(4), 608–619 (2018). https://doi.org/10.1111/bjet.12628
15. Grammenos, D., Savidis, A., Stephanidis, C.: Designing universally accessible games. Mag. Comput. Entertain. (CIE) 7, 29 (2009). https://doi.org/10.1145/1486508.1486516. SPECIAL ISSUE: Media Arts and Games
16. Grammenos, D., Savidis, A., Stephanidis, C.: Unified design of universally accessible games. In: Stephanidis, C. (ed.) UAHCI 2007. LNCS, vol. 4556, pp. 607–616. Springer, Heidelberg (2007). https://doi.org/10.1007/978-3-540-73283-9_67
17. Gregory, J.: Game Engine Architecture, 2nd edn. A K Peters/CRC Press, Boca Raton (2014)
18. Lieberman, H., Paternò, F., Klann, M., Wulf, V.: End-user development: an emerging paradigm. In: Lieberman, H., Paternò, F., Wulf, V. (eds.) End User Development. Human-Computer Interaction Series, vol. 9, pp. 1–8. Springer, Netherlands (2006). https://doi.org/10.1007/1-4020-5386-X_1
19. Liu, P., Ding, X., Gu, N.: Helping others makes me happy: social interaction and integration of people with disabilities. In: Proceedings of the 19th ACM Conference on Computer-Supported Cooperative Work & Social Computing, CSCW 2016, pp. 1596–1608. ACM, New York (2016). https://doi.org/10.1145/2818048.2819998
20. Marchiori, E.J., Torrente, J., del Blanco, Á., Moreno-Ger, P., Sancho, P., Fernández-Manjón, B.: A narrative metaphor to facilitate educational game authoring. Comput. Educ. 58(1), 590–599 (2012). https://doi.org/10.1016/j.compedu.2011.09.017
21. Mørch, A.: Three levels of end-user tailoring: Customization, integration, and extension. In: Computers and Design in Context, pp. 51–76 (1997)
22. Muller, M.J., Haslwanter, J.H., Dayton, T.: Participatory practices in the software lifecycle. In: Helander, M., Landauer, T.K., Prabhu, P. (eds.) Handbook of Human-Computer Interaction, 2nd edn, pp. 255–297. Elsevier Science Inc., Amsterdam (1997)
23. Porter, J.R.: Understanding and addressing real-world accessibility issues in mainstream video games. SIGACCESS Access. Comput. 108, 42–45 (2014). https://doi.org/10.1145/2591357.2591364
24. Pozzi, S., Bagnara, S.: Individuation and diversity: The need for idiographic HCI. Theo. Issues Ergonomics Sci. 14(1), 1–21 (2013). https://doi.org/10.1080/1464536X.2011.562564
25. Repenning, A., Ioannidou, A.: What makes end-user development tick? 13 design guidelines. In: Lieberman, H., Paternò, F., Wulf, V. (eds.) End User Development. Human-Computer Interaction Series, vol. 9, pp. 51–85. Springer, Netherlands (2006). https://doi.org/10.1007/1-4020-5386-X_4
26. Rodrigues, K., Garcia, F.E., Bocanegra, L., Gonçalves, V., Carvalho, V., Neris, V.P.A.: Personas-driven design for mental health therapeutic applications. SBC J. Interact. Syst. 6(1), 18–34 (2015)

27. Urbanek, M., Güldenpfennig, F., Schrempf, M.T.: Building a community of audio game designers - towards an online audio game editor. In: Proceedings of the 2018 ACM Conference Companion Publication on Designing Interactive Systems, DIS 2018 Companion, pp. 171–175. ACM, New York (2018). https://doi.org/10.1145/3197391.3205431

28. Westin, T., Dupire, J.: Design of a curriculum framework for raising awareness of game accessibility. In: Miesenberger, K., Bühler, C., Penaz, P. (eds.) ICCHP 2016. LNCS, vol. 9758, pp. 501–508. Springer, Cham (2016). https://doi.org/10.1007/978-3-319-41264-1_68

29. Yuan, B., Folmer, E., Harris, F.: Game accessibility: a survey. Universal Access Inf. Soc. **10**(1), 81–100 (2011). https://doi.org/10.1007/s10209-010-0189-5

# Exploring the Effect of Game Premise in Cooperative Digital Board Games

Supara Grudpan[1]([✉]), Dmitry Alexandrovky[1], Jannicke Baalsrud Hauge[2,3], and Rainer Malaka[1]

[1] Digital Media Lab, TZI, University of Bremen, Bremen, Germany
{sgrudpan,dimi,malaka}@uni-bremen.de
[2] BIBA-Bremen Institute for Production and Logistics Gmbh, Bremen, Germany
baa@biba.uni-bremen.de
[3] KTH-Royal Institute of Technology, Stockholm, Sweden, Mariekällvägen 3, 151 81 Södertälje, Sweden

**Abstract.** The design of cooperative games is challenging due to the requirements of cooperation between the players. The major need of the design is to provide an environment that enables players to achieve the game goal in a cooperative fashion. The game premise which is the story behind the game is one of the dramatic elements and impacts the engagement of players. In this paper, we investigate the effect of game premise on the engagement of the players and the cooperation between the players. Hence, to understand this effect, we developed three versions of the Pandemic game with three premises namely positive, negative, and neutral. Using these game versions, we conducted an experiment to see how game premise affects the player experience. The results show that premise can significantly influence the players' intrinsic motivation, the connection with the game and the cooperation strategies.

**Keywords:** Cooperative games · Game premise · Player experience · Players' cooperation

## 1 Introduction

Cooperative and collaborative games are rapidly increasing on the market. Similar trends are observed with board games [26] such as Pandemic and The Lord of the Rings [9,29]. These board games facilitate the players to have fun together while assisting each other in achieving the goals of the game, which they might not be able to solve individually. This characteristic of cooperative and collaborative games not only engage players to collaborate during the game but also train a player's social skills and abilities to work as a team. This makes cooperative games widely used in the context of serious games, which can be stated as the games that focus on learning and training purposes while also serving as entertainment [23,29]. However, the design of cooperative or collaborative games is challenging as the games require proper mechanics that foster collaboration. One of the challenges is to set specifiable outcomes that can motivate players

© IFIP International Federation for Information Processing 2019
Published by Springer Nature Switzerland AG 2019
E. van der Spek et al. (Eds.): ICEC-JCSG 2019, LNCS 11863, pp. 214–227, 2019.
https://doi.org/10.1007/978-3-030-34644-7_17

to help each other and to improve their performance. The unspecified outcomes lead to players not being able to understand the consequences of their actions. Hence, they might not want to play it again.

Literature on game experience often attempts to formalize features of games that engage players. Fullerton defines games by its formal and dramatic elements. While formal elements describe a strong interplay of boundaries and technology, dramatic elements formalize elements that affect the players' emotions providing context to the gameplay and give a meaningful experience [8]. The elements make the game more emotionally engaging. The complicated dramatic techniques such as premise, character, and story are used in many games to explain the abstract elements of the formal system which can create a deeper connection with player experience [8,27].

In this paper, we report on a user study that employed a custom "Pandemic"-like video game, with three different premises of positive, neutral and negative player roles to investigate the influence of dramatic elements on player experience (pX) in cooperative games. Our study is motivated by two research questions: (i) *Do the game premises affect the players' experience in cooperative games?* (ii) *How do three different premises affect the player cooperation in cooperative games?* Our work suggests that premise has an essential impact on pX and players' cooperation and that the negative premise provides most engagement. This work can help researchers and developers to apply premise more effectively into game design.

## 2    Related Literature

### 2.1    Game Premise

Dramatic elements can be used as a set of tools for game designers for elicitation of emotional reaction from players. Fullerton's definition of games include premise as a dramatic element [9]. Premise establishes meaning to the players' actions through a setting or metaphor [8] and its base-level effect is to make players easily understand and operate essential features in the games [1,6,8,15,17]. Game premise differs from the story in narrative aspect. A premise stays the same throughout the game unchanged by players' actions whereas the game story builds upon the setting or theme (i.e., premise) and unfolds throughout the progression of the game. For example, the premise of "Simcity" [11] is to build a city from scratch using limited financial resources. For the whole game, player actions mainly focus on construction of the city, while the story of the game consists of the small events that affect a player's decision.

Psychologists define behavioural intentions as "instructions that people give to themselves to behave in certain ways" [24] as the intentions have a strong relationship with behaviours. We have utilized this concept in developing our game premise. We define a game with "Negative" premise that asks the players to employ negative behaviours (to kill the rival gangsters). In contrast, "Positive" premise sets the goal with the positive behaviours (discovering the cure of diseases) with the positive intention to save the world. For the neutral version, we created the game with an abstract environment (without any context). We had not set any background story for the players in the neutral version and they just complete the game mission. Research focus on studying the effect of game premise with the pX has been considerably limited in the literature. However, quite many examples are found in literature that employ dramatic elements such as premise, characters and story in order to operationalize pX [9]. Birk et al. [5] showed that identification and customization with an avatar can increase the intrinsic motivation of the players. Iten et al. [12] showed the impact of meaningful choices in a narrative-rich game which leads to the players having more appreciation for the narrative in addition to winning the game. Holmes et al. [10] studied the effect of game narrative and theme on pX. They found preferences towards "Horror" and "Sanitized" themes whereas higher curiosity was observed in the horror scenario. In contrast to Holmes et al., our paper manipulates the premise of the players' role rather than comparing different aesthetic elements of the game.

## 2.2   Cooperative Games

Sedano et al. [23] define cooperative games as games where players have individual actions but a common goal to be achieved together. Designing cooperative games are complex as the game requires mechanics enabling cooperation in a meaningful way [29]. Beznosyk et al. [4] identified closely- and loosely- coupled collaboration patterns and they found that close collaboration provides higher enjoyment while increasing the communication challenges between the players. Emmerich et al. [7] analyzes pX and social interaction of three game patterns: player interdependence, time pressure and shared control. They found that high player interdependence indicates more communication and less frustration, whereas shared control results in lower competence and autonomy. Similarly, Johnson et al. [13], compares the impact of teammate on pX in cooperative game. They found that playing with human teammates was associated with greater sense of relatedness, but less competence and flow than playing with computer-controlled bots. The presented literature identified important factors and patterns of cooperation in games. Our work investigates which aspects of cooperation are affected by the game's premise.

## 2.3   Good and Bad Roles in Games

Peter [20] pointed out that video games allow a discussion about morality in a unique manner, since they allow experiencing unethical content. Liebrand et al. [16] studied how the social values of self relate to the interpretation of the others. They classified subjects into four types on social values: altruistic, cooperative, individualistic and competitive and also asked subjects to rate other's behavior. The authors found that cooperators attached more significance to factors like sincere, fair, just, dishonest (evaluative dimension) whereas the individualists attached more significance to factors like weak, self-assured, purposeful, naive (potency dimension). Weaver et al. [25] examined how moral decision of players affect their emotional response. The results showed that antisocial behavior increases without an impact on the enjoyment. In our paper, we focus on exploring how dramatic elements influence on pX in a cooperative game. We developed games which asked players to cooperate in three different objectives: to save the world (positive), to eliminate the boss (negative), and to remove all cubes (abstract). We compared the effect of these game settings by measuring the pX of the games, observing players' behavior, and asking semi-structured interview questions.

### 2.4   Gender in Video Games

Further, there are various discussions on gender differences in video game characters [2,14,19]. Miller and Summers showed that significant differences of gender exist in portrayal of video game characters such as the males having a high likelihood to be heroes and main characters while females more often tend to be supplemental characters [19]. Bergstrom et al. discusses the relation between gender and professions in non-player characters (NPCs) games and the results show that the characters in the game world have been chosen to reflect the real world demography [2]. Similarly, Kivikangas et al. showed that males prefer competition over cooperation while females choose cooperation over competition [14]. In our game design, we kept the characters in the game gender neutral to avoid biases of gender in our study.

## 3   Study

To investigate the effect of premise on pX we designed a simplified version of the Pandemic game with three different premises and an additional setting to dynamically enable and disable special abilities mechanics. Our prototype implements $3 \times 2$ versions of the game. First, we explain the original Pandemic game and its features followed by our game design of the modified versions for the experiment. Next, we present the measurements and the procedure of the comparative study.

### 3.1   Pandemic Game

Originally, Pandemic [28] is a multi-player cooperative game where the goal is to stop spreading of a diseases on a map by discovering the cure of the diseases before the pandemic occurs. The players have to work cooperatively in order to win the game. The game begins with spreading of the infection. In turns, the player take actions, which consist of the following three phases: Action phase: The player needs to execute movement actions and actions for treating/discovering. Draw phase: The player draws cards that allow movement and cure actions from the player deck. Infection phase: The player draws two cards from infection deck and the infection progresses on the map. The game has a non-zero-sum outcome and ends if any of the following lose conditions occur: (i)

The players run out of cards from player deck. (ii) all infection markers are set on the map. (iii) an outbreak (a city has more than three infection items and hence, leads to a cascade spreading to adjacent cities) occurs more than eight times. To win the game, the players need to discover a cure for all diseases. The game is designed in such a way that the more turns the players use, higher are the chances to lose the game by running out of cards or by outbreak. The game design forces players to work cooperatively in order to achieve the goal of discovering cures for the diseases within limited game turns. A typical play session takes at least 45 min. The original version is available as a board game and also as a mobile application.

## 3.2  Game Design

For our experiment, we developed three variants of simplified version of the original Pandemic game and reduced it to only the core mechanics. Consequently, we took out some game elements, downsized the map from 48 cities to 24 cities and decreased the number of diseases from 4 to 2. The game was developed as a multi touch game in Unity3D. During our design process we iteratively play-tested a paper prototype of the downsized modified game to estimate the play-time and identify the game strategies. And to develop strategies for the tutorials, which will be discussed later in this section. Figure 1 shows screenshots of the final prototype. We intentionally kept the visual design simplistic as we were concerned that advanced graphics would interfere with the three variants.

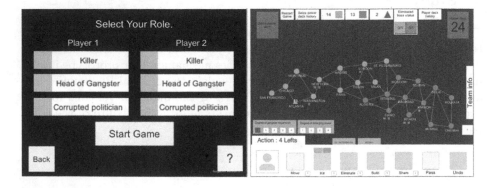

**Fig. 1.** Screenshots of the game prototype

## 3.3  Additional Game Element

Due to the complexity of the game and in order to establish a stronger connection of the premise with players' actions we added an option to introduce a subset of the additional game mechanics from the original. These mechanics are not required in order to make the game playable, but add dramatic elements that improve the dynamics of the gameplay (cards that affect infection rate, reshuffle the infection deck and resort infection markers on the map) and mechanics that give players roles with special abilities. Namely, we used the: operations expert, dispatcher and medic roles. The researcher and scientist roles were discarded as they were loosely coupled with the game mechanics for the downsized game.

### 3.4   Game Versions with Different Premises

For the study, we developed three premises, that put players into specific roles.

*Positive Premise:* Two diseases are spreading around the world. The plot involves a group of two heroes, who cooperate in traveling around the world to discover the cures for the two diseases (red and blue cubes) and save the world.

*Negative Premise:* Two groups of gangsters intend to expand their criminal enterprises around the world. The bosses of both teams try to send their gangsters to seize power over the other networks in the cities of the world. The players from the team of greatest head of gangsters, have to stop the other gangsters from increasing their power by killing their members (red and blue cubes). Then, the players need to bring down the other gangsters by taking over their criminal businesses and evacuating their bosses.

*Neutral Premise:* Two colors of cubes are spreading on the map. The players have to remove the cubes (red and blue) and stop the spreading of the cubes.

   In our design process, we ensure that all three game versions have the same game mechanics but the naming of the game elements such as the name of actions, roles of players as well as the tutorials are phrased differently depending on the game premise. Table 1 lists the different naming of game elements and the roles of players in the three versions of the game.

**Table 1.** Game elements in three different game versions.

| Game elements | Naming of game element in different versions of games | | |
|---|---|---|---|
| | Positive premise | Negative premise | Neutral premise |
| Game actions | Treat | Kill | Remove |
| | Cure disease | Eliminate bosses | Stop spreading |
| | Build research station | Build enterprise | Build triangle |
| | Share knowledge | Share license for gambling enterprise | Share card |
| Other elements | Outbreaks rate | Degree of enlarging the gang's power | Spreading rate |
| | Infection rate | Degree of gangster expansion | Explosion rate |
| | Epidemic card | Expanding power card | Spreading cube card |
| Roles | Medic | Killer | Remover |
| | Dispatcher | Head of gangster | Transporter |
| | Operations expert | Corrupted politician | Builder |

### 3.5    Measures

To measure pX we employed Player Experience of Needs Satisfaction (PENS) [21] on a 7-point Likert scale 1 (strongly disagree) to 7 (strongly agree). PENS assess intrinsic motivation on the dimensions competence (how players are able to produce their wanted outcome), autonomy (willingness to do a task) and relatedness (need of being connected to others) from Self-Determination Theory [22] and on two additional game related subscales presence/immersion (how are player are "in the game" [21]) and intuitive control (usability of the game controls).

To assess player cooperation we used observation metrics established by Bernard et al. [3]. During the play session, we logged the actions of players and we recorded their conversations. To explore the effect of premise, we conducted a semi-structured interview with 8 questions regarding the participants' attitude towards the premises and player roles.

### 3.6    Procedure

In each session, two participants were randomly paired, as a team and randomly assigned to one of the three premise version of the game. First, the participants were informed about the study and asked to complete a consent form followed by a demographics questionnaire that assesses, their experience with board games, digital games and their current gaming habits. Subsequently, they performed a two part tutorial which taught them the basic game rules. After they completed the tutorial, the participants played the game in normal mode, then with special abilities. After they finished playing two modes of the game, the subjects filled out the PENS. Finally, the examiner conducted a semi-structured interview and the subjects were debriefed.

### 3.7    Participants

30 Participants (18 female) volunteered to participate in our study. Most subjects were between 23 and 34 years old. Most (n = 20) participants had experience in playing board games and 6 participants stated they knew the Pandemic board game. 11 participants stated that they play video/mobile game daily.

## 4    Results

Our measures consist of subjective self-reports on the PENS, audio recordings during gameplay and game logs. There were 54 game sessions in total. 24 pairs finished the game successfully, 20 pairs lost and 10 groups restarted the game because it was impossible to finish. A Kruskal-Wallis Test didn't show any differences of number of wins between the conditions.

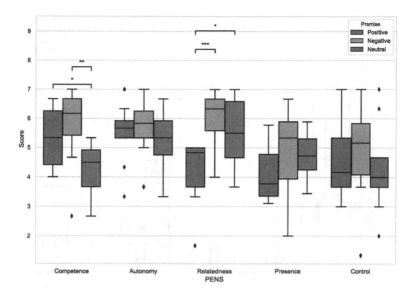

**Fig. 2.** Boxplots of the PENS results.

## 4.1 Game Premise and Player Experience

We conducted a one-way analysis of variance (ANOVA) on the subscales competence, autonomy, relatedness, presence/immersion, and intuitive controls of PENS with the premise as factor. The analysis revealed a significant differences on the sub-scales relatedness ($F_{2,27} = 7.667$, $p = .002$) and the competence ($F_{2,27} = 5.34$, $p = .011$). A plot of the sub-scales and detailed view subsequent post-hoc tests with Bonferroni correction is presented in Fig. 2. A multivariate analysis of variance (MANOVA) of PENS with premise and gender as factors did not show any significant differences for gender ($F_{5,20} = 1.767$, $p = .166$) nor an interaction effect of premise*gender on player experience ($F_{10,40} = 0.985$, $p = .471$). A Pearson correlation between gender and the PENS subscales revealed a significant correlation on relatedness ($r = -0.386$, $p < .05$) and presence ($r = -0.378$, $p < .05$). With females showing higher ratings on both subscales. However, there was no significant correlation between prior experience with Pandemic and PENS.

## 4.2 Player Actions

From the game logs we extracted *number of turns, game ending, usage of special abilities* and *sharing knowledge actions*. A one-way ANOVA revealed a significant effect of condition on number of sharing knowledge actions ($F_{2,51} = 3.91$, $p < 0.05$). Figure 3 shows a chart of the accessed game logs.

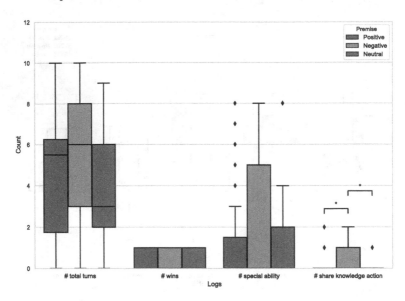

**Fig. 3.** Boxplots of the game logs per condition

## 4.3   Cooperation

We applied Mayring's content analysis method [18] to cluster the the conversations and summarized them into two categories: cooperation approaches and cooperation tasks.

*Cooperation Approaches for Decision Making:* Most players were trying to cooperate and to plan their actions together. However, half of the players decided to take the actions without asking their partners. We identified five pairs (G1p, G2n, G6p G10p, G14o) that always asked their partner's opinion to find the consensus before taking actions. In contrast, in the negative and neutral conditions, decisions were dominated by the players who had more leadership skills (G2n, G7n, G8n, G9n, G12o, G15o). G2n, G5p, G7n started to cooperate for treating/killing/removing actions in different continents. In addition, we observed that all groups that lost the game in the first round adapted their strategies and cooperated closer in the subsequent rounds.

*Cooperation Tasks:* Based on Bernard et al.'s [3] model we identified *divisible*, *disjunctive* and *conjunctive* cooperation tasks.

*Divisible Tasks:* The tasks that can be divided between players in one team, and then integrated together. The example of the scenarios of our games, we found one player from (G2n, G9n, G10o, G11o, G12o) moved to different continents to kill gangsters/remove cubes in their responsible continents in order to avoid the cubes in the storage from running out.

*Disjunctive Tasks:* The tasks that the players completed by assigning more responsibility to one person who has more potential than the other. For our game, we found that in the game with special ability mode, 11 of 15 groups implemented this strategy by using the concept of disjunctive tasks.

*Conjunctive Tasks:* The tasks that require everyone to contribute unique pieces to a puzzle. The conjunctive tasks only succeed when all members succeed. One such scenario involves sharing card action. We found that the players (G1p, G7n, G12o, G14o, G15o) tried to share their cards but did not succeed while (G2n, G9n) were able to use this action.

### 4.4  Premise and Cooperation

To analyze the effect of game premise on players' cooperation, we asked specific questions related to the dramatic elements in the interviews as well as observed cooperation behaviours of players during the gameplay. The difference among three versions are game premise, roles, and special abilities.

*Positive Premise:* 7 of 10 participants like a positive game premise while 3 of 10 participants (P5, P6, P11) mentioned that the premise did not affect their feelings. P7, P8 and P12 highlighted that they enjoyed playing hero, especially when using special abilities. P11 did not feel related to the game as there was no personal relation with the cites. G6 referred to keywords related to game premise when cooperated and mentioned that they feel proud to be a team of heroes. Additionally, G1, G3 and G6 showed more engaged discussions in urgent situations (e.g., when the Epidemic card has been drawn) than groups from other conditions.

*Negative Premise:* 8 of 10 like a negative role. 4 subjects (P4, P13, P16, P17) mentioned a higher sense of achievement. P4, P16, P17 stated they could take a role they cannot take in real-life, but they do not need to handle the consequences of their moral decisions. Also, P16 mentioned that the negative actions was more exciting. Although, P3, P17, P18, P25 liked the negative premise, they preferred to play a positive role. P15, P25, P26 feel related to the cities on the map. P16, P14 were excited to cooperate as gangsters. G2, G7 like cooperative special abilities. Especially "Corrupted politician" and "Killer" were stated as powerful and helpful.

*Neutral Premise:* 7 of 10 participants liked a neutral game premise. Due to this version has an abstract premise, we asked more specific questions to ensure that the players gave opinions based on the game premise and not the gameplay. We asked the players to choose among different roles which are, hero, gangster or being neutral. Only P20 preferred to play with positive premise while (P23, P24, P27, P28, P29, P30) preferred to play an abstract role, since it allows for imagination (P23, P30). P30 also stated, that players just focus on completing the game mission. In contrast to other conditions, G10, G11, G15 used abstract terms to describe their cooperation actions. Further, they mentioned to focus on finding cooperation strategies without concerning the name of actions or the background story.

## 5    Discussion

All participants perceived the game as enjoyable. This is fully supported by the moderate PENS ratings, as well as by many positive comments. Further, the comparable number of turns and winnings indicate that the conditions were comparable and that premise did not affected performance. We identified different cooperative approaches for planning and decision making during gameplay. The players performed divisible, disjunctive and conjunctive cooperative tasks in all conditions, indicating that our game design was successive. Also, the results from the interviews show that all three game versions received positive feedback regarding to the game premise. All subjects agree that the premises fits well with the gameplay. Even though, the results from PENS show that negative premise has the highest ratings for relatedness and competence, most subjects stated that they preferred to play a positive role. The reasons mentioned were related to guiltiness and responsibility for actions. However, subjects from the neutral condition responded that they preferred an abstract role (neutral premise) as it frees space up for imagination and allows to focused on the gameplay itself as well as for exploration of different cooperation strategies.

The results from PENS show that the game premise impacts the pX on relatedness and competence. As the Pearson correlation between gender and PENS shows, females felt more competent and related than males. The negative game version makes players feel most connected with the game and the team members. This is also underpinned by the statements from the interviews where the participants mentioned to be more excited in by the negative premise. The logs show a higher number of share actions in the negative condition, indicating that the negative premise was most effective at fostering cooperative activities. However, there were only 11 share actions in total. Thus these results needs to be interpreted with caution. With special abilities we observe a similar trend, however the data failed to reach significance.

Negative premise showed highest ratings on competence. This is inline with the qualitative results. The participants in negative version mentioned that the goal (eliminating bosses) and actions (killing) provided a high sense of achievement while in positive condition they felt more responsible for the consequence of their mistakes (i.e., failed to save the world). Similarly, participants who played the neutral version mentioned that winning the game had no meaning for them since the game has no context.In contrast, in the positive version, the participants perceived more competence than the neutral groups. In the interviews, some participants stated to feel proud of being heroes.

Our results suggest, that premise has a significant impact on player experience and player cooperation. This can be operationalized in game design in order to achieve specific needs of satisfaction or particular cooperative activities.

## 6    Limitations and Future Work

Although our study shows main effects of premise on player experience and cooperation, we could not identify any specific patterns between the game premise and cooperation strategies. In the future we aim to link how different types of premise can foster specific cooperation patterns and actions considering demographic factors. Further, we asked the participants how they liked their respective premise. These statements are biased by the exposure to the game itself. Future work should investigate unbiased opinions on premise design in cooperative games. Due to small sample size and different distribution of gender in the conditions our findings are not conclusive. Also personality traits were neglected in this study. Future work will investigate how different personalities can be addressed by premise.

However, the results suggest that premise is an easy to use and effective design option to enforce cooperation. This can be useful for game designer, especially improving the engagement of players in serious games. Future research should investigate more specific types of premises and validate these findings in conjunction with learning mechanics in the context of serious games.

## 7 Conclusion

Game premises are deeply anchored into game design. However, so far their impact on player experience and how the players' role affects cooperation in games is under-investigated. We argue, that the framing of players' actions is a simple and effective way to operationalize involvement and sense of competence as well as to push players towards specific cooperation tasks. In this paper, we report on a study that investigates the effect of game premises on player experience and cooperation in a cooperative turn-based game. From our results, we conclude that the game premises can changes players' relatedness and perceived competence in a cooperative game setting. Although a positive role is more attractive in the first place, an antagonistic roles allow a deeper discussion with the game's content. On the other hand, abstract designs with a neutral premise fosters exploration and creativity, however the meaning of the players' actions becomes attenuated. Moreover, our results show that negative roles foster a closer cooperation. Our game design suggest that cooperative games can easily be reframed to positive, negative and neutral premises by defining the respective goals and phrasing of the game mechanics. Designers should consider these options in the development of cooperative games to emphasize the players' role and the relation with the game content. These findings should help researchers and designers to organize the motivational aspects of game premises and provide a starting point for a taxonomy.

## References

1. The effects of adding premise and backstory to psychological tasks. Tech. rep
2. Bergstrom, K., McArthur, V., Jenson, J., Peyton, T.: All in a day's work: a study of world of warcraft npcs comparing gender to professions. In: Proceedings of the 2011 ACM SIGGRAPH Symposium on Video Games, pp. 31–35. ACM (2011)

3. Bass, B.M., Avolio, B.J.: Improving Organizational Effectiveness Through Transformational Leadership. SAGE Publications Inc., Thousand Oaks (1994)
4. Beznosyk, A., Quax, P., Coninx, K., Lamotte, W.: The influence of cooperative game design patterns for remote play on player experience. In: Proceedings of the 10th Asia Pacific Conference on Computer Human Interaction, APCHI 2012, pp. 11–20. ACM, New York (2012)
5. Birk, M.V., Atkins, C., Bowey, J.T., Mandryk, R.L.: Fostering intrinsic motivation through avatar identification in digital games. In: Proceedings of the 2016 CHI Conference on Human Factors in Computing Systems, CHI 2016, pp. 2982–2995. ACM, New York (2016)
6. Clemson, H., Coulton, P., Edwards, R.: A serendipitous mobile game. In: Proceedings of the 4th Annual International Conference in Computer Game Design and Technology (GDTW 2006), pp. 130–134 (2006)
7. Emmerich, K., Masuch, M.: The impact of game patterns on player experience and social interaction in co-located multiplayer games. In: Proceedings of the Annual Symposium on Computer-Human Interaction in Play, CHI PLAY 2017, pp. 411–422. ACM, New York (2017)
8. Fullerton, T.: Game Design Workshop: A Playcentric Approach to Creating Innovative Games. AK Peters/CRC Press, Boca Raton (2014)
9. Fullerton, T.: Game Design Workshop: A Playcentric Approach to Creating Innovative Games. AK Peters/CRC Press, Boca Raton (2018)
10. Holmes, J.R., et al.: A good scare: leveraging game theming and narrative to impact player experience. In: Extended Abstracts of the 2019 CHI Conference on Human Factors in Computing Systems, p. LBW0178. ACM (2019)
11. Electronic Arts Inc.: SimCity. Online (1982)
12. Iten, G.H., Steinemann, S.T., Opwis, K.: Choosing to help monsters: a mixed-method examination of meaningful choices in narrative-rich games and interactive narratives. In: Proceedings of the 2018 CHI Conference on Human Factors in Computing Systems, p. 341. ACM (2018)
13. Johnson, D., Wyeth, P., Clark, M., Watling, C.: Cooperative game play with avatars and agents: differences in brain activity and the experience of play. In: Proceedings of the 33rd Annual ACM Conference on Human Factors in Computing Systems (2015)
14. Kivikangas, J.M., Kätsyri, J., Järvelä, S., Ravaja, N.: Gender differences in emotional responses to cooperative and competitive game play. PloS one 9(7), e100318 (2014)
15. Krause, M., Takhtamysheva, A., Wittstock, M., Malaka, R.: Frontiers of a paradigm: exploring human computation with digital games. In: Proceedings of the Acm Sigkdd Workshop on Human Computation, pp. 22–25. ACM (2010)
16. Liebrand, W.B., Jansen, R.W., Rijken, V.M., Suhre, C.J.: Might over morality: social values and the perception of other players in experimental games. J. Exp. Soc. Psychol. 22(3), 203–215 (1986). https://doi.org/10.1016/0022-1031(86)90024-7
17. Malaka, R.: How computer games can improve your health and fitness. In: Göbel, S., Wiemeyer, J. (eds.) GameDays 2014. LNCS, vol. 8395, pp. 1–7. Springer, Cham (2014). https://doi.org/10.1007/978-3-319-05972-3_1
18. Mayring, P.: The qualitative content analysis process. Forum: Qualitative Social Research (FQS) 1(2, Art. 20) (2000). https://doi.org/10.1111/j.1365-2648.2007.04569.x. http://www.qualitative-research.net/fqs/
19. Miller, M.K., Summers, A.: Gender differences in video game characters' roles, appearances, and attire as portrayed in video game magazines. Sex roles 57(9–10), 733–742 (2007)

20. Rauch, P.E.: Playing with good and evil: videogames and moral philosophy (2007)
21. Rigby, S., Ryan, R.: The player experience of need satisfaction (PENS) model. Immersyve Inc., pp. 1–22 (2007)
22. Ryan, R.M., Rigby, C.S., Przybylski, A.: The motivational pull of video games: a self-determination theory approach. Motiv. Emot. **30**(4), 344–360 (2006)
23. Sedano, C.I., Carvalho, M.B., Secco, N., Longstreet, C.S.: Collaborative and cooperative games: Facts and assumptions. In: Proceedings of the 2013 International Conference on Collaboration Technologies and Systems, CTS 2013 (2013). https://doi.org/10.1109/CTS.2013.6567257
24. Triandis, H.C.: The self and social behavior in differing cultural contexts. Psychol. Rev. **96**(3), 506 (1989)
25. Weaver, A.J., Lewis, N.: Mirrored morality: an exploration of moral choice in video games. Cyberpsychol. Behav. Soc. Netw. **15**(11), 610–614 (2012). https://doi.org/10.1089/cyber.2012.0235
26. Wendel, V., Göbel, S., Steinmetz, R.: Collaborative learning in multiplayer serious games. Clash Realities Proc. **2012** (2012)
27. Wendel, V., Gutjahr, M., Göbel, S., Steinmetz, R.: Designing collaborative multiplayer serious games: escape from wilson island-a multiplayer 3d serious game for collaborative learning in teams. Educ. Inf. Technol. (2013). https://doi.org/10.1007/s10639-012-9244-6
28. Leacock, M.: Pandemic. Z-Man Games, Board game (2008)
29. Zagal, J.P., Rick, J., Hsi, I.: Collaborative games: lessons learned from board games. Simul. Gaming (2006). https://doi.org/10.1177/1046878105282279

# Procedural Content Generation in Competitive Multiplayer Platform Games

Georg Volkmar[✉], Nikolas Mählmann, and Rainer Malaka

Digital Media Lab, TZI, University of Bremen, 28359 Bremen, Germany
{gvolkmar,nikmaehl}@uni-bremen.de, malaka@tzi.de
https://www.uni-bremen.de/

**Abstract.** Procedural content generation (PCG) techniques have become increasingly established over the years in the context of video games. In terms of generating level layouts, PCG has proven to be a cost-efficient alternative to handcrafted design processes. However, previous research is mostly concerned with singleplayer experiences only. Since multiplayer games differ strongly in regards to the requirements that have to be met by map layouts, we addressed the following question: Which PCG approaches are suited best to ensure qualities relevant in the area of level creation for competitive multiplayer platform games? We conclude that a combination of constructive and grammar-based methods serves as a viable solution. We developed a PCG prototype which was integrated into a competitive platform game. Results of a user study indicate that a constructive-grammar PCG algorithm can be used to generate map layouts that are perceived to be fun and compelling.

**Keywords:** Game design · Procedural content generation · Multiplayer platform games

## 1 Introduction

In recent years, the use of procedural content generation (PCG)[1] has risen in popularity, especially in the context of video game content generation [7]. PCG has become highly attractive for game development studios in terms of cost-efficiency since it offers a more time- and money-saving alternative [5]. Various elements of video games are suited to be generated procedurally. One established application domain in the field of video game related PCG is the construction of levels for platform games such as *Super Mario Bros.* [15,19]. However, previous research heavily focused on the utilization of such methods for singleplayer experiences. Since multiplayer games differ immensely in terms of structure and

---

[1] In the domain of games, procedural content generation can be defined as "the algorithmical creation of game content with limited or indirect user input." [20].

© IFIP International Federation for Information Processing 2019
Published by Springer Nature Switzerland AG 2019
E. van der Spek et al. (Eds.): ICEC-JCSG 2019, LNCS 11863, pp. 228–234, 2019.
https://doi.org/10.1007/978-3-030-34644-7_18

gameplay, it is questionable whether these established methods can be applied without alteration. Thus, the first problem addressed in this paper is concerned with the identification of quality requirements for procedurally generated multiplayer platform maps. Additionally, we review a number of various commonly used PCG techniques in terms of suitability to satisfy these demands. Aside from covering the technical aspects of PCG-based level generation, we have to bear in mind, that games are ultimately developed to be enjoyable forms of entertainment. Though it has been shown that PCG can lead to higher replayability and new forms of gameplay [18], it remains unclear if an entertaining experience can be provided in the context of competitive multiplayer platform games. Therefore, we evaluate whether procedurally generated maps provide a satisfying player experience. This paper is a contribution to the research domain of procedural content generation and the empiric validation of PCG methods.

## 2 Identification of Quality Requirements

In this section, we compile a list of quality requirements that have to be met for the generator to be a viable solution. How to evaluate the quality of video games in a standardized way is a topic of debate as the consumption of games is highly subjective leading to different preferences based on personality and experience [10]. However, literature in the domain of video game design has brought up a variety of quality criteria that can be considered when evaluating games [1,2,6, 8,13,14]. For the purpose of evaluating the quality of the procedurally generated maps used in a multiplayer platform game, we have derived a number of criteria from the mentioned literature:

**Internal Completeness**: In an internally complete game, the player never reaches a point that leads to compromising gameplay or functionality [6]. For that purpose, unreachable areas and dead ends[2] should be avoided in any case. This property is especially relevant in a multiplayer scenario since dead ends might lead to the feeling of unfair level design. Reaching a dead end as one player might give the opponent a competitive edge and the opportunity to strike the other player down.

**Flow**: Traditionally, the concept of *Flow* describes a mental state of being fully involved in an activity while the proportion of the task's challenge to the operator's skills is perfectly balanced [3]. In video games, *Flow* strongly correlates with immersion and player enjoyment [6,14]. In the context of multiplayer games, an applicable level generator shouldn't create obstacles that act as hindrances for the players and reduce *Flow*. Therefore, lethal gaps, spikes, traps and the likes should be used scarcely and gaps should be designed smaller than the maximum jumping range of players.

**Risks and Rewards**: Having meaningful and impactful choices spread throughout a game can increase player enjoyment immensely [6]. To have a positive effect,

---

[2] "A dead end occurs when a player gets stranded in the game and cannot continue toward the game objective [...]" [6].

choices need to be designed in proportion to *Risks and Rewards*. In competitive platform games, risks can be designed as gaps or spikes whereas rewards typically take the form of power-ups. Both should be spread over the map in a way that gives meaning to player choices (e.g. placing a power-up in an area that's hard to reach). For multiplayer games, *Risks and Rewards* face the challenge of providing a fair distribution of items such as power-ups.

**Diversity**: As mentioned before, increasing the level of replayability is one core motivational factor to utilize PCG methods. For this purpose, generated map layouts should provide a certain *Diversity* in level structure. For multiplayer games, this factor gains even more relevance as playing the same or similar map over and over again would lead to boredom and players using the same tactics that have proven to work on the map layout.

**Performance**: According to a recent survey conducted by *Electronic Entertainment Design and Research (EEDAR)*, 72% of the interviewed PC players stated that reasonable loading times are a key factor when it comes to enjoyment in playing video games [4]. In multiplayer games, players already spend many seconds or even minutes before the actual game starts by waiting for other players in a lobby or contents to be downloaded [11]. For the *Performance* requirement to be fulfilled, we define a threshold of 15 s, as loading times below that time span are generally considered "good" [9].

**Determinism**: Modern games such as *Minecraft* [12] allow players to share randomly generated maps with others by providing a seed. For competitive multiplayer games, *Determinism* plays a vital role as it allows to repeat a match on a specific map multiple times, ensuring fairness among all players for tournament-like game modes.

## 3   Review of PCG Methods for Level Generation

PCG techniques can be divided into the following categories: optimization, constraint satisfaction, grammars, content selection and constructive [18]. Algorithms based on optimization generate content iteratively based on quality evaluation. The generative process endures until a sufficient result is achieved [16]. The evaluation can be conducted by humans or the algorithm itself. If conducted by the algorithm, optimization is computationally expensive, especially if the generated content ought to be playable [21]. Since we have identified *Performance* as a vital requirement, optimization-based approaches might not be the perfect solution. Constraint satisfaction requires a level designer to formulate properties that a generated map should provide which in turn are fed into a constraint solver algorithm. This method of content generation has been utilized before to create solvable tile-based mazes [17] and might proof suitable for multiplayer platformers as well. Content selection describes a method of generating content by assembling smaller pieces into larger segments. Despite fulfilling the *Performance* requirement, it is rather questionable if generated maps will entail the needed level of *Diversity* as players might notice repeating patterns

[18]. Grammars can be used in the context of PCG with the help of production rules. If these rules are well defined, content does not require additional evaluation leading to an increased *Performance* [18]. Constructive generators combine building blocks that represent small pieces of content to create levels. Often, they are tailored to fit a specific game and do not need any additional evaluation, similar to grammars [18].

## 4   Prototype Implementation

From reviewing existing literature, we conclude that constraint satisfaction, grammars and constructive approaches may provide the qualities we identified as vital in multiplayer platformer levels. For a first prototype, we developed a constructive-grammar algorithm combining the advantages of both techniques in Haskell. As a basic principle, the approach described here fills up an empty map by combining pre-authored building blocks until the area is occupied entirely. As a starting point, we have defined the following set of building blocks or tiles, commonly used in platform games: *air* - players can move freely, *border* - define the frame of each level, *spike* - kill players upon contact, *surface* - provide platforms for players to stand on and finally *any* - tiles in an unfinished map that need to be filled by other types of tiles. With the help of these building blocks, we have created a standard empty map, consisting of a large area of *any* tiles, confined by *border* tiles. At the bottom, *spike* tiles are placed to kill players that fall off the screen. This basic layout served as an initial input for our PCG algorithm to build a level from. Next up, as the map shall be filled with sets of tiles, we had to define a collection of building blocks for the generator to choose from and combine. For this purpose, we have grouped standard tiles into larger segments that served as building blocks. Combining these blocks randomly can lead to malformed level structure which is clearly a violation of the *Internal Completeness* requirement we identified before. This is where grammars and production rules come into play. A single rule could be described as follows: "Building blocks are only to be inserted if they do not overwrite existing tiles in the process." While making sure that all rules are respected, the algorithm integrates building blocks into the map until no insertions can be performed anymore. As a final step in level generation, power-ups and player-spawns were spread over the map. Ultimately, the level generator was integrated into a competitive multiplayer game. The structure of the game was kept rather simple, two players spawn at dedicated positions and aim to hit each other with flying disks that have to be thrown in the other player's direction (see Fig. 1).

## 5   Evaluation

After the development of the constructive-grammar prototype had been concluded, we conducted an evaluation based on quality requirements that were defined beforehand.

**Fig. 1.** Screenshots taken from *Diskophoros*, which was played in the study.

## 5.1 Performance Assessment

To get quantitative measures rating performance, we ran the algorithm 1000 times and noted the time individually for each round. Execution times varied between 0.43 and 6.47 s ($M = 0.43$) while about 99% of recorded times lie below 3 s. Since we had defined the threshold of operation time as a maximum of 15 s, we argue that our approach fulfills the *Performance* requirement sufficiently.

## 5.2 Explorative Pre-study

To get a first insight regarding the remaining requirements *Flow*, *Risk and Rewards* and *Diversity*, we conducted a small-scale user study. For this purpose, we integrated the constructive-grammar PCG algorithm into the existing multiplayer platform game *Diskophoros*.

**Participants.** The experiment consisted of two trials in which two subjects competed against each other. In the first group, two male software developers, aged 39 and 30 years participated. The second group contained two male students, both aged 22 years studying computer science and teaching.

**Procedure.** Before being exposed to procedurally generated maps, subjects were playing a test run on handcrafted levels. When they felt comfortable with the game's controls and overall gameplay, participants were asked to play on random maps, created by the constructive-grammar algorithm, for 20 min. During the procedure, the examiner took notes of observations and feedback given by the players. Ultimately, all subjects filled in a short questionnaire.

**Material.** The study was conducted using a PC with Windows 10 and standard game controllers. For data collection, a questionnaire was compiled that contained questions aimed to examine certain qualities of the game such as *Diversity*, *Flow*, overall impression and wishes for improvements.

**Results.** Three participants explicitly stated that they liked the game in terms of *Diversity*. No subjects mentioned monotony or repetition to be a problem. All players agreed that the game felt enjoyable and playable. As for suggestions for improvement, some pointed out that gaps between platforms were sometimes too large and that maps felt a little empty. Moreover, players criticized cavities that emerged in some maps leading to unescapable death traps and a distortion of *Flow*. Being asked regarding the collection of power-ups, all subjects agreed that they didn't feel like they had to pay extra attention to them and just picked them up. Hence, *Risks and Rewards* felt like they were balanced properly.

**Discussion.** We need to address some limitations of the study and its reliability in general. It is important to note that this user study served as a first evaluation of the constructive-grammar approach in terms of playability. The objective of this study was to gather qualitative data in order to collect user insights that shall help to improve the map generator. It should be taken into consideration that our study involved a very small sample which is sufficient to obtain qualitative data but shouldn't be misinterpreted as a representative group. Additionally, since only male subjects took part in the study, results are gender-biased, potentially leading to skewed effects.

## 6   Conclusion and Future Work

The aim of this paper was to examine the applicability of PCG techniques in the context of multiplayer platform games under consideration of quality criteria that are required in this genre. For the purpose of addressing this topic, we identified a set of quality requirements (*Internal Completeness, Flow, Risks and Rewards, Diversity, Performance* and *Determinism*) and concluded that a combination of constructive and grammar-based methods have the potential to satisfy those needs. Furthermore, we investigated if PCG-based levels offer a satisfying player experience in a competitive multiplayer platform game. To analyze this problem, we conducted an explorative user study and came to realize that procedurally generated map layouts can indeed provide a fun and engaging experience for the players involved.

Concerning future developments, we plan to address the following remaining issues. Regarding the empiric validation of our approach, we rely on a few heavily gender-biased samples, limiting the reliability of the user study immensely. On top of that, only qualitative data has been gathered so far. Therefore, we will conduct another study involving more participants and standardized questionnaires to compare PCG-based levels with hand-crafted ones.

**Acknowledgements.** We would like to thank all participants of the study for their time and effort. This work was partially funded by the EU-project *first.stage*.

## References

1. Costkyan, G.: I have no words & i must design: toward a critical vocabulary for games. In: Proceedings of the Computer Games and Digital Cultures Conference, Finland (2002)
2. Crawford, C.: The art of computer game design (1984)

3. Csikszentmihalyi, M., Csikszentmihalyi, I.: Beyond Boredom and Anxiety, vol. 721. Jossey-Bass, San Francisco (1975)
4. Electronic Entertainment Design and Research: Gaming infrastructure survey (2017). https://www.akamai.com/uk/en/multimedia/documents/report/akamai-eedar-gaming-infrastructure-survey.pdf
5. Franklin-Wallis, O.: Games of the future will be developed by algorithms, not humans, January 2016. https://www.wired.co.uk/article/games-developed-by-algorithms
6. Fullerton, T.: Game Design Workshop: A Playcentric Approach to Creating Innovative Games. AK Peters/CRC Press, Natick (2014)
7. Hendrikx, M., Meijer, S., Van Der Velden, J., Iosup, A.: Procedural content generation for games: a survey. ACM Trans. Multimed. Comput. Commun. Appl. (TOMM) **9**(1), 1 (2013)
8. Hunicke, R., LeBlanc, M., Zubek, R.: MDA: a formal approach to game design and game research. In: Proceedings of the AAAI Workshop on Challenges in Game AI, vol. 4, p. 1722 (2004)
9. Ip, B., Jacobs, G.: Quantifying game design. Des. Stud. **25**(6), 607–624 (2004)
10. Johnson, D., Gardner, J.: Personality, motivation and video games. In: Proceedings of the 22nd Conference of the Computer-Human Interaction Special Interest Group of Australia on Computer-Human Interaction, pp. 276–279. ACM (2010)
11. King, D., Delfabbro, P., Griffiths, M.: Video game structural characteristics: a new psychological taxonomy. Int. J. Ment. Health Addict. **8**(1), 90–106 (2010)
12. Mojang: Minecraft. Game [PC], May 2009
13. Salen, K., Tekinbaş, K.S., Zimmerman, E.: Rules of Play: Game Design Fundamentals. MIT Press, Cambridge (2004)
14. Schell, J.: The Art of Game Design: A Book of Lenses. AK Peters/CRC Press, Natick (2014)
15. Shaker, N., Nicolau, M., Yannakakis, G.N., Togelius, J., O'neill, M.: Evolving levels for Super Mario Bros using grammatical evolution. In: 2012 IEEE Conference on Computational Intelligence and Games (CIG), pp. 304–311. IEEE (2012)
16. Shaker, N., Togelius, J., Nelson, M.J.: Procedural Content Generation in Games. Springer, Cham (2016). https://doi.org/10.1007/978-3-319-42716-4
17. Smith, A.M., Mateas, M.: Answer set programming for procedural content generation: a design space approach. IEEE Trans. Comput. Intell. AI Games **3**(3), 187–200 (2011)
18. Smith, G.: Understanding procedural content generation: a design-centric analysis of the role of PCG in games. In: Proceedings of the 32nd Annual ACM Conference on Human Factors in Computing Systems, pp. 917–926. ACM (2014)
19. Snodgrass, S., Ontañón, S.: Player movement models for video game level generation. In: Proceedings of the Twenty-Sixth International Joint Conference on Artificial Intelligence, IJCAI 2017, pp. 757–763 (2017). https://doi.org/10.24963/ijcai.2017/105
20. Togelius, J., Kastbjerg, E., Schedl, D., Yannakakis, G.N.: What is procedural content generation?: Mario on the borderline. In: Proceedings of the 2nd International Workshop on Procedural Content Generation in Games, p. 3. ACM (2011)
21. Togelius, J., Yannakakis, G.N., Stanley, K.O., Browne, C.: Search-based procedural content generation: a taxonomy and survey. IEEE Trans. Comput. Intell. AI Games **3**(3), 172–186 (2011)

# Interaction Technologies

# Creating Layouts for Virtual Game Controllers Using Generative Design

Gabriel F. Alves, Anselmo A. Montenegro⬤, and Daniela G. Trevisan$^{(\boxtimes)}$⬤

Universidade Federal Fluminense, Niteroi, Rio de Janeiro, Brazil
gabrielferreiraalves@id.uff.br, {anselmo,daniela}@ic.uff.br
http://www.ic.uff.br

**Abstract.** Video game controllers have a high influence factor on play-ers, as they are responsible for the fun, motivation, and personality of a game. The organization and arrangement of the buttons are one of the relevant factors when developing new controllers since they are respon-sible for serving as an input of actions within the games. This work presents the construction of a generative design model to support game designers finding different and innovative layouts of virtual controllers for their games. The generative design produces many valid designs or solu-tions instead of one optimized version of a known solution. This solution was developed by linking genetic algorithms to generate a large number of layouts and machine learning techniques (SVN) to classify individu-als between valid and invalid, seeking to facilitate the exploration of the design space by the designer. The tests performed sought to measure the variability of the results generated by the proposed model, showing that several solutions of different controllers with different configurations can be developed for a game.

**Keywords:** Generative design · Gamepad · Virtual controller · Genetic algorithm · Machine learning

## 1 Introduction

With the advancement of technology and thanks to its dynamism, touchscreen devices like smartphones and tablets have also become game controllers: the vir-tual gamepads. They are dynamic because they have components and devices such as Bluetooth and wireless, accelerometers, gyroscopes and cameras. These components may contribute to the development of different forms of interaction with digital games [2], either in games played on the mobile devices themselves or in games played on another device. Because these controllers can access device components by touching the screen and/or by moving and rotating the device, the buttons on the virtual controller can follow the rules of the game, so it is not necessary to include several buttons that will not be used during the gameplay.

---

Granted by CAPES, Brazil.

E. van der Spek et al. (Eds.): ICEC-JCSG 2019, LNCS 11863, pp. 237–249, 2019.
https://doi.org/10.1007/978-3-030-34644-7_19

Unfortunately, this is not possible in physical controllers, because once the controller has been built, all the buttons will always be available to the user, even if they have no use in certain games. Each game has a finite number of actions and interactions that are not necessarily the same as in other games and can vary between different genres of games, such as action and adventure games; sports and shooting; race and platform; and even within the same genre of games. These actions are usually associated with a single button on the controller. Therefore, there will be a maximum number of buttons required to perform all interactions in the game. On the other hand, generative design is a promising approach to solve various aspects related to User Interface [15]. It offers new opportunities for conception and creation problems in areas such as engineering, architecture, and design, making it possible, through the use of meta-heuristics, to determine the layout of UI components, informing only a limited amount of parameters and producing new and sometimes, unexpected results [15].

Based on all this knowledge, the goal of this work is to develop a tool that can help game designers to find different and innovative layouts of virtual controllers for their games, since a virtual controller can be implemented especially for a specific game, containing only the actions necessary for it. Therefore, it is not the purpose of this paper to provide layouts for physical video game controllers. Thus, we defined a generative design model [4], where the designer must tell to the system what actions the player should be able to perform within the game, the number of layouts he/she wants the model to deliver as output and how many iterations the algorithm will perform before constructing these layouts. A genetic evolution-based approach has been used to generate a huge variety of layouts and, based on information added to a pre-trained database, the model can generate and suggest a set of valid controller configurations for the desired game. A machine learning approach has been applied to filter the most usable and appropriate set of layouts to be presented to the game designer. This approach was chosen because the generative design provides a wide range of solutions, but it is not feasible for the professional to analyze all of them. Based on the generated and filtered results, the designer will be able to choose which one suits his/her game and, if necessary, make adjustments and refinements to its design. A generative design-based solution can be used as a robust starting point where the results can be refined by software engineers and artists [15]. Therefore, it is important to point out that this tool is a software that provides creative support to the designer, the true responsible for the development of the controller of his/her game.

## 2    Related Work

In order to help game designers to develop one or more layouts of ideal and innovative virtual controllers for their games, we sought to find approaches, techniques, and methodologies that would aid in the process of creating ideas and supporting the design process. After researching in academic libraries such as Google Scholar and the ACM library, no results were found on the use of

Generative Design applied in the area of digital game controllers, so this section will present works and knowledge that have been served as the basis for the development of our solution.

Usually, the virtual gamepads follow some rules and are created based on existing organizational elements in physical controllers, such as the grouping of directional buttons, the possibility of incorporation of d-pads, the existence of buttons action, among others. Looking for solutions to support the design process of game controllers, some researchers have tried to use a set of Design Thinking techniques, such as a day in the life, empathy map, persona, ideation workshop and paper prototyping to design a game controller that pleases its players [1]. The developed prototypes have sought to soften and even eliminate the problem of the lack of tactile feedback in touchscreen devices by using personalized skins over smartphones. However, although the work relates to this in the way they look for new solutions that support the design process, no software support for the design process has been provided. Baldauf et al. [3] has developed four virtual controllers based on existing controllers configurations. A comparative laboratory study was conducted where four gamepad smartphone designs were selected. Each was tested in two popular games: Pac-Man and Super Mario Bros. The construction of different configurations of virtual controllers for games is the main relationship between our work and that of the authors, although our work aims to assist and give creative support to the designer, and not to create the controller itself. Regarding approaches that use artificial intelligence techniques to support the design of game controllers, we point out the work of Torok et al. [14] that deals with the design of adaptive game controllers for touchscreen devices. Their solution introduces an adaptation that derives the user's personal preferences from a series of basic events, such as button presses or internal gameplay changes. The main disadvantage of this approach is that the controller layout adaptation takes place during the player interaction time. At times, many changes on the fly to the controller layout may confuse the player, but on the other hand, this can be used by the designer as a way of adding different levels of difficulty to their game. Our work bears similarities to the work of Torok et al. [14], mainly in the quest to find solutions for virtual controllers. However, his work builds the solutions in interaction time, while this work produces them in time of design.

In his work, Krish [8] proposes a Computer-Aided Design (CAD) Generative Design model suitable for complex multi-criteria design problems in which important performance criteria are incomputable. This method is based on the construction of a genotyping project within a parametric CAD system based on history and then its parameters undergo random variations within predefined limits to generate a set of distinct projects. After the designs are generated, they are filtered through multiple constraint envelopes, representing geometric feasibility, manufacturability, cost, and other performance-related constraints, thus reducing the design space in a smaller, feasible design space, represented by a set of different designs.

By contrast, many of the technologies that masquerade as generative design such as topology optimization, lattice optimization, parametric optimization or similar technologies are focused on improving a preexisting design, not creating new design possibilities as in the generative design. The confusion arises because the inputs to generative design are similar to the inputs to many optimization tools. However, generative design produces many valid designs or solutions instead of one optimized version of a known solution. Genetic Algorithms are metaheuristic methods inspired by natural selection [5] and are unquestionably the most dominant in computational design exploration [8].

## 3    Methodology and Implementation

The architecture of the proposed model consists of three stages: parameter specification, exploring the design space (by the genetic algorithm) and filtering the most relevant solutions (by machine learning). In the first part, the user - a game designer - informs the model of the essential parameters for the creation of layouts that will be given as results. The model, in its current state, receives the following parameters: the number of buttons, the actions that these buttons execute within the game, the number of layouts that should be generated by the model and the number of iterations it should run. The second part is responsible for creating layouts based on the parameters entered by the user. These layouts will be randomly defined at the beginning of the model execution, pass through genetic operators, will be evaluated by a fitness function and some of the selected individuals will generate the next population. The algorithm will perform these operations $n$ times, where $n$ is the number of iterations defined by the designer. At the end of the iterations, the final set of layouts, also called the final population, will be defined. Many individuals may be produced at this time. The third and last part of the model was precisely defined so that it was possible to present to the designer just those who had some use for him/her. Therefore, the machine learning Support Vector Machine (SVM) algorithm was used to classify individuals between valid and invalid, separating them so the user could analyze a smaller range of results.

The solution development was done using the Java-based language called 'Processing' [11], highly recommended in the generative design community because it is a free, easy-to-use and flexible software sketchbook and language. Figure 1 illustrates the pipeline of the proposed generative design model which is detailed in the following subsections.

### 3.1    Input Parameters

In order to start the model's development, it was necessary to carry out a previous study on games, their styles and the ways of controlling them. It is said by Rogers [12] that all games fit into a previously established genre, and a game can fit into one or more genres, where one is dominant. An example is the game

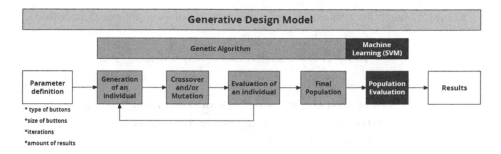

**Fig. 1.** The proposed generative design model pipeline.

The Last of Us [10] released for PlayStation3 and remastered for PlayStation4, classified as an action game containing features of a puzzle and shooting game.

To classify a game in a given genre, it must be possible to perform some specific actions during gameplay. For example, one of the genres that a game can be classified is the "Platform" genre. In Platform games, the player must be able to perform the actions "walk", "run", "jump" and "act", the latter being a variable determined by the game designer, such as throwing an item, triggering a device or performing a hit.

With the knowledge about game genres, it was possible to list the actions that can be performed within them. These actions - from moving to pausing a game - are the first input parameters that the designer must inform the model. Other defined parameter is related to the genetic algorithm: population size and the number of iterations.

### 3.2 Exploring the Design Space

In order to explore the design space for the creation of virtual controllers, we used a genetic algorithm. To understand the logic of the system, it is necessary to understand some terms, such as 'population', 'individual', 'fitness' and 'roulette'. A population consists of two or more individuals, while an individual consists of a set of configurations of a controller. By controller configuration, we are talking about a layout and its components, such as the number of buttons, button types, button classifications and their positions (X and Y axes) on the screen. For the development of the system, some data structures were defined. In the data structure associated with each individual, we define three arrays called chromosomes, and each of them stores essential information for the creation of individuals:

- chromosomeX: contains the X-axis positions of all buttons requested by the designer;
- chromosomeY: contains the Y-axis positions of the buttons;
- classification: contains the classification of the button (the role that such button assumes within a control, what action it assumes).

The most basic button classes defined in the model are presented in Table 1.

**Table 1.** Basic button classes and actions.

| Classes | Buttons | | | |
|---|---|---|---|---|
| Directional buttons | Up | Down | Left | Right |
| Action buttons | Jump | Shoot | Run | Defend |
| Extra buttons | L1 | L2 | R1 | R2 |
| System buttons | Start | Select | – | – |

The size of the chromosomes is defined at the beginning of the process, when the user informs the number of buttons that the controller should have, making it possible to perform the actions within the game. In addition to these three vectors, each individual also carries some attributes:

- fitness: a numerical value responsible for representing how apt an individual is to follow to a new population;
- fitnessPercent: the fitness value represented in percentage;
- rouletteTrack: the range that the individual holds over the roulette of individuals' selection. This will be detailed later.

When an individual is created, the position chromosomes containing the X and Y positions of the buttons are filled with random values, causing each button to assume a random position within the controller area and the classification chromosome is filled with labels for the actions listed on Table 1. The value of the fitness attribute is defined by the fitness that an individual has to maintain in the next generations of the algorithm. Let $L$ be a layout candidate, i.e., an individual in the population, with $n$ buttons. Let $bx$ and $by$ be two arrays that store, respectively, the x and y coordinates of each button $i$, $0 \leq i < n$. Moreover, let us define $bt$ as an array that identifies the type or class of a given button $i$. The objective function that defines the fitness value of a layout $L$ is given by:

$$f(bx, by, bt) = \sum_{i=0}^{n-1} \sum_{j=i+1}^{n-1} \left[ \left( \frac{1 - \delta(bt_i, bt_j)}{l} dist(bx_i, by_i, bx_j, by_j) \right) \right.$$
$$\left. + \alpha\delta(bt_i, bt_j) \left( \frac{1}{1 + dist(bx_i, by_i, bx_j, by_j)} \right) \right] \quad (1)$$

where $\delta(bt_i, bt_j)$ is 1 if buttons $i$ and $j$ belong to the same class and 0 if they are in different classes. The Euclidean distance between two buttons is given by $dist(bx_i, by_i, bx_j, by_j)$, $l = \sqrt{(w+h)}$ is a normalization factor, where $w$ and $h$ are the width and height of the layout, and $\alpha$ is a weight. In our model, we set the $\alpha$ value as six. The first term in the sum is responsible for creating a separation between buttons from different classes, and the second term tries to approximate buttons in the same class. Having defined a fitness value for the individual, the percentage relative to his fitness is calculated and, according to it, the rouletteTrack is defined. The roulette is a technique of selecting individuals. Through it, all individuals have attached to them a range of a roulette wheel, this range is defined based on their fitness: individuals with higher fitness values will have larger range bands in it, thus having a greater chance of being selected to be part of the new population. Although individuals with lower fitness scores have smaller roulette intervals, they still have a chance of being selected to participate in the new population, causing diversity among individuals. Determining the roulette tracks for each individual is done using the fitnessPercent value to assign the ranges: (1) the first step is to sort the population in ascending order using the fitnessPercent values; (2) after that, each individual is linked to a roulette track - the first receives the initial range, which ranges from zero to his fitnessPercent. The next individual will go from the fitnessPercent value of the previous individual to the sum of this value with their percentage; (3) until 100% of the roulette wheel is distributed. With fitness and fitnessPercent values calculated and having defined the ranges of roulette that each individual possesses, the execution of the genetic operations are triggered. By the number of iterations required, the following steps will be performed: (1) a new population is defined; (2) for each individual in the population, a value between 0 and 100% will be drawn. The individual whose track in the roulette contains such value will be selected to undergo the following operations; (3) mutation operators may be triggered to modify the individual; (4) the individual will be added in this new population and old individuals will be removed.

In this work, we did not use any Crossover operators. Instead, we used two mutation operators with 50% probability of a mutation type 1 to occur, while the probability of a mutation type 2 occurring is 80%. The first mutation is responsible for changing the position of any button within the generated layout. This operation calculates an offset vector in any direction and moves the button to a maximum distance of 100 pixels from its original position. The second mutation is responsible for exchanging the position of one or more buttons with other buttons on the same layout - for example, the directional button 'up' exchanges its position with the 'jump' action button.

Finally, it is necessary to check if there is no collision between the buttons, that is if one button does not overlap another within a layout. At the end of $n$ iterations, the final population will be defined and can proceed to the next step: filtering the design space using the Support Vector Machine (SVM) algorithm.

## 3.3    Filtering the Design Space

The search for a solution that applied labels to the results given by the genetic solution was necessary because evaluating all the generated layouts is a tiresome task and the objective function used in the genetic algorithm does not capture all aspects of good design. This was a strategy used to keep the originality and variability of the individuals generated. By embedding too much rules and constraints in the objective function we could drastically reduce the variability of the individuals.

Each button in a controller carries with it a semantics that gives a meaning to its presence in the layout. An 'up' directional button is expected to be positioned above the other directional buttons, which makes the interaction between player and controller more dynamic, easy, and intuitive. Thus, the classification of individuals from different populations was performed considering the position of the buttons in the controller area, the groupings between them and the distances between the buttons of the same class - directional, action or system buttons. This knowledge, orginated in the designer rationale, is learned by the Support Vector Machine (SVM) classifier during the training set.

Based on a previously trained database *(training set)*, the SVM algorithm can classify other databases *(test set)*, automating the process of selecting individuals. For the model, two classifications are made: valid individuals and invalid individuals. The first are those that may be chosen by the designer as candidates for game controller configurations, given the position of the buttons in the controller area, while the second classification is formed by layouts that do not represent configurations that can be used by the final user. After that, the model displays the results for the designer, separating them according to the classification that the SVM has produced. To training the dataset to classify three-button layouts, 301 individuals were labeled manually by a designer, where 150 were labeled 'valid' and 151 as 'invalid'. The SVM training resulted in correct classification of 259 individuals, 86.05% of the entire population. Another population with 306 individuals were manually classified to construct the dataset responsible for classifying controllers configurations with nine buttons. From that, 131 individuals were classified as 'valid' and 175 as 'invalid'. At this case, 273 individuals were correctly classified, corresponding to 89.21% of the settings.

## 4 Tests and Results

The experiments were carried out to find out if there is any relation between the number of iterations and the number of valid individuals generated by the model and, in addition, to measure the variability of the results. It is important that the model provides a range of useful results for the designer and that the layouts are not all similar to each other.

First, it was necessary to define which genre of games we will generate the layouts of the controllers. We assume that the game designer wants to build virtual controllers for games of the platform genre, where some specific actions must be made available to be executed in it. One of the controllers should have only three buttons: two directional buttons (left and right) and one action button (jump) and another controller setting should have nine buttons: the four directional buttons (up, down, right and left), four other action buttons (jump, shoot, defend and run) and a system button (start). After chosing the configurations as a function of the number of buttons we define the number of iterations of the evolutionary algorithm and the number of individuals in the final population. Ten different types of iterations were defined: 1000, 2000, 3000, up to

10,000 iterations. The number of individuals was established as 1000, 2000 and 3000 individuals for each controller configuration with three and nine buttons. A total of 60 populations were obtained. After creating all the settings, each population was submitted to the evaluations of the SVM classifier that, according to a previously trained database, classifies each layout between 'valid' or 'invalid'. In this case, specific classification databases were used for three and nine buttons (Fig. 2).

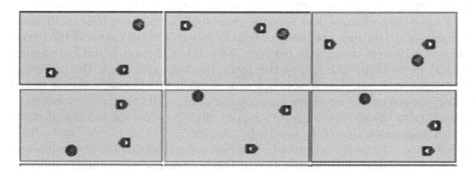

**Fig. 2.** Samples of layouts with three buttons classified as 'valid' (first row) and invalid (second row).

## 4.1  Variability of Layouts

The variability implies the diversity of results so that it is possible to test several valid configurations and to find those that better suit the designer's need to create an ideal controller for his game. That said, we seek to find a solution that can group similar layouts to make it possible to measure the variability of the valid results generated. The K-means [7] clustering algorithm proved to be a possible solution to our problem because it is an algorithm that partitions data into clusters. The K-means clustering algorithm is a commonly used method for automatically partitioning a data set into $k$ groups [16]. The purpose of data grouping is to discover the natural grouping of a set of patterns, points or objects so that it is possible to do analyzes and absorb knowledge intrinsic to the data [7]. The more traditional definition of this technique is not able to determine the ideal number of clusters, and it is necessary to previously inform the number of clusters that it is desired to separate the data. To define the number of clusters and find the number of clusters that might be ideal for measuring the variability of results, we use a K-means extension that uses the Bayesian Information Criterion (BIC) [6]. It is based in part on the likelihood function and can be used to compare models with different parametrizations, with different number of components, or both. Therefore, we use this technique to find the ideal number of clusters and, finally, to separate layouts into similar clusters. As an input to the algorithm, we provide a CSV file containing the positions on the x and y axes of each button, concatenated with the distances between each of the buttons. The algorithm performs clustering and organizes layouts that have been output by the machine learning classifier. It has been observed that both the number of clusters and the number of valid individuals oscillate when the number of iterations varies for each population. This can be explained in part by the fact that the objective function is not able to capture all aspects of a good layout, so this result justifies the use of machine learning to help the designer identify a good design. The stochastic nature of the selection of the individuals can propagate, albeit less likely, individuals with low fitness for subsequent generations, which can then be wrongly classified as valid by the SVM since the technique does not guarantee 100% accuracy in the classification of individuals. One measure that can help us understand the nature of the layout generation process is the ratio between the number of clusters and the number of valid individuals. The largest the ratio, the more efficient is the process is in creating variability inside a group of high quality individuals. As we stated earlier, we are interested in presenting a range of results that are distinct from each other to the end-user. Figure 3 graphically illustrates the calculated ratios in each population created by the model. Analyzing the graphs, we can see that, in most cases, the ratio of clusters by valid individuals is higher in the population of 1000 individuals. This happens in all two configurations containing different amounts of buttons, except in the following iterations: iteration 4000 in layouts with three buttons; iterations 4000, 6000, 7000, and 10,000 in the layouts with nine buttons. As this behavior occurred in a few cases, most likely caused by the randomness of the genetic algorithm when generating and selecting individuals, we realized that a population with 1000 individuals is sufficient to generate sets of valid individuals with greater variability.

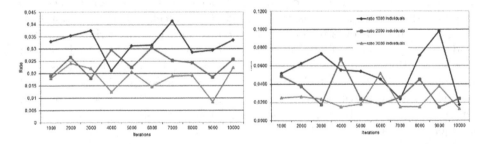

**Fig. 3.** Graphical representation of the value of the ratio between the number of clusters and the number of individuals classified as valid in a population of 1000, 2000 and 3000 individuals - layouts containing three (on the left) and nine (on the right) buttons.

Figure 4 shows examples of layouts generated by the model and grouped into certain clusters (smaller figures) and its potential layout proposed by a designer (bigger figure) after analyzing those results. At the end of the tests, we look for other designers' opinions about the 'ideal layouts' constructed after analyzing the model outputs. Five game designers, four male and one female, aged 18–30 years analyzed the four candidate layouts. Those designers have between one and five years of experience with game design. The layouts were presented to them on a smartphone ASUS Zenfone 3 Zoom with a 5.5-inch screen. Their opinion was requested about those layouts, asking them to consider the arrangement and grouping of the buttons in the virtual controller area. In short, the layouts that separated the directional buttons into two groups divided opinions among the designers. The position of the action button in the three-button settings has been reported as too far away, making it difficult to combine with other actions. There were also comments on the user's finger range and button height.

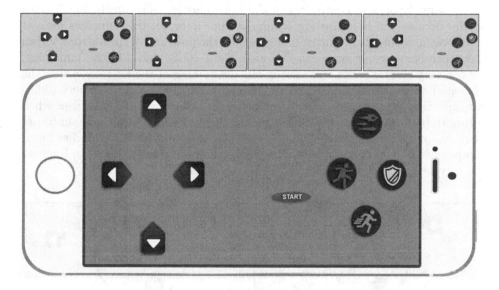

**Fig. 4.** Layouts with different semantic values inserted in the same cluster because of geometric proximity.

## 5   Conclusion and Future Work

In this work, we addressed the problem of assisting a game designer in the process of creating different gamepad layouts using generative design. The main contribution of this work is a generative design pipeline for gamepad design based on evolutionary algorithms and machine learning techniques. The evolution algorithm is responsible for creating a large number of gamepad configurations based on the inputs provided by the user: the number of layouts to be generated, the number of iterations to be executed, quantity, and type of buttons that should be present in the final layout. After execution, the model outputs the exact number of layouts requested by the user. As this is generally a large number, it becomes impractical for the designer to analyze them all. As certainly many of these will be discarded by him because video game controllers must respect some organizational rules, we a Support Vector Machine classifier to divide individuals as 'valid' or 'invalid'. In addition, we propose a way of measuring the variability of the candidate solutions using an extended version of the K-means algorithm, which can automatically determine the number of clusters in the group of individuals. Static database training can be seen as a limitation. Since the data that fed the training base of the SVM classifier have been classified only once, the outputs of the generative design model are, to a certain extent, restricted to those that the classifier knows to be valid or not. In future works we intend to implement a self-feeding of the classifier training base so that it is possible to further increase the variety of results that can be classified as valid. Regarding the analysis of the variability of layouts, the technique used may erroneously group some layouts of controllers in the same cluster, as shown in Fig. 5. This occurs because the K-means algorithm does not interpret the semantics present in videogame controllers since it analyzes only the positions of the buttons within the controller's layout space. In this case, the layouts placed in the same cluster are very similar when considering the positioning of the buttons within the gamepad area, but in the context of the player experience they are very different, and that can generate a high cognitive effort on the part of the user when trying to perform actions within a game. Looking to address this issue, in future work, we intend to apply techniques such as graph matching approaches [9] or computational vision-based techniques (e.g image subtraction) [13], to improve the way we can measure variability of the solution.

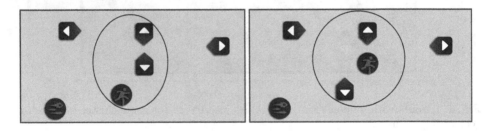

**Fig. 5.** Individuals inserted in the same cluster, however these layouts are not similar because they have buttons with different semantics.

# References

1. Alves, G.F., Souza, E.V., Trevisan, D.G., Montenegro, A.A., de Castro Salgado, L.C., Clua, E.W.G.: Applying design thinking for prototyping a game controller. In: Clua, E., Roque, L., Lugmayr, A., Tuomi, P. (eds.) ICEC 2018. LNCS, vol. 11112, pp. 16–27. Springer, Cham (2018). https://doi.org/10.1007/978-3-319-99426-0_2
2. Baldauf, M., Adegeye, F., Alt, F., Harms, J.: Your browser is the controller: advanced web-based smartphone remote controls for public screens. In: Proceedings of the 5th ACM International Symposium on Pervasive Displays, pp. 175–181. ACM (2016)
3. Baldauf, M., Fröhlich, P., Adegeye, F., Suette, S.: Investigating on-screen gamepad designs for smartphone-controlled video games. ACM Trans. Multimed. Comput. Commun. Appl. (TOMM) **12**(1s), 22 (2015)

4. Bentley, P.: Evolutionary Design by Computers. Morgan Kaufmann, Burlington (1999)
5. Bjørlykhaug, E., Egeland, O.: Mechanical design optimization of a 6DOF serial manipulator using genetic algorithm. IEEE Access **6**, 59087–59095 (2018)
6. Fraley, C., Raftery, A.E.: How many clusters? Which clustering method? Answers via model-based cluster analysis. Comput. J. **41**(8), 578–588 (1998)
7. Jain, A.K.: Data clustering: 50 years beyond k-means. Pattern Recogn. Lett. **31**(8), 651–666 (2010)
8. Krish, S.: A practical generative design method. Comput. Aided Des. **43**(1), 88–100 (2011)
9. Oliveira, A., et al.: An efficient similarity-based approach for comparing XML documents. Inf. Syst. **78**, 40–57 (2018)
10. PlayStation: The last of us (2018). https://www.playstation.com/en-us/games/the-last-of-us-remastered-ps4/. Accessed 30 Dec 2018
11. Reas, C., Fry, B.: Processing (2018). https://processing.org/. Accessed 21 Dec 2018
12. Rogers, S.: Level Up! The Guide to Great Video Game Design. Wiley, Hoboken (2014)
13. Russ, J.C.: The Image Processing Handbook. CRC Press, Boca Raton (2016)
14. Torok, L., Pelegrino, M., Trevisan, D., Montenegro, A., Clua, E.: Designing game controllers in a mobile device. In: Marcus, A., Wang, W. (eds.) DUXU 2017. LNCS, vol. 10289, pp. 456–468. Springer, Cham (2017). https://doi.org/10.1007/978-3-319-58637-3_36
15. Troiano, L., Birtolo, C.: Genetic algorithms supporting generative design of user interfaces: examples. Inf. Sci. **259**, 433–451 (2014)
16. Wagstaff, K., Cardie, C., Rogers, S., Schrödl, S., et al.: Constrained k-means clustering with background knowledge. In: ICML, vol. 1, pp. 577–584 (2001)

# Enhancing Communication and Awareness in Asymmetric Games

Christophe Bortolaso[1], Jérémy Bourdiol[1,2], and T. C. Nicholas Graham[1(✉)]

[1] School of Computing, Queen's University, Kingston, ON K7L 2N6, Canada
christophe.bortolaso@gmail.com, jeremy.bourdiol@laposte.net,
nicholas.graham@queensu.ca
[2] Université Toulouse III – Paul Sabbatier, Toulouse, France
http://equis.cs.queensu.ca

**Abstract.** Asymmetric games rely on players taking on different game-play roles, often with associated different views of the game world and different input modalities. This asymmetry can lead to difficulties in establishing common referents as players collaborate. To explore communication and group awareness in asymmetric games, we present a novel asymmetric game, combining a tablet presenting a 2D top-down view and a virtual reality headset providing an immersive 3D view of the game-world. We demonstrate how communication can be afforded between the two types of views via interaction techniques supporting deixis, shared reference, and awareness. These techniques are bi-directional, enabling an equitable collaboration. A pilot study has shown that players adapt well to the system's two roles, and find the collaborative interaction techniques to be effective.

**Keywords:** Game design · Asymmetric games · Virtual reality

## 1 Introduction

Modern computer hardware affords a wealth of new styles of gaming. An emerging style is *asymmetric* games, where cooperating players take on different roles, sometimes using different forms of interaction, different hardware, and different views of the game world. For example, in *Maze Commander*, two players collaborate to traverse a dangerous maze [20]. One player can see the entire maze, using a virtual reality headset, but cannot navigate. The other sees only a small part of the maze, represented by connected Sifteo Cubes, and can manipulate the cubes to move the avatar. The key behind this game is that each player's views and interaction affordances support part of the gameplay task, and the players must cooperate closely to win the game.

---

**Electronic supplementary material** The online version of this chapter (https://doi.org/10.1007/978-3-030-34644-7_20) contains supplementary material, which is available to authorized users.

© IFIP International Federation for Information Processing 2019
Published by Springer Nature Switzerland AG 2019
E. van der Spek et al. (Eds.): ICEC-JCSG 2019, LNCS 11863, pp. 250–262, 2019.
https://doi.org/10.1007/978-3-030-34644-7_20

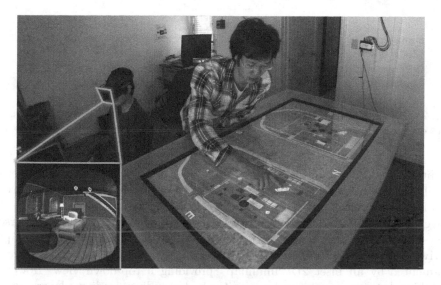

**Fig. 1.** The *Our Virtual Home* game: One player decorates a house on a large tablet device and the other uses immersive VR to assess the result.

Asymmetric games frequently require players to engage in tightly-coupled collaboration [10], despite having often radically different ways of interacting with the game. Such collaboration can be difficult if players have different views of the game world. Players may lack consistent frames of reference, and may have difficulty understanding what the other player can see.

In this paper, we explore the problems of group awareness and communication in asymmetric games. Through *Our Virtual Home*, a novel house decoration mini-game (Fig. 1), we show examples of potential breakdown in collaboration. *Our Virtual Home* combines a large 2D touch tablet and a VR headset, enabling tablet players to view and position furniture in a house while a VR player explores how the furniture will appear to people. This mini-game is inspired by the house decoration features found in games as varied as Bethesda's *The Elder Scrolls V: Skyrim* and Microsoft's *Minecraft*.

This choice of hardware is based on the strengths of the tablet and VR headset devices used. Tablets naturally support planning around 2D representations of physical space such as maps and architectural plans. Example applications support design of interior spaces [13], exploration for oil and gas [22], emergency response planning [4], and determining routes for military vehicles through hostile terrain [3]. However, some situations require a full understanding of the space represented in the map or plan, and in such cases, a top-down 2D view may not be sufficient. For example, when arranging furniture in a room, it is necessary to have a realistic perception of depth and distance to create an aesthetic and enjoyable space [14]. Adding the use of a VR headset, however, seriously compromises group awareness. The player using the headset cannot see where tablet player is looking or pointing, and may not see when the tablet player is moving

| | Same Perspective | Different Perspective |
|---|---|---|
| **Same Input Modalities** | League of Legends, World of Warcraft | Natural Selection, Savage, Nuclear Dawn |
| **Different Input Modalities** | Frozen Treasure Hunter | Beam Me 'Round Scotty!, Maze Commander, Tabula Rasa |

**Fig. 2.** Examples of how asymmetric games can provide players with differing perspectives on the gameworld and different input modalities supported by different hardware.

furniture. To address this problem, *Our Virtual Home* provides a novel set of collaborative widgets supporting communication between tablet and VR players.

3D views can help with such tasks by presenting the space directly to the player. For this reason, many commercial games combine immersive first-person views with an additional top-down view for establishing context. For example, Activision's *Call of Duty* game provides a first-person 3D view of the scene, augmented by an inset 2D "minimap" providing a top-down view. However, switching between views can be cognitively demanding, leading players not to take full advantage of all available perspectives [27].

Recent advances in virtual reality (VR) technology have made immersive views of 3D spaces widely available. Immersive VR goes beyond the desktop by providing stereoscopic 3D views that can be explored using natural movements. Compared to desktop computers, VR headsets have been found to provide a more accurate sense of distance [19], support spatial cognition through the use of natural head movements [18] and provide a more satisfactory experience [21].

This paper makes two contributions. First, we illustrate a novel combination of a large tablet device with a VR headset in an asymmetric game. Second, we show how communication and group awareness can be supported despite the different perspectives of tablet and VR players.

## 2    Related Work

Asymmetric games provide players with different roles, possibly providing different perspectives on the game world, and possibly using different hardware. For example, in *Frozen Treasure Hunter*, two players attempt to capture trophies while being attacked by snowball-wielding enemies [29]. The players cooperatively control a single avatar, where one moves the avatar by pedaling a bicycle, and the other swats away the snowballs by swinging a Wii Remote. Asymmetric games allow players to experience a variety of gameplay, allow people with different interests to play together, and provide a form of game balancing by allowing people to choose a role that plays to their strengths [11].

Figure 2 lists examples of asymmetric games. In the simplest case, games such as Riot Games' *League of Legends* and Blizzard's *World of Warcraft* allow players to take on different roles in games (character classes), while sharing the same hardware and same perspective on the game's action. As described earlier, *Frozen Treasure Hunter* is an example of a game where players share the same third person view of their avatar, while playing different roles using different hardware (Wii Remote vs bicycle.) Several commercial games have explored the provision of different perspectives to different players. Unknown World Entertainment's *Natural Selection*, S2 Games' *Savage: The Battle for Newerth*, and Iceberg Interactive's *Nuclear Dawn* all involve a player in a commander's role, using a real-time strategy interface to direct players on the ground who play as individual units.

A more radical form of asymmetric games offers players different playstyles involving both different perspectives on the gameworld and different hardware interfaces to the game. For example, *Beam Me 'Round Scotty!* allows one player to use a game controller and PC to guide an avatar through a level, while the other player uses a touch tablet to enable special effects that aid the player [10]. Similarly, in *Tabula Rasa*, one player uses a standard PC and game controller to navigate platformer levels, while the other player uses a digital tabletop to create and modify these levels on the fly [7]. This form of asymmetric gameplay allows interesting forms of collaboration, where players are responsible for different parts of the gameplay task (e.g., building a level vs playing it). The differing visual perspectives allow players to see the gameworld in ways that are appropriate to their tasks, and the different input modalities are customized to the tasks the players perform (e.g., touch to build a level, controller to navigate it).

Research outside the realm of gaming has shown how collaborative tasks require people to perceive and manipulate physical spaces, and how these tasks can benefit from a system in which some users manipulate the space using a top-down view while others are immersed in the space using a VR headset. This form of work has been termed *mixed-space collaboration* [8,17,24]. For example, when designing the layout of an apartment, architects draw the floor plan from a top-down perspective and also draw sketches of the space from a first person perspective [13]. The floor plan is useful for exploring spatial constraints and helps the architect to share design decisions with other stakeholders. The first-person sketches help with perception of volumes and of the space's look and feel. In military route planning, officers collaboratively plan how their troops will travel through hostile terrain via discussion over a large map [3]. To plan safe routes, commanders determine the visibility of units along the road, from multiple strategic points. A first-person view can help assess the potential of ambush of units following a proposed route. The common element between these collaborative tasks is that planning and design is discussed using a top-down overview of the space, while specific features are verified at a human scale. Top-down views are used to arrange elements, to resolve spatial constraints and to obtain an overview of the space. Conversely, a first-person view helps in understanding distances, volumes and sightlines. Work benefiting from these two perspectives is referred to as mixed-space collaboration.

The benefit of 2D and 3D perspectives on design tasks was identified as early as 1997 in a modeling interface combining both perspectives [5]. More recently, systems have explored the combined use of a virtual reality headset with a traditional desktop PC display. One user is immersed in the space with the headset while the other controls an overview of the space on a screen. Systems have

| | Tabletop to VR | VR to Tabletop |
|---|---|---|
| **Deixis** | Glowing green column | Blue laser pointer |
| **Shared Reference** | Cardinal direction display | Compass bar |
| **Awareness** | Avatar and vision cone | See-through effect; side-icon; dragging sound |

**Fig. 3.** Interaction techniques used in *Our Virtual Home* to support bi-directional collaboration between tablet and VR players.

been created for search and rescue [1,23], authoring of virtual environments [12], guided navigation [26], and exploring museum exhibits [25]. This decomposition has been shown to improve efficiency in searching and traveling tasks [8,30].

A central problem in systems mixing touch tablets and virtual reality is that the hardware can block communication between the two types of players. The virtual reality headset covers the player's eyes, blocking their view of the physical world around them. Consequently, a VR player cannot see the tablet player or where they are looking or pointing, and cannot see the shared artifact displayed on the table. Similarly, the tablet player cannot see where the VR player is looking. Interaction techniques have been proposed to help players overcome this barrier, some of which are summarized by Stafford et al. [24]. For example, in the context of disaster relief, Bacim et al. allow a "commander" (PC user) to place waypoints to guide a "responder" (VR player), and allow the responder to place virtual markers to alert the commander to places of interest [1]. Holm et al. [12] and Stafford et al. [23] provide similar "god-like" techniques. These allow the PC user to guide the VR player, where the actions of the PC user are illustrated through movements of a giant hand in the VR view. Nguyen et al. demonstrate a range of cues that a "helping user" can provide for an "exploring user", including directional arrows, a light source to flag paths, and an over-the-shoulder camera to allow the helper to see the world from the exploring user's point of view. In the *ShareVR* game, non-VR players maintain awareness of the virtual world through projection of the world onto the floor [9].

## 3    Enhancing Communication in Asymmetric Gameplay

To better understand communication in asymmetric games involving different perspectives and input modalities, we introduce the *Our Virtual Home* house decorating mini-game (Fig. 1). The system is composed of a large interactive touch tablet and a VR headset. The tablet shows a top-down view, allowing players to position furniture by dragging and rotating. The headset provides an immersive view where players can change their perspective by moving their head, and can walk through the house using a game controller. This supports a natural division of duties. The tablet player maintains a large-scale view of the house design, allowing them to conceptualize the global layout, and to easily reposition furniture through touch gestures. The VR player can see the furniture

**Fig. 4.** The sky-laser technique supports deixis from tablet to VR. A tablet player's pointing action is shown in the virtual world as a glowing column of light. (Color figure online)

layout in place, getting a clearer idea of scale, sightlines and movement through the space. The tablet player may try a decoration idea, and ask the VR player to evaluate it. Equally, the VR player may request modifications to the design based on their first-person view. This means that it must be possible for either player to initiate and guide communication. As discussed earlier, however, the fact that the VR players' eyes are covered by the headset forms a barrier to collaboration. As suggested by Dix' framework [6], users require three forms of communication, all of which are hindered by their different perspectives on the gameworld, and particularly through the reduced visibility of the VR hardware:

- *Deixis* to establish explicit referents in conversation (e.g., "try putting that chair over there").
- *Shared reference* (e.g., "what do you see to your left?").
- *Awareness* (e.g., realizing that a table is being moved).

*Our Virtual Home* shows how it is possible to support all three forms of communication, originating either from the touch or the VR player. As summarized in Fig. 3, *Our Virtual Home*'s collaboration techniques support bi-directional deixis, shared reference and awareness. The techniques are designed to match the capabilities and conventions of the devices. Some techniques have been proposed by others (e.g., Stafford et al.'s "god-like" pointing [23]); others are new. The key novelty of *Our Virtual Home* is to demonstrate that this combination of interaction techniques allows all three forms of communication to originate from either player. This affords an equitable collaboration where both the tablet and VR and VR player have the same communication opportunities.

## 3.1 Deixis

Deixis is almost as important as words for face-to-face communication [2]. Traditional finger pointing is hindered when one player wears a VR headset, as that

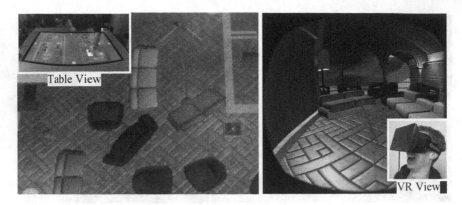

**Fig. 5.** The laser pointer supports deixis from VR to tablet. Here, the VR player is pointing at a sofa. (Color figure online)

player cannot see the other person's hands or the touch device itself. To help VR players see where tablet players are pointing, we designed and implemented a two-way pointing system.

When the tablet player touches the screen, a glowing, green marker appears below their finger (Fig. 4: left). This feedback is immediately reflected in the VR player's view as a column of green light (Fig. 4: right), showing the location of the touch. The green feedback follows the tablet player's touch gestures, and its position is updated in real-time in the VR view. This technique, inspired by Stafford's "god-like" pointing technique [23], enables the tablet player to communicate locations to their VR partner. Deixis is therefore provided via touch. The glowing green marker is important to show the tablet player that the touch is being communicated to the VR player.

In the other direction, the VR player can hold a button on their game controller to trigger a blue laser pointer (Fig. 5: right). When the laser pointer appears in the VR view, it also becomes immediately visible on the tablet surface (Fig. 5: left). The laser's end point is marked with a lightning ball in order to disambiguate which object is being referenced. Lasers have proven to be users' preferred technique when pointing in collaborative virtual environments [28]. This enables a VR player to point at objects and locations in the space to communicate with their tablet partner. As with physical deixis, this mechanism can be used to disambiguate references to elements in the space.

Together, these techniques enable deixis in both directions, allowing both tablet and VR players to reference locations or objects for the other to see.

## 3.2 Shared Reference

Another advantage of face-to-face collaboration lies in the establishment of shared references. For example, people working on a map typically have a shared understanding of which direction is north, allowing the use of cardinal references when discussing directions. Similarly, when working side-by-side, it is easy to reference elements using phrases such as "to your left" or "the chair behind the

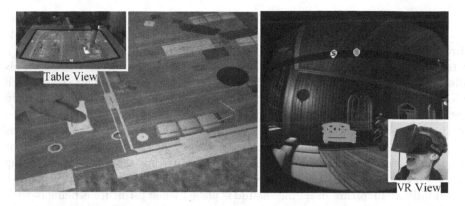

**Fig. 6.** Left: The tablet player is moving a bench. The blue avatar shows the position and orientation of the VR player. Right: The bench is highlighted with the see-through effect in the VR view. The compass on the top shows that the player is facing south and shows the direction of the selected bench. (Color figure online)

table". In an asymmetric game like *Our Virtual Home*, these referencing mechanisms are broken because players do not see the space from the same point of view. Müller et al. recognized the importance of shared reference through the inclusion of shared virtual landmarks [16].

To afford absolute reference, we designed and implemented a compass widget that is visible using the VR headset. As shown in Fig. 6 (right), the compass is a bar at the top of the VR view showing the four cardinal directions. (In the figure, the player is oriented in roughly the southerly direction.) The compass rotates with the player's direction of view. Cardinal directions are also displayed on the tablet, with north pointing toward the top.

To aid with relative references, the position and orientation of the VR player is shown on the tablet. As shown in Fig. 6 (left), the VR player is represented as a small avatar (a blue circle) whose current field of view is shown as an open cone (delineated by two white lines). This shows the tablet player the direction in which the VR player is looking, allowing references such as "look to your left".

### 3.3 Awareness

Shared spaces such as our table-sized tablet afford awareness by allowing people to see the actions of others through direct and peripheral vision. VR players cannot see others' work if that work is out of their field of view. For example, if a tablet player moves a piece of furniture behind the VR player or behind a wall, the VR player may not be aware that the movement has taken place. In *Our Virtual Home*, we addressed this problem via (1) a see-through effect that extends the VR player's sight through obstructions, (2) a "side-icon" indicating activity out of the field of view, and (3) an audio "furniture dragging" sound that is activated when a tablet player moves furniture.

As shown in Fig. 6 (right), when a tablet player touches a piece of furniture, it takes on a glowing, green appearance in the VR view, and becomes visible through obstructions such as walls or other furniture. This draws the VR player's attention to furniture that is being moved, even if it is not directly visible. This allows the VR player to see the movement of occluded objects. This see-through effect requires the object to be within the VR player's field of view. To help with this, as an object is moved, a green marker appears on the compass aligned to the horizontal position of the moved object (Fig. 6 (right)). If the object is outside the VR player's field of view, this green marker appears on the left or right hand side of the display ("side-icon"), indicating that activity is taking place, and showing the direction in which the VR player should turn their head.

Finally, a "furniture dragging" sound is played when furniture is being moved, providing a second cue to the presence of activity that the VR player may not be able to see.

Thus, the VR player's awareness of group activity is enhanced by the ability to see through walls, the highlighting of furniture selected by tablet players, the side-icon visual cue indicating activity out of the field of view, and the use of an audio cue representing furniture being moved. Meanwhile, the tablet player is provided with cues to help show the location and orientation of the VR player. As seen in Fig. 4 (left), the position of the VR player is shown on the tablet as a blue circle. White lines delimit the VR player's field of view. This blue-circle avatar and vision cone help the tablet player to understand what the VR player can currently see.

In sum, this section has presented interaction techniques used to support bi-directional communication between tabletop and VR players in an asymmetric house decorating mini-game. As summarized in Fig. 3, these techniques support deixis, shared reference, and awareness. The implementation of these techniques in *Our Virtual Home* shows that it is possible to support all three forms of communication in a bi-directional form. This is key to allowing equitable collaboration, where both players have the ability to lead and respond to the group's activity.

## 4   Early Evaluation

To gain feedback about the usability of our combination of techniques, we carried out a qualitative pilot study. We recruited four pairs of participants (7 males, 1 female, 18–31 years old). The participants were asked to arrange furniture in a two-story house to create a functional and aesthetic layout. The participants were provided with the techniques described above, supporting deixis, shared reference and awareness. Participants were assigned to use either the tablet or the VR headset and were directed to rearrange the first floor of the house. They then switched roles, and were directed to rearrange the second floor. On average, each participant spent 10 min using each device ($M = 10{:}26$, $SD = 1{:}32$). The sessions were video-recorded and participants were interviewed at the end of the task. We performed a video analysis to identify interesting behaviours and communication issues between players.

## 4.1   Results

All groups completed the task without problems and reported in the interviews that they had no difficulty in playing the game and in collaborating. The combination of our interaction techniques with verbal communication supported effective communication. Exchanges between the two players were mostly verbal, supported by our collaboration widgets. For example, the VR player could call the attention of the tablet player to a furniture item and then disambiguate the object referenced by using the laser pointer: "Hey look! Let's put that ⟨*points at furniture item*⟩ over here ⟨*points at location*⟩". Participants reported that the cardinal references were useful at the beginning of the session when exploring the house.

Not surprisingly, the tablet provided better awareness than the VR view. As stated by group 1, "When you are on the tablet you have full awareness of what the other person is doing", but when using the VR headset, "I was aware that something was going on but not exactly what". The dragging sound was successful in alerting VR players to activity, but players easily overlooked the side-icon indicating the direction of the activity.

All participants reported that the two views were complementary. Tablet players repeatedly asked the VR player how the space felt. Interestingly, not only were the use of space and distance important, but lighting was also frequently discussed. For instance, a tablet player asked a VR player: "Are there enough lamps in the eating area?" When changing from the tablet to the VR headset, participants expressed surprise at how the space looked from the inside. This highlights the complementarity of the two views.

The study showed the importance of bi-directional support for communication. Both tablet and VR players made use of pointing gestures (through the laser pointer and the column of light). The position and orientation of the avatar was used to determine what the VR player was seeing, helping to disambiguate conversation. The see-through movement of furniture objects helped the VR player quickly locate the tablet player's activity.

The video analysis also highlighted interesting behaviours and situations where the techniques were successful, and areas where future work could improve the approach.

*Path Finding.* Although not designed for this purpose, the sky-laser was used to direct the VR player's movement. We observed multiple instances where the tablet player dragged the laser from one location to another to guide the VR player to a specific area. This usage is similar to Bacim et al.'s more explicitly-provided waypoint feature [1].

*Missed Eye Contacts.* While talking, some tablet players sporadically looked at the VR player even though the VR player couldn't see them. This is a good indicator that the tablet player felt the presence of the VR player and felt the need for non-verbal communication. This hints that while deixis is useful, communication of the tablet player's gaze could helpful to indicate specific instances where the tablet player is attending to the VR player.

*Missed Gestures above the Table.* Several participants performed gestures above the table even though the VR player could not see them. For example, one tabletop participant asked the VR player: "is this whole thing roofed?" while gesturing in a circle with his hand above the table. Marquardt et al. have stressed the importance of providing awareness of activities above the table [15]; such awareness could be provided to the VR player for example through finger tracking.

In sum, both tablet and VR players made use of interaction techniques for deixis, shared reference, and awareness. Participants played the game as expected, with the tablet player taking advantage of the spatial presentation afforded by the top-down view, while the VR player focused on the immersive 3D presentation of the furniture layout. Participant response was positive, with all dyads successfully completing the task. While this study was based around the specific hardware of a tabletop-sized tablet and a VR headset, these approaches could be applied to other hardware. For example, the touch device could be replaced by a smaller tablet such as an iPad. This would extend awareness difficulties, as the tablet would be harder for two people to view. A VR headset could be replaced by an augmented-reality (AR) headset, such as Microsoft's *Hololens* product. This could allow the VR player to be more aware of the tablet player's actions; however, current AR headsets obscure the eyes of the wearer, and so awareness cues would still be required.

## 5    Conclusion

In this paper, we have explored an asymmetric implementation of a house decorating mini-game, using a touch tablet and a VR headset. We described a set of interaction techniques to support non-verbal communication between the two players. These interaction techniques support equitable collaboration in which both players can take the lead. An informal study revealed that players were able to carry out an interior design task using this asymmetric collaboration, and that they understood and used the widgets supporting communication and group awareness. Opportunities for improvement were identified, such as the use of gaze detection and tracking of the finger above the table, but the lack of these features did not inhibit the players from completing the task.

**Acknowledgements.** We gratefully acknowledge the support of the SURFNET Strategic Network and the GRAND Network of Centres of Excellence for this research.

## References

1. Bacim, F., Ragan, E.D., Stinson, C., Scerbo, S., Bowman, D.A.: Collaborative navigation in virtual search and rescue. In: Proceedings of the IEEE Symposium on 3D User Interfaces (3DUI), pp. 187–188 (2012)
2. Bekker, M.M., Olson, J.S., Olson, G.M.: Analysis of gestures in face-to-face design teams provides guidance for how to use groupware in design. In: Proceedings of the First Conference on Designing Interactive Systems: Processes, Practices, Methods and Techniques (DIS 1995), pp. 157–166 (1995)

3. Bortolaso, C., Oskamp, M., Graham, T.C.N., Brown, D.: OrMiS: a tabletop interface for simulation-based training. In: Proceedings of the ACM International Conference on Interactive Tabletops and Surfaces (ITS), pp. 145–154 (2013)
4. Chokshi, A., Seyed, T., Marinho Rodrigues, F., Maurer, F.: ePlan multi-surface: a multi-surface environment for emergency response planning exercises. In: Proceedings of the Ninth ACM International Conference on Interactive Tabletops and Surfaces (ITS 2014), pp. 219–228. ACM (2014)
5. Coninx, K., Reeth, F.V., Flerackers, E.: A hybrid 2D/3D user interface for immersive object modeling. In: Proceedings of Computer Graphics International (CGI), pp. 47–55 (1997)
6. Dix, A.: Computer supported cooperative work: a framework. In: Rosenberg, D., Hutchison, C. (eds.) Design Issues in CSCW, pp. 9–26. Springer, London (1994). https://doi.org/10.1007/978-1-4471-2029-2_2
7. Graham, T.C.N., Schumann, I., Patel, M., Bellay, Q., Dachselt, R.: Villains, architects and micro-managers: what Tabula Rasa teaches us about game orchestration. In: Proceedings of the SIGCHI Conference on Human Factors in Computing Systems (CHI 2013), pp. 705–714 (2013)
8. Grasset, R., Lamb, P., Billinghurst, M.: Evaluation of mixed-space collaboration. In: Proceedings of the International Symposium on Mixed and Augmented Reality (ISMAR), pp. 90–99 (2005)
9. Gugenheimer, J., Stemasov, E., Frommel, J., Rukzio, E.: ShareVR: enabling co-located experiences for virtual reality between HMD and non-HMD users. In: Proceedings of Human Factors in Computing Systems (CHI 2017), pp. 4021–4033. ACM (2017)
10. Harris, J., Hancock, M.: To asymmetry and beyond!: improving social connectedness by increasing designed interdependence in cooperative play. In: Proceedings of Human Factors in Computing Systems (CHI 2019), pp. 1–12. ACM Press, Glasgow (2019)
11. Harris, J., Hancock, M., Scott, S.D.: Leveraging Asymmetries in Multiplayer Games: Investigating Design Elements of Interdependent Play. In: Proceedings of the 2016 Annual Symposium on Computer-Human Interaction in Play (CHI PLAY 2016), pp. 350–361. ACM Press, Austin (2016). https://doi.org/10.1145/2967934.2968113
12. Holm, R., Stauder, E., Wagner, R., Priglinger, M., Volkert, J.: A combined immersive and desktop authoring tool for virtual environments. In: Proceedings of Virtual Reality (VR), pp. 93–100 (2002)
13. Kirkpatrick, B.M., Kirkpatrick, J.M., Assadipour, H.: AutoCAD 2015 for Interior Design and Space Planning. Peachpit Press, San Francisco (2014)
14. Laseau, P.: Graphic Thinking for Architects and Designers. Wiley, Hoboken (2000)
15. Marquardt, N., Jota, R., Greenberg, S., Jorge, J.A.: The continuous interaction space: interaction techniques unifying touch and gesture on and above a digital surface. In: Campos, P., Graham, N., Jorge, J., Nunes, N., Palanque, P., Winckler, M. (eds.) INTERACT 2011. LNCS, vol. 6948, pp. 461–476. Springer, Heidelberg (2011). https://doi.org/10.1007/978-3-642-23765-2_32
16. Mueller, J., Rädle, R., Reiterer, H.: Remote collaboration with mixed reality displays: how shared virtual landmarks facilitate spatial referencing. In: Proceedings of the 2017 CHI Conference on Human Factors in Computing Systems, pp. 6481–6486. ACM (2017)
17. Nakanishi, H., Koizumi, S., Ishida, T., Ito, H.: Transcendent communication: location-based guidance for large-scale public spaces. In: Proceedings of Human Factors in Computing Systems (CHI 2014), pp. 655–662 (2004)

18. Pausch, R., Proffitt, D., Williams, G.: Quantifying immersion in virtual reality. In: Proceedings of SIGGRAPH, pp. 13–18 (1997)

19. Ruddle, R.A., Payne, S.J., Jones, D.M.: Navigating large-scale virtual environments: what differences occur between helmet-mounted and desk-top displays? Presence: Teleoperators Virtual Environ. **8**(2), 157–168 (1999)

20. Sajjadi, P., Cebolledo Gutierrez, E.O., Trullemans, S., De Troyer, O.: Maze Commander: a collaborative asynchronous game using the Oculus Rift & the Sifteo cubes. In: Proceedings of the ACM SIGCHI Symposium on Computer-Human Interaction in Play (CHIPLAY 2014), pp. 227–236. ACM Press, Toronto (2014)

21. Santos, B.S., et al.: Head-mounted display versus desktop for 3D navigation in virtual reality: a user study. Multimedia Tools Appl. **41**(1), 161–181 (2008)

22. Seyed, T., Sousa, M.C., Maurer, F., Tang, A.: SkyHunter: a multi-surface environment for supporting oil and gas exploration. In: Proceedings of the ACM Conference on Interactive Tabletops and Surfaces (ITS 2013), pp. 15–22 (2013)

23. Stafford, A., Piekarski, W., Thomas, B.H.: Implementation of god-like interaction techniques for supporting collaboration between outdoor AR and indoor tabletop users. In: Proceedings of the International Symposium on Mixed and Augmented Reality (ISMAR), pp. 165–172 (2006)

24. Stafford, A., Thomas, B.H., Piekarski, W.: Comparison of techniques for mixed-space collaborative navigation. In: Proceedings of the Australasian User Interface Conference (AUIC), pp. 61–70 (2009)

25. Sundén, E., Lundgren, I., Ynnerman, A.: Hybrid virtual reality touch table: an immersive collaborative platform for public explanatory use of cultural objects and sites. In: Eurographics Workshop on Graphics and Cultural Heritage, pp. 109–113. Eurographics-European Association for Computer Graphics (2017)

26. Nguyen, T.T.H., Duval, T., Fleury, C.: Guiding techniques for collaborative exploration in multi-scale shared virtual environments. In: Proceedings of the GRAPP International Conference on Computer Graphics Theory and Applications, pp. 327–336 (2011)

27. Tory, M., Kirkpatrick, A.E., Atkins, M.S., Moller, T.: Visualization task performance with 2D, 3D, and combination displays. IEEE Trans. Vis. Comput. Graph. **12**(1), 2–13 (2006)

28. Wong, N., Gutwin, C.: Support for deictic pointing in CVEs: still fragmented after all these years. In: Proceedings of Computer-Supported Cooperative Work (CSCW), pp. 1377–1387 (2014)

29. Yim, J., Graham, T.C.N.: Using games to increase exercise motivation. In: Proceedings of the 2007 Conference on Future Play (Future Play 2007), pp. 166–173. ACM Press, Toronto (2007)

30. Zhang, X., Furnas, G.W.: The effectiveness of multiscale collaboration in virtual environments. In: Proceedings of Human Factors in Computing Systems (CHI), pp. 790–791 (2003)

# LoRattle - An Exploratory Game with a Purpose Using LoRa and IoT

Marko Radeta[1](✉), Miguel Ribeiro[2], Dinarte Vasconcelos[2],
and Nuno Jardim Nunes[2]

[1] ITI/LARSyS, Universidade da Madeira, Tigerwhale, Funchal, Portugal
marko.radeta@m-iti.org
[2] ITI/LARSyS, Instituto Superior Técnico, Lisbon, Portugal
{jose.miguel.ribeiro,dinarte.vasconcelos,nunojnunes}@tecnico.ulisboa.pt
https://iti.larsys.pt
https://tecnico.ulisboa.pt/

**Abstract.** The Internet of Things (IoT) is opening new possibilities for sensing, monitoring and actuating in urban environments. They support a shift to a hybrid network of humans and things collaborating in production, transmission and processing of data through low-cost and low power devices connected via long-range (LoRa) wide area networks (WAN). This paper describes a 2-player duel game based on IoT controllers and LoRa radio communication protocol. Here we report on the main evaluation dimensions of this new design space for games, namely: (i) game usability (SUS) leading to an above average score; (ii) affective states of the players (SAM) depicting pleasant and engaging gameplay, while players retain control; (iii) radio coverage perception (RCP) showing that most participants did not change their perception of the radio distance after playing. Finally, we discuss the findings and propose future interactive applications to take advantage of this design space.

**Keywords:** LoRa · Internet of Things · Tangible User Interfaces · Games with a purpose · Ubiquitous computing · Radio coverage

## 1 Introduction

Technologies like the Internet of Things (IoT), long-range (LoRa) wide areas networks (WAN) and tangible user interfaces (TUI) are opening new design possibilities in domains from home-automation to urban environments, industry 4.0 and precision agriculture. Mostly titled "smart" applications these range from smart-houses to smart-grids, smart-cities, smart-retails and smart-supply-chain among many others. Generally, they offer the ability to measure, infer and understand environmental indicators, from delicate ecologies and natural resources to urban environments. A critical component of IoT platforms is the evolution of the Internet into a networked of interconnected objects uniquely

© IFIP International Federation for Information Processing 2019
Published by Springer Nature Switzerland AG 2019
E. van der Spek et al. (Eds.): ICEC-JCSG 2019, LNCS 11863, pp. 263–277, 2019.
https://doi.org/10.1007/978-3-030-34644-7_21

addressable based on standard communication platforms. This is a radical evolution of the current Internet but also potentially a change in how we as users and citizens understand the environment around us. When new technologies undergo widespread popularization, it is frequently an exciting opportunity to address open questions about the topic and its broader implications.

While HCI communities and citizen scientists are turning towards IoT and ubiquitous computing technologies [12], interactive applications based on IoT and long-range wireless communication remain greatly unexplored. In this study, we make a contribution into this new design space through a game with a purpose (GWAP), which was used to both study how people perceive these new technologies, as well as to explore how they could drive new interactive applications and games that span to the physical world around us taking advantage of IoT and LoRa technologies.

## 1.1 Study Motivation and Contributions

The main motivation behind our work is to explore the possibilities provided by IoT platforms and long-range communication protocols to support novel interactions. As these technologies become widespread new applications will move beyond personal devices into tangible computing devices based on IoT technologies and long distance communication. For this purpose, we test these new conditions with a GWAP which also serves to measure the performance of the game using the LoRa protocol and impact the knowledge of wide area network communication. Our study contributions are threefold: (i) we design and implement the first GWAP using LoRa and IoT devices, acting as a tangible user interface (TUI); (ii) using the provided apparatus, we study what kind of novel interactions emerge when exposing the participants to such technologies; and (iii) we perform the user study with these participants. With these motivations and contributions in mind, in this study we provide insights into the following research questions:

- **[RQ1]**. How IoT and LoRa combined can be used for GWAP and entertainment?
  In proposed GWAP, we study the feasibility to crowdsource the LoRa radio coverage using the game participants as an alternative tool to outline the limitations of LoRa signal strength. We collect the Received Strength Indicator (RSSI) between two players.
- **[RQ2]**. Which novel interactions emerge from such technologies?
  In this question, we study how participants will actually play the game. We observe whether they will play it indoor or outdoor setting, and if they will be hindering the signal to protect themselves, or exploring the greater distance by using it.
- **[RQ3]**. How user perceive such GWAPs?
  Using usability and affective scales, we study the players' difficulties and engagement in such game. Moreover, we observe whether or not the radio coverage perception would significatelly increase after participating LoRa-based game.

# 2    Related Work

In this section, we describe the state of the art in IoT and usage of LoRa protocols in HCI (Sect. 2.1), suggesting the need for their coupling. Also, to raise awareness of the game and HCI communities about the potential of LoRa technology we provide an outline of this new standard, its potential and limitations (Sect. 2.2). Finally, we analyze the potential of IoT devices connected via LoRa to be used as Tangible User Interfaces (TUIs), in particular when applied in real-world gaming settings (Sect. 2.3).

## 2.1    Towards Interactive IoT on LoRa

In general, IoT's main drive is to "do more with less" [6] and its main focus is to enable the communication between devices while impacting the memory usage, processing power, bandwidth, and energy consumption. Previous work discussed the guidelines for embedding IoT interfaces in daily routines [20]. Others investigated the social side of the IoT [5], using social networking as a metaphor to provide solutions to mechanical problems. Interactive IoT embedded devices offer sophisticated methods to provide users with services to make use of the information and to interact with objects in the real world. Also, some scholars used identification radio technology for interactive purposes [16, 26]. However, to the best of our knowledge the work described here is the first to explore long-range IoT protocols for interactive communication and gameplay. However, high-frequency radio communication is commonly used for many interactive devices such as gamepads, wireless mice and keyboards. Other interactive experiences supporting virtual reality use headsets, motion-capture devices, gloves and other engaging simulators [14]. In this case, motion capture devices use technology based on infrared waves and LEDs discreetly mounted around the perimeters of a display. Conversely, these systems have disadvantages, as they require highly specialized and expensive hardware/software (e.g. simulators or virtual reality environments). Also, in some games, impaired users may have difficulties actually allocating the specific information [15].

Finally, these devices are outside of the industrial, scientific and medical (ISM) radio bands assigned to the open radio spectrum. LoRa belongs to ISM using frequencies surrounding 868 MHz in Europe. Moreover, most other devices are still dependent on the physical connection and wiring with the gaming console and/or computer. Popular devices, such as the Wii Remote or PlayStation Move, were developed to improve the interaction between the user and game consoles, reducing the needs for cumbersome wiring. Work reported by Wilson et al. [30] used handheld pointing devices (using Bluetooth radio communication) for interaction. However, most of these devices have a high cost and are limited as participants have to remain in a predetermined physical space or to be constrained with additional wiring. LoRa is not just the solution to battery autonomy but it also challenges traditional communication methods (Bluetooth, wi-fi, etc). This study depicts more opportunities how LoRa can be brought to entertainment (opening new doors) and how it can overcome aforementioned limitations.

## 2.2 Brief Overview of LoRa for Game and HCI Communities

The growing widespread availability of IoT deployments is leading to an emergence of long-range communication protocols, which comply with the requirement of IoT platforms (wide area connectivity, low power consumption, and low data rate). Among the most popular are Low-Power Wide Area Networks (LPWANs) which offers radio coverage over large geographical areas. LP-WANs can have a range greater than 1000 m [6], and use base stations with adaptive transmission rates, transmission power, modulation, duty cycles, with two ultimate goals: (i) to keep very low energy consumption and (ii) to allow more end-devices to be connected. Between Sigfox and Weightless, LoRa is one of the LPWAN candidate protocols which use low-cost transceivers (with features not available for the majority of IoT applications [9]). They contain embedded crystals, which do not need to be manufactured to perform the extreme accuracy [6]. This makes LoRa a well-situated protagonist for low-power and long-range transmissions [6] and its' modulation is capable of extracting the data from weak signals found in noisy environments.

However, the features of LoRa come at the cost of important constraints: (i) maximum payload size (maximum 256 bytes, including the header); (ii) Bandwidth (BW 125 kHz, 250 kHz or 500 kHz); (iii) Spreading Factors (SF from 7 to 12, where the lower number has less time on air) [1]; (iv) number of channels (which are carefully designed to minimize the probability of collisions, while offering a quick alternative channel for nodes to retransmit the collided packets) [8]; and (v) maximum distance (which varies from urban to landscape to sea settings). Other limitations include the size of the network [21], reliability caused by the type of applications [2], throughput [1], etc. LoRa is certainly not ideal for every application scenario. Each network protocols have their pros and cons. Cellular networks provide high throughput and range, high power and high cost. Wi-Fi provides a high throughput, short range, and moderate power with relatively high cost [23]. A typical application scenario for LoRa technologies is citywide sensor collection where devices send readings at very low frequencies over longer distances. In our study, we argue that LoRa transceivers are useful to construct more generic IoT networks, incorporating not just bidirectional communication enabling only sensing and sharing the sensed information, but also interactive applications in the context of HCI and gaming.

## 2.3 Potential of TUIs in Outdoor GWAPs

Historically, physical games use tangible objects handled by the players (e.g. chess, rolling a dice, etc.) to support the game interaction. With the advent of computing devices new games emerged but also physical games were mapped into the digital interaction capabilities (e.g. keyboard, cursor control device) [4,25]. Aside from the popularity of exergames [27], Tangible User Interfaces

(TUIs) are known to be used in interactive real-world games for educational and in-the-wild environments. They are also increasingly important in children learning [24]. Moreover, reports show that physical tangible interactions can stimulate learning and allow participants to play games through natural interaction with objects in the real world [17]. Also, mobile location-based games in outdoor settings are gaining popularity [7]. Their expansion is due to the widespread use of smartphones with sensing capabilities, leveraging the GPS satellite positioning. These games are also known as "urban games" or "street games" and are typically in a multiplayer setting, played out on streets and urban environments. One of the games that made use of this approach is the Pokemon Go, where scholars study the motivational factors for walking [3,13,22]. Inherent in this type of games is also Augmented Reality (AR). Underpinning the fact that the activities take place in the real physical world, while games are seen through the lens of the mobile device. However, TUIs and AR geolocation games also have a big constraint which is the network connection, as gaming should avoid expensive mobile data usage. This poses a challenge for the network, especially in urban areas. In the remainder of this study, we will be focusing on the potential of using the TUIs as IoT LoRa devices, supporting our GWAP design.

When understanding GWAPs, they were commonly used for security, computer vision, content filtering, and traditionally seen as computer video games. Their goals were to impact the productivity while adding the gamification to the given tasks [28,29]. They emerged from the need to solve demanding computational problems which could be in return seem effortless for humans. These games have been also seen in crowdsourcing the data. Simple tasks for humans would be to classify or identify specific data, and these games would contain the proper incentives and rewards. The work reported by [18], focused on different rewarding strategies for engaging more users in the gameplay where the authors created the theoretical model of rewarding the users who classify the images on the web using the ESP game. To the best of our knowledge, there are no prior works creating GWAPs and combining them with LoRa and IoT. In our approach, we step away from the traditional computer GWAPs and focus on providing them as Tangible User Interfaces (TUIs), capable of real-time interaction using long-range wireless protocols. Our GWAP experience consists from a real-world setting game, LoRa protocol, and an IoT device acting as a TUI.

## 3  Methodology

In this section, we describe the design of our tangible IoT GWAP, used for leveraging the LoRa open radio protocol. In the next subsections, we describe our tangible GWAP apparatus (Sect. 3.1) as well as the game mechanics and the main interactions occurring throughout the game (Sect. 3.2). We then provide the information regarding our LoRa study setup (Sect. 3.3), describing the sample size, location, and methods for collecting the data inquiry using pre and post surveys, collected data used for monitoring and logging. From these data, we gain understanding about the LoRa performance and the game strategies used by the game participants.

## 3.1  GWAP Apparatus

Our design concept for the tangible GWAP interface encompasses two LoRa enabled interactive rattles. These devices embed IoT microcontrollers, their expansion boards containing sensors, additionally mounted actuators, as well as the antennas used to increase the range of LoRa communication. We opted for the metaphor of a rattle due to its familiar interaction usage. Moreover, contrary to the typical usage of antennas, we flipped the antennas upside-down to act as rattle holders, hindering the radio signal on purpose. While IoT LoRa enabled devices can be used without the antennas, in our design we flipped the antenna to provide game participants a more comfortable handling of the IoT device. Also, we were interested in understanding the performance of LoRa communication in a scenario where the antennas are integrated in the tangible device. In addition, the known shaking motion in rattles was used in our prototypes to take the full advantage of the accelerometers, serving as a sensory input to the microcontroller. More details of the sensors and actuators are described in the game mechanics section below. Our tangible IoT GWAP rattles are designed to act as low-power transceivers and to provide the peer-to-peer connection using LoRa (868MHz). The microcontrollers used were based on two low-cost 2 PyCom LoPy4[1] boards, coupled with 2 PySense expansion boards[2], used for power supply and sensory input. In addition, we also mounted the vibration actuator for the purpose of causing additional haptic feedback to the game participants. To each rattle, we also mounted external buttons, which will be used as the fire action. Also, each rattle was equipped with additional external GPS modules, serving to portray the outdoor location of participants during the gameplay. We mounted the GPS to deduce the understanding of the radiation coverage and players' game strategies. Lastly, each rattle was equipped with the rechargeable Li-Po 3.3 V battery, providing the power autonomy throughout the whole gameplay. The batteries were easily rechargeable using the external mini USB cable. Figure 1 depicts the apparatus and how participants used the IoT device for interaction in diverse settings.

## 3.2  GWAP Mechanics and Interactions

Two participants play the GWAP by carrying the IoT rattles. They start the game by facing back from each other while doing the countdown from 10 to 0, then participants go for 1 min in opposite directions of each other. These rules have been taken from previous known games, by merging Hide-and-seek and Pistol Duel games. Afterwards, participants are invited and instructed to explore larger distances from each other and hide behind the urban obstacles found around the campus used in the experiment. The rationale for instructing the participants to hide was to avoid being shot by the other opponent, as the radio signal should get weaker. After receiving the instructions, participants

---

[1] https://pycom.io/product/lopy4/.
[2] https://pycom.io/product/pysense/.

**Fig. 1.** LoRa IoT TUI GWAP apparatus (image to the left) and GWAP participants in outdoor and indoor settings exchanging payloads with IoT device (image to the right)

start to run and charge their devices by performing the shake gestures, which are captured by the microcontrollers' accelerometer. The LED indicator displays the current state of charge, using the variable intensity of the shake, being depicted from red (discharged), passing by yellow, to the green color (fully charged). Once the device is fully charged, the players can proceed to shoot by pressing the button on the rattle at the moment they find more appropriate for the signal to reach the opponent. This action sends the data using the LoRa protocol. Payload size used in our experiment varied between 3 to 10 bytes, relative to the type of action and words used (e.g. "hit", "got_hit|<life>"). Once a player receives a hit from the opponent, it also receives the haptic (e.g. 1 s of constant vibration actuator) followed with the visual feedback (constant red LED indicator). The participant who successfully manages to send the payload and hit the other opponent receives solely the visual feedback (constant blue LED indicator). For the purpose of this study, we did not focus on providing the acoustic feedback, nor we did focus on the payload size. The game is played until one of the participants receives a total of 10 shots. When this happens, both of the opponents receive the visual and haptic indicators of the end of the game (LED and vibration feedback lasting for 10 s). Video of the gameplay can be found on-line[3].

### 3.3 Study Setup and Data Inquiry

Our tests were conducted in the urban area around the main campus building, as well as inside the corridors of a research institute. Our GWAP was successfully played by 20 participants (mainly from XYZ), with an average age of 32 (SD = 10). 12 participants were females, 6 were males and 2 participants preferred not to share their gender.

**Pre and Post Surveys.** Before the start of the game, we briefed the participants about the game rules, explaining that they will be wearing an object and

---

[3] https://goo.gl/dVnvaV.

using open radio communication for interaction, and that their goal is to choose a strategy weather or not they will play in attack or defense. Afterwards, we collected the demographic data. Participants were then invited to complete the pre-study, where we asked them to report their current understanding of long-range radio communication. We asked the users questions regarding the LoRa radio coverage range: "Using LoRa, which is the expected range of communication?". Participants were offered to select one of the following options: below 1 m, 1 m, 10 m, 50 m, 100 m, 1000 m, above 1000 m. Once the game was completed, we asked the participants to report back once again the range during the post-study. We also asked participants to report if they discovered something about the radio coverage during their gameplay. Additional questions were also given where we asked which of the game strategies they used. Finally, we asked the participants to complete the set of predetermined scales: (i) System Usability Scale (SUS) [11], a 7 point scale used for understanding the usability of the game; and (ii) Self-Assessment Manikin (SAM) [10], a 9 point scale used for measuring the arousal, valence and dominance of the game players. The purpose of collecting these data was to compare the affective states of the players and to understand their influence on the usability of our GWAP.

**Data Monitoring and Logging.** Using our GWAP IoT devices during the game, we obtained four different types of data: (i) Events, recorded upon game start, including charging payload, attempting to shoot, shoot, hitting the opponent, getting hit by the opponent, winning and losing the game; (ii) Timelines, used for all parameters throughout the gameplay, including life, charge load, pending shoot and charge shake counter; (iii) LoRa statistics, including rxtimestamp, rssi, snr, sfrx, sftx, txtrials, txpower, txtimeonair, txcounter, txfrequency; and (iv) Geographical information including the GPS timestamp, latitude and longitude. The purpose for collecting these data was to understand the power signal and the feasibility of using the GWAP players to crowdsource the signal strength.

## 4    Results

In this section, we report the several findings obtained through data inquiry techniques described in Sect. 3. We describe how game players evaluate their perception of range before and after the game. Also, we report results on usability and affective states of the GWAP players, and we depict the radiation coverage.

**Usability.** Using the System Usability Scale (SUS), we first modified the word "website" to "game" used in SUS scale to match our GWAP. Concerning the system usability, the final score obtained was 70.88/100. 75% (n = 20) of players reported the wish to frequently use this game. 95% of the participants found the game not to be complex, while 85% suggested that the game was easy to use. 40% of participants would use this game frequently, while 55% did not find anything complex during the game. Moreover, 75% of them, rated the game to be easy to use, while 80% of participants reported no need for any assistance of external persons using the GWAP game. Also, 70% of participants were in favor of the game not containing any inconsistencies, while all participants suggested that most people would learn to use this game very quickly.

**Affective States of the Game Players.** Using the Self-Assessment Manikin Scale (SAM), we asked the game players to rate their affective states after completing the game. They rated the valence (level of game being pleasant), arousal (level of game being exciting) and dominance (level of providing control of the game dominant feeling). We find: (i) valence score (AVG 7.0/9, SD 1.48) keeping the game very pleasant; (ii) arousal score (AVG 5.55/9, SD 2.14) suggesting the game to be slightly above average in terms of being exciting; and (iii) dominance score (AVG 6.10/9, SD 2.34) suggesting that players felt confident using the GWAP system.

**Radio Coverage Perception (RCP).** We asked the game participants to rate the expected radio coverage using LoRa before and after playing the game Our hypothesis was that the perception of the participants will change after playing the GWAP and influence the participants to select the higher coverage. Results indicate that the radio coverage perception increased to 35% of participants, remaining the same for 50%, while decreasing to 15%.

**LoRa Performance Analysis [RQ4].** We compared the number of times the participants were charging and releasing the payload (shooting) against the geographical location (GPS) of the persons. We also analyzed: (i) the ratio of attempts to shoot (when the player does not have a full charge, resulting in an unsuccessful shot) versus effective shoots (resulted with sending the payload); – to understand if the players kept on always trying to shoot no matter what; (ii) the attempt to charge when the charge was already at maximum – to see if the users payed attention to the LED indicator (iii) Lastly, by observing the GPS and places from which participants were sending and receiving the payloads, we get the insight of the game strategies of our players. Observing the Received signal strength (RSSI) from signals of the players, we notice a tendency for a close range ($>= -70$) with a mode = median = $-68$.

**Gameplay Analysis and Strategies.** Using the storage on microcontrollers, we gathered the event logs from the played games, counting the numbers of reset parameters, shoot trials, shots, successful shots, received hits and shake counters. From the device logs, Fig. 2 depicts the location of the events using the GPS, where the color range represents the signal strength (in RSSI) and the circle size represents the number of events occurred in that location. It is worth mentioning that some of the marks are located inside of the building, where GPS accuracy may not be precise. Also some of the other points should be accounted as potential errors due to the game participants being located near the walls of the building, which may interfere with the GPS reception. Among all game players, only one participant decided to explore the distance (red circles at the lower right), and unlike the others, went even further away. Some participants managed to receive and send consecutive shots, while nearby buildings did not interfere much with the signal, nevertheless having the RSSI clearly weaker. Players varied their speeds in some game plays, while in other, players were more passively walking, focusing in charging and shooting, and trying to hide and to obtain a greater distance from each other. Most relevant parameters registered were: (1) play time (min) (AVG 2:34, STD 1:18); (2) RSSI (−64.14, SD 22.49); message time on air (ms) (AVG 36.02, SD 6.24);

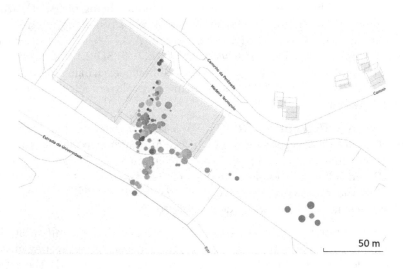

**Fig. 2.** Game heatmap - logged events during the gameplay in indoor and outdoor settings. Line in bottom right corner indicates the scale ruler of 50 m. Color range (green to red) represents the signal strength (in RSSI). Circle size represents the number of events occurred in that location. (Color figure online)

Regarding the game strategies, throughout the game, participants reported diverse game strategies: (i) using walls of the building to hide (12 participants); (ii) getting a bigger distance from the opponent (13 participants); (iii) (playing in attack mode, by shooting as fast as possible (13 participants); Also, 1 participant tried to cover the antenna and 2 participants did not have any strategy, reporting "...I did not have a strategy, nor I was thinking. I was just shaking and shooting". All of these reports we tried to compare against the collected data, however, we were not able to obtain more insights. Moreover, our field observations during the GWAP gameplay underpin that most of the strategies were in fact, for participants not to run nor hide, but rather to shake and shoot as fast as possible. What we also observed, is that the toy aspect of the IoT device seemed to inspire curiosity in most of the participants, inviting them to explore more the device than to explore the surrounding areas around them.

## 5   Discussion

Long range radio technology supports smart IoT applications to solve some of the biggest challenges on our planet such as energy management, natural source reduction, pollution control, infrastructure efficiency, disaster prevention, etc. In our case, we use LoRa for a real-world GWAP. In our study, we use the Internet of Things (IoT) as TUI devices capable of communicating through LoRa. Moreover, we use crowdsourcing to leverage the knowledge and awareness of LoRa technology. We ask participants to play a real-world GWAP and use our designed LoRa IoT devices for interactions. We study: (i) whether participants' perception of LoRa coverage range changes after participating the GWAP; (ii) system evaluation, including usability and affective states of the game players; and (iii) identification of LoRa coverage during the events of the game, depicted in the game heatmap (Fig. 2), understanding the game strategies of the players.

**Usability and Affective States.** Our implemented prototype shows that IoT devices can be used to design GWAPs by engaging the users in an open world physical gameplay. As reported by the SUS scale, the players found the game to be fairly easy to use and play, avoiding any potential inconsistencies. From the SAM scale, focusing on effective responses from our game participants, we found that players tend to fully enjoy the experience throughout the whole game. From the gathered inquires and post-study analysis, the participants shared with research authors couple of suggestions as follows: (i) hit counter would help them to improve the understanding of the game timeline; (ii) red LED indicator should be shown promptly after the hit success, as participants were expecting to have the blue LED indicator. This is intended to be corrected during the future release of our GWAP; (iii) to some participants, rattles were perceived to be more of fragile toys than a robust IoT devices, used as TUIs for interactions.

**Coverage Perception and Performance.** As it was aforementioned, LoRa protocol is using long range communication and frequencies which can obtain high distances. By default, we were aware of the challenge whether it would be actually possible for participants to use the urban obstacles to hinder the signal and thus to avoid getting hit. However, we were surprised in finding out that most of the participants did not actually explore the objects and terrain surrounding them, and instead rather chose to be within the vicinity of each other and observe what actually happens on the other rattle device. This also explains the phenomenon that most of the participants did not have the notion of the real radio range of LoRa protocol. Nevertheless, 35% of participants reported an increase of the radio range perception, while 15% experienced a decrease of the radio range perception. Observing the game results, all participants who reported the decrease in the radio range, fully coincide to participants who lost the game (both indoors and outdoors, as depicted in red in Fig. 2). This can be explained as their performance during the game was not successful. Thus, the perception of the decreased range is the byproduct of them losing the game, due to the amount of times being shot. As for the LoRa performance, from our metadata analysis, we found that two major groups were playing in close vicinity (RSSI $\geq -40$) or farther against each other (RSSI $\leq -90$). All game players stated that the interaction with the opponent was possible in most of the locations they were. We also find that flipped antennas allowed the interactions on longer range (within 100 m), as RSSI signal has been successfully caught by the opponents at greater distances. This suggests that more studies should be performed, with diverse other designs of the LoRa IoT devices, used for GWAP, where antennas can be hindered in other ways.

**Field Observations.** Our LoRa IoT devices (in further, rattles) seemed to have raised interest in participants causing the start of the GWAP as soon as they were instructed with the rules of the game, leaving no space for most of the players to run, but rather focus on fast shaking. We also noticed that our rattles were used for exploration of other interaction gestures. For instance, some participants did not just shake, but also used other curious techniques to charge the payload, including: (i) a metaphor and gestures used for magic wand, when casting a spell; (ii) turning the rattle into a pendulum by grabbing the edge of the antenna, allowing the rattle to hang and rotate; (iii) rolling the rattles between their hands causing them to rotate faster and trigger the accelerometers, using the centrifugal force. It was also interesting to see that some participants who were literate with telecommunication technologies tried to apply the principles of Faraday Cage [19], by placing our rattles inside of a trash bin. There were also participants who expressed the wish to play the GWAP several times (outside of the experiment), which we gladly accepted. Also, one pair of participants was very immersed in the game that they did not notice the game being completed several times, causing them to repeatedly play (also outside of the collected results).

**Contributions.** To the best of our knowledge, this study presents the first game with a purpose based on IoT and LoRa technologies. We use IoT as TUIs, and use them to communicate through LoRa protocol to raise its awareness and gather the radio coverage signal. We believe that this kind of GWAPs in real-world setting may find large appreciation due to the potential of interaction between more people in same physical environments. Our results from the questionnaires and conversation with the players support that the feasibility to engage and inform citizens about these technologies using GWAPs. In this study, we melded these technologies together and embedded them into a game. A game that allows the players to get both the insights of LoRa technology, as well as to gain awareness of how LoRa can be easily integrated in ubiquitous devices and environments. Ultimately, our GWAP empowers citizens to create solutions for their custom problems using long range communication without the need of any third party entities providing the expensive data plan coverage, and with a standardized open-access protocol. By showcasing this kind of GWAPs to citizens, in a concrete application using the different technologies, we are enabling the potential of novel ideas that can be implemented.

**Limitations.** However, it is also important to outline several technical and design constraints for future studies. Current indoor activities are subject to the errors in GPS location. The antenna used in our IoT device which was used as a rattle holder might not be the best practice when understanding the radio coverage. In addition, constant shaking caused damage to the wiring of the external modules (GPS, button, accelerometer) and our rattles had to be re-soldered again. Furthermore, we learned that our IoT devices needed to be more robust in order to resist the direct collision with the ground, as this was the case with one of the game participants being very excited and immersed in the gameplay. Therefore, more long-lasting encapsulation methods and designs should be more thoroughly explored. Also, haptic feedback obtained from the vibration actuator did not provide as much of force it could, as the participants during the shaking gesture sometimes reported not to have received any feedback, occurred when understanding if the opponent was shooting them. Moreover, the current version does not give higher rewarding incentives.

**Future Studies.** In our GWAP, rewarding is solely the sense of winning the game against another human player, and defeating the opponent as many times as the two players can play. In future studies, we envision the possibility of adding multi-step winnings that culminate in a larger victory, i.e. giving the players a sense of progression. We also plan a multiplayer version of the game, allowing the players to be in a radio mesh network from all-to-all instead of one-to-one. This will make it possible to get more metadata regarding the radio coverage from a larger population at once. It will also lead to more detail radiation heat map and can be used for identification of blind spots. Moreover, the multiplayer scenario will be used to test the mechanics allowing the possibility of forming diverse teams. We believe that this IoT GWAP and its design is useful not only for raising awareness and mapping signal coverages but could also be used for other types of applications, including other sensory input such as the interactive way of understanding the health of crops or preventing the fire.

**Conclusion.** The Internet of Things (IoT) is opening new possibilities for sensing, monitoring and actuating in urban environments. They support a shift from mostly human-centric connected devices into a hybrid network of humans and things collaborating in production, transmission and processing of data through low-cost and low power devices connected via long-range wide area networks. This paper explores the design possibilities provided by technologies such as IoT and LoRa and tangible computing in moving beyond traditional egocentric applications based on high cost, power and computing personal mobile devices. To illustrate and test this approach we designed a 2-player duel game based on IoT controllers and the LoRa communication protocol. Here we report on the main evaluation dimensions of this new design space: (i) game usability (SUS) leading to an above average score; (ii) Affective states of the players (SAM) depicting pleasant and engaging gameplay, while players retain control; (iii) Radio coverage perception (RCP) showing that most participants did not change their perception of the radio distance after playing.

**Acknowledgements.** Reported study is part of LARGESCALE project with grant no. 32474 by Fundação para a Ciência e a Tecnologia (FCT) and Portuguese National Funds (PIDDAC). It is also supported by MITIExcell grant M1420-01-0145-FEDER-000002 and LARSyS grant UID/EEA/50009/2019. In further, two FCT grants SFRH/BD/135854/2018 and SFRH/DB/136005/2018 assisted the study.

# References

1. Adelantado, F., Vilajosana, X., Tuset-Peiro, P., Martinez, B., Melia-Segui, J., Watteyne, T.: Understanding the limits of LoRaWAN. IEEE Commun. Mag. **55**(9), 34–40 (2017). https://doi.org/10.1109/MCOM.2017.1600613
2. Al-Kashoash, H., Kemp, A.H.: Comparison of 6LOWPAN and LPWAN for the internet of things. Aust. J. Electr. Electron. Eng. **13**(4), 268–274 (2016)
3. Althoff, T., White, R.W., Horvitz, E.: Influence of Pokémon GO on physicalactivity: study and implications. J. Med. Internet Res. **18**(12), e315 (2016)
4. Antifakos, S., Schiele, B.: Bridging the gap between virtual and physical games using wearable sensors. In: Proceedings of Sixth International Symposium on Wearable Computers, (ISWC 2002), pp. 139–140. IEEE (2002)
5. Atzori, L., Iera, A., Morabito, G.: SIoT: giving a social structure to the internet of things. IEEE Commun. Lett. **15**(11), 1193–1195 (2011)
6. Augustin, A., Yi, J., Clausen, T., Townsley, W.M.: A study of lora: long range & low power networks for the internet of things. Sensors **16**(9), 1466 (2016)
7. Avouris, N.M., Yiannoutsou, N.: A review of mobile location-based games for learning across physical and virtual spaces. J. UCS **18**(15), 2120–2142 (2012)
8. Bankov, D., Khorov, E., Lyakhov, A.: On the limits of LoRaWAN channel access. In: Proceedings of the 2016 International Conference on Engineering and Telecommunication (EnT), Moscow, Russia, pp. 29–30 (2016)
9. Bor, M., Vidler, J.E., Roedig, U.: LoRa for the internet of things (2016)
10. Bradley, M.M., Lang, P.J.: Measuring emotion: the self-assessment manikin and the semantic differential. J. Behav. Ther. Exp. Psychiatry **25**(1), 49–59 (1994)
11. Brooke, J., et al.: SUS-a quick and dirty usability scale. Usabil. Eval. Ind. **189**(194), 4–7 (1996)
12. Burke, J.A., et al.: Participatory sensing (2006)
13. Colley, A., et al.: The geography of Pokémon GO: beneficial and problematic effects on places and movement. In: Proceedings of the 2017 CHI Conference on Human Factors in Computing Systems, pp. 1179–1192. ACM (2017)
14. Cruz-Neira, C., Sandin, D.J., DeFanti, T.A., Kenyon, R.V., Hart, J.C.: The CAVE: audio visual experience automatic virtual environment. Commun. ACM **35**(6), 64–73 (1992)
15. de la Guía, E., Lozano, M.D., Penichet, V.M.: Interacting with objects in games through RFID technology. In: Radio Frequency Identification from System to Applications. InTech (2013)
16. Hinske, S., Langheinrich, M.: Using a movable RFID antenna to automatically determine the position and orientation of objects on a tabletop. In: Roggen, D., Lombriser, C., Tröster, G., Kortuem, G., Havinga, P. (eds.) EuroSSC 2008. LNCS, vol. 5279, pp. 14–26. Springer, Heidelberg (2008). https://doi.org/10.1007/978-3-540-88793-5_2
17. Ishii, H.: Tangible bits: beyond pixels. In: Proceedings of the 2nd International Conference on Tangible and Embedded Interaction, pp. xv–xxv. ACM (2008)
18. Jain, S., Parkes, D.C.: A game-theoretic analysis of games with a purpose. In: Papadimitriou, C., Zhang, S. (eds.) WINE 2008. LNCS, vol. 5385, pp. 342–350. Springer, Heidelberg (2008). https://doi.org/10.1007/978-3-540-92185-1_40
19. King, D.R., Rowan, J.C., Johnson, D.D., Reis, B.E.: Faraday cage. US Patent 5,761,053, 2 June 2 1998
20. Kranz, M., Holleis, P., Schmidt, A.: Embedded interaction: interacting with the internet of things. IEEE Internet Comput. **14**(2), 46–53 (2010)

21. Marais, J.M., Malekian, R., Abu-Mahfouz, A.M.: LoRa and LoRaWAN testbeds: a review. In: 2017 IEEE AFRICON, pp. 1496–1501. IEEE (2017)
22. Prandi, C., Salomoni, P., Roccetti, M., Nisi, V., Nunes, N.J.: Walking with geo-zombie: a pervasive game to engage people in urban crowdsourcing. In: 2016 International Conference on Computing, Networking and Communications (ICNC), pp. 1–5. IEEE (2016)
23. Qin, Z., McCann, J.A.: Resource efficiency in low-power wide-area networks for IoT applications. In: 2017 IEEE Global Communications Conference, GLOBECOM 2017, pp. 1–7. IEEE (2017)
24. Radeta, M., Cesario, V., Matos, S., Nisi, V.: Gaming versus storytelling: understanding children's interactive experiences in a museum setting. In: Nunes, N., Oakley, I., Nisi, V. (eds.) ICIDS 2017. LNCS, vol. 10690, pp. 163–178. Springer, Cham (2017). https://doi.org/10.1007/978-3-319-71027-3_14
25. Robbins, S.J., Westerinen, W.J., Hanson, L.M., Son, S.H., Wattles, R.J.: Augmented reality and physical games. US Patent 9,717,981, 1 August 2017
26. Römer, K., Domnitcheva, S.: Smart playing cards: a ubiquitous computing game. Pers. Ubiquit. Comput. 6(5–6), 371–377 (2002)
27. Sinclair, J., Hingston, P., Masek, M.: Considerations for the design of exergames. In: Proceedings of the 5th International Conference on Computer Graphics and Interactive Techniques in Australia and Southeast Asia, pp. 289–295. ACM (2007)
28. Von Ahn, L.: Games with a purpose. Computer 39(6), 92–94 (2006)
29. Von Ahn, L., Dabbish, L.: Designing games with a purpose. Commun. ACM 51(8), 58–67 (2008)
30. Wilson, D.E.: Designing for the pleasures of disputation-or-how to make friends by trying to kick them! IT University of Copenhagen, Innovative Communication (2012)

# Noise-Canceling Music: Reducing Noise by Mixing It with Suitable Music

Hiroki Tokuhisa[✉], Kenta Sato, Kohei Matsuda, Keiji Matsui, and Satoshi Nakamura

Graduate School of Advanced Mathematical Sciences,
Meiji University, Tokyo, Japan
cs182023@meiji.ac.jp

**Abstract.** Ambient noise is part of our daily life, and sometimes such noise can be bothersome. To reduce noise exposure, people usually listen to music through headphones and earphones or use noise-canceling devices. However, these measures can block some important information that the users do not want to miss. We propose a method called *"noise-canceling music"* that reduces the subjective sound magnitude of the noise when it is mixed with suitable music. The results of the experimental tests confirm that the perceived sound magnitude of noise decreases when it is mixed with suitable music. However, the method was not effective when perceptions of music were different.

**Keywords:** Noise · Music · Entertaining · Noise-canceling-music · Discomfort

## 1 Introduction

We are surrounded by noise in our daily lives. There are many kinds of noise that come from machines (for example, vacuum cleaners, washing machines, police cars, passing trains and aircraft), and noise that comes from people and animals (for example, the sounds of leg shaking, keyboard tapping, mastication, barking dogs, crying children, and electoral campaign loudspeakers), all of which are often annoying.

To protect themselves from noise, people often listen to music at high volume using headphones or earphones. However, this leads to problems such as deterioration of hearing ability and sound leakage. Another way of reducing the exposure to noise is by using hermetically sealed or noise-canceling headphones. However, while these devices can alleviate stress from the ambient noise, using them may cause the wearer to miss important sounds such as train announcements, doorbells, alarms, or the voices of people speaking to us from behind.

We propose a method of protection from the ambient noise by distracting the user's attention from annoying noise instead of covering it up with some other sound. We hypothesize that mixing appropriate music with noise can reduce the negative perception of noise. Specifically, when a particular sound causes negative impressions in a user, our method transforms that impression of the noise to a positive one by playing suitable music and reducing the subjective sound.

We call this method *"noise-canceling music."* In our research, we implement and test a prototype system to check the usefulness of our method through experiments.

© IFIP International Federation for Information Processing 2019
Published by Springer Nature Switzerland AG 2019
E. van der Spek et al. (Eds.): ICEC-JCSG 2019, LNCS 11863, pp. 278–284, 2019.
https://doi.org/10.1007/978-3-030-34644-7_22

## 2  Related Work

Various studies have reported on measures to environmental noise in our daily lives.

Haiyan et al. [1] proposed a method that creates a masking effect by using natural, relaxing sounds such as the flowing of a river or the chirping of a bird. The masking sound is superimposed on the noise and is limited to natural sounds. Music was not at the center of the discussion in Haiyan et al.'s paper. Also, Bolin et al. [2] focused on wind turbine noise in a quiet area and investigated the effect of using natural sound (wind or waves) as masking sounds. The results showed that the perceived loudness of the noise was reduced. In our research, we do not aim to create a masking effect, but our attempt to lower the attention to noise by superimposing another noise over it is similar. If the same effect is confirmed for music, we feel it would be possible to utilize the user's favorite music to cope with noise.

Vawter [3] proposed a method called "*ambient addition*," which applies digital signal processing to noise in devices such as headphones and blends it into the music being listened to. Although this approach is similar to ours in that it removes the discomfort from noise without blocking the surrounding information, our goal is also to change noise to a positive impression. This can significantly improve the quality of users' lives.

Various studies have already investigated the effect of music and noise on human perception and behavior.

Fiegel et al. [4] investigated the influence of the background music genre (hip-hop, jazz, classical, and rock) on the taste of food. The results showed that the impressions of the four music genres alter the impression of emotional stimuli in foods such as chocolate. Yamasaki et al. [5] investigated the effects of music on the perception of the environment. The results showed that the evaluation of the environment affected the characteristics of the music, especially in conditions where the perceived characteristics of the music and environment were incongruent. From these reports, it can be expected that an environment of unpleasant noise will be transformed into the opposite impression by mixing music.

Newbold et al. [6] investigated the effect of natural noise on the performance of work, such as study and office work. The result showed that natural noise creates a gentle feeling but suggests that if the volume change is large, it is harmful to the performance of the work. In our method, we expect there to be a positive effect on psychological impressions of various noise levels by manipulating the sound to feel small to the hearer.

## 3  Noise-Canceling Music

The aim of our work is to reduce the subjective sound magnitude of the noise by mixing the noise with suitable music. We hypothesize that mixing appropriate music with noise can reduce the perceived magnitude of the sound. The *noise-canceling music* method is based on this hypothesis. Below are some examples of how the method works.

- The sound of cicadas is one of the loud noises heard in Japan in summer. When the user feels annoyed by this noise, suitable music evoking images of summer will play (for example, "Summer" composed by Joe Hisaishi) (see Fig. 1).
- The sound of construction is very loud and distracting. When the user feels annoyed by this noise, appropriate music evoking images of people working at a construction site will play (for example, "The star of our planet" by Chijo no Hoshi in Japanese, composed by Miyuki Nakajima).

The sounds surrounding the user should be continuously sensed. If user feels annoyed, suitable music will play automatically, reducing the subjective sound magnitude of the noise psychologically and changing the impression gained from the noise.

The music in our method can be presented in two ways. One is by using smart speakers such as *Google Home* and *Amazon Echo*, which are becoming widespread. The other is by using a wearable acoustic device such as *Xperia Ear Duo* [7]. With smart speakers installed in the environment, it should be possible to reduce the discomfort for all people on the spot by presenting the music selected for a particular kind of noise, but there is also a possibility that for some people that particular music will be undesirable. In contrast, when wearable an acoustic device, the music can be presented according to individual preferences, although it might be inconvenient to wear the device at all times.

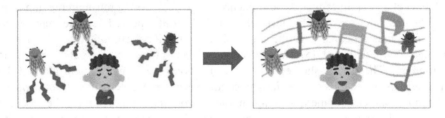

**Fig. 1.** Concept of proposed method

## 4 Experiments and Discussion

The *noise-canceling music* which we propose is based on the hypothesis that "mixing appropriate music with noise can reduce the perceived magnitude of the sound". We conducted an experiment to verify whether the noise remains bothersome when it is mixed with appropriate music.

We presented the participants with noise and music at the same time, for 30 s. Then, the music playback stopped and only the noise was played. The participants operated the system to reproduce the same sound magnitude of the noise as when it was played with the music. Based on this reproduced volume, we defined the subjective volume evaluation of the noise as the sound volume evaluation value and performed analysis to determine the effect of the proposed method.

To test our hypothesis, we selected noises frequently heard in daily life that were deemed by the authors to be bothersome. We then selected music that was deemed to be suitable for each noise. In addition, we decided on noise and music that could be placed in the same category, and then combined them. Table 1 lists the noise and music used in our experiment and the categories determined to be common for them. The participants tested all of the combinations of noise and music in this table randomly (ten kinds of music and nine kinds of noise). Also, when the category was "silence", only noise was reproduced. In this case, the participant evaluated the volume of the noise, assuming that the music without sound was playing. After the experiment, we asked all the participants to answer the question: "What do you associate with each example of music?" There were 16 participants (seven male and nine female).

**Table 1.** Correspondence table of noise and music.

|   | Category | Noise | Music/Composer |
|---|----------|-------|----------------|
| 0 | Silence | | Silence |
| 1 | Summer | Cry of a Cicada | "Summer"/Joe Hisaishi |
| 2 | Car | Car Running | "TRUTH"/Masahiro Ando |
| 3 | Children | Children's Screeches | "Electrical Parade"/Gershon Kingsley, etc. |
| 4 | Bad weather | Strong Wind | "He's a Pirate"/Klaus Badelt |
| 5 | Speaking | Crowd | "Moanin"/Bobby Timmons |
| 6 | Machine operation | Air Conditioner Running | "Battaille Decisive"/Shiro Sagisu |
| 7 | Construction | Rock drill | "Tijo no Hoshi"/Miyuki Nakajima |
| 8 | Sound leakage | Sound Leakage from Earphone | "One More Time"/Thomas Bangalter, etc. |
| 9 | Meal | Mastication Sound | "Attack on Titan"/Hiroyuki Sawano |

Before analyzing the results, we normalized the evaluation value based on the result of noise in no music (silence) category. Then, we compared the same category with a different category and analyzed the answers to the question to see whether the music associations of the participants were the same as ours or not.

Table 2 summarizes the average volume evaluation values for each combination of noise and music, where the noise is listed in rows and the music is listed in columns. Table 2 shows that the volume of the noise heard together with the music of the same category was evaluated as small in five categories: "summer", "children", "bad weather", "driving sound", and "construction".

**Table 2.** Average volume evaluation value.

| Music / Noise | Summer | Car | Children | Weather | Speaking | Driving | Construction | Leakage | Eating |
|---|---|---|---|---|---|---|---|---|---|
| Summer | 0.81 | 0.89 | 1.00 | 1.10 | 0.82 | 0.84 | 0.83 | 0.97 | 0.86 |
| Car | 1.04 | 0.85 | 0.94 | 0.94 | 0.76 | 0.82 | 0.91 | 0.92 | 0.94 |
| Children | 0.90 | 1.05 | 0.82 | 1.31 | 1.24 | 1.38 | 1.04 | 0.97 | 1.11 |
| Weather | 0.88 | 0.77 | 0.92 | 0.72 | 0.95 | 0.89 | 0.81 | 0.86 | 0.80 |
| Speaking | 0.90 | 0.90 | 0.81 | 0.83 | 0.91 | 0.97 | 0.91 | 0.95 | 1.00 |
| Driving | 0.82 | 0.91 | 0.99 | 0.93 | 0.92 | 0.81 | 0.82 | 0.85 | 0.81 |
| Construction | 0.94 | 0.96 | 0.97 | 0.89 | 0.88 | 0.91 | 0.87 | 0.92 | 0.91 |
| Leakage | 0.97 | 0.86 | 0.96 | 0.95 | 0.81 | 0.88 | 0.99 | 0.91 | 0.82 |
| Eating | 0.95 | 0.84 | 0.74 | 0.62 | 1.03 | 0.79 | 0.84 | 0.68 | 0.76 |

The average of all volume evaluation values in the same category (e.g. noise category was summer and music category was also summer) was 0.82, and the average in a different category (e.g. noise category was summer and music category was speaking) was 0.94. Figure 2 shows a comparison of the volume evaluation average with the averages of the same and different categories. Also, the left diagram shows the cases where the associations of the participants were the same as ours, and the right diagram shows the cases where the associations were different from ours. These results reveal that the sound volume evaluation value of the same category was significantly lower, regardless of whether the music associations were the same as, or different to ours (p < 0.05).

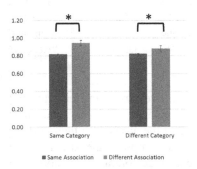

**Fig. 2.** The difference of the sound volume evaluation.

The results of the experiment demonstrate that our method can reduce the subjective sound magnitude of the noise by presenting music suitable for the noise, thus confirming our hypothesis. Moreover, even if associations from the music were different to ours, our method worked effectively with the music selected by us. The results show that even if the images evoked by the music do not match the noise, the tone and the atmosphere of the music blend with the images of the participants, so the noise can be well integrated.

However, in the "Children" category in Table 2, the sound volume is rated very high when presenting the music of another category. This may mean that presenting music unsuitable for the noise makes the noise feel louder, which confirms the importance of presenting music appropriate for the noise. We believe that the effectiveness of our method will increase greatly if we present music that will evoke the same images in as many people as possible.

In the future, we will investigate different kinds of music appropriate for reducing the perceived volume of other types of noise. If wearable acoustic devices like the *Xperia Ear Duo* become more common, it will be possible to present to the user the music he or she likes without having to seal the ears.

# 5    Conclusion and Future Work

In this paper, we proposed a method called "*noise-canceling music*" which protects users from everyday noises by mixing the noise with appropriate music. We conducted experiments combining multiple kinds of noise and music and discovered that the noise tended to be evaluated as less obtrusive when it evoked the same images as the music.

In our experiments, all participants were Japanese, so we used music familiar to Japanese people. However, even in areas other than Japan, the method is expected to have similar effects because it focuses on matching the images evoked by music and noise. Music can be selected according to the specific region and culture.

There are still many aspects of the proposed method that have not been clarified yet. For example, it is not clear whether the effect depends on the context of the music, the frequency, or something else altogether. We intend to clarify these points by conducting more experiments in the future.

In our research, we focused on matching the noise and the music, but the method in which the impression of noise is transformed can also be considered. Sounds in movies, dramas, and animations are often artificial: for example, the sound of a wave is made by shaking red beans in a box, and the footsteps of a horse can be made using a box, a bowl, and wood. In other words, by manipulating the noise to make it seem like something else, it is possible to eliminate the negative influence of the noise. The possibility of this impression transformation will be explored in our future work.

In addition, we also plan to implement a system which can sense the noise surrounding the user and select and play from the user's music archive a type of music suitable for the noise. We plan to assess the usefulness of our system in daily life.

**Acknowledgments.** This work was supported in part by JST ACCEL Grant Number JPMJAC1602, Japan.

# References

1. Haiyan, S., Ying, S., Huan, Z.: High annoyance noise masking. In: IEEE 2nd International Conference on Signal and Image Processing, pp. 380–384 (2018)
2. Bolin, K., Nilsson, M.E.: The potential of natural sounds to mask wind turbine noise. Acta Acust. Unit. Acust. **96**, 131–137 (2010)
3. Vawter, N.: Ambient addition: how to turn urban noise into music. MIT, School of Architecture and Planning, Program in Media Arts and Sciences (2006)
4. Fiegel, A., Meullenet, J.F., Harrington, R.J., Humble, R., Seo, H.S.: Background music genre can modulate flavor pleasantness and overall impression of food stimuli. Appetite **76**, 144–152 (2014)
5. Yamasaki, T., Yamada, K., Petri, L.: Viewing the world through the prism of music: effects of music on perceptions of the environment. Psychol. Music **43**, 61–74 (2013)
6. Newbold, J.W., Luton, J., Cox, A.L., Gould, S.J.J.: Using nature-based soundscapes to support task performance and mood. In: Proceedings of the 2017 CHI Conference Extended Abstracts on Human Factors in Computing Systems, pp. 2802–2809 (2017)
7. Sony: Xperia Ear Duo(2018). https://www.sonymobile.com/global-en/products/smart-products/xperia-ear-duo/. Accessed 23 June 2019

# Measurement and Effects

# Arousal Measurement Reflected in the Pupil Diameter for a Decision-Making Performance in Serious Games

Petar Jerčić[✉][iD]

Department of Computer Science, Blekinge Institute of Technology,
371 79 Karlskrona, Sweden
petar.jercic@bth.se

**Abstract.** This paper sets out to investigate the potentials of using pupil diameter measure as a contactless biofeedback method. The investigation was performed on how the interdependent and competing activation of the autonomic nervous system is reflected in the pupil diameter and how it affects the performance on decision-making task in serious games. The on-line biofeedback based on physiological measurements of arousal was integrated into the serious game set in the financial context. The pupil diameter was validated against the heart rate data measuring arousal, where the effects of such arousal were investigated. It was found that the physiological arousal was observable on both the heart and pupil data. Furthermore, the participants with lower arousal took less time to reach their decisions, and those decisions were more successful, in comparison to the participants with higher arousal. Moreover, such participants were able to get a higher total score and finish the game. This study validated the potential usage of pupil diameter as an unobtrusive measure of biofeedback, which would be beneficial for the investigation of arousal on human decision-making inside of serious games.

**Keywords:** Serious games · Physiology · Pupil diameter · Heart-rate variability · Arousal · Decision-making

## 1 Introduction

*Emotions* in humans are defined as states of readiness that are used to prepare behavioral responses, foster interactions with the socioeconomic environment, and enable us for making advantageous decisions [19]. Nevertheless, emotions are not always accurately processed, and people overwhelmed by them may take disadvantageous decisions. Therefore, it is no surprise that previous research established that emotions impair or facilitate advantageous *decision-making* performance [8]. Such emotions may be classified through their two independent

---

Supported by the xDelia research project (FP7-ICT-231830).

E. van der Spek et al. (Eds.): ICEC-JCSG 2019, LNCS 11863, pp. 287–298, 2019.
https://doi.org/10.1007/978-3-030-34640-7_23

components, which Russell defined as *valence* and *arousal* [18]. In such a model, valence is defined as an emotional experience of certain situations, and those situations are evaluated in a positive or negative aspect. On another hand, arousal defines the level of excitement in certain situations. In that regard, difficulty and performance on the decision task have been correlated with physiological arousal, which has been generally validated in the models of emotions [4].

Previous investigations have found that economic decision-making may be considered biased through high emotions and arousal [1]. Such investigations were found to be highly context-dependent. Thus *serious games* emerged as a useful tool that can deliver the needed context [20]. Serious games may be defined as games whose purpose is other than entertainment alone, and it can be considered as a 'serious' investigation of certain aspects of human endeavor [12]. Through their inherent ability to provide decision choices with immediate feedback [22], such decision-making choices in serious games could be designed with the financial context in mind. Furthermore, they could provide an application for practicing *emotion-regulation* through psychophysiology that can be implemented as a method of *biofeedback* [17]. Therefore, serious games might provide an interactive context for the on-line perception of emotional responses through biofeedback, which reflects the changes in the individuals' physiology [25].

In contrast to the traditional methods of applying sensors to the skin, eye-tracking enables the collection of physiological data unobtrusively and remotely [16]. The expensive hardware and sensing conditions required, restrict the application of directly-attached sensors in the industrial domain [15]. Taking this limitation into consideration, contactless, non-invasive, and unobtrusive methods for acquiring physiological signals are required to evaluate human behavior in such applications [23]. Therefore, this paper sets out to investigate the potentials of using pupil diameter (PD) measure as a remote device that has the benefits of providing contactless biofeedback for serious games.

## 2  Background

It is argued that the underlying activation of *autonomic nervous system* (ANS) is a part of the generative process of emotions and that physiology allows for the investigation of the complex concept of arousal, which is reflected in the underlying mechanism of the activation of *sympathetic nervous system* (SNS) and *parasympathetic nervous system* (PNS) [21]. The authors emphasize the interdependence of such activation in the underlying mechanism of emotions. Both of the mentioned ANS branches are associated with specific modalities of physiology, such as heart rate (HR) and PD [5]. Nevertheless, it is unique that the underlying activation of ANS is observed clearly and separately in the physiological measure of PD. Therefore, pupillometry and PD are associated with both the SNS (dilation) and PNS (constriction) tonus and their balance [5]. Similarly, HR is also associated with both branches of ANS activation and allows for their investigation [13]. Both of these mechanisms have been illustrated on Fig. 1.

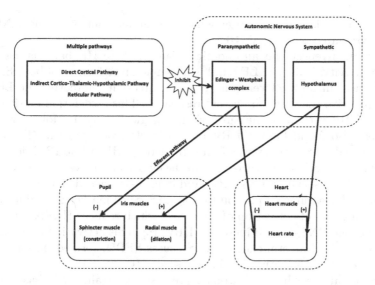

**Fig. 1.** The underlying mechanism of the activation of SNS and PNS on the PD and HR physiology [9].

There are two independent muscles controlling PD, and both are associated with the two competing branches of the ANS [10]. More specifically, the iris sphincter muscle is innervated by the PNS, while the SNS innervates the iris dilator muscle. Therefore, evidence suggests that PD is a measure of the activation of both the SNS and PNS influencing the contraction of the sphincter and dilator muscles. Therefore, the minimal constricted PD is associated with SNS activity, while the maximal dilated PD is associated with PNS activity [24]. Nevertheless, evidence suggests a complex interdependence of PNS and SNS influence on pupillary muscles, as the PD might be associated with the effect of inhibition of the PNS tone together with the SNS activation [5]. Previous research found strong correlations between PD and *heart-rate variance* (HRV) spectrum in the low-frequency (LF) (0.04–0.15 Hz) and high-frequency (HF) (0.15–0.45 Hz) bands [16].

HR and its measure of HRV have been validated as suitable physiological measures of arousal, commonly used in serious games. The information regarding health, emotional, and cognitive state of a person could be inferred through physiological measurements [16]. Therefore, the possibility of acquisition of such measurements with a contactless method might have an important application in many fields, one of which is in serious games [16]. Ample evidence suggests that PD changes reflect higher cognitive processes, such as information-processing load, and physiological arousal in reaction to the stimuli [3]. Contactless sensors offer an added advantage over the traditional ones because they eliminate the possibility of motion artifacts that may occur with electrode measurements [16]. *Spontaneous fluctuations in pupillary diameter* (SFPD) are innervated by the pupillary contraction and dilation which are under control of the ANS, and therefore correlated with HRV [16].

HRV indices reflect the autonomic balance, where HF band is associated with PNS activity, while the LF band is a complex interference of both SNS and PNS influences in both efferent and afferent direction. Moreover, the LF band is associated with the vascular system resonance. This association motivates the usage of LF/HF ratio as a measure of physiological arousal. Moreover, similar effects were also found for the HRV indices in electrocardiogram (ECG) data, where increased SNS activity was found to increase HR, while PNS decreases it [10], as illustrated on Fig. 1. Variations in the interbeat intervals of the successive heartbeats were associated with HRV, and it has been regarded as a quantitative marker of cardiovascular regulation by the ANS. Such marker is used in physiology as the measure of activation of the SNS - which reduces HRV, and with the activation of the PNS - which increases HRV [16]. This activation and inhibition mechanism of the two branches of ANS causes SFPD, termed 'hippus,' which are the target of the investigation in this study [16].

Physiological recordings of arousal are assessed against the baseline measurements before the onset of the task, and they reflect the resting-state of the ANS [11]. It is accepted that bodily states shape emotions, and their physiological responses provide an objective insight into their workings [6]. This renders physiology as an objective measure for evaluating decision performance in games [14].

More specifically, this paper sets out to investigate how the interdependent and competing activation of the two branches of ANS, mainly PNS and SNS, are reflected on the pupillary muscles and affect the performance on decision-making task in serious games, through the measurements of PD and HR. The proposed question will be validated through the usage of ground truth ECG device measuring arousal through HRV. Furthermore, the effects of such arousal inferred through PD will be investigated in the financial decision-making task in the serious game.

## 3    Methodology

The 21 students of Blekinge Institute of Technology were randomly-recruited and participated in the study. They were aged between 20–24 years, while 14 were males and 7 females. No major psychiatric, medical disorders or ophthalmological problems other than corrected vision was reported. The participants signed the informed consent to take part in the experiment after they received complete information on the aims and experimental conditions of the study.

### 3.1    Experimental Setup

A constant temperature of $23\,°C \pm 1\,°C$ and artificial fixture light were controlled throughout the experiment. The experiment was performed in the sound-attenuated room, where the participants were seated in a fixed chair in front of

**Fig. 2.** The screenshot of the challenging decision-making task in the Auction Game, depicting the players' physiological arousal state through biofeedback meter at the top right [2].

a screen at a 50–60 cm distance. The screen was equipped with the *Tobii T60* eye-tracker recording PD data with a frequency of 60 Hz. Furthermore, physiological *Movisens ekgMove* sensor was applied using a chest band holding two contact electrodes positioned at the left and right lowest rib points, which provided a minimal obtrusive measurement of ECG data. Biofeedback arousal data based on HRV was transferred to the serious game application using Bluetooth. Baseline period for both of the physiological modalities was recorded for five minutes in a resting state before the onset of the game. Both of the physiological datasets were analyzed offline.

The serious game used in this study was the Auction Game [2] since it presents a challenging financial decision-making task to the participants, see Fig. 2. The game was connected with the ECG sensor for the on-line biofeedback based on physiological arousal, inferred from the HRV data. Such coupling provided a reliable measure of physiological arousal in a stressful environment [2], which was used as the ground truth for the data analysis. The inferred physiological arousal continuously adjusted the difficulty of the decision-making task in the game through the biofeedback method.

In the game, the participants were presented with a buy or sell decision for given trading stock. To make a decision, participants had to calculate the mean value from three given price estimations and click on the buy or sell button based on the offered price for a stock. Price estimations were directly linked to the physiological arousal level, such that they deviated from the correct price with higher variance, the more aroused the participant was. Thus, lower physiological arousal would make the variance of price estimations closer to the correct price, so that a buy or sell decision could have been easier. The serious game was linear, which meant that there was always just one possible correct decision to be made in each trial. To promote a more significant challenge, higher physiological arousal also reduced the decision time, while the task became more challenging at subsequent trials as the decision period was further reduced, forcing a quick decision.

## 3.2  Data Analysis

Regarding ECG data, the raw signal from the device was amplified, after which it was band-pass filtered at 10–40 Hz with 16-bit digitization. Furthermore, the signal was then smoothed using a 10 ms moving average window, while the R-peaks (heartbeats) were identified using the OSEA algorithm [7]. The heuristic rules were applied in detection to avoid missing R-peaks or detecting multiple peaks for a single heartbeat. The final data consisted of interbeat intervals measured between successive heartbeats to obtain the HR and HRV parameters accordingly.

Regarding PD data, offline analysis of the eye-tracker data in millimeters was used to obtain the power of LF and HF bands that correlate to HRV parameters. The data were corrected for the short and long blink periods. A linear interpolation was then applied to the short blink periods. Both HRV and PD values were normalized for each participant by subtracting the data from the resting-state baseline measurements before the task. Following the method given by Park et al. [15] for extracting HRV indices of LF/HF ratio, the PD data were band-pass filtered for the LF range (0.04–0.15 Hz) and the HF range (0.15–0.4 Hz). Afterward, the signal was processed using FFT analysis (i.e., using the Hanning window of size 180 samples and the resolution of 1 sample) to extract the powers in the LF and HF bands, which were used to infer the HRV index of LF/HF.

## 4  Results

In order to investigate the potentials of using PD as a remote measure for providing contactless biofeedback for serious games based on physiological arousal, PD and HR values were recorded during the performance on decision-making task in serious games. Pearson product-moment correlation and ANOVA comparisons were used to determine the relationship between several variables determining performance in the Auction Game and normalized PD values during the task. Decision performance was assessed throughout the game as: time needed to reach a decision; final game score (money earned); and the level reached in the game.

Regarding the relationship between arousal parameters of LF/HF acquired through PD data and the ground truth HRV acquired through ECG data, there was a significant difference between the arousal levels ($F(4,1509) = 11.5157$, $p < .001$), as depicted on Fig. 3. A Tukey posthoc test revealed that the LF/HF ratio for the highest arousal condition 5 based on the ground truth ECG data

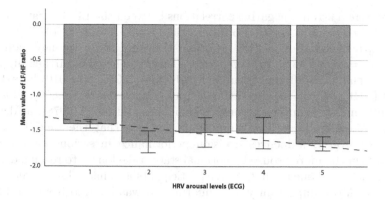

**Fig. 3.** The difference between the arousal levels based on the ground truth HRV data, in regards to the LF/HF ratio acquired through PD, on a decision-making task in the Auction Game. There is a significant difference between the highest and the lowest arousal condition with 95% confidence interval at the <.001 probability level. The line illustrates a significant negative correlation between the mentioned data.

$(-2.004 \pm 1.321, p < .001)$ was significantly different than the ratio for lowest one 1 $(-1.675 \pm 1.014)$. There was no statistically significant difference between the other groups $(p = .169)$. Furthermore, a significant negative correlation between the LF/HF ratio and the arousal conditions was found $(r = -.112, n = 1514, p < .001)$, as illustrated with a line on Fig. 3. These results provided evidence for validation that the PD data, more specifically the LF/HF parameter, indeed provides a measure of physiological arousal. More specifically, the higher LF/HR ratio is correlated with lower arousal, and therefore, a relaxed emotional state.

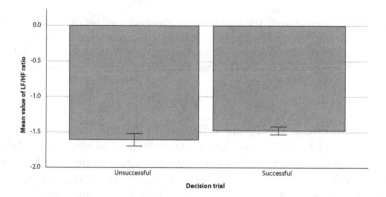

**Fig. 4.** The difference between the successful and the unsuccessful decision trials arousal, in regards to the LF/HF ratio acquired through PD, on a decision-making task in the Auction Game. The successful trials had significantly higher LF/HF ratio, than the unsuccessful ones with 95% confidence interval at the .010 probability level.

There were a strong, negative correlations between the LF/HF ratio and the time needed to reach a decision on each trial ($r = -.118$, $n = 1477$, $p < .001$), as well as, between the LF/HF ratio and the total score (money gained) in the game ($r = -.069$, $n = 1477$, $p < .008$). This evidence was further supported through a significant difference found ($F(1,1475) = 6.576$, $p = .010$) between the arousal LF/HF ratio on the successful decision trials ($-1.476 \pm 0.899$), which was significantly higher than on the unsuccessful ones ($-1.607 \pm 0.978$), as depicted on Fig. 4. These findings lend support to the idea that the LF/HF ratio as an index of arousal influences decision performance in serious games, where participants in the more aroused emotional states take longer to reach a decision, and an unsuccessful one at that. These participants also had a lower overall score in the game. More importantly, this information was inferred from the LF/HF ratio acquired from the PD, which gives further evidence for its usage as a remote measure of the emotional state of arousal.

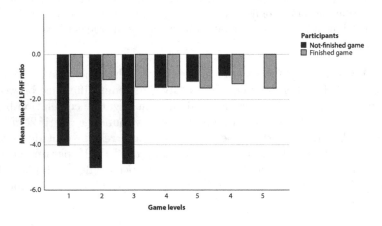

**Fig. 5.** The difference between the participants who had successfully finished the game and the ones that have not, in regards to the LF/HF ratio acquired through PD, on different levels in the Auction Game. The participants who had successfully finished the game had significantly higher LF/HF ratio than the ones that had not, at the < .001 probability level.

Finally, there was a significant difference in LF/HF ratio found ($F(1,51) = 11.344$, $p < .001$) between the participants who had successfully finished the game ($-1.024 \pm 0.415$, $p < .001$), compared to a lower value for the ones that have not ($-1.924 \pm 1.174$), as illustrated in Fig. 5. This finding suggests that the participants who managed to finish this challenging game were able to put themselves in a different emotional state of arousal throughout the game, which enabled them to succeed in the game, compared to the ones that have not reached the end.

# 5  Discussion

The PD data suggests that physiological arousal influences human financial decision-making, as has been previously validated in the economic field, as well as in the field of serious games through the use of other physiological sensors. This study found that the participants in lower arousal states reach their decisions faster, and make more correct decisions which result in higher overall score (money gained) throughout the game. This evidence gives support to the previous finding, as well as gives evidence that PD may be used as a remote contactless measure of arousal to observe the similar effects. If one considers that such remote measure is less obtrusive and has a lower impact on human behavior in the experimental sessions, one can argue that this might be a more ecologically valid measure to infer arousal in user experiments on decision-making in serious games.

The suggestion that PD might be used as a reliable measure of arousal is further supported through the evidence on ground truth validation between the PD and ECG data. Previous evidence suggested synchronicity between human cardiac rhythm and SFPD through neural pathways [15]. They have found that the power in LF (0.04–0.15 Hz) and HF (0.15–0.4 Hz) bands in the ANS were found to be synchronized with the SFPD rhythm in the same frequency ranges respectively, which was validated in this study as well.

The evidence from neuroscience indicates that the same activation of the ANS should be observable on both ECG and PD data, which was validated through the findings in this study. Nevertheless, due to the interdependence of the PNS and SNS activation with their effect on physiological responses, PD provides a rare opportunity to observe distinct activation of the two different pupillary muscles. This information coupled with other evidence suggesting that also higher cognitive functions (e.g., memory load and cognitive processing) are also observable on the pupil data, gives a clear direction on the PD usage in a well-rounded biofeedback modality which provides a window into the mental processes.

Furthermore, it was observed that the participants in a lesser aroused states throughout the game were able to finish the game until the end, compared to the ones that were in a more aroused emotional state throughout the game. Since the stimuli for arousal states throughout the game were variable, due to biofeedback controlling the difficulty, it is unclear if the regulation of arousal made participants more successful at decision-making. Nevertheless, this finding lends further support to the evidence that physiological arousal influences the decision performance, but it also gives motivation that the participants who were able to regulate their emotional arousal were able to reach further in the game due to more advantageous decision performance.

The evidence suggests that both PD and HRV data on the task were correlated with decision performance in the serious game set in the financial context. As previous research established that both of these physiological measures are associated with the balance between activation of PNS and SNS, it can be suggested that both these physiological measures would be a useful measure to asses the decision-making performance of participants. These underlying factors contribute to arousal, which has already been validated as an influencing factor in decision-making performance and task difficulty [2]. As the complex inter-dependent activation of PNS and SNS is reflected in both PD and HR data, these findings validate the notion that these modalities are inferring the same activation and its effects on the decision performance scores in serious games.

## 6    Limitations

In biofeedback-enhanced serious games, it is hard to distinguish if the partici-pants performed better on the decision-making task, or if the task got easier by regulating emotions and subsequently reducing the task difficulty. Such ambi-guity in the experimental data is known as the biofeedback loop, and it applies to the evidence given in this study. One of the aspects of this ambiguity is reflected on how the differences in decision-making time affect the arousal states in participant since this time was controlled by the same arousal states elicited. Nevertheless, the inference of physiological arousal on decision performance in the Auction Game was found, regardless of its nature.

Moreover, inferring arousal through PD has a limitation where the SFPD activity during blinking periods is not available. Linear interpolation was applied to mitigate this limitation, but more extended blink periods greater than one second are going to have this limitation.

Furthermore, systematic carryover effects between the trials are observable in the physiological data, where the arousing stimuli of one trial influences pupil size on the next trial. Therefore, future work should study the duration of these carryover effects to design independent trials, as well as try to mitigate this limitation by providing emotion-regulation training before the task.

## 7    Conclusion

This paper gives evidence that PD might be used as a reliable measure of phys-iological arousal by enabling the collection of physiological data unobtrusively and remotely in serious games set in the financial decision-making context. This evidence has been compared against the ground truth ECG data. Moreover, it suggests that the interdependent and competing activation of the two branches of ANS, mainly PNS and SNS, are observable on both the ECG and PD data. The Auction Game in this study used an electrode contact ECG device as a biofeedback measurement. Nevertheless, this study validated the potential usage of a more unobtrusive PD measure for biofeedback, which would be beneficial to observe the significant effects of arousal on human decision-making inside of the serious game. Therefore, one might argue that potential future biofeedback could be implemented using the PD physiological modality for such serious games.

Furthermore, this paper gives evidence that physiological arousal inferred through the PD modality affects the performance on decision-making task in serious games set in the financial context. It was found that the participants with lower arousal took less time to reach their decision, and those decisions were more successful in comparison to the participants in high arousal. Therefore, such lower arousal participants were able to get a higher total score in the game. The evidence also suggested that the participants who were able to regulate emotions and have lower arousal throughout the game were able to reach the final level and finish the game.

Taking these finding together, it is suggested that PD might be reliably used as a biofeedback method for arousal in serious games. Future work should investigate this direction of application, as well as providing a method that would provide information on memory load, cognitive processing, and emotional states, all inferred from PD data. Furthermore, if one considers eyetracking as a device capable of inferring attention information, one can see how this modality is a promising device for an excellent biofeedback method on the workings of the mind.

# References

1. Adam, M.T.P., Krämer, J., Jähnig, C., Seifert, S., Weinhardt, C.: Understanding auction fever: a framework for emotional bidding. Electron. Markets **21**(3), 197–207 (2011). https://doi.org/10.1007/s12525-011-0068-9
2. Astor, P.J., Adam, M.T.P., Jerčić, P., Schaff, K., Weinhardt, C.: Integrating biosignals into information systems: a neurois tool for improving emotion regulation. J. Manag. Inf. Syst. **30**(3), 247–278 (2013)
3. Attard-Johnson, J., ó Ciardha, C., Bindemann, M.: Comparing methods for the analysis of pupillary response. Behav. Res. **51**, 83–95 (2019). https://doi.org/10.3758/s13428-018-1108-6
4. Cohen, R.A.: Yerkes-Dodson law. In: Kreutzer, J.S., DeLuca, J., Caplan, B. (eds.) Encyclopedia of Clinical Neuropsychology, pp. 2737–2738. Springer, New York (2011). https://doi.org/10.1007/978-0-387-79948-3
5. Eren, O.E., Ruscheweyh, R., Schankin, C., Schöberl, F., Straube, A.: The cold pressor test in interictal migraine patients - different parasympathetic pupillary response indicates dysbalance of the cranial autonomic nervous system. BMC Neurol. **18**(1), 1–9 (2018). https://doi.org/10.1186/s12883-018-1043-2
6. Fenton-O'Creevy, M., et al.: A learning design to support the emotion regulation of investors. In: OECD-SEBI International Conference on Investor Education, pp. 1–16 (2012)
7. Hamilton, P.: Open source ECG analysis software documentation. Comput. Cardiol. **29**, 101–104 (2002)
8. Hu, Y., Wang, D., Pang, K., Xu, G., Guo, J.: The effect of emotion and time pressure on risk decision-making. J. Risk Res. **18**(5), 637–650 (2015). https://doi.org/10.1080/13669877.2014.910688
9. Jerčić, P., Sennersten, C., Lindley, C.: Modeling cognitive load and physiological arousal through pupil diameter and heart rate. Multimedia Tools Appl., 1–15 (2018). https://doi.org/10.1007/s11042-018-6518-z
10. Kaltsatou, A., Kouidi, E., Fotiou, D., Deligiannis, P.: The use of pupillometry in the assessment of cardiac autonomic function in elite different type trained athletes. Eur. J. Appl. Physiol. **111**(9), 2079–2087 (2011). https://doi.org/10.1007/s00421-011-1836-0

11. Kreibig, S.D., Wilhelm, F.H., Roth, W.T., Gross, J.J.: Cardiovascular, electrodermal, and respiratory response patterns to fear- and sadness-inducing films. Psychophysiology **44**(5), 787–806 (2007). https://doi.org/10.1111/j.1469-8986.2007.00550.x

12. Liu, D., Li, X., Santhanam, R.: Digital games and beyond: what happens when players compete? MIS Q. **37**(1), 111–124 (2013)

13. Lynch, G.T., James, S.M., VanDam, M.: Pupillary response and phenotype in ASD: latency to constriction discriminates ASD from typically developing adolescents. Autism Res. **11**(2), 364–375 (2018). https://doi.org/10.1002/aur.1888

14. Nacke, L., Lindley, C.: Flow and immersion in first-person shooters: measuring the player's gameplay experience. In: Proceedings of the 2008 Conference on Future Play: Research, Play, Share, Future Play 2008, pp. 81–88. ACM, New York (2008). http://doi.acm.org/10.1145/1496984.1496998

15. Park, S., Won, M.J., Lee, D.W., Whang, M.: Non-contact measurement of heart response reflected in human eye. Int. J. Psychophysiol. **123**(2018), 179–198 (2018). https://doi.org/10.1016/j.ijpsycho.2017.07.014

16. Parnandi, A., Gutierrez-Osuna, R.: Contactless measurement of heart rate variability from pupillary fluctuations. In: Proceedings - 2013 Humaine Association Conference on Affective Computing and Intelligent Interaction, ACII 2013, pp. 191–196. IEEE (2013). https://doi.org/10.1109/ACII.2013.38

17. Parnandi, A., Gutierrez-Osuna, R.: Visual biofeedback and game adaptation in relaxation skill transfer. IEEE Trans. Affect. Comput. **3045**(c), 1–15 (2017). https://doi.org/10.1109/TAFFC.2017.2705088

18. Posner, J., Russell, J.A., Peterson, B.S.: The circumplex model of affect: an integrative approach to affective neuroscience, cognitive development, and psychopathology. Dev. psychopathol. **17**(3), 715–734 (2005). https://doi.org/10.1017/S0954579405050340

19. Seo, M.G., Barrett, L.: Being emotional during decision makinggood or bad? An empirical investigation. Acad. Manag. J. **50**(4), 923–940 (2007)

20. Sliwinski, J., Katsikitis, M., Jones, C.M.: A review of interactive technologies as support tools for the cultivation of mindfulness. Mindfulness **8**(5), 1150–1159 (2017). https://doi.org/10.1007/s12671-017-0698-x

21. Steinhauer, S.R., Siegle, G.J., Condray, R., Pless, M.: Sympathetic and parasympathetic innervation of pupillary dilation during sustained processing. Int. J. Psychophysiol. **52**(1), 77–86 (2004). https://doi.org/10.1016/j.ijpsycho.2003.12.005

22. Sütterlin, S., Herbert, C., Schmitt, M., Kübler, A., Vögele, C.: Frames, decisions, and cardiac-autonomic control. Soc. Neurosci. **6**(2), 169–177 (2011). https://doi.org/10.1080/17470919.2010.495883

23. Tarassenko, L., Villarroel, M., Guazzi, A., Jorge, J., Clifton, D.A., Pugh, C.: Non-contact video-based vital sign monitoring using ambient light and auto-regressive models. Physiol. Meas. **35**(5), 807–831 (2014). https://doi.org/10.1088/0967-3334/35/5/807

24. Yamaji, K., Hirata, Y., Usui, S.: A method for montitoring autonomic nervous activity by pupillary flash response. Syst. Comput. Jpn. **31**(4), 2447–2456 (2000)

25. Yannakakis, G.N., Martinez, H.P., Garbarino, M.: Psychophysiology in games. In: Karpouzis, K., Yannakakis, G.N. (eds.) Emotion in Games. SC, vol. 4, pp. 119–137. Springer, Cham (2016). https://doi.org/10.1007/978-3-319-41316-7_7

# Identifying Influences of Game Upgrades on Profitable Players Behavior in MMORPGs

Luiz Bernardo Martins Kummer[1]([✉])(iD), Hiroyuki Iida[2]([✉])(iD),
Julio Cesar Nievola[1]([✉])(iD), and Emerson Cabrera Paraiso[1]([✉])(iD)

[1] Pontificia Universidade Catolica do Parana,
Rua Imaculada Conceicao, 1155, Curitiba, PR, Brazil
{luiz.kummer,nievola,paraiso}@ppgia.pucpr.br
[2] Japan Advanced Institute of Science and Technology,
Asahidai 1-1, Nomi, Ishikawa, Japan
iida@jaist.ac.jp

**Abstract.** Players can change their interest in continuing playing due
to many reasons, such as the game content available to them. Therefore, game upgrades play an important role as they have the potential
to influence players, being it a "double-edged sword", as players may
like the new challenges or not. Among the active players, "whales" are
those players that are the most profitable ones. The goal of this paper
is to answer the following research question: "What are the influences
of game upgrades on profitable players behavior?". To do that, we propose to apply and jointly interpret the results of four metrics (or KPIs):
Commitment, Key Risk Indicator, Available Motivational Growth, and
Game Refinement Value. This approach was applied to an MMORPG
dataset that contains four kinds of upgrades. As results, the proposed
joining identified three key influences and two players aspects, showing
the potential to be used by game producers to evaluate the acceptance
and influences of their upgrades in real situations.

**Keywords:** Game Analytics · Profitable players · Players'
commitment · Players' KPIs · Players' metrics · Game Refinement
Theory

## 1 Introduction

The game producers' role can be portrayed by two main challenges: the acquisition of new players, and the maintenance of the active ones. The acquisition of
new players is usually done through advertisements, while the maintenance of
the active ones is done through releases of new game contents (known as game
upgrades) [14], that affect the players' interest in continuing playing [2,5,17]. In
addition, some players can be more profitable than others [14], being the very

© IFIP International Federation for Information Processing 2019
Published by Springer Nature Switzerland AG 2019
E. van der Spek et al. (Eds.): ICEC-JCSG 2019, LNCS 11863, pp. 299–310, 2019.
https://doi.org/10.1007/978-3-030-34644-7_24

profitable players named as "whales" [9]. This fact highlights the importance of game producers being able to identify, comprehend, and satisfy this kind of players, as the more pleased they are, the more profitable a game is. The problem is, satisfaction aspects of players are usually interpreted empirically through raw metrics that consider only the amount of played time, like MAU (monthly active users), which can lead them to risk situations (e.g., due to misinterpretations of a new upgrade acceptance) [5,7,14].

In academia, the research field that focuses on modeling players' behavior is the Game Analytics [3]. One of its approaches regards the identification of changes in players' engagement to help producers identifying risk situations, being it usually based on two features present on usage data, the amount of time spent playing and the obtained score [5,7,12]. As examples, one can cite the Commitment metric and Key Risk Indicator (KRI) from Kummer et al. [5].

The Commitment metric was proposed to give an alternative to the empirical analyses done by game producers in reference to the "how motivated are the active players?" concern. This metric splits the active players into three different groups regarding low, average, and high commitment degrees. Moving to the KRI, this metric is based on the Commitment one, where positive and negative transitions of players between the commitment degrees are identified and then a view of it is presented in a comparative perspective.

An analogous approach is the called Game Refinement Theory (GRT) of Iida et al. [4], which regards the measurement of the players' entertainment based on the game rules, the players' strength, and the outcome uncertainty. Its concepts are represented by the called Game Refinement Value (GRV).

In this work, the aforementioned metrics are studied and improved, resulting in changes of the GRV, KRI and the proposition of a new metric, named Available Motivational Growth (AMG). It was proposed then to jointly apply the Commitment, KRI, GRV, and AMG metrics and use their values as an answer to the following research question (RQ): "What are the influences of game upgrades on profitable players behavior?". As results, three key influences and two players aspects were identified. Players' behavior is a complex universe, where different points of view can be used to try to understand it. In this approach, the influences of upgrades are interpreted in the engagement (increase or decrease) and enjoyment (considering the uncertainty aspect) contexts.

This paper is organized as follows: Sect. 2 presents the adopted metrics, Sect. 3 shows the metrics' previous applications, Sect. 4 depicts the metrics' improvements, Sect. 5 presents the dataset, experiments and discussions, and Sect. 6 concludes the paper with the RQ answer and future works.

## 2 Metrics

This section presents how each metric used in this work was conceived.

### 2.1 Commitment

The Commitment metric was initially proposed by Kummer et al. in [5], being improved by themselves in [7]. Its motivation regarded the fact that analyses over the number of active players may hide risk situations, such when there is a high number of active players and they are not engaged in continuing playing, leading game producers to a false sense of "comfort", while in fact, it is a dangerous situation. To deal with that, this metric segregates the active players into three degrees of commitment (low, average, and high), highlighting when players are disengaged to a considered game (e.g., when the majority of players has a low commitment degree).

This metric is generated through a Machine Learning approach that contains unsupervised and supervised steps, where the amount of time spent playing and the obtained score are used considering a sense of speed progress. The method to generate it requires a definition of a time-span size, which can be weekly or monthly. For each time-span and for each player, his/her commitment degree is identified, and then a sum of all players on each degree is presented as the final result, usually being compared with metrics like MAU.

The Commitment input is represented by the following vector: $V_i = \{id_i, d_i, S_{i-min}, S_{i-max}, \Delta S_i\}$, where $id_i$ is the identification of the player $i$, $d_i$ the number of days played in a week (or in a month; it depends on the adopted time-span size), $S_{i-min}$ the minimum obtained score, $S_{i-max}$ the maximum obtained score, and $\Delta S_i$ the number of times that the score was increased.

The Commitment metric assumes that if a player likes a game, he/she will play for longer, improving his/her abilities. According to this rationale, the commitment to a game is something built and maintained over time. The definitions of low, average, and high degrees are updated based on all time-spans, therefore, the method presents tolerance to outliers and also the capacity to adapt to new and stable behaviors (due to an Ensemble with the majority vote policy).

The low committed profile is understood as players that started to play and are usually in a learning phase about the game mechanisms. The average profile represents the players that are evolving their performance and spending more time playing than the low committed ones, however, with a yet different behavior compared to the high profile. Lastly, the high profile represents the players who play for the longest period of time and present the best performances.

## 2.2  Key Risk Indicator - KRI

The KRI metric aims at depicting the general increase or decrease in players' commitment over time [5]. Its application starts considering the first pair of consecutive time-spans (e.g., two consecutive months or weeks), where the players that increased or decreased their commitment are identified. Next, each player is grouped according to definitions of Table 1. Then, the members of each group are summed up and the RawKRI value is computed through the (1) application. Finally, after computing the RawKRI value for each consecutive time-spans, the normalized and final value is obtained through the (2) application.

$$RawKRI = (LA + AH + LH) - (AL + HA + HL) \tag{1}$$

$$KRI = RawKRI/max(RawKRI) \tag{2}$$

**Table 1.** Possible changes in commitment

| Change group | Label | Engagement |
|---|---|---|
| Low to average | LA | Increase |
| Average to high | AH | Increase |
| Low to high | LH | Increase |
| Average to low | AL | Decrease |
| High to average | HA | Decrease |
| High to low | HL | Decrease |

Where $max(RawKRI)$ is the biggest RawKRI of the series. This metric's range is from 0 to 1, where 0 means the worst decrease in players' engagement, while 1 is the best increase. It is interesting to highlight that every-time a new time-span presents a new $max(RawKRI)$, this time-span receives the value 1 and all the other time-spans have their values updated according to it.

### 2.3 Game Refinement Value - GRV

The GRT was initially proposed by Iida et al. in [4] to try to measure a degree of excitement of board games. It is interesting to notice that this theory avoids the empirical considerations about interest, founding its concepts on the classical mechanic physics of Newton [10]. In the same way that a roller-coaster can provide more or less fun according to settings of G-force, speed, and height, a board game may have a similar structure, as we have interests in both kinds of activities. On the one hand, the roller-coaster applies an acceleration into our body which affects our sensation of pleasure, on the other hand, a board game also provides such sensation which can be the result of an acceleration, but in that case, applied to our minds. This is the essential idea behind the GRT (physics in mind).

The acceleration in mind was modeled as the variations of the outcome uncertainty of a match, therefore, it is assumed that in an exciting game, the winner must be unknown until the very end. Based on this concept, the comprehension about the game result is a function of time (number of moves) $t$, as the result becomes more determined as time passes. Therefore, the amount of solved uncertainty can be represented by the function $x(t)$ (the game information progress model). Let B and D be the average branching factor and the average depth of a game respectively. If B and D are known for a match, the game information progress $x(t)$ will be given as a linear function of time $t$ with $0 \leq t \leq D$ and $0 \leq x(t) \leq B$, as presented in (3).

$$x(t) = (B/D)t \tag{3}$$

However, the game information progress is usually unknown during a match. Hence, it is assumed to be exponential, due to its uncertainty until the very end of a game. Therefore, a more realistic model is given by (4).

$$x(t) = B(t/D)^n \tag{4}$$

where $n$ is a constant given by an observer of the considered game. In this new model, the acceleration of the game information progress can be obtained applying the second derivative of (4). Solving it at $t = D$ (the end game period).

$$x(D)" = (Bn(n-1)/D^n)D^{n-2} = (B/D^2)n(n-1) \tag{5}$$

It is assumed that when a match is happening, the acceleration of game information is happening somehow in our minds, being it enjoyable or not. The physics in mind is not yet fully understood, but according to Newton's laws, if there was an acceleration, there was a force acting, so when there is an acceleration in our minds (i.e., stimulus-response), there is also a force acting. Therefore, it is expected that the larger the value $B/D^2$, the more exciting a game is, due to the outcome uncertainty. Lastly, the GRV is assumed as described in (6).

$$GRV = \sqrt{B}/D \tag{6}$$

The key concept to apply the GRT to a game consists of identifying the game information progress model, i.e., game features that contain uncertainty. For example, in the Soccer and Basketball cases, the average values regarding the number of shots and the number of successful shots are used [15], while for the RPG case, the values of options available and turns can be used [11]. All of these values are conceptually applied somehow to the structure proposed in (6).

According to the applications of GRT [4,11,15,16], there is a common agreement that regards the called "Sophisticated Zone", which is the GRV between 0.07 and 0.08. Games in this zone tend to be more enjoyable than games outside of it. Moreover, values lower than 0.07 mean that a game is more competitive (more based on players' skill), while values above 0.08 mean that a game is more stochastic (i.e., more based on chance), therefore, the Sophisticated Zone is a balance between players' skill and chance. Another aspect regards the game length, where games too long can be seen as boring (lower GRV) while games too short as unfair (higher GRV). As a final remark, the same game may have different GRVs. For example, in an MMORPG, it is possible to compute the GRV for PvP battles, loot boxes, and the reforging system.

## 3    Metrics' Previous Applications

Starting with the Commitment metric, it was applied by Kummer et al. [7] to identify when a game enters in its last stage of the usage lifecycle, known as the Niche stage [2]. In this approach, the authors identified an increasing trend of the number of high committed players together with a decreasing trend of the low committed ones in an MMORPG. Proposing the Niche occurrence when a game has a number of high committed players greater than the number of low committed ones.

In the KRI case, Kummer et al. [5] applied it in an MMORPG to identify variances on players' behavior according to game upgrades. It was possible to identify situations where the MAU did not highlight a risk situation while the KRI did. For example, when the MAU increased due to a game upgrade but the players' commitment decreased (i.e., an initial expectancy that was not attained after the new content consumption). In addition, this approach did not distinguish the characteristics of each upgrade.

Moving to the GRT applications, even though it was successfully applied to several game genres [4,11,15,16], it has never been applied to MMORPGs. Thus this paper has the opportunity to assess the theory's concepts in a new context.

It is interesting to notice that none of these metrics were applied to the profitable players perspective. In addition, this perspective is usually linked to the predictions of players' churn, remaining lifetime, and lifetime value [1,6,8,13].

In conclusion, even though there are interesting approaches to deal with usage lifecycle risks, none of them focused on the identification and interpretation of the influences of game upgrades on profitable players' behavior. Therefore, as far as our knowledge goes, this paper proposal is improving the state-of-art.

## 4   Metrics' Improvements

This section presents the proposed improvements of the GRV and KRI metrics, and also the proposition of a new one, named Available Motivational Growth.

Starting with the GRV metric, it was proposed to join it with the Commitment approach, allowing in that way to interpret the GRVs of low, average, and high committed players. Moving to the KRI metric, it shows the variations of players' commitment over time, however, it is not clear when the majority of players increased or decreased their commitment degree. In view of it, we propose to expand the metric's range from $-1$ to $1$, where negative values regard the case when the majority of players decreased their commitment degree, while the positive ones the opposite of it. The updated KRI Equation is depicted in (7).

$$\text{KRI} = RawKRI/max_{positive}(RawKRI) \veebar max_{negative}(RawKRI) \quad (7)$$

In view of the Eq. (1), when the sum $(LA + AH + LH)$ is bigger than the sum $(AL + HA + HL)$, the $max_{positive}(RawKRI)$ is used, being the $max_{negative}(RawKRI)$ used otherwise.

Another point regards the idea of potential growth of commitment per timespan. As it is neither depicted by Commitment nor by KRI, it was proposed to represent it through a new metric named Available Motivational Growth (AMG), which consists of a sum of the number of players that are not in the high commitment degree, such as depicted in (8) and normalized in (9).

$$\text{RawAMG} = P_{low} + P_{average} \quad (8)$$

$$\text{AMG} = RawAMG/max(RawAMG) \quad (9)$$

Where $P_{low}$ and $P_{average}$ are the number of players with low and average commitment respectively, and $max(RawAMG)$ is the biggest RawAMG of the series. The metric's range is from 0 to 1, where 0 means no potential growth (i.e., all players already have a high commitment) and 1 the opposite.

As final remarks, the Commitment, KRI, and AMG metrics demand data containing players' identification, obtained score, and the time-stamp associated to each score, while the GRV one requires the total number of attempts, the total number of successes, and the associated time-span linked to a game feature.

# 5    Experiments and Discussions

This section shows the metrics' applications to an MMORPG that aim at identifying behavioral changes of players through different game upgrades to answer the proposed RQ. As the dataset is divided in weeks, all metrics were applied considering this perspective. All computations were performed through SQL queries in a MySql database and Machine Learning algorithms written in Java.

## 5.1    The Blade&Soul Dataset

The proposed metrics were applied to the Blade&Soul game, an MMORPG that presents four game upgrades (see Table 2). This dataset was provided by a Data Mining competition [8] and is divided into three subsets. Table 3 summarizes each subset aspects, such as the number of players (all selected by its game producer; all whales), the number of instances (each instance refers to one action did by a player in a given time), the collection period, and the number of weeks.

**Table 2.** Blade&Soul upgrades summary

| Date | Subset | Week | Observations |
|---|---|---|---|
| 2016-04-27 | 1 | 5 | New PvP mode |
| 2016-07-20 | 2 | 8 | More acts (stories) |
| 2016-08-24 | 2 | 13 | PvP improvements |
| 2017-01-18 | 3 | 21 | Cosmetic and item drop modifications |

**Table 3.** Summary of the Blade&Soul dataset

| Subset | # Players | # Instances | Collection period | # Weeks |
|---|---|---|---|---|
| 1 | 4000 | 175,139,564 | 2016-03-30 until 2016-05-10 | 6 |
| 2 | 3000 | 197,661,989 | 2016-07-13 until 2016-09-13 | 9 |
| 3 | 3000 | 206,758,995 | 2016-12-14 until 2017-02-07 | 8 |

Note that there are gaps between the total of 23 weeks. However, regardless of these gaps, the weeks are numbered as a sequence. The 15th-week presents a very distinct behavior compared to the others, as it has only one day of usage. Thus, to not add a bias in the overall analysis, we opted to not consider it.

## 5.2  Metrics' Results and Analysis

All findings presented in this section are understood as detailed answers to the proposed RQ, where each metric contributes in terms of its concepts. Starting with the Commitment one, the input vector $V_i$ was configured such as follows: $id_i$ as the player identification, $d_i$ as the number of days played in a week, $S_{i-min}$ as the minimum level, $S_{i-max}$ as the maximum level, and $\Delta S_i$ as the amount of "level up" occurrences. As we can see in Fig. 1, all weeks presented a number of high committed players greater than the other degrees. This disposition highlights the whales characteristic of this dataset, where it is expected that the majority of players will be from the high commitment profile.

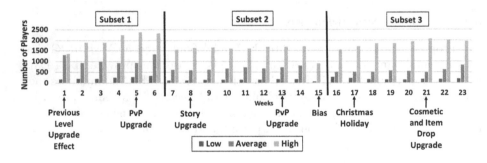

**Fig. 1.** Commitment assignment

The first week had a similar number of average and high committed players due to a previous upgrade that improved the players' max level. This week can be seen as a "rush" to achieve the new highest level, entailing in a greater number of level up events per player. Moving to the Christmas holiday, it presented an increase of the high committed players. We understand this increase as the players' enjoyment due to the opportunity to play longer than usual.

Unpaired $t$ tests were applied (considering $p < 0.05$) over the percentage of players on each commitment degree of each week per subset to identify if their distribution (i.e., mean value) changed from one subset to another. The identified significant differences regarded the low committed players between subsets 1 and 2, and the average and high ones between subsets 1 and 3 and also between 2 and 3. In conclusion, these differences highlight the fact that upgrades and holidays can influence the players' commitment over time. Next, the KRI and the AMG values are presented in Fig. 2.

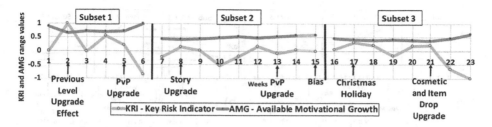

**Fig. 2.** KRI and AMG assignments

In the KRI perspective, it is possible to notice that the 4th-week presents an improvement of players' commitment, which can be seen as a positive expectancy regarding the upcoming upgrade. However, it was not kept in the following two weeks. We found two possible reasons for that, (1) after the players consuming the new content, they lost motivation, or (2) their expectancy was not attained. In the next upgrade (8th-week), the players' commitment increased compared to the previous week, but again, it decreased in the following weeks, due to game content consumption or expectancies not attained. The 13th-week and 21st-week upgrades can be considered as unsuccessful because the players' commitment dropped, in addition, the 21st-week is the starting point of the worst decrease of players' engagement. Even though the level upgrade week is not present in the dataset, its effects could be measured 2 weeks after its release as the best improvement of players' commitment (2nd-week).

Moving to the AMG perspective, none of the upgrades was engaging enough to have an AMG value lower than 0.4 (the lower, the better). The highest value was identified in the week after the first upgrade (6th-week), highlighting the drop of players' engagement in this time-span. Additionally, the best KRI value happened together with an AMG value of 0.66. It means that even though it was the best increase in players' engagement, there was a hidden potential to get better results. As a final remark, the AMG mean value was 0.55, it means that there was a chance to captivate players to higher degrees of commitment over the whole dataset period, highlighting the opportunity to promote upgrades.

Turning to the GRV perspective, we could manage to apply it to two game features, which were the PvP battles and the Reforging system. For the PvP case, we used conceptually the number of fought battles as $D$ and the number of won battles as $B$, while for the Reforging case, the number of attempts was assumed as $D$ and the number of successes as $B$. Next, Fig. 3 shows their results.

Firstly observing the PvP perspective (Fig. 3 a), it is possible to see that the identified GRVs are not in the Sophisticated Zone. After assimilating the zone's concepts to the current data, the PvP battles can be seen as unfair and based on chance due to the high GRVs. However, we understand that it is not fully true in this case, as the PvP battles in the considered game have an extra aspect attached to the players' skill that we named "evolutionary strength". During a battle, the players' skill can be seen as the players' effectiveness and efficiency in using the options available to them (i.e, playing well), while the evolutionary

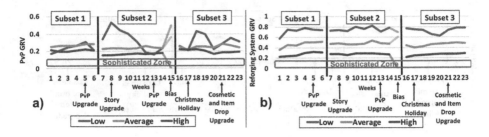

**Fig. 3.** (a) PvP GRVs assignments; (b) Reforging GRVs assignments

strength is the players' acquired level until a given moment. In addition, the evolutionary strength is accumulative, thus once it is acquired (i.e., a "level up" event) it is not possible to lose (i.e., there is no "level down" event), what does not happen to the players' skill, that may improve with training or reduce due to a lack of practice. As an example, the combination of such characteristics can generate situations were a very skilled player may lose a battle against a less skilled one if the other player's level is higher. We understand that this kind of situation influences the concepts around the Sophisticated Zone, for example, the fact of a player having more levels than the other does not mean that the battle is based on chance, therefore, we considered the PvP of the Blade&Soul game as possibly unfair and based on a combination of players' skill and evolutionary strength. As a final remark, unpaired $t$ tests with $p < 0.05$ were performed on each subset (considering the GRV of each commitment degree per week) and statistically significant differences were identified between all degrees for all subsets (except by the low and the average groups).

Moving to the Reforging perspective (Fig. 3 b), it was not possible to distinguish the effects of the different kinds of upgrades to any commitment degree, being a possible explanation for that the lack of improvements in the Reforging system. However, as occurred to the PvP battles, all the GRVs identified are not in the Sophisticated Zone. A reason for that regards the general success rate of approximately 94% that reduced the sense of outcome uncertainty. Moreover, all means of the commitment degrees presented statistically significant differences between them (unpaired $t$ tests with $p < 0.05$). Thus, according to the identified values, we consider the Reforging system of Blade&Soul as stochastic.

## 6   Conclusions and Future Works

This work improved the state-of-art in four main points: (1) by improving the GRV and KRI metrics, (2) by proposing a new metric (AMG), (3) by identifying new points of analysis through the metrics combinations, and (4) by assessing the Sophisticated Zone concepts to the MMORPG context.

According to the Blade&Soul dataset, the KRI indicates that PvP upgrades tend to improve the players' commitment before the upgrade, presenting then a drop of engagement after the new content consumption, while story upgrades can keep players motivated for longer compared to the PvP ones, presenting picks of motivation during the upgrade week. Moreover, the upgrade regarding cosmetic and item drop modifications presents an initial increase before the upgrade and a strong decrease after it, similar to the PvP one. According to these influences we could point three reasons: (1) new PvP battles are opportunities to players became in evidence by winning the most battles as possible, thus an initial preparation is a good idea to have a good performance when the new competition starts, moreover, the competitions seem to excite or demotivate players fast (i.e., one week); (2) there is no preparation to accomplish story upgrades, therefore players become more committed only when the new content is available; and (3) cosmetic and item drop upgrades generate initial expectancies or preparation, but after players obtaining their new costumes or desired items, their engagement drops as the objectives were achieved.

In the GRT perspective, the higher a GRV, the more stochastic, while the lower, the more competitive. Thus, it is possible to state that high committed players present a more competitive behavior than the lower committed ones. Moreover, even though there were different kinds of upgrades, their GRVs kept similar. We rationale two possible reasons for that: (1) the degree of challenge offered to them keeps the same over time, or (2) the players were able to adapt and maintain their performance. By contrast, low and average committed players present more changes in their sense of entertaining considering PvP battles and the Reforging system, which means that they are more sensitive to changes.

The summarized answer to the RQ can be represented by the following three key influences: (1) different upgrades entail in expectations to consume the new content, moreover, some kinds of them allow a preparation while others do not; (2) depending on the considered upgrade, players can increase their commitment to the game for longer; and (3) upgrades that present a preparation aspect tend to keep players engaged for less time than the ones that do not allow it. Also, two aspects of players were identified: (1) the more committed a player is, the more resilient he/she is to changes on game features, and (2) the higher the commitment of a player, the more competitive his/her behavior is.

In conclusion, we understand that the proposed combination of metrics can be used by game producers to better evaluate the acceptance of their upgrades. As future works, we wish to: replicate these measurements considering players besides the whales and compare the results (validating with game producers a possible generalization over the findings), and propose new metrics to explore other aspects not covered in this paper, such as the players' motivations.

**Acknowledgments.** We would like to thank NCSOFT for turning the dataset of Blade&Soul available, and CAPES-Brazil (Coordenação de Aperfeiçoamento de Pessoal de Nível Superior) and Fundação Araucária (CP 09/2016) for their support in this research.

# References

1. Chen, P.P., Guitart, A., del Río, A.F., Periáñez, Á.: Customer lifetime value in video games using deep learning and parametric models. In: 2018 IEEE International Conference on Big Data (Big Data), pp. 2134–2140. IEEE (2018)
2. Cook, D.: The circle of life: an analysis of the game product lifecycle, May 2007. https://www.gamasutra.com/view/feature/129880/the_circle_of_life_an_analysis_of_.php
3. El-Nasr, M.S., Drachen, A., Canossa, A.: Game Analytics. Springer, Heidelberg (2016)
4. Iida, H., Takeshita, N., Yoshimura, J.: A metric for entertainment of boardgames: its implication for evolution of chess variants. In: Nakatsu, R., Hoshino, J. (eds.) Entertainment Computing. ITIFIP, vol. 112, pp. 65–72. Springer, Boston, MA (2003). https://doi.org/10.1007/978-0-387-35660-0_8
5. Kummer, L.B.M., Nievola, J.C., Paraiso, E.C.: A key risk indicator for the game usage lifecycle. In: The Thirtieth International Flairs Conference (FLAIRS), pp. 394–399. AAAI Publications (2017)
6. Kummer, L.B.M., Nievola, J.C., Paraiso, E.C.: Applying commitment to churn and remaining players lifetime prediction. In: 2018 IEEE Conference on Computational Intelligence and Games (CIG), pp. 213–220. IEEE (2018)
7. Kummer, L.B.M., Nievola, J.C., Paraiso, E.C.: Identifying niche stage in MMORPGs using ensemble classifier. In: The Thirty first International Flairs Conference (FLAIRS), pp. 288–293. AAAI Publications (2018)
8. Lee, E., et al.: Game data mining competition on churn prediction and survival analysis using commercial game log data. IEEE Trans. Games (2018)
9. McAloon, A.: Analyst: 'whale' spenders aren't as crucial to F2P mobile games as they once were, September 2018. http://www.gamasutra.com/view/news/326173/Analyst_Whale_spenders_arent_as_crucial_to_F2P_mobile_games_as_they_once_were.php
10. Newton, I.: Philosophiae Naturalis Principia Mathematica, vol. 1. G. Brookman (1833)
11. Panumate, C.: Various approaches to improving entertainment impact in games. Ph.D. thesis, Japan Advanced Institute of Science and Technology (2016)
12. Periáñez, Á., Saas, A., Guitart, A., Magne, C.: Churn prediction in mobile social games: towards a complete assessment using survival ensembles. In: 2016 IEEE International Conference on Data Science and Advanced Analytics (DSAA), pp. 564–573. IEEE (2016)
13. Runge, J., Gao, P., Garcin, F., Faltings, B.: Churn prediction for high-value players in casual social games. In: 2014 IEEE Conference on Computational Intelligence and Games (CIG), pp. 1–8. IEEE (2014)
14. Speller III, T.H.: The business and dynamics of free-to-play social-casual game apps. Ph.D. thesis, Massachusetts Institute of Technology (2012)
15. Sutiono, A.P., Purwarianti, A., Iida, H.: A mathematical model of game refinement. In: Reidsma, D., Choi, I., Bargar, R. (eds.) INTETAIN 2014. LNICST, vol. 136, pp. 148–151. Springer, Cham (2014). https://doi.org/10.1007/978-3-319-08189-2_22
16. Xiong, S.: A new paradigm in game design using game refinement theory and cross media. Ph.D. thesis, Japan Advanced Institute of Science and Technology (2017)
17. Zhu, L., Li, Y., Zhao, G.: Exploring the online-game life cycle stages. In: 2010 International Conference on E-Business and E-Government (ICEE), pp. 2436–2438. IEEE (2010)

# An Exploration of the Relationship Between Personality and Strategy Formation Using Market Farmer: Using a Bespoke Computer Game in Behavioural Research

Andrew Reilly[1]([✉]) [iD], Dirk Van Rooy[1] [iD], and Simon Angus[2] [iD]

[1] The Australian National University, Canberra, Australia
andrew.reilly@anu.edu.au
[2] Monash University, Melbourne, Australia

**Abstract.** A computer game was designed for use in a study examining the relationship between facets of the personality trait openness to experience and exploration of a dynamic environment where initial knowledge is limited. A total of 38 females and 56 males aged between 18 and 62 completed a measure of openness to experience and exploration-exploitation before playing *Market Farmer*: a game specifically designed to engage players and record strategy formation behaviour over time. As expected, exploration increased initially and then fell as players learned successful strategies. It was hypothesised that openness to experience would positively moderate the relationship between exploration and score in the latter part of the game, through adventurousness and intellect. As expected adventurousness did positively moderate the relationship between exploration and score, however intellect did not, and liberalism did. These results may reflect differences in ambiguity tolerance and flexibility in expectations when establishing strategies and indicate that *Market Farmer* offers a promising tool for the examination of personality and strategy formation.

**Keywords:** Serious games · Personality · Openness to experience · Exploration · Strategy · Research

## 1 Introduction

### 1.1 Games as Tools for Research

Over the last decade there have been a number of calls for the use of games in psychological research [1–3] as a means of placing participants in semi-controlled situations where changes in behaviour can be recorded over time [2]. In the broader context of methodology, they complement existing approaches by offering a trade-off between the kind of mundane realism of observational studies and the high levels of experimental control available in laboratory experiments [4]. Furthermore, where studies require participants to be motivated to complete a given task, games engage participants in a way that can produce more authentic behaviour [5]. By deliberately

© IFIP International Federation for Information Processing 2019
Published by Springer Nature Switzerland AG 2019
E. van der Spek et al. (Eds.): ICEC-JCSG 2019, LNCS 11863, pp. 311–323, 2019.
https://doi.org/10.1007/978-3-030-34644-7_25

incorporating elements that motivate players' needs for competence, autonomy and relatedness [6], players experience a desire to continue playing the game.

However, as with any approach, games have their drawbacks as research tools. Developing a game is a resource-intensive process and the focus on engagement often comes at the cost of external validity, particularly when mechanisms unrelated to the target phenomena are introduced [5]. For example, a number of approaches have used commercially available games, but validity and cross-platform reliability are limited by the existing constraints of the selected game [7]. One way of resolving this is to select or produce games that can easily be modified according to the demands of individual studies [8]. This leads to a design sciences approach, where a platform is created that is capable of producing a wide variety of games with a common theme or genre relevant to a broad field of research, thus reducing the need to "reinvent the wheel" every time a game is produced [9]. The aim of this pilot study is to develop an online game that is sufficiently open-ended to offer the potential for further development into such a platform, while also displaying sufficient utility as a research tool. In order to demonstrate this utility, the game is used to examine the relationship between personality and strategic cognition.

## 1.2    Individual Differences in Strategic Cognition

Studies in strategic cognition examine the role of cognitive structures and processes in the formation of strategies that can occur, for example, in a business environment [10]. In this context, the conclusions drawn can differ according to the type of environment that managers work in, and recent years have seen a particular focus on the use of the *doing first* approach to strategy formation as a result of disruptive change in the technology sector [11]. In an environment where there is little understanding of an optimal strategy, this approach advocates action as a means of generating responses from the environment that are then evaluated. Actions that produce positive results are retained and others are discarded, and strategies are thus derived through a process of trial and error [12].

The trade-off between exploration and exploitation is fundamental to strategic cognition, as the exploitation of existing information or resources may be compromised by exploration that results in new sources [13]. An optimal model of an exploration-exploitation strategy produced by Berger-Tal, Nathan, Meron, and Saltz [14], suggests that in environments where there is little or no existing knowledge, individuals acquire strategies by initially exploring the environment and gradually acquiring information through feedback. Over time, however, the costs of exploration outweigh the returns from exploiting information gained in the past, and individuals gradually transition to an approach dominated by exploitation.

Considerable interest has been shown in understanding the antecedents of exploration and exploitation related to individual differences. In particular, the Five Factor Model (FFM) personality trait of openness to experience, which reflects a willingness to change and try new approaches [15], appears to naturally align with behaviours associated with exploration. Although studies have found small but positive correlations between openness to experience and exploration [16, 17], these focus on establishing relationships between dispositional variables measured through self-report scales rather than on behavioural observation. Furthermore, openness to experience is composed of a number of subfactors, or facets [15], each of which may contribute to differences in the way individuals use exploration. Therefore, studies examining relationships between exploration and openness to experience may result in weak or nonexistent correlations because different facets of openness to experience may impact on exploration and exploitation at different points in time.

Conventional approaches to examining exploration have been valuable in developing an understanding of individual differences in strategic cognition. However, these approaches have not been able to give us much insight into how individual differences in personality affect the strategic use of exploration over time. As argued at the start, the use of computer games as research tools to gather behavioural data in real time can address this, as they are ideal for capturing data on the dynamic employment of exploration in strategy formation. A combination of approaches, where personality traits are measured before gathering behavioural data, could yield insights into the relationship between personality and the transition from exploration to exploitation. The use of a bespoke game would also allow for the development of a game specifically designed to capture this behaviour, while ensuring that participants begin with little or no knowledge of optimal strategies, thus simulating an environment where these are unknown.

## 2    Examining Strategic Cognition with *Market Farmer*

### 2.1    Development of *Market Farmer*

Strategic cognition is a process that includes exploration of the environment and the exploitation of information gathered through feedback [18]. Activities designed to capture this behaviour over time must provide participants with the opportunity to make decisions regarding the acquisition and use of this information. As our focus is not on decision-making behaviour under time pressure [19], the game is structured in a way that allows participants to control the advancement of the game. Game time was divided into 1200 ticks, with each tick activated by a button or the space bar that triggered game events related to that tick. This allowed players time to deliberate over decisions, though players were limited to a maximum of two hours to complete the game.

Games that succeed in engaging players draw on fundamental motivations of competence and autonomy [6]. Players enjoy facing and overcoming challenges that fit their skill level, as well as the sense of control in setting and meeting game goals [20]. This can be achieved by creating a system of rewards and punishments within the game that motivates players to form and improve on strategies. These considerations resulted in the game *Market Farmer*, based on a simple mechanic where players plant crops in fields when the price of the crop is low and then wait for the crops to grow while the price changes. When the crops mature, they are automatically sold at the current price, and thus the only control players have over their ability to make a profit is to gauge the best time at which to plant the crops. This provides players with an opportunity to observe changes in crop prices and learn from past mistakes in selecting the right time to plant crops through a system of rewards and punishments that occur when players make a profit or loss. For example, when players plant at the wrong time, the crop will sell at a low price and the return will be less than the cost of planting the crop, thus incurring a loss.

This simple mechanic provides a low-level decision-making process. However, meaningful gameplay that sustains interest over longer periods requires a macro-level decision-making context that interacts with these micro-level decisions in a way that increases the tension experienced by the player [21]. Therefore, the concept of improvements was created to allow players the ability to increase profits and prevent losses. In order to incur more dramatic potential losses, floods that destroy crops and birds that eat them were introduced. This provided the player with the opportunity to install improvements to prevent losses incurred from floods and birds, and increase profits from fields, while constraining the number of improvements in each field forced the player to make decisions regarding which fields improvements should be installed in.

To create further tension in making these decisions, crop varieties were given different qualities according to predictability of price volatility and levels of investment and return, such that varieties with more unpredictable volatility required a larger investment, thus increasing the potential loss, but offering an equally large potential for profit. Thus, players were able to offset the risk of more volatile higher value varieties using improvements, while small differences in volatility between varieties offered players the opportunity to experiment with varying levels of risk. The combination of crop varieties with varying levels of risk and return, floods, birds, and improvements offered players many ways to achieve a high score, with the values, timing, and offsets of each game element carefully balanced to ensure that on average, preferences for a particular improvement type, for example, would not result in a difference in overall score.

Finally, to distract players from the use of the game as a research tool and create an enjoyable experience that would hold their interest for the duration of the game, common game elements such as bright, colourful graphics and lively animations were used to create a sense of action and movement in the game, along with cartoon-like auditory cues to provide feedback to the player. To control for differences in ability, a tutorial was included at the beginning of the game using a narrative to engage the player in a purposeful understanding of what was required, and to show examples of the game mechanics. To maintain motivation, the ability to acquire new crop varieties, fields, and improvements as rewards was staggered throughout the game to encourage goal-setting. Pop-up alerts and hints were also used throughout the game to ensure that players were aware of their options, particularly as new elements were being introduced, or rewards provided.

## 2.2 Playing *Market Farmer*

On loading the game, the player is presented with an introduction screen showing two farmers of the same gender as the player, who provide instructions on how to play the game in the tutorial that follows. The farmers state the broad aim of the game in terms of maximising the amount of money made, and the player clicks through further screens with each farmer presenting aspects of gameplay from positive and negative perspectives: one stating a problem and the other offering a suggestion for solving it. For example, players are told that they can plant new crops and make improvements, but that some crops are expensive and risky. Players are then given an opportunity to sow and harvest a crop of potatoes, which provides very little profit, but is also very low risk. After this, the option to sow potatoes is removed and replaced with broccoli, thus signalling the beginning of the game. The player begins with $1000, and if this amount falls below $20, it is automatically topped up to $20, thus allowing the player to sow broccoli crops and continue playing the game. Features of the game such as floods and improvements are explained to the player as they appear in the game in a similar manner to the tutorial. Figure 1 shows a screenshot from the game with a farmer explaining how to access improvements.

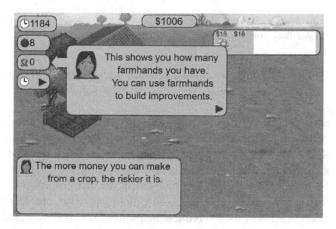

**Fig. 1.** A farmer explains how to access improvements in the *Market Farmer* tutorial.

Over time, the player receives more fields at predetermined points unknown to the them, until they have a maximum of eight fields. Players also receive access to more crop varieties based on the cumulative total of crops sown, i.e. the more crops the player sows, the faster they gain access to new varieties. Players also purchase improvements using farmhands that accrue over time, with a total of 32 farmhands available throughout the game. Information relating to these and other aspects of gameplay is available at the top left of the screen, where the number of ticks remaining, the number of crops that need to be sown in order to gain the displayed variety, the number of farmhands accrued, and a button that advances the game to the next tick are displayed. The amount of money available to the player (score) is displayed at the top centre of the screen. When clicking on the farmhands icon, the screen shown in Fig. 2 is displayed, allowing the player to select an improvement when there are farmhands available to pay for it.

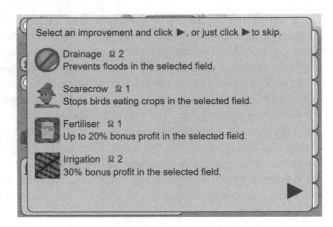

**Fig. 2.** A screen in *Market Farmer* showing the selection of improvements available to the player, the advantages they confer, and the cost in farmhands.

Once installed in a field, improvements produce a given benefit in that field for the remainder of the game and cannot be removed. The following improvements are available for purchase:

*Drainage* prevents floods from occurring in a field and costs two farmhands. A total of 27 floods are scheduled to occur at regular intervals throughout the game, and the more often a player sows a crop in a given field, the more likely it is that a flood will occur in that field. When a flood occurs in a field with a crop, the crop is removed from the field and the player loses their entire investment for that crop.

*Scarecrow* prevents birds from landing in a field and costs one farmhand. Birds land on crops at regular intervals and reduce the profit of the crop by a random amount of up to 20%.

*Fertiliser* adds a random amount of up to 20% of the profit from a crop when it is sold, but has no effect on crops that are sold at a loss. Fertiliser costs one farmhand.

*Irrigation* adds 30% of the profit from a crop when it is sold but has no effect on crops that are sold at a loss. Irrigation costs two farmhands.

These improvements are balanced so that the use of drainage and scarecrows, for example, will have the same mean effect on overall profits as irrigation and fertiliser, respectively.

Figure 3 shows the screen in the second half of a game where all of the seven crop varieties are available. Players sow each crop by dragging the relevant icon into a field. The fixed cost of sowing each crop is displayed above the respective icon, while the figure to the right of this shows the amount of money the player would gain if the crop were harvested in this tick. The recent history of these values is displayed in the accompanying chart, which illustrates the increasing volatility of each variety.

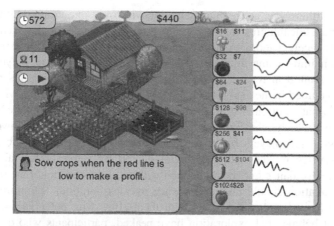

**Fig. 3.** The screen in Market Farmer showing all of the crop varieties available to the player by the end of the game and their price volatility.

The combination of increasing volatility and profitability with each crop and the advantages offered by the improvements affords players a number of different strategies for success when defined as the amount of money made at the end of the game. As players are limited to two improvements per field, choices must be made regarding the potential losses and gains provided by a combination of improvements, and the effect this has on mitigating the risk inherent in planting more volatile crops. Initially, there is a strong incentive for players to explore by experimenting with different combinations, and once a successful strategy has been established, players may then continue to exploit that strategy, or explore other strategies. However, players are not forced to choose between these approaches, and it is possible for players to pursue a given strategy in some fields while exploring alternatives in others, or to adopt a broad strategy within which there may be some room for exploration.

## 3 The Current Study

### 3.1 Introduction

We now demonstrate how Market Farmer can be used to understand the relationship between openness to experience and behavioural patterns of exploration performed in the game, and game performance. These patterns of behaviour are identified according to the extent to which players repeat strategies by trying new crop varieties and improvements, and varying the combination of these (behavioural exploration), or by planting the same crop varieties in fields with the same combination of improvements (behavioural exploitation).

The game consists of 1200 ticks, during which the game pauses so that players can perform actions, but there are a number of phases that occur during the course of the game. Initially, players learn about how to play the game, during which separate elements are introduced in a staggered fashion to prevent overwhelming the player with information. Furthermore, as the player begins with only one crop and one field, the ability to extract meaningful information regarding strategies undertaken is limited until the player receives more crops and fields. As the crop growing times increasingly exceed the remaining game time in the last 100 ticks of the game, players' choices become more limited in regard to the crops that can be sown. For this reason, this period is not included in the analysis. Given that players begin the game with very little knowledge of what an optimal strategy might be, a period of behavioural exploration is expected, during which behavioural exploitation should be quite low. However, as the game progresses and players begin to acquire successful strategies, the situation is expected to reverse in line with the model offered by Berger-Tal et al. [14]. This suggests that performance may be associated with an understanding of the optimal time at which exploitation should take precedence over exploration. Therefore, once participants have had enough time to acquaint themselves with potential strategies, and mean levels of behavioural exploration have peaked, participants who decrease their levels of behavioural exploration while increasing behavioural exploitation should experience a concurrent increase in score (in-game money).

Facets of openness to experience likely to moderate the negative relationship between behavioural exploration and score in the latter part of the game include: intellect, as participants scoring higher on this measure may be more likely to recognise and select successful strategies rather than needlessly continuing to explore; and adventurousness, as participants scoring higher on this may be more likely to continue exploring increasingly successful strategies. Also, the lack of a moderating effect of imagination, artistic interests, emotionality, and liberalism on the relationship between behavioural exploration and score means that the overall relationship between openness to experience and behavioural exploration remains low. On the basis of this, it is hypothesised that once mean levels of behavioural exploration have peaked, higher levels of openness to experience facets intellect and adventurousness will positively moderate the negative relationship between behavioural exploration and score, while imagination, artistic interests, emotionality, and liberalism will not moderate the relationship between behavioural exploration and score.

## 3.2   Method

**Participants.** Participants were recruited through an online recruitment service and remunerated for their time. Only participants aged at least 18 and using devices with screen dimensions of at least 640 pixels were able to take part in the study. Due to compatibility issues, participants were not able to complete the study using the Firefox browser. A total of 94 participants completed the study, including 38 females and 56 males with ages ranging from 18 to 62 ($M = 31$, $SD = 9.93$).

**Procedure.** After providing demographic information, participants completed a number of surveys as part of a wider study before playing the game, with the time taken to play the game ranging from 21 to 129 min ($M = 51$, $SD = 20.81$). At the end of the game, participants were shown their score and asked a series of questions on how much they enjoyed playing the game.

Participants completed the IPIP-NEO-120, a short-form adaptation of a longer scale developed as a measure of factors and facets of the FFM. Participants were asked to indicate the extent to which statements accurately described their personality on a 5-point Likert scale from 1 (strongly disagree) to 5 (strongly agree). Statements related to facets of openness to experience include "I have a vivid imagination" (imagination), "I love to read challenging material" (intellect) and "I believe that there is no absolute right or wrong" (liberalism). Chronbach's alpha for openness to experience is .83, with alphas for facets ranging from .64 (liberalism) to .76 (imagination and artistic interests).

While dispositional measures use conventional self-report approaches, behavioural exploration-exploitation is measured using participants' activity in playing the game. For each tick, there exists a matrix representing the player's strategy in terms of the number of improvement-crop combinations in use at that point. These strategic instances are then compared to determine the extent to which a player is repeating a previous strategy (exploitation) or creating a new strategy (exploration) that can include combinations of previous strategies or alterations to them. A simplified example of how exploration is calculated in a game with five fields; crop varieties, $a$, $b$ and $c$; and improvements, $x$ and $y$, is shown in the matrix below.

$$
\mathbf{M}_t = 
\begin{array}{c|cccc}
 & - & x & y & xy \\
a & 1 & 0 & 0 & 0 \\
b & 0 & 0 & 2 & 0 \\
c & 0 & 0 & 0 & 1 \\
\end{array}
$$

This indicates that at $t$, there was a field with no improvements containing variety $a$, two fields with improvement $y$ containing $b$, and one field with both improvements $x$ and $y$ containing $c$. This matrix $\mathbf{M}_t$ is then compared to all previous matrices by subtracting it from each matrix and summing the absolute values of the differences to derive a single value, $d$, representing the difference between both matrices. For example, the matrix at $t - 1$:

$$
\mathbf{M}_{t-1} = 
\begin{array}{c|cccc}
 & - & x & y & xy \\
a & 1 & 0 & 0 & 0 \\
b & 0 & 0 & 1 & 0 \\
c & 0 & 1 & 0 & 0 \\
\end{array}
$$

indicates that, at $t$, the player has added a $b$ crop to a field with improvement $y$, along with the $c$ crop in a field with improvements $x$ and $y$. Meanwhile, a crop of $c$ in a field with improvement $x$ has harvested. Subtracting $\mathbf{M}_t$ from $\mathbf{M}_{t-1}$ yields:

$$
\begin{array}{c|cccc}
 & - & x & y & xy \\
a & 0 & 0 & 0 & 0 \\
b & 0 & 0 & -1 & 0 \\
c & 0 & 1 & 0 & -1 \\
\end{array}
$$

the summed absolute values of which is $d = 3$. The exploration value for $\mathbf{M}_t$ is the lowest value of $d$ obtained after iterating over all previous matrices, multiplied by 1 divided by the number of fields in the game at $t$ to control for the expansion of fields as the game progresses. Therefore, in a game with 5 fields:

$$exploration = d_{min}\frac{1}{n} = 3 \times .2 = .6$$

This value, calculated once at the end of each tick, provides an indication of the players' level of behavioural exploration at that point in the game. Taken together, these values provide a record of changes to the players' use of exploration as a strategy over time, with higher values at the beginning of the game suggesting a stronger preference for a *doing first* strategy.

**Results.** Table 1 shows descriptive statistics and correlations for dispositional variables included in the analysis. Note that values of score are calculated as the square root of the in-game value to resolve issues related to differences in magnitude and normality that occurred during analysis.

**Table 1.** Descriptive statistics and correlations for dispositional variables.

|      | SC    | OP    | IM    | AI    | EM    | AD    | IN   | LB   |
|------|-------|-------|-------|-------|-------|-------|------|------|
| SC   |       |       |       |       |       |       |      |      |
| OP   | −.05  |       |       |       |       |       |      |      |
| IM   | −.00  | .70** |       |       |       |       |      |      |
| AI   | −.16  | .68** | .39** |       |       |       |      |      |
| EM   | −.18  | .61** | .46** | .26*  |       |       |      |      |
| AD   | .06   | .60** | .29** | .28** | .18   |       |      |      |
| IN   | −.13  | .63** | .27** | .39** | .25*  | .25*  |      |      |
| LB   | .25*  | .47** | .15   | .16   | .02   | .30** | .19  |      |
| M    | 85.23 | 3.42  | 3.57  | 3.54  | 3.68  | 2.94  | 3.54 | 3.26 |
| SD   | 35.21 | 0.49  | 0.82  | 0.86  | 0.85  | 0.76  | 0.77 | 0.73 |

$*p < .05, **p < .01$
SC = Score; OP = Openness to Experience; IM = Imagination; AI = Artistic Interests; EM = Emotionality; AD = Adventurousness; IN = Intellect; LB = Liberalism; M = Mean; SD = Standard Deviation

As expected, there were two broad phases in the game. The first of these occurs from tick 250 and extends to 550, when behavioural exploration increases while behavioural exploitation decreases as players extend their strategies to include more crops and improvements as they become available. Once behavioural exploration peaks at around 550, it then declines as successful strategies have been identified, and behavioural exploitation increases as these selected strategies are increasingly exploited.

Table 2 shows results from multilevel regression models, with score as the dependent variable, behavioural exploration as a level 1 predictor, and both openness to experience and its facets as level 2 predictors. As the study focuses on the influence of dispositional variables (level 2) on the slope between behavioural exploration (level 1) and score over time ($\gamma_{10}$), slope values are presented for level 2 on score controlling for level 1 ($\gamma_{01}$), and the moderation of level 2 on the slope between level 1 and score ($\gamma_{11}$).

**Table 2.** Multilevel regression models with personality traits and facets at level 2, behavioural exploration as a level 1 independent variable, and score as the level 1 dependent variable.

| Level 1 | $\gamma_{10}$ | Error | | |
|---|---|---|---|---|
| Exploration | −5.10*** | 1.05 | | |

| Level 2 | $\gamma_{01}$ | Error | $\gamma_{11}$ | Error |
|---|---|---|---|---|
| Openness | −0.45 | 3.59 | −4.30* | 2.06 |
| Imagination | 0.72 | 2.15 | −1.32 | 1.28 |
| Artistic Interests | −1.93 | 2.06 | −0.93 | 1.23 |
| Emotionality | −4.58* | 2.02 | −0.39 | 1.21 |
| Adventurousness | 1.47 | 2.33 | −3.83** | 1.37 |
| Intellect | −1.19 | 2.29 | −1.29 | 1.29 |
| Liberalism | 6.42** | 2.34 | −2.90* | 1.39 |

*p < .05, **p < .01, ***p < .001

Multilevel regression analysis shows that on average, there was a significant negative slope between behavioural exploration and score ($\gamma_{10} = -5.10$, p < .001) following the peak in exploration at 550 ticks. Openness to experience reduced the negative slope between behavioural exploration and score ($\gamma_{11} = -4.63$, p < .05) through the facets of adventurousness ($\gamma_{11} = -3.83$, p < .01) and liberalism ($\gamma_{11} = -2.90$, p < .05). However, when controlling for behavioural exploration, Emotionality was negatively related to score ($\gamma_{01} = -4.58$, p < .05), while Liberalism was positively related to score ($\gamma_{01} = -6.42$, p < .01).

## 3.3   Discussion

The aim of this study was to assess whether or not theoretical relationships between personality dispositions and behaviours associated with strategy formation could be examined using a game that simulates this in a dynamic environment, where initial knowledge is limited. However, results were mixed. We were expecting that higher levels of openness to experience facets intellect and adventurousness would positively moderate the negative relationship between behavioural exploration and score, while imagination, artistic interests, emotionality, and liberalism would not moderate the relationship between behavioural exploration and score. Although adventurousness moderated the negative relationship between behavioural exploration and score as expected, intellect did not, but liberalism did. This suggests that the ability to recognise successful strategies and curtail further exploration is not related to intellect, and thus the task is not as cognitively demanding as it might be in real-word contexts. However, intellect focuses on reading challenging material, philosophical discussions, and abstract ideas, and may not reflect the kind of pragmatic application of cognition required by this task. For example, entrepreneurs, who tend to operate in environments with initial levels of low information, are more likely to exhibit lower levels of cognitive motivation and rely more on heuristics and advice from others when solving cognitive tasks [22]. This ability to make decisions in the absence of information is also related to entrepreneurs' higher levels of ambiguity tolerance, which may account for the role of liberalism in reducing the negative relationship between behavioural exploration and score.

One surprising result was the significant relationship between liberalism and score after controlling for behavioural exploration, as expectations were that traits related to openness to experience would maintain higher levels of exploration at a time in the game when the focus should be shifting to exploitation in order to achieve a high score. However, this result suggests that liberalism is one of the more significant aspects of personality that contributes to success during this period of the game. Liberalism focuses on the rejection of moral absolutes and greater latitude in the use of punishment for crimes. Therefore, it may be that participants with a preference for ambiguity accurately sense that there is no right or wrong strategy to pursue, and are happy to assume this in exploring new strategies.

### 3.4   Conclusion

The current study demonstrates the advantages of using a game to examine behaviours associated with dispositional constructs over time in combination with multilevel modelling. However, it is often difficult to predict how players will respond to different, interacting features of a game, such that any data generated should inevitably lead to the further development and improvement of the game. This blurs the line between development and research, as an iterated development process, where successive versions of the game are produced based on feedback generated by the previous version [23], lends itself well to the successive gathering and analysis of data needed to establish validity. From this perspective, a game may never be truly finished, as further development can occur to improve validity, or to branch off into a different study. In order to engage players and examine more complex interactions between individuals and behaviours, games could incorporate greater functionality, which requires iterative testing for validity. Although the use of games in research is still in its early stages, these possibilities highlight their huge potential.

## References

1. Coovert, M.D., Winner, J., Bennett Jr., W., Howard, D.J.: Serious games are a serious tool for team research. Int. J. Serious Games 4(1), 41–55 (2017)
2. Schönbrodt, F.D., Asendorpf, J.B.: Virtual social environments as a tool for psychological assessment: dynamics of interaction with a virtual spouse. Psychol. Assess. 23(1), 7–17 (2011)
3. Szell, M., Thurner, S.: Measuring social dynamics in a massive multiplayer online game. Soc. Netw. 32(4), 313–329 (2010)
4. Blascovich, J., Loomis, J., Beall, A.C., Swinth, K.R., Hoyt, C.L., Bailenson, J.N.: Target article: immersive virtual environment technology as a methodological tool for social psychology. Psychol. Inq. 13(2), 103–124 (2002)

5. Washburn, D.A.: The games psychologists play (and the data they provide). Behav. Res. Methods Instrum. Comput. **35**(2), 185–193 (2003)
6. Boyle, E.: Psychological aspects of serious games. In: Moreno-Ger, P., Baxter, G., Boyle, E., Connolly, T.M., Hainey, T. (eds.) Psychology, Pedagogy, and Assessment in Serious Games, pp. 1–18. Information Science Reference, Hershey (2014)
7. Williams, D.: The mapping principle, and a research framework for virtual worlds. Commun. Theory **20**(4), 451–470 (2010)
8. Elson, M., Quandt, T.: Digital games in laboratory experiments: controlling a complex stimulus through modding. Psychol. Pop. Media Culture **5**(1), 52–65 (2016)
9. Reilly, A.: Design sciences in social psychological research: using computational models and serious games to complement existing methods. Manuscript submitted for publication, Department of Psychology, The Australian National University, Canberra, Australia (2019)
10. Narayanan, V.K., Zane, L.J., Kemmerer, B.: The cognitive perspective in strategy: an integrative review. J. Manag. **37**(1), 305–351 (2011)
11. Mintzberg, H., Westley, F.: Decision making: it's not what you think. MIT Sloan Manag. Rev. **42**(3), 89–93 (2001)
12. Gibcus, P., Vermeulen, P.A.M., Radulova, E.: The decision-making entrepreneur: a literature review. In: Vermeulen, P.A.M., Curseu, P.L. (eds.) Entrepreneurial Strategic Decision-Making: A Cognitive Perspective, pp. 11–40. Edward Elgar, Cheltenham (2008)
13. Hills, T.T., Todd, P.M., Lazer, D., Redish, A.D., Couzin, I.D., Cognitive Search Research Group: Exploration versus exploitation in space, mind, and society. Trends Cogn. Sci. **19**(1), 46–54 (2015)
14. Berger-Tal, O., Nathan, J., Meron, E., Saltz, D.: The exploration-exploitation dilemma: a multidisciplinary framework. PLoS One **9**(4), e95693 (2014)
15. Johnson, J.A.: Measuring thirty facets of the Five Factor Model with a 120-item public domain inventory: development of the IPIP-NEO-120. J. Res. Pers. **51**, 78–89 (2014)
16. Keller, T., Weibler, J.: Behind managers' ambidexterity—studying personality traits, leadership, and environmental conditions associated with exploration and exploitation. Schmalenbach Bus. Rev. **66**(3), 309–333 (2014)
17. Keller, T., Weibler, J.: What it takes and costs to be an ambidextrous manager: linking leadership and cognitive strain to balancing exploration and exploitation. J. Leadersh. Organ. Stud. **22**(1), 54–71 (2014)
18. Cohen, J.D., McClure, S.M., Yu, A.J.: Should I stay or should I go? How the human brain manages the trade-off between exploitation and exploration. Philos. Trans. R. Soc. Lond. Ser. B Biol. Sci. **362**(1481), 933–942 (2007)
19. Maule, A.J., Hockey, G.R.J., Bdzola, L.: Effects of time-pressure on decision-making under uncertainty: changes in affective state and information processing strategy. Acta Physiol. **104**, 283–301 (2000)
20. Sweetser, P., Wyeth, P.: GameFlow: a model for evaluating player enjoyment in games. ACM Comput. Entertain. **3**, 3 (2005)
21. Salen, K., Zimmerman, E.: Rules of Play. The MIT Press, Cambridge (2004)
22. Curseu, P.L., Vermeulen, P.A.M., Bakker, R.M.: The psychology of entrepreneurial strategic decisions. In: Vermeulen, P.A.M., Curseu, P.L. (eds.) Entrepreneurial Strategic Decision-Making: A Cognitive Perspective, pp. 41–67. Edward Elgar Publishing, Cheltenham (2008)
23. Braad, E., Žavcer, G., Sandovar, A.: Processes and models for serious game design and development. In: Dörner, R., Göbel, S., Kickmeier-Rust, M., Masuch, M., Zweig, K. (eds.) Entertainment Computing and Serious Games. LNCS, vol. 9970, pp. 92–118. Springer, Cham (2016). https://doi.org/10.1007/978-3-319-46152-6_5

# Using Game-Based Environments to Measure Cognitive Decision Making

Laura A. Waters[✉] and Karen L. Blackmore

The University of Newcastle, Callaghan, NSW 2308, Australia
laura.a.waters@uon.edu.au

**Abstract.** Within the area of serious games research, there is significant potential for researchers and other stakeholders to use serious games to gain more fundamental understanding of the underlying cognitive processes of individual users or participants. In this research, we present the results of an experiment to benchmark a visual search task presented in a 3d game-like environment with a standard, controlled, lab based implementation. Our results show similar trends in performance measures across experimental conditions in the two environments, however, participants were faster and more accurate overall in the 3d game-like environment. There is significant potential for researchers and other stakeholders to utilise serious games platforms as a means of measuring human cognition within environments that are visually more closely related to 'real-life' than those used in cognitive psychology.

**Keywords:** 3D environment · Cognition · Visual search task · Decision making

## 1 Introduction

Serious games (SGs), or games that are used for a purpose other than purely entertainment, are being used more frequently within industries for assessment and training of specific skills and abilities. While some performance measures may be captured, there is great benefit in understanding the types of cognitive processes that underlie abilities. One important research area of cognitive psychology is decision-making; that is, how we process information to make a judgment. This is often done through lab-based experiments that ask participants to make simple cognitive judgments about simple perceptual stimuli.

Many SG models acknowledge that at the crux of any learning activity, there is a cognitive process occurring [7,15]. However, the incorporation of robust measures of cognitive performance in game based environments is not currently done, even though the captured data might shine a light on understanding the processes underlying their cognitive abilities [3,7,11]. Within the field of computer science, there has been extensive research into 2D environments and evidence has shown that visual search abilities improve with gaming [2], however these findings

© IFIP International Federation for Information Processing 2019
Published by Springer Nature Switzerland AG 2019
E. van der Spek et al. (Eds.): ICEC-JCSG 2019, LNCS 11863, pp. 324–330, 2019.
https://doi.org/10.1007/978-3-030-34644-7_26

were often incidental outcomes and visual search abilities have not been explicitly considered in an immersive game-based environment in a way the relates to the more formal, constrained approach used in cognitive psychology [6].

In this work we present the results of a pilot study to compare visual search task performance, as measured through reaction time (RT), between a standard 2D constrained lab based task, and a 3D game-like visual environment. The focus here is to assess whether the deviations in RTs that occur when the number of visual stimuli change maps between the 2D lab based task and the 3D counterpart. We begin by providing a brief background to the measurement of human cognition, followed by an outline of our research focus, the experimental methodology and the results of our pilot study. Lastly, we provide some concluding discussion, and outline potential avenues for future work.

## 2   Background

### 2.1   Measuring Human Cognition

Cognitive psychology uses robust methodological approaches to test an individuals underlying processing abilities and capacity when performing particular cognitive tasks. There are a number of robust tools and tasks that are used to understand cognitive performance that can provide this broader understanding of capability; for example, surveys, psychometrics, observation, randomised controlled trials (RCTs). One key difficulty in being able to generalise task performance to real world behaviours lies in the highly constrained nature of lab-based environments and artificial stimuli used [5], such as simple shapes. These concerns relate to the overall context of the results, and the potential impact of this context on performance [8]. On the other hand, studies of entertainment games and SGs tend to use quasi-experimental designs and surveys and largely tend to measure post-intervention activity engagement [12]. While studies using quasi-experimental designs and surveys have added to our understanding of the outcomes and impacts of playing games, RCTs provide more rigorous evidence about the impacts of games. Although, laboratory-based tests provide a robust foundation for our understanding of decision making processes, more research is required for conversion of highly constrained lab based tasks and measures into other contexts such as more realistic virtual games-based environments. The rise of SGs and immersive simulation environments provides a platform for a more 'realistic' and variable environment which could be used for cognitive testing and training purposes. Simplistically, performance data can be used to profile players or measure competency [1], and there is promise for game environments to be used to capture more cognitive level data to assess cognitive processing architecture and capacity.

### 2.2   Research Focus

At the higher level, the purpose of this research is to develop the foundations of a theoretical framework that uses the strengths of two currently separate research areas to address some of their respective limitations. On one hand, cognitive psychology uses robust methodological approaches to design, measure performance, empirically analyse, and make inferences about the underlying cognitive processes and abilities that people use to complete a task or make decisions. We understand that human cognition plays a role in nearly every aspect of every day life, however, due to the highly constrained nature of lab-based tasks, it can be difficult to generalise results to how an individual might approach tasks in their everyday environment. On the other hand, the gaming industry has conducted extensive research into human-computer interaction, engagement and player typing/preferences. By combining aspects of SGs with cognitive lab-based approaches, we aim to develop a framework which provides guidelines to both researchers and game designers on (a) how to increase engagement and realism when developing experiments in cognitive psychology, and (b) how to embed robust cognitive methodology in a SG. This would allow for finer grain data and a greater depth of understanding about how individuals are processing and engaging within the environment. This can help us to adapt or optimally design games for learning to accommodate cognitive styles. This is particularly relevant for SGs, where these games are typically deployed across a cohort of individuals with different player profiles and styles.

One overall end-goal of this research will consider how virtual environments impact users; that is, do people behave and make decisions in a more realistic and virtual environment in the same way they would in standard artificial lab-based environments. However, in order to retain the robustness and validity of any cognitive measures used in a game-based environment, we first need to lay the groundwork for ensuring reliable measures of in-game performance by benchmarking performance on simple tasks using the highly constrained approach of cognitive psychology. Although we are restricting participant interaction with the 3D game-like environment, the goal of this pilot study is to ensure that the more visually immersive environment is still capturing valid and reliable data that can be used as a performance baseline for future studies in which we allow greater interactive possibilities for participants. As a means of benchmarking performance on a cognitive task between a standard 2D lab-based cognitive psychology test and a 3D game-like environment, we elect to design and pilot a simple visual search task and replicate this in a restricted game-like environment. Python programming language was used to create the 2D lab-based task whereas we used Virtual Battlespace 3 (VBS3) [4], a visually realistic game environment with scenario creation tools, to create the 3D game-like environment.

We hypothesise that participants will have a preference for the mechanics used in the immersive environment of VBS3, and that this will be reflected in this pilot experiment through faster RTs and greater accuracy even though the cognitive processes involved should remain the same. If we find evidence to support the hypothesis that game-based environments are a valid way to deliver cognitive tasks and assess underlying cognitive processes, then we are developing the capacity to re-deploy this back into the design of SGs and potentially allow for greater flexibility in the realism of environments used for cognitive testing.

# 3   Methodology

In this pilot study, we designed a simple visual search task [14] within a 3D virtual environment (Virtual Battlespace 3) which replicated the experimental design of a typical 2D laboratory-based task requiring participants to make a simple decision. Further details on the environments and visual stimuli are provided in the materials section below. The research was conducted under the University of Newcastle's Human Research Ethics Committee approval number H-2018-0227.

## 3.1   Participants

Participants were undergraduate students from the University of Newcastle. Of the 41 students who completed the experiment, there were 28 males (M = 22.23 years, SD = 3.71) and 13 females (M = 25.38 years, SD = 9.91) ranging from 18 to 52 years of age. Participants were enrolled in either a second year software engineering course (28 males and 2 females respectively) or a first year introductory psychology course (11 females) and received course credit for their participation.

## 3.2   Materials and Design

The experiment was conducted in one of the University of Newcastle HCI labs using an Alienware 17 R3 laptop. PsychoPy2 (v1.90.3) was used to develop and run the 2D laboratory-based task, while the 3D game-based task was run using VBS 3.7.0.

*Design.* In each of the environments, participants were presented with either 5, 10, 15 or 20 items (stimuli) in a single 4 second trial and required to make a simple decision on whether a target item was present or not. The desired target depended on the presented colour arrangement of an item. Stimuli used in standard cognitive experiments are often highly constrained shapes or letters which are varied visually through the use of colours, location, or rotation [14]. Replication of our task in a 3D game-like environment meant that to achieve a higher level of realism, abstract visual stimuli could not be used in both conditions. As such, this experiment used human avatars in VBS3 to address the criteria of perceptual salience between targets and distractor items, relying on colour arrangement of clothing to provide distinction. In each environment, the target (2D: a rectangular, two toned shape, and 3D: a human avatar, see Figs. 1 and 2 for example trials) would be tan on top and red on the bottom, while both distractor types would be tan on the bottom half, and either red or yellow on top.

For each task, a practice block with feedback (correct or incorrect response) was completed prior to undertaking 10 experimental blocks, each containing 40 trials (no feedback). We counterbalanced task and response key orders to account for any potential ordering effects. We also asked participants to complete two (2) questionnaires; one pre-test demographic survey containing additional questions regarding gaming preferences and behaviours, and one post-test where we asked participants about the difficulty of the two tasks and whether they were aware of using a particular search strategy to reach their decision.

**Fig. 1.** An example 15-item set presented in the 2D environment. The target item is absent from this trial. (Color figure online)

**Fig. 2.** An example 20-item set from the VBS3 (3D) environment. The target avatar is present on this trial. (Color figure online)

## 4    Results

### 4.1    Preliminary Analysis

Surface level analysis of this pilot experiment revealed a significantly faster mean RT ($M = 0.74$s) in the 3D environment compared to the 2D environment ($M = 1.02$s), $t = 74.515$, $p < .001$, as well as higher accuracy overall ($M = 99\%$ and $M = 97\%$ for 3D and 2D respectively), $t = -9.191$, $p < .001$. At first glance it could be proposed that in each task participants respond 'yes' as soon as the target item has been identified (self-terminating cognitive architecture) on target present trials, or exhaustively search all items in target absent trials before responding 'no'. [13]. This is reflected in both 2D and 3D environments by the slower average RTs on trials where no target item was present (see below figure).

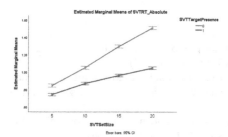
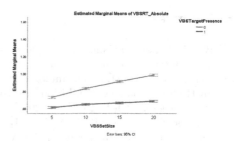

**Fig. 3.** The absolute RTs averaged across participants can be shown in the two graphs above (Left graph: RTs for the 2D environment, Right graph: RTs for the 3D VBS3 environment). Participants were significantly faster when completing the task in VBS3 compared to the 2D python environment, however in both tasks were participants tended to respond slower to trials without a target present.

## 5    Discussion

Two main arguments in favour of using game-like or scenario based platforms for teaching and training purposes are that firstly, they are more engaging and therefore more effective as a training tool [9], and secondly, they can be more closely related to the 'real world' meaning an individuals performance is more likely to reflect actual behaviour [10]. Unfortunately, the reported benefits and effectiveness of these training approaches are often mostly subjective rather than objectively measured, and assumptions are often made about generalisability to real world behaviours.

The findings of this simple pilot experiment indicate that embedding cognitive tasks within virtual training environments with high levels of 'realism' hold promise as a comparative environment for the capture of robust measures of underlying cognitive processes. The group level trends of slower RTs on trials where target item was absent or when there was a greater number of items to be processed (as seen in Fig. 3), indicates that participants were engaging similar underlying cognitive decision-making processes despite the different environments. While the design of the task itself was highly constrained, it is worth noting that the faster response times and improved accuracy in the VBS3 environment may be impacted by additional factors such as a discrepancy in the perceived perceptual planes of the two environments. This factor warrants further investigation and as such, future experimentation will focus on adjusting the locations of the avatars as well as the viewing angle of the 'player avatar' so the spatial locations are more closely aligned with the 2D plane presented in the comparative environment. By further researching performance measures within these 2D and 3D comparative environments, we aim to develop a foundation for designing and implementing tasks within SGs that can provide rich, robust and valid measures of a users cognitive processing abilities. This would also provide researchers, educators, or game designers with greater insight into the cognitive abilities, interactions and learning styles of specific SG users.

# References

1. Busch, M., et al.: Using player type models for personalized game design-an empirical investigation. Interact. Des. Archit. **28**, 145–163 (2016)
2. Castel, A.D., Pratt, J., Drummond, E.: The effects of action video game experience on the time course of inhibition of return and the efficiency of visual search. Acta Psychologica **119**(2), 217–230 (2005)
3. Gunter, G., Kenny, R.F., Vick, E.H.: A case for a formal design paradigm for serious games. J. Int. Digit. Media Arts Assoc. **3**(1), 93–105 (2006)
4. Bohemia Interactive. Virtual Battlespace 3. 2015. https://bisimulations.com/products/virtual-battlespace. Accessed 2019
5. Ladouce, S., et al.: Understanding minds in real-world environments: toward a mobile cognition approach. Front. Hum. Neurosci. **10**, 694 (2017)
6. Lee, M.-S., et al.: Characteristics of internet use in relation to game genre in Korean adolescents. CyberPsychol. Behav. **10**(2), 278–285 (2007). https://doi.org/10.1089/cpb.2006.9958. PMID: 17474846
7. Mayer, I., et al.: The research and evaluation of serious games: toward a comprehensive methodology. BJET **45**, 502–527 (2014)
8. Norman, G.: Generalization and the qualitative-quantitative debate. Adv. Health Sci. Educ. **22**(5), 1051–1055 (2017). https://doi.org/10.1007/s10459-017-9799-5. ISSN 1573-1677
9. Quinn, C.N.: Engaging Learning: Designing E-Learning Simulation Games. Wiley, Hoboken (2005)
10. Ritterfeld, U., Cody, M., Vorderer, P.: Serious Games: Mechanisms and Effects. Routledge, Abingdon (2009)
11. Shute, V.J.: Learning Processes and Learning Outcomes. English. Distributed by ERIC Clearinghouse, Washington, D.C., 38 p. (1992). https://eric.ed.gov/?id=ED366660
12. Smith, S.P., Blackmore, K., Nesbitt, K.: A meta-analysis of data collection in serious games research. In: Loh, C.S., Sheng, Y., Ifenthaler, D. (eds.) Serious Games Analytics. AGL, pp. 31–55. Springer, Cham (2015). https://doi.org/10.1007/978-3-319-05834-4_2. ISBN 978-3-319-05834-4
13. Townsend, J.T.: Serial vs. parallel processing: sometimes they look like tweedledum and tweedledee but they can (and should) be distinguished. Psychol. Sci. **1**(1), 46–54 (1990). https://doi.org/10.1111/j.1467-9280.1990.tb00067.x
14. Wolfe, J.M.: Visual attention. In: Seeing, pp. 335–386. Elsevier (2000)
15. Yusoff, A., et al.: A conceptual framework for serious games. In: 2009 Ninth IEEE International Conference on Advanced Learning Technologies, pp. 21–23, July 2009. https://doi.org/10.1109/ICALT.2009.19

# Towards Cognitive Adaptive Serious Games: A Conceptual Framework

Andrew J. A. Seyderhelm$^{(\boxtimes)}$ ⓘ, Karen L. Blackmore ⓘ, and Keith Nesbitt ⓘ

School of Electrical Engineering and Computing, University of Newcastle, Callaghan, Australia
Andrew.Seyderhelm@uon.edu.au

**Abstract.** Games and immersive training environments frequently rely on user performance measures to adapt the difficulty of tasks and behaviors, responding dynamically to changes in performance. However, users may maintain task performance while experiencing increasing levels of cognitive load. These high levels of load mean the user has no spare capacity and may fail to get the maximum benefit from the training task. While other adaptive mechanisms exist, they do not account well for cognitive load and thus may not be optimal for training tasks. In this paper we outline a conceptual framework for using real-time measures of cognitive load to dynamically adapt immersive environments. We argue that these measures have the benefit of providing a richer mix of data to base adaption on beyond simple performance metrics, and additionally provide further metrics to assess both the learner and the training material. To this end, a Cognitive Adaptive Serious Game Framework (CASG-F) is presented that draws on frameworks and theories of cognitive load and serious games. We additionally outline the range of potential mechanics and environment parameters that could potentially be adjusted to modify difficulty.

**Keywords:** Serious games · Conceptual model · Cognitive load · Adaptive

## 1 Introduction

### 1.1 Overview

Serious games are used for many purposes; throughout this paper reference to serious games will adopt a definition specific to the purposes of education and training: "A serious game is an experience designed using game mechanics and game thinking to educate individuals in a specific content domain" [1, p. 15]. It has been suggested that serious games provide a number of advantages over traditional learning or instructional approaches, including flexibility, creative problem solving, greater engagement and enjoyment in the material [2, 3] and the ability to produce metrics that are valuable to debriefing learners and informing ongoing serious game development [4, 5].

However, many serious games fail to leverage their full advantages, and this is particularly true in respect of adaptive mechanisms and dynamic difficulty adaption (DDA). Adaptive training in serious games has the benefit of being a cost-effective

© IFIP International Federation for Information Processing 2019
Published by Springer Nature Switzerland AG 2019
E. van der Spek et al. (Eds.): ICEC-JCSG 2019, LNCS 11863, pp. 331–338, 2019.
https://doi.org/10.1007/978-3-030-34644-7_27

method of providing training that closely approximates one-on-one tutoring and increases the overall effectiveness of training [6]. Traditional games have explored DDA in 3D games for well over a decade, and have demonstrated the efficacy of these systems on player enjoyment and engagement [7, 8]. Serious games have an additional purpose to provide a learning outcome for players. Thus, the mechanisms for adaption may need to be different as the foci is on learning outcomes rather than purely entertainment, although enjoyment and engagement are crucial components of effective learning.

A range of approaches have the potential for being useful for adapting serious games. This includes, but is not limited to, inventory and pick-up adaption [7], pedagogical agents [9], and a wide range of AI implementations. Serious games that adjust the challenge level in-line with the growing capability and knowledge of the learner are ideal for maintaining engagement, motivation and learning outcomes [3]. In this paper, we discuss DDA for adapting serious games, and extend this to consider approaches for measuring cognitive load that could be used to drive the adaptive mechanism in serious games. From this, we present a conceptual framework for cognitive adaptive serious games based on cognitive load theory and discuss future research plans to develop and assess this approach.

## 2    Core Components for Cognitive Adaptive Serious Games

### 2.1    Dynamic Difficulty Adjustment and Adaptive Techniques

The purpose of an adaptive framework is to assess the current state of the individual learner and adjust the training to better suit their needs within the constraints of the training requirements. In a commercial video games context, there has been significant research into developing systems to implement DDA [10, 11]. The aim of DDA is to provide the player with the correct level of challenge in order to make the game neither too hard nor too easy, thus increasing enjoyment [11, 12]. This concept of optimal challenge for the purpose of enjoyment is implemented with the aim of assisting the player achieve a flow state [11, 13]. Ideally, the benefit of DDA is that it will continuously adapt to player skill in an appropriate and subtle manner.

As previously indicated, the primary aim of a serious game is to deliver instructional, learning, or development outcomes. As a result, DDA in this context needs to relate to the performance of the participant against the serious games purpose rather than solely to enhance entertainment through amplification of flow states. Our conceptual model adopts a three-part framework towards engagement that encompasses flow along with other aspects suited to serious games [14]. One of the crucial aspects we consider is the role of cognitive load in the learning process, acknowledging the role of cognitive load levels in providing insights into schema integration amongst learners [15].

### 2.2    Measuring Cognitive Load

Cognitive load is the degree to which a learning task meets, exceeds, or fails to reach the processing capacity of a learner's cognitive system [16]. This is explained through Cognitive load theory (CLT), which originated in the 1980s [17]. It is a widely accepted concept that describes three states of the cognitive processes involved in learning; intrinsic, extraneous and germane cognitive load [18]. There are a number of methods of measuring cognitive load, principally subjective and objective measures. Subjective measures are typically completed by participants after undertaking an activity, for example the NASA Task Load Index (NASA-TLX) [19, 20]. In contrast, objective measures are undertaken during an activity, measuring an observable occurrence, affect, or physiological system, and interpreting that data for cognitive load.

The conceptual framework detailed in this paper proposes the use of an adapted version of the detection-response task (DRT) [21] embedded within a serious game. The DRT has been chosen as it is registered through the International Organization for Standardization in ISO 17488:2016 as a proven and effective measure [22]. A virtual DRT, termed the "Remote DRT", has been previously tested in-simulation, and proven to be effective [21]. An updated version of the "Remote DRT" is proposed here, potentially making a cognitive load based adaption an accurate, effective and affordable method for wide scale adoption.

### 2.3 Adapting Serious Games Through the Frame of CLT

CLT provides three aspects of cognitive load that can be manipulated to establish a sophisticated and theoretically sound adaptive framework. A practical description of how these adaptions may be implemented serious game tasks is outlined in Table 1.

**Table 1.** Adaptive examples tailored to CLT

| Cognitive load element | Method for adjustment |
| --- | --- |
| Intrinsic Cognitive Load (interaction elements) | Alter the task complexity [23] by increasing or decreasing the number steps at each stage e.g. making a car automatic rather than manual until the driver has grasped steering etc. |
| Extraneous Cognitive Load (presentation of material) | The way material is presented can lead to an increase, or decrease, in extraneous load, e.g. light or weather effects may increase or decrease cognitive load |
| Germane Cognitive Load (development of schemas) | The introduction of a "pedagogical agent" who assists the student may assist the learning process [9] |

Using CLT as a framework provides a structured way for a combination of cognitive load and various performance metrics to be used to dynamically adapt a serious game to optimize learning.

## 3 Conceptual Framework

The conceptual framework detailed here is an extension of the serious games conceptual model proposed by Yusoff et al. [24]. However, the Yusoff et al. model does not incorporate learner motivation, affect, and prior knowledge as described in the cognitive-affective theory of learning with media (CATLM) [9]. Yusoff et al. define a range of factors, and the conceptual model outlined below adopts their definitions and adds the following components by drawing on CATLM and others [25]:

1. *Learner Knowledge & Experience* – understanding the learner's current state of intrinsic motivation, knowledge and experience is essential [6]. It is important to assess the player's ability with the serious game controls to avoid the learner struggling with the controls, rather than the learning content within it.
2. *Review, Iterate* – post-game review otherwise termed after-action review. This is critical to the learning process and is often underutilized in serious games [4, 5]. It is important for the facilitator to assess the performance of the serious game itself.
3. *Play Game* – forms the start/finish of the cognitive and performance measure loop.
4. *Cognitive load and performance measures* – a constant loop driven by the cognitive measure. This process includes a performance measure, this is separate to the cognitive measure loop however they are combined to inform the DDA mechanism.
5. *Feedback* – is similar to Reflection described by Yusoff et al. [24] and by Moreno and Mayer [9]; this is in-game feedback to help and inform the player.
6. *DDA ±/−* – This is the point at which an adaption mechanism is implemented making the game easier, harder or the same as described in Table 2.
7. *Game Performance* – outputs the player performance and cognitive load measures to inform the debrief process and other course requirements [4, 5].

**Table 2.** Performance and cognitive load (CL) adaption template

| Achievement | Adaption | Description |
|---|---|---|
| Pass assessment with low CL | DDA increase (+) | Player is finding the task easy, so increase the challenge |
| Pass assessment with mid CL | DDA static | Player is in the correct level of difficulty. No change |
| Pass assessment with High CL | DDA static | Player is passing but finding it hard, provide in-game feedback |
| Fail assessment with low CL | DDA Static | Player has failed but not being mentally challenged, in-game feedback |
| Fail assessment with mid CL | DDA - | Cognitive load is ideal but failed assessment, indicating a lack of knowledge, reduce the difficulty slightly and add a hint |
| Fail assessment with high CL | DDA- | Player is struggling, make it easier and reduce complexity |

Table 2 presents the various proposed DDA adaptions including concepts discussed in the preceding section (Sect. 2.3). This follows on from the identification of how difficulty may be adjusted (Table 1). Together, the existing serious game conceptual models, extended to incorporate the inclusion of an adaptive mechanism based on cognitive load, results in a new Cognitive Adaptive Serious Game Framework (CASG-F) (Fig. 1). Performance measures and cognitive load will work together to adapt the in-game tasks. However cognitive load will form an adaption mechanism in its own right, e.g. making a simulated car automatic instead of manual to reduce interaction elements (intrinsic cognitive load), or increasing challenge by introducing additional tasks (intrinsic) or weather effects (extraneous cognitive load).

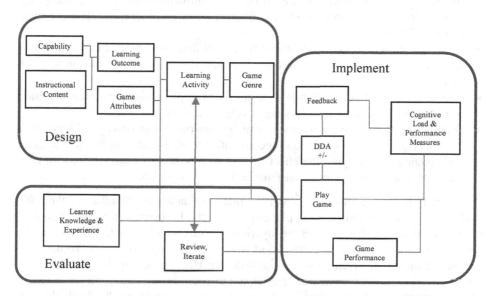

**Fig. 1.** The Cognitive Adaptive Serious Game Framework (CASG-F)

## 4   Future Research

The CASG-F proposed here has three broad stages in order to encompass instructional design concepts [26] and the triadic theoretical framework [27]. The CASG-F provides a roadmap for future experiments to incorporate these principles as best practice, and to outline how they are being integrated into the design and development process. The overarching aim of this research is to create an adaptive framework that can work flexibly and effectively using cognitive load as a key adaption measure.

Moving forward, robust experimental studies to validate the proposed adaptive process, and also to provide efficacy for the approach, are planned. Firstly, an experimental study is required to assess the in-game use of the DRT cognitive load measure, and to further validate its authenticity using a triangulation approach with an EEG combined with the NASA-TLX. The first experiment enables statistical validation of the affect different interventions have on the participants' cognitive load, providing a 'toolbox' of adaptive techniques for future experiments. Later experimental studies will then be required to compare adaptive serious game performance to non-adaptive variants in order to corroborate the assumption that adaptive serious games are more effective in enhancing human performance.

The first experiment involves a driving task in a 3D game environment. This has the benefit of using a task where the real-world efficacy of the DRT has already been established [21]. The proposed experiment will:

- Present three levels with the same driving track layout; the surrounding virtual environment will be different in each layout minimizing repetition for participants, and also provide information on how different visual environments affect cognitive and visual load.
- Using a randomized approach, participants will drive two loops of the track; one loop will have the DRT and the other will not, the EEG will remain on for both loops.
- The levels will include challenge sections, for example navigating a narrow section of road, observation tasks, following a vehicle, and more.
- Qualities of the visual environment will be manipulated in order to observe how these changes relate to visual load and cognitive load, e.g. altering in-game weather and lighting. Quantifying the effect of visual environment manipulations on cognitive load will then further contribute to the adaption 'toolbox'.

A study following this design will facilitate evaluation of the effect of the DRT itself on the cognitive load of the player participants. Experimental designs based on the CASG-F should also consider the layering of primary and secondary tasks to allow for robust measurement of cognitive load using the DRT approach [28]. To this end, the player should be given an additional task to perform requiring different cognitive processes. For example, asking the participant to count or respond to certain assets in the environment, requiring visual and cognitive discrimination, will effectively alter cognitive load [28]. Together, the CASG-F and the proposed experimental design provides an authentic first step toward a generalizable framework for developing serious games that respond dynamically to improve learning outcomes.

## 5   Conclusion

In this paper we propose a framework to realize the value of DDA and cognitive measures as applied to serious games. We then discussed how an adaptive framework can be applied through the lens of CLT. Extending existing theoretical frameworks, a conceptual model for Cognitive Adaptive Serious Games was presented that incorporates and recognizes different learning design approaches. Additionally, the proposed model has the potential to deliver real-time personalized training environments to move serious game implementations closer to the overall aim of enhancing human performance. Lastly, a comprehensive experimental design for future studies was presented where in-game cognitive load will be measured and verified by a variety of methods against a range of stimuli. This experiment design provides a roadmap for validating the real-time DRT as a cognitive load measure, and to establish a toolbox of validated methods to manipulate cognitive load based on a robust understanding of the impact of different game mechanics and mechanisms on the cognitive load of end users. Once established, this toolbox can then be applied to serious game implementations to assess the efficacy of adaptive serious games for education and training.

# References

1. Kapp, K.M.: The Gamification of Learning and Instruction: Game-Based Methods and Strategies for Training and Education. Wiley, San Francisco (2012)
2. Connolly, T.M., Boyle, E.A., MacArthur, E., Hainey, T., Boyle, J.M.: A systematic literature review of empirical evidence on computer games and serious games. Comput. Educ. **59**(2), 661–686 (2012). https://doi.org/10.1016/j.compedu.2012.03.004
3. Hamari, J., Shernoff, D.J., Rowe, E., Coller, B., Asbell-Clarke, J., Edwards, T.: Challenging games help students learn: an empirical study on engagement, flow and immersion in game-based learning. Comput. Hum. Behav. **54**, 170–179 (2016). https://doi.org/10.1016/j.chb.2015.07.045
4. Loh, C.S., Sheng, Y., Ifenthaler, D.: Serious games analytics: theoretical framework. In: Loh, C.S., Sheng, Y., Ifenthaler, D. (eds.) Serious Games Analytics. AGL, pp. 3–29. Springer, Cham (2015). https://doi.org/10.1007/978-3-319-05834-4_1
5. Crookall, D.: Serious games, debriefing, and simulation/gaming as a discipline. Simul. Gaming **41**(6), 898–920 (2010). https://doi.org/10.1177/1046878110390784
6. Landsberg, C.R., Astwood, R.S., Van Buskirk, W.L., Townsend, L.N., Steinhauser, N.B., Mercado, A.D.: Review of adaptive training system techniques. Mil. Psychol. **24**(2), 96–113 (2012). https://doi.org/10.1080/08995605.2012.672903
7. Hunicke, R.: The case for dynamic difficulty adjustment in games. In: Proceedings of the 2005 ACM SIGCHI International Conference on Advances in Computer Entertainment Technology, pp. 429–433. ACM (2005)
8. Xue, S., Wu, M., Kolen, J., Aghdaie, N., Zaman, K.A.: Dynamic difficulty adjustment for maximized engagement in digital games. In: Proceedings of the 26th International Conference on World Wide Web Companion, pp. 465–471. International World Wide Web Conferences Steering Committee (2017)
9. Moreno, R., Mayer, R.: Interactive multimodal learning environments. Educ. Psychol. Rev. **19**(3), 309–326 (2007). https://doi.org/10.1007/s10648-007-9047-2
10. Zohaib, M.: Dynamic difficulty adjustment (DDA) in computer games: a review. Adv. Hum.-Comput. Interact. **2018**, 1–12 (2018). https://doi.org/10.1155/2018/5681652
11. Dziedzic, D., Włodarczyk, W.: Approaches to measuring the difficulty of games in dynamic difficulty adjustment systems. Int. J. Hum.-Comput. Interact. **34**(8), 707–715 (2018). https://doi.org/10.1080/10447318.2018.1461764
12. Alexander, J.T., Sear, J., Oikonomou, A.: An investigation of the effects of game difficulty on player enjoyment. Entertain. Comput. **4**(1), 53–62 (2013). https://doi.org/10.1016/j.entcom.2012.09.001
13. Burns, A., Tulip, J.: Detecting flow in games using facial expressions. In: 2017 IEEE Conference on Computational Intelligence and Games (CIG), pp. 45–52. IEEE (2017)
14. Hookham, G., Nesbitt, K.: A systematic review of the definition and measurement of engagement in serious games. Paper presented at the Proceedings of the Australasian Computer Science Week Multiconference on - ACSW 2019 (2019)
15. Greitzer, F.L., Kuchar, O.A., Huston, K.: Cognitive science implications for enhancing training effectiveness in a serious gaming context. J. Educ. Resour. Comput. (JERIC) **7**(3), 2 (2007). https://doi.org/10.1145/1281320.1281322
16. Mayer, R.E., Moreno, R.: Nine ways to reduce cognitive load in multimedia learning. Educ. Psychol. **38**(1), 43–52 (2003). https://doi.org/10.1207/S15326985EP3801_6
17. Paas, F., Van Gog, T., Sweller, J.: Cognitive load theory: new conceptualizations, specifications, and integrated research perspectives. Educ. Psychol. Rev. **22**(2), 115–121 (2010). https://doi.org/10.1007/s10648-010-9133-8

18. Paas, F., Renkl, A., Sweller, J.: Cognitive load theory and instructional design: recent developments. Educ. Psychol. **38**(1), 1–4 (2003). https://doi.org/10.1207/S15326985EP3801_1
19. Hart, S.G., Staveland, L.E.: Development of NASA-TLX (Task Load Index): results of empirical and theoretical research. In: Advances in Psychology, vol. 52, pp. 139–183. Elsevier (1988)
20. Hart, S.G.: NASA-task load index (NASA-TLX); 20 years later. In: 2006 Proceedings of the Human Factors and Ergonomics Society Annual Meeting, vol. 9, pp. 904–908. Sage publications Sage CA, Los Angeles (2006)
21. Harbluk, J.L., Burns, P.C., Tam, J., Glazduri, V.: Detection response tasks: using remote, headmounted and Tactile signals to assess cognitive demand while driving (2013). https://doi.org/10.17077/drivingassessment.1470
22. Stojmenova, K., Sodnik, J.: Detection-response task-uses and limitations. Sensors (Basel) **18**(2) (2018). https://doi.org/10.3390/s18020594
23. Liu, P., Li, Z.: Task complexity: a review and conceptualization framework. Int. J. Ind. Ergon. **42**(6), 553–568 (2012). https://doi.org/10.1016/j.ergon.2012.09.001
24. Yusoff, A., Crowder, R., Gilbert, L., Wills, G.: A conceptual framework for serious games. In: 2009 Ninth IEEE International Conference on Advanced Learning Technologies, pp. 21–23. IEEE (2009)
25. Annetta, L.A.: The "I's" have it: a framework for serious educational game design. Rev. Gen. Psychol. **14**(2), 105–113 (2010). https://doi.org/10.1037/a0018985
26. Keller, J.M.: Development and use of the ARCS model of instructional design. J. Instr. Dev. **10**(3), 2 (1987). https://doi.org/10.1007/BF02905780
27. Rooney, P.: A theoretical framework for serious game design: exploring pedagogy, play and fidelity and their implications for the design process. Int. J. Game-Based Learn. (IJGBL) **2**(4), 41–60 (2012). https://doi.org/10.4018/ijgbl.2012100103
28. Conti, A., Dlugosch, C., Vilimek, R., Keinath, A., Bengler, K.: An assessment of cognitive workload using detection response tasks. In: Advances in Human Factors and Ergonomics Series. Advances in Human Aspects of Road and Rail Transportation, pp. 735–743 (2012). https://doi.org/10.1201/b12320-82

# Serious Game Applications

# Designing Gamified Interventions for Autism Spectrum Disorder: A Systematic Review

Murilo C. Camargo(✉), Rodolfo M. Barros, Jacques D. Brancher,
Vanessa T. O. Barros, and Matheus Santana

State University of Londrina, Londrina, PR 86057 970, Brazil
murilocrivellaric@gmail.com,
rodolfomdebarros@gmail.com,
ss.matheus.94@gmail.com, {jacques,vanessa}@uel.br

**Abstract.** Serious games and gamified interventions have become increasingly popular among researchers and therapists dealing with the autistic audience. The number of studies on technology for autism has multiplied, with the aim to foster independence and improve learning outcomes. Nevertheless, designing interventions for Autism Spectrum Disorder is challenging, due to the complex clinical conditions and the broad range of symptoms covered by the disturbance. Thus, this systematic review investigates the current status of gamification resources for autism, with a special interest in the gamification elements and the User Interface design. We describe the planning and the searching procedures and present the data extracted from 30 primary sources. The studies analyzed show a multitude of gamification elements and a plethora of methods and strategies to support decision-making and improve accessibility in the development of autism-specific software. It is concluded that the existence of methodological gaps related to the definition of the target audience and the conduction of testing may impose additional challenges to the development process, whilst the combination of gamification elements is generally positive.

**Keywords:** Gamification · Autism Spectrum Disorder · Systematic review

## 1 Introduction

According to the Diagnostic and Statistical Manual of Mental Disorders – DSM-5 [1], autism is characterized by persistent limitation in social communication/interaction, restrictive and repetitive behavioral patterns, and (verbal and non-verbal) communication deficits. As the autism diagnosis evolved to cover a broader spectrum of symptoms, there is emerging evidence of increasing epidemic rates. Numbers may vary depending on the metrics used for evaluation, but there are studies reporting on rates as high as 1 in 150 children being diagnosed with Autism Spectrum Disorder (ASD) [2].

Accessibility has played an important role in providing autistic individuals with opportunities to overcome their limitations by fostering independence and assisting them in social relationships [3]. Despite the fact that much information on autism etiology remains to be uncovered, accessibility advocates (researchers, psychologists, therapists, teachers, among others) have been thriving to propose feasible and

E. van der Spek et al. (Eds.): ICEC-JCSG 2019, LNCS 11863, pp. 341–352, 2019.
https://doi.org/10.1007/978-3-030-34644-7_28

interesting intervention solutions, which can be confirmed by the growing number of computer-based resources published and available to the community.

Serious games and gamification strategies have been largely used in the treatment of psychiatric conditions, such as depression, eating disorders, substance use, dementia, and, also, Autism Spectrum Disorder [4]. Gamification is a powerful resource to increase motivation and engage participants, thus favoring the teaching-learning process or training for specific situations. Design elements of serious games and/or gamified interfaces often include storylines, mid-term and long-term goals, increasing level of difficulty, feedback and/or rewards, and provision of choice [5].

Recent studies suggest improvements in handling disorder-related symptoms through the use of serious games or gamified interventions [6]. The same applies to autism: gamification may be a potentially effective approach due to the high visual processing skills the ASD individuals possess. On the other hand, developers may face challenges. According to [5], little evidence exists that ASD individuals subjected to computer-based interventions are able to apply such learning to real life. This can be partly explained by the lack of fundamental gamification elements during the design process.

In light of this situation, there is an undeniable need to understand the current status of serious gaming targeted to Autism Spectrum Disorder. Through a systematic review, this paper collects data on serious games and/or gamified interventions for autism, with a focus on the gamification elements used and their visual representation in terms of the User Interface design. We believe that this study may help uncover best practices used and shed light on the graphic design approach to deliver them at the same time.

This paper is organized as follows: in Sect. 2, the review protocol is presented, including research questions, inclusion criteria, search strings, and databases; in Sect. 3, results from the review are described and discussed; finally, Sect. 4 brings conclusions and future perspectives regarding the design of gamified interventions for the autistic audience.

## 2    Review Protocol

This systematic review applies a three-phase process, including the design of the review protocol, the conducting of the search, and the data extraction [7]. We search, identify, analyze, and summarize evidence on computer-based gamification resources targeted to the ASD audience. In order to prevent biased or mixed results, the scope is limited to resources in which the User Interface is the primary output channel. Robotics, hardware-only ubicomp solutions, or any interface-less devices are not included in this study, because their examination would require a completely alternative approach.

Preliminary studies and consultations with field experts helped pilot the review protocol. The protocol was designed to provide comprehensive guidance through the review process, with respect to the inclusion criteria and the nature of the results. It intends to promote the identification of all relevant primary sources and assist the data extraction process at the same time. The research questions are: what is/are the learning objectives? What is the development process/methodology/approach employed? Who is the target audience? What gamification elements are used to improve learning skills? What representation methods are applied in the User Interface design?

Then, a list of keywords was defined to support the searching process. Keywords should cover three aspects of major importance, namely: (1) the target audience, that is, autistic individuals; (2) the object of study – software development; and (3) the intervention approach – computer-based serious games or gamified interventions. Similar keywords were grouped to form a search string, using Boolean "ANDs" and "ORs": ("Autism spectrum disorder" OR "autistic individuals" OR "autism" OR "high-functioning autism") AND ("computer-assisted learning" OR "computer-assisted intervention" OR "computer-enhanced learning" OR "therapy software") AND ("serious games" OR "gamification" OR "gamified resources").

In order to be included, papers had to adhere to the sensitivity inclusion criteria: describe a novel contribution to computer-based serious games for ASD; have the software development as the primary object of study; provide relevant information on the gamification elements used during development; and rely on the User Interface as the main output channel. Secondary studies and hardware-only interventions were not considered. Also, publications older than 10 years were discarded, thus prioritizing the recent literature.

Six sources were selected in this study: (1) IEEE Xplore Digital Library, (2) ACM Digital Library, (3) SpringerLink, (4) SCOPUS, (5) ScienceDirect, and (6) Google Scholar. Together, they grant access to a large collection of relevant resources for Software Engineering. Besides, important journals on autism research can be accessed through these sources, such as the Journal of Autism and Developmental Disorders (Springer) and the Autism (SCOPUS).

Searching was performed using a combination of the search string described previously. Multiple trials of the keywords were performed in order to reach as many primary studies as possible. The search resulted in a combined total of 2,995 papers, which were downloaded. After the exclusion of duplicated papers, the total narrowed down to 2,642 studies. Then, two assessors examined titles and abstracts to determine the relevance of the subject matter. Papers that failed to meet the inclusion criteria were eventually withdrawn from this review, resulting in 30 eligible studies.

## 3 Results and Discussion

All 30 selected papers were carefully examined according to the review protocol. Data extracted was compiled in quality reports and double-checked whenever assessors had conflicting recommendations. Quality reports included data on the learning objectives, the team organization, the software development process applied, the target audience, gamification elements, and the User Interface design.

The selected papers present a variety of learning objectives. Many aim to improve communication skills (46.6%), mostly by teaching new vocabulary and phrases while improving semantic meaningfulness. Other learning objectives are social interaction

(13.3%), basic education (10%), and daily activities (10%). Two studies focused on facial recognition [14, 18] and only one aimed at refining motor skills [10]. Six of them (20%) presented multiple learning purposes [9, 13, 17, 19, 25, 32]. All of them involved the major impairments faced by ASD individuals: difficulty of socialization, imagination impairment, communication deficit, and behavioral issues [12] (Fig. 1).

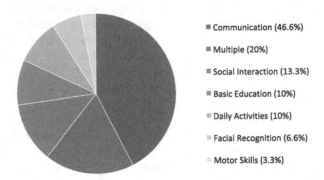

■ Communication (46.6%)

■ Multiple (20%)

■ Social Interaction (13.3%)

■ Basic Education (10%)

■ Daily Activities (10%)

■ Facial Recognition (6.6%)

■ Motor Skills (3.3%)

**Fig. 1.** Learning objectives extracted from primary studies.

Popular development approaches are the Participatory Design [15, 17, 30, 32] and the User-Centered Design [22–24, 31]. Both are techniques that aim to involve external help (experts, parents, teachers, and/or end-users) to assist the development process. Other approaches mentioned are the Applied Behavior Analysis [12], the ADDIE approach (Analysis, Design, Development, Implementation, Evaluation) [33], and the Extreme Programming [20]. Some studies reported on the use of an "iterative" [13, 14, 16, 21, 27, 29, 35] and/or "agile" approach [21, 27, 36], although they did not provide detailed information on it.

The team organization is either cross-functional or participatory. *Cross-functional teams* are composed by the development staff and stakeholders, who are deeply involved in the development lifecycle. On the other hand, *participatory teams* also engage stakeholders, but they are involved only in specific moments during the process (requirements specification or testing, for example). In any case, this reveals an effort to understand the needs and preferences of the end-user. Two studies did not provide any information on the methodological approach or the team organization [10, 34].

The vast majority of studies analyzed (76.6%) refer to their target audience simply as "autistic children" or some variation of the term. Only four studies report on the development of software for severity-specific audiences – that is, high-functioning and/or low-functioning autism [24, 28, 32, 36]. Two studies (6.6%) referred to the audience as "autistic individuals", claiming that the proposed intervention would serve for ASD adolescents or adults as well [16, 34]. There is also one study [20] that designed an intervention for children with "specific disorders", such as ASD, Down syndrome, mental retardation, etc. According to the author, this is possible due to the use of the PECS (Picture Exchange Communication System), which is an educational resource largely used in interventions for several disturbances, including autism.

**Table 1.** Gamification elements and user interface design.

| Reference | Gamification elements | | | | | | | | | | User Interface design | | | | | | | Objective |
|---|---|---|---|---|---|---|---|---|---|---|---|---|---|---|---|---|---|---|
| | Feedback | Rewards | Virtual reality | Level of difficulty | Personalization | Multimedia | Storytelling | Monitoring | Custom learning | Othezr | Illustration | Photographs | Words / Text | Use of colors | Sounds | Voice | Video / VR | |
| [11] | | | ✓ | ✓ | | ✓ | | | | | | | ✓ | ✓ | | | ✓ | |
| [12] | | | ✓ | | | | | ✓ | ✓ | | ✓ | | ✓ | | | | ✓ | |
| [15] | | | | ✓ | ✓ | ✓ | | | | | | ✓ | ✓ | ✓ | | | | |
| [16] | ✓ | | | ✓ | | | | | | ✓ | ✓ | | ✓ | | | | | |
| [20] | | ✓ | | ✓ | | | | ✓ | ✓ | | ✓ | | ✓ | ✓ | | | | |
| [21] | ✓ | | | | | | | ✓ | ✓ | | ✓ | ✓ | ✓ | | | | | |
| [22] | ✓ | | | ✓ | | | | | | | ✓ | | ✓ | ✓ | ✓ | | | C |
| [23] | | | | ✓ | ✓ | | | ✓ | ✓ | | ✓ | ✓ | ✓ | ✓ | | | | |
| [24] | | ✓ | | ✓ | ✓ | | | ✓ | ✓ | | | ✓ | ✓ | | | ✓ | | |
| [26] | | | | ✓ | ✓ | | | ✓ | ✓ | | ✓ | ✓ | ✓ | ✓ | | | | |
| [29] | | | | ✓ | | ✓ | ✓ | ✓ | ✓ | ✓ | ✓ | | ✓ | | ✓ | | | |
| [30] | ✓ | | | ✓ | | | | ✓ | ✓ | | ✓ | ✓ | ✓ | | | ✓ | | |
| [31] | ✓ | | ✓ | ✓ | | | | | | | ✓ | | ✓ | ✓ | | | | |
| [35] | ✓ | | | ✓ | | | | ✓ | ✓ | | ✓ | ✓ | ✓ | ✓ | ✓ | | ✓ | |
| [9] | | ✓ | ✓ | ✓ | | ✓ | | | | | | | | ✓ | | | ✓ | |
| [13] | ✓ | | | | | ✓ | | ✓ | ✓ | ✓ | ✓ | | ✓ | ✓ | ✓ | | | |
| [17] | | ✓ | | ✓ | | | ✓ | | | | ✓ | | ✓ | ✓ | ✓ | | | M |
| [19] | | ✓ | | | | | | ✓ | ✓ | | ✓ | | ✓ | | | ✓ | | |
| [25] | ✓ | ✓ | | ✓ | ✓ | | | | | | ✓ | | ✓ | ✓ | ✓ | | | |
| [32] | | ✓ | | ✓ | | | | | | | | ✓ | ✓ | ✓ | | | ✓ | |
| [16] | ✓ | | | ✓ | | | | | | ✓ | ✓ | | ✓ | | | | | |
| [26] | | | ✓ | ✓ | | | | ✓ | ✓ | | ✓ | ✓ | ✓ | ✓ | | | | SI |
| [27] | ✓ | | | ✓ | | ✓ | ✓ | ✓ | ✓ | | ✓ | ✓ | ✓ | | ✓ | | | |
| [34] | | ✓ | | ✓ | | | | ✓ | | ✓ | ✓ | | ✓ | ✓ | | | ✓ | |
| [8] | | | | | ✓ | | | ✓ | ✓ | | ✓ | | ✓ | ✓ | | | | |
| [28] | | | ✓ | ✓ | | | | ✓ | | | ✓ | | ✓ | ✓ | | | | BE |
| [37] | ✓ | | | ✓ | | ✓ | | | | | ✓ | | ✓ | ✓ | | | | |
| [30] | ✓ | | | ✓ | | | | ✓ | ✓ | | ✓ | ✓ | ✓ | | | ✓ | | |
| [33] | ✓ | | ✓ | ✓ | ✓ | | | | | | ✓ | | ✓ | ✓ | | | ✓ | DA |
| [36] | ✓ | ✓ | | ✓ | | | | ✓ | ✓ | | ✓ | ✓ | ✓ | ✓ | ✓ | | | |
| [14] | ✓ | | | ✓ | | | | | | | | ✓ | | ✓ | ✓ | ✓ | ✓ | FR |
| [18] | ✓ | | ✓ | ✓ | | | | ✓ | | ✓ | ✓ | | ✓ | ✓ | | | ✓ | |
| [10] | ✓ | ✓ | ✓ | ✓ | | | | | | | | ✓ | ✓ | ✓ | | | ✓ | MS |

Table 1 summarizes data on the gamification elements applied in the software and the User Interface design, that is, what visual representation methods were used to deliver the interface. Also, it clusters the primary studies according to the learning objective(s) they aim to achieve. "C" stands for Communication; "M" is Multiple, meaning that the study intended to cover more than one learning objective at the same time; "SI" means Social Interaction; "BE" means Basic Education; "DA" stands for Daily Activities; "FR" means Facial Recognition; and "MS" is an abbreviation for Motor Skills.

## 3.1 Gamification Elements

According to Table 1, many of the studies use feedback (50%) and/or rewarding systems (33%) to appeal to the audience. Those can be either virtual output stimuli, such as visual cues or auditory feedback, or real-life tokens (a fruit, a game, or anything that the user would associate with having positively accomplished a task). Rewards have been largely used in ASD-specific interventions, often applied immediately after the task completion, in order to reinforce certain behavioral patterns [36].

Four studies applied Virtual Reality environments within the software [9–12]. There has been increasing interest in using VR for autistic intervention, since this technology provides an immersion environment that improves interventionist control and promotes engagement [10]. In addition to that, many studies (60%) increased the level of difficulty as the user progresses. This feature includes either mid-term or long-term goals, and is used to foster motivation and interest in using the software.

Most of the studies also include some degree of personalization to the software they propose. This allows the child (or teachers, or parents) to customize the graphics and/or the content according to their particular needs and preferences. On the top level, it may allow for changes in the color scheme, graphics size, and layout arrangement. Besides that, it may include changes in content presentation: photographs instead of cartoon-like illustrations, text messages or picture-only content, background music on and off, etc. A few studies combine personalization with a multimedia approach, including text, audio and video options [8, 9, 11, 13, 15, 37]. These features are particularly interesting if we take into account that each ASD individual has unique interests and preferences, and that the autism covers a broad range of symptoms [8].

In terms of monitoring, many studies apply strategies to customize learning outcomes and provide parental control (56.6% combined). This is often reached by synchronizing child-parent/child-teacher devices or having multiple interface profiles. These studies report on the use of an integrated system that allows teachers, therapists or parents to monitor their children progress, and select custom learning objectives depending on individual cognitive responses. Again, ASD individuals can benefit from having tasks tailored specifically for each of them and, at the same time, teachers and parents are entitled with more control over the learning outcomes.

A few studies also reported on the use of storytelling [15, 17, 27, 29, 33]. This method uses multiple media formats (text, images, sounds, animation, and video) in order to encourage students to create their own narratives. In ASD children, this may help improve their communication skills and the symbolic function, thus promoting an autonomous attitude [27]. Other features found on the studies include familiarization (pictures of the surroundings and/or voice recording) [18, 34], information sharing [16], use of virtual avatars [13], active experimentation [27], and remote control [29].

By clustering the information in relation to the game objective, a few more insights emerge. When dealing with communication, there is a preference to work with personalization, monitoring, custom learning, and increasing level of difficulty. This may be explained by the communication process itself, which requires a certain vocabulary level in order to make sentences, and so on. The same applies to Social Interaction, since it involves cognitive skills rather than physical abilities. In fact, objectives that cope with physical development, such as Daily Activities and Motor Skills, tend to apply feedback, rewards, and also personalization strategies, which provides a more immediate response to the user. In turn, games that included multiple objectives often used a wide variety of strategies (although rewards and level of difficulty are more frequent), perhaps because a single approach would not be sufficient to comply with all the objectives at once.

## 3.2  User Interface Design

The User Interface design methods reported by the studies include visual presentation (colors, illustration, photographs, video), textual elements (words or phrases) and even sounds, voice/narration, and virtual 3D environments. The most popular approaches, however, are the use of illustrations (76.6%), words/text (80%), and colors (73.3%) to express feelings and guide the user through the interface. The items check-marked (refer to Table 1) represent the topics described in more detail in the papers, which does not mean unmarked items were not covered by the study.

In relation to illustrations, there are multiple approaches available. Reports range from the use of simple, sketchy, basic shapes (squares, triangles, and circles) [9, 16, 17, 22, 37] to more sophisticated illustrations [25, 26, 31]. None of them report on the use of realistic drawings. Instead, whenever the authors wanted a more realistic style, they would rely on real-life pictures or photographs. The main explanation provided in those cases is that real-life pictures would be easier to recognize, especially if the parents/teachers use the built-in camera to upload their own images. It would also look more familiar to the user, and may, in some cases, be more effective [38].

The use of colors appeared as one of the major concerns in the development process. Again, there are various approaches. Some of the studies inform on the use of more vibrant colors [16, 22, 25, 28], while others suggest a calm and half-toned color scheme [23, 36]. There is no apparent revaluation of colors based on users' feedback. A similar situation arises from the use of words/text: there is not much information on why authors chose one strategy over another. The differences in communication deficits experienced by ASD individuals impose a challenge because some of them are able to read while others are not [1]. Thus, using an amount of written information that fits the communication skills of the target audience is of major importance to achieve success.

The use of sounds is also reported in many of the studies (56.6%), though voice recording features or narration are much scarcer (10%). Sounds, in this case, include background music and/or other sound effects (clicking a button, for instance). Sounds can be interesting decorative strategies to increase motivation and reinforce learning activities [39]. A few studies report on the use of voice recording or narration in order to add customization attributes or improve familiarization [14, 24, 30]. Around 30% of the studies also include video (self-recorded or not) and virtual environments as means to promote immersion experiences.

Once again, clustering the information according to the objectives leads to other insights. Games with communication objectives largely apply illustration, photographs, and words/text. Surprisingly, however, not many of the studies use sounds, voice recording or video modeling, which could potentially help users become familiar with the sounds of the words and practice pronunciation. The same applies to Social Interaction and Basic Education – they could greatly benefit from having sound reinforcing positive behavior. In turn, video modeling and Virtual Reality appears in all of the studies handling Facial Recognition and Motor Skills, probably because those strategies offer opportunities to simulate real situations – which could also be applied to Daily Activities.

## 4 Conclusions and Future Perspectives

The objective of this review was to investigate the current status of research on ASD-specific gamified interventions, emphasizing gamification elements and design representation methods applied in the software development process. Data were also collected on the target audience, the learning objectives, and the software development process. As results show, there are a good number of studies addressing the topic, which suggests more awareness of the disturbance and a willingness to move toward accessibility.

Clinically, the causes of autism are unclear, and as medicine advances more complexity is added to its diagnosis, treatment, and prognostic. On the one hand, parents find it difficult to handle autism inside their homes, because many times they have little or no assistance on how to behave with their autistic children. On the other, accessibility is often seen as unnecessary and expensive in the corporate environment. That is precisely why it became so important: development teams endure the task to develop effective solutions for autism and, at the same time, prove they are feasible from a productive, financial, and corporate perspective.

In this context, this review shows a wide collection of gamification strategies to cope with the development of autism-specific software. Despite that, many challenges emerge from dealing with the ASD audience. Studies included in this review share some common characteristics. Overall, they provide information on the development process, although the procedures are often not described in full detail (with only a few exceptions). We believe this does not mean the development process was neglected, but rather that the authors decided to highlight some of the aspects they assumed to be the most relevant. However, the lack of information is disappointing, since a more detailed description would add consistency to the studies, and also help readers understand and replicate the methods and strategies used.

The target audience is, most of the cases, referred to simply as "autistic children" or "autistic individuals". As mentioned before, autism covers a broad spectrum, that is, different symptoms appear in different severity levels in ASD individuals [1]. For this reason, it is hard to assume a single software product would be equally effective to the entire spectrum. Having a specific target audience (including the comprehensive description of symptoms) would potentially help optimize the development process and also serve as guidance for therapists in managing the software. Furthermore, this has a negative impact on testing, since results may reflect mixed ASD profiles.

In relation to the development process/design approach, there is a clear focus on applying methodologies that prioritize the end-user. On the one hand, cross-functional teams often present a better performance, since their particular expertise helps improving the software product in terms of usability. On the other, involving external agents (teachers, parents, and the ASD users) is fundamental to collect feedback and confirm its efficiency on a User Experience level. Even though most studies did not present the design process comprehensively, they surely reveal an effort to meet the end-user's needs and preferences.

Despite the issues with the process detailing, all of the studies show a good use of multiple techniques (gamification elements and UI design strategies). The combination of such methods for the development of serious gaming applications often results in better usability and acceptance levels [30]. We should remember, once more, that ASD individuals have complex clinical conditions. Thus, combining multiple strategies and forms of presentation may have a huge impact on how they use and benefit from the software.

Unfortunately, most of the studies analyzed did not provide consistent testing procedures or clear results achieved with the games. Many studies used indirect forms of assessment, which is valuable, but hardly represents the end-user realistically. In cases when authors did test the software with autistic children [8, 9, 11, 12, 22, 23, 25, 27, 28], samples were often small, revealing fragility in the results achieved. In addition to that, none of the studies reported having used control groups within the testing procedures. This leaves us with no reference for comparison on how the audience would have behaved with and without the serious game. Of course, the testing efforts are important but, most of the cases, it is hard to assume they are unquestionable evidence of success.

Results, in turn, are generally presented in a superficial manner. Mostly, they are described as "good/not good" or "positive/negative", without providing further information on the analysis criteria, reference metrics, or a comprehensive review process. Only a small number of studies inform on the specific positive/negative feedback received, as well as how they would apply the suggestions on later improvements [9, 13, 16, 17, 26, 32]. Exclusively negative or unsuccessful outcomes have not been found.

The path towards accessibility for autism is obviously not straightforward. Since the clinical literature is still limited, practitioners are also learning from empirical evidence. In this sense, one of the main challenges in developing serious games for autism is to reach out the end-user, in order to understand the complexity of conditions they have. In addition to that, the development process must be scrutinized. As showed in this systematic review, there are issues related to the selection of the target audience (which may lead to a poor definition of learning objectives), and the conduction of testing procedures (which may lead to biased or mixed results). Finally, developers must be aware of the user-centered approaches – involving autism advocates along the process may be a good strategy to prevent usability disasters.

The studies included in this review are undeniably valuable, and we believe the authors did their best with the limitations they might have faced and with the resources they had available at the time. Results achieved and presented in the studies reinforce that. Notwithstanding, scientific and methodological procedures must be taken seriously given the complexity of the subject matter. This review also intends to open future discussions on scientific rigor and integrity involving the development of ASD-specific software. Efforts must continue toward accessibility, effective learning, and social inclusion.

# References

1. American Psychiatric Association: Diagnostic and Statistical Manual of Mental Disorders, DSM-5, 5th edn. Artmed (2013)
2. Venkatesh, S., Greenhill, S., Phung, D., Adams, B.: Cognitive intervention in autism using multimedia stimulus. ACM Multimedia (2011)
3. United Nations: Accessibility and development: mainstreaming disability in the post-2015 development agenda. Department of Economics and Social Affairs Division for Inclusive Social Development (2013)
4. Chandran, S., Prakrithi, S.N., Kishor, M.: Gamifying education and mental health. Arch. Med. Health Sci. 6(2), 284–289 (2018)
5. Whyte, E.M., Smyth, J.M., Scherf, K.S.: Designing serious game interventions for individuals with autism. J. Autism Dev. Disord. 45(1), 3820–3831 (2015). https://doi.org/10.1007/s10803-014-2333-1
6. Lau, H.M., Smit, J.H., Fleming, T.M., Riper, H.: Serious games for mental health: are they accessible, feasible, and effective? A systematic review and meta-analysis. Front. Psychiatry 7(1), 1–13 (2017). https://doi.org/10.3389/fpsyt.2016.00209
7. Kitchenham, B.: Procedures for performing systematic reviews. Kelee, UK, Kelee University, vol. 33, no. 2004, pp. 1–26 (2004)
8. Kamaruzaman, M.F., Ranic, N.M., Norb, H.M., Azaharia, M.H.H.: Developing user interface design application for children with autism. Soc. Behav. Sci. 217(1), 887–894 (2016). https://doi.org/10.1016/j.sbspro.2016.02.022
9. Cai, Y., Chia, N.K.H., Thalmann, D., Kee, N.K.N., Zheng, J., Thalmann, N.M.: Design and development of a virtual dolphinarium for children with Autism. Trans. Neural Syst. Rehabil. Eng. 21(2), 208–217 (2013). https://doi.org/10.1109/TNSRE.2013.2240700
10. Finkelstein, S., Nickel, A., Barnes, T., Suma, E.: Astrojumper: motivating children with autism to exercise using a VR game. In: 28th ACM Conference on Human Factors in Computing Systems, pp. 4189–4194 (2010)
11. Winoto, P., Xu, C.N., Zhu, A.A.: "Look to remove": a virtual reality application on word learning for chinese children with Autism. In: Antona, M., Stephanidis, C. (eds.) UAHCI 2016. LNCS, vol. 9739, pp. 257–264. Springer, Cham (2016). https://doi.org/10.1007/978-3-319-40238-3_25
12. da Silva, C.A., Fernandes, A.R., Grohmann, A.P.: STAR: speech therapy with augmented reality for children with Autism spectrum disorders. In: Cordeiro, J., Hammoudi, S., Maciaszek, L., Camp, O., Filipe, J. (eds.) ICEIS 2014. LNBIP, vol. 227, pp. 379–396. Springer, Cham (2015). https://doi.org/10.1007/978-3-319-22348-3_21
13. Konstantinidis, E.I., Hitoglou-Antoniadou, M., Luneski, A., Bamidis, P.D.: Using affective avatars and rich multimedia content for education of children with Autism. In: Pervasive Technologies Related to Assistive Environments (PETRA) (2009)

14. Tan, C.T., Harrold, N., Rosser, D.: Can you CopyMe?: An expression mimicking serious game. In: 40th International Conference on Computer Graphics and Interactive Techniques SIGGRAPH 2013 (2013)
15. Wadhwa, B., Jianxiong, C.: Collaborative tablet applications to enhance language skills of children with autism spectrum disorder. In: 11th Asia Pacific Conference on Computer Human-Interaction - APCHI 2013, pp. 39–44. http://dx.doi.org/10.1145/2525194.2525297
16. Zhang, L., Fu, Q., Swanson, A., Weitlauf, A., Warren, Z., Sarkar, N.: Design and evaluation of a collaborative virtual environment (CoMove) for Autism spectrum disorder intervention. Transaction on Accessible Computing 11(2) (2018). https://doi.org/10.1145/3209687
17. Hourcade, J.P., Bullock-Rest, N.E., Hansen, T.E.: Multitouch tablet applications and activities to enhance the social skills of children with Autism spectrum disorders. Pers. Ubiquitous Comput. 16(1), 157–168 (2012). https://doi.org/10.1007/s00779-011-0383-3
18. Washington, P., et al.: SuperpowerGlass: a wearable aid for the at-home therapy of children with Autism. In: ACM on Interactive, Mobile, Wearable and Ubiquitous Technology 1(3) (2017). https://doi.org/10.1145/3130977
19. Venkatesh, S., Phung, D., Duong, T., Greenhill, S., Adams, B.: TOBY: Early intervention in Autism through technology. In: Conference on Human Factors and Computing Systems - CHI 2013, pp. 3187–3196 (2013)
20. Fotjik, R.: Agile methodology and development of software for users with specific disorders. In: International Multiconference on Computer Science and Information Technology, pp. 687–691 (2010)
21. Shminan, A.S., Adzani, R.A., Sharif, S., Lee, N.K.: AutiPECS: mobile based learning of picture exchange communication intervention for caregivers of autistic children. In: International Conference on Computer and Drone Applications, pp. 49–54 (2017)
22. Alvarado, C., Munoz, R., Villarroel, R., Acuña, O., Barcelos, T.S., Becerra, C.: Valpodijo: developing a software that supports the teaching of Chilean idioms to children with autism spectrum disorders. In: 12th Latin American Conference on Learning Technologies (LACLO) (2017)
23. De Leo, G., Gonzales, C.H., Battagiri, P., Leroy, G.: A smart-phone application and a companion website for the improvement of the communication skills of children with Autism: clinical rationale, technical development and preliminary results. J. Med. Syst. 35 (1), 703–711 (2011). https://doi.org/10.1007/s10916-009-9407-1
24. Winoto, P., Cao, V.L., Tang, E.M.: A highly customizable parent-child word-learning mobile game for Chinese Children with Autism. In: Antona, M., Stephanidis, C. (eds.) UAHCI 2017. LNCS, vol. 10277, pp. 545–554. Springer, Cham (2017). https://doi.org/10. 1007/978-3-319-58706-6_44
25. Yan, F.: A sunny day: Ann and Ron's world an iPad application for children with Autism. In: International Conference on Serious Games Development and Applications, pp. 129–138 (2011)
26. Wojciechowski, A., Al-Musawi, R.: Assistive technology application for enhancing social and language skills of young children with Autism. Multimed. Tools Appl. 76(1), 5419–5439 (2017). https://doi.org/10.1007/s11042-016-3995-9
27. Chatzara, K., Karagiannidis, C., Mavropoulou, S., Stamatis, D.: Digital storytelling for children with Autism: software development and pilot application. In: Karagiannidis, C., Politis, P., Karasavvidis, I. (eds.) Research on e-Learning and ICT in Education, pp. 287–300. Springer, New York (2014). https://doi.org/10.1007/978-1-4614-6501-0_19
28. Iradah, I.S. Rabiah, A.K.: EduTism: an assistive educational system for the treatment of autism children with intelligent approach. In: International Visual Informatics Conference, pp. 193–204 (2011)

29. Zaffke, A., Jain, N., Johnson, N., Alam, M.A.U., Magiera, M., Ahamed, S.I.: iCanLearn: a mobile application for creating flashcards and social Stories™ for Children with Autism. In: Bodine, C., Helal, S., Gu, T., Mokhtari, M. (eds.) ICOST 2014. LNCS, vol. 8456, pp. 225–230. Springer, Cham (2015). https://doi.org/10.1007/978-3-319-14424-5_25

30. Hayes, G.R., Hirano, S., Marcu, G., Monibi, M., Nguyen, D.H., Yeganyan, M.: Interactive visual supports for children with autism. Pers. Ubiquit. Comput. **14**(1), 663–680 (2010). https://doi.org/10.1007/s00779-010-0294-8

31. Signore, A., Balasi, P., Yuan, T.: You Talk! – YOU vs Autism. In: Miesenberger, K., Fels, D., Archambault, D., Peňáz, P., Zagler, W. (eds.) ICCHP 2014. LNCS, vol. 8547, pp. 506–512. Springer, Cham (2014). https://doi.org/10.1007/978-3-319-08596-8_79

32. Malinverni, L., Mora-Guiard, J., Padillo, V., Valero, L., Hervás, A., Pares, N.: An inclusive design approach for developing video games for children with autism spectrum disorder. Comput. Hum. Behav. **71**(1), 535–549 (2017). https://doi.org/10.1016/j.chb.2016.01.018

33. Kurniawan, R., Purnamasari, W.M., Rakhmawati, R., Jalaputra, D.P.E.: Development of game for self-help toilet learning for children with Autism. CommIT (Commun. Inf. Technol.) J. **12**(1), 1–12 (2018)

34. Tsiopela, D., Jimoyiannis, A.: Pre-vocational skills laboratory: designing interventions to improve employment skills for students with autism spectrum disorders. Univers. Access. Inf. Soc. **16**(1), 609–627 (2016). https://doi.org/10.1007/s10209-016-0488-6

35. Cabielles-Hernández, D., Pérez-Pérez, J.-R., Paule-Ruiz, M.P., Fernández- Fernández, S.: Specialized intervention using tablet devices for communication deficits in children with autism spectrum disorders. Trans. Learn. Technol. **10**(2), 182–193 (2016). https://doi.org/10.1109/TLT.2016.2559482

36. de Oliveira Barros, V.T., de Almeida Zerbetto, C.A., Meserlian, K.T., Barros, R., Crivellari Camargo, M., Cristina Passos de Carvalho, T.: DayByDay: interactive and customizable use of mobile technology in the cognitive development process of children with autistic spectrum disorder. In: Stephanidis, C., Antona, M. (eds.) UAHCI 2014. LNCS, vol. 8514, pp. 443–453. Springer, Cham (2014). https://doi.org/10.1007/978-3-319-07440-5_41

37. Hulusic, V., Pistoljevic, N.: LEFCA: learning framework for children with Autism. Virtual Worlds for Serious Applications (VS-GAMES 2012), **15**(1), 4–16 (2012). https://doi.org/10.1016/j.procs.2012.10.052

38. Harrold, N., Tan, C.T., Rosser, D.: Towards and expression recognition game to assist the emotional development of children with autism spectrum disorders. In: 7th International Conference on Wireless Algorithms, Systems and Applications, WASA 2012, pp. 33–37 (2012)

39. Banire, B., Jomhari, N., Ahmad, R.: Visual hybrid development learning system (VHDLS) framework for children with autism. J. Autism Dev. Disord. **45**(1), 3069–3084 (2015). https://doi.org/10.1007/s10803-015-2469-7

# Analytical Design of Clinical Cases for Educational Games

Marcos Felipe de Menezes Mota[1]([⊠]), Fagner Leal Pantoja[1],
Matheus Silva Mota[1], Tiago de Araujo Guerra Grangeia[2],
Marco Antonio de Carvalho Filho[2], and André Santanchè[1]

[1] Institute of Computing, University of Campinas, São Paulo, Brazil
marcos.mota@students.ic.unicamp.br,
{fagner.pantoja,matheus.mota,santanche}@ic.unicamp.br
[2] Faculty of Medical Sciences, University of Campinas, São Paulo, Brazil
tiagoguerra35@gmail.com, macarvalhofilho@gmail.com

**Abstract.** Preparing medical students to provide emergency care is one of the biggest challenges in health education, as novices must articulate a wide spectrum, ever-growing knowledge of a generalist physician in the shortest possible time. Previous experience has shown that a problem-based e-Learning environment, presenting clinical cases to be solved by students, has several benefits in the learning process. This paper describes the design and development of an approach to produce health learning games. The approach focuses on combining student engagement with realistic narratives. The central component is a narrative scripting language that enables rapid prototyping and integration with a data analysis backed authoring process. Our method has been materialized in an educational game authoring environment that allows the creation of complex cases and automatic generation of simpler ones. The analytical design provides a scalable method to create medical learning experiences based on well-defined medical education theories and health data.

**Keywords:** Health education · e-Learning · Serious games

## 1 Introduction

Training doctors to find the best diagnostic and treatment for each clinical case is one of the biggest challenges in medical education. To become a good clinician, medical students need to apply the best scientific evidence in caring for patients. Medical educators need to design pedagogical strategies that offer medical students the opportunity to repeat the clinical tasks to develop expertise while guaranteeing the safety of patients. Among the main competencies, medical students need to foster is clinical reasoning, the mental strategies to reach a diagnosis and plan a therapeutic intervention. Developing reasoning skills is particularly important for emergency physicians who work under time pressure in situations potentially fatal. In summary, emergency training requires the student to master the spectrum of knowledge of a generalist physician in the shortest possible time.

© IFIP International Federation for Information Processing 2019
Published by Springer Nature Switzerland AG 2019
E. van der Spek et al. (Eds.): ICEC-JCSG 2019, LNCS 11863, pp. 353–365, 2019.
https://doi.org/10.1007/978-3-030-34644-7_29

In a previous successful experience, which is the starting point of this research [6], an e-learning environment directed to teach emergency medicine through the solution of clinical cases has shown to improve the engagement of students and their performance.

However, this solution lacks support in three main aspects: narrative, evidence, and evaluation/feedback. The environment to build the narrative of clinical cases, presented to the students, was adapted in an e-learning platform (Moodle), being limited to the possibilities offered by its forum and quiz tools. Clinical cases are manually crafted by tutors (physicians) based on evidence of real-world cases, their own experience, and facts reported in the literature. The system pipeline is still highly dependent on the action of professors to evaluate and give feedback to each answer or decision of the students, hampering the scalability of the system.

Building the narrative of a game for clinical cases training is a challenge encompassing two dimensions. On the one hand, there is a real dimension, as the game aims at training real doctors, each scenario – with diseases, symptoms, medications, etc. – must be supported by real-world phenomena. On the other hand, there is a fantasy dimension, in which the author is not constrained by preexisting evidence, having the freedom of introducing elements of an engaging narrative that do not compete with the real dimension.

In this paper, we present our approach to align these two dimensions through a scripting language that combines the freedom of composing narratives, blending them with data backed by scientific evidence. It is the kernel of an environment for authoring and playing educational health games.

The remainder of the paper is organized as follows: Sect. 2 introduces the main challenges and background of this research; Sect. 3 summarizes the health education scenario based on narratives and simulations of clinical cases; Sect. 4 explains how narrative scripting languages are used in the game industry in order to help authoring of stories; Sect. 5 proposes a pipeline using analytical design principles and narrative languages to produce realistic cases aided with data; Sect. 6 details implementation of a system that materializes our proposed design approach; and Sect. 7 presents the discussion of main results and future work.

## 2   Motivation

Real-world cases are the best source to build possible and reliable scenarios, given the complexity of a human body and its interaction with the environment. However, clinical experience and data from the literature are fundamental to enrich the case with alternative paths to the solution and assess student decision-solving capabilities.

The amount of tutor work to build the cases is paramount and relying on data-driven solutions would boost the capacity of the system to generate clinical cases while saving tutoring time. To address the real dimension we have been building an analytical design backed system, in which the authoring process is the result of an interaction between a human author and an information system.

Following a data-driven approach, the system extracts, combines and analyzes health data coming from different data sources. It helps the enrichment of the case, suggesting and advising; the verification of consistency on information; and the production of machine-interpretable outputs to automatize students tracking, evaluation and feedback.

Tufte in 2006 coined the six principles of analytical design [15]. According to Tufte, allowing the viewer to establish: comparisons, causality or mechanism, multivariate analysis, integration of evidence, documentation and rich content, in graphical data is the main quality of good evidence display and reliable scientific data exposition [15]. A clinical case writer needs to gather evidence from different medical data sources, understand the mechanisms governing the diseases in the case, compare a case with many others used in class, and provide feedback based on a narrative content known by the student. Therefore, although these analytical design principles were originally asserted for graphics, they can be transported to measure the quality of a well written clinical case and guide the development of data-driven e-learning system that allows effective creation of such cases.

There is a tight coupling between the narrative and the computational resources necessary to render it in rich interactive scenarios. This demands a close interaction among health professionals (authors of cases), IT professionals, and designers.

One of the challenges in such interaction is the lack of common ground among health professionals, IT professionals, and designers. In several authoring systems, health professionals can produce a great narrative on their cases but are not able to transform them on interactive learning experiences. Such challenge of integrating the creator (author), the developer, and the designer is also tackled by the computer game industry [8]. An effort to soften the gap between the content creator and the game development process is the introduction of a narrative scripting language, for example, Ink [14] or March22 [8] languages. Such languages allow the writer to build a narrative closer to a natural language but with lightweight markups that can be compiled in an interactive game ready for the user.

In this work, we have blended elements of Analytical Design with a narrative scripting language, which is the kernel of our authoring and execution system. A third central component is a template-based authoring process. It addresses a natural problem of decision-based games that produces an alternative scenario for each action of the player. The consequence is an unmanageable explosion of alternative scenarios, which are even harder to produce when the alternatives must be backed by evidence data. To circumvent such problem we have developed an authoring method, in which the creative process is conducted by templates. Templates guide the author, avoiding the explosion of alternatives, and also embed the experience of several years in health education from physicians.

Following this approach, we were able to produce case scripts and to turn them into playable cases, following proved educational templates. The developed application can be improved using more data sources, better human-computer interaction and better artificial intelligence. Nevertheless, the design pipeline has shown to be consistent with the goals of physicians health education.

## 3    Narrative and Simulation in Health Education

We consider three main components in an approach to support producing clinical scenarios to train doctors: (i) a proper analogy to real-world health phenomena; (ii) an engaging narrative; (iii) rich interactive content to present the case. Components (i) and (ii) have been explored in health education and they are detailed in this section; components (ii) and (iii) have been explored in games development, presented in the next section.

Flexnerian education [3] refers to the actual health care education approach, in which students start by receiving science-based medical knowledge, usually through traditional lectures and/or problem-based learning approaches. Frenk et al. [5] consider the introduction of Problem-based Learning (PBL) and disciplinarily integrated curricula the second generation of reforms in health care education. It moves the focus to the problem and the patient, early promoting the articulation among several disciplines, usually through focusing on real-life scenarios. In fact, throughout the diversity of PBL methods, the usual approach consists of a small group of students working in a real-life based case, evaluating the problem and making decisions [10]. Case-based learning techniques – i.e., based on the resolution of clinical cases – have been a widespread PBL approach to learn clinical reasoning [7]. The narrative of each case is the key to blend technical health aspects and engaging properties.

PBL introduced the concept of Standardized Patients – i.e., individuals trained to act as real patients, simulating their behaviors and complaints [5]. Simulated patients offer the possibility of bringing complexity to students in a stepwise fashion, adapting the task to students developmental level, optimizing the cognitive load.

The information technology has been contributing to the advance of analogies and simulations through the introduction of computer-based clinical scenarios – the Virtual Patients (VP) [2] – as well as high-fidelity Human Patient Simulators (HPS) [1], based on automated mannequins. A VP runs a clinical scenario behind a computer screen, with variable interaction levels – from textual narratives accompanied by static images to 2D or 3D interactive simulations. An HPS simulates physical characteristics that resemble real persons – one can auscultate the mannequin; inject drugs; try cardiopulmonary resuscitation, etc.

The route of a case in a VP or a simulation in an HPS is still authored manually by a specialist, which is not ready yet due to the complexity of creating algorithms that properly simulate the dynamics of a human body and possible variations. This route usually takes the form of a graph, with nodes representing case states and edges representing transitions triggered according to actions. State nodes will contain free-text descriptions, for those VPs based on narratives, and will contain structured data that drive HPSs or VPs with interactive simulations.

As shown in Fig. 1, these instructional modalities can be seen as complementary in a continuum of competency [2]. Narratives and the analogy to real-world health phenomena will play important roles in each modality.

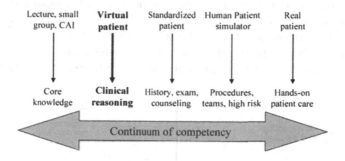

**Fig. 1.** Instructional modalities with desired outcomes [2].

Narratives usually come from specialists that write PBL cases, VP scenarios or Standardized Patient scripts; the analogy to real-world phenomena can be seen as part of a bigger scenario, comprising data collected from the real-world to drive predictions, inferences, and discoveries. Even though they are treated as distinct and sometimes alternative disciplines [4], in the Analytical Design perspective, proposed here, both are treated as interdependent.

Our focus in this paper is in the VP tools context. Existing tools are still highly limited in the support to author engaging narratives when compared to game authoring approaches and lack support to add rich interactive content. In the next section, it will be presented with game authoring approaches, which we exploited to enrich our solution.

## 4   Narrative Scripting Languages

Many aspects of clinical cases authoring, described in the previous session, are shared with the development of interactive narratives for games. One of the challenges is the entry barrier of the case writer and the software-based platform that executes it. Also, effective approaches in problem-based learning rely on a narrative format [6], therefore common tools can be used. Complex narratives have the drawback of not being suitable for tools like cognitive maps and stories on sticky labels because they branch exponentially for each decision point a user can make.

In Fig. 2-A (left), we can see a standard pipeline performed by an author to insert their clinical cases in a web-based e-Learning system, adapted from Lynch et al. [8]. First, the writer gathers information about real clinical cases, the diseases in such cases and relevant references. After the complete case is written, the script is sent to a developer that turns it into an interactive code.

Web-designers or game artists create the environment and animations necessary for an interesting learning experience. If the developer does not fulfill the requirements of the author or produce a code with errors the interaction with the author/physician continues. Looking at this pipeline, we can see that the author is decoupled of the game production environment, possibly raising the following problems: many errors can arise due to the difference in the background of the physician and the developer; the feedback in the authoring cycle is too slow, i.e., writers cannot preview the result of their narrative decisions, therefore, they are not able to try different ways to present the case during its conception.

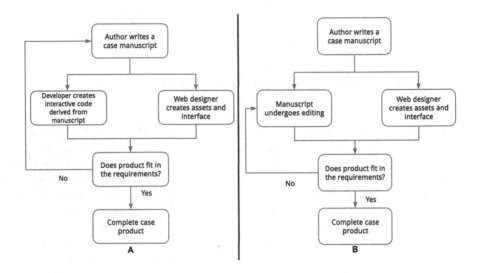

**Fig. 2.** Pipelines for clinical case writing in e-Learning systems.

Some initiatives, like Ink [14], March22 [8] and INDIeAuthor [12] rely on textual languages that bridge the narratives with the control of the flow according to decisions. More specifically, in [14] and [8] is created a narrative scripting language. It is a markup language that allows the writer to script a narrative in a way closer to a natural language but with a structure machine-interpretable, so it can be compiled into a software. In the game context, it can be compiled to an interactive game ready for the player. Usually, these languages are lightweight markup languages enriched with common narrative directives like branching, variables, choices and conditional content. In Fig. 2-B (right), we see how a narrative language changes the pipeline of case writing. The main change is more integration of the author through the process of editing and compiling of the narrative language and development team more free to focus on graphical design issues.

## 5   Analytical Design of Clinical Cases

Even though the adoption of narrative scripting languages is a design improvement to create clinical cases, the existing approaches, coming from the game
development context, are geared towards fantasy stories. Therefore, they lack
proper support to represent structured technical information, fundamental to
create realistic clinical cases.

### 5.1   Information Layers

To address this limitation we have designed a system backed by a language[1]
that blends the three components mentioned in Sect. 3. They are organized in
information layers as presented in Fig. 3.

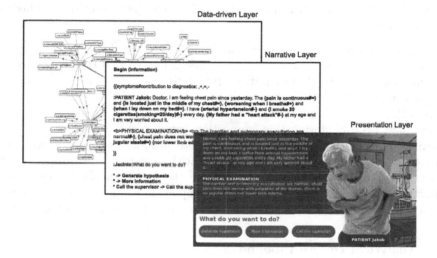

**Fig. 3.** Information layers of our system.

**Narrative Layer** - We designed a language derived from Markdown, which adds
elements that represent an extra semantics to build scenarios and the control flow
of the game. This language has some structures based on Ink [14]. We further
present some elements of the language in Table 1.

**Data-Driven Layer** - Elements from the Narrative Layer are annotated and
connected to structured data and knowledge structures defined in the Data-
driven Layer, as dictionaries and ontologies. These structures are connected with
external knowledge bases, e.g., MeSH - Medical Subject Headings. This layer is
designed to be consumed by machines to support the automation of tasks as

---

[1] Full language reference at https://github.com/datasci4health/harena-space/tree/
master/src/adonisjs/public/translator.

**Table 1.** Main narrative language constructs for case writing.

| Symbol | Action |
|--------|--------|
| # or === | Markdown headers delimit scene nodes |
| -> | Node transitions triggered user actions, e.g., a button pressed |
| {? } | Player inputs that are further matched with lists, dictionaries or knowledge structures defined in the Data-driven layer |
| { } | Annotate terms inside the narrative and connect them with the Data-driven Layer |
| {{ }} | Defines a semantic context for the narrative and the respective annotations. The context guides the interpretation of parts of the narrative |

evaluation and feedback. It is also part of a future project to build a full fledged intelligent tutor.

**Presentation Layer** - The document in the Narrative Layer is compiled to the final product, which is a game. Each node is related to a theme that guides its conversion to the final presentation. Interactive elements are mapped to web components, based in the Digital Content Component Model (DCC) developed by us [13].

We have been exploring this connection between the Narrative and Data-driven Layers to provide automatic support to produce and enrich cases. The analyses of existing cases and their bridge with structured data supports the discovery of patterns of narrating, for example, the symptoms of a disease and the respective treatment. These patterns can be applied in finding extra knowledge to enrich the case in narrative-based data sources, as scientific papers repositories.

### 5.2   Analytical Design Pipeline

To generalize the concepts presented in the previous section, we propose an analytical design pipeline (Fig. 4), which fulfills most of the requirements of an application to write clinical cases. Besides a method based on the three layers model, another key feature in this pipeline is the introduction of a case template. A template is a previously defined pattern in the system that guides the creation of new scenes or groups of scenes. It defines a fixed backbone structure with spots to be filled or elements to be configured by the author. In the health context, the doctors of our team developed templates based on their long term experience in medical education, as described by [6].

Our pipeline has as design guidance the principles of analytical design as specified in [15]. We enumerate below the principles and how they are ensured by our pipeline:

1. Comparisons - The author can start a case choosing from many different templates or cases to derive. Results achieved from previous adoptions of

cases/templates will enable to choose which case is better for her educational intention.

2. Causality, Mechanism, Explanations - The Data-driven Layer enables the production of cases derived from Evidence-based Medicine, which unveils the mechanisms of relating symptoms to diagnostics. Such mechanisms could be useful to increment the case realism even in a fantasy story, once able to mix narrative and data coming from scientific literature, The system also tracks all actions of the users during a case. From its analysis, the author can understand the mechanism for presenting a concept.

3. Multivariate Analysis - The proposed design generates three types of data: medical, player and educational. Each type has multiple dimensions that must be shown to the author.

4. Integration of Evidence - Our three information layers model enables to integrate into a narrative different type of data and makes accessible to the authoring process the best scientific foundation to the case.

5. Documentation - Each case is indexed by its authors, keywords, and data coming from the data-driven layer, as each medical evidence the case is based (e.g. papers, study cases).

6. Content - A template ensures that the case has a health education theory as background and it has educational efficacy proven. Moreover, annotations connected with external bases enable to track their provenance.

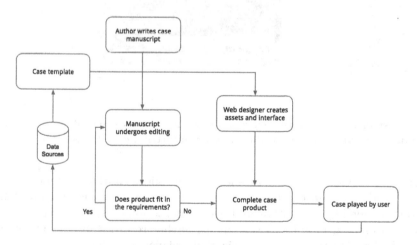

**Fig. 4.** Analytical Design pipeline for clinical case writing in e-Learning systems.

In the next section, we describe how we implemented the Analytical Design pipeline and our continuous effort to develop a system that allows easy creation of clinical cases for medical educational games.

# 6   Implementation

The analytical pipeline was materialized under a system called *Harena*[2,3]. The system is a web-based application following microservice architecture where every microservice is a REST API. The system allows authoring cases and the generation of games built from the cases.

The system has two main environments: the author and the player. In the author mode, scenes can be edited in the visual or textual mode. In Fig. 5 we see the visual authoring mode of the system. In this mode, the user can see: the structure of the case in a tree form (left); a preview of the scene node as it will be presented to the player (middle); and attributes of the currently selected scene or element inside it (right). The textual authoring mode switch the preview for a text box where the same scene can be edited using the narrative scripting language. Every change in the narrative script is automatically updated in the visual mode, therefore, we provide two ways of editing one more visual suitable to beginners and a textual mode for advanced users.

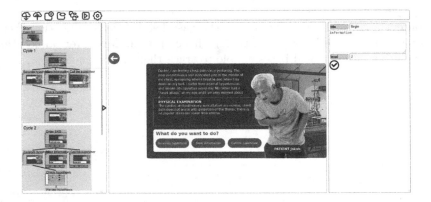

**Fig. 5.** System visual authoring view of a case. In the left the narrative scenes tree, in the middle the current scene to edit and on right attributes of the scene.

The player view has the same look of the visual authoring mode preview because both are compilations of a narrative script. The player mode follows the route defined by the author and every interaction of the player is converted to messages stored in a JSON document, further recorded in a database. Such approach allows further data analysis of the player behavior.

The authoring environment and respective games produced on it were tested in workshops developed at the Interactive Science Museum of Unicamp. We have conducted 3 workshops where we tested two modalities of the games. One of the games was manually crafted in conjunction with doctors and the second one was automatically generated, as further described.

---

[2] https://github.com/datasci4health/harena.
[3] https://ds4h.org/.

## 6.1   Automatic Generation of Cases

The first experiment we performed with the Analytical Design approach was a test for the narrative scripting language, case templates, and the communication between the three information layers. The output was a children's game that confronted them with simple clinical reasoning. Thus, we developed the game *ZombieHealth*, which is a decision game where the player is a doctor who needs to treat zombies examining their symptoms to identify a disease to be treated.

The generated game was derived from a causal model and its goal was to verify if the children will learn the correlation between causes (diseases) and effects (symptoms) modeled in the game.

Each zombie in the game has a generated name and disease. Each disease is based on a causal model, as defined in [11], so the disease is the cause of a set of symptoms (effects). The model is as simple as possible but each disease entails a different probabilistic distribution of symptoms from its model. Three diseases and six symptoms were modeled for the game using the probabilistic programming framework Pyro[4]. In the game, a zombie has an equal probability of having one of the three diseases and each disease has its symptoms distribution. A set of case attributes were generated from a set of samples following the probabilistic distribution. Thus, models and case attributes form the Data-driven Layer for this experiment.

Provided the case attributes set that form the Data-driven layer in this game, we can proceed to the Narrative Layer. Therefore, we wrote a template in the narrative scripting language and defined multimedia assets to be compiled for the complete game on the Presentation Layer. The script of every case has the same pattern of symptom inquiry, so features of the case can be substituted in the narrative script placeholders. In Fig. 6 we can see a scene of an automatically generated case.

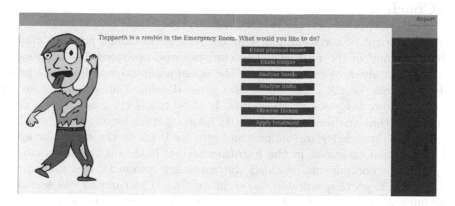

**Fig. 6.** Player view of an automatic generated case for *ZombieHealth* game.

---

[4] http://pyro.ai/.

Despite the simple interaction, the narrative setup and the uncertainty aspect of each case were enough to engage the children on playing and fostering clinical reasoning of cause and effect.

## 6.2  Authoring of Complex Cases

Besides automatically generated cases, we tested the system in much more complex scenarios. Health professionals were able to translate the interaction of [6] to the new system. Figure 4 shows a scene of one of these cases written using *Harena*. An important new feature of this transition is the possibility of organizing the inner structure of cases as cycles of evidence gathering and a case as a composition of these cycles. Such approach can guide the creation of complex cases in progressive levels of detail. This structure follows the best practices of medical education. New elements as gamified reward, leaderboard or interactive media can be added given tested benefits in medical education. More complex cases are being written to be organized in a course structure to integrate class curriculum at the University of Campinas.

There is an ongoing effort in defining how to assess students performance using Harena. There is an increasing interest in psychometrics in health education and, in the context of this work, it needs to be integrated with game-based assessment. Therefore, future work includes student assessment using complex cases. Harena currently has the infrastructure for evidence-centered assessment, capturing and storing data concerning students evolution suitable for assessment – known in the educational assessments as work products [9]. It can also store in data stream log files, case-specific data using variables and contextual data like timestamp, identifier, actions, and game state. Defined the assessment methodology, these logs can be used for rigorous assessment and psychometrics.

## 7  Conclusion

The development of a system, following the Analytical Design pipeline, allowed us to test many of the pipelines characteristics and produced a new potential for the development of serious games. The use of a narrative scripting language bridges the role of the case author and game development, as shown by the creation of complex cases by specialists. It also bridges the cases with a data-driven layer that enables their automatic interpretation by machines, which in turn use this knowledge to evaluate and give feedback to the user. The application of transformations in the narrative script, based on themes combined with software components, enabled the automatic production of a final web product and a preview suitable for visual editing. The complex cases created using our pipeline indicate that templates help manage the narrative complexity and physicians can focus more on the learning goals than the narrative. Users interaction are captured and stored by our system, as defined in the Analytical Design pipeline. Future work will explore techniques of user assessment, template enhancement, automated feedback and gamification testing in the system.

The Analytical Design pipeline and its principles can enable computer scientists and physicians to jointly conduct research under the same system and context in medical education, serious games, data-intensive applications, and artificial intelligence.

# References

1. Bremner, M.N., Aduddell, K., Bennett, D.N., VanGeest, J.B.: The use of human patient simulators: best practices with novice nursing students. Nurse Educ. **31**(4), 170–174 (2006)
2. Cook, D.A., Triola, M.M.: Virtual patients: a critical literature review and proposed next steps. Med. Educ. **43**(4), 303–311 (2009). https://doi.org/10.1111/j.1365-2923.2008.03286.x
3. Flexner, A.: Medical education in the united states and canada: a report to the Carnegie foundation for the advancement of teaching. Technical report, New York (1910). http://www.ncbi.nlm.nih.gov/pubmed/12163926
4. Frasca, G.: Simulation versus narrative: introduction to ludology. In: The Video Game Theory Reader, chap. 10, pp. 243–258. Routledge, New York, October 2013. https://doi.org/10.4324/9780203700457-17
5. Frenk, J., et al.: Health professionals for a new century: transforming education to strengthen health systems in an interdependent world. Lancet **376**(9756), 1923–1958 (2010). https://doi.org/10.1016/S0140-6736(10)61854-5, http://www.ncbi.nlm.nih.gov/pubmed/21112623
6. Grangeia, T.D.A.G., et al.: Cognitive load and self-determination theories applied to e-learning: impact on students' participation and academic performance. PLOS ONE **11**(3), e0152462 (2016). https://doi.org/10.1371/journal.pone.0152462, http://dx.plos.org/10.1371/journal.pone.0152462
7. Kassirer, J.P.: Teaching clinical reasoning: case-based and coached. Acad. Med. **85**(7), 1118–1124 (2010). https://doi.org/10.1097/ACM.0b013e3181d5dd0d, https://insights.ovid.com/crossref?an=00001888-201007000-00011
8. Lynch, S., Hargood, C., Charles, F.: Textual authoring for interactive narrative (2017)
9. Mislevy, R.J., et al.: Psychometrics and game-based assessment. In: Technology and Testing: Improving Educational and Psychological Measurement, pp. 23–48 (2016)
10. Neville, A.J.: Problem-based learning and medical education forty years on. A review of its effects on knowledge and clinical performance. Med. Princ. Pract. **18**(1), 1–9 (2009). https://doi.org/10.1159/000163038, http://www.ncbi.nlm.nih.gov/pubmed/19060483
11. Pearl, J.: Causal inference in the health sciences: a conceptual introduction. Health Serv. Outcomes Res. Method. **2**(3–4), 189–220 (2001)
12. Pérez-Berenguer, D., García-Molina, J.: INDIeAuthor: a metamodel-based textual language for authoring educational courses. IEEE Access **7**, 51396–51416 (2019)
13. Santanchè, A., Medeiros, C.B., Pastorello Jr., G.Z.: User-author centered multimedia building blocks. Multimedia Syst. **12**(4), 403–421 (2007)
14. Studios, I.: Ink - inkle's scripting language for writing interactive narrative (2019). https://github.com/inkle/ink
15. Tufte, E.R.: Beautiful Evidence, vol. 1. Graphics Press, Cheshire (2006)

# Evaluation of Informative Content of Health Data Submitted Through a Mobile Serious Game

Konrad Peters[1](✉), Stephanie Bührer[2], Marisa Silbernagl[1], Fares Kayali[3], Helmut Hlavacs[1], and Anita Lawitschka[2]

[1] Research Group Entertainment Computing, University of Vienna, Vienna, Austria
{konrad.peters,marisa.silbernagl,helmut.hlavacs}@univie.ac.at
[2] St. Anna Children's Hospital, Vienna, Austria
{stephanie.buehrer,anita.lawitschka}@stanna.at
[3] Vienna University of Technology, Vienna, Austria
fares@igw.tuwien.ac.at
https://ec.cs.univie.ac.at/

**Abstract.** In the presented study, the informative content of health data of a handwritten health diary was compared with health data submitted through a serious game. Physicians are able to derive a better and more complete health status of patients with higher informative content in health reports. The serious game was implemented in the project Interacct, in which patients submit health data through a mobile app on a daily basis to receive in-game rewards. The main hypothesis is, that the informative content of health data, which was submitted through a serious game, is higher than the informative content of hand written health diaries. Statistical results confirm this hypothesis significantly. This is especially important for young and adolescent cancer patients, where the results were even more conclusive than in the control group of students. Considering positive side effects of the serious game (such as high engagement, compliance and pleasure reporting health data through a serious game), the proposition of the authors is to conduct further studies and experiments regarding this topic.

**Keywords:** Serious games · Serious games for health · Health reports · Informative content · Cancer outpatient treatment · m-health

## 1 Introduction

There are various ways of remotely recording health-related data, facilitated by the development of new technologies [30]. However, the usage of these technological applications are not always backed by scientific evaluations and thus the safety of users can be at risk [20]. This is especially true if the users are members of a vulnerable group, such as chronically ill cancer patients. Further, it is hard

© IFIP International Federation for Information Processing 2019
Published by Springer Nature Switzerland AG 2019
E. van der Spek et al. (Eds.): ICEC-JCSG 2019, LNCS 11863, pp. 366–376, 2019.
https://doi.org/10.1007/978-3-030-34644-7_30

to quantify the benefits of new technologies, especially when compared to analog methods of gathering data (e.g. through handwritten health diaries).

The project Interacct has the aim to foster communication between young leukaemia patients and their treating physicians using a mobile serious game. The project is conducted by the St. Anna Children's Hospital Vienna[1], in cooperation with the University of Vienna (Research Group Entertainment Computing)[2] the University of Applied Arts Vienna[3] and T-Systems Austria[4]. Interacct includes a serious game for patients with a health reporting function, as well as a web-interface for physicians to evaluate and observe the submitted data.

The target group of project Interacct consists of children and adolescents who have been treated by an allogeneic hematopoietic stem cell transplantation (HSCT). This method is used to cure diseases like red-cell disorder or leukemia. After treatment, patients struggle with a variety of symptoms, risks, and sequelae [3,26]. Although many symptoms occur independently of the cancer type and the treatment method [6,31], no screening tool exists that can be used to query symptoms in a standardized way [8].

At the St. Anna Children's Hospital, health monitoring of HSCT patients in childhood and adolescence is currently based on a paper diary. In this paper diary, the young patients document health-related changes on a daily basis. Once they visit the clinic, they hand over the diary to their aftercare physician. This procedure is accompanied by two major disadvantages. First, the adherence of patients regarding paper diaries is low [19,27]. Second, the diaries are often filled later and not regularly, which is partly caused by the low adherence [16, 25]. These disadvantages may be prevented by real-time electronic symptom checking, for example via smartphone app [7,18]. If information about symptoms is transmitted daily and directly to the physician, negative changes in health can be detected quickly without visiting the hospital. Therefore, patients can receive an immediate response after symptoms have been reported and can seek medical care or initiate coping strategies [14]. Due to the timestamps of electronic data, it is furthermore easy to arrange and evaluate data according to the date of entries [25]. Another advantage of mobile applications is that children and adolescents feel more comfortable with the electronic exchange of sensitive information [1,2, 15].

Although a lot of health-related software is available, a review published in 2015 revealed only four pilot-tested smartphone applications for young cancer patients [28]. Often medical professionals are not included during the development of health-related software [14], but these four apps are theoretically based and evaluated scientifically. Currently, no study exists that has developed as well as evaluated such an app and compared its content directly with the traditional paper method. It is also unclear, whether a meaningful health profile can be

---

[1]  https://www.stanna.at/, accessed 21.06.2019.
[2]  https://ec.cs.univie.ac.at, accessed 21.06.2019.
[3]  https://www.dieangewandte.at, accessed 21.06.2019.
[4]  https://www.t-systems.com/de/at, accessed. 21.06.2019.

conveyed via electronic data transmission without seeing the patient personally, due to the rare involvement of physicians in the development of those apps.

Therefore, this study aimed to develop and test a serious game for HSCT patients that provides information about the health condition of treated children and adolescents. Physicians evaluated the information content delivered through the serious game and compared it with the information obtained from the paper diary. The information content of the serious game was expected to be significantly higher than the one derived from the diary.

## 1.1    Related Work

Hochstenbach et al. tested the feasibility of a mobile and web-based self-management tool for outpatients with cancer pain. Patients (n = 11) and nurses (n = 3) used the tool for pain monitoring, medication monitoring, and educational sessions. Results show, that patients and nurses were positive about using the tool. The authors conclude, that the system demonstrates feasibility in everyday practice [11]. A similar system is *PainBuddy*, which is discussed by Fortier et al.: young cancer patients keep track of their pain during cancer treatment using tablet computers. The provided app uses an animated avatar and gamification components, as well as remote symptom monitoring. A pilot study has shown, that patients (n = 12) were highly satisfied [10]. In *PainSquad*, adolescent cancer patients keep track of their pain during therapy through an iPhone app. The app was found to be appealing to the patients, which resulted in high compliance rates [24]. A more specific approach was investigated by Rodgers et al. by implementing *EAT!*, which should assist adolescents with self-management of eating-related issues during HSCT recovery. While patients (n = 16) initially embraced the app, the use decreased extensively over time. Authors suggest further development and studies [22]. Baggott et al. implemented an electronic diary for adolescent cancer patients. In a 3-week trial, patients (n = 10) showed high adherence ($\geq$90%) [2]. Wesley and Fizur reviewed several studies dealing with cancer treatment with app support. They conclude positively but state the demand for more empirical data and further research effort [29].

Outside of the field of cancer patient aftercare, Charlier et al. conducted a meta-analysis on the effect of serious games for improving knowledge and self-management in young people with chronic conditions. The authors conclude, that using serious games can significantly improve self-management as well as knowledge transfer [4]. Fishbein et al. give suggestions for the design and development of mobile applications to promote oral drug adherence and symptom management during chemotherapy [9]. Klaassen et al. have evaluated a coaching and gamification platform for the self-management of young diabetes patients. They give concise suggestions for the development of coaching and gamification platforms in medical practice [13]. Price et al. developed *Painpad*, a tangible device to self-log pain, and have shown increases in both frequency and compliance with pain logging [21]. They further note that data self-reported this way is more faithful than data reported to nurses.

# 2   Methods

## 2.1   Study Design and Statistical Methods

Patients and students between ages 7–18 participated in this study to compare the Interacct serious game app with a paper health diary. All participants were asked to use the diary as well as the serious game for 5 days (Monday-Friday) and to document given body function parameters (e.g.: tiredness, appetite, pain, etc.) as conscientiously as possible. Only participants who used both, paper diary and app, for at least one day were included. Due to this criterion, 10 students were excluded prior to the analyzes and the final sample consisted of 15 patients and 27 students. Due to organizational reasons, a completely balanced design (crossover between starting with the diary or the app) could not be realized and the diary was always used before the app.

The information content of the diary entries and the app data was checked by two independent, blinded physicians. The physicians used a scale ranging from 1 to 5 points to evaluate the information. One point reflects low information, whereas 5 points indicate a high information content. The interrater-reliability was evaluated by calculating the intraclass correlation coefficient (ICC), which was based on a two-way mixed model and the absolute agreement. Subsequently, a one-way repeated-measures ANOVA was used to check whether the information content of the app differs from the diary. Also, the between-subject-factor *group* was included to examine any differences between patients and students. T-tests for associated samples were conducted post-hoc to calculate contrasts between the groups.

After participation, the children were asked to answer a usability questionnaire regarding general user satisfaction as well as the suitability of the app design. User satisfaction was measured on a 5-point Likert scale, where 1 represented low values ("not at all") and 5 high values ("extraordinary"). To evaluate the app design, participants could award 3 points for each app-function, with 3 points being the most positive rating. The median and the interquartile range (IQR) were calculated for each item. Additionally, participants had the opportunity to write down feedback to reveal additional ideas for the improvement of the app.

## 2.2   Technical Components

The technical components used in the study were a *Unity 3D*[5] app for the patients and an *ASP.net*[6] web-interface for the physicians. The persistence layer was implemented through the *ASP.net*-backend, accessing a *Microsoft* SQL database, running in a secure *Windows Server 2016* environment. The connection between clients and server was established using *Secure Socket Layer - SSL*. Basic authentication and cross-site request forgery (CSRF) tokens were used to ensure data integrity and security.

---

[5] https://unity3d.com/, accessed 21.06.2019.
[6] https://dotnet.microsoft.com/apps/aspnet/, accessed 21.06.2019.

## 2.3    Interacct Client

The Interacct client is a native smartphone application for Android and iOS, developed in Unity 3D. It was used as the main tool for the presented study. The main components of the client app are remote medical data entry as well as the game content itself. Completing the medical data entry survey, users were rewarded with virtual in-game currency, used to progress in the main game. Registration of new users was only possible through the administrative team of the project.

The following subchapters will describe the main components of project Interacct. A detailed project description, as well as design considerations, are covered by Kayali et al. in [12].

**Game Design.** The core game idea of Interacct is to collect *avatars* and complete procedurally generated levels. The avatar explores an island and needs to fight off hostile NPC (*non-player characters*) monsters to complete a level. Fights with the NPC monsters are easier for the player, once the avatar has reached a certain level or skill set. To upgrade an avatar, the player can spend *science points*, which are earned through the completion of health reports. At the end of each island, a boss monster is encountered and has a chance of dropping an *egg shell*, which eventually allowed the player to hatch a new avatar. The levels come in different graphical settings and with different NPC monsters to provide variety.

**Health Reports/Remote Data Entry.** Within the Interacct serious game, users can to report a set of health parameters. The parameters mostly follow a 0–3 scale and were adapted to match LOINC[7] codes, where possible. The parameters are listed and explained in Table 1. The health report data could be submitted several times per day by each user and was accumulated by the backend for each full day. For completing the report for the first time each day, the user was rewarded with *science points*, a virtual in-game currency, which could be used to extend the capabilities of the user's avatar. Fig. 1 shows the health report UI with all health parameter categories. Fig. 2 shows the input for fluid intake amount and if the patient felt any pain during fluid intake.

## 3    Results

A high degree of interrater-reliability was found between the physicians. The average measure ICC was .867 (95% confidence interval [CI] from .733 to .932, $F(41,41) = 8.530$, $p \leq .001$) for the paper diary and .912 (95% CI from .794 to .958, $F(41,41) = 14.001$, $p \leq .001$) for the app. Over the entire sample, the physicians gave an average of 3.77 ($\pm$ .91) points for the information content of the diary and 4.14 ($\pm 1.14$) points for the app. The repeated measures ANOVA

---

[7] https://loinc.org/, accessed 21.06.2019.

**Fig. 1.** Interacct serious game client with the health report categories

**Fig. 2.** Interacct serious game client showing input for fluid intake amount and fluid intake pain

revealed a significant difference between information content of the diary compared to the app ($F(1, 40) = 5.571$, $p = .023$, $\eta = .12$). This means that the app provided significantly more information than the diary. The between subject factor group was not significant ($F(1, 40) = .522$, $p = .474$) and also no significant interaction effect was found ($F(1, 40) = 1.807$, $p = .186$).

Although there were no group-differences shown in the ANOVA, post-hoc t-tests revealed that the significant main effect was primarily driven by the patients (Fig. 3). Patients received an average of 3.73 ($\pm.63$) points for the paper diary and 4.43 ($\pm1.07$) points for the app. This difference was significant ($t(1,14) = -2.941$, $p = .011$), while there was no significant difference in information content for students ($t(1,26) = -.772$, $p = .447$). The information content of their diaries was rated with 3.78 ($\pm1.05$) points and the app with 3.98 ($\pm1.17$) points. The information content of the students' diary and app was very similar to the information given by the patients in the diary. These results indicate that only the patients, who were probably the more intrinsically motivated group, documented the body function parameters conscientiously. It is quite possible that the students revealed rather superficial information.

**Table 1.** Health parameters and their meaning, used by the Interacct serious game/ health report tool

| Health parameter | Meaning |
|---|---|
| Fluid intake amount | Amount of fluid intake |
| Fluid intake pain | Pain during drinking |
| Food intake amount | Amount of food intake |
| Appetite | Appetite before food intake |
| Stool consistency | Consistency of stool (soft/normal/hard) |
| Stool frequency | Frequency of defecation |
| Stool pain | Pain during defecation |
| Playtime duration | Amount of playing in minutes |
| Walking duration | Amount of walking in minutes |
| Physical exercise duration | Amount of physical exercise in minutes |
| Urine frequency | Frequency of urination |
| Nausea | Level of nausea |
| Vomiting | Amount of vomiting |
| Anxiety | Level of anxiety |
| Rage | Level of rage |
| Fear | Level of fear |
| Tiredness | Level of tiredness |
| Mouth pain | Level of mouth pain |
| Body temperature | Body temperature in °C |
| Localized skin pain | Level of skin pain + localization |

This assumption is supported by considering the number of days participants used the diary and the app. Patients used the paper diary for an average of 5.67 (±1.23) days, which was more than the required 5 days. The app was used by this group for 4.67 (±2.53) days, but the difference to the diary was not significant (t(1,14) = 1.479, p = .161). The students used the diary as long as patients (5.89 ± 1.31 days), but there was a significant difference in the use of the app (t(1,26) = 6.138, p ≤.001), which they used only 3.41 (±1.69) days. As mentioned in the introduction, it is easy to fill the diary afterward, which is impossible with the app. Therefore, the probability is quite high that especially the students did not keep the diary up to date.

Furthermore, user satisfaction, as well as the evaluation of the app-design, were positive (Table 2). There was no evidence that the diary was preferred to the app.

**Table 2.** User satisfaction and evaluation of the app design

| User satisfaction | Median score (IQR) |
| --- | --- |
| | *[1 = not at all; 5 = extraordinary]* |
| I was bored | 3.00 (IQR: 3.00) |
| I was impressed | 3.00 (IQR: 3.00) |
| I felt frustrated | 1.00 (IQR: 1.00) |
| I found it tiring | 2.00 (IQR: 2.00) |
| I was irritated | 1.00 (IQR: 1.00) |
| I felt skillful | 3.00 (IQR: 3.00) |
| I was satisfied | 4.00 (IQR: 4.00) |
| I felt challenged | 2.00 (IQR: 2.00) |
| I had to put a lot of effort into playing | 1.00 (IQR: 1.00) |
| I felt good | 4.00 (IQR: 4.00) |

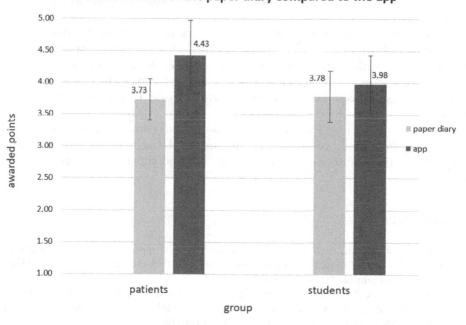

**Fig. 3.** Main result: awarded points for paper diary and app compared between patients and students (error bars: 95% CI)

## 4 Discussion

### 4.1 Main Findings

High usability of an app is not sufficient to motivate patients to enter data in the long term [23]. In addition to usability, illness experience, information technology infrastructure, emotional activation, degree of burden caused by the app and relevance of symptom monitoring are important factors for patient motivation [5]. Especially children and adolescents who are not interested in health-related symptom tracking and changes, such as the students participated in this study, are quickly demotivated if they must enter a large amount of data every day [17]. The fewer data users are asked to enter, the greater is the level of adherence in general [18].

## 5   Conclusion

In the presented study, the informative content of health data of a handwritten health diary was compared with health data submitted through a serious game. The serious game was implemented in the project Interacct, in which patients can submit health data through a mobile app on a daily basis to receive in-game rewards. Patients and students submitted 2 weeks of consecutive health reports, first with the Interacct serious game, eventually with the paper diary. Two independent, blinded physicians reviewed the health reports and rated the informative content.

The main hypothesis is, that the informative content of health data, which was submitted through a serious game, is higher than the informative content of handwritten health diaries. The statistical results confirm this hypothesis significantly. This is especially important for young and adolescent cancer patients, where the results were even more conclusive than in the control group of students.

Considering the positive side effects of the serious game (such as high engagement, compliance, and pleasure reporting health data through a serious game), the authors propose to conduct further studies and experiments regarding this topic.

## References

1. Aiello, E.J., et al.: In a randomized controlled trial, patients preferred electronic data collection of breast cancer risk-factor information in a mammography setting. J. Clin. Epidemiol. **59**, 77–81 (2006)
2. Baggott, C., Gibson, F., Coll, B., Kletter, R., Zeltzer, P., Miaskowski, C.: Initial evaluation of an electronic symptom diary for adolescents with cancer. J. Med. Internet Res. (2012). https://doi.org/10.2196/resprot.2175
3. Bhatia, S., Davies, S.M., Baker, S., Pulsipher, M.A., Hansen, J.A.: NCI, NHLBI first international consensus conference on late effects after pediatric hematopoietic cell transplantation: etiology and pathogenesis of late effects after HCT performed in childhood - methodologic challenges. Biol. Blood Marrow Transplant. **17**, 1428–1435 (2011)
4. Charlier, N., Zupancic, N., Fieuws, S., Denhaerynck, K., Zaman, B., Moons, P.: Serious games for improving knowledge and self-management in young people with chronic conditions: a systematic review and meta-analysis. J. Am. Med. Inform. Assoc. (2016). https://doi.org/10.1093/jamia/ocv100

5. Cohen, D.J., Keller, S.R., Hayes, G.R., Dorr, D.A., Ash, J.S., Sittig, D.F.: Developing a model for understanding patient collection of observations of daily living: a qualitative meta-synthesis of the Project HealthDesign Program. Pers. Ubiquitous Comput. **19**, 91–102 (2015)
6. Collins, J.J., Collins, J.J., et al.: The measurement of symptoms in children with cancer. J. Pain Symptom Manag. **19**, 363–377 (2000)
7. Dale, O., Hagen, K.B.: Despite technical problems personal digital assistants outperform pen and paper when collecting patient diary data. J. Clin. Epidemiol. **60**, 8–17 (2007)
8. Dupuis, L.L., Ethier, M.C., Tomlinson, D., Hesser, T., Sung, L.: A systematic review of symptom assessment scales in children with cancer. BioMed Central Cancer **12**, 430 (2012)
9. Fishbein, J.N., et al.: Mobile application to promote adherence to oral chemotherapy and symptom management: a protocol for design and development. JMIR Res. Protoc. **6**(4), e62 (2017). https://doi.org/10.2196/resprot.6198, http://www.researchprotocols.org/2017/4/e62/
10. Fortier, M.A., Chung, W.W., Martinez, A., Gago-Masague, S., Sender, L.: Painbuddy: a novel use of m-health in the management of children's cancer pain. Comput. Biol. Med. **76** (2016).https://doi.org/10.1016/j.compbiomed.2016.07.012
11. Hochstenbach, L.M., Zwakhalen, S.M., Courtens, A.M., van Kleef, M., de Witte, L.P.: Feasibility of a mobile and web-based intervention to support self-management in outpatients with cancer pain. Eur. J. Oncol. Nurs. **23**, 97–105 (2016). https://doi.org/10.1016/j.ejon.2016.03.009, http://dx.doi.org/10.1016/j.ejon.2016.03.009
12. Kayali, F., et al.: Design considerations for a serious game for children after hematopoietic stem cell transplantation. Entertain. Comput. **15**, 57 73 (2016)
13. Klaassen, R., Bul, K.C., Op Den Akker, R., Van Der Burg, G.J., Kato, P.M., Di Bitonto, P.: Design and evaluation of a pervasive coaching and gamification platform for young diabetes patients. Sensors (Switzerland) **18**(2), 1–27 (2018). https://doi.org/10.3390/s18020402
14. Lalloo, C., Jibb, L.A., Rivera, J., Agarwal, A., Stinson, J.N.: "There's a pain app for that": review of patient-targeted smartphone applications for pain management. Clin. J. Pain **31**, 557–563 (2015)
15. Lane, S.J., Heddle, N.M., Arnold, E., Walker, I.: A review of randomized controlled trials comparing the effectiveness of hand held computers with paper methods for data collection. BMC Med. Inform. Decis. Mak. **6**, 1–10 (2006)
16. Lauritsen, K., et al.: Symptom recording in a randomised clinical trial: paper diaries vs. electronic or telephone data capture. Control Clin. Trials **25**, 585–597 (2004)
17. Marceau, L.D., Link, C., Jamison, R.N., Carolan, S.: Electronic diaries as a toll to improve pain management: is there any evidence? Pain Med. **8**, 101–109 (2007)
18. Morren, M., van Dulmen, S., Ouwerkerk, J., Bensing, J.: Compliance with momentary pain measurement using electronic diaris: a systematic review. Eur. J. Pain **13**, 354–365 (2008)
19. Palermo, T.M., Valenzuela, D., Stork, P.: A randomized trial of electronic versus paper pain diaries in children: impact on compliance, accuracy, and acceptability. Pain **107**, 213–219 (2004)
20. Pandey, A., Hasan, S., Dubey, D., Sarangi, S.: Smartphone apps as a source of cancer information: changing trends in health information-seeking behavior. J. Cancer Educ. **28**, 138–142 (2013)

21. Price, B.A., Kelly, R., Mehta, V., McCormick, C., Ahmed, H., Pearce, O.: Feel my pain: design and evaluation of painpad, a Tangible device for supporting inpatient self-logging of pain. In: Proceedings of the 2018 CHI Conference on Human Factors in Computing Systems, CHI 2018, pp. 169:1–169:13. ACM, New York (2018). https://doi.org/10.1145/3173574.3173743

22. Rodgers, C.C., Krance, R., Street, R.L.J., Hockenberry, M.J.: Feasibility of a symptom management intervention for adolescents recovering from a hematopoietic stem cell transplant. Cancer Nurs. (2013). https://doi.org/10.1097/NCC.0b013e31829629b5

23. Scott, A.R., Alore, E.A., Naik, A.D., Berger, D.H., Suliburk, J.: Mixed-methods analysis of factors impacting use of a postoperative mHealthapp. JMIR mHealth uHealth 5(2), e11 (2017)

24. Stinson, J.N., et al.: Development and testing of a multidimensional iphone pain assessment application for adolescents with cancer. J. Med. Internet Res. (2013). https://doi.org/10.2196/jmir.2350

25. Stone, A.A., Shiffman, S., Schwartz, J.E., Broderick, J.E., Hufford, M.R.: Patient compliance with paper and electronic diaries. Control Clin. Trials **24**, 182–199 (2003)

26. Tamari, R., Castro-Malaspina, H.: Allogeneic haematopoietic stem cell transplantation for primary myelofibrosis and myelofibrosis evolved from other myeloproliferative neoplasms. Curr. Opin. Hematol. **22**, 184–190 (2015)

27. Walker, I., Sigouin, C., Sek, J., Almonte, T., Carruthers, J., Chan, A., Heddle, N.: Comparing hand-held computers and paper diaries for haemophilia home therapy: a randomized trial. Heamophilia **10**, 698–704 (2004)

28. Wesley, K.M., Fizur, P.J.: A review of mobile applications to help adolescent and young adult cancer patients. Adolesc. Health Med. Ther. **6**, 141–148 (2015)

29. Wesley, K., Fizur, P.: A review of mobile applications to help adolescent and young adult cancer patients. Adolesc. Health Med. Ther. **6**, 141 (2015). https://doi.org/10.2147/AHMT.S69209

30. Wilcox, A.B., Gallagher, K.D., Boden-Albala, B., Bakken, S.R.: Research data collection methods: from paper to tablet computers. Med. Care **50**, 68–73 (2012)

31. Wolfe, J., et al.: Symptoms and distress in children with advanced cancer: prospective patient-reported outcomes from the PrediQUEST study. J. Clin. Oncol.: Off. J. Am. Soc. Clin. Oncol. **33**, 1928–1935 (2015)

# Designing Game-Inspired Applications to Increase Daily PA for People with ID

Ingrid Evensen[1], Jens Brandsgård Omfjord[1], Juan Carlos Torrado[1(✉)], Letizia Jaccheri[1], and Javier Gomez[2]

[1] Department of Computer Science,
Norwegian University of Science and Technology, Trondheim, Norway
{ingriev,jensbom}@stud.ntnu.no,
{juan.c.t.vidal,letizia.jaccheri}@ntnu.no
[2] Computer Science and Engineering Department,
Universidad Autónoma de Madrid, Madrid, Spain
jg.escribano@uam.es

**Abstract.** People with intellectual disabilities are less likely to meet the recommended daily levels of physical activity. Meeting these requirements can lower the risk of serious health problems and life threatening diseases. To address this problem, the idea is to exploit mobile applications designed specifically to help increase daily levels of physical activity.

The results are: guidelines developed by a literature review and lessons learned during the development of a prototype application. Evaluation issues are based on focus group and usability test.

**Keywords:** Physical activity · Intellectual disabilities · Mobile applications · Gamification · e-Health

## 1 Introduction

Cognition is the "mental action or process of acquiring knowledge and understanding through thought, experience, and the senses" [3]. Intellectual disabilities (ID) falls under the term cognitive disabilities, but there is no international standard to what it means to have an ID. The Diagnostic and Statistical Manual of Mental Disorders 5th edition (DSM-V) says intellectual disability means a significant deficit in adaptive skills and carrying out age-appropriate daily tasks [19]. The World Health Organization (WHO) uses IQ and defines intellectual disability as having an IQ under 70, although meeting this requirement is not enough for a diagnosis. A diagnosis requires further tests in motor and social skills, language and social interaction and the handling of everyday tasks [24].

Among people with IDs, studies has discovered very low levels of physical activity [14,20,21] with only a small percentage meeting recommended levels of physical activities set by both global and national health organizations [1,2]. According to the WHO, all adults between the age of 18–64 years old have the

© IFIP International Federation for Information Processing 2019
Published by Springer Nature Switzerland AG 2019
E. van der Spek et al. (Eds.): ICEC-JCSG 2019, LNCS 11863, pp. 377–382, 2019.
https://doi.org/10.1007/978-3-030-34644-7_31

same recommendation for minimal level of physical activities per week; *at least 150 min of moderate-intensity aerobic physical activity throughout the week or do at least 75 min of vigorous-intensity aerobic physical activity throughout the week* [1]. Evidence shows that meeting these requirements can result in an overall lower rate of life-threatening diseases such as coronary heart disease, high blood pressure, stroke, different types of cancer and depression. Physical activity will also help reduce the risk of becoming overweight and the increased health risks that brings [15].

Among technologies used to create and support solutions for health benefits (eHealth) the use of mobile technology is growing fast [13,16]. The term mHealth (mobile health) covers *The use of mobile and wireless technologies to support the achievement of health objectives* [16]. Mobile phones are a potential platform for serious games, which in recent years have become an increasingly valid medium for solving challenges in the fields of education and healthcare [11,23]. Serious games have been used to support rehabilitation, to promote healthy lifestyles and have shown effectiveness as a training program [12]. *The practice of making activities more like games in order to make them more interesting or enjoyable is called gamification* [4]. Mechanics from gamification used in eHealth are for example rewards, feedback and socialization [18].

## 2    Related Work

In this section we are going to present the most relevant work that address the problem of physical activity of people with ID.

As people with IDs are more sedentary than people without IDs, several studies have examined the motivators and barriers for physical activity in this population [9,10,17,20,21]. These factors are very individual and varied, but certain common motivators and barriers has been identified and should be considered:

- **Motivators;** Social interaction, working towards a goal, feeling healthy, having work that requires PA & competition
- **Barriers;** Lack of facilities for PA, lack of support from key support persons, cost of activities, enjoying unhealthy food and activities & lack of guidance.

The Web Accessibility Initiative (WAI) [6] has examples on potential barriers for people with cognitive disabilities when using technology. Their guidelines WCAG 2.0 (Web Content Accessibility Guidelines) [7] have several requirements to fulfil in order to create an accessible application.

When designing applications for people with disabilities, accessibility (i.e operating the application, perception of events and requirements of use) needs to be considered [22]. Another point to keep in mind should be that when designing applications for adults, one should avoid designing the application as if it is intended for children [5].

The DSM-V [8] describes different levels of intellectual disabilities and the impact on conceptual, social and practical domain. Understanding written communication and abstract ideas can be difficult in varying degrees for people with IDs, meaning abstract thinking and executive function is impaired.

"Information for all" [5] is an European standard helping anyone trying to communicate information to make it accessible to everyone. The standards are describing how to use words, sentences, fonts and images. As many can find it hard to read text, the standards suggests the use of images to support the information trying to be communicated.

## 3  Application Proposal

The applications should focus on supporting the motivators and counteracting the barriers outlined in previous sections. By having the option to interact with family and friends, social interaction and competition can be achieved. At the same time strengthening the support and guidance from key support persons. Rewards in the form of medals or achievements is also encouraged to further promote social interaction and working towards a goal. Where possible, developers should attempt to limit the required hardware to devices the users already have access to, in order to decrease the cost of activities. The level of customisation should also be considered. Having key support persons be able to suggest or decide what activities are available to the disabled user, could have a positive impact on the daily level of physical activity as they are performing activities they enjoy.

**Design.** The design of the applications should focus on conveying clear, unambiguous information to the users. Information should be presented in limited quantities per view, considering font size, colour-use and contrast, as discussed previously and outlined by WCAG [7].

**Communication.** The *European standards for making information easy to read and understand* [5], provides a high number of rules to consider. Many of which can be directly included into development of applications designed for people with IDs. Highlighting a selection of them, it is suggested to keep sentences short and to use simple words. Larger numbers and percentages should be avoided. Images are a good way of conveying information, either alongside text, or alone.

### 3.1  Initial Prototype

Figures 1, 2 and 3, illustrates the main flow of an early prototype application considering the guidelines presented.

Figure 1 shows the screen that would greet the user before the daily activity goal is reached. As suggested by WAI [6], the amount of information provided is limited in order to make the main objectives of the view clear. The available activities are described using a single word, accompanied by an image as suggested in *Information for all* [5].

Instead of using a step-counter or progress-bar, the progress of the daily activity is symbolised using a flower that blooms as you get closer to the daily activity goal. Figure 3 shows the flower in full bloom, symbolising that you have met your daily goal.

Figure 2 is displayed while the user is active and shows the flower changing, in order to motivate them to keep going. The data is also displayed in a similar way throughout the application in order to make it easier to understand.

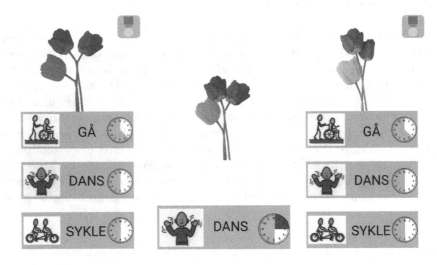

**Fig. 1.** Before activity    **Fig. 2.** During activity    **Fig. 3.** After activity

## 4    Conclusions and Future Work

In this paper we present the initial prototype of a game-inspired application to promote physical activity among people with intellectual disabilities. The application design and interaction is based on guidelines extracted from the literature and design standards.

The prototype and the guidelines will be evaluated in a focus group, and later tested with a selection from the user group. Based on this first evaluation, the design will be refined and further developed. The improved prototype will then be tested with a selection of the user group.

The results and observations gathered from this test will be the basis of data in the larger project, that will attempt to answer the question of whether or not such applications can be a motivating factor towards an increased level of daily physical activity in the user group.

**Acknowledgement.** This work is part of a collaboration with the Artic University of Norway (UiT) under grant number HNF 1353-17 from The North Norwegian Health Authorities.

# References

1. Physical activity and adults, June 2015. https://www.who.int/dietphysicalactivi ty/factsheet_adults/en/
2. Anbefalinger fysisk aktivitet, July 2016. https://helsedirektoratet.no/folkehelse/ fysisk-aktivitet/anbefalinger-fysisk-aktivitet
3. Definition of cognition in English (2018). https://en.oxforddictionaries.com/ definition/cognition
4. Definition of gamification in English (2018). https://dictionary.cambridge.org/us/ dictionary/english/gamification
5. European standards for making information easy to read and understand (2019). https://easy-to-read.eu/european-standards/
6. W3, wai, funtamentals; accessibility intro (2019). https://www.w3.org/WAI/ fundamentals/accessibility-intro/
7. Web content accessibility guidelines (wcag) 2.0 (2019). https://www.w3.org/TR/ WCAG20/
8. American Psychiatric Association, et al.: Diagnostic and Statistical Manual of Mental Disorders (DSM-5®). American Psychiatric Pub, Philadelphia (2013)
9. Bodde, A.E., Seo, D.C.: A review of social and environmental barriers to physical activity for adults with intellectual disabilities. Disabil. Health J. **2**(2), 57 66 (2009). https://doi.org/10.1016/j.dhjo.2008.11.004
10. Bossink, L., van der Putten, A.A., Vlaskamp, C.: Understanding low levels of physical activity in people with intellectual disabilities: a systematic review to identify barriers and facilitators. Res. Dev. Disabil. **68**, 95–110 (2017). https:// doi.org/10.1016/j.ridd.2017.06.008
11. Crookall, D.: Serious games, debriefing, and simulation/gaming as a discipline. Simul. Gaming **41**(6), 898–920 (2010)
12. Graafland, M., et al.: How to systematically assess serious games applied to health care. JMIR Serious Games **2**(2), e11 (2014). https://doi.org/10.2196/games.3825. http://games.jmir.org/2014/2/e11/
13. Gurman, T.A., Rubin, S.E., Roess, A.A.: Effectiveness of mHealth behavior change communication interventions in developing countries: a systematic review of the literature. J. Health Commun. **17**(sup1), 82–104 (2012)
14. Hilgenkamp, T.I., Reis, D., van Wijck, R., Evenhuis, H.M.: Physical activity levels in older adults with intellectual disabilities are extremely low. Res. Dev. Disabil. **33**(2), 477–483 (2012). https://doi.org/10.1016/j.ridd.2011.10.011. http://linkinghub.elsevier.com/retrieve/pii/S0891422211003908
15. Kohl III, H.W., Cook, H.D. (eds.): Educating the Student Body: Taking Physical Activity and Physical Education to School. The National Academies Press, Washington, DC (2013). https://doi.org/10.17226/18314, https://www.nap.edu/ catalog/18314/educating-the-student-body-taking-physical-activity-and-physical -education
16. Kay, M., Santos, J., Takane, M.: mHealth: new horizons for health through mobile technologies. World Health Organ. **64**(7), 66–71 (2011)

17. Kuijken, N.M.J., Naaldenberg, J., Nijhuis-van der Sanden, M.W., van Schrojenstein-Lantman de Valk, H.M.J.: Healthy living according to adults with intellectual disabilities: towards tailoring health promotion initiatives: perspectives of people with ID on healthy living. J. Intellect. Disabil. Res. **60**(3), 228–241 (2015). https://doi.org/10.1111/jir.12243

18. Sardi, L., Idri, A., Fernández-Alemán, J.L.: A systematic review of gamification in e-Health. J. Biomed. Inf. **71**, 31–48 (2017)

19. National Academies of Sciences, E., Medicine, et al.: Mental Disorders and Disabilities Among Low-income Children. National Academies Press, Washington, D.C. (2015)

20. Temple, V.A.: Barriers, enjoyment, and preference for physical activity among adults with intellectual disability. Int. J. Rehabil. Res. **30**(4), 281–287 (2007). https://doi.org/10.1097/mrr.0b013e3282f144fb

21. Temple, V.A.: Factors associated with high levels of physical activity among adults with intellectual disability. Int. J. Rehabil. Res. **32**(1), 89–92 (2009). https://doi.org/10.1097/mrr.0b013e328307f5a0

22. Wiemeyer, J., et al.: Recommendations for the optimal design of exergame interventions for persons with disabilities: challenges, best practices, and future research. Games Health J. **4**(1), 58–62 (2015). https://doi.org/10.1089/g4h.2014.0078

23. Wilkinson, P.: A brief history of serious games. In: Dörner, R., Göbel, S., Kickmeier-Rust, M., Masuch, M., Zweig, K. (eds.) Entertainment Computing and Serious Games. LNCS, vol. 9970, pp. 17–41. Springer, Cham (2016). https://doi.org/10.1007/978-3-319-46152-6_2

24. World Health Organization: International statistical classification of diseases and related health problems, Chap. v; mental and behavioural disorders, pp. f00–f99 (2016)

# An Educational Game About Math and Magic

Tiago Lemos[1], Teresa Romão[1], Nuno Correia[1(✉)], and Miguel Pedro[2]

[1] NOVA LINCS, FCT/UNL, Campus Caparica, 2829-516 Caparica, Portugal
t.lemos@campus.fct.unl.pt, {tir,nmc}@fct.unl.pt
[2] Watizeet - Unipessoal Lda, 2685-190 Portela, Portugal
miguel.pedro@watizeet.com

**Abstract.** This paper presents a mobile game to be played by fifth and sixth grade students during their free time, to improve the knowledge they obtain at school. The game uses a unique story and various interaction mechanisms (e.g., drawing on the screen, tilting the phone) to take the focus away from the educational aspects, so that the players feel like they are playing, not studying. User tests have been performed, showing that most students improved their knowledge and providing feedback for future developments.

**Keywords:** Mobile game · Educational game · Interaction mechanisms · Shape recognition · Accelerometer

## 1 Introduction

Students spend a considerable portion of their time interacting with their phones. Mobile games are enjoyable for being simple and fun. However, most of them have no educational purpose. Meanwhile, most students struggle with some school subjects and end up losing the motivation to study. Therefore, we decided to create a mobile game that would be appealing while helping to strengthen math knowledge. We aimed at taking the focus away from the educational aspects, so that the players don't feel like they're studying. Math questions are answered in different ways, like leaning the phone, drawing on the screen or even having a math duel with a wizard.

In recent years, there has been more focus on using videogames as a learning method, mostly because of their ability to captivate attention and hold it for long. Educational games use interactivity to transmit knowledge, by requiring players to strategize, test hypothesis, or solve problems. These games usually include a system of rewards to motivate the player, a context to the activities, and learning content [1]. A handheld math facts game [2] for second graders made those who played it solve three times more problems in the same time as those using paper worksheets.

Mobile games recently started being used in support of student learning, both in formal and informal settings [3]. Since these games can be played anytime and anywhere [6], they don't necessarily need to be used in the classroom [4] and have the potential to improve efficiency and effectiveness in teaching and learning [5] while also offering various unique and contemporary learning opportunities and promoting collaboration and interaction between players [3].

These games also help to develop a whole other set of important skills, such as creativity, decision-making, abstract thinking and visual and spatial processing.

E. van der Spek et al. (Eds.): ICEC-JCSG 2019, LNCS 11863, pp. 383–389, 2019.
https://doi.org/10.1007/978-3-030-34644-7_32

A study [8] found that students tend to be more motivated to play games that challenge them to utilize higher order thinking skills, where a strong narrative with fitting and tightly coupled learning tasks help motivate players to learn [9], and that giving the player goals of different levels to achieve helps them being more engaged [10].

## 2   Game Description

We created a mobile game to be played by fifth and sixth grade students during their free time aiming at reinforcing the knowledge they obtain at school, while using techniques to move the focus away from the educational aspects of the game. We do this by having not only different ways of answering questions, but also by adding decision-making and minigames, which helps the students enjoy playing and also obtain helpful knowledge. We focused on math, because it is a fundamental topic which is not naturally understood by all the students, but the game can be expanded in the future. During the design process we counted with the informal feedback of a fifth-grade student.

In the game, an evil wizard stole all the math in the world and hid in his magic mansion. The player's mission is to find and defeat him. The game consists in walking through the corridors and rooms of the mansion, overcoming the challenges that come up by using different interaction mechanisms. The game ends when the player reaches the wizard's room and defeats (or is defeated) by him in a math duel, consisting in a series of math questions answered by both the player and the wizard simultaneously.

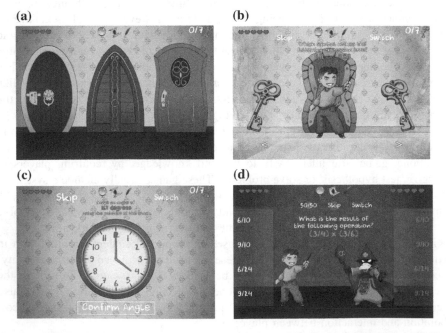

**Fig. 1.**  (a) Example corridor. (b) Example tilting question. (c) Example clock question. (d) Final duel.

When the game starts, the player is asked to choose their school year and difficulty level, so the experience is tailored to their choices. By increasing the difficulty, the player will start the game with less lives available, and the evil wizard will become smarter, answering correctly more often during the final duel.

After a short introductory story to engage the player in the context of the game, the player enters the magic mansion through a first corridor (Fig. 1a). Each corridor has three different doors to choose from, each one leading to a different room. The player will find a different corridor every time they leave a room, which helps providing a feeling of choice and variety. There are several kinds of rooms available.

*Key Room:* In these rooms the player finds a key. The wizard's room is protected by magical wards, preventing the player to find and unlock it until they have all seven keys. In a key room, the player must click the key to collect it.

*Question Room:* Here the player finds the wizard, who escapes, locking the way out with a spell. To be able to exit the room the player must answer a math question related to a school subject. If they fail, they lose a life. The game has four kinds of questions:

**Multiple-choice:** A question with four predefined answers from which the player must choose one, with no time limit but only one chance.

**Drawing:** A question to which the player must answer with a simple character (e.g. a one-digit number) by drawing it on the screen. Time limit of thirty seconds, with no limit of tries.

**Tilting** (Fig. 1b): A question with two possible answers. The player must tilt their phone and guide their character to the correct answer.

**Clock** (Fig. 1c): A question that requires the player to form an angle with the hands of a clock. The player is able to control only one of the hands, by tilting their phone, while the other hand is fixed.

After answering a question, the player receives feedback about the correct answer. The player then proceeds to another corridor, if they have not lost the game.

*Treasure Room:* Here, the player finds a chest they can decide to open. It contains one of the following artefacts:

- **Crystal Ball:** Remove two wrong answers in a multiple-choice question.
- **Portal Scroll:** Skip a question.
- **Feather Pen:** Change a question to another of the same kind.
- **Life Medallion:** Grants the player an extra life.
- **Cursed Medallion:** Takes a life from the player.

All the artefacts have the same chance of appearing. The player is only able to carry one of each artefact at a time (except lives) and will keep them until used. The artefacts can be seen on the top center of the screen (Fig. 1c).

*Minigame Room:* This room allows the player to get an artefact of their choice by completing a minigame. Currently the minigame requires the player to tilt their phone in order to help the character move and catch potions falling from the sky. Catching the required number of potions within the time limit completes successfully the minigame. These minigames contribute to highlight the entertaining aspects of the game.

When the player obtains all seven keys, the magic wards are broken, and they'll find and face the wizard in a math duel. Both the player and the wizard must answer a series of multiple-choice questions (Fig. 1d). The player starts the duel with the lives they saved during the game, while the evil wizard always starts with full (five) lives. When the player answers a question, the evil wizard answers it too, and each wrong answer makes them lose a life. The wizard uses a simple algorithm to answer a question, where he can either choose the correct answer, or choose one of the answers at random. The chance of choosing the right answer increases with the difficulty level. Whoever manages to survive the longest wins the game.

## 3 User Study

To evaluate the game, two testing sessions were performed. The educational effectiveness of the game (through a math test), and the interest and enjoyment of the children were evaluated while playing (through observation, a small questionnaire and an informal conversation).

The first prototype had only one difficulty level, no minigames, no tilting or clock questions, and the drawing detection was not calibrated. Its evaluation provided us with valuable feedback to validate requirements and guide further developments. With this feedback a second prototype was implemented and evaluated, comprising all major features described in the previous section.

Two different classes of sixth-grade students participated in each of the sessions. Both sessions occurred in a classroom and lasted around 1 h 30 m for each class, with a post-session one week later that lasted for 20 min. The same methodology was used in both test sessions:

- First the students answered a math test, about their knowledge prior to playing the game. The test lasted for 20 min.
- After the test, we let them play the game. The participants installed the game on their phone or tablet and played it for 50 min while the research team members moved around the classroom, observing their behaviour and assisting when needed.
- In the end, we offered a questionnaire to fill in and had an informal conversation with them. This lasted 20 min.
- We then let them play the game on their own for a week.
- One week later we met again in the classroom to repeat the same math test they had done the previous week, so we could see if they had improved their math knowledge (they had no information the test would be the same, nor did they have the solutions). This lasted 20 min.

The test and questionnaire were individual, but the participants were allowed to join their friends and play together, as we wanted them to feel free and act as naturally as possible. A total of 29 sixth grade students (17 boys and 12 girls) with ages between 10 and 11, from two classes participated in the first evaluation. The test used to evaluate their improvement consisted in 16 open answer questions addressing both fifth and sixth grade subjects (as they were at the end of the sixth grade). The questions were based on subjects in the game. We obtained the following results:

- On average, students increased their scores by 10% and the highest score increased by 12%.
- In a total of 29 students, 20 improved their score after playing the game, while 6 maintained it and 3 lowered it.
- The student with the biggest improvement had an improvement of 44%.

To evaluate the players enjoyment, we gave them a questionnaire with a few questions, using the Smileyometer [11] technique. From the first prototype, we learned that:

- Most students use their phone to play while using their computer to study. This supports our decision of creating a mobile educational game, as they can play on their phone and learn from it.
- When asked about the game, 91% enjoyed playing it, while 78% showed interest in playing it again, which were quite positive results.
- When asked if they had trouble understanding the game, 57% answered "never" or "almost never", while 37% answered "sometimes" and 6% answered "very often". This was concerning, as it meant the interface wasn't as simple to understand as we thought. Thus, we decided to improve it according to the observations and the informal conversations.
- When asked about the game questions' difficulty, 77% found it to be appropriate, so there didn't seem to be reason for concern.

During play time, we observed that while the children started by playing alone, as time passed, they begin to interact with each other, helping their friends or challenging them to a speed run of the game. We also observed that the players were having some trouble with parts of the interface. During the whole session the children were very enthusiastic about the game and eager to collaborate. They provided us with plenty of ideas, like the possibility of choosing between difficulty levels, and the minigames.

The second prototype was tested by 30 students (11 boys and 19 girls) from two sixth grade classes, with ages between 10 and 11. This time we gave them a test consisting of 14 questions covering only fifth grade subjects (as the students were only starting the sixth grade). From this second prototype we obtained the following results:

- On average, students increased their scores by 11% and the highest score increased by 22%.
- From 30 students, 18 improved their score after playing the game, while 10 maintained it and 2 lowered it.
- The students with the biggest improvement had an improvement of 36%.

These results, as the ones from the first evaluation, show that the game was effective at helping students obtain and retain math knowledge. We were not able to relate the playing time with their performance in the math test, as we couldn't collect data regarding the students' usage of the game outside the classroom. We can, however, assume they had their usual study patterns during that week, as they had no exams planned.

From the second prototype's questionnaire we learned that:

- Most students use their phone to play. In this case they reported using the computer to play and study, and most of them also used a tablet to play.

- About the game, 96% enjoyed playing it while 92% showed interest in playing it again. These were improvements from the already good results of the first session.
- When asked if they had trouble understanding the game, 84% answered "never" or "almost never" while 12% answered "sometimes" and 4% answered "constantly". This is also an improvement over the first prototype, as now a majority of players seems to understand the game easily.
- When asked about the questions' difficulty, 60% found it to be appropriate. While the percentage of players finding the questions' difficulty level appropriate has gone down, it can be justified as different kinds of questions were added to the game and the increased difficulty that was detected on the clock questions, something we have later improved.
- When asked the participants to sort the various parts of the game in terms of enjoyment, we found out the part that needed more improvement were the clock questions. We also found out that the players seem to enjoy more the parts that don't involve math questions, with the final duel being an exception to this. The favourite interaction was drawing the answer.

Again, the players were very excited, proposing new features to the game, including a labyrinth minigame. We can conclude we were successful in incorporating the educational aspects in a game that is fun while transmitting knowledge.

## 4   Conclusions

We created a game with the objective of helping students of the fifth and sixth grades obtain and retain math knowledge, while still having fun. Overall, we obtained good results from the tests we conducted, as a majority of players improved their knowledge after one week of playing the game, and also enjoyed the game. Thus, we can conclude we created a game that shifts the focus to its ludic aspect, while promoting learning. We plan to add new features to engage players as, for example, new unlockable characters to play with, and new kinds of challenges.

**Acknowledgments.** This work is funded by FCT/MCTES NOVA LINCS PEst UID/CEC/ 04516/2019.

## References

1. Dondlinger, M.: Educational video game design: a review of the literature. J. Appl. Educ. Technol. **4**(1), 21–31 (2007)
2. Lee, J., Luchini, K., Michael, B., Norris, C., Soloway, E.: More than just fun and games: assessing the value of educational video games in the classroom. In: Proceedings of CHI '04 Extended Abstracts on Human Factors in Computing Systems, Vienna, Austria, pp. 1375–1378. ACM, New York (2004)
3. Koutromanos, G., Avraamidou, L.: The use of mobile games in formal and informal learning environments: a review of the literature. Educ. Media Int. J. **51**(1), 49–65 (2014)

4. Seppala, P., Alamaki, H.: Mobile learning in teacher training. J. Comput. Assist. Learn. **19**, 330–335 (2003)
5. Dubendorf, V.A.: Wireless Data Technologies. Wiley, New York, NY (2003)
6. Jeong, E.J., Kim, D.J.: Definitions, key characteristics, and generations of mobile games. In: Taniar, D. (ed.), Mobile computing: concepts, methodologies, tools, and applications, pp. 289–295. Idea Group, Hershey (2009)
7. Amory, A., Naicker, K., Vincent, J., Adams, C.: The use of computer games as an educational tool: identification of appropriate game types and game elements. Br. J. Edu. Technol. **30**(4), 311–321 (1999)
8. Waraich, A.: Using narrative as a motivating device to teach binary arithmetic and logic gates. In: Proceedings of 9th Annual SIGCSE Conference on Innovation and Technology in Computer Science Education, Leeds, United Kingdom, pp. 97–101. ACM, New York (2004)
9. Swartout, W., van Lent, M.: Making a game of system design. Commun. ACM **46**(7), 32–39 (2003)
10. Dix, A., Finley, J., Abowd, G., Beale, R.: Human-Computer Interaction, 2nd edn. Prentice Hall Europe, London (1998)
11. Read, J.: Validating the Fun Toolkit: an instrument for measuring children's opinions of technology. Cogn. Technol. Work **10**(2), 119–128 (2008)

# Poster Papers

# "Aedes Vs. Repellents": Applying Tower Defense Dynamics in a Digital Game to Combat the Mosquito

Gabriel Azevedo(iD) and Victor Sarinho(✉)(iD)

Laboratório de Entretenimento Digital Aplicado (LEnDA),
State University of Feira de Santana, Av. Transnordestina, s/n, Novo Horizonte,
Feira de Santana, Bahia, Brazil
gabrielsilvadeazevedo@gmail.com, vsarinho@uefs.br

**Abstract.** Serious games represent a computational resource that can be used as a tool to create new ways of raising awareness of digital natives. In this sense, this paper presents current results with the *"Aedes vs. Repellents"*, a 3D tower defense game that aims to promote the interaction and learning of the population in the prevention and combat of the Aedes aegypti mosquito. For this, mechanics and dynamics of the well-known *"Plants vs. Zombies"* game will be reuse, being applied in a scenario capable of providing a context of public health learning in the prevention of the mosquito.

**Keywords:** Game design · Aedes aegypti · Serious games

## 1 Introduction

Aedes aegypti is a mosquito that acts as a vector for the transmission of recurrent diseases in public health with alternating outbreaks and difficult-to-combat epidemics, such as dengue fever, yellow fever, chikungunya and zika virus [3]. As a result, several educational campaigns have been developed and increased over the years in mosquito prevention and control involving science, education and coordinated arts activities with schools, students, parents and teachers [5].

Educational games, also known as serious games, are types of software primarily aimed at educational purposes [7]. It is a computational resource that can be used as a tool to create new forms of dissemination, as well as implement educational actions capable of increasing the public interest in combating the mosquito [8].

However, there are evidences that define serious games as a boring alternative for their players, being focused on learning aspects instead of promoting pleasure and enjoyment for the player [1]. In fact, promoting the relationship between

Supported by FAPESB and Kamikan.

E. van der Spek et al. (Eds.): ICEC-JCSG 2019, LNCS 11863, pp. 393–397, 2019.
https://doi.org/10.1007/978-3-030-34644-7_33

playfulness and learning is a major challenge during the process of designing and building a serious game [1].

In this sense, and considering the reuse of mechanics and dynamics of successful games to be applied in a scenario that provides a health learning context, this article presents the *"Aedes vs. Repellents"* project. It is a game that seeks to apply available mechanics and dynamics of the *"Plants vs. Zombies"* [2] game in a context where the player has to protect a house suffering from constant waves of mosquito attacks.

## 2    Related Work

Different types of serious games have been developed in the context of combating the Aedes aegypti mosquito. As an example, the Mission Aedes [1] features a 2D platform style game that seeks to: remember which is a mosquito focus; understand and analyze the life cycle of the mosquito; apply knowledge acquired regarding mosquito outbreaks; and evaluate the development cycle of the mosquito. Following the graphic quiz style the *Aedes Game* [6] aims to inform the Brazilian population about their social responsibility in the fight against Aedes aegypti, providing a set of questions and answers that seek to inform the player by feedback of the given responses. Finally, the *Aedes in the Sights* game [4] uses virtual reality to propitiate an immerse backyard of a house full of dengue spots, where the player must eliminate all the mosquito larvae found.

## 3    The "Aedes vs. Repellents" Game

The general objective of the proposed game is to avoid the player house invasion by mosquitoes (Fig. 1). In this sense, as a protection strategy, the player must build defense towers, in this case repellents, able to avoid mosquitoes but with an energy consumption each one.

**Fig. 1.** Initial menu of the "Aedes vs. Repellents" game.

To use energy, the player needs to build solar panels and batteries to generate and store more energy as soon as possible. These resources are necessary to allow the player to be protected at night, when the wave of mosquitoes begins to attack the player residence.

The game difficulty will increase according to the subsequent mosquitoes waves, along with the mosquito variations that can both destroy the towers more easily and also offer more resistance to player damages.

As examples of game modeled characters: the insecticide is the base attack structure (Fig. 2(a)) to kill mosquitoes; the plug repellent and the grid protection work as defense units (Fig. 2(c) and (b)) against the mosquito wave; and the special mosquito that does not fly provides a hull that gives a greater resistance to damage promoted by repellents (Fig. 2(d)).

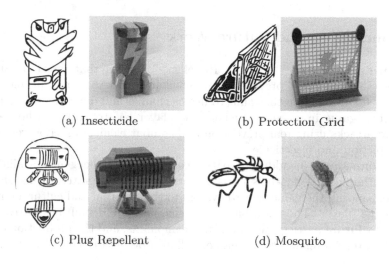

(a) Insecticide                (b) Protection Grid

(c) Plug Repellent             (d) Mosquito

**Fig. 2.** Designed characters of the "Aedes vs. Repellents" game.

The initial scenario of the game play presents a 3D environment, containing the tracks where the elements of the game will be placed to avoid the invasion of the mosquitoes to the residence (Fig. 3). New mosquitoes are applied in each track per night wave, being increased by amount, speed and resistance in each mosquitoes attack, according to the continuous survivor state of the player.

**Fig. 3.** Initial game play of the "Aedes vs. Repellents" game.

## 4    Conclusions and Future Work

This paper presented the "Aedes vs. Repellents", a game that aims to apply digital entertainment in the prevention and combat of the Aedes aegypti mosquito. It is a playful application that aims to use mechanics and dynamics of the Plants vs. Zombies game in a scenario where the player has to protect a house from mosquito attacks using real prevention and combat elements such as repellents, grid protection and insecticide.

As future work, in addition to the completion of the game (available at https://github.com/lenda-uefs), it is important to be integrated with social networks, expanding the game reward system to the external and cultural environment of the player. The addition of new characters and multimedia resources, followed by future participation in health campaigns, and the production of educational materials related to the game, will also be performed in the future.

**Acknowledgments.** The authors are grateful for the financial support provided by FAPESB and Kamikan for the development of the "Aedes vs. Repellents" project.

## References

1. Araújo, D., Rodrigues, A., Lacerda, P., Dionísio, M., Santos, H.: Processo de desenvolvimento do jogo série missão aedes: relações entre objetivos pedagógicos, ludicidade e implicações de design. In: Brazilian Symposium on Computers in Education (Simpósio Brasileiro de Informática na Educação-SBIE), vol. 27, p. 597 (2016)
2. Games, P.: Plants vs. zombies. PopCap Games (2009)
3. Kikuti, M.: Distribuição espacial e determinantes ecológicos para dengue em uma comunidade urbana de salvador, Bahia (2014)
4. Moura, J.V.C., Sarinho, V.T.: Aedes na mira - aplicando realidade virtual no combate a focos de mosquitos (2017)
5. Pitta, Á.M., Oliveira, V.C.D.: Estratégias de comunicação frente ao desafio do aedes aegypti no brasil. Ciência & Saúde Coletiva 1, 137–146 (1996)

6. Portella, F.F., Tubelo, R.A., Zanatta, E.J., Pinto, M.E.B.: Experiência da una-sus/ufcspa no desenvolvimento de jogos educacionais (2017)
7. Silva, A.C.B.D., Gomes, A.S.: Conheça e utilize software educativo: avaliação e planejamento para a educação básica. Recife: Pipa Comunicação (2015)
8. Silva, T.D., et al.: Jogos virtuais no ensino: usando a dengue como modelo. Revista Brasileira de Ensino de Ciência e Tecnologia 1(2) (2008)

# Quimi-Crush: A Digital Game
# for the Teaching of Inorganic Chemistry

Oto A. L. Cunha(iD), Joimar B. Gonçalves(iD), and Victor T. Sarinho(✉)(iD)

Laboratório de Entretenimento Digital Aplicado (LEnDA),
State University of Feira de Santana,
Av. Transnordestina, s/n, Novo Horizonte, Feira de Santana, Bahia, Brazil
otoengc@gmail.com, joimarbgf@gmail.com, vsarinho@uefs.br

**Abstract.** Traditional teaching strategies have become increasingly unattractive and demotivating for students in general. Students of inorganic chemistry usually have difficulties in learning the atomicity of the elements during the composition of the chemical compounds, as well as in the understanding of the characteristics and functions of such compounds. This work presents Quimi-Crush, a tile-matching digital puzzle capable of stimulating students to learn and participate in the understanding of inorganic chemistry concepts in a playful and fun way.

**Keywords:** Chemistry teaching · Educational game · Tile-matching puzzle

## 1 Introduction

The teaching of chemistry provides students a basic knowledge on specific phenomena in nature [4]. However traditional strategies of chemistry teaching are often seen as discouraging by students, since such strategies are based on memorization of formulas and calculations making the learning process less enjoyable [5].

As a result, more dynamic and attractive new approaches need to be incorporated into the chemistry learning and teaching process, in order to create a friendly and welcoming environment to promote a playful approach to learn inorganic chemistry [1].

Regarding serious games, "they combine the entertainment value of games with additional objectives such as players acquiring knowledge or skills, receiving guidance and feedback on tasks to perform, or contributing partial solutions to problems" [2]. They are "intentionally designed to attract, engage, and retain (even addict) players by applying psychology principles" [2], whose impact for educational purposes has received considerable attention.

This paper presents *Quimi-Crush*, a tile-matching puzzle serious game capable of stimulating apprenticeship and participation of high school students in inorganic chemistry learning-teaching process.

© IFIP International Federation for Information Processing 2019
Published by Springer Nature Switzerland AG 2019
E. van der Spek et al. (Eds.): ICEC-JCSG 2019, LNCS 11863, pp. 398–401, 2019.
https://doi.org/10.1007/978-3-030-34644-7_34

## 2   The Quimi-Crush Game

Quimi-Crush is similar to famous match-3 puzzle games, like "Fat Princess - Piece of Cake" [6] and "Candy Crush - Soda Saga" [3] (Fig. 1). One of the main objectives in "Candy Crush - Soda Saga" is making a certain quantity of combinations containing objects that look like soda bottles. In order to reach that aim it is necessary to keep combining "candies" to create opportunities to release the "soda bottles" objects. In "Fat Princess-Piece of Cake", the player must defend himself from waves of enemies that increase according the progress of the player in the game. The player team has characters that perform attack and defense actions from the combination of pieces on the board.

(a) Candy Crush

(b) Fat Princess - Piece of Cake

**Fig. 1.** Images from the games "Candy Crush - Soda Sag" (a) and "Fat Princess - Piece of Cake" (b).

Regarding Quimi-Crush, the player controls actions of a hero by combining chemical components in order to perform attacks on the villain, and the player character suffers a damage when compounds that are not oxides are combined. In principle, the spot where combinations occur has a six by six dimension, initially containing five chemical elements: Hydrogen (H), Carbon (C), Sodium (Na), Nitrogen (N) and Oxygen (O) (Fig. 2).

The dynamics of the game consists of turns, in which player searches for basic chemical elements that are able to combine with each other (Hydrogen, Carbon, Sodium, Nitrogen and Oxygen) according to a catalog of combinations (Fig. 3). For each combination of basic elements that does not generate an oxide, the hero of the game will take damage in the turn and consequently lose a heart. When

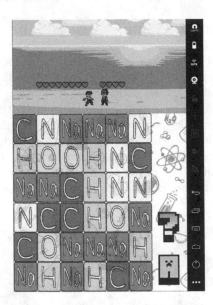

**Fig. 2.** Game play screen where chemical combinations occur.

the combination of components produces an oxide, the hero will attack and the villain will lose a heart.

If the player manages to combine enough oxides to destroy all hearts of the enemy, he wins the match. The player loses the match when the number of simple combinations that do not generate oxides is greater than the total number of hero hearts. In case of victory, a new level is unlocked, otherwise, the player will have to try to play the same level again or return to the initial menu.

If the player delays to find a possible item to be combined, the game signals a possible match that can be performed, but this combination will not be necessarily the best for the victory. However, if there are really no combinations, the component area is scrambled again. An introductory tutorial is also provided by the game, thus facilitating the explanation of the basic dynamics of the game itself.

## 3    Conclusions and Future Work

Quimi-Crush presents an innovative approach to the teaching of inorganic chemistry. Through the blending of rules and goals of tile-matching puzzle games known to young audiences, the game is able to dynamically exercise the knowledge of atomicity of proposed base chemical elements. As a result, there is an interesting didactic resource in the teaching of inorganic chemistry, which can easily be extended to different inorganic chemical compounds and other known chemistry concepts.

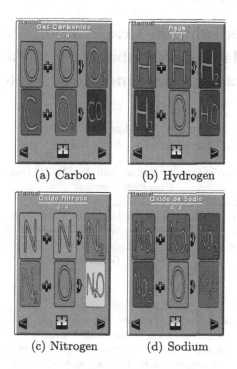

(a) Carbon          (b) Hydrogen

(c) Nitrogen        (d) Sodium

**Fig. 3.** Combination catalogs of basic elements applied in the game.

As future work, besides extra improvements and corrections to become more aesthetically attractive for the players, it is intended to evaluate the game usability in the process of teaching public high school students. For this, the game will be applied in both the mobile version and in public school PCs in the region. Mobile and desktop versions of the game, together with developed source code, will also be available at https://github.com/lenda-uefs after the necessary fixes and adjustments.

## References

1. de Barros, C.F.: Jogos no ensino de química: um estado da arte sobre a revista química nova na escola (2016)
2. Dalpiaz, F., Cooper, K.M.: Games for requirements engineers: analysis and directions. IEEE Softw. (2018)
3. Dockterman, E.: Candy crush saga: the science behind our addiction. http://business.time.com/2013/11/15/candy-crush-saga-the-science-behind-our-addiction/ Novembro 2013. Accessed 01 July 2019
4. de Fátima Rocha, M., de Lima, I.C., Victor, C.M.B., Iany Silva de Santana, L.P.D.S.: Jogos didáticos no ensino de química. Formação de Professores: interação Universidade (2011)
5. Oliveira, L.M.S., da Silva, O.G., da Silva Ferreira, U.V.: Desenvolvendo jogos didáticos para o ensino de química. Holos, U.V. (2010)
6. One Loop Games LLC: Fat princess: Piece of cake. https://www.playstation.com/pt-br/games/fat-princess-piece-of-cake-psvita/

# PDPuzzleTable: A Leap Motion Exergame for Dual-Tasking Rehabilitation in Parkinson's Disease. Design and Study Protocol

Augusto Garcia-Agundez[1]([⊠]), Mareike Goosses[2], Robert Konrad[1], Manuel Stork[1], Hagen Becker[1], Stefan Göbel[1], and Elke Kalbe[2]

[1] Multimedia Communications Lab (KOM), TU Darmstadt,
Darmstadt, Germany
Augusto.garcia@kom.tu-darmstadt.de
[2] Medical Psychology, Neuropsychology and Gender Studies and Center
for Neuropsychological Diagnostics and Intervention (CeNDI),
Faculty of Medicine and University Hospital Cologne Cologne,
Cologne, Germany

**Abstract.** In this paper, we present PDPuzzleTable, our exergame framework for dual-tasking rehabilitation exercises for patients with Parkinson's Disease (PD). It is our aim to create a home monitorization scenario for the Leap Motion Sensor together with a specific set of exercises designed for PD, that allows us to follow upon disease progression by inferring motor-cognitive skills remotely and passively.

**Keywords:** Parkinson's disease · Cognitive impairment · Motor impairment · Rehabilitation · Exergames · Serious games · Leap motion

## 1 Introduction

Parkinson's Disease (PD) is a neurodegenerative disease primarily caused by the idiopathic degeneration of the dopaminergic neurons in the substantia nigra pars compacta. The core symptoms of PD are bradykinesia, tremor, rigor and postural instability. Besides motor symptoms, cognitive symptoms are also typical of PD [1], particularly executive dysfunction [2]. Once objectified, it is called Mild Cognitive Impairment in PD (PD-MCI) and presents itself as a subtle difficulty on complex functional tasks. The prevalence of PD-MCI is around 25% [3] and it is a risk factor for decline into PD Dementia (PDD). PDD excludes PD patients from certain treatments such as deep brain stimulation, and currently has no approved pharmacological intervention.

However, recent research shows cognitive training may improve or stabilize the cognitive skills of affected patients [4]. This research also indicates that transfer effects can be expected, that is, cognitive training may improve motor symptoms and vice versa [5]. An excellent way to combine cognitive training with motor rehabilitation is the use of exergames, i.e. games that require the player to perform physical movements. Another advantage of this approach is the sensory feedback provided by game

© IFIP International Federation for Information Processing 2019
Published by Springer Nature Switzerland AG 2019
E. van der Spek et al. (Eds.): ICEC-JCSG 2019, LNCS 11863, pp. 402–406, 2019.
https://doi.org/10.1007/978-3-030-34644-7_35

controllers and sensors [6]. A recent systematic review [7] indicated the significant progress of exergames for PD patients in the recent years, also pointing to the requirements of future work, mainly the standardization of outcome evaluation and the inclusion of new sensors and control techniques to train unaddressed areas, such as fine motor skills.

For this purpose, the Leap Motion Sensor (LMS) seems to be a highly promising approach, since it provides an intuitive, natural interface while providing sensory feedback on motor skills. The LMS has already been shown to have potential in evaluating the motor performance of PD patients [8, 9], particularly for hand opening and closing exercises or finger tapping [10]. In fact, researchers have already begun developing LMS based exergames or LMS-digitalized version of traditional motor skill assessment methods such as the Fugl-Meyer test or the Box and Blocks test [11].

## 2   Methods

As a first step, we considered the diverse cognitive symptoms of PD and how they can be trained via LMS Exercises. Table 1 summarizes our observations in this regard.

**Table 1.** Cognitive Symptoms of PD and potential training in LMS scenarios

| PD symptom | Treatment intent |
|---|---|
| Resting tremor | Fine motor training in ADL-context |
| Reduction of joint mobility | Grab and drop exercises, writing |
| Coordination/speed issues | Training in a virtual scenario |
| Executive function | Calculation and manipulation exercises with increasing difficulty |
| Concentration problems | Search and differentiate, sorting, simplification exercises |
| Memory disturbances | Memorization techniques (systematic repetition, method of Loci). Memory games/word puzzles |
| Delay in cognitive processes | Awareness exercises, speed exercises |

In order to create our exergaming framework, we accessed the LMS data directly by using LeapC, a C-style Application Programming Interface (API) for the LMS. This API was connected to our application, developed under Kha, a Haxe-based open source multimedia framework. By using LeapC, it is possible to access the raw data of the LMS directly, as presented in Table 2. Besides palm and finger coordinates, the LMS is capable of measuring "pinch" and "grab" parameters, which determine the degree of closure of a pinching motion (that is, grabbing an object with the index finger and thumb) and grabbing motion (closing the fist) respectively. This provides a great advantage when developing scenarios for people with varied fine motor mobility, since the pinch and grab parameter thresholds can then be adjusted to adapt to users with limited mobility, as it occurs in PD.

The main advantage of the LMS, besides acquiring hand position with a sampling rate of 200 Hz, is precisely this grabbing and pinching motion detection, since it allows developers to adapt their environments to the varied motor skills of their target group [11]. For this purpose, we implemented to unitary parameters, one for pinching and one for grabbing, 1 being a completely closed pinch or grab. This permits us to demand specific movements for patients with determinate degrees of hand closure, which we can quickly change to ease playability or increase difficulty with time to further improve the motor skills of players.

 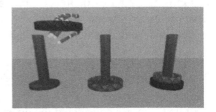

**Fig. 1.** Example images of the TOH game

Considering our observations, we decided to create two scenarios. Firstly, the Tower of Hanoi (ToH), also called tower of London (Fig. 1). The goal in this game is to move a set of n discs from the left to either the middle or right columns in the shortest possible time. It is only possible to place a disc over an empty tower or a larger disc, one by one, which limits the possible movements. The game can be adapted to operate with pinching motions, grabbing motions, or both. This task combines motor skills with problem solving and sequencing, two important cognition areas.

Secondly, we decided to include a Simon-based Memory Game (SMG), in which the player has to follow a visual and musical sequence by clicking on blocks. This allows the training of working memory and sequencing. For the SMG, the goal is to grab or pinch the blocks, following a randomized music and color sequence generated by the game, that is one element longer for every successfully completed sequence. The sequence can be limited to music or color exclusively and it may be requested from the player to repeat the sequence forwards or backwards. This interaction pattern was chosen purposely to mimic a hand opening/closing test. Figure 2 presents the SMG game.

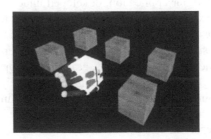

**Fig. 2.** Example image of the SMG game

**Table 2.** LMS and game extracted parameters

| Hand parameters (200 Hz) | Game parameters (Per play through) |
|---|---|
| Fingertip position (x, y, z) of each finger | Number of movements/max sequence length |
| Hand palm position (x, y, z) | Elapsed time (s) |
| Hand palm rotation (x, y, z) | Input timelapse (s) |
| Pinch ratio (0–1) | Number of disks (TOH)/number of elements (SMG) |
| Grab ratio (0–1) | |

For every game session, relevant game data as well as finger data are saved for future processing. This data is described in Table 2, and is saved both locally (as a .csv file) and remotely using a Rest API if desired. The data can be then automatically processed in Matlab and relevant parameters can be extracted, for example detected tremor (if any), variations in elapsed time or number of movements across different sessions, or maximum fist closing/pinching achieved across different sessions. On a future pilot test, we plan to link these game and sensor parameters to relevant PD assessment scores, such as UPDRS-III (motor examination) to create difficulty adaptation algorithms as well as a potential home monitoring scenario [12]. To evaluate the scenario, we firstly plan to analyze its feasibility, considering its technical, therapeutic and patient-centered outcomes. Followed by this is a cross-over evaluation, meaning the PD patient sample will be divided into two groups: Group 1 will first test a physically demanding but cognitively lenient version and then a cognitively demanding but physically easy one, while group 2 will test the same versions in the opposite order. A diagram of the study protocol is presented on Fig. 2. The goal of this phase is to determine whether the order in which the cognitive or motor task is presented plays a role (Fig. 3).

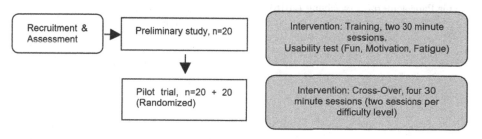

**Fig. 3.** Study protocol

# References

1. Muslimović, D., Post, B., Speelman, J.D., Schmand, B.: Cognitive profile of patients with newly diagnosed Parkinson disease. Neurology **65**(8), 1239–1245 (2005)
2. Kalbe, E., et al.: Subtypes of mild cognitive impairment in patients with Parkinson's disease: evidence from the LANDSCAPE study, pp. jnnp-2016-313838 (2016)
3. Aarsland, D., Brønnick, K., Fladby, T.: Mild cognitive impairment in Parkinson's disease. Curr. Neurol. Neurosci. Rep. **11**(4), 371–378 (2011)
4. Leung, I.H., Walton, C.C., Hallock, H., Lewis, S.J., Valenzuela, M., Lampit, A.J.N.: Cognitive training in Parkinson disease a systematic review and meta-analysis (2015). https://doi.org/10.1212/wnl.0000000000002145
5. Walton, C.C., Shine, J.M., Mowszowski, L., Naismith, S.L., Lewis, S.J.: Freezing of gait in Parkinson's disease: current treatments and the potential role for cognitive training. Restor. Neurol. Neurosci. **32**(3), 411–422 (2014)
6. Garcia-Agundez, A., Folkerts, A.-K., Robert Konrad, R.P.C., Göbel, S., Kalbe, E.: PDDanceCity: an exergame for patients with idiopathic parkinson's disease and cognitive impairment, Mensch und Computer 2017-Tagungsband (2017)
7. Garcia-Agundez, A., Folkerts, A.-K., Konrad, R., Caserman, P., Tregel, T., Goosses, M., Göbel, S., Kalbe, E.: Recent advances in rehabilitation for Parkinson's Disease with exergames: a systematic review. J. Neuroeng. Rehabil. **16**(1), 17 (2019)
8. Butt, A.H., Rovini, E., Dolciotti, C., Bongioanni, P., De Petris, G., Cavallo, F.: Leap motion evaluation for assessment of upper limb motor skills in Parkinson's disease. In: 2017 International Conference on Rehabilitation Robotics (ICORR), pp. 116–121. IEEE (2017)
9. Kaji, H., Sugano, M.: A noncontact tremor measurement system using leap motion. In: Proceedings of the 6th International Conference on Informatics, Environment, Energy and Applications, pp. 76–79. ACM (2017)
10. Butt, A., et al.: Objective and automatic classification of Parkinson disease with leap motion controller, vol. 17, no. 1, p. 168 (2018)
11. Oña, E.D., Balaguer, C., Cano-de la Cuerda, R., Collado-Vázquez, S., Jardón, A.: Effectiveness of serious games for leap motion on the functionality of the upper limb in Parkinson's disease: a feasibility study. Comput. Intell. Neurosci. **2018**, 17 (2018)
12. Garcia-Agundez, A., Sharma, S., Dutz, T., Göbel, S.: Ein smartphone-basiertes framework für Patientenfernüberwachung (2016)

# UGC Generator: An Open Access Web Tool to Model Unified Game Canvas

Bruno C. Matias⬛, Victória O. Gomes⬛, and Victor T. Sarinho⁽⊠⁾⬛

Laboratório de Entretenimento Digital Aplicado (LEnDA),
State University of Feira de Santana, Av. Transnordestina, s/n,
Novo Horizonte, Feira de Santana, Bahia, Brazil
brunoclaudinomatias@gmail.com, victoria.oliveiragomes@gmail.com,
vsarinho@uefs.br

**Abstract.** Game Design Canvas (GDC) is a framework that can be used to define fundamental game elements, and is able to provide a general view of a game designer idea. Unified Game Canvas (UGC) combines common GDC characteristics in a 5W2H perspective, increasing the design possibilities for a GDC creation of a desired game. This paper presents the UGC Generator, a simple and interactive open access web tool that helps game designers to fill UGC panels and to provide UGC models in a fast and dynamic way.

**Keywords:** Game design canvas · UGC · Open access web tool

## 1 Introduction

Game design can be defined as "the act of deciding what a game should be" [6]. It is an important step to view the game as many perspectives as possible [6], working as a planning/documentation step in the process of creating desired analog/digital games.

Among the different ways of creating game design documents, Game Design Canvas (GDC) is a framework that can be used to define fundamental game elements [8]. It allows a quick synthesis of game ideas that will be developed, showing the game project overview in a unique design panel [7]. GDC also describes the information in a systemic, integrated and quick way, showing perceptions about how the developer team should act to compose the desired game [7].

Several types of design canvas were proposed to define the necessary information to model a GDC, being a little exhausting to choose which fits better in a desired game project. As a result, the Unified Game Canvas (UGC) [5] was proposed to provide an unified canvas model for game designers. It organizes the modeling information found on available GDCs in a 5W2H perspective [1–3], achieving as a result a fast modeling of fundamental game elements available in important GDC models [5].

© IFIP International Federation for Information Processing 2019
Published by Springer Nature Switzerland AG 2019
E. van der Spek et al. (Eds.): ICEC-JCSG 2019, LNCS 11863, pp. 407–411, 2019.
https://doi.org/10.1007/978-3-030-34644-7_36

This paper presents the UGC Generator, an open access web tool for the production of desired UGC models. It is a simple and interactive modeling tool that helps game designers to fill UGC panels and to provide UGC models in a fast and dynamic way.

## 2    The Unified Game Canvas (UGC)

5W1H is described [3] as a document that, through questioning, identifies actions and responsibilities able to guide what should be developed. Those questions are: "What?", "Why?", "Where?", "When?", "Who?" and "How?" [2]. Later, Candeloro [1] suggest the inclusion of another questioning: "How much?" (the cost), generating the 5W2H tool.

For the UGC model, 5W2H is used as a game design information classifier, which should be related to: representation (*what*); responsibility (*who*); decision making (*when*); motivation (*why*); execution (*where*); production approach (*how*); and business (*how much*) [5]. This information is organized in panels, that must be fulfilled by the game designer to start the development of a game.

Eight panels are proposed by the UGC [5], which should be filled in the following way:

- **Game Impact:** defines what the game must bring to the player, highlighting motivations and reasons of emotion, fun and learning;
- **Game Concept:** seeks to attend the demand in identify the game responsibility, highlighting their name, objective, intention and inspiration to the game being created;
- **Game Player:** describes the information about who is playing the game, varying from player ages to possible community involved;
- **Game Play:** describes the game representation, highlighting their start, middle and end steps according limitations and rules inside a defined game space;
- **Game Flow:** seeks to represent the game time experience of the player, highlighting the repetition loop, the permanence in the playing act and the concept of "my turn to play";
- **Game Core:** indicates elements for the game building, describing mechanics for the game rules, dynamics for game systems and the aesthetics for modeled game components;
- **Game Interaction:** presents the execution environment of the game itself, varying in platforms, implementation resources and technology involved; and
- **Game Business:** indicates financial concerns and the market view of the game.

## 3    The UGC Generator

Developed by the integration of web technologies, the UGC Generator, which is available at https://ugc-generator.herokuapp.com/, starts on a screen that

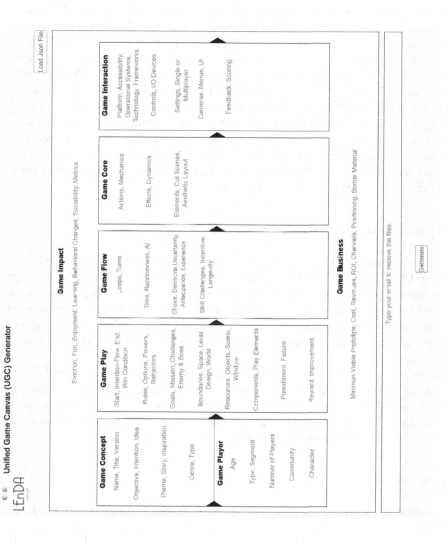

**Fig. 1.** UGC generator website.

shows UGC panels waiting to be filled (Fig. 1). Each UGC panel contains fields with placeholders that give hints about the information that is expected to be filled by the user. The user is free to fill the panel with any necessary information for the game design.

If a UGC panel has too many information, the application will reduce the text font size to fit all in the respective panel, when the PDF is generated. The "*Generate*" button (end of the page) produces the respective UGC PDF with all panel information, which can be download immediately. The user can also provide an email to receive the UGC PDF, together with an extra JSON file.

A JSON file represents each subsection that the user can fill in a UGC panel. It provides the necessary content to load the UGC model and perform desired changes on it. To upload an UGC JSON file for edition, is necessary to press the "*Load JSON file*" button (top of the page) and select the desired file to upload.

Regarding the UGC Generator usage, it was successfully applied in the *Master of Process* game design [4]. It is a paper-based board game developed to teach how to take decisions during software project phases, where you can hire, fire and train employees in development activities. The filled UGC for this game can be checked in https://ibb.co/8B8qwjJ.

## 4    Conclusions and Future Work

This paper presented the UGC Generator, an open access web tool able to create and edit UGC models in a fast and dynamic way. For that, the UGC design canvas was described, together with the main functionality of the proposed tool.

The UGC Generator is in an initial development version, but already presents a useful resource to optimize the time of anyone who needs to design games and their features, without having to worry about small details and the canvas formatting.

As future work, some features will be changed to make it more suitable and comfortable for their users, such as personal user account, usage monitoring and usability assessment, for example. The integration with game patterns, game elements and game features, showing possible contents to be filled in a respective panel, will be also performed in the future.

## References

1. Candeloro, R.: Não tenha dúvidas: método 5w2h. Portal Administradores, São Paulo (2008)
2. de Oliveira, S.T.: Ferramentas para o aprimoramento da qualidade. Pioneira (1996)
3. Rossato, I.d.F.: Uma metodologia para análise e solução de problema. Dissertação de Mestrado apresentada ao Programa de Pós-Graduação em Engenharia de Produção e Sistema da Universidade Federal de Santa Catarina (1996)
4. Sarinho, V.T.: Masters of the process: a board game proposal for teaching software management and software development process. In: XXXIII Brazilian Symposium on Software Engineering (SBES) (2019)

5. Sarinho, V.T.: Uma Proposta de Game Design Canvas Unificado. In: XVI Simpósio Brasileiro de Jogos e Entretenimento Digital (SBGames) (2017)
6. Schell, J.: The Art of Game Design: A book of lenses. AK Peters/CRC Press, Natick (2014)
7. da Silva, I.C.S., Bittencourt, J.R.: Game thinking is not game design thinking! Uma proposta de metodologia para o projeto de jogos digitais. In: Proceedings of the XV SBGames, pp. 295–304 (2016)
8. Vargas, V.C.L.: Uma extensão do Design Thinking Canvas com foco em Modelos de Negócios para a Indústria de Games (2015)

# Avatars: The Other Side of Proteus's Mirror

## A Study into Avatar Choice Regarding Perception

Charly Harbord[(⊠)] and Euan Dempster

Abertay University, Bell Street, Dundee DD1 1HG, UK
{c-a.harbord,c-a.harbord}@abertay.ac.uk

**Abstract.** The trend for online interactions, can be regarded as being 'anti-socially social', meaning that a great deal of time is spent playing, working and socializing with the internet serving as the communication conduit. Within that Virtual Social Environment very deep relationships are formed and maintained without the parties ever having met each other face-to-face. Raising the question how much does the physical appearance of an avatar influence the perception of the person behind it? Are relationships informed by appearance even in the virtual world and what implications does that have for second language acquisition? This paper leads to a small-scale research project where a selection of avatars with various racially identifiable characteristics were used to identify which avatars a second language speaker would feel more at ease interacting with in the target language. The resultant research aims to test three hypotheses regarding preferred avatar choice for second language users based solely on perceptions.

**Keywords:** Avatars · Second language acquisition · Proteus Effect · Perception · Chinese concept of face · RPGs

## 1 Literature Study

### 1.1 Proteus Mirror

Yee and Bailenson [13] coined the term 'The Proteus Effect' to define the way in which in-game behaviors are influenced by the appearance of a player's avatar. These self-perceptions and resulting actions can be seen as independent from perceptions of other players. It is important to the future planned research on RPGs and second language acquisition to ascertain whether interaction with other avatars is based on cultural aesthetics and perceived personality. This paper aims to look through the other side of Proteus's mirror to examine what the viewer sees and how that affects their online in-game interactions.

### 1.2 Avatars

Avatars are endemic throughout online communities and modern culture [1]. High levels of personalization allow players to select exactly how they wish to present themselves and therefore how they wish to be perceived by others; creating a virtual

© IFIP International Federation for Information Processing 2019
Published by Springer Nature Switzerland AG 2019
E. van der Spek et al. (Eds.): ICEC-JCSG 2019, LNCS 11863, pp. 412–416, 2019.
https://doi.org/10.1007/978-3-030-34644-7_37

mask [2–4]. When a new avatar is encountered, impulse judgements are often made regarding the personality of the user informing the type of interpersonal relationship that may be formed and acting a predictor of the behavioral profile of the user; known as the 'Thin-Slice Effect' [10]. The high level of avatar customization freely available now to users, means that the thin-slice style of judgement has greater validity [4]. However, the 'thin-slice' may be open to a certain level of bias with the viewer superimposing how honestly, they themselves self-represent as an avatar. The study aims to investigate how avatar perception affects relationships in general and specifically as second language interlocutors. It is intended that the focus of this small-scale research will be purely on the aesthetics of avatar perception and the level of subjectivity held by the viewer towards the visual cues.

### 1.3 Face and Second Language Acquisition

When relationships are formed and maintained entirely online via the medium of avatars, the player is likely to feel less anxiety due to the 'faceless' anonymity of the interaction. Additionally, the lack of visible social prompts based on context that may otherwise cause interference, allow for a freer interaction without anxiety or inhibition [8]. This is particularly prevalent cross-linguistically between English and Mandarin. The use of a racially neutral avatar can help to alleviate the anxiety that can be felt when communicating with a native speaker in the target language [7]. The concept of 'Face' resonates quite strongly with Chinese native speakers [9, 11]. Face is intrinsic to Chinese culture; it holds that the perception of a person and how they present themselves is potentially more important than the actual reality. Avatars allow a degree of freedom within the interactions as there is no perceived loss of face [11]. Feeding into the negation of face is a sense of impermanence and reduction of responsibility with avatar relationships; should a major mistake or social faux pas happen instead of trying to make amends a new avatar can be created, and the cycle starts over [5].

## 2 Avatar Small Scale Study

The main area of research in the small-scale study was directed at second language speakers and how willing or not they are to interact with avatars that represent the cultural and racial background of the target language. Participants were shown a selection of avatars representing a potential target language interlocutor. They were then asked to express what their perception of the character is and what level of interaction they would take.

It was predicted that the choice of avatar for in game interactions would mimic those in real life; that the second language speakers would feel more at ease interacting in the target language with a more culturally neutral character. Within the classroom environment students are quite happy to use the target language to converse and feel less pressure to be perfect at the language, thereby creating a rapport and a safe space with peers of similar ability [9]. However, when faced with a native speaker, students reported feeling anxious and reluctant to interact in the target language [9]. It was predicted that players would feel more comfortable interacting in the second language if their avatar looks more culturally representative to the target language and the interlocutor's avatar looks more generic.

In order to test the hypothesis as a proof of concept, 16 avatars were designed to represent multiple racial identifiers and fantasy styles (see Fig. 1). The participants were 20 Chinese students who have English as a second language and 20 home students who learn Mandarin. They were asked to select which of the avatars they would choose in three different scenarios. The scenarios are based on the participant being a second language user interacting with native speakers in the target language in an RPG. (1) Which avatar that they would feel comfortable interacting with in the target language with. (2) Which avatar that they would feel uncomfortable speaking in the target language with. (3) Which avatar would they choose for themselves as the second language speaker. The preferred avatars will inform the choices given in the resultant RPG that is being created by the author for the larger scale research project into the use of RPG for the mutual enhancement of both Mandarin and English.

**Fig. 1.** Avatars designed for the study.

**Hypothesis 1:** Participants are more likely to choose an avatar that resembles a native speaker. Players will select an avatar to look more racially appropriate to the target language and be more comfortable interacting with avatars that present as less racially stereotypical.

**Hypothesis 2:** Participants are more likely to be comfortable interacting with a more racially neutral character. Avatars with a lower level of racial and cultural identifiers act as the interlocutor helps to negate the levels of anxiety that a second language speaker may have when interacting with a native speaker.

**Hypothesis 3:** Participants are more likely to experience increase lack of inhibition and increased motivation due the anonymity of using an avatar. Avatars enhance not only the immersion and emotional investment also the role-play and communication between players [6]. The use of an avatar can help negate the anxiety that a learner may feel within face-to-face conversation in the target language [8].

# 3   Preliminary Results

The first round of testing was the Chinese participants carried out via an anonymous online questionnaire (http://tiny.cc/e74adz).

**1** shows the avatars that the Chinese participants were most likely to choose to represent themselves. The reasons given for these choices were: "the Chinese boy looks most like me" "this avatar is the most neutral" and "she is really pretty so more people may choose to talk to me".

**2** shows the avatars that the Chinese participants would choose to interact with in the target language. The reasons given for these selections were "She is the prettiest", "I like her smile", "She looks Scottish and I want to go to Scotland".

**3** shows the avatars that the Chinese participants would not want to interact with. The reasons given for these selections were "This avatar is too ugly", "I don't like it's face".

Whilst the chosen avatars for each scenario reflected the author's predictions the reasonings veered from the original hypotheses. The Chinese participants demonstrated aesthetics to be the main driving force behind their choices. When considered with the burgeoning "*meinü jingji*, beauty economy" [12] in China the justifications are not surprising. Closely linked to face; beauty is intrinsically connected to success and prestige.

# 4   Conclusion

The results have allowed the avatar choice given to the Chinese players to be narrowed down to the top three from 1 & 2. The home participants questionnaire will be carried out in September 2019; informing the avatar choices given to players of the finalized RPG for the larger study. Further research will focus on the investigating the socio-cultural implications of avatar choice and how aesthetics of perception affects player interactions in the target language. Additionally, connections will be drawn between the historical culture of mask use and the Chinese concept of 'Face'.

# References

1. Dunn, R., Guadagno, R.: My avatar and me - Gender and personality predictors of avatar-self discrepancy. Comput. Hum. Behav. **28**(1), 97–106 (2012). https://doi.org/10.1016/j.chb. 2011.08.015. Accessed 29 May 2019
2. Leding, J., Horton, J., Wootan, S.: The contrast effect with avatars. Comput. Hum. Behav. **44**, 118–123 (2015). https://doi.org/10.1016/j.chb.2014.11.054. Accessed 29 May 2019
3. Li, D., Liau, A., Khoo, A.: Player-avatar identification in video gaming: concept and measurement. Comput. Hum. Behav. **29**(1), 257–263 (2013). https://doi.org/10.1016/j.chb. 2012.09.002. Accessed 29 May 2019
4. Lin, H., Wang, H.: Avatar creation in virtual worlds: behaviors and motivations. Comput. Hum. Behav. **34**, 213–218 (2014). https://doi.org/10.1016/j.chb.2013.10.005. Accessed 29 May 2019
5. Nylund, A., Landfors, O.: Frustration and its effect on immersion in games, Umea University, Masters (2015)
6. Peterson, M.: Learner interaction management in an avatar and chat-based virtual world. Comput. Assist. Lang. Learn. **19**(1), 79–103 (2006). https://doi.org/10.1080/ 09588220600804087. Accessed 24 Jan 2019
7. Peterson, M.: Digital gaming and second language development: Japanese learners interactions in a MMORPG. Digit. Cult. Educ. **3**(1), 56–73 (2011)
8. Rankin, Y.A., McNeal, M., Shute, M.W., Gooch, B.: User centered game design: evaluating massive multiplayer online role playing games for second language acquisition. In: Proceedings of the 2008 ACM SIGGRAPH Symposium on Video Games, pp. 43–49. ACM (2008)
9. Rublik, N.: Chinese cultural beliefs: implications for the Chinese learner of English. Sino-US Engl. Teach. **15**(4) (2018). http://dx.doi.org/10.17265/15398072/2018.04/001. Accessed 4 June 2019
10. Shin, M., Kim, S., Biocca, F.: The uncanny valley: no need for any further judgments when an avatar looks eerie. Comput. Hum. Behav. **94**, 100–109 (2019). http://dx.doi.org/10.1016/ j.chb.2019.01.016. Accessed 27 May 2019
11. Wen, W., Clement, R.: A Chinese conceptualisation of willingness to communicate in ESL. Lang. Cult. Curriculum **16**(1), 18–38 (2003). https://doi.org/10.1080/07908310308666654. Accessed 30 May 2019
12. Xu, G., Feiner, S.: Meinu Jingji/China's beauty economy: buying looks, shifting value, and changing place. Feminist Econ. **13**(3–4), 307–323 (2007). https://doi.org/10.1080/ 13545700701439499. Accessed 21 June 2019
13. Yee, N., Bailenson, J.: The proteus effect: the effect of transformed self-representation on behavior. Hum. Commun. Res. **33**(3), 271–290 (2007). https://doi.org/10.1111/j.1468-2958. 2007.00299.x. Accessed 23 Jan 2019

# Presenting the Key Ideas of Fractions Through MathFractions: A Game Based Learning

Manuel J. Ibarra[1]($\boxtimes$), Wilber Jiménez[1], Carolina Soto[2],
Eduardo Chavez[2], Edison Chiclla[2], Antonio Silva Sprock[3],
and Leônidas de Oliveira Brandão[4]

[1] National University of Micaela Bastidas Apurímac, Garcilazo Av. s/n,
Abancay, Apurímac, Peru
manuelibarra@gmail.com, wjimenezmendoza@yahoo.es
[2] Technological University of the Andes, Perú Av. 700,
Abancay, Apurímac, Peru
caro7001@hotmail.com, eduardochavezv@hotmail.com,
paelle2@hotmail.com
[3] School of Computation, Central University of Venezuela,
Caracas 1043, Venezuela
asilva.sprock@gmail.com
[4] Institute of Mathematics and Statistics, University of São Paulo,
São Paulo, SP 05508–090, Brazil
leo@ime.usp.br

**Abstract.** This paper describes a Game Based Learning tool to teach fractions. It was designed for children from 6 to 10 years old. It was developed considering the six facets framework to serious game. For the purpose of the study, 66 videos recorded were analyzed. On the other hand, the game was played by 34 students and it has been observed that 76% of them were able to complete three activities without problems, 24% of them completed only one or two activities.

**Keywords:** Serious game · Fractions · Learning · Math learning · Games

## 1 Introduction

There are changes necessary to implement in classrooms the usage of new ICT [1], the first one is to rethink the pedagogical practice in classrooms. It is necessary to research on the influence of digital games on learning, the importance of virtual learning environments in distance learning and the use of ICT [2].

In mathematics, fractions are one of the basic concepts in which learners present difficulties in their understanding. The points as the most frequent problems in the fractions learn are: (a) the learners focus on the counting of parts prioritizing the number of parts and not the relation between the part and the whole; (b) do not work with fractions larger than unity; (c) there is no emphasis on the ratio number of parts and total size; (d) fractions are not represented in the same scale; and (e) comparing heterogeneous fractions [3, 4]. Some studies have shown that teaching with computer tools have better results than teaching using only verbal communication. It is also

E. van der Spek et al. (Eds.): ICEC-JCSG 2019, LNCS 11863, pp. 417–421, 2019.
https://doi.org/10.1007/978-3-030-34644-7_38

relative effectiveness of Video Mediated Instruction and Classroom Demonstration Technique on the performance of students [5–7]. In mathematics, many concepts and processes could be linked to visual interpretations, the reason why researchers used the potential of visualization and simulations in teaching [8, 9].

## 2    Related Works

Gresalfi et al. [10], investigated the effects of design in fractions games, the goal of the study was to contribute to understand how particular types of digital games can support student learning and engagement. It was focused on commercially available educational apps that focused on similar content (fraction comparison and equivalence) but represented extremes in how game-like they were (games vs. worksheets). Third-grade students (n = 95) worked on the apps for an hour in their math classrooms. Students preformed equally well on a paper and pencil assessment, but students' enjoyment of the games was significantly higher. Student interviews indicated that students who played the games noticed the mathematics content in the games, sometimes linking it to the game mechanics, noticed the relevance of the game for the assessment and talked about enjoying the games. Findings suggest that exploratory games that implicitly support mathematics knowledge can improve students' math knowledge outside of the game context and improve student engagement.

Sevinc and Brady [11], investigated a tradition in mathematics education research which produced a genre of activities known as model-eliciting activities. They show two story-based model-eliciting activities aimed at kindergarten and first-grade (K − 1) students' development of length measurement and an estimation of area measurement. The study highlights not only that young learners were capable of developing models on numbers representing length and area but also that engaging story narratives and parallel whole-class and small-group activities were the main resources to support the model development of young learners.

Dube et al. [12], they reviewed the published research papers indexed in databases such us Scopus, Web of Science, Google Scholar and others. The focus of searching was the use of tablets as elementary mathematics education tools. The goal of this study is to discuss whether tablet computers are useful for mathematics learning. The three more important tasks were: engaging children with mathematics, improving children's attitudes towards mathematic and improving children's mathematic achievements.

## 3    The Six Facets of the Game Design

Marne et al. [13] developed a non-sequential and flexible framework with 6 facets of serious game design. These facets were adapted and used in this serious game.

(a) *Pedagogical Objectives*
Learn fractions 1/2, 1/4, 3/4 with a visual approach

(b) *Domain Simulation*

The game was designed considering the student's context (culture aspects, geographical sceneries, society thinking). For example, the cultural thinking of a child from the mountain range of Peru (rain, mountains, clouds) and different to the cultural thinking of a child form the country of Brazil (trees, rivers, animals).

(c) *Interactions with the Simulation*

Considering the mathFractions with all models (it is possible to use only one or more game models). The learner starts the game selecting the flag of his country, to select automatically the language and the context (Peru, Brazil, USA or France).

(d) *Problems and Progression*

The problem means that, the game has 9 options to solve problems, and they are grouped in 3 sectors: *Quadrilaterals* (filling quadrilateral blocks to pave the floor), *Circles* (representation of circles over the Cartesian plane) and *Fractions comparison* (visualizing the equivalence between two fractions). The progression means that each selected option of the game has 5 difficulty levels. The progression is from the easiest level to the difficulty level. Additionally, the game has 3 options to play: add (right arrow), subtract (left arrow), and combine add and subtract operations (left and right arrows).

(e) *Decorum*

The game uses computer animation approach to engage the student's motivation.
In addition, when student completes correctly the task, there is a winning sound and icon representation, and when the student fails the task, there is a sound indicating fail and the correspondent icon representation.

(f) *Conditions of use*

Students from six years old on could play this game. Most of the time, the game does not need assistance from the teacher or high ICT skills, but maybe young children need an explanation about the rules of the game. Only one player could play the game, it is not multiplayer.

# 4  MathFractions Design and Implementation

The game was developed considering the six facets methodology [13] and designed mostly for children from 6 to 10 years old. The game has some flexible characteristics of configuration for the user: the language selection, the image and the sound could be contextualized according the country. In addition, each level has a progressive difficulty. The software was developed using some tools like HTML5, JavaScript, Mysql, and phaser.io framework. Currently, the mathFractions serios game are hosted under the URL http://educatics.org/mathfractions/.

The software was developed by undergraduate students of the Academic School of Computer Science at the National University Micaela Bastidas of Apurimac. The agile methodology of extreme programming was applied, in which the User Stories were created and then the programming tasks were assigned to programmers. It was very important to have graphic designers to create the scenes, the characters, and the images of the game; also, sound designers were needed to create the different sounds of the game. The tests were carried out by the programmers (alpha tests) and later by the children who collaborated with the project (beta tests) and after the corrections. Both tests allowed corrections and improvements to the software. The software game is multiplatform (Windows, Linux, Mac), multilanguage (English, Spanish, French) and easy to maintain.

## 5   Evaluation and Analysis

Initially, evaluations were made to the software product, through 5 children 10 years of age, this allowed us to improve the software and served as a pilot test before formally launching the product; then, two types of evaluation were carried out: evaluation by children and evaluation by video recording analysis.

**Analysis of Children's Playing.** This game was tested by undergraduate students, From January-2016 to October-2016, the system registered 34 children from 2 different schools; they acceded remotely to play the serious game. They played on freely, but their teachers recommended to follow the interface order (first is the top leftmost, the last one the bottom right). Considering the game model used, 75% played filling quadrilateral blocks on the floor, 19% played the representation of the circle on the Cartesian Plane, and 6% played the equivalence between two fractions.

**Video Recording Analysis.** The software was evaluated by 29 math prospective teachers (enrolled in four years graduation program to math teacher preparation) of the Institute of Mathematics and Statistics of the University of São Paulo. They worked in one session of about half an hour with mathFractions, each student with an individual computer desktop. There was no explanation about the software; they only received the Web address where the game was hosted. Previously free screencast software was installed in every computer of the laboratory (the *RecordMyDesktop* to Linux/Debian). The teacher and two assistants watched the group and their screen during the working session were registered in the video. A total of 66 videos were recorded, since some of them had no experience with *RecordMyDesktop* software, starting it more than once.

## 6   Conclusions and Future Work

This Game was developed to enhance fractions teaching and learners comprehension of the fraction concepts, directed to children from 6 to 10 years old. The tool was developed under the six facets framework to design serious games. The software is hosted and available at http://educatics.org/mathfractions/. In this interface and didactical evaluation of mathFractions 66 screen sessions were recorded and analyzed.

It has been observed that: 76% of master degree students were able to complete three activities without problems; 24% of the students completed; and 24% of them completed only one or two activities, probably because they did not read the instructions correctly or did not recorded the activity completely.

In addition, we analyzed others 34 children that used mathFractions, indicated by 2 math teachers in 2 different schools in Peru and Brazil used the game, 75% of them played filling quadrilateral blocks on the floor, 19% played the representation of the circle on the Cartesian Plane, and 6% played the equivalence between two fractions.

For the future, the tool will be applied in real class sessions environment and will be measured the qualitative punctuation obtained by the students.

# References

1. Spies, L.: Integrando informática nas aulas dos anos iniciais do ensino fundamental (2013)
2. Aguiar, E.V.B.: As novas tecnologias e o ensino-aprendizagem. Vértices **10**, 63–72 (2008)
3. Pazos, L.: Las fracciones son un problema (2009)
4. Perera, P.B., Valdemoros, M.E.: Fracciones en cuarto grado de educación primaria. In: Comunicaciones de los grupos de investigación del XI Simposio de la SEIEM, pp. 209–218 (2007)
5. Chuang, Y.-R.: Teaching in a multimedia computer environment: a study of the effects of learning style, gender, and math achievement. Interact. Multimed. Electron. J. Comput. Learn. **1**, 1999 (1999)
6. Baukal Jr., C.E.: Learning strategy preferences, verbal-visual cognitive styles, and multimedia preferences for continuing engineering education instructional design. Oklahoma State University (2014)
7. Ominowa, O.T., Bamidele, E.F.: Effectiveness of video-mediated instruction on teaching secondary school practical chemistry in Akure South Local Government Area of Ondo State, Nigeria. Eur. J. Educ. Stud. (2016)
8. Woolner, P.: A Comparison of a visual-spatial approach and a verbal approach to teaching mathematics. In: Proceedings of 28th Conference on International Group for the Psychology of Mathematics Education, vol. 4, pp. 449–456 (2004)
9. Rahim, M.H.: From visualization to computer animation approaches in mathematics learning: the legacy throughout history of human endeavours for better understanding. Res. Math. Educ. **17**, 279–290 (2013)
10. Gresalfi, M.S., Rittle-Johnson, B., Loehr, A., Nichols, I.: Design matters: explorations of content and design in fraction games. Educ. Technol. Res. Dev. **66**, 579–596 (2018)
11. Sevinc, S., Brady, C.: Kindergarteners' and first-graders' development of numbers representing length and area: stories of measurement. In: Robinson, K.M., Osana, H.P., Kotsopoulos, D. (eds.) Mathematical Learning and Cognition in Early Childhood, pp. 115–137. Springer, Cham (2019). https://doi.org/10.1007/978-3-030-12895-1_8
12. Dubé, A.K., Alam, S.S., Xu, C., Wen, R., Kacmaz, G.: Tablets as elementary mathematics education tools: are they effective and why. In: Robinson, K.M., Osana, H.P., Kotsopoulos, D. (eds.) Mathematical Learning and Cognition in Early Childhood, pp. 223–248. Springer, Cham (2019). https://doi.org/10.1007/978-3-030-12895-1_13
13. Marne, B., Wisdom, J., Huynh-Kim-Bang, B., Labat, J.-M.: The six facets of serious game design: a methodology enhanced by our design pattern library. In: Ravenscroft, A., Lindstaedt, S., Kloos, C.D., Hernández-Leo, D. (eds.) EC-TEL 2012. LNCS, vol. 7563, pp. 208–221. Springer, Heidelberg (2012). https://doi.org/10.1007/978-3-642-33263-0_17

# "Ultimate Food Defense": A Serious Game for Healthy Eating Behavior Awareness

Bruno C. Matias[ID], Victória O. Gomes[ID], and Victor T. Sarinho[✉][ID]

Laboratório de Entretenimento Digital Aplicado (LEnDA),
State University of Feira de Santana,
Av. Transnordestina, s/n, Novo Horizonte, Feira de Santana, Bahia, Brazil
brunoclaudinomatias@gmail.com, victoria.oliveiragomes@gmail.com,
vsarinho@uefs.br

**Abstract.** Taking into account the importance of developing a healthy eating behavior, which starts in childhood, this work presents the *Ultimate Food Defense*. It is a tower defense digital game designed to help players acquire healthy eating habits. As a result, a playful and entertaining approach has been obtained that can present the harm caused by fatty foods when consumed in excess.

**Keywords:** Tower defense · Healthy eating · Blood glucose level

## 1 Introduction

The learning of eating behavior is a process that already begins in childhood of an individual. Thus, the family and sociocultural context have an indispensable role in the process of structuring the child eating habits [1].

One of the main ways of accessing technology for children is digital games [4]. Those can be defined as "attractive and interactive environments that captures the player attention, offering challenges that require increasing level of dexterity and skill" [9]. In addition, *serious games* are often characterizes as games that the main purpose is to transmit knowledge [6], something that represents a window of opportunity for the insertion of fun, pleasant and enjoyable elements to play.

This paper presents the *Ultimate Food Defense*, a digital game where the player assumes the role of a defense cell to protects the body against caloric and greasy food, being helped by health food available for consumption.

## 2 Related Work

*Tower defence* is a strategy game subgenre whose objective is prevent that the enemy crosses the map and arrives in a specific reference spot in the game. As an example of tower defense game in health thematic, *Smile Battle* [8] is a game

© IFIP International Federation for Information Processing 2019
Published by Springer Nature Switzerland AG 2019
E. van der Spek et al. (Eds.): ICEC-JCSG 2019, LNCS 11863, pp. 422–425, 2019.
https://doi.org/10.1007/978-3-030-34644-7_39

developed with the purpose of transmitting oral health knowledge, where the player has the duty of defend its mouth of the poor hygiene bacterium's attack.

Another tower defense for health game is the *DigesTower*, designed to help prevent childhood obesity [2]. The scenario is the Elise digestive system, who is the main character in the game, where the foods are the "enemies" and the digestives enzymes represents the player tower defense.

## 3   The Ultimate Food Defense Game

The game main menu (Fig. 1) was designed as a child friendly representation of a sales stall containing healthy fruits to eat. For the menu buttons, five options are provided to the player: *New Game*, *Load Game*, *Instructions*, *Options* and *Credits*.

**Fig. 1.** Initial screen of the game.

When starting a new game, the players will see a human mouth, the greasy and caloric food that advances into our organism, and a barrier in the end of the tong that must be defended by the player to avoid health problems caused by bad feeding (Fig. 2). To defend the body against the enemies and prevent blood glucose increase, there is a defense cell controlled by the player that attempts to avoid the advance of the bad food through the throat by shooting them.

Some healthy food were also chosen to help the player during the game play. The **strawberry** for example helps in the blood glucose control [3], as it has a substance called *anthocyanin* in its composition. For this reason, in the game, this fruit helps the player to decrease the organism blood glucose level in 2 mg/dL. The **grape** impact in blood glucose level happens because, besides the *anthocyanin* presence, there is the *resveratrol* existence. This substance promotes a blood glucose drop, improving cells sensibility to insulin [10], increasing as a result the defense cell velocity attack to the unhealthy foods in the game. Finally, the **lemon** fruit has a substance called *pectin*, a soluble fiber that, besides help

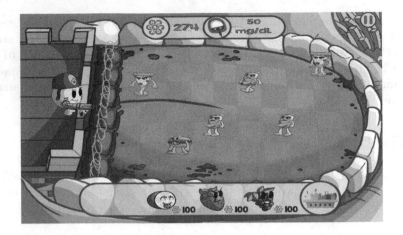

**Fig. 2.** Ultimate Food Defense game play scene.

in the digestion, it decelerates the absorption of sugar in the body [5]. For this reason, in the game, this fruit makes the enemies attacks slow down.

To maintain a pleasant game, free use of fruits is not allowed during the game. To control it, the game has a coin (the vitamins), which are received after certain regular intervals of time or when an enemy is defeated. When the player does not have enough vitamins to buy fruits, they remains blocked.

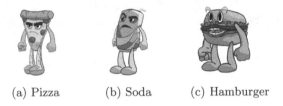

(a) Pizza        (b) Soda        (c) Hamburger

**Fig. 3.** Caloric and greasy game enemies.

About the caloric and greasy game enemies, Pizza, Soda and Hamburger (Fig. 3) were chosen because they are commonly found in fast-food stores and, therefore, consumed in large scale. When the enemies get as closer as possible to the defense cell tower, they start to attack the wall that defends the organism, and the attacks make the blood glucose increase gradually. For every enemy attack against the wall, the blood glucose increases in 2 mg/dL.

The player blood glucose level always starts in 50 mg/dL. Considering that the blood glucose values comprehended between 100 mg/dL and 125 mg/dL are already considered a pre-diabetes indicative [7], the player will loose the match if he were unable to conserve your blood glucose level at a value lower than 99 mg/dL. If this happens, the end game screen will be displayed to the player, which will have the option of try again or go back to the initial menu.

# 4    Conclusions and Future Work

This paper presented the Ultimate Food Defense, a digital game for the awareness of the healthy eating importance. For this, a focus has been placed on the body glucose level, giving the player the possibility to verify the impact that healthy and unhealthy foods have on the sugar in our blood.

Regarding the game metaphor, besides the cartoon design to encourage the consumption of healthy foods, the tower defense style reinforce the long-term incentive for good nutrition. Its is possible to observe as the player must keep avoiding the excessive consumption of caloric and greasy foods to cross the barrier, together with the consume of nutritious food to balance the body glycemic level.

As future works, more game levels will be provided, along with the addiction of new enemies and nutritious food. It is also planned to perform a game usability test to identify possible aspects that can be improved, making the game more effective and attractive as possible.

# References

1. Aparício, G.: Ajudar a desenvolver hábitos alimentares saudáveis na infância. Millenium, pp. 283–298 (2010)
2. Dias, J., et al.: Digestower: serious game como estratégia para prevenção e enfrentamento da obesidade infantil. In: Anais dos Workshops do Congresso Brasileiro de Informática na Educação, vol. 5, p. 167 (2016)
3. Giampieri, F., Tulipani, S., Alvarez-Suarez, J.M., Quiles, J.L., Mezzetti, B., Battino, M.: The strawberry: composition, nutritional quality, and impact on human health. Nutrition 28(1), 9–19 (2012)
4. Gros, B.: The impact of digital games in education. First Monday 8(7), 6–26 (2003)
5. Jenkins, D.J., Jenkins, A.L.: Dietary fiber and the glycemic response. Proc. Soc. Exp. Biol. Med. 180(3), 422–431 (1985)
6. Michael, D.R., Chen, S.L.: Serious Games: Games that Educate, Train, and Inform. Muska & Lipman/Premier-Trade (2005)
7. Millani, L.V.: Humanização e acolhimento no instituto da criança com diabetes/hospital-dia (2017)
8. Rodrigues, A., Cordeiro, H., da Silva, J.A.S., Silva, R., Barboza, B.: Batalha do sorriso: Processo de desenvolvimento de um jogo sério para a saúde bucal. In: Anais dos Workshops do Congresso Brasileiro de Informática na Educação, vol. 7, p. 1089 (2018)
9. Savi, R., Ulbricht, V.R.: Jogos digitais educacionais: benefícios edesafios. Renote 6(1) (2008)
10. Zunino, S.J.: Type 2 diabetes and glycemic response to grapes or grape products. J. Nutr. 139(9), 1794S–1800S (2009)

# The Concept and Development of a Serious Game „Alter Eco" as Part of Creating a Digital Twin of a Smart City

Robert Olszewski[1]([⊠]) [ID], Mateusz Cegiełka[1], and Jacek Wesołowski[2]

[1] Faculty of Geodesy and Cartography, Warsaw University of Technology,
Warsaw, Poland
robert.olszewski@pw.edu.pl, mateusz_cegielka@wp.pl
[2] Wonderland Engineering, Vaughan, Canada
jzwesolowski@gmail.com

**Abstract.** An essential way to lifelong learning in the modern information society is using ICT, geoinformation, and the concept of the so-called serious games, as well as gamification mechanisms. The „Smart City Alter Eco" game is a solution that not only facilitates social education for sustainable development but is also part of creating a so-called digital twin of a smart city. The authors propose an approach that enables creating a virtual model of a city, which reflects spatial, economic, social, and legal relations, as well as testing various versions of the city's development. The objective of the game is not as much creating an operative biogas plant but making it an attractive solution to the environmental, economic, and social problems of the town of Żuromin in central Poland.

**Keywords:** Serious game · Gamification · Digital twin · Smart city · Sustainable development · Geoinformation · Information society · Geoparticipation

## 1 Introduction

For the modern information society moulded in the era of civilisational transformation associated with the spread of IT, games and gamification not only constitute a platform for virtual entertainment, but are, or perhaps may become, a tool for responsible and participatory shaping of the surrounding space. Sustainable development and shaping of the so-called smart cities [1, 2] by their inhabitants require the ability to process available information (including spatial data) and the needs or expectations of the local community, as well as the extraction and use of the acquired knowledge of those participating in the creation of an information society. One of the most effective ways to educate society on sustainable development is to utilise the techniques of gamification and the so-called serious games [3–7].

The primary purpose for creating serious games is not merely entertainment; "serious games" help the players in obtaining, developing and consolidating specific skills, as well as problem-solving [8].

© IFIP International Federation for Information Processing 2019
Published by Springer Nature Switzerland AG 2019
E. van der Spek et al. (Eds.): ICEC-JCSG 2019, LNCS 11863, pp. 426–430, 2019.
https://doi.org/10.1007/978-3-030-34644-7_40

A variety of areas [9–15] uses serious games and serious games analytics [16–20]. The authors of this article aim to use serious games in the participative process of shaping a smart city, the development of (geo)information society, as well as solving complex social, economic, and environmental problems. Such a goal stems from the Warsaw University of Technology's implementation of the Ministry of Investment and Economic Development's project within the "Human Smart City" program. The project is entitled "Increasing the participation of residents of Żuromin in the process of managing, environmental monitoring, and creating a vision for the town's development by stimulating social geoparticipation." It is carried out by an interdisciplinary scientific team that supports the authorities and the local community of Żuromin – a town and commune located in central Poland, around 100 km north of Warsaw.

## 2   Problem Definition and Research Area

The crux of the problem of creating and developing a smart city in Żuromin lies in the residents' low level of engagement in the process of co-deciding about the town's development, and their low activity in social consultations, civic shaping of the spatial order or responsibility for the environment. Żuromin's specific problem is an inconvenient neighbourhood in the form of a massive number of pig and poultry farms in its immediate vicinity. Around this town with a population of 10 000, there is the largest poultry "basin" in Poland, with annual production exceeding 20 million chickens and 600 000 pigs. Such intensive agricultural production condensed within a few kilometres around Żuromin creates an extremely offensive odour. Standards for the concentration of substances, such as sulphur compounds, nitrogen compounds, and mercaptans, are far exceeded in this area. An additional problem lies in the excessive fertilisation of the soil with liquid manure, which degrades the soil and increases the odour offensiveness. This process also results in social conflicts between agricultural producers, residents, and town authorities; the local community accuses the authorities of being passive towards environmental degradation.

The construction of a biogas plant may solve this problem. It would also enable advanced processing of agricultural production waste, as well as reduce the odour and soil degradation, enable the generation of significant amounts of energy, and the commercialisation of the project. According to the authors, developing and popularising a serious game and running a social campaign, which shows that building a biogas plant would be beneficial for all the parties, may not only be an extremely innovative, but also an effective means of solving this problem.

## 3   Concept and Test Implementation of the „Smart City Alter Eco" Game

What is crucial in solving the problems of Żuromin is the issue of social education on sustainable development. The inhabitants of the commune (about 15 000 people), owners of poultry and pig farms (several hundred people), and town authorities (dozens of officials) should be made aware that only joint actions to shape a smart city may bring the desired results. The construction of a biogas plant, in which odorous waste from agricultural production will be processed, may solve environmental, economic, and social problems. However, the issue of the location of the biogas plant, its power, funding sources, environmental effects and, above all, the sense behind its construction – have all sparked controversy in the town. The authors believe that the practical solution to this problem is creating a so-called digital twin of the town of Żuromin and testing different variants of its development. An excellent tool for solving this problem is building a virtual model of the town to develop a serious game so that a person may play as town authorities, agricultural producers or residents. This game would also enable virtual cooperation of all the parties and help them realise that cooperation is a win-win solution.

To develop a prototype version of the „Smart City Alter Eco" game, a tool environment of the engine of the strategic and economic computer game "Cities: Skylines" (based on the modified version of Unity3D) was used in cooperation with the game's producers from Paradox Interactive company. Using this engine is intentional: the open programming interface in "Cities: Skylines" uses C# language; therefore, it is possible to modify and develop the game's basic functionalities. The tool environment of "Cities: Skylines" enables using the Unity – UnityScripting API's programming interface, as well as modifying the content of maps, objects, rules, and scenarios for the development of a virtual town by using Map Editor, Theme Editor, Asset Editor, and Scenario Editor. The following are the underlying conceptual assumptions of the „Smart City Alter Eco" game:

- The application should display enough information about the commune so that users are able to find their place of residence and the main facilities in the town of Żuromin. Thanks to the engine from "Cities: Skylines" and 3D models of buildings, a digital twin called Żuromina was developed, where every object has its digital equivalent in the game.
- The application should ensure that the functions of particular buildings are recognised at first glance, e.g. distinguishing residential structures from industrial installations. This means that the 3D model should have contrasting textures in different positions so that a residential building is different from an office or a farm.
- Without any loss of efficiency, users should be able to zoom out on the entire municipality or to bring it closer to focus on a specific object. The view at the maximum close-up does not have to be very detailed, but it is necessary that at the maximum distance, one can still find a place, focus on it and approach it. It is permissible that only a few terrain elements are seen at maximum distances.
- All farms in the commune are marked on the model. Clicking on a farm brings up a window with available information on the farm, such as its size, the number of farm animals, and the number of generated pollutants.
- When users locate a biogas plant in the commune, the "connect", or "disconnect" button becomes available. Pressing the button enables or disables the use of a biogas plant by a given farm. The statistics of a farm change when it "connects" to the biogas plant. Connecting a farm to a biogas plant may require additional data, such as the cost of waste collection and transport, energy production profits, as well as the positive public perception by the residents of the commune.

- What is crucial to the effectiveness of the game is the visualisation of the environmental effects of building a biogas plant. The devised game enables the visualisation of two types of pollution: soil contamination and air pollution in the form of the odour. Connecting to a biogas plant causes the decrease of the level of air pollution (fast) and soil (much slower) in a given area of the town and commune.
- Users may place exactly one biogas plant in the commune; it cannot be located on a farm or in the town of Żuromin. Its location may influence the results of the simulation, mainly the estimation of the costs of waste transport.
- In the game, there are several variants of financing the biogas plant (commune investment, European Union funds, private investment, public-private partnership), but users may select and implement only one of the options in a given game. Naturally, the power and efficiency of the biogas plant can be modified during the game as subsequent farms are connected. The economic and social effects of making decisions are visualised on a map and in the form of a set of information tables indicating costs, profits, savings, environmental changes, and so on.
- Pollutants are assigned to a specific farm. In a given point of the town or commune, pollution comes from many farms. When it happens, the game engine and a proprietary spatial interpolation algorithm, which uses the GIS calculation engine, estimates how much pollution comes from which farm. When users switch the farm over to the use of a biogas plant, the change in the environmental impact becomes immediately visible in the digital view of the town.

## 4  Summary

According to the authors, using clear rules and the mechanics of gamification may enable large-scale public consultations, but – above all – may also contribute to the awareness of the social consequences of actions, and, indirectly, to the development of a knowledge- and morality-based open information society. There seems to be an interesting parallel [21] between the development of technology (including the use of games in the educational process), the emergence of an information society, and the formation of an open society defined by Karl Popper in 1945; a society characterised by a balance of proponents of various historicist theories [22]. Social participation for sustainable development may constitute an essential element of the public discourse in an information society (implemented, e.g., through properly built gamification tools), understood as a free exchange of opinions on shaping the surrounding space.

## References

1. BSI Group: PAS 181 Smart city framework. https://www.bsigroup.com/en-GB/smart-cities/Smart-Cities-Standards-and-Publication/PAS-181-smart-cities-framework
2. Manville, C.: Mapping Smart Cities in the EU (2014)
3. Kapp, K.M.: The Gamification of Learning and Instruction: Game-Based Methods and Strategies for Training and Education, 1st edn., p. 336. Pfeiffer, San Francisco (2012)
4. Kapp, K.: The Gamification of Learning and Instruction. Pfeiffer/Wiley (2012)

5. Abt, C.: Serious Games. University Press of America (1970)
6. Aldrich, C.: The Complete Guide to Simulations and Serious Games. Pfeiffer/Wiley (2009)
7. Bartle, R.: Designing Virtual Worlds. New Riders (2003)
8. Loh, C.S., Sheng, Y., Ifenthaler, D. (eds.): Serious Games Analytics. AGL. Springer, Cham (2015). https://doi.org/10.1007/978-3-319-05834-4
9. Ifenthaler, D., Eseryel, D., Ge, X.: Assessment in Game-Based Learning. Springer, Heidelberg (2012). https://doi.org/10.1007/978-1-4614-3546-4
10. BankersLab: A smart guide to serious gaming (2013). http://bankerslab.com/blogposts/a-smart-guide-to-serious-gaming-part-1/
11. Arnab, S., et al.: Mapping learning and game mechanics for serious games analysis. Br. J. Educ. Technol. **46**(2), 391–411 (2015). https://doi.org/10.1111/bjet.12113
12. Carvalho, M.B.: Serious games for learning: a model and a reference architecture for efficient game development. Technical report (2017)
13. Bogost, I.: Persuasive Games. MIT Press, Cambridge (2007)
14. Gee, J.P.: Good Video Games + Good Learning, pp. 18–19. Peter Lang, New York (2007)
15. Ifenthaler, D.: Learning analytics. In: Spector, J.M. (ed.) The SAGE Encyclopedia of Educational Technology. Sage, Thousand Oaks (2015)
16. Canossa, A., Seif El-Nasr, M., Drachen, A.: Benefits of game analytics: stakeholders, contexts and domains. In: Seif El-Nasr, M., Drachen, A., Canossa, A. (eds.) game analytics, pp. 41–52. Springer, London (2013). https://doi.org/10.1007/978-1-4471-4769-5_3
17. Kim, T.W.: Gamification ethics: exploitation and manipulation. Published in Proceedings of the ACM SIGCHI Gamifying Research Workshop (2015)
18. Bellotti, F., Kapralos, B., Lec, K.. Moreno-Ger, P., Berta, R.: Assessment in and of serious games: an overview. In: Advances in Human-Computer Interaction (2013). https://doi.org/10.1155/2013/136864
19. Carvalho, M.B., et al.: An activity theory-based model for serious games analysis and conceptual design. Comput. Educ. **87**, 166–181 (2015)
20. Olszewski, R., Pałka, P., Turek, A.: Solving smart city transport problems by designing carpooling gamification schemes with multi-agent systems: the case of the so-called "Mordor of Warsaw". Sensors **18**, 1–25 (2018). https://doi.org/10.3390/s18010141
21. Olszewski, R., Wieszaczewska, A.: The application of modern geoinformation technologies in social geoparticipation. In: Gotlib, D., Olszewski, R. (eds.) Smart City. Spatial Information in Smart Cities Management. PWN, Warszawa (2016)
22. Popper, K.: The Open Society and Its Enemies. Complete, 5th edn., vol. I–II (1962). Revised (1966)

# "BDD Assemble!": A Paper-Based Game Proposal for Behavior Driven Development Design Learning

Victor T. Sarinho(✉)

Laboratório de Entretenimento Digital Aplicado (LEnDA),
State University of Feira de Santana, Av. Transnordestina, s/n, Novo Horizonte,
Feira de Santana, Bahia, Brazil
vsarinho@uefs.br

**Abstract.** Game-based learning represents a promising alternative to teach computing in higher education. This paper presents "BDD Assemble!", a paper-based game proposal for teaching Behavior Driven Development (BDD) competences. For this, the proposed game and the evaluation approach with software engineering students are described. As a result, a simple, interactive and colaborative game was provided, able to teach BDD concepts in a practical, competitive and fun way.

**Keywords:** Behavior Driven Development · Educational game · Paper-based game

## 1 Introduction

Originally developed by North [8], Behavior Driven Development (BDD) is an "increasingly prevailing agile development approach in recent years, and has gained attentions of both research and practice" [10]. It is focused on defining fine-grained specifications of the behaviour of the targeting system, in a way that they can be automated as executable specifications of a system [8,10]. It is also an outside-in agile software development process for agile teams that helps in a cooperative way to reduce this type of rework and regain time for new development work [9].

BDD uses the Gherkin language to describe software behaviors [5], providing a specific ubiquitous language that helps stakeholders to specify their system tests [10]. It starts with textual descriptions of the requirements using specific keywords that tag the type of sentence (*Given, When, Then*), indicating how the sentence is going to be treated in the subsequent development phases [1,5].

Regarding serious games, "they combine the entertainment value of games with additional objectives such as players acquiring knowledge or skills, receiving guidance and feedback on tasks to perform, or contributing partial solutions to problems" [2]. They are "intentionally designed to attract, engage, and retain

© IFIP International Federation for Information Processing 2019
Published by Springer Nature Switzerland AG 2019
E. van der Spek et al. (Eds.): ICEC-JCSG 2019, LNCS 11863, pp. 431–435, 2019.
https://doi.org/10.1007/978-3-030-34644-7_41

(even addict) players by applying psychology principles" [2], whose impact for educational purposes has received considerable attention.

Considering the relationship between BDD and serious games, BDD has been used to document user stories as an approach to identify game rules [3]. Stakeholders who are exposed to gamified elements can produce more BDD user stories in better quality and with more creative ideas [6]. Moreover, as a cooperative game, BDD can be used to demonstrate how issues can arise when requirements are not communicated effectively or clarified with other team members [4].

This paper presents the "BDD Assemble!", a paper-based game proposal able to complement the list of BDD game options, as well as improve the BDD design competence among agile development students.

## 2   Related Work

Regarding BDD usage to design a game, *BDD Warriors* [3] is a card game that describes fictional scenarios as sets of *Given-When-Then* constructs that must be completed by the players to get points and win the game. Players score collaboratively by completing scenarios, which should make sense for the other players to consider them as complete.

By the application of gamification strategies, the *UserStory Game* [6] is a game on BDD-based requirements elicitation with diversified game elements. It is an online gamified platform for eliciting requirements through user stories and acceptance tests, which was developed to test the effect of gamification on engagement and on performance in requirements engineering (Fig. 1).

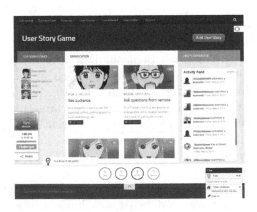

**Fig. 1.** UserStory Game example [6].

Finally, focusing on the agile perspective, and without face-to-face communication, software teams playing the *BDD Game* rely on their interpretation of a set of instructions - while under the pressure of time and resources, which are based on a drawing in a booklet that represents a set of user requirements that need to be implemented [4].

## 3   Methodology

"BDD Assemble!" is a competition among player teams to combine in short time proposed Gherkin sentences. Each team receives a story and 4 possible scenarios related to it. Similar pieces of Gherkin sentences for *Given*, *When* and *Then* are distributed for each team to be fit into their respective scenarios. Teams are challenged to produce correct sentences using the distributed pieces in each scenario, under the pressure of time against the other players. The team wins if it can complete more correct scenarios before the other competitors. Figure 2 illustrates some prepared Gherkin sentences for possible scenarios in a ATM (Account is in credit, Account is overdrawn past the overdraft limit, Deposit money and Transfer between accounts) to be combined by each player team.

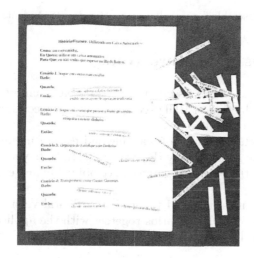

**Fig. 2.** BDD sentences for the "BDD Assemble!" gameplay.

As a verification approach for the game, the same was used by master degree students in a Software Engineering (SE) classroom (Fig. 3). In this activity, the students participated in a game match with 4–5 players each team, which was performed after the conclusion of the Acceptance Test class.

**Fig. 3.** "BDD Assemble!" gameplay by master degree students in a SE class.

## 4   Conclusions and Future Work

This paper introduced "BDD Assemble!", a paper-based entertainment approach that allows the production of BDD scenarios by proposed Gherkin sentences in a colaborative and competitive way.

Satisfaction, usefulness, ease of learning and ease of use attributes was also identified during the game play by the evaluated students via USE questionnaire [7], confirming that the proposed game can combine fun and engaging with BDD learning.

As future work, it is intended to produce a digital version of the proposed game, as well as more BDD scenarios together with the application and evaluation of the game in different SE classes.

## References

1. de Carvalho, R.A., Manhaes, R.S., et al.: Mapping business process modeling constructs to behavior driven development ubiquitous language. arXiv preprint arXiv:1006.4892 (2010)
2. Dalpiaz, F., Cooper, K.M.: Games for requirements engineers: analysis and directions. IEEE Software (2018)
3. Hermann, A.C.: BDD warriors & other games, December 2016. https://pt.slideshare.net/inovacaoDBServer/bdd-warriors-and-other-games. Accessed 31 May 2019
4. Hindsight: Try our BDD game. https://www.hindsightsoftware.com/bdd-game
5. Kudryashov, K.: The beginner's guide to BDD. Dan North Q & A. https://inviqa.com/blog/bdd-guide (2015)
6. Lombriser, P., Dalpiaz, F., Lucassen, G., Brinkkemper, S.: Gamified requirements engineering: model and experimentation. In: Daneva, M., Pastor, O. (eds.) REFSQ 2016. LNCS, vol. 9619, pp. 171–187. Springer, Cham (2016). https://doi.org/10.1007/978-3-319-30282-9_12

7. Lund, A.M.: Measuring usability with the use questionnaire12. Usability Interface **8**(2), 3–6 (2001)
8. North, D.: Introducing BDD, March 2006. https://dannorth.net/introducing-bdd/. Accessed 31 May 2019
9. Rahman, M., Gao, J.: A reusable automated acceptance testing architecture for microservices in behavior-driven development. In: 2015 IEEE Symposium on Service-Oriented System Engineering, pp. 321–325. IEEE (2015)
10. Solis, C., Wang, X.: A study of the characteristics of behaviour driven development. In: 2011 37th EUROMICRO Conference on Software Engineering and Advanced Applications, pp. 383–387. IEEE (2011)

# A Health Point-Based Dynamic Difficulty Adjustment Strategy for Video Games

Juan Suaza$^{(\boxtimes)}$, Edwin Gamboa$^{(\boxtimes)}$, and María Trujillo$^{(\boxtimes)}$

University of Valle, Cali, Colombia
{juan.suaza,edwin.gamboa,maria.trujillo}@correounivalle.edu.co

**Abstract.** Commonly, video games make a clear division on the difficulty offered (e.g. Easy, Medium, Hard), causing that players often do not experience what game designers intended. In this document, we propose a dynamic difficulty adjustment strategy for health point-based video games based on a heuristic evaluation performed at play time. This means that a video game may change its difficulty based on players' performance while they play. To test our strategy, we implement a fighting video game and perform an evaluation with $10^{th}$ grade students from Institución Educativa Multipropósito. Based on our results, the students considered that the game is balanced, suggesting that this strategy is a viable choice to implement and test in other video games.

**Keywords:** Video games · Dynamic difficulty adjustment · Heuristics

## 1 Introduction

Game balance is key to provide a fun and engaged experienced to players [2]. It is defined as a state where the game is fair for a player, providing him/her with challenges that match their skill. Commonly, video games make a clear division on the difficulty offered,e.g. Easy, Medium, Hard, being these difficulties subjective and unclear, specially to new players. Therefore, players do not often experience what game designers intended. On the other hand, there are video games that have a single difficulty, to deliver the intended experience designed. In some cases, causing players to quit because it is too hard.

In this document, we propose a dynamic difficulty adjustment strategy composed of two components: a playing agent with multiple difficulties and a heuristic function that swaps between them by measuring players' performance. To test our strategy, we implement a fighting video game and perform a Player Experience (PX) evaluation. The results show that the students considered the game is balanced and each component of the strategy serves its purpose.

## 2 Methodology

Our Dynamic Difficulty Adjustment (DDA) mechanism is based on the work done by [1] and [3], and extended to support more video games. It is composed

© IFIP International Federation for Information Processing 2019
Published by Springer Nature Switzerland AG 2019
E. van der Spek et al. (Eds.): ICEC-JCSG 2019, LNCS 11863, pp. 436–440, 2019.
https://doi.org/10.1007/978-3-030-34644-7_42

of two core components: a heuristic function and a playing agent with multiple difficulty levels that will be swapped based on the heuristic value.

## 2.1 Playing Agent

The playing agent is the character players face during their play-through. This agent has difficulty levels that are interchanged based on a heuristic. A playing agent should have at least three difficulties: easy, intended, and hard.

The most common types of agents are Finite State Machines (FSMs) which allow an easy difficulty adjustment since FSMs rely on parameter values that can be changed to increase or decrease the difficulty.

## 2.2 Heuristic Function

A heuristic function is in charge of selecting the difficulty of the agents a player will face. To address this task, we identify two different scenarios: an immediate evaluation and a episodic evaluation:

**The immediate heuristic function** measures the *aggression of a player* using a proportion of the character's Health Point (HP) difference. Equation 1 shows the proposed heuristic's equation.

$$H(PHP_c, EHP_c, PHP_m, EHP_m) = \frac{PHP_c}{PHP_m} - \frac{EHP_c}{EHP_m} \tag{1}$$

$H \in [-1, 1]$ and it is calculated every $T$ time-steps. $PHP_c$, $PHP_m$, $EHP_c$, $EHP_m$ are the current and maximum HP levels for both characters. $H = 1$ means the player has won and vice versa. The goal is to keep $H \approx 0$, meaning that both characters have similar HP such that they reach the end of a fight in similar conditions. For each difficulty level, different selection intervals need to be established to switch between them. For example, for three playing agents, the intervals would be: $[-1, -\alpha)$, $[-\alpha, \alpha]$, and $(\alpha, 1]$.

**The episodic heuristic function** measures how well a player has performed in the past levels, or gameplay episodes, of a video game. This heuristic's equation is shown in Eq. 2.

$$H(P) = Count(Successful\ \ episodes) - Count(Player's\ \ deaths) \tag{2}$$

$H$ is calculated after an episode has finished, $H \in \mathbb{Z}$. The count of successful episodes and player's deaths are natural numbers, including zero. If $H > 0$, means a harder difficulty should be selected and viceversa. An episode can be interpreted as a level, task, enemies defeated, among others, depending on the game.

# 3    The Forest of the Guardians

The Forest of the Guardians is a 2.5D fighting mobile video game developed to test the DDA proposed. The game consists on a 1 Vs. 1 fight against an agent. The agent uses a FSMs with three difficulty levels and the immediate heuristic.

## 3.1    Finite State Machine

The enemy uses a FSM that has four core combat states, described below:

- The *base attack* state casts $k$ long-range attacks in the direction of the player.
- In the *move towards the player* state, the agent moves towards the player.
- The *melee attack* state is triggered once the agent is close enough to the player's character.
- Finally, in the *move away* state, the agent moves to the farthest corner/wall from the player's character. While in this state, if the player's character is close enough, the agent will transition to the *melee attack* state.

## 3.2    Difficulties

The three levels of difficulty proposed are: easy, medium, and hard difficulty. All of the FSMs variations have the same parameters. The parameters are shown in Table 1. These values were chosen experimentally.

**Table 1.** Difficulties' parameter values

| Difficulty | Attack speed (attacks/second) | Movement speed (units/action) | Armour points |
|---|---|---|---|
| Easy | 0.8 | 4 | 0 |
| Medium | 1 | 6 | 2 |
| Hard | 1.5 | 6 | 5 |

# 4    Strategy Evaluation

## 4.1    Participants

Nineteen $10^{th}$ grade students from Institución Educativa Multipropósito were involved in the evaluation process (58% are males and 42% are females). All the students were asked to play the game once. The students' age ranged from 15 to 18 years-old (Mean = 16.5, SD = 1.3).

## 4.2   Methods

**Player Experience Inventory** is a standardised questionnaire proposed by [4]. Player Experience Inventory (PXI) incorporates two sub-scales: the functional level, which evaluates the dynamics situated at the usage level, i.e., immediate consequences experienced; and at the psycho-social level, i.e., which exceed the usage level and focuses on the consequences at the psycho-social level.

## 4.3   Results and Discussion

**Immersion** presents positive results: 73.7% of students were not aware of their surroundings, 79% were immersed in the game, and all of the students were focused on the game. Even though there was another student playing another video game, students were focused on the fight; indicating that the Flow channel was achieved in some of them.

**Challenge.** This dimension presents positive results, 63.1% of the students considered that the game was not too easy nor too hard to play; the remaining students show a neutral agreement. Similarly, 73.8% agree that the was challenging but not too challenging; the remaining students have a neutral agreement.

Besides from the questions, a 74% win-rate is reported and an average remaining HP of 26%. Even though the remaining HP is low, which is one goal of the heuristic, the high win-rate shows that the game was probably too easy.

Considering these results we can argue that the game is considered balanced by a group of students. This means that the difficulty level assigned by the heuristic is adequate.

## 5   Conclusions and Future Work

As a result of this work, a dynamic difficulty adjustment strategy for HP-based video is proposed, including two heuristics that address different scenarios. One of the heuristics proposed was implemented in a video game and tested by $10^{th}$ grade students. Our results show that students considered the video game balanced, therefore it might provide a solution to motivate students to play a video game. In general, this strategy may be a viable solution to implement in other scenarios and video games. However, to fully establish if the strategy motivates students, longer evaluations with students are needed to corroborate that fact.

Based on our results, the immediate heuristic served its purpose: get both player to low health at the end of the fight, averaging a 26% HP remaining at the end of the fight. However, we are aware that the players' win rate is still too high (74%) implying that the FSM used was probably too easy for players.

As future work, longer evaluations are needed to validate if the proposed balancing strategy motivates students to play the game in the long-term. Moreover, the episodic heuristic should also be tested. Additionally, combining both heuristic functions is still a task to do.

# References

1. Brown, R., Guinn, C.: Developing game-playing agents that adapt to user strategies: a case study. In: 2014 IEEE Symposium on Intelligent Agents (IA), pp. 51–56. IEEE (2014)
2. Csikszentmihalyi, M.: Beyond Boredom and Anxiety. Jossey-Bass (2000)
3. Silva, M.P., do Nascimento Silva, V., Chaimowicz, L.: Dynamic difficulty adjustment through an adaptive AI. In: 2015 14th Brazilian Symposium on Computer Games and Digital Entertainment (SBGames), pp. 173–182. IEEE (2015)
4. Vanden Abeele, V., Nacke, L.E., Mekler, E.D., Johnson, D.: Design and preliminary validation of the player experience inventory. In: Proceedings of the 2016 Annual Symposium on Computer-Human Interaction in Play Companion Extended Abstracts, pp. 335–341. ACM (2016)

# "University Universe": A Mobile Game to Simulate the University Student Life

Matheus Teixeira, Victor Munduruca, and Victor Sarinho(✉)

Laboratório de Entretenimento Digital Aplicado (LEnDA),
State University of Feira de Santana, Av. Transnordestina s/n, Novo Horizonte,
Feira de Santana, Bahia, Brazil
teixeirista@gmail.com, victormunduruca@gmail.com, vsarinho@uefs.br

**Abstract.** Nowadays, there are different reasons why a student leaves a course, a university, or the higher education system. This article presents the University Universe, a playful digital game that simulates in practice the difficult task of concluding the semesters of higher education. For this, game dynamics, scenarios and design approach were presented, together with the developed game prototype. As a result, there is a game that can simulate the difficult task of completing the semesters in a university course, something particularly challenging, but capable of being transformed into a gamified activity for students awareness.

**Keywords:** Higher education · Student retention · Serious game

## 1 Introduction

Nowadays, there are a lot of reasons why a student might drop out of university. Among the usual reasons for this phenomenon, some of them stand out, such as methodology disagreement, comprehension difficulty, monetary problems, bad college infrastructure, no adaptation to the academic environment, etc. They also come along with different types of personal problems, such as, diseases, home moving and psychological problems, for example [1].

The lack of information during the first year, the student unsuitability with the university system, and the inability of create new friendships are also pointed as the main reasons of college evasion [2]. This is also attributed to the lack of communication and information faced by the university environment [3], something that could be solved by appropriated information systems as a whole.

Undergraduates are deeply in touch with digital games, bringing the game play to a new purpose level, such as education and spread knowledge [4]. In this sense, this paper presents *University Universe*, a digital game that simulates the hard task of finishing semesters during a university course. It aims to represent the tension of a university student life, showing common problems found by them in a fun and casual way that must be solved during the game play.

© IFIP International Federation for Information Processing 2019
Published by Springer Nature Switzerland AG 2019
E. van der Spek et al. (Eds.): ICEC-JCSG 2019, LNCS 11863, pp. 441–444, 2019.
https://doi.org/10.1007/978-3-030-34644-7_43

## 2  The University Universe Game

Designed to be a mobile game that could be played with only one hand, the University Universe game dynamic is to balance the essential attributes of a university student: health, money, social life and grades (Fig. 1). These attributes are modified by the execution of campus activities according to the game map (Home, Library, Cafeteria and Academic Research Facility) (Fig. 2), which must be kept at a certain minimum value to continue playing. Each level represents a semester and the difficulty increases as the semesters advance, simulating what students face in a real course.

**Fig. 1.** HUD displaying the current player status.

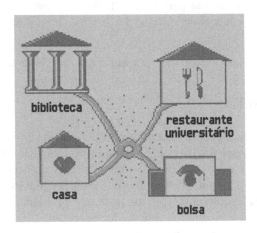

**Fig. 2.** Map of the University Universe game.

By the usage of a game design canvas approach [5], important features were identified to develop an initial game prototype, such as:

- Initial menu and gameplay scenarios (Fig. 3);
- HUD with the following attributes: health, grades, money, social life and the semester time indication (Fig. 1);
- Automatic decrease of player attributes as the time goes during the semester;
- Verification of the minimum attribute value required to go to the next semester;

- Representation of the current scene the player is on;
- Definition of which location affects the attributes in a certain way, during the time and as the player clicks the scene;
- Change location according to the map selection;
- Record of the semester reached by the player; and
- End game when the player does not have the minimum attribute value required or if an attribute reaches zero.

**Fig. 3.** General overview of the game scenes.

At the beginning of the game, the player has all attribute values maxed out (100 points). The player character starts at Home (Fig. 3), and, when the scene is touched, attributes are increased or decreased according to the context defined for the respective campus activity:

- **Home** increases health in 3 points, decreases grades in 2 points;
- **Library** increases study in 4 points, decreases health in 2 points and social life in 1 point;
- **Cafeteria** increases health and social life in 2 points, decreases money in 1 point; and
- **Academic Research Facility** increases grade and money in 2 points, decreases health in 2 points and social in 1 points.

The location-based effects were defined by personal experiences during the academic life. For instance, it was verified that productivity decreased at home, due to the number of possible distractions. On the other hand, health increases, due to the rest and procrastination possibilities. Conversely, a long time procrastinating might cause the opposite effect. So, in the game, if the player stays in a location for a long time, it will be harmful.

The first semester introduces the player to the gameplay and mechanics, working as a game tutorial. It lasts 60 s while the following semesters are 100 s long. This game design decision was made during beta testing, where all semesters were 200 s long. This duration was considered too long by the initial players who tested the game.

When a semester ends, the attributes need to be more or equal to the minimum values required to keep playing. In the first semester, the minimum value of all attributes is 30 points and, as the following semesters advance, this value is increased by 5 points.

There are 4 ways to lose the game, one for each attribute to convey a message about academic reality. For example, when the health attribute ends, a funny message warning is displayed about the importance of mental and physical health care during college years. When the grade attribute reaches zero, the player is warned that he can not leave his academic life behind.

## 3   Conclusions and Future Work

This paper presented University Universe, a mobile game developed to the player faces the difficult task of finishing semesters in a university. It is a challenge that has a significant impact on the reality of student retention, which has been turned into a gamified activity that introduces a funny perspective on the current life status of most undergraduates.

As future work, new functionalities will be implemented, such as adding random events that could turn out to be beneficial or harmful for the university student (surprise tests, dating, etc). The correct balance between the attributes and scenes for new implemented events, resources and scenes will also be performed, together with an online ranking able to share obtained results in social networks as a viral marketing strategy for the game.

Finally, the University Universe arcade is under construction to be placed in a popular university environment, where students opinions and suggestions about the game, especially about how the game has changed their life prospects as an undergraduate student, will be collected by them.

## References

1. Paredes, A.S.: A evasão do terceiro grau em Curitiba. NUPES (1994)
2. Cunha, A.M., Tunes, E., Silva, R.R.D.: Evasção do curso de química da Universidade de Brasília: a interpretação do aluno evadido. SciELO Brasil (2001). https://doi.org/10.10007/1234567890
3. da Silva, E.R., de França, T.C., de Oliveira Sampaio, J.: Aumento da Adesão e do Engajamento de Usuários do Campus Social com Uso de Mecanismos de Gamificação. In: Proceedings of the III Regional School on Information Systems of Rio de Janeiro, Brasil (2016)
4. da Silva, L.M.: Ludicidade e matemática: Um novo olhar para aprendizagem. Psicologia Saberes 4(5), 10–22 (2018)
5. Sarinho, V.T.: Uma Proposta de Game Design Canvas Unificado. XVI Simpósio Brasileiro de Jogos e Entretenimento Digital (SBGames) (2017)

# Demonstrations

# GaZone: VR Image Browsing System Providing Feelings of Happiness

Sho Sugimoto[✉] and Hisashi Miyamori[✉]

Division of Frontier Informatics, Graduate School of Kyoto Sangyo University,
Motoyama, Kamigamo, Kita-ku, Kyoto-shi 603-8555, Japan
{i1888097,miya}@cc.kyoto-su.ac.jp

**Abstract.** In this paper, we propose GaZone, a system providing happiness through unusual immersive experiences surrounded by their favorite images. GaZone provides a function to search images on the Web and easily collect them in the VR environment realized by the head mounted display. The user immerses in the unusual environment surrounded by many images suited to their preference, resulting in experiencing the happiness that cannot be obtained by the conventional systems. From the user study, it was confirmed that users felt happiness and their hearts were moved by being surrounded by their favorite things.

**Keywords:** Happiness · Image search · Possession · Virtual reality · Entertainment

## 1 Introduction

Realization of happiness is important for humans to live a fruitful life [4,9]. One of the ways for human beings to get the feelings of happiness is to gather goods that match their tastes and arrange them around themselves. Knutson et al clearly indicated that one's mere imagination of buying something makes the state in the head almost the same as when he or she actually bought it [3]. Simple look at the images of one's favorite goods strongly stimulate the nucleus accumbens, which is the pleasure center of the brain, and the brain gets filled with dopamine. That is, it is assumed that our viewing of the favorite things arranged around us will bring us the similar effect. In this paper, we focus on the happiness that can be felt by users when they collect their favorite goods and put them around themselves.

However, anyone cannot always put it into action easily. There are restrictions on securing necessary economic strength for collection (economic constraints) and on ensuring necessary physical space for installation (spatial constraints).

In this paper, we propose GaZone, a system which allows users to feel happiness without being bound by economic or spatial constraints. First, in order to reduce the economic constraints when collecting things, GaZone introduces a means of "obtaining images of user's favorite things". Also, it utilizes

© IFIP International Federation for Information Processing 2019
Published by Springer Nature Switzerland AG 2019
E. van der Spek et al. (Eds.): ICEC-JCSG 2019, LNCS 11863, pp. 447–451, 2019.
https://doi.org/10.1007/978-3-030-34644-7_44

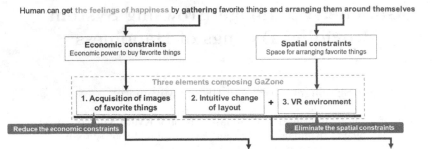

**Fig. 1.** Concept of GaZone

"VR environment" to eliminate the spatial constraints when arranging things, and has the function of "changing layout by intuitive operations" such as grasping with a controller, to provide the feelings that users can actually arrange things with their own hands as shown in Fig. 1.

In addition, it is expected that the users can feel a kind of possession[1] of favorite things from the elements of "acquisition of images of favorite things" and "intuitive change of layout". Similarly, it is expected that the users can feel a kind of unreality from the elements of "VR environment" and "intuitive change of layout". It is thought that these feelings also contribute to form the "happiness" that GaZone brings about.

## 2    Related Research

Conventionally, systems allowing any 3D objects to be displayed and freely browsed have been proposed [1], in contrast, GaZone, the proposed system in this paper, provides the immersive experience including elements as size and distance because it displays the objects in the VR environment.

Ichikawa et al. proposed VR Safari Park as the interface with interactivity using the VR environment [7]. This is a system where users combine the previously prepared block-like objects, resulting in inflating imagination and promoting new discoveries, whereas GaZone utilizes a large number of images on the Web being freely displayed around the user and provides the feeling of happiness. There is another existing service which has a function of image search in the VR environment, called "COMOLU"[2]. Meanwhile, GaZone aims to make the user feel happier by interface providing certain feedbacks.

In addition, recent investigations have demonstrated that VR environment can be effectively used to alleviate pain and discomfort in medical care [2,6]. In these studies, the VR environment was used to alleviate the pain and discomfort felt by humans, whereas in GaZone is used to induce human happiness.

---

[1] The feeling of possession refers to the feeling when we can handle or arrange them freely. It does not necessarily include the ownership towards the target thing.

[2] http://comolu.info/.

# 3   Proposed System

We propose GaZone, a VR system where users can fetch many images of their favorite things and arrange them freely in their surroundings for browsing evoking happiness (Fig. 2). We made the promotion video for explanation [8].

**Fig. 2.** A user experiencing GaZone

GaZone is a new system providing users the feelings of happiness, and composed of three elements, namely, the function to obtain a set of images of user's favorite things, the VR environment where the set of images are displayed around the user, and the function allowing the user to intuitively change the layout of the displayed images. Specifically, when the users' favorite keyword is received by voice, the images on the Web are searched and the obtained group of images are displayed around the user (acquisition of images). After that, users can pull images of interest closer to them in the VR environment, and perform operations such as selection, movement, scaling, and so on (intuitive layout change). Users can freely repeat these operations, and an environment where the feeling of happiness can be obtained is developed.

As a user of GaZone, ordinary people over junior high school students are mainly assumed who have experience in image search on the Web and has no hesitation in using the VR environment. In addition, it is expected to be particularly effective for users who have economic difficulty in freely purchasing their favorite things, or difficulty in securing a space for physically arranging them.

# 4   Evaluation Experiment

Here, we have the users experience the proposed system in the following three ways, and discuss the effect of the system.

First, we underwent the assessment by Qualification trial[3] at an academic conference, Entertainment Computing 2018, in order to confirm whether GaZone

---

[3] Framework of the value standard in the field of Entertainment Computing research. The applicants describe how they want the users' minds to be moved and what kind of approach was taken for that in the Entertainment Data Asset (EDA). The Qualification committee members judge the validity of the system's approach based on the EDA and their experience using the system [5].

provides the feeling of happiness and possession. As a result of having undergone the assessment, the Qualification committee qualified the usefulness. It was confirmed that the "feeling of happiness" was evoked by being surrounded by the favorite images. In addition, the opinions were divided among the judges about the "feeling of possession", and comments were obtained that one of the reasons for this could be because they had not always experienced the intuitive change of layouts of the favorite images sufficiently due to the limited amount of qualification time.

Next, we took advantage of open campus to get various opinions from many users unfamiliar with VR contents. We summarized the feedbacks from about 180 high school students who visited the open campus and experienced GaZone. It was confirmed that nearly 90% of the participants enjoyed the system. Some participants talked with their friends after leaving the demonstration booth, saying "I felt happiness" and "I wanted to stay longer and more immersed".

Finally, after securing about 15 min as experience time, we interviewed two students to obtain their impressions and to confirm the changes happening in the subject's feelings after the experience. As a result, both users expressed that it was unrealistic and enjoyable about the immersive experience where they were surrounded by their favorite images. The user also noted that he felt he held the images by himself, and that the impression he got when looking at the images with GaZone was different from the one when looking at them with PCs or smartphones. It was observed that they were often surprised or felt joy in the process of freely moving images of favorite things with the controllers. That is considered to be one of the major factors that evokes the feelings of possession.

## 5   Conclusion

In this paper, we proposed GaZone, a VR system providing the feelings of happiness. GaZone focuses on the feelings of happiness that can be evoked when collecting and putting things that match with the users' tastes around themselves, and reduces and eliminates the economic and spatial constraints associated with this behavior, respectively. In the evaluation experiment, users were asked to experience GaZone, and their opinions on the system and changes in feelings after the experience were collected. As a result, it was verified that the experience of GaZone actually evokes the feeling of happiness. In the future, we plan to improve the system so that the feelings of happiness can be evoked more surely, as well as to extend the function so that the feelings being evoked can be remembered continuously even after the experience.

**Acknowledgment.** A part of this work was supported by JSPS KAKENHI Grant Number 18K11557.

# References

1. Asuka, S., Tetsu, N.: An intuitive placing system for virtual collection cases. EC2017 (2017)
2. Hoffman, H.G., Patterson, D.R., Seibel, E., Soltani, M., Jewett-Leahy, L., Sharar, S.R.: Virtual reality pain control during burn wound debridement in the hydrotank. Clin. J. Pain **24**(4), 299–304 (2008)
3. Knutson, B., Rick, S., Wimmer, G.E., Prelec, D., Loewenstein, G.: Neural predictors of purchases. Neuron **53**(1), 147–156 (2007)
4. Masao, S., Shigehiro, O.: Research frontiers on subjective well-being. Kanjou shin-rigaku kenkyuu **21**(2), 92–98 (2014). https://doi.org/10.4092/jsre.21.92
5. Mitsuru, M.: Proposal of framework of value standard in entertainment computing research. In: Entertainment Computing Symposium 2018 proceedings, vol. 2018, pp. 57–64, september 2018. (in Japanese)
6. Patterson, D., Hoffman, H., Palacios, A.G., Jensen, M.: Analgesic effects of posthyp-notic suggestions and virtual reality distraction on thermal pain. J. Abnorm. Psy-chol. **115**(4), 834 (2006)
7. Shotaro, I., Kazuki, T., Yoshifumi, K.: Development of "VR Safari Park" using the explorative interface with metaphor of world tree and blocks. EC2017 (2017)
8. Sugimoto, S.: Gazone: VR image browsing system providing feelings of happiness (2018). https://www.youtube.com/watch?v=yD7g1eQ76_s
9. Thomson, J., Tredennick, H., Barnes, J.: The Nicomachean Ethics. Penguin Classics, Westminster (2004). https://books.google.co.jp/books?id=iBoqmEvavawC

# AutomataMind: A Serious Game Proposal for the Automata Theory Learning

Manuella Vieira(iD) and Victor Sarinho(✉)(iD)

Laboratório de Entretenimento Digital Aplicado (LEnDA),
State University of Feira de Santana, Av. Transnordestina, s/n,
Novo Horizonte, Feira de Santana, Bahia, Brazil
manuellavr7@gmail.com, vsarinho@uefs.br

**Abstract.** Digital games facilitate the teaching-learning process, arousing the interest of students in various areas of competence. This paper introduces AutomataMind, a game that seeks to stimulate the player logical thinking skills, while presenting the concepts of Computer Theory with emphasis on Automata Theory in a playful and challenging way.

**Keywords:** Game based learning · Automata theory · Serious games

## 1 Introduction

Educational software is a significant element in the construction of a knowledge base for students [1]. In addition, digital games have been designed for teaching purposes to engage and motivate the players into learning activities [3].

Studies have shown that many difficulties experienced by students when learning Theory of Computation are related to the lack of logical thinking and problem-solving skills [5], as well as a sense of monotony [6] that is caused by the great number of complex and abstract concepts involved [2].

As a gamified approach to introduce concepts related to the Automata Theory in a playful way, this paper presents "*AutomataMind*", an educational game based on the *Mastermind* board game that seeks to stimulate the player logical reasoning skills through proposed automata challenges.

## 2 Related Work

As an example of digital game related to the Automata Theory learning, *Automata Defense 2.0* [6] is a tower defense game whose objective is to stop a variety of creatures, each one associated with a word, from reaching the map exit. To achieve this goal, the player must design an automaton and assign it to a tower. Each creature that carries a word accepted by a tower automaton

© IFIP International Federation for Information Processing 2019
Published by Springer Nature Switzerland AG 2019
E. van der Spek et al. (Eds.): ICEC-JCSG 2019, LNCS 11863, pp. 452–455, 2019.
https://doi.org/10.1007/978-3-030-34644-7_45

is attacked when it moves inside of that tower coverage area. The player is able to position towers in a strategic way, so that they can either attack or slow the creatures movements.

Another game example is the *"Chomsky's Mountain"* [4], where the player goal is to reach the top of a mountain by solving problems that represent the "enemies" that the user must defeat. To do this, the player must build a computing model that matches the theme of the current level of the game. Each level refers to languages associated with two types of grammar from Chomky's Hierarchy: Regular Languages and Context Free Languages.

Regarding the *Mastermind* game, whose game dynamics will be applied in AutomataMind game, it is a code-breaking game that challenges the players by prompting them to guess a specific pattern - also referred to as "the code" - usually composed of a combination of pegs with different colors. Every time the player takes a guess about the code, a feedback is provided showing how close the player's attempt to the actual code was.

## 3   The AutomataMind Game

AutomataMind was designed by integrating Mastermind game play aspects with Automata Theory concepts. The game was structured in the following manner: each level of the game starts with an automaton being shown on the screen. Then, a string - a sequence of characters - that can be accepted by that automaton is generated. This sequence remains hidden and represents the code that should be "broken" by the player.

The player must try to guess what the secret sequence is, based on the automaton that is being presented on the current level screen. Every time the player takes a guess on what the code might be, a certain amount of information regarding the current guess is provided, so that the player next guess can be improved based on that feedback.

There is a limited number of guesses that can be made during a level. Therefore, if the player reaches the limit without having guessed the correct sequence, the stage restarts from the beginning, with a new code that may or may not be similar to the prior one (the sequence selection process is random).

## AutomataMind

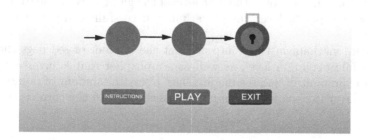

**Fig. 1.** Title screen of the AutomataMind game.

The game main menu (Fig. 1) was designed as a graphic representation of a finite automaton that has a lock as its final state, implying that in order to find the correct code, the player guesses must necessarily be able to reach the automaton accept state. For the menu buttons, three options are provided to the player: *Read* the instructions, *Play* and *Exit* the game.

Figure 2 illustrates one game level, where the automaton at the top of the screen is used as the player reference to discover the hidden sequence. The pegs in the right side of the screen are used to provide feedback about the player guess, where a **red peg** is placed for each character that is in the same position as a similar character on the secret code. The **white peg** indicates the presence of a matching character - a character that can be found in both the guess and the secret code - but that is placed in the wrong position. The **green confirmation** indicates that the string inserted by the player is accepted by the automaton (meaning it ends in a final state) even though it might not be the correct code.

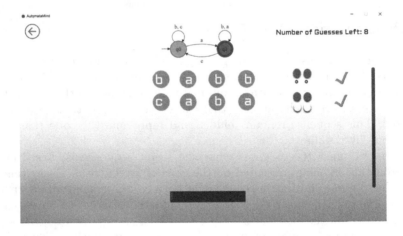

**Fig. 2.** Game play screen of the AutomataMind game.

AutomataMind is also divided into levels with increasing degrees of difficulty, ranging from: number of characters used in the secret code; number of symbols belonging to the automaton alphabet; and number of states and transitions the automaton has. Initially, only the first level of the game is available to the player, and to unlock a specific level, the player must successfully complete the previous one (Fig. 3).

The score mechanism takes into account the number of red pegs the player obtained while playing a level, as well as a multiplier that is inversely proportional to the amount of guesses made. Thus, a greater amount of points is given when the player takes a less amount of guesses to get to the correct sequence.

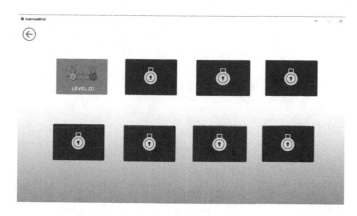

**Fig. 3.** Level selection screen of the AutomataMind game.

# 4  Conclusion and Future Work

This paper presented the AutomataMind, an educational game capable of helping students to develop logical reasoning skills while learning about the Theory of Computation. The developed game is a simple solution that has the possibility of contributing to the scenario of games aimed at teaching topics related to the theoretical aspects of computing.

As AutomataMind is an on-going project (available at https://github.com/lenda-uefs), an usability evaluation with undergraduates related to computer science will be performed in the future. The inclusion of Pushdown automata and Turing machines topics in future levels of the game will also be performed for challenging and learning purposes.

# References

1. Bernardi, S.T.: Utilização de softwares educacionais nos processos de alfabetização, de ensino e aprendizagem com uma visão psicopedagógica. Revista REI, Getúlio Vargas **5**(10) (2010)
2. Devedzic, V., Debenham, J.: An intelligent tutoring system for teaching formal languages. In: Goettl, B.P., Halff, H.M., Redfield, C.L., Shute, V.J. (eds.) ITS 1998. LNCS, vol. 1452, pp. 514–523. Springer, Heidelberg (1998). https://doi.org/10.1007/3-540-68716-5_57
3. Klopfer, E., Osterweil, S., Salen, K.: Moving learning games forward: Obstacles, opportunities & openness: an educational arcade paper (2009)
4. Leite, L., Sibaldo, M., Carvalho, T., Souza, R.: Montanha de chomsky: jogo tutor para auxílio no ensino de teoria da computaç ao. In: XXII Workshop sobre Educaç ao em Informática (WEI 2014), Brasília, DF (2014)
5. Pillay, N.: Learning difficulties experienced by students in a course on formal languages and automata theory. ACM SIGCSE Bull. **41**(4), 48–52 (2010)
6. Silva, R.C., Binsfeld, R.L., Carelli, I.M., Watanabe, R.: Automata defense 2.0: reedição de um jogo educacional para apoio em linguagens formais e autômatos. In: Brazilian Symposium on Computers in Education (Simpósio Brasileiro de Informática na Educação-SBIE), vol. 1 (2010)

# Designing Serious Mobile Location-based Augmented Reality Games

# Smiling Earth - Citizens' Awareness on Environmental Sustainability Using Energy and Transport Data

Sobah Abbas Petersen[1]([✉]), Peter Ahcin[2], and Idar Petersen[2]

[1] Department of Computer Science, Norwegian University of Science and Technology, Trondheim, Norway
sap@ntnu.no
[2] SINTEF Energy, Trondheim, Norway
{Peter.Ahcin, Idar.Petersen}@sintef.no

**Abstract.** This paper describes the design and implementation of a mobile app, Smiling Earth, to support citizens to contribute to climate change by being aware of their carbon footprint and making changes in their daily energy consumption and transportation. One of the main aims of this work is to explore the ways in which ICT could help raise awareness and educate citizens about their actions and their consequences on the environment. The Smiling Earth app is designed to visualise data about citizens' activities and to motivate citizens to change their behavior to reduce their $CO2$ emissions by changing their transportation habits. The app takes a broader perspective of $CO2$ emissions, bringing together the transport and energy sectors. The design process and a preliminary evaluation of Smiling Earth is presented in the paper. This work has been conducted as a part of the EU DESENT project.

**Keywords:** $CO2$ emissions · Green transportation · Urban mobility · Carbon footprint · Behavior change · Gamification

## 1 Introduction

Global warming is one of the biggest and most urgent issues facing the world today. Transportation, electricity consumption and domestic heating are responsible for a large part of greenhouse gas emissions, which contribute to climate change. One of the biggest contributors to Carbon Dioxide ($CO2$) emissions is transportation. Savings can be made with better energy and transportation management transport is the sector where most emissions cuts will be made in the near future [1]. While physical activity such as walking or cycling for short trips are possibilities, many still choose to drive to work to save time and for flexibility [2], or out of habit [3]. The main motivations for the work presented in this paper is to explore the use of ICT to motivate citizens to reduce their carbon footprint by changing their behavior. We believe that this is a relevant step towards taking action to combat climate change and its impacts and for responsible and sustainable societies, in line with the United Nations' Sustainable Development Goals (SDG). One of the areas in which ICT could contribute towards

© IFIP International Federation for Information Processing 2019
Published by Springer Nature Switzerland AG 2019
E. van der Spek et al. (Eds.): ICEC-JCSG 2019, LNCS 11863, pp. 459–465, 2019.
https://doi.org/10.1007/978-3-030-34644-7_46

achieving the SDGs is to help citizens perceive them as goals they will contribute to as a part of their daily lives. Indeed technologies are most effective when they help people to achieve the goals they have already decided upon [4].

The success of smart urban mobility needs integrated solutions about energy, transport, service and governance with the full involvement of multiple stakeholders, such as governments, public and private enterprises and citizens. The European project, DESENT, focuses on providing a smart decision support tool for urban energy and transport, by developing innovative approaches and utilizing cutting-edge technologies using co-creation. The DESENT consortium includes municipalities, universities, research institutes, enterprises and private companies from Austria, The Netherlands and Norway, and tackles the various challenges by implementing innovative solutions in demo cities. One of the focus areas of DESENT is to support smart decision making for policy makers and personalized services for citizens.

The aims of this paper are to describe a gamified pervasive mobile app, Smiling Earth, designed to create awareness about carbon footprints and affect individuals' behavior change towards more sustainable choices and actions in their daily lives. The overall research question addressed is the paper is: Can the combination of energy and transport data and individual energy consumption in terms of CO2 emissions motivate people to manage energy better and reduce CO2 emissions? Smiling Earth, is designed to (i) increase citizens' awareness about their CO2 emissions through visualising data about their daily activities; and (ii) motivate citizens to change their behavior to reduce their CO2 emissions by adopting a healthier lifestyle. Smiling Earth takes a broader perspective of CO2 emissions, bringing together the transport and energy sectors as well as the lifestyle (e.g. transportation modes) of individuals. A few earlier examples of mobile apps that address green transportation and sustainable urban mobility are reported in the literature; *UbiGreen* tracks an individual's transport options, e.g. carpooling and walking, and provides feedback using a metaphor from nature as the "wall paper" for the mobile app [2]. Another app is the MUV which encourages people to adopt sustainable mobility modes livability [5, 6].

The rest of this paper is organised as follows: Sect. 2 describes the design process; Sect. 3 describes the Smiling Earth app; Sect. 4 describes the evaluations and provide an overview of the main results; Sect. 5 concludes the paper.

## 2  Design Process

The user group for the Smiling Earth are the general citizens and electricity consumers in urban areas. Since the project consortium included energy companies and we had easy access to them, we chose to work closely with them to leverage on their knowledge of their customers. The design and development team also included researchers with engineering, ICT and economics backgrounds. A participatory design approach was followed. Several formative evaluations and design iterations were conducted using sketches and the rapid prototyping tool Proto.io.

Designs to affect behavior change require an understanding of how humans adopt or change behaviors. We have based our work on the Transtheoretical Model of Behaviour Change (TTM), developed in the health sector [7]. TTM posits that behaviour change progresses through six stages of change: Precontemplation, Contemplation, Preparation, Action, Maintenance and Termination. The first stage is to inform users to raise awareness and then to educate and persuade them to contemplate and take action.

## 3  Description of Smiling Earth

The central concepts that influence the design of Smiling Earth are CO2 emissions, health benefits, environmental impact and economic profit. The Graphical User Interface (GUI) for the main page is designed to reflect these concepts and draw the user's attention to the concept of CO2 emissions and how that affect the world we live in; see Fig. 1. Metaphors have been used to create emotional attachments to concepts such as the environment; e.g. [8–10]. We have used the earth as a metaphor to show the impact of a high carbon footprint (global warning) which may be caused by the user's actions. The dashboard for the app, shown in Fig. 1(a) and (b), show the daily values of CO2 emissions by an individual, from transportation and domestic heating. The circular indicator informs the user about the current value emissions in kg of CO2. The number indicated in the circle is the daily value. The circular progress bar for each circular indicator shows the user's value relative to the maximum allowed level of emissions; i.e. the target for the user must be less than this maximum amount. The daily goal for the CO2 limit is 4 kg CO2 for the carbon footprint.

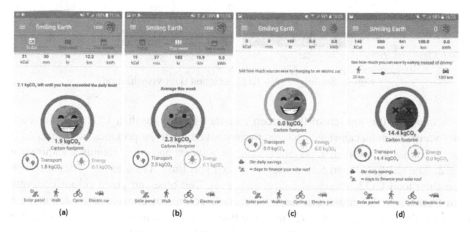

(a)          (b)          (c)          (d)

**Fig. 1.**  Smiling earth concept and GUI

The screen shots in Fig. 1 show three possible states (out of five); (a) shows a very happy earth due to low emissions with respect to the maximum level; (b) shows a happy face, but less happy than (a) as the CO2 emissions are reaching close to the maximum; (d) shows a very dismal picture of the earth due to a high level of emission, far above the maximum level. The colour code used in the GUI are blue for values that are related to housing (such as the household heating and electricity consumption) and green, which is related to transportation, such as walking, cycling or EVs.

Figures, (c) and (d), show estimations of CO2 values, when the user selects a transportation or heating mode. The symbols on the bottom of the screen are "estimation buttons" which are for solar panels, walking, cycling and an electrical vehicle, from left to right. By clicking on the "estimation buttons", the relevant values will be displayed. For example, in Fig. 1(c), the estimated CO2 emission by selecting an electrical vehicle is shown as 0.0 kg. On the other hand, the estimation for walking while either sometimes driving a combustion engine vehicle or using conventional heating means could lead to a higher CO2 emission as shown in (d). These values are based on statistical data [11] and analyses conducted by SINTEF Energy and the DESENT partners.

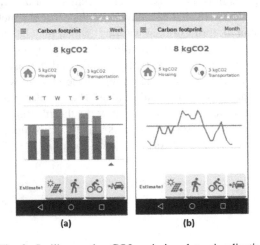

**Fig. 2** Smiling earth - CO2 emission data visualization

A menu on the top left of the screen enables users to see their CO2 emissions and other values such as calories burnt and money saved, over the previous week, month or year. The visualisation of CO2 emissions for a week and for a month are shown in Fig. 2. The red horizontal line marks the maximum limit; i.e. users are encouraged to keep their total CO2 emissions below that level. The blue and green colour coding is used to indicate the emissions due to household actions or transportation actions; e.g. Fig. 2(a) shows that 5 kg of Co2 out of the total of 8, are from household activities. Bar graphs are used to visualise the data for a week while the continuous graph shown in (b) is another visualisation of the data for a longer time period such as a month or a year.

Two approaches are used to calculate the carbon footprint and costs related to the energy consumption. In the first phase of development, users provide a monthly value of their electricity consumption. A typical yearly energy consumption profile is then calibrated to fit this value. The carbon footprint and costs from driving are estimated on user provided data for fuel consumption and a conversion value of 2348 gCO2e/L [12] and the distance travelled captured by the mobile device.

# 4   Evaluation

The focus of the evaluations were the concept and overall design and the GUI. Questionnaires were used to obtain systematic feedback. Screenshots of the design were presented with brief explanations, followed by discussions and a questionnaire, designed to evaluate the general concept, usability, motivations and behaviour change of the users through using Smiling Earth. The main feedback was about the values that were shown on each screen so as to minimize the cognitive load on a user to remember information across the different screens. One concern was the quality of the data that is displayed as this was important for the users to gain trust in the data and the app.

This paper reports the responses to the questionnaire for the specific questions related to the motivation of the user. There were five participants, who were university students. The participants were asked to install Smiling Earth on their mobile devices and use it for 8 days. The questionnaire included a set of statements (42 in total), where the users were asked to agree or disagree, based on a Likert scale: 0: Strongly disagree, 1: Disagree, 2: Neither agree or disagree, 3: Agree and 4: Strongly agree. The set of statements that are relevant for evaluating if the concept of Smiling Earth is understandable and if it can motivate citizens to affect their behaviour are shown in Table 1.

**Table 1.** Statements on motivation and concept (the number of the statements in the evaluation questionnaire have been used)

| Questions | Related to behaviour change and concept |
|---|---|
| Q3 | Viewing the data visualized in the app made me want to make some changes to reduce my emissions |
| Q6 | The app motivated me to change my behavior to a more sustainable one |
| Q7 | My concern for the environment has increased after using the app |
| Q15 | I understand clearly the purpose of the app |
| Q16 | The link between energy, carbon footprint, activity, and expenses is motivating |
| Q17 | I am more curious about energy and environment after using the app |
| Q19 | I find the earth metaphor engaging |

The responses to the statements in Table 1 are shown in Fig. 3. The responses to Q15: "I understand clearly the purpose of the app" has a score > 3.5 (between agree and strongly agree) and there was general agreement that the earth metaphor teaches the impact of a high carbon footprint. The users also agreed to the statement about the overall concept, Q16, (the link between energy, carbon footprint, activity and expenses is motivating). These are encouraging results, considering that several participants from the formative evaluations had found the concept complicated and difficult to understand. Furthermore, the threshold of relating energy consumption data to one's own carbon footprint and contribution to the CO2 emissions was high. The users neither agreed or disagreed to the statement that Smiling Earth raised curiosity about energy and environment, Q17.

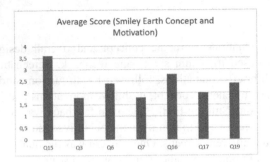

**Fig. 3.** Smiling earth evaluation - concept and motivation

The responses to Q3 and Q7 suggest that the users' concerns for the environment were not increased after using Smiling Earth. Through the discussions after the questionnaires, it appears that they were aware of the climate problem and want to do something about it and they wanted to engage others. The discussions also indicated that the users' knowledge about $CO_2$ emissions were improved and the awareness among them about the impacts of their everyday activities on the environment was increased. The responses to Q6 show that the users neither agreed nor agreed to the statement that Smiling Earth motivated them to change their behavior. This is perhaps related to the responses to Q3 and Q7 and could be interpreted as the users assuming that they already had a sustainable behavior and transportation habits.

The main feedback from the evaluations indicated that the concepts were interesting and motivating. The overall results look positive and convincing enough to continue developing the concept and the Smiling Earth app and the evaluations have provided valuable feedback to enhance as well as simplify the app.

## 5   Conclusion and Future Work

This paper describes a mobile app Smiling Earth, designed to create awareness about carbon footprints and affect individuals' behavior change towards more sustainable actions in their daily lives. The overall research question addressed is the paper is: Can the combination of energy and transport data and individual energy consumption in terms of $CO_2$ emissions motivate people to manage energy better and reduce $CO_2$ emissions? The evaluations show that Smiling Earth has the potential to contribute to raising the awareness of users and motivating them to learn more about how their daily activities could impact the environment through $CO_2$ emissions. The results from the evaluations of the prototype show that the concept of Smiling Earth is interesting and understandable for the users and that it motivates users to change their behaviour to environmentally sustainable habits. However, work remains to get users to actively use Smiling Earth and sustain behaviours that emit less $CO_2$.

The future plans for this work include further development of the concept and prototype based on the users' feedback and enhancing capabilities such as the social aspects, user communities and enhancing the gamification aspects for intrinsic motivation and raising the users' curiosity to support behaviour change. We also plan to conduct more evaluations with other user groups; e.g. car owners.

**Acknowledgements.** This work has been funded by the Norwegian Research Council and the European Union through the DESENT project. Smiling Earth was implemented and evaluated by 2 MSc students, Celine Minh and Ragnhild Larsen, and a summer student at NTNU.

# References

1. Granell, C., et al.: Future internet technologies for environmental applications. J. Environ. Model. Softw. **78**, 1–15 (2016)
2. Froehlich, J., et al.: UbiGreen: investigating a mobile tool for tracking and supporting green transportation habits. In: CHI, pp. 1043–1052. ACM (2009)
3. Nyblom, Å., Eriksson, E.: Time is of essence - changing the horizon of travel planning. In: 2nd International Conference on ICT for Sustainability (ICT4S 2014). Atlantis Press, Amsterdam (2014)
4. Fogg, B.J.: Persuasive Technology: Using Computers to Change What We Think and Do. Morgan Kaufmann Publishers, San Francisco (2003)
5. Caroleo, B., Morelli, N., Lissandrello, E., Vesco, A., Di Dio, S., Mauro, S.: Measuring the change towards more sustainable mobility: MUV impact evaluation approach. Systems **7**(2), 30 (2019)
6. Di Dio, S., Lissandrello, E., Schillaci, D., Caroleo, B., Vesco, A., D'Hespeel, I.: MUV: a game to encourage sustainable mobility habits. In: Gentile, M., Allegra, M., Söbke, H. (eds.) GALA 2018. LNCS, vol. 11385, pp. 60–70. Springer, Cham (2019). https://doi.org/10.1007/978-3-030-11548-7_6
7. Prochaska, J.O., Velicer, W.F.: The transtheoretical model of health behavior change. Am. J. Health Promot. **12**(1), 38–48 (1997)
8. Dillahunt, T., Becker, G., Mankoff, J., Kraut, R.: Motivating environmentally sustainable behavior changes with a virtual polar bear. In: Foth, M., Satchell, C., Paulos, E., Igoe, T., Raasch, C. (eds.) Workshop on Pervasive Persuasive Technology and Environmental Sustainability, pp. 18–22 (2008)
9. Shiraishi, M., Washio, Y., Takayama, C., Lehdonvirta, V., Kimura, H., Nakajima, T.: Using individual social and economic persuasion techniques to reduce CO2 emissions in a family setting. In: Proceedings of the 4th International Conference on Persuasive Technology 2009, Claremont, California, USA (2009)
10. Takayama, C., Lehdonvirta, V.: EcoIsland: a system for persuading users to reduce CO2 Emissions. In: Workshop on Pervasive Persuasive Technology and Environmental Sustainability, pp. 73–76 (2008)
11. Statistics Norway. Emissions of greenhouse gases, 1990–2015, final figures. Accessed 28 June 2017. https://www.ssb.no/en/natur-og-miljo/statistikker/klimagassn/aar-endelige/2016-12-13?fane=tabell&sort=nummer&tabell=287212
12. Greenhouse Gas Emissions from a Typical Passenger Vehicle. Office of Transportation and Air Quality, EPA (2014)

# Using a Location-Based AR Game in Environmental Engineering

Heinrich Söbke[1]([⊠]), Jannicke Baalsrud Hauge[2,3], Ioana A. Stefan[4],
and Antoniu Stefan[4]

[1] Bauhaus-Universität Weimar, Bauhaus-Institute
for Infrastructure Solutions (b.is), Coudraystr. 7, 99423 Weimar, Germany
heinrich.soebke@uni-weimar.de
[2] BIBA – Bremer Institut für Produktion und Logistik GmbH,
Hochschulring 20, 28359 Bremen, Germany
baa@biba.uni-bremen.de
[3] Royal Institute of Technology, Kvarnbergagatan 12, Södertälje, Sweden
jmbh@kth.se
[4] Advanced Technology Systems, Str. Tineretului Nr 1,
130029 Targoviste, Romania
{ioana.stefan,antoniu.stefan}@ats.com.ro

**Abstract.** Location-based AR games have experienced a tremendous rise. With Ingress (2013) and later Pokémon GO (2016), the two games have established a new genre on the one hand and set new bench-marks in popularity on the other. The specific characteristics, like multiplayer mode, integration of authentic places, and ubiquitous accessibility, make it likely that these games may have a potential as learning tools, i.e., being used in a game-based learning setting. In education for engineering disciplines, such as Environmental Engineering, authentic on-site experiences can be provided using location-based games. The study presented herein analyzes the application of a serious location-based AR game in the course Urban Water Management of the Master's programme Environmental Engineering. Methodologically, the application was evaluated with the help of questionnaires (N = 7, 9, 17, pre- and posttest, perceptions and preferences of the students). Despite the advanced level of education, there was a high acceptance of the game-based learning setting. The study supports the hypothesis that location-based AR games can be well-suited learning tools in higher education.

**Keywords:** Augmented Reality · Serious game · Location-based · Higher education · Environmental Engineering

## 1 Introduction

In recent years, the popularity of location-based Augmented Reality (AR) games is increasing. For example, 2013 Ingress [1] has generated a hype that was surpassed by 2016 Pokémon GO [2] with an even larger player base. From a didactic perspective, location-based AR apps, which encompass Ingress and Pokémon GO, have a number of characteristics that make their use as learning tools very appealing: they lead learners

© IFIP International Federation for Information Processing 2019
Published by Springer Nature Switzerland AG 2019
E. van der Spek et al. (Eds.): ICEC-JCSG 2019, LNCS 11863, pp. 466–469, 2019.
https://doi.org/10.1007/978-3-030-34644-7_47

to real objects on location and supplement these objects with information to be learned. One of the principles supported is the contiguity principle: learning effects are reinforced by the temporal and/or spatial combination of object and information [3]. Location-based mobile apps may be also suitable as social interaction triggers for the joint development of learning content in groups or for making decisions and achieving goals as a team.

## 2  Study

The main objective of this small-scale study was to investigate to what extent the usage of a location-based AR game could increase the engagement, as well as the learning outcome related to the technical topic (i.e. the core objective of the course). The 18 participants of the study are enrolled in a course on management of urban water, which is a part of the master programme Environmental Engineering at Bauhaus-University Weimar offered as distance education with some on-site workshops. As a part of the first on-site workshop in Weimar, the students experienced a customized scenario using a location-based AR game, allowing the students to explore both touristic Points of Interests (POIs), as well as information related to water management. The theoretical foundations of the scenario are described in [4]. PlayVisit [5], the location-based game works on the principle of a scavenger hunt: it leads the students to the next POI by continuously indicating the current distance. Specific, customized information can be displayed for each of the POIs, and questions can be integrated in the location-based experience to allow checking the students' knowledge, to establish a competition and to capture students' interest. The scenario contained a total of 16 POIs, 6 of which were exclusively of a touristic nature. The differentiation between technical and touristic POIs was based on the subject of the related question (Table 1). For example, the Kirms Krakow House, a touristic location, served as a setting for a question on the role of water in epidemics and therefore was considered a technical POI. Each POI was associated with one multiple choice question that had to be answered. Each questions was preceded by an introductory text, and the answer was followed by an explanatory text. Table 2 shows an example sequence of these texts.

The participants were divided into groups, using three different paths (set in the personalization of the game play) to avoid a joint tour in a single large group. Each group consisted of three participants, each of whom was asked to perform one of three tasks: (1) operating the mobile app, (2) coordination and documentation of the city tour, and (3) ensuring road safety for the group. Two outcomes were requested to encourage students to participate in the activity: The achieved score in PlayVisit and the handwritten completion of a protocol form in which, for each POI visited, the name of the POI, its key information from the students' point of view, as well as further remarks regarding the POI had to be entered. The tour was expected to last 70 min, and all groups had to return within 90 min. At the end there was a combined debriefing and feedback session of 15 min, where the winning group determined by the highest point score in PlayVisit, was rewarded with a box of sweets. A pre-test and a post-test in the days before and after the event, a feedback questionnaire, as well as a feedback round within the debriefing were used as measuring instruments. Pre- (N = 17) and posttest

(N = 7) as well as the questionnaire (N = 9) were provided online via Moodle. The voluntary response resulting from the field study explains the large variation in the number of participants. Pre- and posttest both consisted of 5 questions, which were randomly selected from a pool of 29 questions and were similar to the questions to be answered via PlayVisit. The feedback questionnaire consisted of 16 questions, out of which three questions each asked several items on a 5-point Likert scale.

**Table 1.** Sample questions (Correct answers underlined)

| Technical | Which groundwater aquifer is most probable in Muschelkalk? (porous aquifer, karst aquifer) |
| --- | --- |
| | How can fine-grained up to colloidal particles be turned into a filterable material? (precipitation, sedimentation, flocculation) |
| | Who is the eponym of the formula for calculating the flow velocity of a watercourse? (Reynold, Manning-Strickler, Pettenkofer) |
| Touristic | To whom does the Poet's Room in the City Palace pay tribute? (Wieland, Herder, Schiller, Goethe) |
| | What was the ox-eye (Ochsenauge, a small pond with fresh water supply) used for in the past? (washing laundry, drinking water supply, tanning) |
| | Which building is on the western side of the market square? (City Hall, Cranach House, Goethe's residence) |

**Table 2.** Information provided at the first POI, the Urban Water Management Laboratory of the university (Correct answers underlined)

| Introductory text | The characteristics of water are described using physical, chemical and microbiological parameters. The concentration of organic material is of great importance for the quality of water. In order to measure the concentration of organic material in the water, there are different sum parameters such as BOD5 and COD |
| --- | --- |
| Question | Which of these two sum parameters ($BOD_5$ and COD) has always a larger value than the other? ($BOD_5$ and COD) |
| Explanatory text | Right! The COD indicates how much oxygen is needed to oxidize the organic ingredients to $CO_2$ and $H_2O$. The $BSB_5$ indicates how much oxygen was consumed by the microorganisms in 5 days to biodegrade the wastewater substances. However, since only a part of the organic wastewater constituents is biodegradable, the following always applies: $COD > BOD_5$ |

## 3 Results

This section describes only a selection of the results. In the feedback session, the participants expressed themselves positively about the game play activity and stated to have learned during the activity. This impression is confirmed by the items referring to the question of how the city tour was perceived: "was fun" (4.1), "a good mixture between technical and touristic POIs" (3.8), and "the technical POIs were interesting"

(3.4). The items "was boring" (1.1), "the questions were too difficult" (2.0), and "was work" (2.4) found the least approval. The item "I prefer a city tour with a human guide" was rated neutral with 2.4. The game was seen as a good support, and the overall conclusion was that also the students found that they learned a lot by taking the tour (both scored 3.3). Interestingly, only 2 out of 9 participants were regular users of commercial location-based AR games, such as Ingress or Pokémon GO. In addition to the closed questions for which we used a 5-point Likert scale, it was also possible for the participants to add their own comments. The overall comments were positive, showed a general acceptance and indicated that the usage led to engagement with the topic. However, some participants had too little time and it was an issue in keeping the spatial orientation without looking at the mobile device continuously. Furthermore, a critical issue was that for some groups the game did not work correctly at the beginning.

## 4  Discussion and Conclusions

This small study showed that even if only a minority of the participants regularly play location-based AR games, the integration of this element in a learning context was perceived as motivating and interesting. The mix of different types of point of interests may have contributed to this success and also the fact that the participants did not know their surroundings well before. The results related to the learning aspects are in line with a similar experiment carried out with a group of engineering students in January 2018, but the fun score is higher in this study. The main reasons for this are most likely the usage of AR and also that the game is now much more stable and less energy consuming. However, work still to be done includes more extensive studies with more participants, dealing with unfavorable conditions such as rain and cold, and an exact effect analysis.

## References

1. Niantic Labs: Ingress. http://www.ingress.com/
2. Niantic Inc.: Pokémon Go. http://www.pokemongo.com/
3. Mayer, R.E., Fiorella, L.: 12 Principles for Reducing Extraneous Processing in Multimedia Learning: Coherence, Signaling, Redundancy, Spatial Contiguity, and Temporal Contiguity Principles. The Cambridge Handbook of Multimedia Learning, pp. 279–315. Cambridge University Press, Cambridge (2014)
4. Baalsrud Hauge, J., et al.: Exploring context-aware activities to enhance the learning experience. In: Dias, J., Santos, P.A., Veltkamp, R.C. (eds.) Games and Learning Alliance 6th International Conference, GALA 2017, Lisbon, Portugal, December 5–7, 2017, Proceedings, pp. 238–247. Springer, Cham (2017)
5. Geomotion Games: PlayVisit. http://www.playvisit.com/

# Incentivise Me: Smartphone-Based Mobility Detection for Pervasive Games

Thomas Tregel[1]([✉]), Felix Leber[2], and Stefan Göbel[1]

[1] Multimedia Communications Lab – KOM, TU Darmstadt,
Darmstadt, Germany
{thomas.tregel,stefan.goebel}@kom.tu-darmstadt.de
[2] TU Darmstadt, Darmstadt, Germany
felix.leber@stud.tu-darmstadt.de

**Abstract.** The ubiquity of smartphones with a plethora of sensors made it possible to develop context-based pervasive games playable by most people without any additional equipment required. However, popular games like Pokémon GO or Zombie, Run! show the minimal influence context has on the gameplay besides the user's position. Furthermore, in the context of movement and mobility the distinction between different modes of transport becomes necessary both for security and for environmental reasons.

In this paper we present a system that uses location information combined with public transport data to detect different types of mobility, especially vehicular mobility and uses this information for adaptation purposes in a prototypical location-based game. Our evaluation shows that our system can be used to reliably differentiate between public transport and driving a car within minutes and is able to adapt content in pervasive games according to the context surrounding the current user.

**Keywords:** Mobility · Mobility detection · Pervasive games · Context detection

## 1 Introduction

With the rise of smartphones, the demand for mobile games has also increased as a result of increased mobile Internet use. As a result, pervasive games that mix the real and fictional world have become more popular. In addition to larger screens, more and more sensors such as GPS receivers or magnetometers are being installed in smartphones. With these sensors it is possible to collect more data, so-called context information, about the user and his environment. One game that uses one of these data types is Pokémon GO, with which pervasive games have experienced a great hype. In 2016, Pokémon GO was the most widely used mobile game, which led to a positive change in behaviour for many users [1].

However, current pervasive games use little to no data about the players' movement, besides velocity threshold based approaches to detection potential vehicle usage. The aim of this paper is to detect the players' mode of transportation and individualize the content of pervasive games accordingly by collecting and analysing contextual

© IFIP International Federation for Information Processing 2019
Published by Springer Nature Switzerland AG 2019
E. van der Spek et al. (Eds.): ICEC-JCSG 2019, LNCS 11863, pp. 470–476, 2019.
https://doi.org/10.1007/978-3-030-34644-7_48

information based on smartphones. This is especially important for serious games in the areas of eco-friendly behaviour.

## 2 Smartphone-Based Context Detection for Mobile Games

Contextual information related to pervasive games has been defined differently by several researchers. [2] and [3] present two well-known definitions for context with the latter being that that: *"Context is any information that can be used to characterize the situation of an entity"*.

Current pervasive games already include different context types exemplarily described in the scenario of Pokémon Go. Besides the player position as a main game input, the time context is used as a day-night cycle for both gameplay reasons and security concerns. Weather is detected via many different online services for the user's position, for which open API can be used [4]. This weather information both influences game mechanics and notifies the user about upcoming weather changes.

Another information of particular interest with regard to pervasive games is the current activity of the user. This includes, walking, cycling, driving a car or the like. This is done by using sensor-fusion with e.g. the accelerometer, gyroscope, magnetometer, GPS, WiFi, pedometer and others [5]. Current games however only use a velocity-based static threshold to differentiate between valid movement and motorized travel.

The differentiation between certain activities is particularly difficult when sensor data hardly differs. In order to distinguish between different modes of vehicular transportation additional logic is required, which we will investigate in the next Section.

### 2.1 Differentiating Between Different Modes of Transportation

The detection of the player's current activity plays an important role in context detection. Data when the user is in a vehicle is quite similar, which makes it difficult to tell whether the user is sitting in the bus or in his own car. We have examined multiple approaches regarding IMU-based modality detection in our previous work [6]. The downside here lies within the distinction between different vehicular modes of transportation, as accelerometer sensor data is influenced by many other aspects like road quality or vehicle suspension.

Enriching a vehicle discrimination by location data can be promising as shown by Thiagarajan et al. who have presented three distinguishing characteristics [7]:

- a car is significantly faster outside rush hours than a bus on its route.
- the mean distance between consecutive stops is significantly greater for cars during rush hour.
- drivers do not tend to stop at stops.

Stenneth et al. use routes of trains and bus stops to identify the means of transport [8]. In addition to that Montoya et al. also use timetables and live information of busses

[7, 9]. Location-based approaches need to incorporate mechanisms that handle variance in location sensor accuracy [10].

However, using position information can lead to significant errors or jumps, especially in large cities. Additionally, bus and train routes often overlap, so a lot of data is needed to distinguish between specific routes.

In Germany the availability of public transport data is very limited, due to the division into different transport associations, which usually do not provide open APIs. However, public transport stop information can usually be downloaded directly from the transport associations [11] or obtained via OpenStreetMap.

## 3    Detecting Public Transport and Game Adaptation

As investigated in [6] using a common API is reliable when detecting basic activities, excluding different modes of transportation. We have evaluated the Google Awareness Transition API [12], which detected the current activity (running, driving in a vehicle or standstill) in 45 tests (15 per activity) within a maximum of two minutes. Especially the change to running was very fast. It was also noticeable that it makes no difference which activity is changed from, but only to which. An overview of the results of the tests is given in Fig. 1.

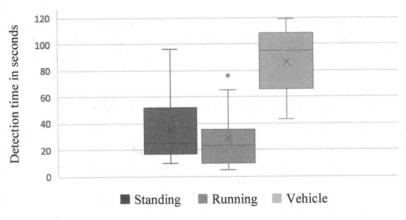

**Fig. 1.** Detection times of Google Transition API.

Thereby our approach starts as soon as the user is recognized by a common API as being in a vehicle. As noted in Sect. 2.1 it is important that all stops are detected. Therefore, we need to determine the minimum sensing frequency for location updates, as stops can be primarily be detected due to no change in player position.

For 30 journeys with bus and train, we have determined ten seconds to be the minimum downtime, which leads us to a required location update every five seconds according to the Nyquist-theorem. Due to higher basic update frequencies in location-based games, this could easily be increased without additional battery consumption.

At each position, route information is determined for the player's surrounding, which includes nearby routes and stops using our OpenStreetMap approach, which we extended by a public transport module. This information is then stored to reduce the number of consecutive network calls.

After obtaining all required information, we check to see whether a possible route is nearby. The procedure is as follows:

(1) A standstill is assumed at a speed of less than one meter per second. In this case, the determined route information is first searched for stops at a distance of $\delta = 50$ meters (step 2). If the speed is higher, only nearby routes are searched (step 4).

(2) If a stop is found, it is saved. If there is the possibility to query departure times, the departures for all stops found will be retrieved (step 3). If no stops were found, the system also searches for nearby routes (step 4).

(3) If a departure is found within the time interval $[-2$ min, 10 min$]$, the departure is also saved. Ten minutes were selected here due to the ten-minute guarantee of the RMV [14]. The two minutes were selected because the times in the timetable are often departure times, and therefore a short standing time is also taken into account. The values of the possible routes are then updated (step 5).

(4) The system searches for routes at a distance of $\delta = 50$ meters around the current position. If one or more routes are found, they will be saved. If no routes are found within a time window of 2 min (represents 12 location updates with a frequency of 1 update per 10 s), the algorithm terminates and outputs the activity *Driving a car*. Then the values of the possible routes are updated (step 5).

(5) Each route that has been detected at least once in the vicinity is assigned a value. This value for a route $r$ is calculated according to the following formula:

$$score_r = \frac{\omega_p * pos_r + \omega_r * stops_r + \omega_d * departures_r}{\#pos}$$

For this formula the weights $\omega_p = 1$, $\omega_r = 3$ and $\omega_d = 7$ have been chosen initially. $pos_r$ represents the number of positions within the vicinity of route $r$. Additionally, $stops_r$ is the amount of correctly detected stops for route $r$ and $departures_r$ the amount of valid departures within the given time window of step 3 for successfully detected stops. This sum is then divided by the number of positions processed so far, so that a value is generated as a function of time.

If a route's value succeeds a give threshold $\tau = 1$ the value and route information of the highest scoring route is returned and the respective route is detected (tram, bus, train, etc.). In case all scores are below threshold $\tau$ the algorithm returns *Driving a car* (Fig. 2).

In addition, active Bluetooth connections and Wi-Fi information are analysed to influence the decision-making process. In case an active Bluetooth connection with a car is detected *Driving a car* is returned. Similarly, when the smartphone is connected to public transport Wi-Fi public transport becomes more likely.

## 3.1    Game Adaptation Based on Mode of Transportation

Game content adaptation for public transport is especially interesting as, given an attractive reward, these could change the player's mobility behaviour. These can be implemented using a quest-based system, similar to quests current location-based games already provide. One exemplary quest for public transport would be to *Use your local public transport for a full workweek in both directions (two times per day)*. As we further want to encourage users to use available public transport options we modify the allowed radius of interaction. This allows users when e.g. sitting in a tram to interact with content on a larger distance than when going by car. Because trams and buses do not take detours this is both required and convenient to allow enough content to be interacted with when going on a pre-determined route.

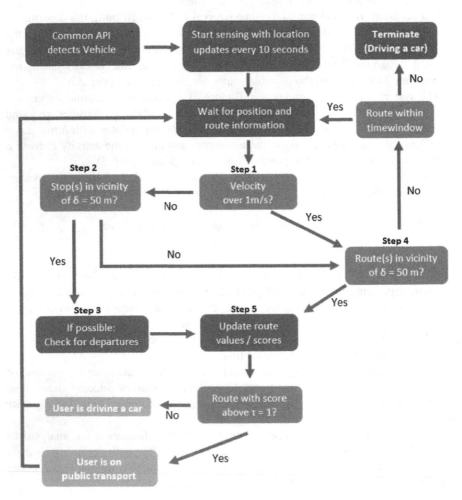

**Fig. 2.** Public transport detection algorithm in a diagram.

## 4   Evaluation

In our evaluation we want to investigate the accuracy of our public transport detection approach and look at the feasibility and outcome of adaptation approaches for content selection and quest generation. The system was implemented within our GEOVis framework first presented in [13].

### 4.1   Public Transport Detection

In order to investigate the temporal aspect of the detection with regard to the means of transport, 20 tests were carried out, half in a car and half in a public transport. The aim was to determine with what accuracy the correct activity was detected and after what time it was valid. The results show that the correct activity or route is detected in 85% of cases during the journey. On average, the correct activity and route is detected after 179 s, having faster detection times for cars.

For 50% of journeys, the algorithm started detecting an incorrect activity or route during the journey before it was correctly detected. This happened on average after 65 s, which can be interpreted as a required time until a stable prediction can be done. It is also noticeable that at least one 'wrong' stop was detected in all car tests where a wrong route was detected during the journey (50%). This happened especially when stops were near traffic lights and the car had to stop. Due to the higher value of stops in the algorithm, this route was detected as wrong first. For this reason, the correct activity was not detected correctly during a journey. The public transport tests, where no correct route was detected, showed that the journey times were too short. Both consisted of only one stop and a maximum of two minutes of travel time. In both cases the correct activity, but not the correct route, was detected because several routes were driving this route.

Stops and departures of the specific routes were detected properly for real stops and departures which were within the defined time window.

## 5   Conclusion

In this paper we presented a concept for context-based adaptation in pervasive games focusing on differentiating between different modes of transportation, which is recognized by a combination of smartphone sensors and openly available APIs. An algorithm was designed to improve the recognition of the user's activity, in particular the distinction between car and bus or train.

The in-game content is customized by player's respective movement context, by both providing him quests that further encourage public transport usage and improve his interaction radius, that allows the access to more content in the vicinity. Our results show that the recognition can be improved with existing departure data of the public local traffic.

**Acknowledgment.** The research presented in this paper was partially funded by the LOEWE initiative (Hessen, Germany) within the research project, Infrastruktur – Design – Gesellschaft" as project mo.de.

# References

1. Althoff, T., White, R.W., Horvitz, E.: Influence of Pokémon Go on physical activity: study and implications. J. Med. Internet Res. **18**, e315 (2016)
2. Schilit, B., Adams, N., Want, R.: Context-aware computing applications. In: Proceedings of IEEE Workshop on Mobile Computing Systems and Applications (1994)
3. Abowd, Gregory D., Dey, Anind K., Brown, Peter J., Davies, N., Smith, M., Steggles, P.: Towards a better understanding of context and context-awareness. In: Gellersen, Hans-W. (ed.) HUC 1999. LNCS, vol. 1707, pp. 304–307. Springer, Heidelberg (1999). https://doi.org/10.1007/3-540-48157-5_29
4. De Pessemier, T., Dooms, S., Martens, L.: Context-aware recommendations through context and activity recognition in a mobile environment. Multimedia Tools Appl. **72**(3), 2925–2948 (2014)
5. Su, X., Tong, H., Ji, P.: Activity recognition with smartphone sensors. Tsinghua Sci. Technol. **19**(3), 235–249 (2014)
6. Tregel, T., Gilbert, A., Konrad, R., Schäfer, P., Göbel, S.: Examining approaches for mobility detection through smartphone sensors. In: Göbel, S., et al. (eds.) JCSG 2018. LNCS, vol. 11243, pp. 217–228. Springer, Cham (2018). https://doi.org/10.1007/978-3-030-02762-9_22
7. Thiagarajan, A., Biagioni, J., Gerlich, T., Eriksson, J.: Cooperative transit tracking using smart-phones. In: Proceedings of the 8th ACM Conference on Embedded Networked Sensor Systems (2010)
8. Stenneth, L., Wolfson, O., Yu, P.S., Xu, B.: Transportation mode detection using mobile phones and GIS information. In: Proceedings of the 19th International Conference on Advances in Geographic Information Systems (2011)
9. Montoya, D., Abiteboul, S., Senellart, P.: Hup-me: inferring and reconciling a timeline of user activity from rich smartphone data. In: Proceedings of the 23rd SIGSPATIAL International Conference on Advances in Geographic Information Systems (2015)
10. Grimes, J.G.: Global positioning system standard positioning service performance standard. Washington, D.C., U.S. Department of Defense (2008)
11. Rhein-Main-Verkehrsverbund: RMV Open Data. https://opendata.rmv.de/site/start.html. Accessed 05 Mar 2019
12. Google: Google Awareness API (2016). https://developers.google.com/awareness/. Accessed 15 June 2018
13. Tregel, T., Raymann, L., Göbel, S., Steinmetz, R.: Geodata classification for automatic content creation in location-based games. In: Alcañiz, M., Göbel, S., Ma, M., Fradinho Oliveira, M., Baalsrud Hauge, J., Marsh, T. (eds.) JCSG 2017. LNCS, vol. 10622, pp. 212–223. Springer, Cham (2017). https://doi.org/10.1007/978-3-319-70111-0_20
14. Rhein-Main-Verkehrsverbund:    RMV-10-Minute-Guarantee.    https://www.rmv.de/c/en/services/passenger-rights/rmv-10-minute-guarantee/. Accessed 05 Mar 2019

# Workshops

# Designing Serious Mobile Location-Based Games

Jannicke Baalsrud Hauge[1,2], Heinrich Söbke[3(✉)], Ioana A. Stefan[4],
and Antoniu Stefan[4]

[1] BIBA – Bremer Institut für Produktion und Logistik GmbH,
Hochschulring 20, 28359 Bremen, Germany
baa@biba.uni-bremen.de
[2] Royal Institute of Technology, Kvarnbergagatan 12, Södertälje, Sweden
jmbh@kth.se
[3] Bauhaus-Universität Weimar, Bauhaus-Institute
for Infrastructure Solutions (b.is), Coudraystr. 7, 99423 Weimar, Germany
heinrich.soebke@uni-weimar.de
[4] Advanced Technology Systems, Str. Tineretului Nr 1,
130029 Targoviste, Romania
{ioana.stefan, antoniu.stefan}@ats.com.ro

**Abstract.** The technical requirements of mobile location-based games have been met sufficiently well to make location-based mobile games an everyday object. Games like Ingress or Pokémon GO have experienced a huge popularity. Hence, the question arises how the obvious attraction of these games can be used to achieve goals other than entertainment, such as learning. This article describes the basic scientific background of a workshop of the ICEC-JCSG 2019 for the development of design principles for serious mobile location-based games. First the game types involved are defined, then relevant design principles are identified and presented providing a basis to substantiate design guidelines in the workshop and contribute to the purposeful design of mobile location-based games.

## 1 Introduction

In recent years, mobile location-based games have experienced the breakthrough to mass media, as the games Ingress [1] and Pokémon GO [2] demonstrate. From a didactic point of view, games have unique advantages that turn them into promising learning tools. For example, as interaction triggers, they can support situated learning just as much as they inherently support principles of multimedia learning [3], such as the contiguity principles or signaling.

Among the aims of this workshop are the identification of design guidelines for serious mobile location-based games, based on phenomena documented in literature [4–6]. Further, it is important to analyze the characteristics of suitable learning content for mobile location-based games [7] and frameworks for the integration of learning content into serious games [8–10]. Additionally, current software frameworks for the creation of serious mobile location-based games, such as PlayVisit [11] need to be

© IFIP International Federation for Information Processing 2019
Published by Springer Nature Switzerland AG 2019
E. van der Spek et al. (Eds.): ICEC-JCSG 2019, LNCS 11863, pp. 479–484, 2019.
https://doi.org/10.1007/978-3-030-34644-7_49

identified. In the following, first the types of games under investigation are outlined. Thereafter, existing design guidelines are presented. The workshop is based, in part, on the experience gained during an earlier workshop [12] and the EU BEACONING project [13].

## 2 Serious Mobile Location-Based Games

This section briefly describes the terms used to denote game types under investigation. For this workshop, the term **game** implies a digital game. **Serious games** are games that serve further purposes in addition to entertainment, such as learning. If learning is the further purpose of a game, then such a game is also called **educational game**. **Mobile games** can be understood as games that are played with the help of mobile devices such as cellphones, smartphones or tablets. A further distinction can be made between games which require an internet connection to play and games which can be played on mobile devices without an internet connection.

**Location-based games** are in the context of this workshop interpreted as games whose game mechanics depend on the awareness of the current position and its temporal changes, i.e. the movement of the player through the space. Location-based games require positioning technology, such as GPS, to track the current position. The vast majority of location-based games are played on mobile devices and require an internet connection, so **mobile location-based games** can almost be considered a synonym to location-based games.

A categorization of **AR games** is provided by Wetzel et al. [14]. They distinguish systematically the dimensions device mobility and content spaces. In their categorization, "true mobile AR games", which is the type of games primarily covered in the workshop, are games that include high device mobility and a wide content space, i.e. players are required to roam through the real world, such as a city. There is no clear definition of how augmentation is to be performed for mobile AR games. For example, both Pokémon GO and Ingress are commonly called AR Games. While Pokémon GO implements true video-see-through AR, Ingress uses augmentations to display additional information about near real-world objects on the screen of the mobile device.

**Pervasive games** are close to mobile location-based games in that they also link their game mechanics with the elements of the real world [15]. Through the intersection of virtual and real world, pervasive games are very closely associated with augmented reality. However, pervasive games are not necessarily relying on location-awareness.

The game types described here are not commonly defined, and many other definitions that differ by nuances exist. For example, De Souza e Silva and Hjorth [16] distinguish between urban games, location-based games and hybrid reality games and state that there is a "range of types of games mediated by mobile technologies". Briefly, the workshop focuses on the design of digital games that are used for learning purposes using notions of location-based, mobile and/or augmented reality.

# 3   A Set of Guidelines

This sections provides an overview of existing guidelines for game design. It serves as a starting point for the workshop and follow a general-to-specific approach is: starting from the design of games in general, guidelines will be presented that complement the aspects of learning, mobile, location-based and augmented reality.

Among the game design guidelines, the work of Schell [17] is well-known and established. When it comes to learning games, Harteveld et al. [18] contribute the model of "1. Fun (game), 2. Learning (pedagogy), and 3. Validity (reality)", which is characterized by inherent tensions and leaves the design process to become a complex problem. The notion of fun is associated with engagement-causing motivation. Peters et al. [19] discuss the options to design for engagement. For location-based games, Kiefer et al. [20] specify the following dimensions of design that have to be considered in game design: dimension of game environmental embedding, game conceptual dimension and game spatial and temporal dimension. Montola et al. [21] describe design guidelines for pervasive games. In the following, three selected design frameworks are described: First, the PGDF identifies the areas that need to be covered during design. Another framework for designing mobile AR Games focuses on entertainment games, while the last framework deals specifically with mobile location-based games for learning.

## 3.1   The Pervasive Game Design Framework (PGDF)

The PGDF [8, 22] names the components of consideration when designing pervasive games for learning (Table 1), but without any specific rules on the implementation.

Table 1. Components of the PGDF

| Component | Description |
|---|---|
| Pervasive context | The Pervasive Context describes the integration of the game into the real world, i.e. the meaningful linkage of game mechanics and real-world objects |
| Pedagogical objectives | Since the aim of the PGDF is the design of pervasive games for learning purposes, a description of learning objectives is required |
| Assessment metrics | Educational technology, is also inevitably tied to measuring the achievement of learning objectives. Therefore, it must be defined how the achievement of learning objectives is measured |
| Difficulty level | A serious game should be able to provide tasks of varying degrees of difficulty |
| User skills | Since the players most probably have different skill levels, it should be determined which requirements are placed on the skills of the players and also how games can respond to different skills |
| Social interaction | Social interaction is one of the key triggers of learning processes. It is therefore rewarding to analyze the extent to which social interactions can be stimulated by the game mechanics in each serious pervasive game |
| Motivation | Motivating players to engage with the game and thus indirectly with the learning objectives is the basic rationale behind using learning games. Therefore, it is essential to describe the game mechanics that should provide motivation |

## 3.2   Mobile AR Games

Wetzel et al. [14] present guidelines for designing mobile AR games. The guidelines in Table 2 also focus on the narrative connection between the objects of the real and the virtual worlds. This aspect is rather neglected in the design of serious games due to the effort involved.

**Table 2.** Guidelines for designing Mobile AR Games [14]

| Category | Guideline |
|---|---|
| General | • Justify the use of AR<br>• Engage players physically |
| Virtual elements | • Create meaningful AR content<br>• Create fully-fledged characters<br>• Create a rich scenery<br>• Go beyond the visual |
| Real world elements | • Make the journey interesting<br>• Comprise atmospheric elements from the reality<br>• Think about security<br>• Plan ahead |
| Social elements | • Use complementing roles<br>• Use non-player characters<br>• Encourage discussions<br>• Avoid crowded areas |
| Technology and usability | • Make the technology part of the game<br>• Keep the interaction simple<br>• Take display properties into account<br>• Take tracking characteristics into account<br>• Avoid occlusion-rich areas<br>• Design seamfully and for disconnection |

## 3.3   Design Guidelines for Location-Based Mobile Games for Learning

Ardito et al. [23] provide guidelines especially for learning games. The guidelines are divided into five categories. Most of the guidelines are generally applicable for learning game design. Table 3 shows an extract of the guidelines especially relevant for designing mobile location-based games. The category "Control/Flexibility" seems to comprise solely guidelines applicable for general game design, thus it has not been included in Table 3.

**Table 3.** Design guidelines focusing on location-based mobile games [23]

| Category | Guidelines (literally cited from [23]) |
|---|---|
| Game general design | • Minimize the changes to the physical places<br>• Consider the social conventions of the place (e.g. not loud speaking in a church)<br>• Consider to include activities/events that are not part of the game, but happen in the real world (e.g. the ceremony of change of the guard at noon) |
| Engagement | • Provide contextual cues linked to specific places or events to convey additional information (e.g. sounds reproducing noises of daily activities in an ancient city)<br>• Minimize the interaction with the game tools. Players' attention should be focused on the game and the environment |
| Learning aspects | • Game should emphasize either vertical or horizontal exploration of a place/topic, i.e., deeply exploring a limited space [...] vs. more superficially exploring a broad space [...])<br>• Tasks should require players to link areas, locations, physical objects to concepts, topics, etc. |
| Social aspects | • Assign responsibilities and tools (e.g. mobile devices, maps, etc.) among team members to induce collaboration. Consider to force, forbid or allow responsibilities exchange among team members |

## 4 Summary

Starting from the positive and engaging experiences of location-based AR entertainment games, this workshop aims to facilitate knowledge transfer towards education communities and set the stage for analyzing key design principles that could guide the creation of serious location-based AR games.

## References

1. Niantic Labs: Ingress. http://www.ingress.com/
2. Niantic Inc.: Pokémon Go. http://www.pokemongo.com/
3. Mayer, R.E., Fiorella, L.: 12 Principles for Reducing Extraneous Processing in Multimedia Learning: Coherence, Signaling, Redundancy, Spatial Contiguity, and Temporal Contiguity Principles. The Cambridge Handbook of Multimedia Learning, pp. 279–315. Cambridge University Press, Cambridge (2014)
4. Rauschnabel, P.A., Rossmann, A., tom Dieck, M.C.: An adoption framework for mobile augmented reality games: the case of Pokémon Go. Comput. Hum. Behav. **76**, 276–286 (2017). https://doi.org/10.1016/j.chb.2017.07.030
5. Hamari, J., Malik, A., Koski, J., Johri, A.: Uses and gratifications of Pokémon Go: why do people play mobile location-based augmented reality games? Int. J. Hum. Comput. Interact. **35**, 1–16 (2018). https://doi.org/10.1080/10447318.2018.1497115

6. Söbke, H., Baalsrud Hauge, J., Stefan, I.A.: Long-term engagement in mobile location-based augmented reality games. In: Geroimenko, V. (ed.) Augmented Reality Games I, pp. 129–147. Springer, Cham (2019). https://doi.org/10.1007/978-3-030-15616-9_9

7. Stefan, I.A., Baalsrud Hauge, J., Gheorge, A.F., Stefan, A.: Improving learning experiences through customizable metagames. In: Gentile, M., Allegra, M., Söbke, H. (eds.) GALA 2018. LNCS, vol. 11385, pp. 418–421. Springer, Cham (2019). https://doi.org/10.1007/978-3-030-11548-7_40

8. Söbke, H., Baalsrud Hauge, J., Stefan, I.A.: Prime example ingress: reframing the pervasive game design framework (PGDF). Int. J. Serious Games 4, 39–58 (2017). https://doi.org/10.17083/ijsg.v4i2.182

9. Habgood, M.P.J., Ainsworth, S.E.: Motivating children to learn effectively: exploring the value of intrinsic integration in educational games. J. Learn. Sci. 20, 169–206 (2011). https://doi.org/10.1080/10508406.2010.508029

10. Arnab, S., et al.: Mapping learning and game mechanics for serious games analysis. Br. J. Educ. Technol. 46, 391–411 (2015). https://doi.org/10.1111/bjet.12113

11. Geomtion Games: PlayVisit. http://www.playvisit.com/

12. Baalsrud Hauge, J., Stanescu, I.A., Stefan, A.: Constructing and experimenting pervasive, gamified learning. In: Entertainment Computing – ICEC 2016 15th IFIP TC 14 International Conference Vienna, Austria, September 28–30, 2016 (2016)

13. Beaconing Consortium led by Coventry University: Beaconing - Breaking Educational Barriers with Contextualized Pervasive and Gameful Learning. http://beaconing.eu/

14. Wetzel, R., Blum, L., Broll, W., Oppermann, L.: Designing mobile augmented reality games. In: Furht, B. (ed.) Handbook of Augmented Reality, pp. 513–539. Springer, New York (2011). https://doi.org/10.1007/978-1-4614-0064-6_25

15. Hinske, S., Lampe, M., Magerkurth, C., Röcker, C.: Classifying pervasive games: on pervasive computing and mixed reality. Concepts Technol. Pervasive Games Read. Pervasive Gaming Res. 1, 11–37 (2007)

16. de Souza e Silva, A., Hjorth, L.: Playful urban spaces: a historical approach to mobile games. Simul. Gaming. 40, 602–625 (2009)

17. Schell, J.: The Art of Game Design: A book of lenses. Morgan Kaufmann Publishers Inc., San Francisco (2008)

18. Harteveld, C., Guimarães, R., Mayer, I., Bidarra, R.: Balancing pedagogy, game and reality components within a unique serious game for training levee inspection. In: Hui, K.-C., et al. (eds.) Edutainment 2007. LNCS, vol. 4469, pp. 128–139. Springer, Heidelberg (2007). https://doi.org/10.1007/978-3-540-73011-8_15

19. Peters, D., Calvo, R.A., Ryan, R.M.: Designing for motivation, engagement and wellbeing in digital experience. Front. Psychol. 9, 797 (2018). https://doi.org/10.3389/fpsyg.2018.00797

20. Kiefer, P., Matyas, S., Schlieder, C.: Systematically exploring the design space of location-based games. In: Proceedings of Pervasive 2006 Work, Poster Present. PerGames2006, pp. 183–190 (2006)

21. Montola, M., Stenros, J., Waern, A.: Pervasive Games: Theory and Design. CRC Press, Boca Raton (2009)

22. Hauge, J.B., et al.: Exploring context-aware activities to enhance the learning experience. In: Dias, J., Santos, P.A., Veltkamp, R.C. (eds.) GALA 2017. LNCS, vol. 10653, pp. 238–247. Springer, Cham (2017). https://doi.org/10.1007/978-3-319-71940-5_22

23. Ardito, C., Sintoris, C., Raptis, D., Yiannoutsou, N., Avouris, N., Costabile, M.F.: Design guidelines for location-based mobile games for learning. In: International Conference on Social Applications for Lifelong Learning, pp. 96–100 (2010)

# Workshop: Towards Inclusive Co-creation of Inclusive Games

Franco Eusébio Garcia[1]($\boxtimes$), Thomas Westin[2], and Jérôme Dupire[3]

[1] Departamento de Computação, Universidade Federal de São Carlos (UFSCar),
São Carlos, SP, Brazil
franco.garcia@dc.ufscar.br
[2] Department of Computer and Systems Science, Stockholm University,
Kista, Sweden
thomasw@dsv.su.se
[3] CNAM/CEDRIC, 292, rue St Martin, 75003 Paris, France
dupire@cnam.fr

**Abstract.** Game creation precedes game play. In this workshop, we describe our efforts towards enabling people with different (dis)abilities to co-create and play digital games. We focus on abilities, skills and knowledge to enable collaborative and inclusive co-creation of inclusive games.

**Keywords:** Game development · Game design · Game accessibility · Serious games · End-User Development

## 1  Introduction

Digital games extend beyond entertainment. Besides professional game development, multiple domains have been benefiting from games. Education (game-based learning, gaming literacy), training (serious games), and therapy and rehabilitation (games for health, therapeutic games), game making and modding, and even game playing as a profession (e-sports) are successful examples of games supporting real world activities.

However, despite applications and importance of games, millions of people are still unable to play (reasons include physical, cognitive, and emotional (dis)abilities; social, cultural, and economic issues; and even access to technology itself). Moreover, intended audiences for game creation are currently limited to young people without physical, cognitive, and emotional disabilities, often living in favorable socioeconomic conditions.

A possible way to enable more people to play is enabling more people to design and implement digital games. If we bring diversity to creation, we can potentially achieve greater diversity to resulting games. In this strategy, creation predates play. In this workshop, we explore the framework defined in [1] to present our ongoing efforts towards enabling inclusive co-creation of inclusive

Published by Springer Nature Switzerland AG 2019
E. van der Spek et al. (Eds.): ICEC-JCSG 2019, LNCS 11863, pp. 485–488, 2019.
https://doi.org/10.1007/978-3-030-34644-7_50

games. The goal of the framework is enabling communities of people with hetero-geneous interaction needs to co-create games for themselves and for people with different interaction needs (currently traditional audiences, hearing disabilities, and low literacy).

The framework has three main pillars to support its goal: (1) a flexible archi-tecture that enabled use-time modification of human-computer interaction; (2) a collaborative work model to transform inclusion into a community problem, which the community could collaborate to address; (3) tools to enable the work-flow. It aims for maximum inclusion, towards approaching game accessibility modding. The main idea is to transform game accessibility into a community problem, on which people contribute based on their abilities, skills, and knowl-edge to enable more people to play and create games. In this strategy, whenever someone provides a new alternative, she/he might enable more people to co-create and play. Once able to co-create, the newly-included may also become able to contribute, transforming accessibility into an iterative process towards maximum inclusion.

To enable the workflow, we provide communities with game creation and modding tools. For instance, a storytelling tool (Lepi) was developed as proof of concept for game creation, considering accessibility to a subset of interaction needs (traditional audiences, hearing disabilities, and low literacy) and a single genre (storytelling) [1,2]. A second example is a support system to aid play-ers with cognitive disabilities to play, exploring community-created content to remove accessibility barriers and enable play [3]. Our intention is defining and expanding solutions to include new audiences, aiming for broader inclusion.

Current evaluation has found that each pillar of the framework enabled the proposed workflow for the initial audience [2]. With the tool, people could co-create story-based games with their abilities; with the collaborative work model, contributors inserted media and content to address other interaction needs of the community; due to architecture, people could insert this new content to the game. This way, people could co-create inclusion as a community – from each according to their abilities, to each according to their needs.

## 2    Call for Participation

Game creation precedes game play. In this half-day workshop, mixing tutorials with participatory activities, we describe our efforts towards enabling people with different interaction needs to co-create and play inclusive digital games. We focus on abilities, skills and knowledge to enable collaborative and inclusive co-creation of inclusive games.

Besides game accessibility professionals and researchers, this workshop can benefit professionals exploring games for serious activities, designers aiming for broader inclusion in interactive systems, digital accessibility researches, meta-designers exploring end-user development for inclusion, researchers designing collaborative systems, or professionals exploring Information and Communica-tions Technologies with people with heterogeneous interaction needs.

The workshop provides resources to accommodate people with different computing backgrounds, as the framework encompasses design and programming for professional developers; meta-design and end-user programming for end-users; and individual and community workflows for collaboration.

# 3   Outcomes for Participants and for the Workshop

Game design is a discipline on which every area of human knowledge can contribute towards a better project. With suitable approaches, everyone could co-create according to their own abilities. In this workshop, co-creation is focused on accessibility, abilities, and skills towards maximum inclusion.

In inclusive environments, there might be people with heterogeneous abilities – including people with and without disabilities. With the framework, they can co-create storytelling games accessible for them all. People can create content based on their own abilities. Then members of the community can enrich the game project based on their own abilities: they can convert existing content into alternatives to enable use. Once they provide a new alternative, more people can play – and potentially create new alternatives for inclusion. Thus, people who could not use the original game may become able to further improve it.

At the end of the workshop, participants should be familiar with design and implementation principles described in [2] to achieve co-creation of inclusion[1]. A desired outcome towards inclusive co-creation and play could be a curated list of game accessibility related efforts based on participants suggestions. Thus, this workshop may be a starting point to gather these existing efforts in one place – for instance, at the International Game Developers Association Game Accessibility Special Interest Group's Open Educational Resources[2]. This could serve as reference for professional developers (for instance, designers, programmers, and artists), and for end-users acting as non-professional developers.

# 4   Program

1. *Welcome and Overview of the Framework.* Participants will learn how each pillar of the framework are combined to promote inclusive co-creation of inclusive games.
2. *The Architecture: Game Interaction as Add-Ons.* Participants will be introduced a different way to think about digital games. We can design and implement games for semantics of use and define commands to represent players' intents. In particular, this enables us to provide different interaction alternatives for game play. These strategies allow development of games with

---

[1] (i) Design for Semantics of Use, (ii) Implement for Modification, (iii) Provide Different Ways to Create and Play, (iv) Compose Interaction, (v) Focus on Abilities and Skills, (vi) Foster Community Inclusion, (vii) Consider Inclusion as a Dynamic Process, (viii) Foster Community Collaboration.

[2] https://igda-gasig.org/oer/.

multiple interaction schemes: we can define multiple ways to enable play by defining how a player should perceive the game content and provide commands to it.

3. *The Collaborative Co-creation of Inclusive Digital Games: End-User Collaboration Towards Inclusion.* Participants will learn how communities of people with heterogeneous abilities can promote inclusion. The collaborative work model describes a process to promote the workflow for inclusive co-creation, on which individuals provide inclusion to a community according to their abilities, and a community provides support to individuals according to their interaction needs.

4. *The Game Co-creation Platform: Enabling People with Heterogeneous Interaction Needs to Create and Play Digital Games.* We will discuss and present tools and strategies to enable inclusive co-creation of inclusive games. Lepi and the support system are explored as case studies, acting as proof of concept for the strategies defined by the first two pillars. Besides game play, inclusive creation tools allow domain experts to explore game creation and play as a support for their professional activities. Thus, this activity showcases how end-users can co-create accessibility features for inclusion according to their own abilities.

5. *Fostering Inclusive Co-creation and Play by People with Disabilities: Approaches for Content Creation and Play.* Aiming to achieve the outcomes for the workshop from Sect. 3, participants could share game accessibility resources that they know, and suggest improvements and directions to enable broader audiences to create and play. What are possible strategies to enable more people to create and play? Which existing content creation tools are designed for people with disabilities? What game genres and mechanics could become more accessible – or even universally accessible??

# References

1. Garcia, F.E.: An inclusive end-user development framework for tailorable games. Phd thesis, Universidade Federal de São Carlos, São Carlos (2019)
2. Garcia, F.E., Brandão, R.P., Mendes, G.C.D.P., Neris, V.P.D.A.: Able to create, able to (self-)improve: how an inclusive game framework fostered self-improvement through creation and play in alcohol and drugs rehabilitation. In: Proceedings of the 17th IFIP TC.13 International Conference on Human-Computer Interaction (INTERACT 2019). Paphos, Cyprus (2019)
3. Yildiz, S., Carlsson, A., Järnbrand, H., Sandberg, T., Westin, T.: Design of a game community based support system for cognitive game accessibility. In: Brooks, A.L., Brooks, E., Vidakis, N. (eds.) ArtsIT/DLI -2017. LNICST, vol. 229, pp. 238–247. Springer, Cham (2018). https://doi.org/10.1007/978-3-319-76908-0_23

# Author Index

Printed in the United States
By Bookmasters